RETRACING THE PAST

RETRACING THE PAST

Readings in
the History of the American People

VOLUME ONE · TO 1877

GARY B. NASH

EDITOR
University of California, Los Angeles

1817

HARPER & ROW, PUBLISHERS, New York

Cambridge, Philadelphia, San Francisco,
London, Mexico City, São Paulo, Singapore, Sydney

Sponsoring Editor: Marianne J. Russell
Development Editor: Johnna G. Barto
Project Editor: Jo-Ann Goldfarb
Text and Cover Design: Robert Bull/Design
Photo Research: Elsa Peterson
Production: Willie Lane
Compositor: ComCom Division of Haddon Craftsmen, Inc.
Printer and Binder: R. R. Donnelley & Sons Company

Cover Illustration: Albert Bierstadt, *The Oregon Trail* (detail), 1869. Butler Institute of American Art, Youngstown, Ohio.

Part-Opening Illustrations: (Part One) L. I. (maker's initials), needlework picture, c. 1740–1760. The Henry Francis DuPont Winterthur Museum, Winterthur, Del.   (Part Two) William P. Chappell, *Tammany Society Celebrating the Fourth of July, 1812,* 1869. New York Historical Society, New York.   (Part Three) Edward Lamson Henry, *The 9:45 A.M. Accommodation,* Stratford, Connecticut, 1867. Metropolitan Museum of Art, New York, bequest of Moses Tanenbaum.

RETRACING THE PAST: Readings in the History of the American People, Volume One, To 1877

Library of Congress Cataloging-in-Publication Data
Main entry under title:

Retracing the past.

  Contents: v. 1. To 1877—v. 2. Since 1865.
  1. United States—History. I. Nash, Gary B.
E178.1.R37   1986   973   85–24893
ISBN 0–06–044719–2 (v. 1)
ISBN 0–06–044721–4 (v. 2)

  86 87 88 9 8 7 6 5 4 3 2

CONTENTS

Preface   **vii**

PART ONE
A COLONIZING PEOPLE

PART TWO
A REVOLUTIONARY PEOPLE

PART THREE
AN EXPANDING PEOPLE

PREFACE

This two-volume reader has been constructed to accompany *The American People: Creating a Nation and a Society* (New York: Harper & Row, 1986), but I hope it will also prove a useful supplement to other textbooks in American history. The essays have been selected with three goals in mind: first, to blend political and social history; second, to lead students to a consideration of the role of women, ethnic groups, and laboring Americans in the weaving of the nation's social fabric; and third, to explore life at the individual and community levels. The book also means to introduce students to the individuals and groups who made a critical difference in the shaping of American history or whose experience reflected key changes in their society.

A few of the individuals highlighted are famous—Benjamin Franklin, Abraham Lincoln, and Thomas Edison, for example. A number of others are historically visible but not quite household names—Daniel Shays, Tecumseh, "Big Bill" Haywood, W. E. B. Du Bois, and Margaret Sanger. Some will be totally obscure to students, such as "Long Bill" Scott, a revolutionary soldier, and Mayo Greenleaf Patch, whose early nineteenth-century misfortunes mirror some of the changes occurring in rural society after the American Revolution. Sometimes the focus is on groups whose role in history has not been adequately treated—the Chinese in the building of the transcontinental railroad, the women of the Southern Farmers Alliance in the late nineteenth century, and the Hispanic agricultural laborers of this century.

Some of the essays chosen take us inside American homes, farms, and factories, such as the essays on the beginnings of industrialization before the Civil War, the transcontinental migrants of the nineteenth century, and the upcountry yeoman farmers of Georgia after the Civil War. Such essays, it is hoped, will convey an understanding of the daily lives of ordinary Americans, who collectively helped shape society. Other essays deal with the vital social and political movements that transformed American society: the revolutionary movement of the eighteenth century; abolitionism in the antebellum period; populism and progressivism in the late nineteenth and early twentieth centuries; and the civil rights and feminist movements of our own times. Finally, some of the essays treat technological and scientific advances that greatly affected society, such as electricity and birth control.

Readability has been an important criterion in the selection of these essays. An important indicator of readability, in turn, is how vividly and concretely the past has been brought alive by the author. The main objective has been a palpable presentation of the past—one that allows students to sense and feel the forces of historical change and hence to understand them.

GARY B. NASH

PART ONE
A
COLONIZING
PEOPLE

1

THE CONQUEST OF UTOPIA

ERIC R. WOLF

The success of the Spanish conquest of Middle America and Peru has long fascinated historians. The very scale of the conquest, accomplished by no more than a few thousand Spanish soldiers and a few dozen priests, has led historians to search for an explanation for the almost effortless Spanish victory. While earlier historians attributed the conquest to the superiority of European technology and culture, the Spanish victory, as Eric Wolf shows in this essay, rested as much on the nature of Indian society as on Spanish military tactics and armaments.

Although he does not use the term here, Wolf uses the anthropological concept of acculturation to explain the transformation of Middle American society. Acculturation is the process of cultural interchange that occurs when two different cultures come into contact with each other. In the process of this interchange a complex borrowing and accommodation of cultural traits takes place. Neither culture was left unaltered, even though European settlers believed that their superior culture would uplift the tribal culture without itself being affected.

Applied to Middle America, the acculturation process can be followed in the use to which the Spanish desire for gold and conquest was put by some of the local Native Americans. Long subjugated to a Mexica tribal hierarchy, local groups of natives used the coming of the Spanish as a means of revolting against their oppression. The conquest, as Wolf points out, was as much a popular revolt against indigenous domination as a Spanish military victory.

It was in the realm of religion, however, that the acculturation process is most apparent. From the beginning of contact, Spanish and Indian priests searched for a mutual understanding between their doctrines and rituals. Their shared belief in baptism, the similarities between the Catholic Virgin and the Indian Coatlícue, and the common use of the cross as a religious symbol gave the Spanish and Native Americans a common language in which elements of the two cultures could be merged.

The Spanish were not alone in the conquest of America. Soon Dutch, Portuguese, French, Swedish, and English adventurers sought to follow the Spanish example and claim colonies of their own. In doing so, they brought themselves into contact with other indigenous peoples and began their own cycle of acculturation. How did the motives of the English colonizers, described by William Cronon in Reading 4, differ from those of the Spanish? How did the nature of the European–Native American interaction differ?

Reprinted from Eric R. Wolf, *Sons of the Shaking Earth* (Chicago: University of Chicago Press, 1959), pp. 152–175, with permission of the author and the University of Chicago Press.

In 1492, Christopher Columbus, sailing under the flag of Castile, discovered the islands of the Caribbean and planted upon their shores the standard of his sovereigns and the cross of his Savior. From these islands, the newcomers began to probe the Middle American coast. In Easter week, 1519, a young adventurer, Hernán Cortés —lawyer by professional training and military man through baptism of fire on Santo Domingo —landed in the vicinity of San Juan de Ulua in Veracruz. He brought with him an army of 508 soldiers—32 of whom were crossbowmen and carried harquebuses—16 horses, and 14 pieces of artillery, together with a navy of 11 ships and 100 sailors. In July and August of that year, Cortés beached his ships and embarked on the conquest of Tenochtitlán. Two years later, on August 13, 1521, Tenochtitlán fell into Spanish hands. One cycle of history had come to an end and another cycle began.

How is one to explain this sudden irreversible change in the fate of Middle America? The entire enterprise of the Spanish Conquest seems shrouded in a curious air of unreality. Hernán Cortés conquers an empire embracing millions of people. For lack of holy water, a Fray Pedro de Gante baptizes hundreds of thousands of Indians with his saliva. A Nuñez Cabeza de Vaca sets out to find the golden cities of Cíbola and the Fountain of Youth, to be shipwrecked, reduced to starvation, nearly eaten by cannibals, only to return to the fray as soon as he is rescued. Actors, acts, and motives seem superhuman: their lust for gold and for salvation, their undivided loyalty to a distant monarch, their courage in the face of a thousand obstacles seem to defy simple psychological explanations. They not only made history; they struck poses against the backdrop of history, conscious of their role as makers and shakers of this earth. The utterances of a Cortés, a Panfilo Narváez, a Garay, are replete with references to Caesar, Pompey, and Hannibal. Cortés plays not only at being himself; he is also the Amadís of Gaul celebrated in the medieval books of chivalry. They were not satisfied with the simple act; they translated each act into a symbolic statement, an evocation of a superhuman purpose.

Struck with admiration of their deeds and postures, their chroniclers took them at their word. In the pages of the history books these men parade in the guise of their own evaluation of themselves: half centaurs, pawing the ground with their hoofs and bellowing with voices like cannon, half gods, therefore, and only half men.

But their image of themselves obscures the real greatness of their achievement, for greatness can be measured only on a human scale, not on a divine. Part of their greatness was undoubtedly due to the military tactics employed by a courageous and cunning general. The Spaniards used cavalry to break through the massed formations of an enemy that had never before encountered horses; they thus avoided hand-to-hand combat in which gunpowder and iron arms would have been of little avail in the face of the wicked Indian swords, beset with obsidian chips. To counteract the Indian firepower of spears and arrows, the Spaniards used the crossbow, the instrument that gained them such a decisive victory in the great battle of Pavia against the remnants of French knighthood. When Spanish cavalry, artillery, and infantry proved impotent against Indian canoes manned by archers in the canals and lagoons surrounding Tenochtitlán, Cortés again carried the battle to the enemy, attacking the embattled capital across the water, from the boards of thirteen ships built on the spot.

None of these military successes would have been possible, however, without the Indian allies Cortés won in Middle America. From the first, he enlisted on his side rulers and peoples who had suffered grievously at the hands of their Mexica enemies. In a decisive way, as Ralph Beals has put it, "the conquest of Tenochtitlán was less a conquest than it was a revolt of dominated peoples." Spanish firepower and cavalry would have been impotent against the Mexica armies without the Tlaxcaltec, Texcocans and others who joined the Spanish cause. They furnished the bulk of the infantry and manned the canoes that covered the advance of the brigantines across the lagoon of Tenochtitlán. They provided, transported, and prepared the food supplies needed to sustain an army in the field. They maintained lines of communication between coast and highland, and they policed occupied and pacified areas. They supplied the raw materials and muscular energy for the construction of the ships that decided the siege of the Mexica capital. Spanish military equipment and tactics carried the day, but Indian assistance determined the outcome of the war.

In an ultimate sense, the time was ripe for a redress in the balance of power in Middle America. Even Moctezuma, in his abode at Tenochtitlán, must have felt this, for we can read in his hesitations, in his hearkening to omens of doom, evidence of the doubt and uncertainty which was gnawing at the vitals of Mexica domination. The Spaniards provided the indispensable additional energy required to reverse the dominant political trend. Yet they were not mere agents of the indigenous will, mere leaders of an indigenous revolt. Cortés' genius lay precisely in his ability to play this role, to surround himself with charisma in the eyes of the Indians. Cortés played this role to the hilt, but with calculated duplicity. For the Spaniards had not come to Middle America to restore an indigenous society. They acted from autonomous motives which were not those of their Indian allies. Accepting the command of a people deeply accustomed to obedience through long participation in a hierarchical social order, they began to enact their own purposes, to realize their own ends, which were those of Spanish society and therefore alien and hostile to those of the Indians among whom they had begun to move.

To understand these ends, we must try to understand Spanish society of that time, a task in which we moderns experience a particular difficulty. The reduced and impoverished Spain of today [1959] obscures our understanding of the once wealthy and powerful empire upon which the sun never set. All too often, we tend to interpret the past by reconstructing it in the image of the present. Again, too often, we view Spain through the lens of a powerful political mythology, a mythology forged both consciously and unconsciously in Protestant countries to advance the liberating cause of Protestantism and republican institutions against Catholicism and monarchical absolutism. According to this mythol-

ogy, a singularly partisan deity ranged himself on the side of human freedom and economic progress against "feudal" Spain. While in northern Europe right-thinking and industrious men put their shoulders to the wheel of the Industrial Revolution, the Catholic South remained sunk in medieval sloth. But the rise and decline of a society is not explained by recourse to political demonology; the truth is at once simpler and more complex.

Let us not forget that the Mediterranean and not the European North is the homeland of capitalism and of the Industrial Revolution. Italy, southern France, Spain, and southern Germany witnessed the rise of the first factories, the first banks, the first great fairs. At the time of the discovery of America, the Iberian Peninsula harbored thriving cities, humming with expanding wealth and trade. The sources of this prosperity were manifold: the sale of wool to England or to Flanders; the sale of iron wares to the Levant; the seizure and sale of slaves from the African coast; the quick raid on a Saracen stronghold or a pirate's lair. These were enterprises which demanded the utmost in individual stamina and personal valor; they were also exceedingly profitable. And in response the culture which fed upon an extension of these enterprises elaborated its peculiar image of the manly ideal: the overweening personality possessed of skill and courage. This ideal belonged as much to the medieval past as to the commercial future. It was inherently contradictory and revealed in its contradiction the opposing forces at work within the social system that gave it birth. Its heroes act; but the cultural forms of their acts are not only rich in the symbolic pageantry of the medieval knight-crusader but also supreme examples of the exaltation of Renaissance man pioneering on new frontiers of thought and human behavior. Covertly, more than once, the goal of the act is profit, conceived as personal enhancement through the acquisition of gold and riches.

There were in reality two Spains, or two tendencies at work in the Iberian Peninsula. The first tendency was aristocratic, oriented toward warfare and the gain of riches by warfare. It was exemplified most clearly by the armies of Castile, composed of a warlike nobility and a warlike peasantry. These armies had been forged in the fight against the Moors, first in raid and counter-raid, later in the systematic reconquest of the Moorish southland. The nobility, partly organized into religious orders of monastic warriors, saw in warfare a ready source of ego enhancement and looted wealth. Its traditional economic interest lay in the extension of grazing range for its herds of cattle and sheep, coupled with a flourishing export trade in wool to northern Europe. The peasantry, on the other hand, consisted of soldier-cultivators, recruited into the army by promises and guaranties of freedom from servile encumbrances and charters of local self-rule. These peasants desired land, free land, to divide among their sons. In warfare, both nobility and peasantry gained their divergent ends.

The other Spain, the other Spanish trend, was less involved in warfare; it pointed toward capital accumulation through rising industry and trade in the hands of a town-based bourgeoisie. Such entrepreneurs existed in all Peninsular towns; but only in eastern Spain, centered in Catalonia, had they gained sufficient power to check the expansionist desires of the aristocratic soldiery. In this part of Spain, a bloody peasant war had smashed the remnants of a feudal system of the classic European kind. Traditional relationships in which a lord exercised economic, judicial, and social control of a group of serfs had given way to new social ties. A free peasantry populated the countryside; a prosperous bourgeoisie, long oriented toward maritime trade, controlled the towns. The country was undergoing incipient industrialization, and the cloth, leather, and iron wares so produced were exchanged in the eastern Mediterranean for the drugs, dyestuffs, and luxury goods of the Orient.

By 1492, these two Spains were headed for collision, a conflict which might well have altered the face of Spain but for the discovery of America. The fall of the last Moorish redoubt put an end to the limitless acquisition of land by conquest and to the easy accumulation of wealth by forceful seizure; 1492 marked the closing of the Spanish frontier. As land became scarce, interests which had run parallel up to that time began to conflict; while the soldier-peasant wanted unencumbered land, the aristocrat wanted open range for sheep and cattle or land for dependent cultivators. With the distribution of the fruits of conquest among the conquerors, moreover, readily available wealth became unavailable. How was new wealth to be produced? To this problem the merchant-entrepreneur of the towns had an answer: capital investment in industry coupled with the reduction of aristocratic power. At this moment, however, the doors to the New World swung wide open to reveal a new frontier: dream cities of gold, endless expanses of land, huge reservoirs of dependent labor. The merchant-entrepreneur receded into obscurity; the knight-adventurer, the visionary of wealth through seizure at sword's point, gained new impetus.

It was this new frontier which settled the fate of Spain. Paradoxically, Spanish industry was to be swamped in a tide of gold from the Indies, which spelled its ultimate ruin; paradoxically, also, the new frontier destroyed the class which might have carried such industrialization to a successful conclusion. For in this New World, all men—peasant, merchant, impoverished noble, noble merchant-prince—could dream of becoming lords of land, Indians, and gold. Men who in Spain might have allied themselves politically and economically with the entrepreneurs and traders of the towns against the aristocrat could in this new venture identify themselves with the ideal of the mounted noble. Men who in Spain might have spurred the growth of the middle classes were here converted into its opponents. The year 1492 might have marked Spain's awakening to a new reality; instead, it marked the coming of a new dream, a new utopia.

Where men of varied pasts and varied interests engage in a common enterprise, belief in a universal utopia renders possible their common action. Utopia asks no questions of reality; it serves to bind men in the service of a dream. Belief in it postpones the day of reckoning on which the spoils will be divided and men will draw their swords to validate their personal utopia against the counterclaims of their comrades-in-arms. Some came to the New World to find gold; others to find order; still others to save souls. Yet in their common dream they asked no questions of one another. For the time being, their dream was validated by their common experience on board ship, by their common sufferings in the face of the enemy, by their common victory.

In the course of their common adventure in utopia they also achieved a set of common usages and understandings which made "the culture of the Conquest" different from their ancestral culture and from the culture still to be in the New World. Their purposes had a transcendental simplicity: gold, subjects, souls. This simplicity patterned their behavior and their thought, some of it conscious, self-imposed. The colonist-to-be in search of his liberty casts off the traditional forms which he has experienced as shackles and encumbrances. The royal official in search of order abhors the tangle of inherited forms of the Old World. The friar leaves behind him a world which is old and corrupt; in utopia he seeks austerity and clarity. The very process of migration produces a simplified stock of cultural forms.

Men drawn from all walks of life, the conquerors were not a complete sample of their ancestral society. They did not bring with them complete knowledge of the gamut of Spanish culture. Some of this age-old heritage they could not reproduce in the New World because they lacked acquaintance with it. Some of it, however, vanished in the crucible of their common experience, in their need to develop a common cultural denominator to facilitate their common task. Spain, but recently unified under one crown, had remained a cultural plural, a mosaic of many parts. Yet the culture of the conquerors was, by contrast, highly homogeneous. This simplification extended to material goods: only one plow, of the many Spanish plows, was transmitted to the New World; only a few techniques of fishing were selected from the plethora of Spanish fishing techniques and transplanted into the new setting. Simplification extended also to symbolic behavior: speech undergoes a leveling, a planing-down of the formalities of Castilian Spanish into a plain and utilitarian idiom. Left behind are the many Spanish folk fiestas in honor of a multitude of beloved local saints; they yield in the New World to the measured and standardized performance of the formal celebrations of way stations in the life of Christ. The culture of the conquest was, as George Foster has pointed out, *sui generis*. In vain one looks in the culture of these men for the rich varied regional heritage of the mother country.

Some of the conquerors wanted gold—gold, the actual tangible substance, not the intangible "promises to pay" of later capitalism. In this they were children of their times, caught in the contradiction between medieval magic and the modern search for profits. All over Europe men longed for gold, encountered gold in dreams, dug for it under trees and in caves, sold their souls to the devil for it, labored over retorts to obtain it from base metals such as iron or lead. It was a kind of illness, and Cortés stated it that way—half cynically and half realistically—in addressing the first Mexica noble he met: "The Spaniards are troubled with a disease of the heart for which gold is the specific remedy." The illness was greed, but beyond greed the desire for personal liberty, escape of the ego from bondage to other men, "spiritual autarchy," as Eliseo Vivas has said, "which is achieved only when you are able to say to another man, *a mi no me manda nadie*—no one bosses me; I am lord because I have land and gold and Indians, and I need not beg any favors from you or any one else." This is the new self-made man talking, the medieval adventurer on the threshold of capitalism, knight-errant in cultural form but primitive capitalist in disguise. The goal is medieval—never again to bend one's will to that of another—but the instrument is modern: the instrument of wealth.

Utopia thus bears at the outset the mark of a contradiction between past and future, a contradiction never wholly overcome. The contradiction is most startlingly illuminated when the Spanish entrepreneur is compared with his contemporary English rival. "The Englishmen," says Salvador de Madariaga, "though on the surface more self-seeking, were in depth more socially minded; the Spaniards, though in appearance more statesmanlike and creative, more intent on 'ennobling' cities and setting up kingdoms, were more self-centered. The Englishman, with his dividends, socialized his adventures, gain, booty; the Spaniard, with his hospitals, foundations, cathedrals, colleges and marquisates, raised a monument to his own self. . . ." The rise of puritanism in the Anglo-American world, so brilliantly analyzed by Max Weber and Richard Tawney, destroyed the contradiction between individual goals and cultural means. For in accepting the Protestant ethic of work and capital accumulation as virtue, the entrepreneur made himself an instrument of production, harnessed himself to the process of capital formation. In Anglo-America, the very means thus became the ends; in Ibero-America, means and ends remained at war with one another, contradictory, unresolved.

If some came in search of gold and its promise of personal liberty, others came in search of order. Their deity was the absolute monarch; their religion the new religion of the reason of state. At the end of the fifteenth century the Spanish crown had just emerged victorious in its political battles against its rivals. With the help of the rising middle classes and the peasantry, it had successfully defeated the attempts of the aristocrats who wished to reduce the king once again to the passive position of a mere *primus inter pares.* Yet this political success but threatened to put the king into the hands of the penny-wise merchants who wished to trade support for a veto over his military and bureaucratic expenditures. The long period of the reconquest had also brought with it a spate of *fueros* or local charters which exempted one or the other local or professional body from the application of the general law; many a king had traded local autonomy for support against the Moorish enemy.

In the conquest of the New World, the crown saw its opportunity to escape the limitations of internal Spanish politics. Gold from the Indies would enrich not only the eager adventurer; a fifth of all gold and silver mined in the New World would be the king's, to finance a royal army, navy, and officialdom, to build the bases of absolutist power upon institutions wholly independent of nobility, middle classes, or peasant cultivators. Wealth from the Indies would underwrite a state standing above all classes, above the endless quarrels of contending interest groups. This state would speak with a new voice, with a new will. It would no longer be bound by precedent; it would set aside solutions which had become traditional, overgrown with the "cake of custom" and with compromise. The New World would not have to grow, piecemeal, in the shadows of ancient complexities: it would be a planned world, projected into reality by the royal will and its executioners. Thus utopia would become law, and law utopian. If Spanish towns had been small, cramped within their rings of fortifications, crowded around small irregular squares, then the towns of the New World would be large, open, unfortified; built upon the gridiron plan; centered upon a spacious square dominated by church and city-hall as twin symbols of sacred and secular power; an architectural utopia conceived by Italian architect-dreamers and built in the New World by royal mandate.

Was it true that many Indians lived in scattered hamlets instead of stationary, circumscribed, concentrated settlements? Then let there be a law to force them to live in nucleated towns, each with its own church, each surrounded by its own fields—within a measured radius of 560 yards from the church steeple—so that they could learn to order their lives to the tolling of church bells and to the commands of royal officers. Land and people of utopia had both been conquered by the sword; but it would be the dry scratching of the goose-quill pen upon parchment that would turn utopia into reality. Let each Indian keep twelve chickens and six turkeys and sell them for no more than 4 reales per turkey and 1½ reales per chicken; let each Indian working in a textile mill receive a daily ration of eighteen tortillas or fourteen tamales, plus chili, chickpeas, and beans. No problem was too insignificant to demand solution, and all solutions were solutions of law. Utopia was to be born also with this fatal deficiency implicit in the contradiction of law and reality. Reality is too protean to be wholly covered by law; it soon grows through, around, and over law, leaving but a hollow shell of words, a gesture of etiquette to gloss over the gap between wish and existence. The Latin American world still bears this legacy of law as a gesture to initiate action, to create a new order, and—when the energy of the gesture is spent—to use the law as wish, to wipe out a reality grown beyond law and order, beyond utopia.

Utopia contained many houses. If some men longed for gold, to build upon it their untrammeled liberty, and if others sought Indian subjects to rule and exercise in the spirit of the new order, so there were men who came to save souls. Upon the ruins of pagan shrines and idols in a new continent filled with souls hungry for salvation, yet uncorrupted by the age-old vices of the Old World, they would erect their own utopia: the prelude on earth of the Kingdom of Heaven. To these prophets of salvation, the conquest of the New World was the call to a great spiritual task: the defeat of Satan in his own redoubt, the redemption of souls languishing in his power, the annunciation of the faith in the one true God. The shock troops of this new faith were the friars, members of the monastic orders, strongly influenced by the reformist religious currents of the times. In some countries, such movements were soon to feed the flames of the Protestant revolution. If this did not happen in Spain, it was not because Spain lacked inflammable intellectual tinder. The economic and political development of the country had given strong impetus to men who began to question long-accepted opinions and to explore new interpretations of Catholicism. Most of these questioners were influenced by Erasmus of Rotterdam (1466–1536), whose teaching de-emphasized the importance of formal ritual and stressed the promptings to piety of an "inner" voice, and by the utopian and reformist thought of Thomas More (1478–1535) and Luis Vives (1492–1540).

The reason that this new religious current did not explode into open rebellion against accepted religious forms is to be found in the character of the Spanish state and the circumstances which surrounded it rather than in the intellectual heterodoxy of the movement. The Spanish state had no need to break with the papacy: it dictated ecclesiastical appointments in its own territory; it possessed the right to read and suppress papal bulls before making them public; it controlled the office of the Inquisition; it even sponsored autonomy in doctrinal matters through its support of the belief in the immaculate conception of the Virgin Mary, long before this belief became official church dogma at the Council of Trent (1545–63). In other European states the hunger for land and capital was one of the chief underlying motives for religious reformation; after the break with Rome, the estates of the church were divided among the members of the Protestant faction. In Spain, the frontiers had not yet closed. Until 1492 land and wealth were still to be had by fighting the Moors in southern Spain in the name of religion, and that year witnessed the opening of the new frontier in the New World, with its promise of gold and glory for all takers.

Under Cardinal Ximénez de Cisneros, the Erasmists received royal approval. The crown saw in their effort to restore the simplicity and austerity of primitive Christianity—in the face of decay and corruption—a spiritual counterpart to its own efforts to centralize Spain and to endow the new empire with a unified sense of mission. Many of the friars who came to the New World had taken part in this religious renewal. The first twelve friars to set foot in New Spain—the so-called Apostolic Twelve—had all worked to spread the gospel of primitive Christendom in southern Spain. Fray Juan de Zumárraga (1461?–1548), the first archbishop of Mexico, was a follower of Erasmus and familiar with the utopian writings of Sir Thomas More. Vasco de Quiroga (1470–1565), the first bishop of Michoacán, actually established a replica of Sir Thomas More's Utopia among the Indian communities of his bishopric. All these soldiers of the faith favored poverty over wealth, communal property over private property. Carefully they labored to purge Catholicism of the accumulation of ritual, selecting from the profusion of religious ritual only the major ceremonials celebrating the way-stations of

Christ's life. This desire for purity and simplicity they also expressed in their great single-naved churches, symbolic of the homogeneity of primitive Christian worship, uncluttered by devotion to smaller altars and lateral naves.

The utopia of gold and liberty crumbled in the tension between exaltation of the self, through valiant deeds, and wealth, the instrument selected for their validation. The utopia of order remained arrested in the legal gesture, attempting to stem the tide of real behavior. The utopia of faith, too, was to founder, hoped-for morality all too often impotent in the face of stubborn secular demand. And yet, conversion proved a success. The romanticists have long delighted in discovering the idols behind altars, the Gods of the Cave transformed into Christs hanging upon the Cross, the earth goddesses disguised as Catholic Virgins, the braziers burning copal gum on the steps of the churches, and other evidences of pre-Conquest heritage in the religious beliefs and practices of modern Indians. There is much that is Indian in the Catholicism of Middle America; but more surprising than the numerous survivals of pre-Conquest ideas and rituals is the organizational success of the Catholic utopia in a country of different religions and languages. Wherever you go in Middle America, you encounter the images of the Catholic saints and the churches built by the conquerors. Christ and the Virgin may have been transmuted by the adoration of men who had worshipped the Sun and the Moon and the Earth and the Lords of the Four Directions; but when an Indian speaks of a human being today, he does not say "a man"; he says "a Christian," a believer.

How is this success to be explained? It is easy to dismember men with cannons; it is more difficult to tame their minds. Certainly military defeat played a part, because it provided a visible demonstration of the impotence and decadence of the Mexica gods. The Children of the Sun had died by the sword as they had lived by the sword. The old gods had failed. When the Spaniards had demanded that the Totonac of Cempoala destroy their idols, the people had recoiled in horror; yet when the conquerors hurled the idols to the

ground and broke them to pieces, the idols had remained mute and defenseless. They had not smitten the foreigners; they had failed to show the power that was in them. When the priests released the stones from the Pyramid of Cholula which held back the magic water that was in the mountain so that it would drown the strange men in a flood, the channel remained dry, and their magic deserted them. When the Children of the Sun, the Toltec rulers of Tenochtitlán, called down the wrath of their terrible idol Hummingbird-on-the-Left upon their enemies, Hummingbird-on-the-Left remained silent. The mutilated idols of their gods now rested on the bottom of the lake from which they had set out to conquer the universe for the sun; and the rubble of their temples served as fill for the new city of Mexico which was to arise upon these ruins. The old gods were dead, and powerless.

Not that these old gods had been so greatly loved. We know—or we can guess—that the will of these gods and the burden of human sacrifice rested heavily upon the land. Worship of warrior gods and human sacrifice were religious activities consonant with the military character of Mexica expansion. Inevitably, however, peace and political consolidation brought to the fore alternative religious explanations of a less militaristic character. Quetzalcoatl, the Shining Serpent, served as a symbolic form through which these new interpretations and longings could find expression. His latter-day attributes as a harbinger of peaceful productivity and human wisdom bear surprising similarity to the ideological dictates of Christianity. Indeed, the Spanish friars came to believe that Quetzalcoatl had been none other than the apostle Thomas, come to the New World to convert the Indians. The longing for peace and for an end to bloodshed provided a fertile soil for the diffusion of the Christian message.

Both religions, moreover, believed in a structured and ordered supernatural world, in which more powerful, unseen, and unfathomable divinities stood above local supernatural mediators of lesser scope and power that were yet more immediately tangible. The Middle American peasant, like his Spanish counterpart, focused his religious interest on these lowlier supernatural helpers. He was more interested in the powers that affected his crops, his children, his family, and the people with whom he was in immediate and personal contact, than in the ultimate powers and their manifestations, which absorbed the interest of the religious specialist. Among the gods of a multi-headed pantheon, his daily concern was with the gods of the earth, fertility, rain and water, with illness, with the immediate short-range future, with the malevolence of his neighbors. Where the Spanish peasant worshipped wooden saints, the Middle American peasant worshipped clay idols; both had recourse to the magical practices of folk medicine; both had a strong sense of omens; and both believed in the reality of witches who could be ordinary everyday people during the day and malevolent spirits in animal disguise at night.

The priests, the specialists of both religions, on the other hand, were the heirs of rich and complex intellectual traditions, trained in the esoteric interpretation of religious symbols whether these symbols concerned multiple incarnations of Tezcatlipoca or the implications of the Revelation of St. John the Divine. The concern of the priest was not the concern of the peasant, and yet the same religious structure could embrace both. As long as the priests remained in command, as ultimate mediators between gods and men and ultimate interpreters of this relationship, men could adapt the manifold religious patterns to suit their personal and local concerns. What was true of religious concerns also held true of gods. A god could be one or triune, unique or multiple, and interpretation could stress his oneness at one time, his multiplicity at another. The Mexica pantheon had embraced many local gods, and the Mexica priesthood had labored to equate these gods with their own inherited deities or with one another. The Catholic Church had a similar tradition of flexibility. Just as the cloak of the Virgin hid many a local Persephone or Isis along the shores of the European Mediterranean, or as an Odin hanging himself from the tree of life became a Christ, so a Hummingbird-on-the-Left became a Spanish St. James riding down upon the hea-

thens; a Tlaloc, a Christian Señor de Sacromonte; a God of the Cave, the Lord of Chalma; and Our Lady Spirit, the Virgin of Guadalupe.

The Catholic Church drove out the priests of the old gods and manned the pivotal points of the religious hierarchy with men ordained in its own cult. It destroyed the old idols and put an end to human sacrifices, burned the sacred picture books and relegated to oblivion much of the calendric and divinatory knowledge of its predecessors; but it also offered the common man a way in which he could cast his traditional attachments into new forms. The Catholic Church, like the solar religion of the Mexica rigid at the heights of command but flexible on the level of the peasant household, built a bridge from the old order to the new. As Frank Tannenbaum has said, "It gave the Indian an opportunity . . . to save his faith in his own gods."

This transition from the old to the new was eased also by an astonishing similarity in ritual and symbol between the old and the new religion. A Nahua or an Otomí would hardly know what to make of a Spanish friar who, hampered by the language barrier, pointed first to the sky to indicate heaven and then to earth to indicate hell, as a first lesson in Catholic catechism. But rituals can be observed and learned by imitation. Both religious traditions had a rite of baptism. In Catholicism, the child was baptized and named, thus including him among the true believers. The Mexica similarly bathed and named the child in a religious rite, and the Maya celebrated with a ceremony the first time the child was carried astride the hip. Both religious traditions had a kind of confession. The Mexica and the inhabitants of the Gulf coast confessed their sexual transgressions to a priest of the earth goddess Filth-Eater; the Zapotec had annual public confessions; and the Maya confessed themselves either to priests or members of their families in case of illness. Both religious traditions possessed a ritual of communion. The Catholics drank wine and swallowed a wafer to symbolize their contact with the divine blood and body of Christ; the Mexica consumed images of the gods made of amaranth and liberally anointed with sacrificial blood. Both people used incense in their churches; both fasted and did penance; both went on pilgrimages to holy places; both kept houses of celibate virgins. Both believed in the existence of a supernatural mother; and both believed in virgin birth. Where Catholics held that Mary conceived immaculately through the power of the Holy Spirit, the Mexica believed that their goddess Coatlícue had given birth to Hummingbird-on-the-Left, impregnated by an obsidian knife which fell from the sky. Both people made use of the cross. A white St. Andrew's Cross, representing the four directions of the universe, often graced the hat and shield of the Shining Serpent, and the Maya made frequent use of the symbol of the foliated cross. The Spaniards represented their sacred stories in passion plays; the Middle Americans represented the annual changes of vegetation and activities in their sacrifices.

The Catholic missionaries well recognized the danger which lay in the maintenance of similar outward forms of ritual upon conversion. Yet they were themselves unable to decide whether these similarities were merely the work of Satan laboring to duplicate in his hellish church the rituals of the church sanctified by God, or whether they might not indeed represent the precipitate of some previous Christian teaching, brought to the New World perhaps by no less a personage than the apostle Thomas. Whatever their doubts, the formal similarities between the two religious traditions permitted an easy transition for the worshipper and gave him continuity precisely in the realm in which continuity was vital: the realm of religious behavior.

Nor did the psychology of Spanish Catholicism differ greatly from the psychology of the Mesoamerican solar cult. The Spanish ideal of the austere knight, defending his honor and the Virgin against Moors or other unbelievers, was not far removed from the Mexica ideal of the jaguar-eagle knight, whose obsidian sword insured victory and sacrificial victims for the hungry deities of war. In both religions cruelty against others in warfare and exalted pride went hand in hand with sacrificial penance—cruelty against the self, performed by a Spanish con-

queror in a hairshirt, by a Mexica noble torturing his flesh with the sharp spikes of the century plant.

True to their hierarchical habits, the Spaniards expended their greatest religious effort in converting the nobles, who became their first converts, partly because of the similarity of motivation, partly because of a desire to achieve a secure place in the new Spanish hierarchy through baptism and Christian vows. At Tlaxcala, the first center of the Spanish missionary effort, the local aristocracy strove mightily to reserve for itself a monopoly of all new religious offices, even those of cook, janitor, and gardener in the new monasteries. Their children were the first beneficiaries of Spanish ecclesiastical schooling. They used their power to set the feet of their own tributaries upon the new road to salvation; these tributaries thus came to church, as Fray Mendieta said, "more for the sake of outer appearance, to follow the orders of the *principales* who wanted to deceive them than to find a remedy for their souls." With the nobles firmly dedicated to the worship of the new religion, the commoners could be converted in mass, often with no more than a token understanding of the new divinities they were to worship. Pedro de Gante, exemplary Franciscan and kinsman of Charles V, baptized Indians in Mexico City at a daily rate of 14,000.

To the task of mass conversion, moreover, the church brought an exemplary table of organization. Like the Middle American religion, it drew a line between religious specialists and lay worshippers. In both traditions, the priests were the final spokesmen of the divine realm, in contact with a world to which ordinary men had no access. In both religions, long training was required to make a man worthy of his special role, and in both religions fasts, penances, self-torture, and sexual abstinence were required of priests to maintain their spiritual worth in the sight of the divine powers. Throughout the exercise of their spiritual role on earth, dress, residence, speech, and comportment marked them off from ordinary men. Such parallelism again eased the transition from the worship of the old gods to the worship of the new, maintaining as it did the hierarchy of channels through which supernatural commands were passed down to the lay believer.

To be sure, the Catholic Church was organized internally to take maximum advantage of the opportunities so offered. Its division into holy orders and secular clergy made for great flexibility in a situation where an advance guard was needed to establish new beachheads of the faith, while a rear-guard took over and consolidated the gains. The friars were the advance guard; the abiding missionary work of the sixteenth century which laid the basis for all later religious efforts was probably carried out by no more than one thousand individuals. Established in fortified churches within the core areas of the newly won land, they spread out in "missions of penetration" into areas where Spanish political control was often still in doubt, sometimes ahead of Spanish armies, sometimes in their wake. Always they linked these outposts with their home bases through "liaison missions," to which they could retreat or where they could seek new strength to carry on their task of penetration. The secular clergy, the ordinary priesthood, carried out the work of consolidation.

Inevitably there were quarrels and conflicts of jurisdiction as the work progressed, as well as conflicts of temperament. The holy orders recruited men whose personalities differed markedly from those characteristic of the regular clergy. The friars favored individuals who were more adventurous and utopian in outlook, as well as less amenable to routine and less adapted to the day-to-day life of a going society. The secular clergy showed more conservatism, less of a tendency to sacrifice reality to otherworldly visions and schemes. Thus the larger church benefited by

its possession of both kinds of men, both kinds of organization. When the task of conversion was completed, the work of shepherding the flock through its daily tribulations could be turned over to men capable of preserving the gains.

The eventual adjustment of the religious dream to mundane reality was less than utopia, and yet it left an impress on the Indian population such as no other religious or political current has done to this day. Ultimately the message of salvation spelled hope for the Indian, not only hope in the transcendental realm of a supernatural life after death but hope on earth, where utopia was yielding to the pressure of all too secular interests. Men would labor to deny him his humanity, to defend his use as a resource, a tool to be used and discarded at will; but against such claims of politicians, lawyers, and theologians, Pope Paul III would in 1537 assert, in his bull "Sublimis Deus":

> The sublime God so loved the human race that He not only created man in such wise that he might participate in the good that other creatures enjoy, but also endowed him with capacity to attain to the inaccessible and invisible Supreme Good and behold it face to face[;] . . . all are capable of receiving the doctrines of the faith. . . . We . . . consider . . . that the Indians are truly men. . . .

To the Indian, the rite of baptism thus proved an assertion of his essential humanity, to be a man with human claims upon other men. Of this right no colonist or royal official could rob him. When the Indian re-emerges from beneath the wreckage of utopia, we find that he has rebuilt and cemented his new life with bonds drawn from the new religion, at once his opium, his consolation, and his hope of ultimate justice.

2

THE PLANTER'S WIFE: THE EXPERIENCE OF WHITE WOMEN IN SEVENTEENTH-CENTURY MARYLAND

LOIS GREEN CARR AND LORENA S. WALSH

To reconstruct the lives of ordinary people, historians must often rely on the use of public records, those places where everyday life intersects the operation of the state. In this essay Carr and Walsh draw upon public records—immigrant lists, court records, and probate reports—to reconstruct the lives of women in seventeenth-century Maryland.

Unlike New England, which was settled by religious dissenters who sought to create a more Godly society in the New World, Maryland was a colony founded with a single purpose: to raise tobacco for planter profit and for royal and proprietary revenue. Thus Maryland attracted a different sort of colonist. Whereas New England towns attracted families of predominantly middling station, the typical Maryland immigrant was a young, unmarried man from the lower ranks of society.

A second important difference between the northern and southern colonies was the presence of malaria-bearing insects in the Maryland tidewater. The Marylander had first to survive a brutal "seasoning" time, during which he fought to overcome the malarial infection. In the event he survived, he then faced the prospect of a life of arduous labor tending, weeding, transplanting, and harvesting tobacco.

What was the place of women in such a society? To answer this question, Carr and Walsh focus on the life course of the women who came to the tobacco colony as indentured servants in the seventeenth century and compare their lives as colonists with those of the sisters, cousins, and female friends they left behind.

Why do you think these English women abandoned the relative comforts of their native England for the primitive and brutal conditions found in Maryland? How do these immigrants compare with those who settled in New England, discussed by Breen and Foster in Reading 3?

Four facts were basic to all human experience in seventeenth-century Maryland. First, for most of the period the great majority of inhabitants had been born in what we now call Britain. Population increase in Maryland did not result primarily from births in the colony before the late 1680s and did not produce a predominantly native population of adults before the first decade of the eighteenth century. Second, immigrant men could not expect to live beyond age forty-three, and 70 percent would die before age fifty. Women may have had even shorter lives. Third, perhaps 85 percent of the immigrants, and practically all the unmarried immigrant women, arrived as indentured servants and consequently married late. Family groups were never predominant in the immigration to Maryland and were a significant part for only a brief time at mid-century. Fourth,

Reprinted from *The William and Mary Quarterly,* Third Series, 34 (1977), 542–571, with permission of the authors.

many more men than women immigrated during the whole period. These facts—immigrant predominance, early death, late marriage, and sexual imbalance—created circumstances of social and demographic disruption that deeply affected family and community life.

We need to assess the effects of this disruption on the experience of women in seventeenth-century Maryland. Were women degraded by the hazards of servitude in a society in which everyone had left community and kin behind and in which women were in short supply? Were traditional restraints on social conduct weakened? If so, were women more exploited or more independent and powerful than women who remained in England? Did any differences from English experience which we can observe in the experience of Maryland women survive the transformation from an immigrant to a predominantly native-born society with its own kinship networks and community traditions? The tentative argument put forward here is that the answer to all these questions is Yes. There were degrading aspects of servitude, although these probably did not characterize the lot of most women; there were fewer restraints on social conduct, especially in courtship, than in England; women were less protected but also more powerful than those who remained at home; and at least some of these changes survived the appearance in Maryland of New World creole communities. However, these issues are far from settled, and we shall offer some suggestions as to how they might be further pursued.

Maryland was settled in 1634, but in 1650 there were probably no more than six hundred persons and fewer than two hundred adult women in the province. After that time population growth was steady; in 1704 a census listed 30,437 white persons, of whom 7,163 were adult women. Thus in discussing the experience of white women in seventeenth-century Maryland we are dealing basically with the second half of the century.

Marylanders of that period did not leave letters and diaries to record their New World experience or their relationships to one another. Nevertheless, they left trails in the public records

that give us clues. Immigrant lists kept in England and documents of the Maryland courts offer quantifiable evidence about the kinds of people who came and some of the problems they faced in making a new life. Especially valuable are the probate court records. Estate inventories reveal the kinds of activities carried on in the house and on the farm, and wills, which are usually the only personal statements that remain for any man or woman, show something of personal attitudes. This essay relies on the most useful of the immigrant lists and all surviving Maryland court records, but concentrates especially on the surviving records of the lower Western Shore, an early-settled area highly suitable for tobacco. Most of this region comprised four counties: St. Mary's, Calvert, Charles, and Prince George's (formed in 1696 from Calvert and Charles). Inventories from all four counties, wills from St. Mary's and Charles, and court proceedings from Charles and Prince George's provide the major data.

Because immigrants predominated, who they were determined much about the character of Maryland society. The best information so far available comes from lists of indentured servants who left the ports of London, Bristol, and Liverpool. These lists vary in quality, but at the very least they distinguish immigrants by sex and general destination. A place of residence in England is usually given, although it may not represent the emigrant's place of origin; and age and occupation are often noted. These lists reveal several characteristics of immigrants to the Chesapeake and, by inference, to Maryland.

Servants who arrived under indenture included yeomen, husbandmen, farm laborers, artisans, and small tradesmen, as well as many untrained to any special skill. They were young: over half of the men on the London lists of 1683–1684 were aged eighteen to twenty-two. They were seldom under seventeen or over twenty-eight. The women were a little older; the great majority were between eighteen and twenty-five, and half were aged twenty to twenty-two. Most servants contracted for four or five years service, although those under fifteen were to serve at least seven years. These youthful immigrants represented a wide range of English society. All were seeking opportunities they had not found at home.

However, many immigrants—perhaps about half—did not leave England with indentures but paid for their passage by serving according to the custom of the country. Less is known about their social characteristics, but some inferences are possible. From 1661, customary service was set by Maryland laws that required four-year (later five-year) terms for men and women who were twenty-two years or over at arrival and longer terms for those who were younger. A requirement of these laws enables us to determine something about age at arrival of servants who came without indentures. A planter who wished to obtain more than four or five years of service had to take his servant before the county court to have his or her age judged and a written record made. Servants aged over twenty-one were not often registered, there being no incentive for a master to pay court fees for those who would serve the minimum term. Nevertheless, a comparison of the ages of servants under twenty-two recorded in Charles County, 1658–1689, with those under twenty-two on the London list is revealing. Of Charles County male servants (N = 363), 77.1 percent were aged seventeen or under, whereas on the London list (N = 196), 77.6 percent were eighteen or over. Women registered in Charles County court were somewhat older than the men, but among those under twenty-two (N = 107), 5.5 percent were aged twenty-one, whereas on the London list (N = 69), 46.4 percent had reached this age. Evidently, some immigrants who served by custom were younger than those who came indentured, and this age difference probably characterized the two groups as a whole. Servants who were not only very young but had arrived without the protection of a written contract were possibly of lower social origins than were servants who came under indenture. The absence of skills among Charles County servants who served by custom supports this supposition.

Whatever their status, one fact about immigrant women is certain: many fewer came than men. Immigrant lists, headright lists, and itemizations of servants in inventories show severe imbalance. On a London immigrant list of 1634–1635 men outnumbered women six to one. From the 1650s at least until the 1680s most sources show a ratio of three to one. From then on, all sources show some, but not great, improvement. Among immigrants from Liverpool over the years 1697–1707 the ratio was just under two and one half to one.

Why did not more women come? Presumably, fewer wished to leave family and community to venture into a wilderness. But perhaps more important, women were not as desirable as men to merchants and planters who were making fortunes raising and marketing tobacco, a crop that requires large amounts of labor. The gradual improvement in the sex ratio among servants toward the end of the century may have been the result of a change in recruiting the needed labor. In the late 1660s the supply of young men willing to emigrate stopped increasing sufficiently to meet the labor demands of a growing Chesapeake population. Merchants who recruited servants for planters turned to other sources, and among these sources were women. They did not crowd the ships arriving in the Chesapeake, but their numbers did increase.

To ask the question another way, why did women come? Doubtless, most came to get a husband, an objective virtually certain of success in a land where women were so far outnumbered. The promotional literature, furthermore, painted bright pictures of the life that awaited men and women once out of their time; and various studies suggest that for a while, at least, the promoters were not being entirely fanciful. Until the 1660s, and to a lesser degree the 1680s, the expanding economy of Maryland and Virginia offered opportunities well beyond those available in England to men without capital and to the women who became their wives.

Nevertheless, the hazards were also great, and the greatest was untimely death. Newcomers promptly became ill, probably with malaria, and many died. What proportion survived is unclear; so far no one has devised a way of measuring it.

Recurrent malaria made the woman who survived seasoning less able to withstand other diseases, especially dysentery and influenza. She was especially vulnerable when pregnant. Expectation of life for everyone was low in the Chesapeake, but especially so for women. A woman who had immigrated to Maryland took an extra risk, though perhaps a risk not greater than she might have suffered by moving from her village to London instead.

The majority of women who survived seasoning paid their transportation costs by working for a four- or five-year term of service. The kind of work depended on the status of the family they served. A female servant of a small planter—who through about the 1670s might have had a servant—probably worked at the hoe. Such a man could not afford to buy labor that would not help with the cash crop. In wealthy families women probably were household servants, although some are occasionally listed in inventories of well-to-do planters as living on the quarters—that is, on plantations other than the dwelling plantation. Such women saved men the jobs of preparing food and washing linen but doubtless also worked in the fields. In middling households experience must have varied. Where the number of people to feed and wash for was large, female servants would have had little time to tend the crops.

Tracts that promoted immigration to the Chesapeake region asserted that female servants did not labor in the fields, except "nasty" wenches not fit for other tasks. This implies that most immigrant women expected, or at least hoped, to avoid heavy field work, which English women—at least those above the cottager's status—did not do. What proportion of female servants in Maryland found themselves demeaned by this unaccustomed labor is impossible to say, but this must have been the fate of some. A study of the distribution of female servants among wealth groups in Maryland might shed some light on this question. Nevertheless, we still would not know whether those purchased by the poor or sent to work on a quarter were women whose previous experience suited them for field labor.

An additional risk for the woman who came as a servant was the possibility of bearing a bastard. At least 20 percent of the female servants who came to Charles County between 1658 and 1705 were presented to the county court for this cause. A servant woman could not marry unless someone was willing to pay her master for the term she had left to serve. If a man made her pregnant, she could not marry him unless he could buy her time. Once a woman became free, however, marriage was clearly the usual solution. Only a handful of free women were presented in Charles County for bastardy between 1658 and 1705. Since few free women remained either single or widowed for long, not many were subject to the risk. The hazard of bearing a bastard was a hazard of being a servant.

This high rate of illegitimate pregnancies among servants raises lurid questions. Did men import women for sexual exploitation? Does John Barth's Whore of Dorset have a basis outside his fertile imagination? In our opinion, the answers are clearly No. Servants were economic investments on the part of planters who needed labor. A female servant in a household where there were unmarried men must have both provided and faced temptation, for the pressures were great in a society in which men outnumbered women by three to one. Nevertheless, the servant woman was in the household to work—to help feed and clothe the family and make tobacco. She was not primarily a concubine.

This point could be established more firmly if we knew more about the fathers of the bastards. Often the culprits were fellow servants or men recently freed but too poor to purchase the woman's remaining time. Sometimes the master was clearly at fault. But often the father is not identified. Some masters surely did exploit their female servants sexually. Nevertheless, masters were infrequently accused of fathering their servants' bastards, and those found guilty were punished as severely as were other men. Community mores did not sanction their misconduct.

A female servant paid dearly for the fault of unmarried pregnancy. She was heavily fined, and if no one would pay her fine, she was whipped.

Furthermore, she served an extra twelve to twenty-four months to repay her master for the "trouble of his house" and labor lost, and the fathers often did not share in this payment of damages. On top of all, she might lose the child after weaning unless by then she had become free, for the courts bound out bastard children at very early ages.

English life probably did not offer a comparable hazard to young unmarried female servants. No figures are available to show rates of illegitimacy among those who were subject to the risk, but the female servant was less restricted in England than in the Chesapeake. She did not owe anyone for passage across the Atlantic; hence it was easier for her to marry, supposing she happened to become pregnant while in service. Perhaps, furthermore, her temptations were fewer. She was not 3,000 miles from home and friends, and she lived in a society in which there was no shortage of women. Bastards were born in England in the seventeenth century, but surely not to as many as one-fifth of the female servants.

Some women escaped all or part of their servitude because prospective husbands purchased the remainder of their time. At least one promotional pamphlet published in the 1660s described such purchases as likely, but how often they actually occurred is difficult to determine. Suggestive is a 20 percent difference between the sex ratios found in a Maryland headright sample, 1658–1681, and among servants listed in lower Western Shore inventories for 1658–1679. Some of the discrepancy must reflect the fact that male servants were younger than female servants and therefore served longer terms; hence they had a greater chance of appearing in an inventory. But part of the discrepancy doubtless follows from the purchase of women for wives. Before 1660, when sex ratios were even more unbalanced and the expanding economy enabled men to establish themselves more quickly, even more women may have married before their terms were finished.

Were women sold for wives against their wills? No record says so, but nothing restricted a man from selling his servant to whomever he wished. Perhaps some women were forced into such marriages or accepted them as the least evil. But the man who could afford to purchase a wife—especially a new arrival—was usually already an established landowner. Probably most servant women saw an opportunity in such a marriage. In addition, the shortage of labor gave women some bargaining power. Many masters must have been ready to refuse to sell a woman who was unwilling to marry a would-be purchaser.

If a woman's time was not purchased by a prospective husband, she was virtually certain to find a husband once she was free. Those famous spinsters, Margaret and Mary Brent, were probably almost unique in seventeenth-century Maryland. In the four counties of the lower Western Shore only two of the women who left a probate inventory before the eighteenth century are known to have died single. Comely or homely, strong or weak, any young woman was too valuable to be overlooked, and most could find a man with prospects.

The woman who immigrated to Maryland, survived seasoning and service, and gained her freedom became a planter's wife. She had considerable liberty in making her choice. There were men aplenty, and no fathers or brothers were hovering to monitor her behavior or disapprove her preference. This is the modern way of looking at her situation, of course. Perhaps she missed the protection of a father, a guardian, or kinfolk, and the participation in her decision of a community to which she felt ties. There is some evidence that the absence of kin and the pressures of the sex ratio created conditions of sexual freedom in courtship that were not customary in England. A register of marriages and births for seventeenth-century Somerset County shows that about one-third of the immigrant women whose marriages are recorded were pregnant at the time of the ceremony—nearly twice the rate in English parishes. There is no indication of community objection to this freedom so long as marriage took place. No presentments for bridal pregnancy were made in any of the Maryland courts.

The planter's wife was likely to be in her mid-twenties at marriage. An estimate of minimum age at marriage for servant women can be made from lists of indentured servants who left London over the years 1683–1684 and from age judgments in Maryland county court records. If we assume that the 112 female indentured servants going to Maryland and Virginia whose ages are given in the London lists served full four-year terms, then only 1.8 percent married before age twenty, but 68 percent after age twenty-four. Similarly, if the 141 women whose ages were judged in Charles County between 1666 and 1705 served out their terms according to the custom of the country, none married before age twenty-two, and half were twenty-five or over. When adjustments are made for the ages at which wives may have been purchased, the figures drop, but even so the majority of women waited until at least age twenty-four to marry. Actual age at marriage in Maryland can be found for few seventeenth-century female immigrants, but observations for Charles and Somerset counties place the mean age at about twenty-five.

Because of the age at which an immigrant woman married, the number of children she would bear her husband was small. She had lost up to ten years of her childbearing life—the possibility of perhaps four or five children, given the usual rhythm of childbearing. At the same time, high mortality would reduce both the number of children she would bear over the rest of her life and the number who would live. One partner to a marriage was likely to die within seven years, and the chances were only one in three that a marriage would last ten years. In these circumstances, most women would not bear more than three or four children—not counting those stillborn—to any one husband, plus a posthumous child were she the survivor. The best estimates suggest that nearly a quarter, perhaps more, of the children born alive died during their first year and that 40 to 55 percent would not live to see age twenty. Consequently, one of her children would probably die in infancy, and another one or two would fail to reach adulthood. Wills left in St. Mary's County during the seventeenth century show the results. In 105 families over the years 1660 to 1680 only twelve parents left more than

three children behind them, including those conceived but not yet born. The average number was 2.3, nearly always minors, some of whom might die before reaching adulthood.

For the immigrant woman, then, one of the major facts of life was that although she might bear a child about every two years, nearly half would not reach maturity. The social implications of this fact are far-reaching. Because she married late in her childbearing years and because so many of her children would die young, the number who would reach marriageable age might not replace, or might only barely replace, her and her husband or husbands as child-producing members of the society. Consequently, so long as immigrants were heavily predominant in the adult female population, Maryland could not grow much by natural increase. It remained a land of newcomers.

This fact was fundamental to the character of seventeenth-century Maryland society, although its implications have yet to be fully explored. Settlers came from all parts of England and hence from differing traditions—in types of agriculture, forms of landholding and estate management, kinds of building construction, customary contributions to community needs, and family arrangements, including the role of women. The necessities of life in the Chesapeake required all immigrants to make adaptations. But until the native-born became predominant, a securely established Maryland tradition would not guide or restrict the newcomers.

If the immigrant woman had remained in England, she would probably have married at about the same age or perhaps a little later. But the social consequences of marriage at these ages in most parts of England were probably different. More children may have lived to maturity, and even where mortality was as high newcomers are not likely to have been the main source of population growth. The locally born would still dominate the community, its social organization, and its traditions. However, where there were exceptions, as perhaps in London, late age at marriage, combined with high mortality and heavy immigration, may have had consequences in some ways similar to those we have found in Maryland.

A hazard of marriage for seventeenth-century women everywhere was death in childbirth, but this hazard may have been greater than usual in the Chesapeake. Whereas in most societies women tend to outlive men, in this malaria-ridden area it is probable that men outlived women. Hazards of childbirth provide the likely reason that Chesapeake women died so young. Once a woman in the Chesapeake reached forty-five, she tended to outlive men who reached the same age. Darrett and Anita Rutman have found malaria a probable cause of an exceptionally high death rate among pregnant women, who are, it appears, peculiarly vulnerable to that disease.

This argument, however, suggests that immigrant women may have lived longer than their native-born daughters, although among men the opposite was true. Life tables created for men in Maryland show that those native-born who survived to age twenty could expect a life span three to ten years longer than that of immigrants, depending upon the region where they lived. The reason for the improvement was doubtless immunities to local diseases developed in childhood. A native woman developed these immunities, but, as we shall see, she also married earlier than immigrant women usually could and hence had more children. Thus she was more exposed to the hazards of childbirth and may have died a little sooner. Unfortunately, the life tables for immigrant women that would settle this question have so far proved impossible to construct.

However long they lived, immigrant women in Maryland tended to outlive their husbands—in Charles County, for example, by a ratio of two to one. This was possible, despite the fact that women were younger than men at death, because women were also younger than men at marriage. Some women were widowed with no living children, but most were left responsible for two or three. These were often tiny, and nearly always not yet sixteen.

This fact had drastic consequences, given the physical circumstances of life. People lived at a distance from one another, not even in villages, much less towns. The widow had left her kin

3,000 miles across an ocean, and her husband's family was also there. She would have to feed her children and make her own tobacco crop. Though neighbors might help, heavy labor would be required of her if she had no servants, until—what admittedly was usually not difficult—she acquired a new husband.

In this situation dying husbands were understandably anxious about the welfare of their families. Their wills reflected their feelings and tell something of how they regarded their wives. In St. Mary's and Charles counties during the seventeenth century, little more than one-quarter of the men left their widows with no more than the dower the law required—one-third of his land for her life, plus outright ownership of one-third of his personal property. (See Table I.) If there were no children, a man almost always left his widow his whole estate. Otherwise there were a variety of arrangements. (See Table II.)

During the 1660s, when testators begin to appear in quantity, nearly a fifth of the men who had children left all to their wives, trusting them to see that the children received fair portions. Thus in 1663 John Shircliffe willed his whole estate to his wife "towards the maintenance of herself and my children into whose tender care I do Commend them Desireing to see them brought up in the fear of God and the Catholick Religion and Chargeing them to be Dutiful and obedient to her." As the century progressed, husbands tended instead to give the wife all or a major part of the estate for her life, and to desig-

Table I

Bequests of Husbands to Wives, St. Mary's and Charles Counties, Maryland, 1640 to 1710

		Dower or less	
	N	**N**	**%**
1640s	6	2	34
1650s	24	7	29
1660s	65	18	28
1670s	86	21	24
1680s	64	17	27
1690s	83	23	28
1700s	74	25	34
Totals	402	113	28

Source: Wills, I–XIV, Hall of Records, Annapolis, Md.

Table II
Bequests of Husbands to Wives with Children, St. Mary's and Charles Counties,
Maryland, 1640 to 1710

	All estate		All or dwelling plantation for life		All or dwelling plantation for widowhood		All or dwelling plantation for minority of child		More than dower in other form		Dower or less or unknown	
N	N	%	N	%	N	%	N	%	N	%	N	%
1640s	3	1	33		33							2	67
1650s	16	1	6	2	13	1	6	1	6	4	25	7	44
1660s	45	8	18	8	18	2	4	3	7	9	20	15	33
1670s	61	4	7	21	34	2	3	3	5	13	21	18	30
1680s	52	5	10	19	37	2	4	2	4	11	21	13	25
1690s	69	1	1	31	45	7	10	2	3	10	14	18	26
1700s	62			20	32	6	10	2	3	14	23	20	32
Totals	308	20	6	101	33	20	6	13	4	61	20	93	30

Source: Wills, I–XIV.

nate how it should be distributed after her death. Either way, the husband put great trust in his widow, considering that he knew she was bound to remarry. Only a handful of men left estates to their wives only for their term of widowhood or until the children came of age. When a man did not leave his wife a life estate, he often gave her land outright or more than her dower third of his movable property. Such bequests were at the expense of his children and showed his concern that his widow should have a maintenance which young children could not supply.

A husband usually made his wife his executor and thus responsible for paying his debts and preserving the estate. Only 11 percent deprived their wives of such powers. In many instances, however, men also appointed overseers to assist their wives and to see that their children were not abused or their property embezzled. Danger lay in the fact that a second husband acquired control of all his wife's property, including her life estate in the property of his predecessor. Over half of the husbands who died in the 1650s and 1660s appointed overseers to ensure that their wills were followed. Some trusted to the overseers' "Care and good Conscience for the good of my widow and fatherless children." Others more explicitly made overseers responsible for seeing that "my said child . . . and the other [expected

child] (when pleases God to send it) may have their right Proportion of my Said Estate and that the said Children may be bred up Chiefly in the fear of God." A few men—but remarkably few—authorized overseers to remove children from households of stepfathers who abused them or wasted their property. On the whole, the absence of such provisions for the protection of the children points to the husband's overriding concern for the welfare of his widow and to his confidence in her management, regardless of the certainty of her remarriage. Evidently, in the politics of family life women enjoyed great respect.

We have implied that this respect was a product of the experience of immigrants in the Chesapeake. Might it have been instead a reflection of English culture? Little work is yet in print that allows comparison of the provisions for Maryland widows with those made for the widows of English farmers. Possibly, Maryland husbands were making traditional wills which could have been written in the communities they left behind. However, Margaret Spufford's recent study of three Cambridgeshire villages in the late sixteenth century and early seventeenth century suggests a different pattern. In one of these villages, Chippenham, women usually did receive a life interest in the property, but in the other two they did not. If the children were all minors, the widow controlled the property until the oldest son came of age, and then only if she did not remarry. In the majority of cases adult sons were given control of the property with instructions for the support of their mothers. Spufford suggests that the pattern found in Chippenham must have been very exceptional. On the basis of village censuses in six other counties, dating from 1624 to 1724, which show only 3 percent of widowed people heading households that included a married child, she argues that if widows commonly controlled the farm, a higher proportion should have headed such households. However, she also argues that widows with an interest in land would not long remain unmarried. If so, the low percentage may be deceptive. More direct work with wills needs to be done before we can be sure that Maryland husbands and fathers gave their widows greater control of property and family than did their English counterparts.

Maryland men trusted their widows, but this is not to say that many did not express great anxiety about the future of their children. They asked both wives and overseers to see that the children received "some learning." Robert Sly made his wife sole guardian of his children but admonished her "to take due Care that they be brought up in the true fear of God and instructed in such Literature as may tend to their improvement." Widowers, whose children would be left without any parent, were often the most explicit in prescribing their upbringing. Robert Cole, a middling planter, directed that his children "have such Education in Learning as [to] write and read and Cast accompt I mean my three Sonnes my two daughters to learn to read and sew with their needle and all of them to be keept from Idleness but not to be kept as Common Servants." John Lawson required his executors to see that his two daughters be reared together, receive learning and sewing instruction, and be "brought up to huswifery." Often present was the fear that orphaned children would be treated as servants and trained only to work in the fields. With stepfathers in mind, many fathers provided that their sons should be independent before the usual age of majority, which for girls was sixteen but for

men twenty-one. Sometimes fathers willed that their sons should inherit when they were as young as sixteen, though more often eighteen. The sons could then escape an incompatible stepfather, who could no longer exploit their labor or property. If a son was already close to age sixteen, the father might bind him to his mother until he reached majority or his mother died, whichever came first. If she lived, she could watch out for his welfare, and his labor could contribute to her support. If she died, he and his property would be free from a stepfather's control.

What happened to widows and children if a man died without leaving a will? There was great need for some community institution that could protect children left fatherless or parentless in a society where they usually had no other kin. By the 1660s the probate court and county orphans' courts were supplying this need. If a man left a widow, the probate court—in Maryland a central government agency—usually appointed her or her new husband administrator of the estate with power to pay its creditors under court supervision. Probate procedures provided a large measure of protection. These required an inventory of the movable property and careful accounting of all disbursements, whether or not a man had left a will. William Hollis of Baltimore County, for example, had three stepfathers in seven years, and only the care of the judge of probate prevented the third stepfather from paying the debts of the second with goods that had belonged to William's father. As the judge remarked, William had "an uncareful mother."

Once the property of an intestate had been fully accounted and creditors paid, the county courts appointed a guardian who took charge of the property and gave bond to the children with sureties that he or she would not waste it. If the mother were living, she could be the guardian, or if she had remarried, her new husband would act. Through most of the century bond was waived in these circumstances, but from the 1690s security was required of all guardians, even of mothers. Thereafter the courts might actually take away an orphan's property from a widow or stepfather if she or he could not find sureties—that is, neighbors who judged the parent responsible and hence were willing to risk their own property as security. Children without any parents were assigned new families, who at all times found surety if there were property to manage. If the orphans inherited land, English common law allowed them to choose guardians for themselves at age fourteen—another escape hatch for children in conflict with stepparents. Orphans who had no property, or whose property was insufficient to provide an income that could maintain them, were expected to work for their guardians in return for their maintenance. Every year the county courts were expected to check on the welfare of orphans of intestate parents and remove them or their property from guardians who abused them or misused their estates. From 1681, Maryland law required that a special jury be impaneled once a year to report neighborhood knowledge of mistreatment of orphans and hear complaints.

This form of community surveillance of widows and orphans proved quite effective. In 1696 the assembly declared that orphans of intestates were often better cared for than orphans of testators. From that time forward, orphans' courts were charged with supervision of all orphans and were soon given powers to remove any guardians who were shown false to their trusts, regardless of the arrangements laid down in a will. The assumption was that the deceased parent's main concern was the welfare of the child, and that the orphans' court, as "father to us poor orphans," should implement the parent's intent. In actual fact, the courts never removed children—as opposed to their property—from a household in which the mother was living, except to apprentice them at the mother's request. These powers were mainly exercised over guardians of orphans both of whose parents were dead. The community as well as the husband believed the mother most capable of nurturing his children.

Remarriage was the usual and often the immediate solution for a woman who had lost her husband. The shortage of women made any woman eligible to marry again, and the difficulties of raising a family while running a plantation must have made remarriage necessary for widows who had

no son old enough to make tobacco. One indication of the high incidence of remarriage is the fact that there were only sixty women, almost all of them widows, among the 1,735 people who left probate inventories in four southern Maryland counties over the second half of the century. Most other women must have died while married and therefore legally without property to put through probate.

One result of remarriage was the development of complex family structures. Men found themselves responsible for stepchildren as well as their own offspring, and children acquired half-sisters and half-brothers. Sometimes a woman married a second husband who himself had been previously married, and both brought children of former spouses to the new marriage. They then produced children of their own. The possibilities for conflict over the upbringing of children are evident, and crowded living conditions, found even in the households of the wealthy, must have added to family tensions. Luckily, the children of the family very often had the same mother. In Charles County, at least, widows took new husbands three times more often than widowers took new wives. The role of the mother in managing the relationships of half-brothers and half-sisters or stepfathers and stepchildren must have been critical to family harmony.

Early death in this immigrant population thus had broad effects on Maryland society in the seventeenth century. It produced what we might call a pattern of serial polyandry, which enabled more men to marry and to father families than the sex ratios otherwise would have permitted. It produced thousands of orphaned children who had no kin to maintain them or preserve their property, and thus gave rise to an institution almost unknown in England, the orphans' court, which was charged with their protection. And early death, by creating families in which the mother was the unifying element, may have increased her authority within the household.

When the immigrant woman married her first husband, there was usually no property settlement involved, since she was unlikely to have any dowry. But her remarriage was another matter.

At the very least, she owned or had a life interest in a third of her former husband's estate. She needed also to think of her children's interests. If she remarried, she would lose control of the property. Consequently, property settlements occasionally appear in the seventeenth-century court records between widows and their future husbands. Sometimes she and her intended signed an agreement whereby he relinquished his rights to the use of her children's portions. Sometimes he deeded to her property which she could dispose of at her pleasure. Whether any of these agreements or gifts would have survived a test in court is unknown. We have not yet found any challenged. Generally speaking, the formal marriage settlements of English law, which bypassed the legal difficulties of the married woman's inability to make a contract with her husband, were not adopted by immigrants, most of whom probably came from levels of English society that did not use these legal formalities.

The wife's dower rights in her husband's estate were a recognition of her role in contributing to his prosperity, whether by the property she had brought to the marriage or by the labor she performed in his household. A woman newly freed from servitude would not bring property, but the benefits of her labor would be great. A man not yet prosperous enough to own a servant might need his wife's help in the fields as well as in the house, especially if he were paying rent or still paying for land. Moreover, food preparation was so time-consuming that even if she worked only at household duties, she saved him time he needed for making tobacco and corn. The corn, for example, had to be pounded in the mortar or ground in a handmill before it could be used to make bread, for there were very few water mills in seventeenth-century Maryland. The wife probably raised vegetables in a kitchen garden; she also milked the cows and made butter and cheese, which might produce a salable surplus. She washed the clothes, and made them if she had the skill. When there were servants to do field work, the wife undoubtedly spent her time entirely in such household tasks. A contract of 1681 expressed such a division of labor. Nicholas Ma-

niere agreed to live on a plantation with his wife and child and a servant. Nicholas and the servant were to work the land; his wife was to "Dresse the Victualls milk the Cowes wash for the servants and Doe allthings necessary for a woman to doe upon the s[ai]d plantation."

We have suggested that wives did field work; the suggestion is supported by occasional direct references in the court records. Mary Castleton, for example, told the judge of probate that "her husband late Deceased in his Life time had Little to sustain himself and Children but what was produced out of ye ground by ye hard Labour of her the said Mary.' Household inventories provide indirect evidence. Before about 1680 those of poor men and even middling planters on Maryland's lower Western Shore—the bottom two-thirds of the married decedents—show few signs of household industry, such as appear in equivalent English estates. Sheep and woolcards, flax and hackles, and spinning wheels all were a rarity, and such things as candle molds were nonexistent. Women in these households must have been busy at other work. In households with bound labor the wife doubtless was fully occupied preparing food and washing clothes for family and hands. But the wife in a household too poor to afford bound labor—the bottom fifth of the married decedent group—might well tend tobacco when she could. Eventually, the profits of her labor might enable the family to buy a servant, making greater profits possible. From such beginnings many families climbed the economic ladder in seventeenth-century Maryland.

The proportion of servantless households must have been larger than is suggested by the inventories of the dead, since young men were less likely to die than old men and had had less time to accumulate property. Well over a fifth of the households of married men on the lower Western Shore may have had no bound labor. Not every wife in such households would necessarily work at the hoe—saved from it by upbringing, ill-health, or the presence of small children who needed her care—but many women performed such work. A lease of 1691, for example, specified that the lessee could farm the amount of land which "he his wife and children can tend."

Stagnation of the tobacco economy, beginning about 1680, produced changes that had some effect on women's economic role. As shown by inventories of the lower Western Shore, home industry increased, especially at the upper ranges of the economic spectrum. In these households women were spinning yarn and knitting it into clothing. The increase in such activity was far less in the households of the bottom fifth, where changes of a different kind may have increased the pressures to grow tobacco. Fewer men at this level could now purchase land, and a portion of their crop went for rent. At this level, more wives than before may have been helping to produce tobacco when they could. And by this time they were often helping as a matter of survival, not as a means of improving the family position.

So far we have considered primarily the experience of immigrant women. What of their daughters? How were their lives affected by the demographic stresses of Chesapeake society?

One of the most important points in which the experience of daughters differed from that of their mothers was the age at which they married. In this woman-short world, the mothers had married as soon as they were eligible, but they had not usually become eligible until they were mature women in their middle twenties. Their daughters were much younger at marriage. A vital register kept in Somerset County shows that some girls married at age twelve and that the mean age at marriage for those born before 1670 was sixteen and a half years.

Were some of these girls actually child brides? It seems unlikely that girls were married before they had become capable of bearing children. Culturally, such a practice would fly in the face of English, indeed Western European, precedent, nobility excepted. Nevertheless, the number of girls who married before age sixteen, the legal age of inheritance for girls, is astonishing. Their English counterparts ordinarily did not marry until their mid- to late twenties or early thirties. In other parts of the Chesapeake, historians have found somewhat higher ages at marriage than appear in Somerset, but everywhere in seven-

teenth-century Maryland and Virginia most native-born women married before they reached age twenty-one. Were such early marriages a result of the absence of fathers? Evidently not. In Somerset County, the fathers of very young brides—those under sixteen—were usually living. Evidently, guardians were unlikely to allow such marriages, and this fact suggests that they were not entirely approved. But the shortage of women imposed strong pressures to marry as early as possible.

Not only did native girls marry early, but many of them were pregnant before the ceremony. Bridal pregnancy among native-born women was not as common as among immigrants. Nevertheless, in seventeenth-century Somerset County 20 percent of native brides bore children within eight and one half months of marriage. This was a somewhat higher percentage than has been reported from seventeenth-century English parishes.

These facts suggest considerable freedom for girls in selecting a husband. Almost any girl must have had more than one suitor, and evidently many had freedom to spend time with a suitor in a fashion that allowed her to become pregnant. We might suppose that such pregnancies were not incurred until after the couple had become betrothed, and that they were consequently an allowable part of courtship, were it not that girls whose fathers were living were usually not the culprits. In Somerset, at least, only 10 percent of the brides with fathers living were pregnant, in contrast to 30 percent of those who were orphans. Since there was only about one year's difference between the mean ages at which orphan and non-orphan girls married, parental supervision rather than age seems to have been the main factor in the differing bridal pregnancy rates.

Native girls married young and bore children young; hence they had more children than immigrant women. This fact ultimately changed the composition of the Maryland population. Native-born females began to have enough children to enable couples to replace themselves. These children, furthermore, were divided about evenly between males and females. By the mid-1680s, in all probability, the population thus began to grow through reproductive increase, and sexual imbalance began to decline. In 1704 the native-born preponderated in the Maryland assembly for the first time and by then were becoming predominant in the adult population as a whole.

This appearance of a native population was bringing alterations in family life, especially for widows and orphaned minors. They were acquiring kin. St. Mary's and Charles counties wills demonstrate the change. (See Table III.) Before 1680, when nearly all those who died and left families had been immigrants, three-quarters of the men and women who left widows and/or minor children made no mention in their wills of any other kin in Maryland. In the first decade of the eighteenth century, among native-born testators, nearly three-fifths mention other kin, and if we add information from sources other than wills —other probate records, land records, vital registers, and so on—at least 70 percent are found to have had such local connections. This development of local family ties must have been one of the most important events of early Maryland history.

Historians have only recently begun to explore the consequences of the shift from an immigrant to a predominantly native population. We would like to suggest some changes in the position of women that may have resulted from this transition. It is already known that as sexual imbalance disappeared, age at first marriage rose, but it remained lower than it had been for immigrants over the second half of the seventeenth century. At the same time, life expectancy improved, at least for men. The results were longer marriages and more children who reached maturity. In St. Mary's County after 1700, dying men far more often than earlier left children of age to maintain their widows, and widows may have felt less inclination and had less opportunity to remarry.

We may speculate on the social consequences of such changes. More fathers were still alive when their daughters married, and hence would have been able to exercise control over the selection of their sons-in-law. What in the seventeenth century may have been a period of comparative

independence for women, both immigrant and native, may have given way to a return to more traditional European social controls over the creation of new families. If so, we might see the results in a decline in bridal pregnancy and perhaps a decline in bastardy.

We may also find the wife losing ground in the household polity, although her economic importance probably remained unimpaired. Indeed, she must have been far more likely than a seventeenth-century immigrant woman to bring property to her marriage. But several changes may have caused women to play a smaller role than before in household decision-making. Women became proportionately more numerous and may have lost bargaining power. Furthermore, as marriages lasted longer, the proportion of households full of stepchildren and half-brothers and half-sisters united primarily by the mother must have diminished. Finally, when husbands died, more widows would have had children old enough to maintain them and any minor brothers and sisters. There would be less need for women to play a controlling role, as well as less incentive for their husbands to grant it. The provincial marriage of the eighteenth century may have more closely resembled that of England than did the immigrant marriage of the seventeenth century.

If this change occurred, we should find symptoms to measure. There should be fewer gifts from husbands to wives of property put at the wife's disposal. Husbands should less frequently make bequests to wives that provided them with property beyond their dower. A wife might even be restricted to less than her dower, although the law allowed her to choose her dower instead of a bequest. At the same time, children should be commanded to maintain their mothers.

However, St. Mary's County wills do not show these symptoms. (See Table IV.) True, wives occasionally were willed less than their dower, an arrangement that was rare in the wills examined for the period before 1710. But there was no overall decrease in bequests to wives of property beyond their dower, nor was there a tendency to confine the wife's interest to the term of her wid-

Table III
Resident Kin of Testate Men and Women Who Left Minor Children, St. Mary's and Charles Counties 1640 to 1710

	Families N	No kin % families	Only wife % families	Grown child % families	Other kin % families
A					
1640–1669	95	23	43	11	23
1670–1679	76	17	50	7	26
1700–1710	71	6	35[a]	25	34[b]
B.					
1700–1710					
Immigrant	41	10	37	37	17
Native	30		33[c]	10	57[d]

Notes: [a]If information found in other records is included, the percentage is 30.
[b]If information found in other records is included, the percentage is 39.
[c]If information found in other records is included, the percentage is 20.
[d]If information found in other records is included, the percentage is 70.
Only 8 testators were natives of Maryland before 1680s; hence no effort has been made to distinguish them from immigrants.
Source: Wills, I–XIV.

Table IV
Bequests of Husbands to Wives with Children, St. Mary's County, Maryland, 1710 to 1776

	N	All estate (%)	All or dwelling plantation for life (%)	All or dwelling plantation for widow-hood (%)	All or dwelling plantation for minority of child (%)	More than dower in other form (%)	Dower or less or unknown (%)	Main-tenance or house room (%)
1710–1714	13	0	46	0	0	23	31	0
1715–1719	25	4	24	4	0	28	36	4
1720–1724	31	10	42	0	0	28	23	3
1725–1729	34	3	29	0	0	24	41	3
1730–1734	31	6	16	13	0	29	35	0
1735–1739	27	0	37	4	4	19	37	0
1740–1744	35	0	40	0	3	23	34	0
1745–1749	39	3	31	8	0	31	28	0
1750–1754	43	2	35	7	0	16	40	0
1755–1759	34	3	41	3	0	41	12	0
1760–1764	48	2	46	10	2	13	27	0
1765–1769	45	4	27	11	2	18	33	4
1770–1774	46	4	26	7	0	37	26	0
1775–1776	19	5	32	26	0	5	32	0
Totals	470	3	33	7	1	24	31	1

Source: Wills, XIV–XLI.

owhood or the minority of the oldest son. Children were not exhorted to help their mothers or give them living space. Widows evidently received at least enough property to maintain themselves, and husbands saw no need to ensure the help of children in managing it. Possibly, then,

women did not lose ground, or at least not all ground, within the family polity. The demographic disruption of New World settlement may have given women power which they were able to keep even after sex ratios became balanced and traditional family networks appeared. Immigrant mothers may have bequeathed their daughters a legacy of independence which they in turn handed down, despite pressures toward more traditional behavior.

It is time to issue a warning. Whether or not Maryland women in a creole society lost ground, the argument hinges on an interpretation of English behavior that also requires testing. Either position supposes that women in seventeenth-century Maryland obtained power in the household which wives of English farmers did not enjoy. Much of the evidence for Maryland is drawn from the disposition of property in wills. If English wills show a similar pattern, similar inferences might be drawn about English women. We have already discussed evidence from English wills that supports the view that women in Maryland were favored; but the position of seventeenth-century English women—especially those not of gentle status—has been little explored. A finding of little difference between bequests to women in England and in Maryland would greatly weaken the argument that demographic stress created peculiar conditions especially favorable to Maryland women.

If the demography of Maryland produced the effects here described, such effects should also be evident elsewhere in the Chesapeake. The four characteristics of the seventeenth-century Maryland population—immigrant predominance, early death, late marriage, and sexual imbalance—are to be found everywhere in the region, at least at first. The timing of the disappearance of these peculiarities may have varied from place to place, depending on date of settlement or rapidity of development, but the effect of their existence upon the experience of women should be clear. Should research in other areas of the Chesapeake fail to find women enjoying the status they achieved on the lower Western Shore of Maryland, then our arguments would have to be revised.

Work is also needed that will enable historians to compare conditions in Maryland with those in other colonies. Richard S. Dunn's study of the British West Indies also shows demographic disruption. When the status of wives is studied, it should prove similar to that of Maryland women. In contrast were demographic conditions in New England, where immigrants came in family groups, major immigration had ceased by the mid-seventeenth century, sex ratios balanced early, and mortality was low. Under these conditions, demographic disruption must have been both less severe and less prolonged. If New England women achieved status similar to that suggested for women in the Chesapeake, that fact will have to be explained. The dynamics might prove to have been different; or a dynamic we have not identified, common to both areas, might turn out to have been the primary engine of change. And, if women in England shared the status—which we doubt—conditions in the New World may have had secondary importance. The Maryland data establish persuasive grounds for a hypothesis, but the evidence is not all in.

3

MOVING TO THE NEW WORLD: THE CHARACTER OF EARLY MASSACHUSETTS MIGRATION

T. H. BREEN AND STEPHEN FOSTER

Emigration to the New World in the seventeenth century was an arduous undertaking. The journey required two to six months at sea, with passengers huddled in cramped quarters with little provision for privacy. During the long voyage one could expect minimal, and at times rotten, provisions. Seasickness, fevers, contagious diseases, and boredom afflicted most sojourners. Death often awaited the very young, the old, and the infirm. Yet, in spite of the rigors and dangers of such a crossing, nearly 16,000 English men, women, and children uprooted themselves between 1630 and 1641 and set sail for the wilderness in New England.

In this article, Breen and Foster take a fresh look at what has come to be called "the Great Migration." Using English Customs records for the year 1637, they attempt to answer three questions: who were these migrants? why did they leave their homes for New England? what happened to them once they arrived? Their answers challenge many other accounts of the Great Migration, providing a clear profile of the early colonizers of New England.

The Great Migration was, above all else, a Puritan migration. While Breen and Foster point to economic changes that might have disposed some to migrate, religion was probably foremost in the minds of most immigrants. From the sixteenth century onward, Protestant beliefs traveled from Europe to England, where they took their firmest roots in the towns and seaports associated with the clothing trade, the same areas from which the bulk of the Great Migration originated. The English Puritans were staunch critics of the established Church of England, which they thought to be insufficiently reformed in structure and doctrine. Taking their beliefs from the French reformer Jean Calvin, the Puritans criticized not only the doctrines of the established church but also its elaborate ceremonials and especially the inclusive nature of its membership. To be born English was to be born into the Church of England, to be expected to pay its tithes and fees, and to accept such ministers as the church hierarchy saw fit to appoint. In doctrine and social practice the Puritans believed in a locally controlled church with a voluntary membership of faithful believers who elected and paid their own ministers. By the 1620s Puritan communities became a growing threat to the established church as well as to Charles I's plans for an absolutist state. Under the tenure of William Laud, Archbishop of Canterbury and titular head of the national church, Puritan ministers and their congregations were harshly persecuted as heretics as well as enemies of the state. It was against this backdrop that the Great Migration to New England took place.

Reprinted from *The William and Mary Quarterly,* Third Series, 30 (1973), 189–222, with permission of the authors.

The early migrants to New England remain a puzzling group. Who were these men and women who crossed the Atlantic to settle Massachusetts Bay? Why did they come? And what effect did the New World have upon the character of their lives?

Often asked, these questions are still difficult to answer with precision, as anyone with experience of seventeenth-century record keeping can testify. Lack of hard statistical data has forced most accounts of the Great Migration to rely heavily on statements drawn from the Puritan leadership. Ordinary folk appear in the story only haphazardly: the contents of some probate inventory or snatches from the odd surviving letters to relatives back in England will be used to give substantiation to the official claims of a Winthrop or a Cotton.

What is needed now, we believe, is a new and systematic analysis of the mass of the ordinary settlers who moved to New England during the 1630s. Such a study should properly begin with the English origins of the migrants and then follow them through their experiences in the New World. Yet with the exception of Sumner C. Powell's work on Sudbury, Massachusetts, the existing literature is surprisingly silent about the migrants' previous life in the mother country. Recent intensive demographic explorations of individual New England towns, valuable as they are in other respects, inevitably slight the migration itself. The new town studies usually begin not with the migrant in England but with the townsman in New England, and, since they focus on a particular village, they cease to follow individual settlers once they leave this town for another locality. These local studies would gain a new dimension from complementary investigations into the experiences of entire groups of migrants irrespective of the place or places in which they happened to settle.

Fortunately, surviving lists of migrants do make possible the systematic study of early Massachusetts immigration. Englishmen departing the realm prior to the Civil War were required to present the royal customs officers with evidence that they had taken the oath of allegiance to the king and conformed to the established church. Some emigrants may well have ignored the regulations, and the records of many more have certainly been lost, but registers giving the names of well over two thousand of the first settlers of New England still exist, and many contain important supplementary information about age, vocation, and place of origin.

Most of these lists were collected and printed by John Camden Hotten in 1874. Fifty years later Col. Charles Edward Banks attempted to rearrange the names on the Hotten lists by family and shipload, publishing the reordered registers with a short analytical introduction as *The Planters of the Commonwealth*. Hotten's version of the lists is the more reliable, but whichever source is used, any attempt to generalize from these lists to the whole of the New England migration can be extremely misleading.

Banks correctly noted that he and Hotten had collected *only* the names of those emigrants appearing on extant registers with whatever biases the accidental survival of one list rather than another may have introduced. The existing lists are not in any sense a random sample, and attempts to treat them as such have led to some dubious conclusions. For example, one attempt to measure changes in the place of origin of New England immigrants during the 1630s discovered an apparent shift away from Essex and Suffolk after 1636 and an increasing predominance of Norfolk migrants in 1637 and 1638. The change in question, however, may actually only be the result of full reporting from the port of London in 1635 but not after and equally full reporting from the Norfolk port of Great Yarmouth in 1637 but not before. Ships, of course, had sailed from Yarmouth before 1637 and continued to sail from London after 1635, but their passenger lists disappeared before either Hotten or Banks could collect them. Similarly, the repeated efforts to assign the bulk of the Great Migration to East Anglia as a whole run afoul of the same difficulty: relatively complete recording for London and the East Anglian ports without equally detailed West and North Country port records, which, if they had survived, might have swelled the roll of emigrants from those parts of England.

Inconsistent recording makes generalizations about vocation equally difficult. On some lists every adult male gave a specific occupation, but on most only ministers, conscious of their status, bothered to record a calling, so that a straightforward count of all the trades listed in Hotten would end with the conclusion that more than one out of every seven adult male emigrants leaving East Anglia for New England were clergymen. Even those who claim that Massachusetts was a theocracy would find this statistic hard to accept.

Yet the lists have much to tell about the Great Migration if they are not abused by uncritical extrapolation from the whole of the record without regard for the varying utility of the different parts. Careful analysis of limited sections of the material can yield conclusions more limited in their turn but more reliable for the specific groups under consideration. In particular, the year 1637 stands out for its relatively complete data. One hundred ninety-three emigrants who departed that year from Great Yarmouth in Norfolk and another eighty who sailed from Sandwich in Kent listed their age, profession, place of origin, and probable destination for the benefit of the royal customs officers. Some passengers leaving in other years gave their occupation or place of origin, but it was only in 1637 that *every* adult who gave his name also gave such full additional information about himself and his family. There had not been such careful recording before and there would not be again.

A total of 273 migrants constitutes too small a number for us to claim with confidence that they reflect the overall character of the Great Migration. But limited as it is, this group may provide some useful suggestions about the types of persons who emigrated before the Civil War as well as about their motives for doing so. Comparison of the experience of these settlers in the New World with their counterparts in the Old can also put to the test various theories about the effect of migration on family structure, vocational patterns, and social relationships. Our conclusions

about the economic and spatial mobility of the 1637 group do challenge some historiographical commonplaces, but further, more extensive studies of seventeenth-century migration will have to determine the representative quality of these particular settlers.

Turning to the lists themselves, even a casual examination calls into question the classic picture of migration to the New World: a predominantly male movement of young, single unattached persons, that is, individuals free both of strong ties to their homes and of constitutional infirmities that would preclude a difficult journey. On the contrary, most of the 1637 emigrants were grouped into relatively small nuclear families consisting of two parents, a few children, and sometimes one or more servants. Men and women were about equal in number, and only a handful of the families included grandparents or in-laws. The Sandwich list consists of twelve male heads of families and their wives, thirty-one children, twenty-two servants, and only three single men (traveling without a family). The comparable figures for Yarmouth are twenty-nine male heads of households and their wives, eighty-six children, thirty-four servants, five single men, and eight single women or female heads of families. Whatever disruptions migration may have inflicted on the nuclear family structure in other times and places, they were not much in evidence in the migration to New England in 1637. Moreover, if this pattern holds true for the rest of the migration, the absence of large numbers of single unattached men in early New England could have contributed to social stability and helped Massachusetts to avoid the type of recurring internal conflict that plagued colonies like Virginia, where, according to one recent historian, women "were scarcer than corn or liquor."

Migration is often assumed to be an affair of the young, but the Yarmouth examiners left enough material about age to establish that this was not a particularly youthful group of colonists. Although among the servants, as might be expected, almost all of the men were between the ages of eighteen and twenty-two, with heads of households the case was quite different. Almost half of the twenty-five men whose ages were recorded were in their thirties, another eight were forty or older, while only five were in their twenties. Nor were the women appreciably younger: a large minority of the wives, in fact, were older than their husbands. Seventeenth-century life spans being what they were, the nine men and women who were fifty or over in 1637 had little reason to suppose that they had many years to live when they removed to America. Nicholas Busby, aged fifty, managed to live until 1657, but Richard Carucar at sixty and Thomas Paine at fifty survived their arrival in Massachusetts by less than three years, and Benjamin Cooper, aged fifty, did not live to see the end of the voyage.

Most migrants fared better. Despite some early deaths among the older settlers, New England (unlike contemporary Virginia) turned out to be an unusually healthy place in which to live. Of the fifty-six men whose death dates are known, thirty-two were alive in 1670 and five were still alive in 1695, fifty-eight years after their voyage to the New World.

Revealing as the lists are about individual settlers, they throw no light on how they came to embark together on the same ships. Groups of prospective colonists may have chartered a ship, or a captain may have announced his intention to sail to New England and then waited for a full contingent of passengers. The manner of putting together boatloads of migrants is still an unsolved problem, but whatever the actual practice, the 1637 emigrants did not have to travel far in order to find a Massachusetts-bound vessel. Virtually all those who left a record of their English home came from towns or parishes close to the port of embarkation. All the passengers on the Sandwich list originated in the northeastern section of Kent: the westernmost came from Faversham, the southernmost from the North Downs. A majority lived in a still smaller area, the triangle bounded by Canterbury, Dover, and the port of Sandwich itself which is traditionally called East Kent. The Yarmouth emigrants originated mainly in the city of Norwich, the lowland regions around Yarmouth, or the port of Yarmouth

itself. Those of the emigrants who came from Suffolk were exclusively residents of the coastal and lowland towns in the north of the shire, which were oriented towards Norwich and Yarmouth across the county line, and only two of the emigrants on the Yarmouth list originated outside East Anglia.

The northeastern part of East Anglia (the light-loam region) and East Kent had a good deal in common. Both regions were located in shires containing disproportionately high percentages of England's town dwellers and industrial workers. In both areas the chief industry was clothworking, particularly the production of the lighter worsteds and "new draperies" introduced into England in the previous century by Protestant refugees from the Low Countries. Yet despite the importance of the cloth trade, Norfolk, High Suffolk, and Kent remained predominantly rural and agricultural, and agriculture meant primarily raising grain rather than dairying in both the East Anglian lightloam and East Kent. Agriculture in both areas was relatively advanced, however, and High Suffolk in particular may have been the most progressive farming region in seventeenth-century England.

With such an agrarian background the Yarmouth and Sandwich colonists might be expected to conform fairly closely to the pattern of occupational distribution noted by a recent study of West Country migration in the latter half of the seventeenth century: few poor laborers, a large majority of husbandmen and yeoman, and a small but significant number of craftsmen. In point of fact, while there were no laborers whatever among those who listed their occupation, the order of occupational frequency differs dramatically from the West Country men. Most of the East Anglians and Kentish men were urban and most were artisans. Excluding servants, forty-two of forty-nine men gave their occupation, and only eleven were farmers as against eight weavers, four cordwainers, four carpenters, two each of joiners, tailors, coopers, and mariners, as well as a brewer, a shoemaker, a grocer, a locksmith, a minister, a butcher, and a calendar. The cities of Norwich and Great Yarmouth between them accounted for well over half the East Anglian emigrants, and Canterbury, Sandwich, and Dover for the majority of the men from Kent. At least thirteen adult males on the 1637 lists and very probably more were freemen of incorporated boroughs.

Freemanship did not necessarily indicate that an individual was more wealthy or prominent than the average yeoman. But many of the urban migrants were clearly reasonably well off, a few more than that. Edward Johnson, a Canterbury joiner, also owned enough land in the county of Kent (let to others) to make him the equal of a very substantial Kentish yeoman. Nicholas Busby, Francis Lawes, and Michael Metcalfe, all freemen weavers of Norwich, merited the distinction of being among the ten individuals cited by name in the Long Parliament's indictment of the former bishop of Norwich for driving into exile the most important tradespeople of his diocese, some of whom had provided work for "an hundred poor people." Wren denied the prominence of most of the ten, Busby and Lawes included, but even he admitted that Metcalfe was "of some estate."

Rich or poor, none of the migrants was hopelessly ruined at the time of his decision to leave England for America. Here again, their ages are worth remembering. Most of the male heads of households were five or more years past their apprenticeship, all were old enough to be launched on a career, most were too young to have been driven to desperation by the incapacities of age or misfortune. Instead of consisting of adventurers or of the dispossessed, the 1637 group was made up mainly of families headed by urban tradesmen somewhere in mid-career who apparently chose to exchange their settled English vocations for life in a pioneer agricultural community of uncertain prospects. So unlikely a choice calls for an explanation, however difficult it may be to discuss the subject of personal motivation with any kind of exactness.

Acting on the assumption that happy people do not emigrate, historians have usually begun their histories of the Great Migration by turning to whatever might have made men unhappy in East Anglia and Kent in 1637. The economy of both regions, it has been noted, depended heavily on the clothtrade, which for some time had suffered severely from the disruption of traditional continental markets and the blunders of government policy. There had been sharp contractions in the volume of the trade in 1618, 1621, and 1629 to 1631, while a serious outbreak of the plague in London, Norwich, Sandwich, and many other cities in 1636 and 1637 had suspended commerce for months at a time, a major setback to a recovery already painfully slow and uneven.

On top of depressions and epidemics came harassment by overzealous church officials. Bishop Matthew Wren held the diocese of Norwich (which comprised the shires of Norfolk and Suffolk) from the fall of 1635 to the spring of 1638. During this brief period he enforced ceremonialism and deprived nonconformist clergy with so much enthusiasm that at the calling of the Long Parliament he was impeached and spent eighteen years as a prisoner in the Tower. Wren's enemies in Parliament claimed among other things that his "rigorous prosecutions and dealings" had driven three thousand families from the diocese of Norwich. Certainly, his policy took a heavy toll among the clergy of his diocese: Wrentham, Norwich, Yarmouth, and Hingham, towns which supplied the bulk of the East Anglian emigrants of 1637, also sent seven ministers into exile in New England and another two to Holland. Nor were the Puritan laity any happier under the bishop's administration: his policy provoked civic discord in both Yarmouth and Norwich as well as an increase in conventicle keeping, and when his officers arrived in Ipswich in 1637 full-scale rioting broke out. Kent had a less spectacular ecclesiastical history in the same period, but the shire did contain well-entrenched nonconformist and Separatist movements dating back to Elizabethan days and still vital at the time of the Civil War; as the diocese of Archbishop Laud himself, Canterbury was hardly a haven for Puritans.

After cataloguing the woes of English society in the 1630s (which were obviously considerable), traditional historiography has turned to a ferocious debate over the primacy of economic as against religious discontents in producing the migration. But put in less abstract terms, in terms of the individual experiences of the migrants rather than of impersonal religious and economic "factors," the whole attempt to separate out one cause from another appears not merely hopeless but unhistorical—a question badly posed. Given the unusually strong appeal of nonconformity to town dwellers and artisans, there was likely to be a marked congruence between disgruntled tradesmen and disgruntled Puritans: people falling into one category would frequently fall into the other, and there is no way to distinguish between them. The traditional either/or dichotomy—*either* religion *or* economics—makes no sense.

Take the case of William Ludkin, a locksmith from the city of Norwich. While we can establish that the Norfolk clothtrade experienced violent fluctuations, we cannot meaningfully argue that Ludkin moved to Massachusetts in 1637 because the impoverished weavers of Norwich could not afford locks. On the other hand, neither can we say persuasively that he left Norwich because he had come to dislike altar railings and ceremonies in his own parish of St. Clements and because a respected preacher named Thomas Allen in a nearby parish had been forced to flee to the Bay Colony for resisting Wren's innovations. Ludkin was one of the better recorded migrants, and yet he has left us only his name, age, occupation, and an inventory taken at the time of his death in 1652. None of this data reveals whether Ludkin the locksmith was also Ludkin the Puritan, and if he was, which role was the more important in his decision to leave England.

Whatever motive was suggested for Ludkin's removal, the assertion would fail for lack of conclusive evidence. But incomplete documentation is only part of the problem. Motivation appears straightforward enough in a man like the Norwich master weaver Michael Metcalfe. Unlike his shipmates, Metcalfe left a detailed memorial of his particular troubles. He was a parishioner of the suspended Thomas Allen and was himself in trouble with the ecclesiastical courts in 1633 and again in 1636 for failing to bow at the name of Jesus. Evidently a strong-willed man, Metcalfe

defended himself with such asperity that a church official threatened him, "Blockhead, old heretic, the Devil made you, I will send you to the Devil." Following this exchange Metcalfe found it prudent to depart the realm and set down his reasons, all religious, in a circular letter addressed "to all the true professors of Christ's gospel within the city of Norwich." "Therefore, seeing what the Lord hath done unto thee," he intoned, "O! Norwich: prepare to meet thy God."

Metcalfe, then, becomes a religious refugee while the absence of a similar statement from Ludkin could permit him to be pictured as an aspiring craftsman moving west in order to move up the social scale. But if it should have turned out that Metcalfe had also left a record of business failure, we might have been tempted to say with a Suffolk episcopal official that "as soon as any one doe purpose to breake or is become much indebted he may flye into new England and be accompted a religious man for leaving of the kingdome because he cannot indure the ceremonies of the church." And by the same token if evidence existed to link Ludkin with Metcalfe's "professors," we could plausibly rank him among the persecuted Puritans whatever his financial situation. Our difficulty is not just that we do not know enough about the Metcalfes and Ludkins, for if the problem of motivation is posed as a choice between two mutually exclusive impulses, religious or economic, then complete records for every individual migrant would not explain the Great Migration. In addition to insufficient evidence, the problem is also one of interpretation.

Rather than seeking to separate the historically inseparable, a more fruitful account of the migration should begin with the actual relationship between religious and economic conditions in the regions which supplied the migrants, and it must consider other possible motives for emigration as well as other possible destinations the emigrants might have chosen. Instead of ending the discussion with general statements about hard times in the clothworking areas, it may legitimately be asked how hard they were and for whom, and what the available alternatives were for those affected by them.

In the case of the 1637 migration the colonists originated in towns which differed from other clothworking centers in that they contained large foreign congregations and were also well on the way to recovery from the earlier depressions. One hundred sixty-four of the 273 migrants came from Norwich, Yarmouth, Canterbury, or Sandwich, all cities which had been the chief refuges (outside of London) for the Fleming, Walloon, and Dutch Protestants who fled the Spanish armies in the Low Countries in the latter half of the sixteenth century. The Protestants from the Continent imported both their religion and their skills into England, accentuating the native nonconformity of their new homes at the same time that they turned them into centers for the manufacture of "new draperies." Coarser but cheaper than the traditional broadcloth, these mixed and worsted fabrics would be the economic salvation of England in the course of the seventeenth century as the market for the "old draperies" declined and new markets opened for light and inexpensive fabrics. Much of the instability in the cloth trade in the 1630s reflected the transition from old to new clothmaking, a transition in which the worsted weaving areas, especially Norfolk, would lead at the expense of large parts of the West Country, Yorkshire, and central East Anglia. To argue, then, that depression was the primary inspiration for the Kentish and East Anglian migration of 1637, and that religion amounted to little more than the social cement that bound the migrants together inverts the actual order of importance of the facts: the 273 colonists in question came from the most Protestant and comparatively the least blighted sections of the clothworking areas. Contemporaries were well aware that tradesmen in the coastal towns made good Puritans and that Puritan tradesmen were especially likely to become New England colonists. And so the hostile, albeit careful, subdean of Westminster Abbey, Peter Heylin, noted acidly that the people "in many great trading towns which were near the sea" were "long discharged from the bond of ceremonies" and already organized into congregations, so that "it was no hard matter for those [suspended] Minis-

ters and Lecturers to persuade them to remove their dwellings and transport their trades . . . New England was chiefly in their eye, a Puritan plantation from the beginning, and therefore fitter for the growth of the Zwinglian or Calvinian gospel than any country whatsoever."

Heylin saw only a portion of the truth, and that hazily. The majority of urban artisans of Puritan sympathies never seriously considered leaving England despite *both* the state of the clothtrade *and* Archbishop Laud. To present economic and religious discontents as mutually exclusive not only obscures their real relationship, but it errs by ignoring additional causes for emigration. Neighborhood squabbles, family quarrels, the sense of adventure and similar personality traits, all of these motives and more figured in the exodus of Englishmen from their native land. Among the 1637 emigrants perhaps Thomas Oliver chose to follow his fellow parishioner Michael Metcalfe out of respect for the latter's courage and integrity, and the three Batchellor brothers of Kent may have left together to keep up their family ties. Such reasons are less accessible today than the more obvious economic and religious discontents, but the men who actually took part in the Great Migration felt their weight when they made up their minds to leave their country.

Having chosen migration, our 273 then made a second and in many ways more remarkable decision, to go to New England, an underdeveloped agricultural colony where few of them would ever again practice the crafts which had given them income and status in the Old World. Their destination was not forced upon them: they could just as easily have moved to the Netherlands, the most economically advanced area in the whole of Europe, where every kind of craft and especially that of worsted weaving was in high demand. Wages in the Netherlands were so much in advance of the prevailing English level that the cynical Bishop Wren thought the Dutch had deliberately bid them up to drain England of its skilled labor, and the government of Charles I, alarmed at the growing size of the English community in Holland, came up with the fantastic plan to resettle the expatriates in New England or Virginia. But in 1637 the real choice was between New England and Holland, and it was no foregone conclusion. In the same six months of that year that 193 people left Yarmouth for Massachusetts, another 414, the bulk of them artisans, sailed from the same port, bound for Holland.

The Netherlands offered employment for skilled craftsmen and even a more palatable form of religion for disgruntled nonconformists, but it was New England which possessed special attraction for men unhappy with the new Laudian regime in the Church of England. By 1637 the eccentricities of Massachusetts church government were well known to interested parties back in England, indeed too well known for some. Moderate nonconformists in the mother country complained that reports of New England Congregationalism had encouraged enthusiastic imitators in England and thereby opened the entire nonconformist movement to the charge of Separatism. One correspondent of Gov. John Winthrop warned him in May 1637 that "the whole kingdome begins, or rather proceeds, to be full of prejudice against you, and you are spoken of disgracefully and with bitterness in the greatest meetings in the kingdome, the Pulpits sound of you both at Visitacions and Assises, and the Judges begin to mention you in theyre charges."

A church way which seemed excessive to the moderates and pure anathema to the Laudians could also have been a powerful magnet to enthusiasts already made restless by episcopal rigor and the slump in trade. There is no sure evidence that the Yarmouth and Sandwich emigrants inclined to congregationalism before their departure, but they certainly found the New England Way appealing once they had arrived. Despite admissions procedures that had grown increasingly more restrictive since 1630, about half and possibly more of the adult males in the migration became church members in Massachusetts, usually within a few years of their arrival. Some carried their religious zeal too far even for the established authorities of the Bay Colony, who were no fonder of schism and heterodoxy than was Peter Heylin. For example, Mary Oliver, for-

merly of Norwich, had been cited with her husband before Bishop Richard Corbett in 1633; once settled in Salem, she took Roger Williams's part against the Bay Colony elders with such vehemence that she quickly ran afoul of the Massachusetts General Court. Later, in 1644, her ardent advocacy of eccentric religious views brought her a public whipping. Less spectacularly but similarly, Adam Goodens, who as a boy living near Great Yarmouth was a frequenter of conventicles as early as 1628, as a young man of twenty in New England found the Providence of Roger Williams more suitable to his constitution than the Massachusetts of John Winthrop and moved there in 1638.

There were undoubtedly some worldlings in the New England migration, even in that select portion of it examined in this essay. But one should not mistake initial indifference for sustained hostility. Reviewing the settlement of the colonies in 1648, John Cotton observed that the churches of New England were the means of conversion "of sundry elder and younger persons, who came over hither not out of respect to conscience, or spiritual ends, but out of respect to friends, or outward inlargements: but have here found that grace, which they sought not for." Cotton in his way was shrewder than some later commentators: he neither denied the mixed motives that brought some people to New England nor much worried about them provided church and state were arranged so that his inadvertent Puritans were likely to find "that grace, which they sought not for."

Perhaps with such cautions about motivation in mind it will become easier to discuss without preconception the experiences of the immigrants once arrived in New England. The impact of the New World on seventeenth-century Englishmen is most easily approached by sticking to specifics, that is, by examining the nature and degree of changes in mobility, social status, and vocation brought on by the Atlantic passage. Seventeenth-century Boston was not half the size of Norwich, nor was it prior to 1700 even as large as Canterbury, and the other New England towns were substantially smaller than Boston, so that dramatic alterations in the life style of the migrants might be expected as a consequence of their new, less populous, more rural environment. In fact, the changes for the first generation do not seem to have been very great.

In their initial choice of New England homes the Kentish and Norfolk groups fell into divergent patterns. The East Anglians tended to bunch together, settling mostly in Essex County at first and then spreading northwards into Old Norfolk County (most of which is now in New Hampshire) or, less frequently, drifting south into Plymouth Colony. The emigrants from Kent were more dispersed from the start and generally began their New England careers in Suffolk or Middlesex counties. Hingham, Dedham, Watertown, Charlestown, and Dorchester all received a portion of the 1637 influx, but no one moved to Cambridge or Roxbury and only a few initially settled in Boston.

Differences in the areas of settlement should not obscure a fundamental similarity between the East Anglian and Kentish colonists: the individuals in both groups moved about a good deal in their first twenty-five years in the New World. Considering the high rate of geographic mobility in Elizabethan and Stuart England, a comparable pattern in Massachusetts is, perhaps, not so surprising. Seventeen of the eighty-one adult males cannot be traced at all, and another five have left such scanty records that they too must be excluded from the count. Of the fifty-nine men remaining, twenty-four moved at least once *after* their original settlement, four twice, three three times, and one particularly peripatetic individual completed four moves. These figures do not include purely nominal removals, such as the legal separation of Malden from Charlestown, Wenham from Salem, or Topsfield from Ipswich, and, if anything, understate the extent of spatial mobility in early New England. The twenty-seven men with only one recorded location include several who did not live long enough to get in a second move and several more whose disappearance from their town's records probably indicates another move rather than an unrecorded death.

Some of the colonists, as might be expected,

made their first move soon after arrival, probably leaving hastily chosen first homes for more attractive locations they had learned of only after settling in or near their port of disembarkation: Robert Page moved to Hampton in Old Norfolk after only a short time in Salem, Jarvis Boykett left Charlestown for New Haven within a few years of his first settlement. But others continued shifting about well into the 1640s. John Yonges, the only minister in the 1637 group, left to found Southold, Long Island (named for his birthplace in Suffolk) in 1646, taking with him another of the Yarmouth emigrants, Philomen Dickinson, an established tanner in Salem. So dramatic a venture as the founding of a new town on Long Island was, however, unusual: on the whole the 1637 migrants confined their moves to previously settled villages or to the lands nearby, and the vast empty acreage of western Massachusetts never seems to have tempted any of them.

Internal migration on this scale did not pass unnoticed even at the time, and not all observers were sympathetic. Giles Firmin wrote bitterly in 1639 of men who "range from place to place on purpose to live upon the Country." Firmin was too jaundiced to see the social significance of the process he was criticizing, but the career of Thomas Dagget, although an extreme instance, throws some light on why so many people took to moving about. Dagget was a servant who made good by dint of the main chance and two rich widows. He was about thirty when he arrived in Salem in 1637 with his master, the Norwich calendar Thomas Oliver, and stayed in his first home for a few years at most; by 1642 at the latest he was living in Concord in Middlesex County, for in that year his wife's death is recorded on the town records. The following year, 1643, he moved to Weymouth (then in Suffolk County) where he promptly married the widow of William Frey. Through his new wife's inheritance from her late husband, Dagget found himself a proprietor of Weymouth, and by 1648 he was respectable enough to be elected selectman, a clear sign of status in any New England community. But four years later Dagget's second wife passed away, and he continued his southward migration, this time settling in Marshfield in Plymouth Colony, where he married another widow in 1654 and finally settled down to spend the rest of his days there as a selectman, tax collector, and leading citizen. Dagget apparently had become an ever bigger fish by seeking ever smaller ponds, a technique which may well account for the attraction comparatively underpopulated areas such as Plymouth and New Hampshire held for the migrants of 1637 who had first settled in the more populous coastal towns.

Men could occasionally remain in one spot, even a well-developed one, and still prosper. Without ever leaving Salem, John Gedney, a Norwich weaver, acquired considerable land, held important town offices, and founded a dynasty a good deal more prominent in early New England history than that of Dagget. Fortune, however, usually favored the mobile, who if they failed in three towns might yet make good in a fourth. While Gedney flourished at Salem, his fellow weaver and fellow parishioner at Norwich, William Nickerson, brought his own stormy career to a more or less triumphant conclusion by methods strikingly similar to those of the ex-servant Dagget, down to a good marriage, except that Nickerson surpassed even Dagget in frequency of removal. Settling first in Ipswich, he moved on to Yarmouth on Cape Cod in 1640, briefly transferred to Boston in 1657 to wind up the estate of his well-to-do father-in-law Nicholas Busby, returned to Yarmouth again two years later and stayed there until 1672 when he trekked even farther out on the Cape to found Chatham. Along the way Nickerson speculated in Indian lands with such relentless energy that he was almost constantly in trouble with the Plymouth Colony authorities. Although his business dealings once landed him in the stocks, he still managed to amass over four thousand acres on the Cape, ending his days as Chatham's leading citizen and, for want of a settled minister, as its religious teacher as well.

Geographic mobility sometimes had less happy consequences. John Roper, a Norfolk carpenter, settled in Dedham and failed, moved to Charlestown and failed, and then decided to try his luck in the frontier town of Lancaster where he seemed to be succeeding at last when in 1676 the Indians wiped out the entire town. Others on the 1637 lists found that ambition involved conflict with the law. Samuel Greenfield, still another of the Norwich weavers, lived briefly in Salem and Ipswich but then moved to more congenial surroundings in Old Norfolk County, settling in Hampton in 1639 and moving to Exeter a few years later. Greenfield too had a taste for land speculation and quickly became a leading citizen of Exeter and one of its selectmen in 1644. He was also in trouble with the Essex County Court in 1639 for illegally appropriating his stepchildren's legacy, and in 1649 he was up before the same court "for singing a lascivious song and using unseemly gestures." Later the same year he made another attempt on his stepchildren's money by forging a bill of sale; this time his misdemeanors landed him in the Boston jail, at which point he disappears from New England history.

Despite their varied fates, Dagget, Nickerson, Roper, and Greenfield had all responded to the same lure, leaving the older, more settled towns for small, outlying villages where they would enjoy the advantages of firstcomers. But others of their shipmates turned to the city of Boston for personal advancement, finding in its steady expansion the same opportunities and more. Jonathan Gill began life in New England as the servant of the Kentish yeoman Nicholas Butler, but while Butler went on to achieve prominence on Martha's Vineyard, Gill took the opposite tack and moved first to Dorchester and then to Boston itself, dying in 1678 as "Mr." Jonathan Gill, millowner, substantial landholder, and prosperous merchant with an estate in excess of £1,600. Boston could be the scene of this provincial variant on the Dick Whittington story because alone among the New England towns it could recreate the urban way of life most of the 1637 migrants gave up in coming to the New World; it was the one community where men trained in a craft might still practice it or at least avoid obligatory farming. William Ludkin, the Norwich locksmith, spent a few years in Hingham and then bought a smith's shop in Boston. At his death in

1652 he left an estate of only £158, but he had distinguished himself by being one of the few 1637 immigrants to maintain his original trade. Another Norwich freeman, the weaver Nicholas Busby, after a brief stay in Newbury, tried his hand at farming in Watertown, but then, still game at the age of fifty-nine, he too moved to Boston, bringing his looms with him, to set up as a merchant trading primarily in cloth. His new life was not quite that of Norwich master weaver, but it was probably close enough: Busby served a turn as Boston constable in 1649 and died in 1657, leaving a substantial £973, although his two looms so carefully transported across the Atlantic were now valued at only £4.

Boston, however, could only accommodate a limited number of colonists. For most of the Norfolk and Kentish emigrants the move to the New World carried with it a change in vocation, usually a transition from a skilled craftsman in England to a farmer in America. The psychological effects of such a shift are not easily determined. Perhaps the freemen artisans in the 1637 group were already prepared to give up their old callings; perhaps the limited vocational opportunities of Massachusetts came as a shock. Whatever the case may have been, most of them found new callings successfully, but the process of adjustment sometimes required time.

The clothworkers as members of the most industrialized sector of the English economy encountered the greatest difficulty in keeping up their trades in Massachusetts, and yet it was these men who made the most stubborn efforts to retain their original vocation. To the end of their lives they proudly called themselves "weaver" on every official document, even if like William Nickerson living far out on Cape Cod they probably had not put their looms to commercial use in years. Busby received a government bounty for making some cloth in 1643 and continued to weave small quantities until his death: his probate record shows £6 of cloth still on his looms. Another former weaver, John Pearce of Watertown, apparently ever hopeful, took on a young apprentice in 1656, promising that "with the trade of weaving, he is . . . to instruct him." Pearce re-

tained a small "shop" with looms in Watertown, but he was primarily a farmer, just as Busby was primarily a merchant.

The failure of clothworking is a mystery. Massachusetts possessed a considerable resource in the persons of so many trained weavers. Its population obviously required cloth. Yet despite repeated encouragement from the General Court, every attempt to establish a textile industry in the Bay Colony ended shortly after it began. The inhabitants of Rowley, many of whom were experienced English weavers, took the lead in the first great drive to create an indigenous textile industry in 1643. Three years later, however, they were still paying premium prices to Boston merchants for imported fabrics. "The greatest want (for the present) if not our only," complained Rowley's minister Ezekiel Rogers, "is Clothing."

One wonders why so much determination produced so little. Part of the trouble may have been a labor shortage. Like all seventeenth-century trades, clothworking was extremely specialized and fragmented, while the "new draperies" in particular were also an unusually "labor intensive" industry. Although Massachusetts had a large body of immigrant weavers, it quite possibly lacked the necessary number of combers, throwers, carders, calendars, and the like to complement their skills. Equally, there probably was never enough wool for them to weave. Ezekiel Rogers boasted in 1646 that "we are about getting sheep, which doe thrive here exceedingly well." It was an empty boast. Sheep appear periodically on Massachusetts inventories (among others, Abraham Toppan, a former Yarmouth cooper, kept twenty-four head at Newbury), but they are far inferior to other types of livestock both in number and assessed value. This lack of interest in sheep, in turn, may be the product of the English origins of the migrants. The 1637 group came from areas where livestock was raised primarily for meat rather than for dairying, and the settlers may have followed their former preferences in the New World. If so, then sheep would probably take up too much land and demand too much care for too little return in meat to make them a viable substitute for cattle or swine as an important source of food.

Whatever the reasons, English clothworkers became New England farmers or occasionally, like Busby, found alternative trades. Coopers, cordwainers, and (surprisingly) shoemakers and tailors had little better luck in keeping their English vocations. The mariners and carpenters possessed skills still very much in demand, but even they used their crafts only to supplement a basically agricultural way of life. In its early years the New England economy was too primitive to support substantial vocational specialization, so that, willing or not, for the artisan emigrant the trip to Massachusetts Bay turned into a movement back to the land.

The eight husbandmen and three yeomen who left England in 1637 were spared this vocational transition, and it is worth noting that they became far and away the single most successful occupational group in New England. Four of the eleven died within a few years of their arrival; all were probably advanced in years and, judging from probate records and the number of their servants, at least three of them were already men of considerable property before their emigration. The surviving seven farmers prospered in New England. Nicholas Butler of Eastwell in Kent became a founder of a settlement on the Vineyard, Henry Smith of Norfolk served Medfield as selectman for thirteen terms, and no less than three of the seven were founders of Hampton, each serving the town in turn as selectman and deputy to the Massachusetts General Court. The most needed skills in New England brought a high reward to those fortunate enough to possess them.

Despite the effects of vocational changes and the potential for social disruption inherent in so much geographic mobility, the status relationships established in the mother country remained basically intact. For the most part the masters on the 1637 lists flourished in the New World while their former servants remained humble. For every Dagget, Gill, or other servant made good, there were several men like Samuel Arres, who came to Ipswich with his master John Baker and

lived there for the next forty years without accomplishing anything of note. By contrast, Baker put his old Norwich trade of grocer to use by keeping an ordinary, acquired a large amount of property in Ipswich and Topsfield, took to calling himself "Mr.," and finally in 1682 attained the office of selectman. The disparity in officeholding is in itself one indication of the difficulty the servants encountered in raising their status. Twenty-seven nonservants were chosen to some post in New England, while only seven former servants could boast the same honor. Six of these nonservants were elected deputies to the Massachusetts General Court, a position of importance in the Bay Colony, but none of the servants ever held an office beyond the village level. Yet in the original migration of 1637 adult male nonservants had outnumbered male servants by a ratio of less than four to three.

The servants provide the darkest element in the entire story of the colonists of 1637. Thirty-six male servants are known by name, but seventeen have left little or no other record of their existence after their initial entry on the ship lists (as against only five nonservants in the same category). Brief entries in probate records reveal that the disappearance of two servants can definitely be ascribed to early deaths, but there is no way of knowing how many others suffered the same fate without leaving an estate to be recorded. The journal of an earlier migrant to New England, however, may be suggestive. Gov. William Bradford of New Plymouth kept a record of the mortality among the Pilgrims in the first awful winter of 1620–1621: in spite of the advantages of youth the death toll was much higher among servants than masters.

Less unhappy explanations for sparse recording of the missing seventeen might include early return to England, removal to another colony, or merely an obscure life in New England. None of these theories, however, indicates much of a success story for almost half the thirty-six men who sailed from Yarmouth or Sandwich as servants. Several of the nineteen remaining who left some record of their life in New England have done so mainly on account of their collisions with the authorities. John Pope was censured for foolery with women in 1640 and presented for excessive wages in 1643. Isaac Hart was bound over for good behavior in 1640 and convicted of stealing a cow in 1656 and again in 1658, while on still another occasion he was admonished "for divers naughty speeches against the Court." The principal achievement of another servant, John Granger, seems to have been the fathering of Thomas Granger, who was executed by the Plymouth Colony government after one of the most bizarre trials on record in the history of early New England.

Even some of the servants who prospered did so mainly with the help of influential relatives already established in Massachusetts before their arrival. Samuel Lincoln of Hingham and William Moulton of Hampton were able to reap the benefits of the dominant positions of their families in their respective towns, but their careers no more bear testimony to New England as a land of opportunity than do the more sordid records of Hart and Pope.

For most of the 1637 migrants prominence in the New World had followed substance in the Old. Edward Johnson, founder of Woburn, power in the lower house of the Massachusetts General Court, and author of the chronicle entitled *Wonder-Working Providence,* had been a substantial landholder in Kent, the son of the clerk of St. Gregory's Parish, Canterbury, and a freeman of that city. John Gedney of Salem was originally a Norwich freeman capable of bringing over four servants, while Nicholas Butler of Martha's Vineyard had been a Kentish yeoman with five.

There were exceptions. Samuel Greenfield proved quite clearly that not every Norwich weaver lived a long happy life in New England. Again, one might have expected more from the pugnacious Michael Metcalfe, who had been bold and learned enough to dispute theology with an episcopal court. Even Bishop Wren thought him an important if seditious inhabitant of his diocese. Yet Metcalfe's career in Dedham was anticlimactic: one term as selectman, a brief turn as town schoolmaster towards the end of his life, and an

estate of £364. Perhaps the cantankerousness that stood him in such good stead in his personal war against prelacy in Norfolk was less useful in the more peaceful environment of Dedham. Metcalfe, in any case, is not typical of the 1637 group. Records of estates, lists of town officers, even the use of honorific titles all point in the same direction: social status could be transferred across the Atlantic without major disruptions.

In summary, several characteristics about the 1637 migration stand out in spite of sometimes inadequate information. The men on the passenger lists were for the most part urban artisans who gave up their English callings to become farmers in New England. Their motives for moving to the New World were mixed, but for most, religion was probably not incidental. Moreover, their patterns of physical and social mobility in America apparently paralleled those of the England of their birth.

Conceivably this group of migrants may have been atypical, but at this stage of research it is not really possible to define what was typical and what eccentric. This much can be said, however: there is no obvious indication that the 1637 group is unique. The passenger lists are not top-heavy with the names of ministers and magistrates; indeed, the most remarkable attribute of most of the men prior to their decision to emigrate was their apparent ordinariness. Nor is there anything singular in their trades or origins. Contemporary commentators on English economic policy knew well enough that the country was losing valuable skilled labor to the Continent and the colonies. Reflecting on the previous two decades, a pamphleteer in 1641 lamented that the tradesmen and artificers of the nation had suffered under a "multiplicity of vexations" which "did impoverish many thousands and so afflict and trouble others that great numbers, to avoid their miseries, departed out of the kingdom, some into New England, and other parts of America, others into Holland, where they have transported their manufacture of Cloth." The author of this complaint knew whereof he spoke: a standard genealogical work lists ninety-one men who identified themselves as clothworkers on Bay Colony records prior to 1650 as well as equally impressive contingents from other crafts. The average migrant may not have been a craftsman, but a significant proportion of the Great Migration must have consisted of men drawn from urban and artisan backgrounds.

A large number of such people among the early colonists might help to answer some of the continuing problems of New England history. New Englanders may have adopted an unusual system of land division, for example, in part because many of them were amateurs at agriculture. The urban origins of so many migrants also suggest one way in which the migration was recruited: from among neighbors already grouped into loosely organized congregations. One Canterbury parish, St. George's, provided a strikingly large number of the Kentish emigrants, and it was the home of Edward Johnson, who had already been to New England once before his return there in 1637. Perhaps he spent his sojourn back in England informing his fellow parishioners about the nature of the American settlement. The proposition is supported by Johnson's own account of the promotion of the New England migration. Often regarded as fanciful rhetoric, he may have intended it as self-description: "This Proclamation [from Christ] being audibly published through the Ile of Great Brittaine by sundry Herraulds, which Christ had prepared for that end: the rumour ran through Cities, Townes and Villages."

We offer these possibilities as suggestions only. The New England migration lasted for twelve years and involved over fifteen thousand people. Conclusions based on the lives of only 273, all of whom arrived in a single year, obviously cannot be too generously applied to the Great Migration as a whole. However, examining this one unusually well-documented group establishes in outline the character of one form of migrant, the urban artisan of Puritan leaning. The frequency of this type of settler and the relevance of his experience to early New England history are questions awaiting further detailed research. At least the men and women who left England in 1637 have had their story told, and this may help us to understand the entire movement of which they formed one part.

4

COMMODITIES OF THE HUNT

WILLIAM CRONON

By the beginning of European colonization in the seventeenth century Native American tribes had inhabited the eastern seaboard of North America for more than 6,000 years. Until recently, historians have paid little attention to the contributions of the Powhatans, the Mahicans, the Abnaki, and the many other tribes in shaping the course of American history. In this essay William Cronon paints a vivid portrait of the complex interaction between the original inhabitants and the Europeans who explored and settled along the New England coastline.

As we have already seen in the case of colonial Maryland, disease environments can play an important historical role. Perhaps the most far-reaching consequence of what one historian has called the European "invasion of America" was the devastation that even relatively minor European diseases, such as measles and chicken pox, wrought upon native populations. As Cronon points out, the horrible decimation of the Native American population that followed European contact had profound effects on those who survived. With mortality rates as high as 80 to 90 percent, normal social relations became impossible, the mixed economy of hunting and planting was disrupted, political alliances were shattered, and longstanding cultural systems were destroyed. Survivors were left vulnerable to the designs of European settlers and to the new economic system they brought with them.

In spite of this devastation and cultural dislocation, however, the history of early European–Native American contact was more than a tale of death and destruction. It was also the story of the several ways in which early settlers depended on the Indian presence: for the sites of their settlements, for their crops, and for the pelts of indigenous animals with which they paid for their imported goods. Without Native Americans there might not have been a "New" England.

In his essay Cronon emphasizes the economic and political aspects of European–Native American contact. Compare this tale of European conquest and settlement with that of Eric Wolf in Reading 1. What were the similarities and differences in the Spanish-Indian and the English–Native American acculturation processes?

The tension between Indian and European property systems did not become instantly apparent the moment the first European visited New England. Indeed, for well over a century before English settlement began in Massachusetts, Europeans and Indians engaged in a largely unrecorded trade which suggested more possibilities for cooperation than for conflict between their respective economies. Hunters and sailors encountering one another on the coasts of Maine, Nova Scotia, and the St. Lawrence discovered very early that they had valuable things to trade:

Reprinted from William Cronon, *Changes in the Land: Indians, Colonists, and the Ecology of New England.* Copyright © 1983 by William Cronon. (New York: Hill & Wang, 1983), pp. 82–107, with permission of Hill & Wang, a division of Farrar, Straus and Giroux, Inc.

metal goods, weaponry, articles of clothing, and ornamental objects on the part of the Europeans; furs and skins on the part of the Indians. For the Europeans, such trade began as a casual adjunct to the cod fisheries, but in the second half of the sixteenth century, with the rising popularity of felt hats and the decline in European fur production, North American furs became a principal object of trade in their own right. For the Indians, that trade marked a new involvement in an alien commercial economy, as well as the onset of complicated shifts in their ecological circumstances.

It is important to underscore how little we know of this early fur trade and its effects: the various Indian peoples of New England undoubtedly started interacting with European visitors neither at the same time nor in the same way. As early as 1524, Verrazzano found Indians along the Maine coast who were only too familiar with the ways of European sailors. Although they actively sought to trade furs for knives, hooks, and other metal goods, they were nevertheless careful to direct Verrazzano's men to meet them at the rockiest and most dangerous part of the shore, where landing was impossible. There, as Verrazzano reported, "they sent us what they wanted to give on a rope, continually shouting to us not to approach the land," and communicating great hostility. This was in marked contrast to the inhabitants of Narragansett Bay, who apparently had had rather less experience with Europeans. They not only welcomed Verrazzano wholeheartedly but seemed indifferent to his offers of trade. "They did not appreciate cloth of silk and gold," Verrazzano wrote, "nor even of any other kind, nor did they care to have them; the same was true for metals like steel and iron, for many times when we showed them some of our arms, they did not admire them, nor ask for them, but merely examined their workmanship." Northern Indians, who lived closer to the fishing banks, learned of European trade goods and military methods before their southern counterparts; likewise, inhabitants of the coast began European contacts before those of interior villages.

Nevertheless, by the beginning of the seventeenth century, every recorded European exploration found Indians in villages all along the New England coast eager for trade. On the island of Cuttyhunk in 1602, Bartholomew Gosnold obtained the skins of beavers, otters, martens, foxes, rabbits, seals, and deer in exchange for knives and what he called "trifles." In 1605, Champlain was greeted on the Penobscot River by thirty Indians led by a sachem named Bashaba, who assured him that "no greater good could come to them than to have our friendship." Champlain was told that "they desired to live in peace with their enemies, and that we should dwell in their land, in order that they might in future more than ever before engage in hunting beavers, and give us a part of them in return for our providing them with things which they wanted." Already in 1605, Bashaba's speech displayed the extent to which Indians were orienting their economic activity to enable them to trade with Europeans. Bashaba made clear that he understood the demand for beaver on European markets, that he and his followers were prepared to increase their production to meet that demand, and that he saw friendship with Europeans as a way both of obtaining trade goods and of shifting military balances among Indian villages.

These were important lessons, to which we must soon return. For the moment, however, the most significant thing about them was that they were learned primarily not from men like Champlain and Gosnold but from dozens of unknown visitors who left no record of their trips. We know next to nothing about most of the Europeans who journeyed to New England in the sixteenth and early seventeenth centuries, and we can make only the crudest of inferences about how Indians responded to them. Yet there can be no doubt that contacts between the two groups were extensive. Explorers who were greeted by Indians speaking French, English, or Basque could have few illusions about being the first European visitors to an area. When the Pilgrims first landed on Cape Cod in 1620, they discovered "a place like a grave" covered with wooden boards. Digging it up, they found layer upon layer of household goods, the personal possessions that Indians ordinarily buried with their dead: mats, bowls, trays, dishes, a bow, and two bundles. In the smaller of the two bundles was a quantity of sweet-smelling red powder in which were the bones of a young child, wrapped in beads and accompanied by an undersized bow. Still, what troubled the grave-robbers were not these Indian things, many of which they took, but the contents of the larger bundle. There, in the same red powder, were the remnants of a man: some of the flesh remained on the bones, and they realized with a shock that "the skull had fine yellow haire still on it." With the bones, "bound up in a saylers canvas Casacke, and a payre of cloth breeches," were a knife, a needle, and "two or three old iron things," evidently the dead man's most personal belongings. A blond European sailor, shipwrecked or abandoned on the Massachusetts coast, had lived as an Indian, had perhaps fathered an Indian child, and had been buried in an Indian grave. His circumstances may or may not have been unusual—even this we cannot know—but they betokened an already long and continuing exchange between peoples on opposite sides of the Atlantic.

It was anonymous Europeans like the dead sailor in the Cape Cod grave who helped bring about the single most dramatic ecological change in Indian lives, one whose full significance historians have only recently come to understand. Of all the many organisms Europeans carried to America, none of them were more devastating to the Indians than the Old World diseases, what W. H. McNeill has called the microparasites. The ancestors of New England Indians had reached North America perhaps twenty or thirty thousand years before the Europeans, arriving via a land bridge at the Bering Straits during the most recent of the glacial epochs. In the course of their migrations, they failed to bring with them many of the illnesses that were common elsewhere in the world. Their low population densities and their having lived for extended periods under semiarctic conditions served to filter out microorganisms which required large host populations and more temperate climates to survive. Their lack of domesticated animals, especially the grazing ungulates, such as swine, cattle, and horses, which share many diseases with humans, also

helped to reduce the number of pathogens they brought with them from Eurasia. As a result, the American Indians were blessed by the absence not only of diseases that Europeans ordinarily experienced in childhood, such as chicken pox and measles, but also of more lethal organisms that were epidemic in the Old World: smallpox, influenza, plague, malaria, yellow fever, tuberculosis, and several others. As William Wood said, the New England Indians were a people of "lusty and healthful bodies, not experimentally knowing the catalogue of those health-wasting diseases which are incident to other countries."

It was, of course, a blessing that proved all too quickly to be a curse. For hundreds of generations, Indian babies had grown to adulthood with no experience of these illnesses, so that Indian mothers transferred to their infants none of the antibodies which might have provided some measure of immunity against them. What the Indians lacked was not so much *genetic* protection from Eurasian disease—though this may have been a partial factor—as the historical experience as a population to maintain *acquired* immunities from generation to generation: each new generation that failed to encounter a disease was left with less protection against it. As a result, European diseases struck Indian villages with horrible ferocity. Mortality rates in initial onslaughts were rarely less than 80 or 90 percent, and it was not unheard of for an entire village to be wiped out. From the moment of their first contact with an Old World pathogen, Indian populations experienced wave upon wave of epidemics as new diseases made their appearance or as new nonimmune generations came of age. A long process of depopulation set in, accompanied by massive social and economic disorganization.

How early this began in New England is impossible to know. The long sea voyage across the Atlantic acted as a disease filter in its own right, since epidemic diseases had usually run their course on board ship before sailors reached North America. Many visits probably occurred with no disease organisms at all being passed on to Indians, and the earliest transfers may well have been of endemic illnesses—diarrheas, dysentery, venereal diseases, respiratory viruses, tuber-culosis—which had remained nonvirulent in the shipboard population. Those Indians who saw the most of European visitors were obviously most at risk to acquire any disease that survived the sea journey, and so the inhabitants of north-ern fur-trading areas probably began to suffer from the new diseases first. By 1616, Pierre Biard could write of disease as being a regular visitor to the Indians of Maine and Nova Scotia. "They are astonished," he said,

> and often complain that, since the French mingle with and carry on trade with them, they are dying fast, and the population is thinning out. For they assert that, before this association and intercourse, all their countries were very populous, and they tell how one by one the different coasts, according as they have begun to traffic with us, have been more reduced by disease.

Biard's description suggests a significant increase in mortality rates among the northern Indians, but does not convey the catastrophic scale of epi-demics that occurred elsewhere. The low popula-tion densities of the northern hunters probably protected them somewhat from certain diseases (cholera, for instance) that needed a minimum host population in order to reproduce themselves, and may also have limited the diseases that did occur to sporadic outbreaks. Nevertheless, north-ern death sentences were postponed rather than annulled, and the effects of disease were simply spread over a long period of slow attrition.

Although the corn-growing Indians of south-ern New England were less involved in the fur trade, their much greater population densities meant that when disease was finally introduced to them, its effects were explosive. The first recorded epidemic in the south began in 1616 and raged for three years on the coast between Cape Cod and Penobscot Bay, reaching villages perhaps twenty or thirty miles inland but sparing both the deeper interior and the coast west of Narragansett Bay. Although contemporary observers describe it as "the plague," New England lacked the rats and human population densities necessary to sustain

that disease. Chicken pox seems a more likely cause, since its virus requires only a small host population in order to remain in circulation; it could have traveled in latent form across the At-lantic in the body of a European sailor who might then have developed shingles from which Indians could easily have become infected. Whichever disease the Indians caught, its effects are well documented. Thomas Morton told of villages in which only a single inhabitant was left alive. So many died that no one remained to bury the corpses, and crows and wolves feasted on them where they lay. When colonists arrived a few years after the epidemic had spent itself, they found such quantities of bleached bones and skulls that, as Morton said, "it seemed . . . a new found Golgotha."

Southern New England Indians continued to experience serious outbreaks of disease during the 1620s, and in 1633 they were visited by smallpox, one of the most lethal of European killers. The 1633 epidemic saw mortalities in many villages reach 95 percent. This time villages in the interior and along the coast west of Narragansett Bay fell victim to the viral fury as much as those else-where, perhaps an indication of the extent to which their trade connections had been expanded since 1616. William Bradford, Governor of the Plymouth Colony, has left the fullest description of the horrors brought by the disease. "For want of bedding and linen and other helps," he wrote,

> they fall into a lamentable condition as they lie on their hard mats, the pox breaking and mattering and running one into another, their skin cleaving by reason thereof to the mats they lie on. When they turn them, a whole side will flay off at once as it were, and they will be all of a gore blood, most fearful to behold. And then being very sore, what with cold and other distempers, they die like rotten sheep.

There was little Indians could do to protect themselves from the epidemics. Whereas they had previously dealt with their sick companions by gathering at their bedside to sit through the illness with them, they quickly learned that the new diseases could be escaped only by casting aside family and community ties and fleeing. "So terrible is their apprehension of an infectious disease," wrote Roger Williams in the 1640s, "that not only persons, but the Houses and the whole Towne takes flight." With only the sick left to help the sick, even those who might otherwise have survived an epidemic were doomed. Bradford said that

> they were in the end not able to help one another, no not to make a fire nor to fetch a little water to drink, nor any to bury the dead. But would strive as long as they could, and when they could procure no other means to make fire, they would burn the wooden trays and dishes they ate their meat in, and their very bows and arrows. And some would crawl out on all fours to get a little water, and sometimes die by the way and not be able to get in again.

Social disorganization compounded the biological effects of disease. Once villages were attacked by a new pathogen, they often missed key phases in their annual subsistence cycles—the corn planting, say, or the fall hunt—and so were weakened when the next infection arrived. Worse, hungry times that had always been normal in precolonial Indian society—for instance, the late winter among northern hunters—became lethal when accompanied by the new diseases. Chronic illnesses gained their foothold in this way, and broke out whenever Indian populations became particularly susceptible to them. Tuberculosis had become common by the end of the seventeenth century, and influenza in combination with pneumonia recurred regularly in epidemic proportions. Measles, typhus, dysentery, and syphilis all became endemic and contributed to the general decline in Indian populations. As a result, in the first seventy-five years of the seventeenth century, the total number of Indians in New England fell precipitously from well over 70,000 to fewer than 12,000. In some areas, the decline was even more dramatic: New Hampshire and Vermont were virtually depopulated as the western Abenaki declined from perhaps 10,000 to fewer than 500.

The epidemics disrupted most of the networks of kinship and authority that had previously organized Indian lives. When Bradford described a village in which "the chief sachem himself now died and almost all his friends and kindred," he was depicting a phenomenon that took place in many Indian communities. Villages which had lost their sachems and whose populations had declined twentyfold were often no longer viable entities; surviving Indians were forced to move to new villages and create new political alignments. Depopulation and alliances with Europeans gave ambitious individuals who had lacked high rank before an epidemic opportunities to assume new leadership roles. Squanto, for instance, later to become the Pilgrims' interpreter, was the only survivor from his village at the end of the 1616–19 epidemic. A man without a community, "whose ends," as Edward Winslow said, "were only to make himself great in the eyes of his countrymen, by means of his nearness and favor with us," he consciously sought to undermine the authority of the neighboring sachem Massasoit. One of his devices for doing this was to convince other Indians that the colonists "had the plague buried in our storehouse; which, at our pleasure, we could send forth to what place or people we would, and destroy them therewith, though we stirred not from home." This was a particularly blatant attempt to use disease to amass political power; the Indians' willingness to believe it testifies to both their fear and their well-grounded suspicion that the new illnesses were of European origin. But the mere fact of depopulation promoted conditions of turmoil which enabled new leaders to emerge in the ensuing political vacuum.

The social disruption brought by the epidemics was not limited to political leaders. Indian doctors, or powwows, found their ordinary healing practices useless against so potent a biological assault. Indeed, as the Puritan historian Edward Johnson said, the "powwows themselves were oft smitten with deaths stroke." European pathogens thus served to undermine the spiritual and religious practices of Indian communities. John Winthrop, in speaking of victims of smallpox in

1633, said that "divers of them, in their sickness, confessed that the Englishmen's God was a good God; and that, if they recovered, they would serve him." Conversions of this sort were often a kind of hedging of bets with little lasting consequence, but they suggest some of the spiritual trauma brought by the enormous mortalities. As Robert Cushman said of the Indians around Plymouth, "Those that are left, have their courage much abated, and their countenance is dejected, and they seem as a people affrighted."

Indian depopulation as a result of European diseases ironically made it easier for Europeans to justify taking Indian lands. If the English believed that cornfields were the only property Indians had improved sufficiently to own, the wiping out of a village—and the subsequent abandonment of its planting fields—eliminated even this modest right. Over and over again, New England towns made their first settlements on the sites of destroyed Indian villages. Plymouth, for instance, was located "where there is a great deal of Land cleared, and hath beene planted with Corne three or foure years agoe"—planted, in fact, just before the 1616 epidemic broke out. More than fifty of the earliest settlements had similar locations, thus saving their inhabitants much initial work in clearing trees. To Puritans, the epidemics were manifestly a sign of God's providence, "in sweeping away great multitudes of the natives . . . that he might make room for us there." John Winthrop saw this "making room" as a direct conveyance of property right: "God," he said, "hath hereby cleared our title to this place."

As Indian villages vanished, the land on which they had lived began to change. Freed from the annual burnings and soon to be subject to an entirely different agricultural regime, the land's transformations were often so gradual as to be imperceptible. But a few changes were directly attributable to the depopulation caused by the epidemics. Fields which had still stood in grass when the Pilgrims arrived in 1620 were rapidly being reclaimed by forest by the time of the 1630 Puritan migrations to Massachusetts. William Wood spoke of places "where the Indians died of

the plague some fourteen years ago" that were covered with "much underwood . . . because it hath not been burned." Between Wessaguscus and Plymouth, the regrowth of forest had already made one extensive area "unuseful and troublesome to travel through, insomuch that it is called ragged plain because it tears and rents the clothes of them that pass." Some Indian fields were rapidly overgrown by the strawberries and raspberries in whose abundance colonists took so much delight, but these were an old-field phenomenon that would not reproduce themselves for long without the growing conditions Indians had created for them. When the Puritan migrations began, the animals that had relied on the Indians to maintain their edge habitats were still abundant beyond English belief, but in many areas the edges were beginning to return to forest. Declining animal populations would not be noticed for many years, but habitat conditions were already shifting to produce that effect.

Because Old World pathogens had such profound effects on Indian lives, any analysis of the fur trade must bear those effects constantly in mind. Changes in the ways Indians organized subsistence, made political alliances, and interacted with the environment stemmed directly from the new market in furs and trade goods, but the larger context was that of a society facing biological havoc. One historian, Calvin Martin, has gone so far as to assert that Indians became involved in the fur trade because they believed that game animals, rather than Europeans, had brought the epidemics upon them. In Martin's view, Indian demand for European trade goods was decidedly secondary to the Indians' belief that they were conducting a holy war against animals that were persecuting them with disease. Elegant as his thesis may be, it is supported by very little evidence, and none of it from New England. Martin is right to note the apparent paradox of Indian participation in the fur trade: by so willingly overhunting the beaver and other game animals, Indians across North America were responsible for attacking one of the major bases of their own subsistence. But to appeal to a spiritual holy war to explain this phenomenon trivializes the social and economic circumstances that led Indians to engage in trade in the first place. The connection between the epidemics and the fur trade was real, but neither so direct nor so purely spiritual as Martin would have us believe.

The fur trade could not have existed without Indians: in order for the English to exploit beavers and other furbearers, it was essential that they have the willing cooperation of Indian partners. This fact sprang from the very hunting skills which English observers regarded as "laziness" in Indian males. Writing of the beaver, William Wood admitted that "these beasts are too cunning for the English, who seldom or never catch any of them; therefore we leave them to those skillful hunters [Indian males] whose time is not so precious." In fact, the Indians' time was not less precious: they simply hunted much more efficiently than the English—even with their supposedly "inferior" technology—and stopped when they were satisfied with what they had caught. (Perhaps their leisure time seemed to them *more* precious than the English thought their own.) No amount of English labor could have yielded so great a return on invested capital as did the Indians' labor in hunting and processing beaver. But to obtain that return, English colonists needed to offer goods that the Indians found as desirable as the Europeans found furs.

Trade was nothing new to the New England Indians. "Amongst themselves," said Roger Williams, "they trade their Corne, skins, Coates, Venison, Fish, etc." Within villages, it was difficult to distinguish such trade from the gift giving that was so important in maintaining political and economic alliance networks. But trade also took place between villages, especially of goods that some possessed in greater quantities by reason of ecological circumstances. An interior village in the upland forest, for instance, which had an abundance of chestnuts, might regularly exchange them with a coastal village that had an abundance of shellfish. Northern New England Indians could obtain a much greater variety and quantity of furs than those in the south, and these could be traded for corn and beans with southern Indians who had agricultural surpluses. But even exchange between villages had important political overtones, since it served as a token of their diplomatic relations. Champlain in 1606 observed a transaction in which one sachem felt he had not received value for value: he "went away very ill-disposed towards them for not properly recognizing his presents, and with the intention of making war upon them in a short time." Most exchanges, whether internal or external to a village, were articulated in the language of gift giving.

In addition to the implicit gift relationship, what distinguished this trade from that of European merchants was its preponderantly local nature. Trade took place largely between adjacent villages; no entrepreneurial class existed whose chief role was to move commodities over long distances. Goods of high value might still travel hundreds of miles, but generally only by being traded from village to village. As John Smith said, villages "have each trade with other so farre as they have society on each others frontiers, for they make no such voyages as from *Pennobscot* to *Cape Cod,* seldome to *Massachset.*" Trade was either between individuals for goods each would personally use, or between sachems for goods that could be redistributed to followers. The European fur trade could come into existence only by being assimilated into this earlier context.

The objects Europeans could offer in trade had certain qualities that were completely new to Indian material culture. Brass and copper pots allowed women to cook over a fire without the risk of shattering their earthen vessels, and were much more easily transported. Woven fabrics were lighter and more colorful than animal skins and nearly as warm. Iron could be sharpened and would hold an edge better than stone, so that European hatchets and knives had advantages over Indian ones. Indians had no firearms, and were unfamiliar with alcohol. But in spite of the newness of these things, it is wrong to see the acquisition of European technology as in itself necessitating a revolution in Indian social life. European tools did not instantly increase Indian

productivity in any drastic way. Most were readily incorporated into subsistence practices and
trade patterns that had existed in precolonial
times. They were in fact often reconverted into
less utilitarian but more highly valued Indian objects: the many early explorers who came across
Indians wearing brass and copper jewelry, for
instance, were probably seeing what Indians believed to be—along with arrowheads—the proper
use of European brass and copper kettles.

Indians had first to learn the uses of European
fabrics and metals before they would trade for
them; as Verrazzano discovered at Narragansett
Bay, this did not always happen automatically.
What Indians valued was often less the inherent
technical qualities of a material object than its
ascriptive qualities as an object of status. (In this,
they were not fundamentally different from Europeans who sought to obtain animal skins so as to
display personal wealth.) A kettle or a metal ar-
rowhead might have virtues that saved labor and
were desirable in their own right, but these did
not become compelling until other Indians owned
them and an individual's importance began to be
measured by their possession. Indians eventually
sought many of the things Europeans offered in
trade, not for what *Europeans* thought valuable
about them, but for what those things conveyed
in *Indian* schemes of value. In effect, they became
different objects. Being rare and exotic, European
goods could function as emblems of rank in Indian society and as gifts in the exchanges that
created and maintained alliance networks. Indian
individuals seeking to increase their political
power, especially in the wake of the epidemics,
often tried to accumulate trade goods that could
be used to gain more allies. Transactions of this
kind involved exchanges of values that were func-
tionally more symbolic than utilitarian; as with
the property systems we have already examined,
Indians and Europeans understood their acquisitions differently, for the simple reason that those
acquisitions were embedded in different social
and ecological contexts.

Some of the most highly desired goods offered
by Europeans in fact had little to do with European technologies at all. After using up their tiny
initial store of trade goods, the Plymouth colonists had, as Bradford said, "little or nothing
else" to offer Indians "but this corn which themselves had raised out of the earth." Agricultural
produce had been the major substance offered by
southern Indians in trade with northern ones, and
Plymouth at first behaved little differently from
an Indian village in trading its maize for furs.
What stimulated the trade was not so much new
European technologies—nothing other than the
sailing ship was necessary to pursue it—as a new
European economic need: the need to find commodities that would repay debts to European
merchants. In this sense, Europeans took hold of
the traditional maize-fur trade network and
transformed it from a system of binary village
exchange to a link in the new Atlantic economy.
Colonial governments reserved the fur trade as a
sovereign right for themselves and the merchants
who served as their agents, and began to amass
corn both by trading with southern Indians and
by taxing the colonists themselves. For a short
while, it seemed as if corn raising would prove a
most profitable enterprise: when Francis Higginson said that it was "almost incredible what great
gaine some of our English Planters have had by
our Indian Corne," he was excited not about the
grain itself but about its easy convertibility into
furs. Transported in English ships from southern
New England to the Maine coast, corn remained
one element of the fur trade throughout the
seventeenth century, but its importance nevertheless declined. Its disadvantages limited its
desirability as a staple commodity: it was bulky,
relatively difficult to transport, and its value fluc-
tuated considerably relative to both the size of the
annual corn crop and the northern Indians' success in hunting for food.

It was another commodity—like maize, more
Indian than European—that revolutionized the
New England fur trade: wampumpeag, the
strings of white and purple beads we know today
as wampum. Made by grinding and drilling the
shells of whelks and quahogs until they were hollow cylinders a quarter of an inch long and an
eighth of an inch in diameter, its manufacture
was ecologically limited to the Long Island

Sound area where these shellfish flourished. Never made in great quantities during pre-colonial times, wampum was a highly valued token of personal power and wealth. It was initially rare outside the coastal villages in which it was made, so that elsewhere, as Bradford noted, only "the sachems and some special persons . . . wore a little of it for ornament." Lesser individuals dared not accumulate too much of it unless they were willing to challenge those with higher prestige. It was exchanged mainly at well-circumscribed ritual moments: in the payment of tribute between sachems, as recompense for murder or other serious crimes, in the transfer of bride-wealth when proposing marriage, as payment for a powwow's magical services, or in gift exchanges to betoken friendship and alliance. It was, in other words, a medium of gift giving whose value was widely accepted among the Indians of southern New England.

To Europeans, wampum was ideally suited to become the medium for a wider, more commercial exchange—to become what John Locke called "money." The Indians' adoption of European metal drills increased their production of wampum, making it more widely available for trade. But, as with corn, the chief European innovation was to introduce a new functional role into Indian economies, that of the merchant who transported goods between communities which, for cultural and ecological reasons, valued those goods differently. The Dutch first discovered wampum's value in 1622, and were astonished at how much it facilitated their trade. Fearing that the Pilgrims would become rivals in the Connecticut fur trade if they found out about wampum independently, the Dutch West India Company's agent, Isaack de Rasieres, decided to introduce them to it himself. He accordingly sold them £50 worth of it in 1627 and encouraged them to try trading it on the Maine coast (rather than on the Connecticut, where the Dutch trading houses were located). Although Maine Indians were initially reluctant to acquire wampum, within two years it had become the single most important commodity Plymouth had to offer. Presumably because of the high prestige that Indians as-

sociated with its possession, Plymouth traders "could scarce ever get enough for them, for many years together," and were able to cut off other traders who lacked wampum and had only European goods to sell.

Control of wampum rapidly became crucial to both Indians and Europeans. The political crisis created by the epidemics made wampum a necessary acquisition for any sachem trying to expand—or even retain—his or her power. As greater and greater quantities became available to more and more individuals, even to those who had once been of low rank, an inflationary cycle in the price of prestige objects fueled trade all the more. Possession of wampum became increasingly common, with widening effects on status systems. Here again, wampum was part of the reorganization of Indian economic and political life which followed in the wake of the epidemics: competition for its acquisition established new leaders, promoted dependence on European traders, and helped shift the tribute obligations which had previously existed among Indian villages. "Strange it was," said Bradford, "to see the great alteration it made in a few years among the Indians themselves."

On the European side, the importance of wampum to the fur trade made it imperative that colonies have a guaranteed supply of it. That meant controlling trade with the Indians of Long Island Sound—Pequots, Mohegans, Narragansetts, and villages on Long Island—who could procure the necessary whelks and quahogs. At first their wampum was obtained by flooding them with high-status European goods such as kettles and firearms; in response, they expanded their production of it and, as Bradford said, "became rich and potent by it." The number of Europeans trying to trade with the wampum makers encouraged the Indians to become shrewd bargainers who played one trader off against another. According to Roger Williams, they "beate all markets and try all places, and runne twenty thirty, yea forty mile, and more, and lodge in the Woods, to save six pence." In part because of the guns which these markets gave the Indians of the south coast, many colonists increasingly feared the Indians' power and sought a less dangerous way of acquiring their wampum. Governor Bradford went so far as to write a poem about the problem:

But now they know their advantage so well,
And will not stick, to some, the same to tell,
That now they can, when they please or will,
The English drive away, or else them kill.

The colonists' economic problem of obtaining a sure supply of wampum and the military problem of dealing with independent Indian arms were finally solved simultaneously by means of armed force: the slaughter of the Pequots in 1637 and the assassination of the Narragansett sachem Miantonomo in 1643. Exacting a regular military tribute in wampum proved a safer and more reliable source of supply than trading guns for it.

The fur trade was thus far more complicated than a simple exchange of European metal goods for Indian beaver skins. It revolutionized Indian economies less by its new technology than by its new commercialism, at once utilizing and subverting Indian trade patterns to extend European mercantile ones. European merchants created an expanded regional economy in New England by shuttling between several different trading partners: wampum producers along Long Island Sound, corn growers—both Indians and colonists—in the south generally, European manufacturers, and the Indians—located primarily in the north—who hunted furs. Trade linked these groups with an abstract set of equivalent values measured in pelts, bushels of corn, fathoms of wampum, and price movements in sterling on London markets. The essential lesson for the Indians was that certain things began to have *prices* that had not had them before. In particular, one could buy personal prestige by killing animals and exchanging their skins for wampum or high-status European goods.

Formerly, there had been little incentive for Indians to kill more than a fixed number of animals. As Nicolas Denys observed of the northern Indians, "they killed animals only in proportion as they had need of them. They never made an accumulation of skins of Moose, Beaver, Otter, or others, but only so far as they needed them for personal use." The one occasion for which furs *were* accumulated in precolonial times—when they were exchanged with southern villages for corn and other goods—was in fact an exception to prove the rule. Aside from limitations on the amount of grain Indians could move overland or by canoe, such precolonial trade was kept to modest levels by two factors. Need—as measured by use and by the success of harvest or hunt—still determined the volume of trade: there was little reason for the inhabitants of a village to trade for more food than they could eat, or more clothes than they could wear. Taking place mainly between villages, the trade was conducted by sachems and other high-prestige individuals, and so was held in check by the status relationships within a village and the diplomatic relations between villages. It had few of the expansionist tendencies of European commerce.

Precolonial trade enforced an unintentional conservation of animal populations, a conservation which was less the result of an enlightened ecological sensibility than of the Indians' limited social definition of "need." One Indian at the end of the eighteenth century remembered that in earlier times his people had not killed "more than necessary." He said this was because "there was none to barter with them that would have tempted them to waste their animals, as they did after the Chuckopek or white people came on this island, consequently game was never diminished." As we have seen, European trade changed all of this. It introduced Indians to a new set of prestige goods which could only be obtained by trade; moreover, the disruption of earlier status systems by the epidemics eliminated many of the social sanctions which had formerly restricted individual accumulation. Indian economies thus became attached to international markets, not for technological, but for social and political reasons. For them, it was a market of much more limited circulation than it was for Europeans: Indian notions of status were measured by a handful of goods, whereas Europeans could accumulate wealth with virtually any material possession.

Nevertheless, even a limited market in prestige was enough to turn Indians into the leading assailants of New England's fur-bearing mammals. Certain animal populations began to decline in consequence, even though the epidemics meant that fewer Indians were hunting them. The commercialization of the Indian's earlier material culture thus brought with it a disintegration of their earlier ecological practices.

Chief among the animals which suffered from the fur trade was of course the beaver, whose low reproductive rates and sedentary habits made it easily threatened by concentrated hunting. Never abundant in southern New England, it was disappearing from Massachusetts coastal regions by 1640 and had ceased to be of much economic significance in the Narragansett country by 1660. The southern trade lasted longest on major rivers that drained extensive regions to the north, where Indian hunters continued to find beavers to kill. On the Connecticut River, European traders established in turn the towns of Wethersfield, Hartford, Windsor, and Springfield as fur posts. Each successive one captured Indian trade from those below it, and the arrival of agricultural settlers eventually brought the fur trade of each to an end. Springfield, established by William Pynchon in 1636, maintained its hold longer than most. Although its trade had declined by 1650 to the point that Edward Johnson could describe it as of "little worth," Pynchon's son John managed between 1652 and 1658 to procure from Indians nearly 9000 beaver pelts, in addition to hundreds of moose, otter, muskrat, fox, raccoon, mink, marten, and lynx skins. Output gradually declined, experienced a sharp drop in the 1670s during the conflicts surrounding King Philip's War, and from then on continued only at much reduced levels. By the end of the century, the fur trade had lost its economic importance to the area. The same fate overtook the string of trading posts—Concord, Chelmsford, and Lancaster—which were established on the Merrimac River.

Other southern animals were also at risk. As Pynchon's records showed, virtually any furbearer could be sold for its pelt. But in the vicinity of denser English settlements, especially Boston, there was also a market for meat, one in which both Indians and colonists participated. In the early 1630s, a male turkey weighing forty pounds brought four shillings in eastern Massachusetts, while other birds—heathcocks, ducks, geese, and so on—cost from four- to sixpence. In Springfield, Pynchon bought venison from the Indians by paying wampum for it. To increase colonial meat supplies, the Massachusetts General Court gave exclusive hunting privileges to designated colonists who improved a pond by setting decoys on it, or who used nets to hunt birds on certain islands. Other colonists used Indian servants to hunt food for them. For their part, Indians found colonial guns particularly helpful in hunting birds and large mammals. They sold enough of what they killed for Governor Bradford to object that

The gain hereof to make they know so well,
The fowl to kill, and us the feathers sell.
For us to seek for deer it doth not boot,
Since now with guns themselves at them can shoot.
That garbage, of which we no use did make,
They have been glad to gather up and take;
But now they can themselves fully supply,
And the English of them are glad to buy.

Bradford's main anxiety was that Indians owned guns at all, but he was also irritated by their killing and selling things which English colonists might otherwise have obtained for nothing.

Overhunting combined with reductions in edge habitats led some of the meat species to decline in numbers even by the end of the seventeenth century. Already in 1672, John Josselyn said of the turkey that English and Indian hunters had "now destroyed the breed, so that 'tis very rare to meet with a wild turkie in the woods." Only domesticated ones could be seen in eastern Massachusetts. A century later, the bird which William Wood had seen in flocks of a hundred had become so rare throughout New England that a popular farmer's manual could define the word "turkey" as "a large domestick fowl, brought from Turkey, and is called by the name of its country." The fact that the domesticated bird of Europe had originally been brought from America by Spanish colonists in the sixteenth century had apparently been forgotten. Other birds would eventually be eliminated as well—the passenger pigeon, which had existed in so many "millions of millions," began to disappear toward the end of the eighteenth century—but the fate of these other species was not finally sealed until the rise of metropolitan markets for fowl in the nineteenth century.

More important to southern Indians was the gradual disappearance of the white-tailed deer and other large herbivores. Deer were threatened by changes in their habitat, augmented numbers of hunters, and competition from domestic livestock. They were so reduced by the end of the seventeenth century that Massachusetts enforced its first closed season on their hunting in 1694, and in 1718 all hunting of them was forbidden for a closed term of three years. By the 1740s, a series of "deer reeves"—early game wardens—were regulating the deer hunt, but to little avail. At the end of the eighteenth century, Timothy Dwight noted that deer were "scarcely known below the forty-fourth degree of north latitude," having vanished from all but the northern stretches of Vermont, New Hampshire, and Maine. With them, save for in the far north, had gone the elk, bear, and lynx. "Hunting with us," said Dwight, "exists chiefly in the tales of other times."

By the time this happened, of course, the colonists no longer relied on hunting for any significant portion of their subsistence. The real losers were the Indians, whose earlier way of life was encountering increasing ecological constraints. Indian settlement patterns began to change in the 1630s. On the south coast, Indians took to occupying coastal sites year-round in order to stockpile shellfish so that they could make wampum on an expanded scale. This new sedentarism was reinforced, and promoted elsewhere in New England, by military conflicts—themselves a consequence of the political turmoil which followed the epidemics and expanding European trade—that led villages to prefer permanently fortified sites inhabited by relatively dense populations. Attacks by colonists and intertribal warfare concen-

trated Indians with particularly dramatic consequences: Gookin described how it forced "many of them to get together in forts; by which means they were brought to such straits and poverty, that had it not been for relief they had from the English, in compensation for labour, doubtless many of them had suffered famine." But even when the threat of violence was not so immediate, Indians were living in fixed locations on a more permanent basis. Earlier subsistence practices which had depended on seasonal dispersal were gradually being abandoned, with important social and ecological effects. Denser settlement patterns encouraged the spread of infectious diseases and increased pressure on adjacent hunting and planting areas. As a result, Indians found themselves relying on a narrowing range of foodstuffs.

As Indians increasingly sold the skins they hunted, they had to have an alternative for their own clothing. Despite some initial reluctance, they found it in European fabric, which, next to wampum, was by mid-century the single most important commodity they bought with fur. At Pynchon's trading post in the 1650s, Indian transactions for textiles outnumbered transactions for metal goods more than fivefold. Elsewhere, the price in beaver skins for a blanket was identical to that for a gun. European clothing was not only high in prestige value but cheaper than fur to own: a large beaver pelt cost nearly twice as much in wampum as a finished cloth coat. Raw cloth, which Indians preferred, was even cheaper. By the 1670s, Daniel Gookin could write:

> The Indians' clothing in former times was of the same matter as Adam's was, viz. skins of beasts, as deer, moose, beaver, otters, raccoons, foxes, and other wild creatures. . . . But, for the most part, they sell the skins and furs to the English, Dutch, and French, and buy of them for clothing a kind of cloth, called duffils, or trucking cloth, about a yard and a half wide.

From duffils they learned to fashion their clothing, and eventually they had no choice but to do so. The decline in deer populations made their reliance on European fabrics inescapable.

By the 1660s, southern New England Indians had for several decades been relying on wampum and furs to trade for textiles, arrowheads, knives, guns, and kettles. Gookin reported that "they generally disuse their former weapons." During the seventeenth century, earlier forms of these implements lost prestige value and young Indians growing up gained less and less experience in making them. Villages thus became vulnerable to changes in their trade base in a way they had not been before. Wampum, which in the 1640s had circulated as legal tender among colonists as well as Indians, lost much of its value in the 1660s when European demand for beaver declined and new supplies of silver coin from the West Indies reduced the scarcity of colonial specie. As a result, although wampum continued to circulate in the Indian trade, the colonists no longer defined it legally as money. "It is but a commodity," declared the Providence Court, and "it is unreasonable that it should be forced upon any man." Demand for wampum fell, and Indians on the south coast suddenly found themselves isolated from markets on which they had come to rely. Indians for whom pelts had been their main access to trade had comparable experiences when their fur supplies gave out. These changes contributed to the conflicts leading up to King Philip's War in 1675–76, but their longer-term effect was to force Indians who depended on trade goods to turn to the only major commodity they had left: their land.

The second half of the seventeenth century saw Indians in southern New England lose most of their land. The colonists accomplished this dispossession in ways which have been recounted at length elsewhere and need not be repeated here. Whether seized as the spoils of war, stolen by colonial subterfuge, or simply sold by Indians to obtain trade goods, the net effect was the same: decreasing quantities of land remained free for the Indians' use. The denser settlement patterns they had adopted earlier became less and less a matter of choice as they found themselves more and more surrounded by colonists. Subsistence practices which had never before had deleterious ecological consequences began gradually to have

them. Planting fields could no longer be so easily abandoned when their fertility declined, and agricultural yields fell, making crops a less reliable source of food. Hunting too became more difficult. Adjacent colonial settlements eventually tried to restrict Indian hunting on English land, and such key food sources as deer became harder to obtain. Toward the end of the seventeenth century, many Indians were actually beginning to keep European livestock. If the evidence from one archaeological site in Connecticut can be generalized, by 1700 some Indian villages were relying on domesticated animals for over half their mammalian meat supply. The keeping of cattle on Indian land further decreased the forage available for wild deer herds and so continued the erosion of hunting resources. From an ecological point of view, Indian subsistence practices were in many ways more and more like those of European peasants. As European trade had done earlier, European agriculture reorganized Indian relationships within both the New England regional economy and the New England ecosystem.

Many of the changes I have been describing apply primarily to southern New England. In the north, where Indian populations were much smaller in relation to their land base and fewer colonists came to settle, pressure on animal populations resulted almost wholly from trade rather than competition over land. Low Indian densities meant fewer hunters and for that reason larger concentrations of the very animals Europeans most desired, so that the fur trade was far more active in Maine and eastern Canada than it was farther south. In response, Indians extended their hunting of furbearers to seasons when those animals had not traditionally been taken, and winter subsistence activities which had earlier relied on a wide range of species turned increasingly to the handful that had become tradeable commodities. When Indians returned to the coast in summer to sell their catch, they sought not only wampum and the preferred European tools, but food as well, including corn, bread, peas, prunes, and alcohol. Because of their larger and more concentrated involvement with the fur trade, their eventual dependence on it was even greater than that of southern New England Indians. Nicolas Denys, writing in 1672, said that they had "abandoned all their own utensils." In effect, furbearers were being asked to supply not only clothing and winter food but many other aspects of subsistence as well.

As in the case of southern New England Indians, certain forms of European technology became integrated into northern subsistence practices, with important effects. Once Indians stopped cutting up brass and copper kettles for jewelry, they were liberated from the large and cumbersome wooden kettles, made from tree stumps, which they had once used for cooking. Denys said that the earlier "immovable kettles were the chief regulators of their lives, since they were able to live only in places where these were." European kettles enabled villages to follow animal populations more readily and without the necessity of resorting to base camps; to Indians, they seemed "the most valuable article they can obtain from us." Likewise, the musket, although rarely used for hunting beaver or the smaller furbearers because of its inaccuracy, made the killing of large herbivores a simpler task. Shooting a moose provided far more food with much less labor than killing many birds or small game animals. A solitary beast which had once been hunted only when deep snows slowed its movements, the moose suddenly became an easier prey. As a result, it was gone from parts of eastern Canada by the mid-seventeenth century, and the same pattern repeated itself in northern New England. At the end of the eighteenth century, the colonial historian James Sullivan said of Maine that "the moose, a monstrous large animal, has been plenty there in former days, but it is rare to see one at the present time."

What encouraged the destruction of the beaver, on the other hand, was less new technologies than new market relations. Because supplies of the animal lasted much longer in the north than in the south, northern Indians developed a new set of institutions for controlling the hunt. Reduction in beaver populations, as well as conflict over who should be permitted to trap where, led

to major shifts in Indian notions of property. Northern villages had formerly divided their hunting territories on a shifting and ad hoc basis; now, as families tried to hang on to their share of a declining beaver hunt, such territories became more and more fixed. By the eighteenth century, Maine Indians had allocated their lands into family hunting territories whose possession was inherited from generation to generation. In 1764, the fur trader Joseph Chadwick wrote that "their hunting ground and streams were all parcelled out to certain families, time out of mind." By turning uncaught beavers into private property, Indian families sought to guarantee their conservation: "it was their rule," said Chadwick, "to hunt every third year and kill two-thirds of the beaver, leaving the other third part to breed." Indians had once conserved their game animals, probably without fully realizing it, by their seasonal rotation from habitat to habitat, moving wherever food could be had with least effort. Now their dependence on trade forced them to control the beaver hunt much more self-consciously in order to assure that there would be animals to bring to market. The beaver, in other words, had ceased to be an object of use, conserved because the need for it was slight; instead, it had become a commodity of exchange, conserved because the need for it was great.

In part because of the family hunting territories, the beaver survived in Maine, albeit in much reduced numbers. The Maine fur trade continued throughout the eighteenth century, but the effects of colonial warfare, overhunting by English trappers, and competition from Canadian furs combined to make it less and less profitable. At the end of the French and Indian Wars, Maine Indians were complaining that "since the late war English hunters kill all the Beaver they find on said streams, which had not only empoverished many Indian families, but destroyed the breed of Beavers." Elsewhere in New England, the beaver barely survived into the nineteenth century; the southern fur trade was no longer very profitable by 1700, and the animal itself remained only in isolated areas. By 1797, Benjamin Trumbull could write of Connecticut's beavers—as well as its otters, foxes, martens, raccoons, minks and muskrats—using the past tense. Samuel Williams, in his *History of Vermont,* said that "the beaver has deserted all the southern parts of Vermont, and is now found only in the most northern, and uncultivated parts of the state." Even there, the animal would be gone before long.

The elimination of the beaver had ecological consequences beyond the loss of the animals themselves. Their passing left New England with a wealth of place names which no longer made much sense: scattered across the map of the region one still finds Beaver Brooks, Beaver Stations, Beaver Creeks, and Beaver Ponds. More importantly, they left behind a series of artifacts that would await European settlers when they came to clear the land. When colonists cut a road through freshly opened countryside, they often went out of their way to cross streams on abandoned beaver dams rather than to build bridges. The sites of old dams were often chosen as preferred mill sites. Some beaver ponds became spawning grounds for shad and salmon, thus providing sites where fish for food and fertilizer could be had with a minimum of labor. But it was when the old dams collapsed for want of maintenance that they conferred their greatest benefit on colonial settlers. Behind them was many years' accumulation of leaves, bark, rotten wood, and rain-washed silt; in addition, their ponds had killed acres of trees which had once stood on the banks of pre-beaver streams. When the pond disappeared with the breaching of its dam, the rich black soil was suddenly exposed to the sun and rapidly became covered with grass that grew "as high as a man's shoulders." Not only did this provide forage for moose and deer—as long as those animals remained to browse there—but it became ideal mowing ground when settlers arrived with their cattle. As the English traveler Henry Wansy remarked, "It is a fortunate circumstance to have purchased lands where these industrious animals have made a settlement. At some of them, there have been four ton of hay cut on an acre." The old pond bottoms, which could be as much as two hundred acres in extent, provided excellent agricultural land as well. As one colonial writer put it, "Without these natural meadows, many settlements could not possibly have been made, at the time they were made." The death of the beaver in fact paved the way for the non-Indian communities that would soon arrive.

By 1800, the joint efforts of Indians and colonists had decimated many of the animals whose abundance had most astonished early European visitors to New England. Timothy Dwight in the early nineteenth century said of Connecticut that "we have hardly any wild animals remaining besides a few small species of no consequence except for their fur." Such animals had fallen victim especially to the new Indian dependence on a market in prestige goods. The Indians, not realizing the full ramifications of what that market meant, and finally having little choice but to participate in it, fell victims too: to disease, demographic collapse, economic dependency, and the loss of a world of ecological relationships they could never find again. No one understood this better than the Indians themselves. In 1789, the Mohegans petitioned the state of Connecticut for assistance, explaining:

> The times are Exceedingly Alter'd, Yea the times have turn'd everything upside down, or rather we have Chang'd the good Times, Chiefly by the help of the White People, for in times past, our Fore-Fathers lived in Peace, Love, and great harmony, and had everything in Great plenty. . . . But alas, it is not so now, all our Fishing, Hunting and Fowling is entirely gone.

Even if they exaggerated the peace, love, and harmony of precolonial Indian life, they did not mistake its plenty. Indian economies had maintained and relied on that plenty, and could not exist without the ecological relationships it implied. But although selling the animals had been the Indians' major contribution to their new circumstances, it was by no means the only reason their world had turned upside down. Ecological changes wrought by the colonists themselves were far more extensive, and needed no Indian partners for their accomplishment.

5

TIME, SPACE, AND THE EVOLUTION OF AFRO-AMERICAN SOCIETY

IRA BERLIN

As English colonists gained a foothold on the mainland of North America and began the process of establishing permanent communities, the need for labor became increasingly acute. The small farmers of New England and the middle colonies needed labor to clear land, harvest crops, and maintain livestock. In the South large plantations required flocks of fieldhands to tend labor-intensive crops such as tobacco and rice. And in the growing seaport cities labor was needed to handle a growing volume of goods, to build houses for a burgeoning population, and to augment the production of local craftsmen. During the colonial period much of this labor was supplied by indentured servants, who exchanged four to seven years of their labor for passage to America.

But by the end of the seventeenth century colonists began to turn to a new source of labor: African slaves. Slavery was not new to the Americas; Spain and Portugal had been conducting a profitable slave trade since the sixteenth century. English mainland colonists could also draw upon the experiences of their West Indian counterparts whose sugar plantations depended upon a constant supply of slaves for their operation. By the early eighteenth century southern plantation owners as well as northern artisans and merchants had turned to large-scale importations of slaves in order to maintain their tobacco and rice plantations, their shops, and their homes.

One consequence of the introduction of slavery into mainland North America was the development of a distinctive Afro-American culture. Historians have long argued about the nature of this culture, some arguing that it retained its African characteristics while others have maintained that its African attributes were quickly submerged within the dominant Anglo-American culture. In this essay Ira Berlin suggests another way of addressing this problem. By surveying the development of mainland slavery on northern farms, in cities, and on southern plantations, he adds the dimensions of time and locale to the ongoing discussion of Afro-American culture. From this perspective he finds that in America African slaves created three—not one—Afro-American cultures.

Time and space are the usual boundaries of historical inquiry. The last generation of slavery studies in the United States has largely ignored these critical dimensions but has, instead, been preoccupied with defining the nature of American slavery, especially as compared with racial bondage elsewhere in the Americas. These studies have been extraordinarily valuable not only in revealing much about slave society but also in telling a good deal about free society. They have

---

Reprinted from *The American Historical Review* 80 (1980): 44–78, with permission of the author and *The American Historical Review*.

been essential to the development of a new under-standing of American life centered on social transformation: the emergence of bourgeois society in the North with an upward-striving middle class and an increasingly self-conscious working class and the development of a plantocracy in the South with a segmented social order and ideals of interdependence, stability, and hierarchy. But viewing Southern slavery from the point of maturity, dissecting it into component parts, comparing it to other slave societies, and juxtaposing it to free society have produced an essentially static vision of slave culture. This has been especially evident in the studies of Afro-American life. From Stanley M. Elkins's Sambo to John W. Blassingame's Nat-Sambo-Jack typology, scholars of all persuasions have held time constant and ignored the influence of place. Even the most comprehensive recent interpretation of slave life, Eugene D. Genovese's *Roll, Jordan, Roll,* has been more concerned with explicating the dynamic of the patriarchal ideal in the making of Afro-American culture than in explaining its development in time and space. None of the histories written since World War II has equaled the temporal and spatial specificity of U. B. Phillips's *American Negro Slavery.*

Recent interest in the beginnings of slavery on the mainland of British North America, however, has revealed a striking diversity in Afro-American life. During the seventeenth and eighteenth centuries, three distinct slave systems evolved: a Northern nonplantation system and two Southern plantation systems, one around Chesapeake Bay and the other in the Carolina and Georgia lowcountry. Slavery took shape differently in each with important consequences for the growth of black culture and society. The development of these slave societies depended upon the nature of the slave trade and the demographic configurations of blacks and whites as well as upon the diverse character of colonial economy. Thus, while cultural differences between newly arrived Africans and second and third generation Afro-Americans or creoles everywhere provided the basis for social stratification within black society, African-creole differences emerged at different times with different force and even different meaning in the North, the Chesapeake region, and the lowcountry. A careful examination of the diverse development of Afro-American culture in the colonial era yields important clues for an understanding of the full complexity of black society in the centuries that followed.

The nature of slavery and the demographic balance of whites and blacks during the seventeenth and first decades of the eighteenth centuries tended to incorporate Northern blacks into the emerging Euro-American culture, even as whites denied them a place in Northern society. But changes in the character of the slave trade during the middle third of the eighteenth century gave new impetus to African culture and institutions in the Northern colonies. By the American Revolution, Afro-American culture had been integrated into the larger Euro-American one, but black people remained acutely conscious of their African inheritance and freely drew on it in shaping their lives.

Throughout the colonial years, blacks composed a small fraction of the population of New England and the Middle Colonies. Only in New York and Rhode Island did they reach 15 percent of the population. In most Northern colonies the proportion was considerably smaller. At its height, the black population totaled 8 percent of the population of New Jersey and less than 4 percent in Massachusetts and Connecticut. But these colony-wide enumerations dilute the presence of blacks and underestimate the importance of slave labor. In some of the most productive agricultural regions and in the cities, blacks composed a larger share of the population, sometimes constituting as much as one-third of the whole and perhaps one-half of the work force. Although many Northern whites never saw a black slave, others had daily, intimate contact with them. And, although some blacks found it difficult to join together with their former countrymen, others lived in close contact.

The vast majority of Northern blacks lived and worked in the countryside. A few labored in highly capitalized rural industries—tanneries, salt works, and iron furnaces—where they often composed the bulk of the work force, skilled and unskilled. Iron masters, the largest employers of industrial slaves, also were often the largest slaveholders in the North. Pennsylvania iron masters manifested their dependence on slave labor when, in 1727, they petitioned for a reduction in the tariff on slaves so they might keep their furnaces in operation. Bloomeries and forges in other colonies similarly relied on slave labor. But in an overwhelmingly agrarian society only a small proportion of the slave population engaged in industrial labor.

Like most rural whites, most rural blacks toiled as agricultural workers. In southern New England, on Long Island, and in northern New Jersey, which contained the North's densest black populations, slaves tended stock and raised crops for export to the sugar islands. Farmers engaged in provisioning the West Indies with draft animals and foodstuffs were familiar with slavery and had easy access to slaves. Some, like the Barbadian émigrés in northern New Jersey, had migrated from the sugar islands. Others, particularly those around Narragansett Bay, styled themselves planters in the West Indian manner. They built great houses, bred race horses, and accumulated slaves, sometimes holding twenty or more bondsmen. But, whatever the aspirations of this commercial gentry, the provisioning trade could not support a plantation regime. Most slaves lived on farms (not plantations), worked at a variety of tasks, and never labored in large gangs. No one in the North suggested that agricultural labor could be done only by black people, a common assertion in the sugar islands and the Carolina lowcountry. In northern New England, the Hudson Valley, and Pennsylvania, the seasonal demands of cereal farming undermined the viability of slavery. For most wheat farmers, as Peter Kalm shrewdly observed, "a Negro or black slave requires too much money at one time," and they relied instead on white indentured servants and free workers to supplement their own labor. Throughout the North's bread basket, even those members of the gentry who could afford the larger capital investment and the

concomitant risk that slave ownership entailed generally depended on the labor of indentured servants more than on that of slaves. Fully two-thirds of the bond servants held by the wealthiest farmers in Lancaster and Chester counties, Pennsylvania, were indentured whites rather than chattel blacks. These farmers tended to view their slaves more as status symbols than as agricultural workers. While slaves labored in the fields part of the year, as did nearly everyone, they also spent a large portion of their time working in and around their masters' houses as domestic servants, stable keepers, and gardeners. Significantly, the wills and inventories of Northern slaveholders listed their slaves with other high status objects like clocks and carriages rather than with land or agricultural implements.

The distinct demands of Northern agriculture shaped black life in the countryside. Where the provisioning trade predominated, black men worked as stock minders and herdsmen while black women labored as dairy maids as well as domestics of various kinds. The large number of slaves demanded by the provisioning trade and the ready access to horses and mules it allowed placed black companionship within easy reach of most bondsmen. Such was not always true in the cereal region. Living scattered throughout the countryside on the largest farms and working in the house as often as in the field, blacks enjoyed neither the mobility nor the autonomy of slaves employed in the provisioning trade. But, if the demands of Northern agriculture affected black life in different ways, almost all rural blacks lived and worked in close proximity to whites. Slaves quickly learned the rudiments of the English language, the Christian religion, the white man's ways. In the North, few rural blacks remained untouched by the larger forces of Euro-American life.

Northern slaves were also disproportionately urban. During the eighteenth century, a fifth to a quarter of the blacks in New York lived in New York City. Portsmouth and Boston contained fully a third of the blacks in New Hampshire and Massachusetts, and nearly half of Rhode Island's black population resided in Newport. Ownership of slaves was almost universal among the urban elite and commonplace among the middling classes as well. On the eve of the Revolution, nearly three-fourths of Boston's wealthiest quartile of propertyholders ranked in the slaveholding class. Fragmentary evidence from earlier in the century suggests that urban slave-ownership had been even more widespread but contracted with the growth of a free working class. Viewed from the top of colonial society, the observation of one visitor that there was "not a house in Boston" that did "not have one or two" slaves might be applied to every Northern city with but slight exaggeration.

Urban slaves generally worked as house servants—cooking, cleaning, tending gardens and stables, and running errands. They lived in back rooms, lofts, closets, and, occasionally, makeshift alley shacks. Under these cramped conditions, few masters held more than one or two slaves. However they might cherish a large retinue of retainers, urban slaveholders rarely had the room to lodge them. Because of the general shortage of space, masters discouraged their slaves from establishing families in the cities. Women with reputations for fecundity found few buyers, and some slaveholders sold their domestics at the first sign of pregnancy. A New York master candidly announced the sale of his cook "because she breeds too fast for her owners to put up with such inconvenience," and others gave away children because they were an unwarranted expense. As a result, black women had few children, and their fertility ratio was generally lower than that of whites. The inability or unwillingness of urban masters to support large households placed a severe strain on black family life. But it also encouraged masters to allow their slaves to live out, hire their own time, and thereby gain a measure of independence and freedom.

Slave hirelings along with those bondsmen owned by merchants, warehouse keepers, and ship chandlers kept Northern cities moving. Working outside their masters' houses, these bondsmen found employment as teamsters, wagoners, and stockmen on the docks and drays and in the warehouses and shops that composed the essential core of the mercantile economy. In addition, many slaves labored in the maritime trades not only as sailors on coasting vessels, but also in the rope walks, shipyards, and sail factories that supported the colonial maritime industry. Generally, the importance of these slaves to the growth of Northern cities increased during the eighteenth century. Urban slavery moved steadily away from the household to the docks, warehouses, and shops, as demonstrated by the growing disproportion of slave men in the urban North. Aside from those skills associated with the maritime trades, however, few slaves entered artisan work. Only a handful could be found in the carriage trades that enjoyed higher status and that offered greater opportunity for an independent livelihood and perhaps the chance to buy freedom.

In the cities as in the countryside, blacks tended to live and work in close proximity to whites. Northern slaves not only gained firsthand knowledge of their masters' world, but they also rubbed elbows with lower-class whites in taverns, cock fights, and fairs where poor people of varying status mingled. If urban life allowed slaves to meet more frequently and enjoy a larger degree of social autonomy than did slavery in the countryside, the cosmopolitan nature of cities speeded the transformation of Africans to Afro-Americans. Acculturation in the cities of the North was a matter of years, not generations.

For many blacks, the process of cultural transformation was well under way before they stepped off the boat. During the first century of American settlement, few blacks arrived in the North directly from Africa. Although American slavers generally originated in the North, few gave priority to Northern ports. The markets to the south were simply too large and too lucrative. Slaves dribbled into the Northern colonies from the West Indies or the mainland South singly, in twos and threes, or by the score but rarely by the boatload. Some came on special order from merchants or farmers with connections to the West Indian trade. Others arrived on consignment, since few Northern merchants specialized in selling slaves. Many of these were the unsalable "refuse" (as traders contemptuously called them) of larger shipments. Northern slaveholders generally disliked these scourings of the transatlantic trade who, the governor of Massachusetts observed, were "usually the worst servants they have"; they feared that the West Indian re-exports had records of recalcitrance and criminality as well as physical defects. In time, some masters may have come to prefer seasoned slaves because of their knowledge of English, familiarity with work routines, or resistance to New World diseases. But, whatever their preference, Northern colonies could not compete with the wealthier staple-producing colonies for prime African field hands. Before the 1740s, Africans appear to have arrived in the North only when a temporary glut made sale impossible in the West Indies and the mainland South. Even then they did not always remain in the North. When conditions in the plantation colonies changed, merchants re-exported them for a quick profit. The absence of direct importation during the early years and the slow, random, haphazard entry of West Indian creoles shaped the development of black culture in the Northern colonies. While the nature of the slave trade prevented the survival of tribal or even shipboard ties that figured so prominently in Afro-American life in the West Indies and the Lower South, it better prepared blacks to take advantage of the special circumstances of their captivity.

Newly arrived blacks, most already experienced in the New World and familiar with their proscribed status, turned Northern bondage to their advantage where they could. They quickly established a stable family life and, unlike newly imported Africans elsewhere on the continent, increased their numbers by natural means during the first generation. By 1708, the governor of Rhode Island observed that the colony's slaves were "supplied by the offspring of those they have already, which increase daily. . . ." The transplanted creoles also seized the opportunities provided by the complex Northern economy, the relatively close ties of master and slave, and, for many, the independence afforded by urban life. In New Amsterdam, for example, the diverse needs of the Dutch mercantile economy induced the West India Company, the largest slaveholder in the colony, to allow its slaves to live out and work on their own in return for a stipulated amount of labor and an annual tribute. "Half-freedom," as this system came to be called, enlarged black opportunities and allowed for the development of a strong black community. When the West India Company refused to make these privileges hereditary, "half-free" slaves organized and protested, demanding that they be allowed to pass their rights to their children. Failing that, New Amsterdam slaves pressed their masters in other ways to elevate their children's status. Some, hearing rumors that baptism meant freedom, tried to gain church membership. A Dutch prelate complained that these blacks "wanted nothing else than to deliver their children from bodily slavery, without striving for piety and Christian virtues." Even after the conquering English abolished "half-freedom" and instituted a more rigorous system of racial servitude, blacks continued to use the leverage gained by their prominent role in the city's economy to set standards of treatment well above those in the plantation colonies. Into the eighteenth century, New York slaves informally enjoyed the rights of an earlier era, including the right to hold property of their own. "The Custome of this Country," bristled a frustrated New York master to a West Indian friend, "will not allow us to use our Negroes as you doe in Barbados."

Throughout the North, the same factors that mitigated the harshest features of bondage in New York strengthened the position of slaves in dealing with their masters. Small holdings, close living conditions, and the absence of gang labor drew masters and slaves together. A visitor to Connecticut noted in disgust that slaveowners were "too Indulgent (especially the farmers) to their Slaves, suffering too great a familiarity from them, permitting them to sit at Table and eat with them (as they say to save time) and into the dish goes the black hoof as freely as the white hand." Slaves used knowledge gained at their masters' tables to press for additional privileges: the right to visit friends, live with their families, or hire their own time. One slaveholder reluctantly cancelled the sale of his slaves because of "an invariable indulgence here to permit Slaves of any kind of worth or Character who must change Masters, to choose those Masters," and he could not persuade his slaves "to leave their Country (if I may call it so), their acquaintances & friends." Such indulgences originated not only in the ability of slaves to manipulate their masters to their own benefit, but also from the confidence of slaveholders in their own hegemony. Surety of white dominance, derived from white numerical superiority, complemented the blacks' understanding of how best to bend bondage to their own advantage and to maximize black opportunities within slavery.

During the middle decades of the eighteenth century, the nature of Northern slavery changed dramatically. Growing demand for labor, especially when European wars limited the supply of white indentured servants and when depression sent free workers west in search of new opportunities, increased the importance of slaves in the work force. Between 1732 and 1754, blacks composed fully a third of the immigrants (forced and voluntary) arriving in New York. The new importance of slave labor changed the nature of the slave trade. Merchants who previously took black slaves only on consignment now began to import them directly from Africa, often in large numbers. Before 1741, for example, 70 percent of the slaves arriving in New York originated in the West Indies and other mainland sources and only 30 percent came directly from Africa. After that date, the proportions were reversed. Specializing in the slave trade, African slavers carried many times more slaves than did West Indian traders. Whereas slaves had earlier arrived in small parcels rarely numbering more than a half-dozen, direct shipments from Africa at times now totaled over a hundred and, occasionally, several times that. Slaves increasingly replaced white indentured servants as the chief source of unfree labor not only in the areas that had produced for the provisioning trade, where their pre-eminence had been established earlier in the century, but in

the cities as well. In the 1760s, when slave importation into Pennsylvania peaked, blacks composed more than three-quarters of Philadelphia's servant population.

Northern whites generally viewed this new wave of slaves as substitutes for indentured labor. White indentured servants had come as young men without families, and slaves were now imported in much the same way. "For this market they must be young, the younger the better if not quite children," declared a New York merchant. "Males are best." As a result, the sex ratio of the black population, which earlier in the century had been roughly balanced, suddenly swung heavily in favor of men. In Massachusetts, black men outnumbered black women nearly two to one. Elsewhere sex ratios of 130 or more became commonplace. Such sexual imbalance and the proscription of interracial marriage made it increasingly difficult for blacks to enjoy normal family lives. As the birth rate slipped, mortality rates soared, especially in the cities where newly arrived blacks appeared to be concentrated. Since most slaves came without any previous exposure to New World diseases, the harsh Northern winters took an even higher toll. Blacks died by the score; the crude death rate of Philadelphia and Boston blacks in the 1750s and 1760s was well over sixty per thousand, almost double that of whites. In its demographic outline, Northern slavery at mid-century often bore a closer resemblance to the horrors of the West Indies during the height of a sugar boom than to the relatively benign bondage of the earlier years.

Whites easily recovered from this demographic disaster by again switching to European indentured servants and then to free labor as supplies became available, and, as the influx of slaves subsided, black life also regained its balance. But the transformation of Northern slavery had a lasting influence on the development of Afro-American culture. Although the Northern black population remained predominantly Afro-American after nearly a century of slow importation from the West Indies and steady natural increase, the direct entry of Africans into Northern society reoriented black culture.

Even before the redirection of the Northern slave trade, those few Africans in the Northern colonies often stood apart from the creole majority. While Afro-American slaves established precedents and customs, which they then drew upon to improve their condition, Africans tended to stake all to recapture the world they had lost. Significantly, Africans, many of whom did not yet speak English and still carried tribal names, composed the majority of the participants in the New York slave insurrection of 1712, even though most of the city's blacks were creoles. The division between Africans and Afro-Americans became more visible as the number of Africans increased after mid-century. Not only did creoles and Africans evince different aspirations, but their life-chances—as reflected in their resistance to disease and their likelihood of establishing a family—also diverged sharply. Greater visibility may have sharpened differences between creoles and Africans, but Africans were too few in number to stand apart for long. Whatever conflicts different life-chances and beliefs created, whites paid such distinctions little heed in incorporating the African minority into their slaveholdings. The propensity of Northern whites to lump blacks together mitigated intraracial differences. Rather than permanently dividing blacks, the entry of Africans into Northern society gave a new direction to Afro-American culture.

Newly arrived Africans reawakened Afro-Americans to their African past by providing direct knowledge of West African society. Creole blacks began to combine their African inheritance into their own evolving culture. In some measure, the easy confidence of Northern whites in their own dominance speeded the syncretization of African and creole culture by allowing blacks to act far more openly than slaves in the plantation colonies. Northern blacks incorporated African culture into their own Afro-American culture not only in the common-place and unconscious way that generally characterizes the transit of culture but also with a high degree of consciousness and deliberateness. They designated their churches "African," and they called themselves "Sons of Africa." They adopted Afri-

can forms to maximize their freedom, to choose their leaders, and, in general, to give shape to their lives. This new African influence was manifested most fully in Negro election day, a ritual festival of role reversal common throughout West Africa and celebrated openly by blacks in New England and a scattering of places in the Middle Colonies.

The celebration of Negro election day took a variety of forms, but everywhere it was a day of great merrymaking that drew blacks from all over the countryside. "All the various languages of Africa, mixed with broken and ludicrous English, filled the air, accompanied with the music of the fiddle, tambourine, the banjo, [and] drum," recalled an observer of the festival in Newport. Negro election day culminated with the selection of black kings, governors, and judges. These officials sometimes held symbolic power over the whole community and real power over the black community. While the black governors held court, adjudicating minor disputes, the blacks paraded and partied, dressed in their masters' clothes and mounted on their masters' horses. Such role reversal, like similar status inversions in Africa and elsewhere, confirmed rather than challenged the existing order, but it also gave blacks an opportunity to express themselves more fully than the narrow boundaries of slavery ordinarily allowed. Negro election day permitted a seeming release from bondage, and it also provided a mechanism for blacks to recognize and honor their own notables. Most important, it established a framework for the development of black politics. In the places where Negro election day survived into the nineteenth century, its politics shaped the politics within the black community and merged with partisan divisions of American society. Slaves elsewhere in the New World also celebrated this holiday, but whites in the plantation colonies found the implications of role reversal too frightening to allow even symbolically. Northern whites, on the other hand, not only aided election day materially but sometimes joined in themselves. Still, white cooperation was an important but not the crucial element in the rise of Negro election day. Its origin in the

1740s and 1750s suggests how the entry of Africans reoriented Afro-American culture at a formative point in its development.

African acculturation in the Northern colonies at once incorporated blacks into American society and sharpened the memory of their African past and their desire to preserve it. While small numbers and close proximity to whites forced blacks to conform to the forms of the dominant Euro-American culture, the confidence of whites in their own hegemony allowed black slaves a good measure of autonomy. In this context it is not surprising that a black New England sea captain established the first back-to-Africa movement in mainland North America.

Unlike African acculturation in the Northern colonies, the transformation of Africans into Afro-Americans in the Carolina and Georgia lowcountry was a slow, halting process whose effects resonated differently within black society. While creolization created a unified Afro-American population in the North, it left lowcountry blacks deeply divided. A minority lived and worked in close proximity to whites in the cities that lined the rice coast, fully conversant with the most cosmopolitan sector of lowland society. A portion of this urban elite, increasingly light-skinned, pressed for further incorporation into white society, confident they could compete as equals. The mass of black people, however, remained physically separated and psychologically estranged from the Anglo-American world and culturally closer to Africa than any other blacks on continental North America.

The sharp division was not immediately apparent. At first it seemed that African acculturation in the Lower South would follow the Northern pattern. The first blacks arrived in the low country in small groups from the West Indies. Often they accompanied their owners and, like them, frequently immigrated in small family groups. Many had already spent considerable time on the sugar islands, and some had doubtless been born there. Most spoke English, understood European customs and manners, and, as their language skills and family ties suggest, had made the difficult adjustment to the conditions of black life in the New World.

As in the Northern colonies, whites dominated the population of the pioneer Carolina settlement. Until the end of the seventeenth century, they composed better than two-thirds of the settlers. During this period and into the first years of the eighteenth century, most white slaveholders engaged in mixed farming and stock raising for export to the West Indian islands where they had originated. Generally, they lived on small farms, held few slaves, and worked closely with their bond servants. Even when they hated and feared blacks and yearned for the prerogatives of West Indian slave masters, the demands of the primitive, labor-scarce economy frequently placed master and slave face-to-face on opposite sides of a sawbuck. Such direct, equalitarian confrontations tempered white domination and curbed slavery's harshest features.

White dependence on blacks to defend their valuable lowland beachhead reinforced this "sawbuck equality." The threat of invasion by the Spanish and French to the south and Indians to the west hung ominously over the lowcountry during its formative years. To bolster colonial defenses, officials not only drafted slaves in time of war but also regularly enlisted them into the militia. In 1710 Thomas Nairne, a knowledgeable Carolina Indian agent, observed that "enrolled in our Militia [are] a considerable Number of active, able, Negro Slaves; and Law gives every one of those his freedom, who in Time of an Invasion kills an Enemy." Between the settlement of the Carolinas and the conclusion of the Yamasee War almost fifty years later, black soldiers helped fend off every military threat to the colony. Although only a handful of slaves won their freedom through military service, the continued presence of armed, militarily experienced slaves weighed heavily on whites. During the Yamasee War, when the governor of Virginia demanded one Negro woman in return for each Virginia soldier sent to defend South Carolina, the beleaguered Carolinians rejected the offer, observing that it was "impracticable to Send Negro Women in their Roomes by reason of the Discontent such

Usage would have given their husbands to have their wives taken from them which might have occasioned a Revolt."

The unsettled conditions that made the low-country vulnerable to external enemies strengthened the slave's hand in other ways. Confronted by an overbearing master or a particularly onerous assignment, many blacks took to the woods. Truancy was an easy alternative in the thinly settled, heavily forested lowcountry. Forest dangers generally sent truant slaves back to their owners, but the possibility of another flight induced slaveholders to accept them with few questions asked. Some bondsmen, however, took advantage of these circumstances to escape permanently. Maroon colonies existed throughout the lowland swamps and into the backcountry. Maroons lived a hard life, perhaps more difficult than slaves, and few blacks chose to join these outlaw bands. But the ease of escape and the existence of a maroon alternative made masters chary about abusing their slaves.

The transplanted African's intimate knowledge of the subtropical lowland environment—especially when compared to the Englishman's dense ignorance—magnified white dependence on blacks and enlarged black opportunities within the slave regime. Since the geography, climate, and topography of the lowcountry more closely resembled the West African than the English countryside, African not European technology and agronomy often guided lowland development. From the first, whites depended on blacks to identify useful flora and fauna and to define the appropriate methods of production. Blacks, adapting African techniques to the circumstances of the Carolina wilderness, shaped the lowland cattle industry and played a central role in the introduction and development of the region's leading staple. In short, transplanted Englishmen learned as much or more from transplanted Africans as did the former Africans from them. While whites eventually appropriated this knowledge and turned it against black people to rivet together the bonds of servitude, white dependence on African know-how operated during those first years to place blacks in managerial as well as

menial positions and thereby permitted blacks to gain a larger share of the fruits of the new land than whites might otherwise allow. In such circumstances, white domination made itself felt, but both whites and blacks incorporated much of West African culture into their new way of life.

The structure of the fledgling lowland economy and the demands of stock raising, with deerskins as the dominant "crop" during the initial years of settlement, allowed blacks to stretch white military and economic dependence into generous grants of autonomy. On the small farms and isolated cowpens (hardly plantations by even the most latitudinous definition), rude frontier conditions permitted only perfunctory supervision and the most elementary division of labor. Most units were simply too small to employ overseers, single out specialists, or benefit from the economies of gang labor. White, red, and black laborers of varying legal status worked shoulder to shoulder, participating in the dullest drudgery as well as the most sophisticated undertakings. Rather than skilled artisans or prime field hands, most blacks could best be characterized as jacks-of-all-trades. Since cattle roamed freely through the woods until fattened for market, moreover, black cowboys—suggestively called "cattle chasers"—moved with equal freedom through the countryside, gaining full familiarity with the terrain. The autonomy of the isolated cowpen and the freedom of movement stock raising allowed made a mockery of the total dominance that chattel bondage implied. Slaves set the pace of work, defined standards of workmanship, and divided labor among themselves, doubtless leaving a good measure of time for their own use. The insistence of many hard-pressed frontier slaveowners that their slaves raise their own provisions legitimated this autonomy. By law, slaves had Sunday to themselves. Time allowed for gardening, hunting, and fishing both affirmed slave independence and supplemented the slave diet. It also enabled some industrious blacks to produce a small surplus and to participate in the colony's internal economy, establishing an important precedent for black life in the lowcountry.

Such independence burdened whites. They

complained bitterly and frequently about blacks traveling unsupervised through the countryside, congregating in the woods, and visiting Charles Town to carouse, conspire, or worse. Yet knowledge of the countryside and a willingness to take the initiative in hunting down cattle or standing up to Spaniards were precisely the characteristics that whites valued in their slaves. They complained but they accepted. Indeed, to resolve internal disputes within their own community, whites sometimes promoted black participation in the affairs of the colony far beyond the bounds later permitted slaves or even black freemen. "For this last election," grumbled several petitioners in 1706, "Jews, Strangers, Sailors, Servants, Negroes, & almost every French Man in Craven & Berkly County came down to elect, & their votes were taken." Such breaches of what became an iron law of Southern racial policy suggest how the circumstances of the pioneer lowcountry life shrank the social as well as the cultural distance between transplanted Africans and the mélange of European settlers. During the first generations of settlement, Afro-American and Anglo-American culture and society developed along parallel lines with a large degree of overlap.

If the distinction between white and black culture remained small in the lowcountry, so too did differences within black society. The absence of direct importation of African slaves prevented the emergence of African-creole differences; and, since few blacks gained their liberty during those years, differences in status within the black community were almost nonexistent. The small radius of settlement and the ease of water transportation, moreover, placed most blacks within easy reach of Charles Town. A "city" of several dozen rude buildings where the colonial legislature met in a tavern could hardly have impressed slaves as radically different from their own primitive quarters. Town slaves, for their part, doubtless had first-hand familiarity with farm work as few masters could afford the luxury of placing their slaves in livery.

Thus, during the first years of settlement, black life in the lowcountry, like black life in the North, evolved toward a unified Afro-American culture. Although their numbers combined with other circumstances to allow Carolina blacks a larger role in shaping their culture than that enjoyed by blacks in the North, there remained striking similarities in the early development of Afro-American life in both regions. During the last few years of the seventeenth century, however, changes in economy and society undermined these commonalities and set the development of lowcountry Afro-American life on a distinctive course.

The discovery of exportable staples, first naval stores and then rice and indigo, transformed the lowcountry as surely as the sugar revolution transformed the West Indies. Under the pressure of the riches that staple production provided, planters banished the white yeomanry to the hinterland, consolidated small farms into large plantations, and carved new plantations out of the malaria-ridden swamps. Before long, black slaves began pouring into the region and, sometime during the first decade of the eighteenth century, white numerical superiority gave way to the lowcountry's distinguishing demographic characteristic: the black majority.

Black numerical dominance grew rapidly during the eighteenth century. By the 1720s, blacks outnumbered whites by more than two to one in South Carolina. In the heavily settled plantation parishes surrounding Charles Town, blacks enjoyed a three to one majority. That margin grew steadily until the disruptions of the Revolutionary era, but it again increased thereafter. Georgia, where metropolitan policies reined planter ambition, remained slaveless until mid-century. Once restrictions on slavery were removed, planters imported blacks in large numbers, giving lowland Georgia counties considerable black majorities.

Direct importation of slaves from Africa provided the impetus to the growth of the black majority. Some West Indian Afro-Americans continued to enter the lowcountry, but they shrank to a small fraction of the whole. As African importation increased, Charles Town took its place as the largest mainland slave mart and the center of the lowland slave trade. Almost all of the slaves in Carolina and later in Georgia—indeed, fully 40 percent of all pre-Revolutionary black arrivals in mainland North America—entered at Charles Town. The enormous number of slaves allowed slave masters a wide range of choices. Lowcountry planters developed preferences far beyond the usual demands for healthy adult and adolescent males and concerned themselves with the regional and tribal origins of their purchases. Some planters may have based their choices on long experience and a considered understanding of the physical and social character of various African nations. But, for the most part, these preferences were shallow ethnic stereotypes. Coromantees revolted; Angolans ran away; Iboes destroyed themselves. At other times, lowland planters apparently preferred just those slaves they did not get, perhaps because all Africans made unsatisfactory slaves and the unobtainable ones looked better at a distance. Although lowcountry slave masters desired Gambian people above all others, Angolans composed a far larger proportion of the African arrivals. But, however confused or mistaken in their beliefs, planters held them firmly and, in some measure, put them into practice. "Gold Coast and Gambia's are the best, next to them the Windward Coast are prefer'd to Angola's," observed a Charles Town merchant in describing the most salable mixture. "There must not be a Callabar amongst them." Planter preferences informed lowcountry slave traders and, to a considerable degree, determined the tribal origins of lowland blacks.

Whatever their origins, rice cultivation shaped the destiny of African people arriving at Charles Town. Although the production of pitch and tar played a pivotal role in the early development of the staple-based economy in South Carolina, rice quickly became the dominant plantation crop. Rice cultivation evolved slowly during the late seventeenth and early eighteenth centuries as planters, aided by knowledgeable blacks, mastered the complex techniques necessary for commercial production. During the first half of the eighteenth century, rice culture was limited to the inland swamps, where slave-built dikes controlled the irrigation of low-lying rice fields. But by mid-century planters had discovered how to regulate the tidal floods to irrigate and drain their fields. Rice production moved to the tidal swamps that lined the region's many rivers and expanded greatly. By the beginning of the nineteenth century, the rice coast stretched from Cape Fear in North Carolina to the Satilla River in Georgia. Throughout the lowcountry, rice was king.

The relatively mild slave regime of the pioneer years disappeared as rice cultivation expanded. Slaves increasingly lived in large units, and they worked in field gangs rather than at a variety of tasks. The strict requirements of rice production set the course of their work. And rice was a hard master. For a large portion of the year, slaves labored knee deep in brackish muck under the hot tropical sun; and, even after the fields were drained, the crops laid-by, and the grain threshed, there were canals to clear and dams to repair. By mid-century planters had also begun to grow indigo on the upland sections of their estates. Indigo complemented rice in its seasonal requirements, and it made even heavier labor demands. The ready availability of African imports compounded the new harsh realities of plantation slavery by cheapening black life in the eyes of many masters. As long as the slave trade remained open, they skimped on food, clothing, and medical attention for their slaves, knowing full well that substitutes could be easily had. With the planters' reliance on male African imports, slaves found it increasingly difficult to establish and maintain a normal family life. Brutal working conditions, the disease-ridden, lowland environment, and the open slave trade made for a deadly combination. Slave birth rates fell steadily during the middle years of the eighteenth century and mortality rates rose sharply. Between 1730 and 1760, deaths outnumbered births among blacks and only African importation allowed for continued population growth. Not until the eve of the Revolution did the black population begin again to reproduce naturally.

As the lowcountry plantation system took shape, the great slave masters retreated to the cities of the region; their evacuation of the countryside was but another manifestation of the growing social and cultural distance between them and their slaves. The streets of Charles Town, and, later, of Beaufort, Georgetown, Savannah, Darien, and Wilmington sprouted great new mansions as planters fled the malarial lowlands and the black majority. By the 1740s, urban life in the lowcountry had become attractive enough that men who made their fortunes in rice and slaves no longer returned home to England in the West Indian tradition. Instead, through intermarriage and business connections, they began to weave their disparate social relations into a close-knit ruling class, whose self-consciousness and pride of place became legendary. Charles Town, as the capital of this new elite, grew rapidly. Between 1720 and 1740 its population doubled, and it nearly doubled again by the eve of the Revolution to stand at about twelve thousand. With its many fine houses, its great churches, its shops packed with luxury goods, Charles Town's prosperity bespoke the maturation of the lowland plantation system and the rise of the planter class.

Planters, ensconced in their new urban mansions, their pockets lined with the riches rice produced, ruled their lowcountry domains through a long chain of command: stewards located in the smaller rice ports, overseers stationed near or on their plantations, and plantation-based black drivers. But their removal from the plantation did not breed the callous indifference of West Indian absenteeism. For one thing, they were no more than a day's boat ride away from their estates. Generally, they resided on their plantations during the nonmalarial season. Their physical removal from the direct supervision of slave labor and the leisure their urban residences afforded appear to have sharpened their concern for "their people" and bred a paternalist ideology that at once legitimated their rule and informed all social relations.

The lowcountry plantation system with its urban centers, its black majority, its dependence on "salt-water" slaves transformed black culture and society just as it reshaped the white world. The unified Afro-American culture and society

that had evolved during the pioneer years disappeared as rice cultivation spread. In its place a sharp division developed between an increasingly urban creole and a plantation-based African population. The growth of plantation slavery not only set blacks further apart from whites, it also sharply divided blacks.

One branch of black society took shape within the bounds of the region's cities and towns. If planters lived removed from most slaves, they maintained close, intimate relations with some. The masters' great wealth, transient life, and seasonal urban residence placed them in close contact with house servants who kept their estates, boatmen who carried messages and supplies back and forth to their plantations, and urban artisans who made city life not only possible but comfortable. In addition, coastal cities needed large numbers of workers to transport and process the plantation staples, to serve the hundreds of ships that annually visited the lowcountry, and to satisfy the planters' newly acquired taste for luxury goods. Blacks did most of this work. Throughout the eighteenth century they composed more than half the population of Charles Town and other lowcountry ports. Probably nothing arrived or left these cities without some black handling it. Black artisans also played a large role in urban life. Master craftsmen employed them in every variety of work. A visitor to Charles Town found that even barbers "are supported in idleness & ease by their negroes . . . ; & in fact many of the mechaniks bear nothing more of their trade than the name." Although most black artisans labored along the waterfront as shipwrights, ropemakers, and coopers, lowcountry blacks—unlike blacks in Northern cities—also entered the higher trades, working as gold beaters, silversmiths, and cabinetmakers. In addition, black women gained control over much of the marketing in the lowcountry ports, mediating between slave-grown produce in the countryside and urban consumption. White tradesmen and journeymen periodically protested against slave competition, but planters, master craftsmen, and urban consumers who benefited from black labor and services easily brushed aside these objections.

Mobile, often skilled, and occasionally literate, urban slaves understood the white world. They used their knowledge to improve their position within lowcountry society even while the condition of the mass of black people deteriorated in the wake of the rice revolution. Many urban creoles not only retained the independence of the earlier years but enlarged upon it. They hired their own time, earned wages from "overwork," kept market stalls, and sometimes even opened shops. Some lived apart from their masters and rented houses of their own, paying their owners a portion of their earnings in return for *de facto* freedom. Such liberty enabled a few black people to keep their families intact and perhaps even accumulate property for themselves. The small black communities that developed below the Bluff in Savannah and in Charles Town's Neck confirm the growing independence of urban creoles.

The incongruous prosperity of urban bondsmen jarred whites. By hiring their own time, living apart from their masters, and controlling their own family life, these blacks forcibly and visibly claimed the white man's privileges. Perhaps no aspect of their behavior was as obvious and, hence, as galling as their elaborate dress. While plantation slaves—men and women— worked stripped to the waist wearing no more than loin cloths (thereby confirming the white man's image of savagery), urban slaves appropriated their masters' taste for fine clothes and often the clothes themselves. Lowcountry legislators enacted various sumptuary regulations to restrain the slaves' penchant for dressing above their station. The South Carolina Assembly once even considered prohibiting masters from giving their old clothes to their slaves. But hand-me-downs were clearly not the problem as long as slaves earned wages and had easy access to the urban marketplace. Frustrated by the realities of urban slavery, lawmakers passed and repassed the old regulations to little effect. On the eve of the Revolution, a Charles Town Grand Jury continued to bemoan the fact that the "Law for preventing the excessive and costly Apparel of Negroes and other Slaves in this province (espe-

cially in *Charles Town*) [was] not being put into Force."

Most of these privileged bondsmen appear to have been creoles with long experience in the New World. Although some Africans entered urban society, the language skills and the mastery of the complex interpersonal relations needed in the cities gave creoles a clear advantage over Africans in securing elevated positions within the growing urban enclaves. To be sure, their special status was far from "equal." No matter how essential their function or intimate their interaction, their relations with whites no longer smacked of the earlier "sawbuck equality." Instead, these relations might better be characterized as paternal, sometimes literally so.

Increasingly during the eighteenth century, blacks gained privileged positions within lowcountry society as a result of intimate, usually sexual, relations with white slave masters. Like slaveholders everywhere, lowland planters assumed that sexual access to slave women was simply another of the master's prerogatives. Perhaps because their origin was West Indian or perhaps because their dual residence separated them from their white wives part of the year, white men established sexual liaisons with black women frequently and openly. Some white men and black women formed stable, long-lasting unions, legitimate in everything but law. More often than other slaveholders on continental British North America, lowcountry planters recognized and provided for their mulatto offspring, and, occasionally, extended legal freedom. South Carolina's small free Negro population, almost totally confined to Charles Town, was largely the product of such relations. Light-skinned people of color enjoyed special standing in the lowcountry ports, as they did in the West Indies, and whites occasionally looked the other way when such creoles passed into the dominant caste. But even when the planters did not grant legal freedom, they usually assured the elevated standing of their mulatto scions by training them for artisan trades or placing them in household positions. If the countryside was "blackened" by African imports, Charles Town and the other lowcountry ports exhibited a mélange of "colored" peoples.

While one branch of black society stood so close to whites that its members sometimes disappeared into the white population, most plantation slaves remained alienated from the world of their masters, physically and culturally. Living in large units often numbering in the hundreds on plantations that they had carved out of the malarial swamps and working under the direction of black drivers, the black majority gained only fleeting knowledge of Anglo-American culture. What they knew did not encourage them to learn more. Instead, they strove to widen the distance between themselves and their captors. In doing so, they too built upon the large degree of autonomy black people had earlier enjoyed.

In the pioneer period, many masters required slaves to raise their own provisions. Slaves regularly kept small gardens and tended barnyard fowl to maintain themselves, and they often marketed their surplus. Blacks kept these prerogatives with the development of the plantation system. In fact, the growth of lowcountry towns, the increasing specialization in staple production, and the comparative absence of nonslaveholding whites enlarged the market for slave-grown produce. Planters, of course, disliked the independence truck gardening afforded plantation blacks and the tendency of slaves to confuse their owners' produce with their own, but the ease of water transportation and the absence of white supervision made it difficult to prevent.

To keep their slaves on the plantation, some planters traded directly with their bondsmen, bartering manufactured goods for slave produce. Henry Laurens, a planter who described himself as a "factor" for his slaves, exchanged some "very gay Wastcoats which some of the Negro Men may want" for grain at "10 Bushels per Wastcoat." Later, learning that a plantation under his supervision was short of provisions, he authorized the overseer "to purchase of your own Negroes all that you know Lawfully belongs to themselves at the lowest price they will sell it for." As Laurens's notation suggests, planters found benefits in slave participation in the low-

country's internal economy, but the small profits gained by bartering with their bondsmen only strengthened the slaves' customary right to their garden and barnyard fowl. Early in the nineteenth century, when Charles C. Pinckney decided to produce his own provisions, he purchased breeding stock from his slaves. By the Civil War, lowland slaves controlled considerable personal property—flocks of ducks, pigs, milch cows, and occasionally horses—often the product of stock that had been in their families for generations. For the most part, slave propertyholding remained small during the eighteenth century. But it helped insulate plantation blacks from the harsh conditions of primitive rice production and provided social distance from their masters' domination.

The task system, a mode of work organization peculiar to the lowcountry, further strengthened black autonomy. Under the task system, a slave's daily routine was sharply defined: so many rows of rice to be sowed, so much grain to be threshed, or so many lines of canal to be cleared. Such a precise definition of work suggests that city-bound planters found it almost impossible to keep their slaves in the fields from sunup to sundown. With little direct white supervision, slaves and their black foremen conspired to preserve a large portion of the day for their own use, while meeting their masters' minimum work requirements. Struggle over the definition of a task doubtless continued throughout the formative years of the lowcountry plantation system and after, but by the end of the century certain lines had been drawn. Slaves generally left the field sometime in the early afternoon, a practice that protected them from the harsh afternoon sun and allowed them time to tend their own gardens and stock. Like participation in the lowcountry's internal economy, the task system provided slaves with a large measure of control over their own lives.

The autonomy generated by both the task system and truck gardening provided the material basis for lowland black culture. Within the confines of the overwhelmingly black countryside, African culture survived well. The continual arrival of Africans into the lowcountry renewed and refreshed slave knowledge of West African life. In such a setting blacks could hardly lose their past. The distinctive pattern of the lowland slave trade, moreover, heightened the impact of the newly arrived Africans on the evolution of black culture. While slaves dribbled into the North through a multiplicity of ports, they poured into the lowcountry through a single city. The large, unicentered slave trade and the large slaveholding units assured the survival not only of the common denominators of West African culture but also many of its particular tribal and national forms. Planter preferences or perhaps the chance ascendancy of one group sometimes allowed specific African cultures to reconstitute themselves within the plantation setting. To be sure, Africans changed in the lowcountry. Even where blacks enjoyed numerical superiority and a considerable degree of autonomy, they could no more transport their culture unchanged than could their masters. But lowcountry blacks incorporated more of West African culture—as reflected in their language, religion, work patterns, and much else—into their new lives than did other black Americans. Throughout the eighteenth century and into the nineteenth, lowcountry blacks continued to work the land, name their children, and communicate through word and song in a manner that openly combined African traditions with the circumstances of plantation life.

The new pattern of creolization that developed following the rice revolution smashed the emerging homogeneity of black life in the first years of settlement and left lowcountry blacks deeply divided. One branch of black culture evolved in close proximity to whites. Urban, often skilled, well-traveled, and increasingly American-born, creoles knew white society well, and they used their knowledge to better themselves. Some, clearly a well-connected minority, pressed for incorporation into the white world. They urged missionary groups to admit their children to school and later petitioned lawmakers to allow their testimony in court, carefully adding that they did not expect full equality with whites. Plantation slaves shared few of the assimilationist

aspirations of urban creoles. By their dress, language, and work routine, they lived in a world apart. Rather than demand incorporation into white society, they yearned only to be left alone. Within the quarter, aided by their numerical dominance, their plantation-based social hierarchy, and their continued contact with Africa, they developed their own distinctive culture, different not only from that of whites but also from the cosmopolitan world of their Afro-American brethren. To be sure, there were connections between the black majority and the urban creoles. Many—market women, jobbing artisans, and boatmen—moved easily between these two worlds, and most blacks undoubtedly learned something of the other world through chance encounters, occasional visits, and word of mouth. Common white oppression continually shrank the social distance that the distinctive experience created, but by the eve of the Revolution, deep cultural differences separated those blacks who sought to improve their lives through incorporation into the white world and those who determined to disregard the white man's ways. If the movement from African to creole obliterated cultural differences among Northern blacks, creolization fractured black society in the lowcountry.

Cultural distinctions between Africans and Afro-Americans developed in the Chesapeake as well, although the dimension of differences between African and creole tended to be time rather than space. Unlike in the lowcountry, white planters did not promote the creation of a distinctive group whose origins, function, and physical appearance distinguished them from the mass of plantation slaves and offered them hope, however faint, of eventual incorporation into white society. And, compared to the North, African immigration into the Chesapeake came relatively early in the process of cultural transformation. As a result, African-creole differences disappeared with time and a single, unified Afro-American culture slowly emerged in the Chesapeake.

As in the lowcountry, little distinguished black and white laborers during the early years of settlement. Most of the first blacks brought into the

Chesapeake region were West Indian creoles who bore English or Spanish surnames and carried records of baptism. Along the James, as along the Cooper, the demands of pioneer life at times operated to strengthen the slaves' bargaining position. Some blacks set the condition of their labor, secured their family life, participated in the region's internal economy, and occasionally bartered for their liberty. This, of course, did not save most black people from the brutal exploitation that almost all propertyless men and women faced as planters squeezed the last pound of profit from the tobacco economy. The blacks' treatment at the hands of planters differed little from that of white bound labor in large measure because it was difficult to treat people more brutally. While the advantages of this peculiar brand of equality may have been lost on its beneficiaries, those blacks who were able to complete their terms of servitude quickly joined whites in the mad scramble for land, servants, and status.

Many did well. During the seventeenth century, black freemen could be found throughout the region owning land, holding servants, and occasionally attaining minor offices. Like whites, they accumulated property, sued their neighbors, and passed their estates to their children. In 1651, Anthony Johnson, the best known of these early Negro freemen, received a two-hundred-and-fifty-acre headright for importing five persons into Virginia. John Johnson, a neighbor and probably a relative, did even better, earning five hundred and fifty acres for bringing eleven persons into the colony. Both men owned substantial farms on the Eastern Shore, held servants, and left their heirs sizable estates. As established members of their communities, they enjoyed the rights of citizens. When a servant claiming his freedom fled Anthony Johnson's plantation and took refuge with a nearby white farmer, Johnson took his neighbor to court and won the return of his servant along with damages against the white man.

The class rather than racial basis of early Chesapeake society enabled many black men to compete successfully for that scarcest of all New World commodities: the affection of white women. Bastardy lists indicate that white female servants ignored the strictures against what white lawmakers labeled "shameful" and "unnatural" acts and joined together with men of their own condition regardless of color. Fragmentary evidence from various parts of seventeenth-century Virginia reveals that approximately one-quarter to one-third of the bastard children born to white women were mulattoes. The commonplace nature of these interracial unions might have been the reason why one justice legally sanctified the marriage of Hester, an English servant woman, to James Tate, a black slave. Some successful, property-owning whites and blacks also intermarried. In Virginia's Northampton county, Francis Payne, a Negro freeman, married a white woman, who later remarried a white man after Payne's death. William Greensted, a white attorney who represented Elizabeth Key, a mulatto woman, in her successful suit for her freedom, later married her. In 1691, when the Virginia General Assembly finally ruled against the practice, some propertied whites found the legislation novel and obnoxious enough to muster a protest.

By the middle of the seventeenth century, Negro freemen sharing and fulfilling the same ideals and aspirations that whites held were no anomaly in the Chesapeake region. An Eastern Shore tax list of 1668 counted nearly a third of black tithables free. If most blacks did not escape the tightening noose of enslavement, they continued to live and work under conditions not much different from white servants. Throughout the seventeenth and into the first decades of the eighteenth century, black and white servants ran away together, slept together, and, upon occasion, stood shoulder to shoulder against the weighty champions of established authority. Thus viewed from the first years of settlement— the relatively small number of blacks, their creole origins, and the initial success of some in establishing a place in society—black acculturation in the Chesapeake appeared to be following the non-plantation pattern of the Northern colonies and the pioneer lowcountry.

The emergence of a planter class and its consolidation of power during a series of political crises in the middle years of the seventeenth century transformed black life in the Chesapeake and threatened this pattern of cultural change. Following the legalization of slavery in the 1660s, black slaves slowly but steadily replaced white indentured servants as the main source of plantation labor. By 1700, blacks made up more than half the agricultural work force in Virginia and, since the great planters could best afford to purchase slaves, blacks composed an even larger share of the workers on the largest estates. Increased reliance on slave labor quickly outstripped West Indian supplies. Beginning in the 1680s, Africans entered the region in increasingly large numbers. The proportion of blacks born in Africa grew steadily throughout the waning years of the seventeenth century, so that by the first decade of the eighteenth century, Africans composed some three-quarters of the region's blacks. Unlike the lowcountry, African imports never threatened the Chesapeake's overall white numerical superiority, but by the beginning of the eighteenth century they dominated black society. Some eighty years after the first blacks arrived at Jamestown and some forty years after the legalization of slavery, African importation profoundly transformed black life.

Slave conditions deteriorated as their numbers increased. With an eye for a quick profit, planters in the Chesapeake imported males disproportionately. Generally men outnumbered women more than two to one on Chesapeake slavers. Wildly imbalanced sex ratios undermined black family life. Physically spent and emotionally drained by the rigors of the Middle Passage, African women had few children. Thus, as in the North and the Carolina lowlands, the black birth rate fell and mortality rate surged upward with the commencement of direct African importation.

The hard facts of life and death in the Chesapeake region distinguished creoles and Africans at the beginning of the eighteenth century. The demands of the tobacco economy enlarged these differences in several ways. Generally, planters placed little trust in newly arrived Africans with their strange tongues and alien customs. While they assigned creoles to artisanal duties on their plantations and to service within their households, they sent Africans to the distant, upland quarters where the slaves did the dull, back-breaking work of clearing the land and tending tobacco. The small size of these specialized up-country units, their isolation from the mainstream of Chesapeake life, and their rude frontier conditions made these largely male compounds lonely, unhealthy places that narrowed men's vision. The dynamics of creole life, however, broadened black understanding of life in the New World. Traveling freely through the countryside as artisans, watermen, and domestic servants, creoles gained in confidence as they mastered the terrain, perfected their English, and learned about Christianity and other cultural modes that whites equated with civilization. Knowledge of the white world enabled black creoles to manipulate their masters to their own advantage. If Afro-Americans became increasingly knowledgeable about their circumstances and confident of their ability to deal with them, Africans remained provincials, limited by the narrow alternatives of plantation life.

As in the lowcountry and the Northern colonies, Africans in the Chesapeake strove to escape whites, while creoles used their knowledge of white society for their own benefit. These cultural differences, which were reflected in all aspects of black life, can be seen most clearly in the diverse patterns of resistance. Africans ran away toward the back country and isolated swamps. They generally moved in groups that included women and children, despite the hazards such groups entailed for a successful escape. Their purpose was to recreate the only society they knew free from white domination. In 1727, Governor William Gooch of Virginia reported that about a dozen slaves had left a new plantation near the falls of the James River. They headed west and settled near Lexington, built houses, and planted a crop before being retaken. But Afro-Americans ran away alone, usually with the hope of escaping into American society. Moving toward the areas of heaviest settlement, they found refuge in the thick network of black kinship that covered the countryside and sold their labor to white yeomen with few questions asked. While the possibility of passing as free remained small in the years before the Revolution, the creoles' obvious confidence in their ability to integrate themselves into American society stands in stark contrast to that of Africans, who sought first to flee it.

As reflected in the mode of resistance, place of resistance, occupation, and much else, Africans and creoles developed distinctive patterns of behavior and belief. To a degree, whites recognized these differences. They stigmatized Africans as "outlandish" and noted how creoles "affect our language, habits, and customs." They played on African-creole differences to divide blacks from each other, and they utilized creole skills to maximize the benefits of slave labor. But this recognition did not elevate creoles over Africans in any lasting way. Over the course of the century following legal enslavement, it had precisely the opposite effect. Chesapeake planters consolidated their class position by asserting white racial unity. In this context, the entry of large numbers of African—as opposed to creole—blacks into the region enlarged racial differences and helped secure planter domination. Thus, as reliance on black labor increased, the opportunities for any black—no matter how fluent in English or conversant with the countryside—to escape bondage and join the scramble for land, servants, and status diminished steadily.

By the middle of the eighteenth century, the size and character of the free Negro population had been significantly altered. Instead of a large minority of the black population, Negro freemen now composed just a small proportion of all blacks, probably not more than 5 percent. Many were cripples and old folks whom planters discarded when they could no longer wring a profit from their labor. While most were of mixed racial origins, few of these free mulattoes of the Chesapeake, in contrast to those of the lowcountry, traced their ancestry to the planter class. Instead, they descended from white servants, frequently women. These impoverished people had little status to offer their children. Indeed, planter-inspired legislation further compromised their liberty by requiring that the offspring of white

women and black men serve their mother's master for thirty-one years. Those who survived the term could scarcely hope for the opportunities an earlier generation of Negro freemen had enjoyed. The transformation of the free Negro caste in the century between 1660 and 1760 measured the change in Chesapeake society as its organizing principle changed from class to race.

The free Negro's decline reveals how the racial imperatives of Chesapeake society operated to lump all black people together, free and slave, creole and African. In the Chesapeake, planters dared not grant creoles special status at the expense of Africans. Since the Africans would shortly be creoles and since creoles shared so much with whites, distinctions among blacks threatened the racial division that underlay planter domination. In the lowcountry, where geography, economy, and language separated white and black, those few blacks who spoke, dressed, acted, and looked like whites might be allowed some white prerogatives. But, if lowcountry planters could argue that no white man could do the work required to grow rice commercially, no one in the Chesapeake could reasonably deny that whites could grow tobacco. The fundamental unity of Chesapeake life and the long-term instability of African-creole differences pushed blacks together in the white mind and in fact.

During the middle years of the eighteenth century, changes in the Chesapeake economy and society further diminished differences within black society and created a unified Afro-American culture. The success of the tobacco economy enlarged the area of settlement and allowed planters to increase their holdings. The most successful planters, anxious to protect themselves from the rigors of the world marketplace, strove for plantation self-sufficiency. The great estates of the Chesapeake became self-contained enterprises with slaves taking positions as artisans, tradesmen, wagoners, and, sometimes, managers; the plantation was "like a Town," as a tutor on Robert Carter's estate observed, "but most of the Inhabitants are black." The increased sophistication of the Chesapeake economy propelled many more blacks into artisanal positions and the

larger units of production, tighter pattern of settlement, and the greater mobility allowed by the
growing network of roads ended the deadening
isolation of the upcountry quarter. Bondsmen increasingly lived in large groups, and those who
did not could generally find black companionship
within a few miles' walk. Finally, better food,
clothing, and shelter and, perhaps, the development of immunities to New World diseases enabled blacks to live longer, healthier lives.

As part of their drive for self-sufficiency, Chesapeake slaveholders encouraged the development
of an indigenous slave population. Spurred by the
proven ability of Africans to survive and reproduce and pressed in the international slave market by the superior resources of West Indian
sugar magnates and lowland rice growers, Chesapeake planters strove to correct the sexual imbalance within the black population, perhaps by importing a large proportion of women or lessening
the burden of female slaves. Blacks quickly took
advantage of this new circumstance and placed
their family life on a firmer footing. Husbands
and wives petitioned their owners to allow them
to reside together on the same quarter and saw to
it that their families were fed, beyond their masters' rations. Planters, for their part, were usually
receptive to slaves' demands for a secure family
life, both because it reflected their own values and
because they profited mightily from the addition
of slave children. Thomas Jefferson frankly considered "a woman who brings a child every two
years as more profitable than the best man on the
farm [for] what she produces is an addition to
capital, while his labor disappears in mere consumption." Under these circumstances, the black
population increased rapidly. Planters relied less
and less on African importation and, by the
1740s, most of the growth of the black population
came from natural increase. Within a generation,
African importation was, for all practical purposes, no longer a significant source of slave
labor. In the early 1770s, the period of the greatest importation into the lowcountry, only five
hundred of the five thousand slaves added annually to the black population of Virginia derived
directly from Africa.

The establishment of the black family marked
the re-emergence of Afro-American culture in
the Chesapeake. Although Africans continued to
enter the region, albeit at a slower pace, the nature of the slave trade minimized their impact on
the development of black society in the region.
Unlike those in the lowcountry, newly arrived
Africans could rarely hope to remain together.
Rather than funnel their cargo through a single
port, Chesapeake slavers peddled it in small lots
at the many tobacco landings that lined the bay's
extensive perimeter. Planters rarely bought more
than a few slaves at a time, and larger purchasers,
usually the great planter-merchants, often acted
as jobbers, quickly reselling these slaves to backcountry freeholders. The resulting fragmentation
sent newly arrived Africans in all directions and
prevented the maintenance of tribal or shipboard
ties. Chesapeake slaveholders cared little about
the origins of their slaves. In their eyes, newly
arrived Africans were not Iboes, Coromantees, or
Angolans, but "new Negroes." While the unicentered slave trade sustained and strengthened
African culture in the low country, the Chesapeake slave trade facilitated the absorption of
Africans into the evolving creole society.

Differences between creoles and Africans did
not disappear with the creation of a self-sustaining Afro-American population. The creoles' advantages—language skills, familiarity with the
countryside, artisanal standing, and knowledge of
the plantation routine—continued to propel them
into positions of authority within the slave hierarchy. In some ways, the growing complexity of the
Chesapeake economy widened the distance between Africans and creoles, at least at first. Most
of the skilled and managerial positions within the
region's expanding iron industry went to creole
blacks as did the artisanal work in flour mills and
weaving houses. On some plantations, moreover,
artisan and house status became lodged in particular families with parents passing privileged positions on to their children. Increasingly, skilled
slaves entered the market economy by selling
their own time and earning money from "overwork," thereby gaining a large measure of freedom. For the most part, Africans remained on

rude, backwoods plantations tending the broad-leaf weed. Since creole slaves sold at a premium price and most great planters had already established self-sustaining slave forces, small planters purchased nearly all of the newly arrived Africans after mid-century. These upward-striving men generally owned the least developed, most distant farms. Their labor requirements remained primitive compared to the sophisticated division of labor on the self-contained plantation-towns.

Over the long term, however, economic changes sped the integration of Africans into Afro-American society. Under the pressure of a world-wide food shortage, Chesapeake planters turned from the production of tobacco to that of foodstuff, especially wheat. The demands of wheat cultivation transformed the nature of labor in the region. Whereas tobacco farming required season-long labor, wheat farming employed workers steadily only during planting and harvesting. The remainder of the year, laborers had little to do with the crop. At the same time, however, wheat required a larger and more skilled labor force to transport the grain to market and to store it, mill it, and reship it as flour, bread, or bulk grain. Economic changes encouraged masters to teach their slaves skills and to hire them out during the slack season. At first, these opportunities went mostly to creoles, but as the wheat economy grew, spurring urbanization and manufacturing, the demands for artisans and hirelings outstripped the creole population. An increasing number of Africans were placed in positions previously reserved for creoles. The process of cultural transformation that earlier in the eighteenth century had taken a generation or more was considerably shorter at mid-century. Africans became Afro-Americans with increasing rapidity as the century wore on, eliminating the differences within black society that African importation had created.

Chesapeake blacks enjoyed considerably less autonomy than their lowcountry counterparts. Resident planters, small units of production, and the presence of large numbers of whites meant that most blacks lived and worked in close proximity to whites. While lowcountry planters fled to coastal cities for a large part of the year, the resident planter was a fixture of Chesapeake life. Small freeholders labored alongside slaves, and great planters prided themselves on regulating all aspects of their far-flung estates through a combination of direct personal supervision and plantation-based overseers. The latter were usually white, drawn from the region's white majority. Those few blacks who achieved managerial positions, moreover, enjoyed considerably less authority than lowland drivers. The presence of numerous nonslaveholding whites circumscribed black opportunities in other ways as well. While Chesapeake slaves commonly kept gardens and flocks of barnyard animals, white competitors limited their market and created a variety of social tensions. If lowcountry masters sometimes encouraged their slaves to produce nonstaple garden crops, whites in the Chesapeake—slaveholders and nonslaveholders alike—complained that blacks stole more than they raised and worked to curb the practice. Thus, at every turn, economy and society conspired to constrain black autonomy.

The requirements of tobacco cultivation reinforced the planters' concern about daily work routine. Whereas the task system insulated lowcountry blacks against white intervention and maximized black control over their work, the constant attention demanded by tobacco impelled Chesapeake planters to oversee the tedious process of cultivating, topping, worming, suckering, and curing tobacco. The desire of Chesapeake masters to control their slaves went beyond the supervision of labor. Believing that slaves depended on them "for every necessity of life," they intervened in the most intimate aspects of black life. "I hope you will take care that the Negroes both men and women I sent you up last always go by the names we gave them," Robert "King" Carter reminded his steward. "I am sure we repeated them so often . . . that everyone knew their names & would readily answer to them." Chesapeake planters sought to shape domestic relations, cure physical maladies, and form personalities. However miserably they failed to ensure black domestic tranquility and reform slave drunkards, paternalism at close quarters in the Chesapeake had a far more potent influence on black life than the distant paternalism that developed in the lowcountry. Chesapeake blacks developed no distinct language and rarely utilized African day names for their children. Afro-American culture in the Chesapeake evolved parallel with Anglo-American culture and with a considerable measure of congruence.

The diverse development of Afro-American culture during the seventeenth and eighteenth centuries reveals the importance of time and place in the study of American slavery. Black people in colonial America shared many things: a common African lineage, a common racial oppressor, a common desire to create the richest life possible for themselves and their posterity in the most difficult of circumstances. But these commonalities took different shape and meaning within the diverse circumstances of the North American mainland. The nature of the slave trade, the various demographic configurations of whites and blacks, and the demands of particular staples—to name some of the factors influencing the development of slave society—created at least three distinctive patterns of Afro-American life. Perhaps a finer analysis will reveal still others.

This diversity did not end with the American Revolution. While African—creole differences slowly disappeared as the centerpole of black society with the closing of the slave trade and the steady growth of an Afro-American population, other sources of cohesion and division came to the fore. Differences between freemen and bondsmen, urban and rural folk, skilled and unskilled workers, and browns and blacks united and divided black people, and made black society every bit as variable and diverse during the nineteenth century as in the eighteenth. Indeed the diversity of black life increased substantially during the antebellum years as political changes abolished slavery in some places and strengthened it in others, as demographic changes set in motion by the Great Migration across the Lower South took effect, as the introduction of new crops enlarged the South's repertoire of staples, and as the kaleidoscopic movement of the world market sent the American economy in all directions.

If slave society during the colonial era can be comprehended only through a careful delineation of temporal and spatial differences among Northern, Chesapeake, and lowcountry colonies, a similar division will be necessary for a full understanding of black life in nineteenth-century America. The actions of black people during the American Revolution, the Civil War, and the long years of bondage between these two cataclysmic events cannot be understood merely as a function of the dynamics of slavery or the possibilities of liberty, but must be viewed within the specific social circumstances and cultural traditions of black people. These varied from time to time and from place to place. Thus no matter how complete recent studies of black life appear, they are limited to the extent that they provide a static and singular vision of a dynamic and complex society.

6

THE SOCIAL CONTEXT OF
DEMOCRACY IN MASSACHUSETTS

MICHAEL ZUCKERMAN

During the 1950s many historians were concerned with demonstrating the colonial origins of American democracy. For them democracy and America were synonymous. The most influential work to come from these historians was Robert E. Brown's *Middle-Class Democracy and the Revolution in Massachusetts* (1955). In his book Brown used a wide variety of sources, both quantitative and nonquantitative, to show that land ownership and the suffrage that it conferred were much more broadly distributed in colonial Massachusetts than had been previously thought. From this Brown argued that colonial Massachusetts, and by implication the other American colonies, were democracies long before the American Revolution.

In this essay Michael Zuckerman accepts Brown's findings but argues that the extent of suffrage was by no means the most important criterion of a democratic society. For Zuckerman the more important consideration is the social context in which political participation takes place. New England towns, he argues, allowed widespread political participation, not so much from democratic principles as from the need to bring about a consensus in all public matters. This need for unanimous agreement derived, in turn, from the Puritan concept of community. The Puritan town was a covenanted community composed of religious saints whose actions were guided by the hand of God. Dissent or discord in such a community would have called into question the omniscience of God and the saintliness of the town's residents. Thus, as Zuckerman shows, the town meeting, while formally democratic, was merely a mechanism for enforcing consent.

For at least a decade now, a debate has passed through these pages on the extent of democracy in the old New England town. It began, of course, with Robert E. Brown, and it did not begin badly: Brown's work was a breath of fresh air in a stale discussion, substituting statistics for cynicism and adding figures to filiopietism. But what was begun decently has degenerated since, and findings that should have provoked larger questions have only produced quibbles and counterquibbles over methodology and quantification. The discussion has not been entirely futile—few

would now maintain the old claim that the franchise was very closely confined in provincial Massachusetts—but neither has its apparent potential been realized. We are, ultimately, as far from agreement as we ever were about whether eighteenth-century Massachusetts was democratic. Somehow, the discussion has stalled at the starting point; a promising avenue of inquiry has not developed beyond its initial promise.

Perhaps a part of that failure was implicit in Brown's initial formulation of the problem; but one man cannot do everything, and Brown did

Reprinted from *The William and Mary Quarterly,* Third Series, 25 (1968): 523–44, with permission of the author.

advance our consideration of the New England town as far as any one man ever has. If he did not answer, or even ask, all the questions which might have been raised, other students could have done so. Brown's work made that possible. But since *Middle-Class Democracy and the Revolution in Massachusetts* (Ithaca, 1955) no comparable advances have been made. Indeed, the discussion seems to have stopped conceptually where Brown stopped, and one is forced to wonder not merely whether the right questions are being asked but whether any significant questions at all are being asked, other than those of how better to compute voting percentages. Certainly the terms of the debate have been, and are, inadequate to its resolution. Most obviously, figures on the franchise simply cannot serve to establish democracy. In our own time we have seen too many travesties on universal suffrage in too many non-democratic regimes to continue to take seriously in and of itself such an abstract calculus. Yet on both sides the discussion of New England town-meeting democracy has often assumed that the franchise is a satisfactory index of democracy, and the recourse to the seeming solidity of the voting statistics has depended, if only implicitly, upon that dubious premise.

Even those few critics who have challenged the contention that the issue of eighteenth-century democracy could be settled by counting heads have generally acquiesced in the far more fundamental assumption that in one way or another the issue of the eighteenth century was what the Browns have declared it to be: "democracy or aristocracy?" But democracy and aristocracy are probably false alternatives in any case for provincial Massachusetts; and in this case they are surely so, because they have been made initial tools of inquiry instead of end terms.

Of course, the Browns have hardly been alone in their strategy of frontal assault. On the contrary, it is indicative of how thoroughly their work established the contours of subsequent study that others have also rushed right into the issue of democracy without even a pause to ponder whether that issue was quite so readily accessible. Yet it would be admitted on most sides that

democracy was hardly a value of such supreme salience to the men of provincial Massachusetts that it governed their conscious motives and aspirations; nor, after all, did it provide the framework for social structure in the towns of the province. In application to such a society, then, a concept such as democracy must always be recognized for just that: a concept of our own devising. It is not a datum that can be directly apprehended in all its immediacy; it is an abstraction—a rather elevated abstraction—which represents a covering judgment of the general tenor or tendency of social relations and institutions. As such, it can carry its own assurance of validity only if it proceeds out of, rather than precedes, analysis of the society to which it is applied. To rip it out of its social context is to risk exactly the disembodied discussion of democracy we have witnessed over the past decade.

If we would study democracy in provincial Massachusetts, we cannot plunge headlong into that issue without sacrificing the context which conferred meaning on whatever degree of democracy did exist. Since democracy was incidental to the prime purposes of provincial society, we must first confront that society. Democracy, to the extent that it existed, was no isolated element in the organization of the political community, and problems of political participation and inclusion cannot be considered apart from the entire question of the nature of the provincial community. Even if most men in eighteenth-century Massachusetts could vote, that is only the beginning, not the end, of inquiry. What, then, was the *function* of a widely extended suffrage, and what was the function of voting itself in the conduct of the community? Who specifically was admitted to the franchise, and who was denied that privilege, and on what grounds? For ultimately, if we are to understand the towns that made the Revolution in Massachusetts, we must find out not only *whether* most men could vote but also *why*.

It is particularly imperative that we place provincial democracy in its social context because nothing else can plausibly account for its development. The founders of the settlement at Massachusetts Bay came with neither an incusive ethos nor any larger notions of middle-class democracy. In 1630 a band of true believers had entered upon the wilderness, possessed of a conviction of absolute and invincible righteousness. Their leaders, in that first generation, proudly proclaimed that they "abhorred democracy," and, as Perry Miller maintained, "theirs was not an idle boast." The spirit of the founders was set firmly against inclusion, with the very meaning of the migration dependent for many on an extension of the sphere of ecclesiastical exclusivity. The right of every church to keep out the unworthy was precisely the point of the Congregationalists' difference with the established church, and it was a right which could not be realized in England. Yet, without any English prodding and within about a decade of the first settlements, the original ideals of exclusion had begun to break down at the local level. Until 1692 the colonial suffrage extended only to freemen, but by that time nonfreemen had been voting in town affairs for almost half a century. The ability of the settlers to sustain suffrage restrictions at the colonial level so long after they were abandoned in the towns not only indicates the incomplete coincidence of intellectual currents and local conduct in early New England but also contradicts any contention that the pressures for democratic participation derived from Puritan theology or thought. The New England Puritans were pressed to the popularization of political authority only in grudging adjustment to the exigencies of their situation.

Their situation, quite simply, was one that left them stripped of any *other* sanctions than those of the group. The sea passage had cut the new settlement off from the full force of traditional authority, so that even the maintenance of law and order had to be managed in the absence of any customarily accepted agencies for its establishment or enforcement. Furthermore, as the seventeenth century waned and settlement dispersed, the preservation of public order devolved increasingly upon the local community. What was reluctantly admitted in the seventeenth century was openly acknowledged in the eighteenth, after the arrival of the new charter: the public

peace could not be entrusted to Boston, but would have to be separately secured in each town in the province. And though this devolution of effective authority to the local level resolved other difficulties, it only aggravated the problem of order, because the towns even more than the central government were without institutions and authorities sanctioned by tradition. Moreover, the towns had relatively limited instruments of enforcement, and they were demonstrably loath to use the coercive power they did possess.

Nonetheless, order was obtained in the eighteenth-century town, and it was obtained by concord far more than by compulsion. Consensus governed the communities of provincial Massachusetts, and harmony and homogeneity were the regular—and required—realities of local life. Effective action necessitated a public opinion approaching if not attaining unanimity, and public policy was accordingly bent toward securing such unanimity. The result was, to be sure, a kind of government by common consent, but government by consent in eighteenth-century Massachusetts did not imply democracy in any more modern sense because it required far more than mere majoritarianism. Such majoritarianism implied a minority, and the towns could no more condone a competing minority by their norms and values than they could have constrained it by their police power. Neither conflict, dissent, nor any other structured pluralism ever obtained legitimacy in the towns of the Bay before the Revolution.

Thus, authority found another form in provincial Massachusetts. Its instrument was the town meeting, which was no mere forum but the essential element in the delicate equipoise of peace and propriety which governed the New England town. In the absence of any satisfactory means of traditional or institutional coercion, the recalcitrant could not be compelled to adhere to the common course of action. Therefore, the common course of action had to be so shaped as to leave none recalcitrant—that was the vital function of the New England town meeting. To oversimplify perhaps, the town meeting solved the problem of enforcement by evading it. The meeting gave institutional expression to the imperatives of peace. In the meetings consensus was reached, and individual consent and group opinion were placed in the service of social conformity. There the men of the province established their agreements on policies and places, and there they legitimized those agreements so that subsequent deviation from those accords became socially illegitimate and personally immoral as well, meaning as it did the violation of a covenant or the breaking of a promise. In the town meetings men talked of politics, but ultimately they sought to establish moral community.

In the context of such a community, the significance of an extended franchise becomes quite clear: governance by concord and concurrence required inclusiveness. In communities in which effective enforcement depended on the moral binding of decisions upon the men who made them, it was essential that most men be parties to such decisions. Not the principled notions of the New Englanders but the stern necessities of enforcement sustained town-meeting democracy in Massachusetts. The politics of consensus made a degree of democracy functional, even made it a functional imperative. Men were allowed to vote not out of any overweening attachment to democratic principles *per se* but simply because a wide canvass was convenient, if not indeed critical, in consolidating a consensus in the community.

Under this incentive to inclusion, most towns did set their suffrage almost as liberally as Brown claimed. To seek the social context of the suffrage, then, necessitates no major quarrel with Brown's figures on franchise democracy; what it may provide is an explanation for them. It also offers the possibility of accounting for more than just the figures. As soon as we see that the high degree of participation permitted in the politics of the provincial town was not an isolated phenomenon but rather an integral aspect of the conduct of the community, we are in a position to go beyond a disembodied study of electoral eligibility and a simple celebration of middle-class democracy in Massachusetts. We are in a position to convert polemics into problems, and to press for answers.

In many communities, for example, a substantial and sometimes an overwhelming proportion of the people were *not* technically entitled to vote. Brown did not discuss some of these places, and the ones he did discuss were added to his evidence only with the special explanation that sometimes even the ineligible were admitted to the ballot box. But in the context of community such lapses would not necessarily invalidate his larger conclusions, nor would such *ad hoc* expedients be required; for the same imperatives impinged on towns where few were legally qualified as on the others, and the same results of wide political participation obtained because of the same sense that inclusiveness promoted peace while more rigorous methods threatened it. The town of Douglas, with only five qualified voters in its first years, flatly refused to be bound by a determination confined to those five, declaring its conviction "that the intent of no law can bind them to such ill consequences." Mendon, in its "infant state" in 1742, voted "to permit a considerable number of persons not qualified by law to vote . . . being induced thereto by an apprehension that it would be a means of preserving peace and unity amongst ourselves." Princeton, incorporated in 1760 with forty-three settlers but only fourteen eligible to vote according to provincial regulations, established a formal "agreement among themselves to overlook" those regulations, and the General Court upheld that agreement. "The poor freeholders" in the early days of Upton were also "allowed liberty to vote in town meeting," and it had produced "an encouraging harmony" in local affairs until 1746, when a few of the qualified voters, momentarily possessed of a majority of the ten in town, sought to upset the customary arrangements and limit the franchise as the law required. The rest of the town at once protested that "such a strenuous method of proceeding would endanger the peace of the town" and begged the General Court "to prevent the dismal damages that may follow" therefrom. The Court did exactly as it was asked, and at the new meeting the town reverted to its old form: "everyone was admitted to vote, qualified or not."

The principle which governed such universalism was not deliberate democracy; it was merely a recognition that the community could not be governed solely by the qualified voters if they were too few in number. Such a situation was most likely to occur in new communities, but it was not limited to them. Middleton had been established for almost a quarter of a century when it was conceded that in the local elections of 1752 "there was double the number of votes to the lawful voters." In a variety of towns and at other times, requirements for the franchise were also ignored and admission of the unqualified acknowledged explicitly. Thomas Hutchinson's wry lament that "anything with the appearance of a man" was allowed the vote may have been excessive, but it was not wholly fabricated. And even towns whose political procedures were more regular resorted to universalism in cases of conflict or of major issues. Fitchburg, for instance, voted in 1767 that "every freholder be a voter in Chusing of a minestr," while twenty years earlier, in a bitterly contested election in Haverhill, "there was not any list of valuation read nor any list of non-voters nor any weighting of what name or nature whatsoever by which the selectmen did pretend to show who was qualified to vote in town affairs."

The question of inclusiveness itself sometimes came before a town, not always without challenge but generally with a democratic outcome. Dudley, more than a decade after the incorporation of the town, voted "that all the freeholder of sd town should be voters by a graet majorytie and all agreed to it." In Needham in 1750 it was also "put to vote whether it be the mind of the town to allow all freeholders in town to vote for a moderator," and there too the vote carried in the affirmative. And that verdict for inclusion was not even as revealing as the method by which that verdict was reached, for in voting *whether* to include all in the election, Needham *did* include all in the procedural issue. Every man did vote on the question of whether every man was to be allowed to vote.

Of course, absolute inclusiveness never prevailed in provincial Massachusetts—women could not vote at all, and neither could anyone

under 21—and property and residence qualifications, introduced in 1692, were probably adhered to as often as they were ignored, so that even the participation of adult males was something less than universal. It was an important part of Brown's achievement to show that, in general, it was not *very much* less than universal, but, by the nature of his research strategy, he could go no further than that. If we are to penetrate to particulars—if we are to ask who was excluded, and why, and why the suffrage standards were what they were—we must consider not only numbers but also the conditions of community.

The men who were not allowed legitimately to vote with their fellow townsmen were commonly tenants or the sons of voters; as Brown discovered, it was these two groups against which the property requirement primarily operated. But where the controversialists seek to *excuse* these exclusions, or to magnify them, a broader perspective allows one to *explain* them, for against these two groups sanctions were available that were far more effective than those of the generalized community. Stringent property qualifications were clearly self-defeating in a society where consensus was the engine of enforcement, but overly generous qualifications were equally unnecessary. Where some men, such as tenants and dependent sons, could be privately coerced, liberality on their behalf, from the standpoint of social control, would have meant the commission of a sin of superfluity.

Similarly, almost nothing but disadvantage could have accrued from a loose residence requirement enabling men not truly members of the community to participate in its decision-making process, since voting qualifications in provincial Massachusetts were connected to the concept of community, not the concept of democracy. The extensions and contractions of the franchise were significant to the townsmen of the eighteenth century primarily as a means of consolidating communal consensus. All those whose acquiescence in public action was necessary were included, and all those whose concurrence could be compelled otherwise or dispensed with were excluded, often very emphatically. Sixty-six citizens of Watertown, for example, petitioned against the allowance of a single unqualified voter in a 1757 election because he was "well known to belong to the town of Lincoln." In many towns such as Sudbury the town clerk "very carefully warned those that were not legally qualified not to vote and prayed the selectmen to be very careful and watchful that nobody voted that was not legally qualified." Even in disputes over specific qualifications, both sides often agreed on the principle of exclusion of the unqualified; contention occurred only over the application of that principle.

Consciousness of voting qualifications colored the conduct of other town affairs as well as elections, as indeed was natural since the meaning of the franchise went so far beyond mere electoral democracy. Protests by men recently arrived in a town could be discredited, as they were in Haverhill in 1748, without any reference to the justice of the protest itself, simply by stating that "many of their petitioners are not qualified to vote in town affairs as may be seen by the selectmen's list of voters, and some of them were never known to reside in town or did we ever hear of them before we saw their petition." Similarly, in the creation of new communities qualification for the franchise could be crucial. Inhabitants of Bridgewater resisted their own inclusion in a precinct proposed by thirty-seven men dwelling in their vicinity by pointing out that "there is not above eleven or twelve that are qualified to vote in town meetings as the law directs." Many towns in their corporate capacity made much the same plea when confronted with an appeal for separation from the community. As Worcester once noted in such a case, more than half the petitioners were "not voters and one is a single Indian."

Such consciousness of qualifications sometimes appeared to be nothing more than an insistence on a "stake in society" in order to participate in the society's deliberations and decisions, but the stake-in-society concept, despite its popularity in the West and its convergence with certain conditions of public life in the province, was not precisely the notion which controlled those restrictions of the franchise which did persist after 1692. It was not out of any intrinsic attachment to that concept, but simply out of a fear that those without property were overly amenable to bribery or other such suasion, that the men of Massachusetts clung to their voting qualifications. As the Essex Result was to state the principle in 1778, "all the members of the state are qualified to make the election, unless they have not sufficient discretion, or are so situated as to have no wills of their own." Participation in community decisions was the prerogative of independent men, of *all* a town's independent men, but, ideally, *only* of those. Indeed, it was precisely because of their independence that they had to be accorded a vote, since only by their participation did they bind themselves to concur in the community's chosen course of action. The town meeting was an instrument for enforcement, not—at least not intentionally—a school for democracy.

This logic of competence governed the exclusion of women and children and also accounted for the antipathy to voting by tenants. The basis of the prohibitions which were insisted upon was never so much an objection to poverty *per se*—the stake-in-society argument—as to the tenant's concomitant status of dependence, the pervasive assumption of which emerged clearly in a contested election in Haverhill in 1748. There the petitioners charged that a man had been "refused as a voter under pretense that he was a tenant and so not qualified, when the full reason was that he was a tenant to one of their [the selectmen's] opposers and so at all hazards to be suppressed," while another man, a tenant to one of the selectmen themselves, had been received as a voter though "rated at much less in the last year's taxes than he whom they refused." The protest was thus directed primarily against the abuses of the selectmen: that tenants would do as their landlords desired was simply taken for granted. And naturally the same sort of assumption controlled the exclusion of sons still living with their parents. The voting age of twenty-one was the most rudimentary expression of this requirement of a will of one's own, but the legal age was not very firm at the edges. Like other laws of the province, it could not stand when it came up against local desires, and the age qualifications were often abrogated when unusual dependence or independence was demonstrable, as in the case of the eighteen-year-old who voted in a Sheffield election of 1751 because his father had died and he had become head of his family. As the town's elected representative could declare on that occasion, quite ignoring the legal age requirement, the lad "had a good right to vote, for his estate rested in him and that he was a town-born child and so was an inhabitant."

Of course, the townsmen of the eighteenth century placed no premium on independence as such. Massachusetts townsmen were expected to be independent but not too independent; ultimately, they were supposed on their own to arrive at the same actions and commitments as their neighbors. Any *genuine* independence, excessive *or* insufficient, was denigrated if not altogether denied a place in the community. Thus, when a number of inhabitants of a gore of land near Charlton faced the threat of incorporation with the town, they submitted "one word of information" about the townsmen who had asked for that incorporation. The note said only:

Baptist signers   —7
Churchmen   —3
Tenants   —4
Neither tenants nor freeholders but intruders upon
    other men's property   —15
The whole of the petitioners in Charlton consisting
    of 35 in number.

In other words, tenants were tainted, but so too were all others who were their own men, such as squatters and those who dared to differ in religion. In denigrating them, the inhabitants of the gore drew no distinctions: tenant and Baptist were equally offensive because equally outside of orthodoxy, beyond the confines of consensus.

Ultimately almost *any* taint on membership in the homogeneous community was a potential basis for derogation. Some inhabitants of Rutland once even attempted to deny the validity of a town decision merely because many of its supporters were "such as were and are dissenters from the public worship of God in the old meet-

ing-house." And though Rutland's religious orthodoxy was a bit exquisite even for eighteenth-century New England, it was so only in degree. For example, when Sutton opposed the erection of a new district out of parts of itself and several other towns in 1772, the town actually deducted the Anabaptists from the number of signatories to the application—Baptists simply did not count as full citizens. Worcester did the same thing and indeed went even further. Several of the signers of the petition for separation were not heads of families but mere "single persons, some of them transient ones," and so, said the town, were not to be "accounted as part of the number of families the petitioners say are within the limits of the proposed district." Whereas excessively reliable bonds confined the tenant, no reliable bonds at all attached a single man to the community, and either alternative evoked suspicion.

Ultimately, however, the insistence on orthodoxy did not directly exclude any excessive number, and neither did the property and residence requirements disqualify any great proportion of the province's adult males. In the perspective of the English villages from which the New Englanders came, these very dimensions of disqualification may be better seen, in fact, as defining a broader qualification than had previously prevailed in English practice. Far more fundamentally, the criteria of exclusion were measures of the inclusiveness of the communities of early Massachusetts.

The most fundamental shift that had occurred was the one from property to residence as the irreducible basis of town citizenship. In England, several classes of property-holders were "technically termed inhabitants even though they dwelt in another town"; property defined political citizenship, and only those who held the requisite property in the community directed its affairs. In provincial Massachusetts such stake-in-society notions never prevailed for reasons that had little to do with any abstract attachment to democracy or antipathy to absentee ownership. They never prevailed because the point of the town meeting was not so much the raising of a revenue as it was political government, especially the maintenance of law and order. In Massachusetts it was necessary to act only on the individuals living in each town, and it was imperative to act upon all of them. Of course, taxation as well as residence provided the basis for the ballot in Massachusetts, but that was of a piece with the residence requirement. As early as 1638 "every inhabitant of a town was declared liable for his proportion of the town's charges," in sharp contrast to the towns of England where only a few were so taxed.

The democracy of the Massachusetts towns was, then, a democracy despite itself, a democracy without democrats. But it was still, so far as anything yet said is concerned, a democracy, at least in the simple sense of a widely diffused franchise. Such democracy is admitted—indeed, required—in the analysis advanced above; the objection urged against the defenders of that democracy is not that they are wrong but that they are right for the wrong reasons, or for no reasons at all. When they examine electoral eligibility apart from its social setting and when they place franchise democracy at the center of provincial social organization instead of in the peripheral position it actually occupied, they do not condemn their findings to invalidity, only to sterility. They may be correct about the degree of diffusion of the vote, but they can go no further. Within their original terms, they cannot systematically study the purposes of participation, the relative importance of inclusiveness when it confronted competing values, the limits of eligibility and the reasons for them, or, more broadly, the particular texture of the electorate as against abstract statistics.

But if the analysis urged thus far has basically buttressed Brown's position by extending and explaining his statistics, that analysis also has another side. For when we see franchise democracy as a mere incident in the central quest for concord and concurrence among neighbors, we must also observe that the same concern for consensus which promoted wide participation also imposed very significant limitations on the democracy of the provincial community, limitations sufficiently serious to suggest that the democratic appellation

itself may be anachronistic when applied to such a society.

For one thing, the ideal of "townsmen together" implied the power of each town to control its own affairs, and that control not only extended to but also depended upon communal control of its membership. From the founding of the first towns communities retained the right to accept only those whom they wished, and that right persisted without challenge to the time of the Revolution. "Such whose dispositions do not suit us, whose society will be hurtful to us," were simply refused admission as enemies of harmony and homogeneity. Dedham's first covenant, "to keepe of from us all such, as ar contrarye minded. And receave onely such unto us as be such as may be probably of one harte," was typical. For inhabitancy was a matter of public rather than private concern, and among the original settlers it scarcely had to be argued that "if the place of our cohabitation be our own, then no man hath right to come in to us without our consent." Consent meant the formal vote of the town or its selectmen, and none were admitted without one or the other. Not even inhabitants themselves could entertain outsiders—"strangers," they were called—without the permission of the town, and any who violated the rule were subject to penalties. And of course the original thrust of congregational Puritanism to lodge disciplinary powers with the individual churches rather than with bishops also aimed at more local control of the membership of the local community.

Most of these practices continued unabated into the eighteenth century. Swansea's "foundation settlement" of 1667 provided that "if any person denied any particular in the said agreement they should not be admitted an inhabitant in said town," and half a century later seventy-eight townsmen reaffirmed their commitment to the ancestral covenant. Cotton Mather's manual of 1726, *Ratio Disciplinae Fratrum Nov-Anglorum* (Boston, 1726), described a process of "mutual Conferences" by which men came to "a good understanding" which might be subscribed to by any applicant. And even in the crisis of the dissolution of a church, as at Bellingham in 1747, the congregation could not simply disperse to the nearest convenient towns. Each of the congregants, for all that he had already met the tests of church membership and partaken of communion, had to be accepted anew into the nearby churches and approved by their towns, and in 1754 Sunderland claimed that this right of prior approval was "always customary."

Another customary instrument for the stringent control of access to the town which was also sustained throughout the provincial era was the practice of "warning out." Under this aegis, anyone who did secure entry to the town and was then deemed undesirable could be warned and, if necessary, lawfully ejected from the community. Such a policy was, in some part, a device to escape undue expenses in the support of paupers, but it was also, and more importantly, the product of the powerful communitarian assumptions of the early settlers, and those assumptions did not decline in the eighteenth century. William Weeden found the invocation of warning procedures so common that "the actual occurrences hardly need particular mention," and he concluded that "the old restrictions on the admission of freemen to the municipality, and on the sale of land to outsiders, do not appear to have been relaxed generally" as late as the era immediately preceding the imperial crisis. Town records such as Worcester's were studded with such warnings, from the time of the town's founding to the time of the Revolution itself. In other towns, too, penalties were still imposed for violation of the rules of inhabitancy.

The result was that fundamental differences in values were rarely admitted within a town, while differences of race, nationality, or culture scarcely appeared east of the Hudson River before the Revolution. Massachusetts was more nearly restricted to white Anglo-Saxon Protestants than any other province in English America, with the possible exception of its New England neighbors, Connecticut and New Hampshire. Less than 1 per cent of the quarter of a million Germans who came to the English colonies between 1690 and 1770 came to New England, and the proportion of Irish, Scotch, and

Scotch-Irish was little larger. There was no welcome whatsoever for French Catholics and very little encouragement, according to Governor Bellomont, even for the Huguenots. Negroes never attained significant numbers at the Bay—by 1780 they accounted for only 2 per cent of the population of the province and a bare 1 per cent of all the Negroes in the Confederation—and the Indians, who once were significant, were on their way to extinction well before the Revolution broke out. Committed to a conception of the social order that precluded pluralism, the townsmen of Massachusetts never made a place for those who were not of their own kind. The community they desired was an enclave of common believers, and to the best of their ability they secured such a society, rooted not only in ethnic and cultural homogeneity but also in common moral and economic ideas and practices. Thus, the character of the community became a critical—and non-democratic—condition of provincial democracy; for a wide franchise could be ventured only after a society that sought harmony had been made safe for such democracy. In that society it was possible to let men vote precisely because so many men were not allowed entry in the first place.

Thus we can maintain the appearance of democracy only so long as we dwell on elections and elections alone, instead of the entire electoral process. As soon as we depart from that focus, the town meetings of Massachusetts fall short of any decent democratic standard. Wide participation did obtain, but it was premised on stringently controlled access to eligibility, so that open elections presupposed anterior constriction of the electorate. Similarly, most men could vote, but their voting was not designed to contribute to a decision among meaningful alternatives. The town meeting had one prime purpose, and it was not the provision of a neutral battleground for the clash of contending parties or interest groups. In fact, nothing could have been more remote from the minds of men who repeatedly affirmed, to the very end of the provincial period, that "harmony and unanimity" were what "they most heartily wish to enjoy in all their public concerns." Conflict occurred only rarely in these communities, where "prudent and amicable composition and agreement" were urged as preventives for "great and sharp disputes and contentions." When it did appear it was seen as an unnatural and undesirable deviation from the norm. Protests and contested elections almost invariably appealed to unity and concord as the values which had been violated; and in the absence of any socially sanctioned role for dissent, contention was generally surreptitious and scarcely ever sustained for long. The town meeting accordingly aimed at unanimity. Its function was the arrangement of agreement or, more often, the endorsement of agreements already arranged, and it existed for accommodation, not disputation.

Yet democracy devoid of legitimate difference, dissent, and conflict is something less than democracy; and men who are finally to vote only as their neighbors vote have something less than the full range of democratic options. Government by mutual consent may have been a step in the direction of a deeper-going democracy, but it should not be confused with the real article. Democratic consent is predicated upon legitimate choice, while the town meetings of Massachusetts in the provincial era, called as they were to reach and register accords, were still in transition from assent to such consent. The evidence for such a conclusion exists in an abundance of votes from all over the province on all manner of matters "by the free and united consent of the whole" or "by a full and Unanimous Vote that they are Easie and satisfied With What they have Done." Most men may have been eligible to vote, but their voting did not settle differences unless most men voted together. In fact, differences had no defined place in the society that voting could have settled, for that was not in the nature of town politics. Unanimity was expected ethically as well as empirically. Indeed, it was demanded as a matter of social decency, so that even the occasional cases of conflict were shaped by the canons of concord and consensus, with towns pleading for the preservation of "peace and unanimity" as "the only occasion of our petitioning."

This demand for unanimity found its ultimate expression in rather frequent denials of one of the most elementary axioms of democratic theory, the principle of majority rule. A mere majority often commanded scant authority at the local level and scarcely even certified decisions as legitimate. In communities which provided no regular place for minorities a simple majority was not necessarily sufficient to dictate social policy, and many men such as the petitioners from the old part of Berwick were prepared to say so quite explicitly. Since its settlement some eighty or ninety years earlier, that town had grown until by 1748 the inhabitants of the newer parts easily outnumbered the "ancient settlers" and wished to establish a new meetinghouse in a place which the inhabitants of the older parts conceived injurious to their interest. Those who lived in the newer parts of town had the votes, but the "ancient settlers" were icily unimpressed nonetheless. Injury could not be justified "merely because a major vote of the town is or may be obtained to do it," the petitioners protested. They would suffer "great hurt and grievance," and "for no other reason than this: a major vote to do it, which is all the reason they have for the same." Equity, on the other hand, required a "just regard" for the old part of town and its inhabitants. They "ought" to retain their privileges despite their loss of numerical preponderance. And that principle was no mere moral fabrication of a desperate minority. Six years earlier the Massachusetts General Court had endorsed exactly the same position in a similar challenge to the prerogatives of numerical power by the "ancient part" of another town, and in the Berwick controversy the town majority itself tacitly conceded the principle upon which the old quarter depended. Accusing the old quarter of "gross misrepresentation," the rest of the town now maintained that there had been a disingenuous confusion of geography and population. There could be no question as to the physical location of the old town, but, as to its inhabitants, "the greatest part of the ancient settlers and maintainers of the ministry do live to the northward of the old meetinghouse and have always kept the same in times of difficulty and danger." The newer townsmen, then, did not deny that ancient settlers were entitled to special consideration; they simply denied that the inhabitants of the old quarter were in fact the ancient settlers.

Antiquity restricted majoritarianism elsewhere as well in demands of old settlers and in determinations of the General Court. In Lancaster as in Berwick, for example, a "standing part" could cite efforts to disrupt the old order which had been rejected by the Court as unreasonable, "and now though they have obtained a vote from the town the case still remains equally unreasonable." In other towns, too, a majority changed nothing. Consensus comprehended justice and history as well as the counting of a vote. In such a society a case could not be considered solely in its present aspects, as the original inhabitants of Lunenburg made quite clear. "What great discouragement must it needs give to any new settler," those old ones inquired,

> to begin a settlement and go through the difficulties thereof, which are well known to such as have ever engaged in such service, if when, so soon as ever they shall through the blessing of heaven upon their diligence and industry have arrived to live in some measure peaceably and comfortably, if then, after all fatigues and hardships undergone, to be cut to pieces and deprived of charter privileges and rights, and instead of peace and good harmony, contention and confusion introduced, there will be no telling what to trust to.

Nor was history the only resort for the repudiation of a majority. Other men offered other arguments, and some scarcely deigned to argue at all. In a contested election in Haverhill, for example, one side simply denied any authority at all to a majority of the moment. It was, they said, nothing but the creature of "a few designing men who have artfully drawn in the multitude and engaged them in their own cause." That, they argued, was simply "oppression." The merchants of Salem similarly refused to accept the hazards of populistic politics, though their refusal was rather more articulate. The town meeting had enacted a tax schedule more advantageous to the farmers than

to themselves, and the merchants answered that they felt no force in that action, because "the major part of those who were present were [farmers], and the vote then passed was properly their vote and not the vote of the whole body of the town." That legitimacy and obligation attached only to a vote of the whole community was simply assumed by the merchants, as they sought a subtle separation of a town ballot—sheer majoritarianism—from a "vote of the whole body of the town"—a notion akin to the general will— for which the consent of every part of the population was requisite.

Disdain for direct democracy emerged even more explicitly and sweepingly in a petition from the west precinct of Bridgewater in 1738. The precinct faced the prospect of the loss of its northern part due to a town vote authorizing the northern inhabitants to seek separation as an independent town, and the precinct feared that the loss would be fatal. Accordingly, the parishioners prayed the General Court's intervention, and after briefly disputing the majority itself, the precinct allowed that, whether or not a majority in the town *had* been obtained, such a majority *could* be contrived. "We own it is easy for the two neighboring parishes joining with the petitioners to vote away our just rights and privileges and to lay heavy burdens upon us, which they would not be willing to touch with the ends of their fingers." Yet for all the formal validity of such a vote, the precinct would not have assented to it or felt it to be legitimate, "for we trust that your Excellency and Honors will not be governed by numbers but by reason and justice." Other men elsewhere urged the same argument; perhaps none caught the provincial paradox of legality without legitimacy any better than the precinct of Salem Village, soon to become the independent town of Danvers. After a recitation of the imposition it had suffered from the town of Salem for no reason but superior numbers, the village came to its indictment of the town: "we don't say but you have had a legal right to treat us so, but all judgment without mercy is tedious to the flesh."

Typically in such cases, the defense against this indictment was not an invocation of majority rights but rather a denial of having employed them oppressively. Both sides, therefore, operated upon an identical assumption. One accused the other of taking advantage of its majority, the other retorted that it had done no such thing, but neither disputed the principle that majority disregard of a minority was indefensible.

This principle was no mere pious protestation. In Kittery, for instance, the parent parish complained that the men who later became the third parish had "long kept us in very unhappy circumstances . . . counter-acting us in all our proceedings" until finally "we were obliged to come into an agreement with them for dividing the then-lower parish of Kittery into two separate parishes," yet it was conceded on both sides that the old inhabitants enjoyed an easy numerical supremacy. Had they been disposed to employ it, almost any amount of "counter-acting" could have been contained and ultimately quashed, so far as votes in public meeting were concerned. But the parish clearly did not rely upon simple majoritarian procedures. It was more than morality that made consensus imperative; it was also the incapacity for coercion without widespread consent. It was the same incapacity which shaped a hundred other accommodations and abnegations across the province, which enabled some "aggrieved brethren" in Rehoboth to force the resignation of a minister, which paralyzed the town of Upton in the relocation of its meetinghouse. "All are agreed that it should be removed or a new one built," a town petition explained, "but cannot agree upon the place." In the absence of agreement they could see no way to act at all on their own account; there was never any thought of constructing a coalition within the town or contending for a majority.

Ultimately almost every community in the province shared Upton's determination "to unite the people." Disputes, when they arose at all, were commonly concluded by "a full and amicable agreement" in which all parties "were in peace and fully satisfied," and the conflicts that did occur evoked no efforts at resolution in a majoritarian manner. "Mutual and general advantage" was the condition of town continuance in "one entire corporate body." But that corporate ethos was something distant indeed from democracy, and electoral eligibility is, therefore, an unsatisfactory index even of political participation, let alone of any more meaningful democracy. Most men may have been able to vote in the eighteenth-century town, but the town's true politics were not transacted at the ballot box so much as at the tavern and all the other places, including the meeting itself, where men met and negotiated so that the vote might be a mere ratification, rather than a decision among significant alternatives. Alternatives were antithetical to the safe conduct of the community as it was conceived at the Bay, and so to cast a vote was only to participate in the consolidation of the community, not to make a choice among competing interests or ideals.

Accordingly, the claim for middle-class democracy in provincial Massachusetts simply cannot be sustained from the figures on electoral eligibility; relevant participation resided elsewhere than in the final, formal vote. And yet, ironically, local politics may have been democratic indeed, at least in the limited terms of political participation, since a politics of consensus required consultation with most of the inhabitants in order to assure accord. In little towns of two or three hundred adult males living in close, continuing contact, men may very well have shared widely a sense of the amenability of the political process to their own actions and attitudes, and the feeling of involvement may well have been quite general. But to find out we will have to go beyond counting heads or tallying the town treasurers' lists.

7

WHO WAS BENJAMIN FRANKLIN?

JOHN WILLIAM WARD

Much like his contemporary George Washington, Benjamin Franklin has become one of the staples of American mythology. As John William Ward makes clear, however, Franklin was in reality no mythological being but a very complex and even contradictory man. The essence of Franklin, according to Ward, was his existence as a symbol of upward mobility. Beginning life as an apprentice printer, Franklin achieved business success before he was 30, earned an international reputation in science through his experiments in electricity, became influential in politics at the state and national levels, and served as one of the new nation's most successful diplomats in the Revolutionary era. The key to Franklin's rise was his ability to separate appearance and reality: to appear to conform to community norms in public life while following his own desires in private affairs. It was this ability, Ward argues, that accounts for the seeming contradictions in Franklin's character.

Ward relies upon Franklin's *Autobiography* to sort out the meaning of his character. Yet one recent historian characterizes the *Autobiography* as the self-justification of a disappointed office seeker. How could this perspective on Franklin's life alter Ward's reading of the evidence? Recent social historians argue that social mobility was extremely limited by the mid-eighteenth century, especially in cities such as Franklin's Philadelphia. How was it possible for Franklin to symbolize upward mobility, as Ward argues, under such circumstances? How would Franklin and his practice of separating the public and private, have fared in communities such as those discussed by Zuckerman in Reading 6.

Benjamin Franklin bulks large in our national consciousness, sharing room with Washington and Jefferson and Lincoln. Yet it is hard to say precisely what it means to name Franklin one of our cultural heroes. He was, as one book about him has it, "many-sided." The sheer variety of his character has made it possible to praise him and damn him with equal vigor. At home, such dissimilar Yankees as the laconic Calvin Coolidge and the passionate Theodore Parker could each find reason to admire him. Abroad, David Hume could say that he was "the first great man of letters" for whom Europe was "beholden" to America. Yet D. H. Lawrence, brought up, he tells us, in the industrial wastelands of midland England on the pious saws of "Poor Richard," could only "utter a long, loud curse" against "this dry, moral, utilitarian little democrat."

Part of the difficulty in comprehending Franklin's meaning is due to the opposites he seems to have contained with complete serenity within his own personality. He was an eminently reasonable man who maintained a deep skepticism about the power of reason. He was a model of industriousness who, preaching the gospel of hard work, kept his shop only until it kept him and retired

Reprinted from the *The American Scholar* 32 (1963): 541–53, with permission of *The American Scholar*.

at forty-two. He was a cautious and prudent man who was a revolutionist. And, to name only one more seeming contradiction, he was one who had a keen eye for his own advantage and personal advancement who spent nearly all his adult life in the service of others. Small wonder that there have been various interpretations of so various a character.

The problem may seem no problem at all. Today, when we all know that the position of the observer determines the shape of reality, we observe the observer. If Franklin, seeing to it that the streets of Philadelphia are well lit and swept clean at a moderate price, that no fires rage, does not appeal to D. H. Lawrence, we tend not to think of Franklin. We think of Lawrence; we remember his atavistic urge to explore the dark and passionate underside of life and move on. Franklin contained in his own character so many divergent aspects that each observer can make the mistake of seeing one aspect as all and celebrate or despise Franklin accordingly. Mr. I. Bernard Cohen, who has written so well on so much of Franklin, has remarked that "an account of Franklin . . . is apt to be a personal testament of the commentator concerning the America he most admires." Or contemns.

Yet there still remains the obstinate fact that Franklin could mean so many things to so many men, that he was so many-sided, that he did contain opposites, that he was, in other words, so many different characters. One suspects that here is the single most important thing about Franklin. Rather than spend our energies trying to find some consistency in this protean, many-sided figure, trying to resolve who Franklin truly was, we might perhaps better accept his variety itself as our major problem and try to understand that. To insist on the importance of the question, "Who was Benjamin Franklin?" may finally be more conclusive than to agree upon an answer.

The place to begin to ask the question is with the *Memoirs,* with the *Autobiography* as we have come to call them, and the place to begin there is with the history of the text. Fascinating in and of itself, the history of the text gives us an initial lead into the question of the elusiveness of Franklin's personality.

The *Autobiography* was written in four parts. The first part, addressed by Franklin to his son, William, was begun during some few weeks in July and August, 1771, while Franklin was visiting with his friend, Jonathan Shipley, the Bishop of St. Asaph, in Hampshire, England. Franklin was then sixty-five years old. As he wrote the first part he also carefully made a list of topics he would subsequently treat. Somehow the manuscript and list fell into the hands of one Abel James who eleven years later wrote Franklin, returning to him the list of topics but not the first part of the manuscript, urging him to take up his story once again. This was in 1782, or possibly early in January, 1783. Franklin was in France as one of the peace commissioners. He wrote the second part in France in 1784, after the achievement of peace, indicating the beginning and the ending of this short second part in the manuscript itself.

In 1785, Franklin returned to America, promising to work on the manuscript during the voyage. Instead he wrote three of his utilitarian essays: on navigation, on how to avoid smoky streetlamp chimneys, and on his famous stove. He did not return to his life's story until 1788. Then, after retiring from the presidency of the state of Pennsylvania in the spring, Franklin, quite sick, made his will and put his house in order before turning again to his own history. This was in August, 1788. Franklin was eighty-three years old, in pain, and preparing for death. The third part is the longest part of the autobiography, less interesting than the first two, and for many years was thought to conclude the manuscript.

In 1789, Franklin had his grandson, Benjamin Franklin Bache, make two fair copies of Parts I, II and III in order to send them to friends abroad, Benjamin Vaughan in England and M. le Veillard in France. Then, sometime before his death in April, 1790, Franklin added the last and fourth part, some seven and one-half manuscript pages, which was not included, naturally, in the fair copies sent abroad. For the rest, Mr. Max Farrand, our authority on the history of the text:

> After [Franklin's] death, the publication of the autobiography was eagerly awaited, as its existence was widely known, but for nearly thirty years the reading public had to content itself with French translations of the first and second parts, which were again translated from the French into other languages, and even retranslated into English. When the authorized English publication finally appeared in 1818, it was not taken from the original manuscript but from a copy, as was the preceding French version of the first part. The copy, furthermore, did not include the fourth and last part, which also reached the public in a French translation in 1828.
>
> . . . The complete autobiography was not printed in English from the original manuscript until 1868, nearly eighty years after Franklin's death.

The story is, as I have said, interesting in and of itself. The tangled history of one of our most important texts has its own fascination, but it also provides us the first clue to our question. Surely, it must strike any reader of the *Autobiography* as curious that a character who speaks so openly should at the same time seem so difficult to define. But the history of the text points the way to an answer. All we need do is ask why Franklin wrote his memoirs.

When the Quaker Abel James wrote Franklin, returning his list of topics and asking "kind, humane, and benevolent Ben Franklin" to continue his life's story, "a work which would be useful and entertaining not only to a few but to millions," Franklin sent the letter on to his friend, Benjamin Vaughan, asking for advice. Vaughan concurred. He too urged Franklin to publish the history of his life because he could think of no "more efficacious advertisement" of America than Franklin's history. "All that has happened to you," he reminded Franklin, "is also connected with the detail of the manners and situation of a rising people." Franklin included James's and Vaughan's letters in his manuscript to explain why he resumed his story. What had gone before had been written for his family;

"what follows," he said in his "Memo," "was written . . . in compliance with the advice contained in these letters, and accordingly intended for the public. The affairs of the Revolution occasioned the interruption."

The point is obvious enough. When Franklin resumed his story, he did so in full self-consciousness that he was offering himself to the world as a representative type, the American. Intended for the public now, his story was to be an example for young Americans, as Abel James would have it, and an advertisement to the world, as Benjamin Vaughan would have it. We had just concluded a successful revolution; the eyes of all the world were upon us. Just as America had succeeded in creating itself a nation, Franklin set out to show how the American went about creating his own character. As Benjamin Vaughan said, Franklin's life would "give a noble rule and example of self-education" because of Franklin's "discovery that the thing is in many a man's private power." So what follows is no longer the simple annals of Franklin's life for the benefit of his son. Benjamin Franklin plays his proper role. He becomes "The American."

How well he filled the part that his public urged him to play, we can see by observing what he immediately proceeds to provide. In the pages that follow James's and Vaughan's letters, Franklin quickly treats four matters: the establishment of a lending library, that is, the means for satisfying the need for self-education; the importance of frugality and industriousness in one's calling; the social utility of religion; and, of course, the thirteen rules for ordering one's life. Here, in a neat package, were all the materials that went into the making of the self-made man. This is how one goes about making a success of one's self. If the sentiments of our Declaration were to provide prompt notes for European revolutions, then Franklin, as the American Democrat, acted them out. Family, class, religious orthodoxy, higher education: all these were secondary to character and common sense. The thing was in many a man's private power.

If we look back now at the first part, the opening section addressed by Franklin to his son, William, we can see a difference and a similarity. The difference is, of course, in the easy and personal tone, the more familiar manner, appropriate to a communication with one's son. It is in these early pages that Franklin talks more openly about his many *errata,* his "frequent intrigues with low women," and displays that rather cool and calculating attitude toward his wife. Rather plain dealing, one might think, at least one who did not know that William was a bastard son.

But the similarity between the two parts is more important. The message is the same, although addressed to a son, rather than to the world: how to go about making a success. "From the poverty and obscurity in which I was born and in which I passed my earliest years," writes the father to the son, "I have raised myself to a state of affluence and some degree of celebrity in the world." A son, especially, must have found that "some" hard to take. But the career is not simply anecdotal: "my posterity will perhaps be desirous of learning the means, which I employed, and which, thanks to Providence, so well succeeded with me. They may also deem them fit to be imitated." The story is exemplary, although how the example was to affect a son who was, in 1771, about forty years old and already Royal Governor of New Jersey is another matter.

The story has remained exemplary because it is the success story to beat all success stories: the runaway apprentice printer who rose to dine with kings; the penniless boy, walking down Market Street with two large rolls under his arms, who was to sit in Independence Hall and help create a new nation. But notice that the story does not deal with the success itself. That is presumed, of course, but the *Autobiography* never gets to the later and more important years because the *Autobiography* is not about success. It is about the formation of the character that makes success possible. The subject of the *Autobiography* is the making of a character. Having lifted himself by his own bootstraps, Franklin described it that way: "I have raised myself." We were not to find the pat phrase until the early nineteenth century when the age of the common man made the style more common: "the self-made man." The char-

acter was for life, of course, and not for fiction where we usually expect to encounter the made-up, but that should not prevent us from looking a little more closely at the act of creation. We can look in two ways: first, by standing outside the *Autobiography* and assessing it by what we know from elsewhere; second, by reading the *Autobiography* itself more closely.

A good place to begin is with those years in France around the end of the Revolution. It is so delicious an episode in plain Ben's life. More importantly—as Franklin said, one can always find a principle to justify one's inclinations—it is in these very years at Passy that Franklin, in response to James's and Vaughan's letters, wrote those self-conscious pages of the second part of the *Autobiography.* Just as he wrote the lines, he played them. As Carl Van Doren has written, "the French were looking for a hero who should combine the reason and wit of Voltaire with the primitive virtues celebrated by Rousseau. . . . [Franklin] denied them nothing." This is the period of the simple Quaker dress, the fur cap and the spectacles. France went wild in its adulation and Franklin knew why. "Think how this must appear," he wrote a friend, "among the powdered heads of Paris."

But he was also moving with equal ease in that world, the world of the powdered heads of Paris, one of the most cosmopolitan, most preciously civilized societies in history. Although he was no Quaker, Franklin was willing to allow the French to think so. They called him *"le bon Quackeur."* The irony was unintentional, a matter of translation. But at the same time that he was filling the role of the simple backwoods democrat, the innocent abroad, he was also playing cavalier in the brilliant salon of Madame Helvétius, the widow of the French philosopher. Madame Helvétius is supposed to have been so beautiful that Fontenelle, the great popularizer of Newton, who lived to be one hundred years old, was said to have paid her the most famous compliment of the age: "Ah, madame, if I were only eighty again!" Madame Helvétius was sixty when Franklin knew her and the classic anecdote of their acquaintance is that Madame Helvétius is said to have reproached him for not coming to see her, for putting off his long anticipated visit. Franklin replied, "Madame, I am waiting until the nights are longer." There was also Madame Brillon, not a widow, who once wrote to Franklin, "People have the audacity to criticize my pleasant habit of sitting on your knee, and yours of always asking me for what I always refuse."

Some, discovering this side of Franklin, have written him off simply as a rather lively old lecher. Abigail Adams, good New England lady that she was, was thoroughly shocked. She set Madame Helvétius down as a "very bad woman." But Franklin, despite his public style, was not so provincial. He appealed to Madame Brillon that he had spent so many days with her that surely she could spend one night with him. She mockingly called him a sophist. He then appealed to her charity and argued that it was in the design of Providence that she grant him his wish. If somehow a son of the Puritans, Franklin had grown far beyond the reach of their sermonizing. Thomas Hooker had thought, "It's a grievous thing to the loose person, he cannot have his pleasures but he must have his guilt and gall with them." But Franklin wrote Madame Brillon, "Reflect how many of our duties [Providence] has ordained naturally to be pleasures; and that it has had the goodness besides, to give the name of sin to several of them so that we might enjoy them the more."

All this is delightful enough, and for more one need only turn to Carl Van Doren's biography from which I have taken these anecdotes, but what it points to is as important as it is entertaining. It points to Franklin's great capacity to respond to the situation in which he found himself and to play the expected role, to prepare a face to meet the faces that he met. He could, in turn, be the homespun, rustic philosopher or the mocking cavalier, the witty sophist. He knew what was expected of him.

The discovery should not surprise any reader of the *Autobiography.* Throughout it, Franklin insists always on the distinction between appearance and reality, between what he is and what he seems to be.

In order to secure my credit and character as a tradesman, I took care not only to be in *reality* industrious and frugal, but to avoid all *appearances* of the contrary. I dressed plain and was seen at no places of idle diversion. I never went out a fishing or shooting; a book, indeed, sometimes debauched me from my work, but that was seldom, snug, and gave no scandal; and to show that I was not above my business, I sometimes brought home the paper I purchased at the stores, thro' the streets on a wheelbarrow. Thus being esteemed an industrious, thriving young man, and paying duly for what I bought, the merchants who imported stationery solicited my custom; others proposed supplying me with books, and I went on swimmingly.

Now, with this famous passage, one must be careful. However industrious and frugal Franklin may in fact have been, he knew that for the business of social success virtue counts for nothing without its public dress. In Franklin's world there has to be someone in the woods to hear the tree fall. Private virtue might bring one to stand before the King of kings, but if one wants to sit down and sup with the kings of this world, then one must help them see one's merit. There are always in this world, as Franklin pointed out, "a number of rich merchants, nobility, states, and princes who have need of honest instruments for the management of their affairs, and such being so rare [I] have endeavoured to convince young persons, that no qualities are so likely to make a poor man's fortune as those of probity and integrity."

Yet if one wants to secure one's credit in the world by means of one's character, then the character must be of a piece. There can be no false gesture; the part must be played well. When Franklin drew up his list of virtues they contained, he tells us, only twelve. But a Quaker friend "kindly" informed him that he was generally thought proud and overbearing and rather insolent; he proved it by examples. So Franklin added humility to his list; but, having risen in the world and content with the degree of celebrity he had achieved, he could not bring himself to be humble. "I cannot boast of much success in acquiring the *reality* of this virtue, but I had a good deal with regard to the *appearance* of it."

He repeats, at this point, what he had already written in the first part of his story. He forswears all "positive assertion." He drops from his vocabulary such words as "certainly" and "undoubtedly" and adopts a tentative manner. He remembers how he learned to speak softly, to put forward his opinions, not dogmatically, but by saying, " 'I imagine' a thing to be so or so, or 'It so appears to me at present.' " As he had put it to his son earlier, he discovered the Socratic method, "was charmed with it, adopted it, dropped my abrupt contradiction and positive argumentation, and put on the humble enquirer." For good reason, "this habit . . . has been of great advantage to me."

What saves all this in the *Autobiography* from being merely repellent is Franklin's self-awareness, his good humor in telling us about the part he is playing, the public clothes he is putting on to hide what his public will not openly buy. "In reality," he writes, drawing again the distinction from appearance, "there is perhaps no one of our natural passions so hard to subdue as *pride;* disguise it, struggle with it, beat it down, stifle it, mortify it as much as one pleases, it is still alive and will every now and then peep out and show itself. You will see it perhaps often in this history. For even if I could conceive that I had completely overcome it, I should probably be proud of my humility." Here, despite the difference in tone, Franklin speaks like that other and contrasting son of the Puritans, Jonathan Edwards, on the nature of true virtue. Man, if he could achieve virtue, would inevitably be proud of the achievement and so, at the moment of success, fall back into sin.

The difference is, of course, in the tone. The insight is the same but Franklin's skeptical and untroubled self-acceptance is far removed from Edwards' troubled and searching self-doubt. Franklin enjoys the game. Mocking himself, he quietly lures us, in his Yankee deadpan manner, with the very bait he has just described. After having told us that he early learned to "put on the humble enquirer" and to affect a self-depreciating pose, he quotes in his support the line from Alexander Pope, "To speak, though sure, with seem-

ing diffidence." Pope, Franklin immediately goes on to say, "might have joined with this line that which he has coupled with another, I think less properly, 'For want of modesty is want of sense.' "

If you ask why *less properly,* I must repeat the lines,

> Immodest words admit of *no defence,*
> *For* want of modesty is want of sense.

Now is not the "want of sense" (where a man is so unfortunate as to want it) some apology for his "want of modesty"? and would not the lines stand more justly thus?

> Immodest words admit *but* this defense
> That want of modesty is want of sense.

This, however, I should submit to better judgements.

Having been so bold as to correct a couplet of the literary giant of the age, Franklin quietly retreats and defers to the judgment of those better able to say than he. Having just described the humble part he has decided to play, he immediately acts it out. If we get the point, we chuckle with him; if we miss the point, that only proves its worth.

But one of the functions of laughter is to dispel uneasiness and in Franklin's case the joke is not enough. Our uneasiness comes back when we stop to remember that he is, as his friends asked him to, writing his story as an efficacious advertisement. We must always ask whether Franklin's disarming candor in recounting how things went on so swimmingly may not be yet another role, still another part he is playing. Actually, even with Yale's sumptuous edition of Franklin's papers, we know little about Franklin's personal life in the early years, except through his own account. The little we do know suggests that his way to wealth and success was not the smooth and open path he would have us believe. This leads us, then, if we cannot answer finally the question who Franklin was, to a different question. What does it mean to say that a character so changeable, so elusive, somehow represents American culture? What is there in Franklin's style that makes him, as we say, characteristic?

At the outset in colonial America, with men like John Winthrop, there was always the assumption that one would be called to one's appropriate station in life and labor in it for one's own good and the good of society. Magistrates would be magistrates and printers would be printers. But in the world in which Franklin moved, the magistrates, like Governor Keith of Pennsylvania who sends Franklin off on a wild-goose chase to England, prove to be frauds while the plain, leather-aproned set went quietly about the work of making society possible at all, creating the institutions—the militia, the fire companies, the libraries, the hospitals, the public utilities—that made society habitable. The notion that underlay an orderly, hierarchical society failed to make sense of such a world. It proved impossible to keep people in their place.

One need only consider in retrospect how swiftly Franklin moved upward through the various levels of society to see the openness, the fluidity of his world. Simply because he is a young man with some books, Governor Burnet of New York asks to see him. While in New Jersey on a job printing money he meets and makes friends with all the leaders of that provincial society. In England, at the coffeehouses, he chats with Mandeville and meets the great Dr. Henry Pemberton who was seeing the third edition of Newton's *Principia* through the press. As Franklin said, diligent in his calling, he raised himself by some degree.

The Protestant doctrine of calling, of industriousness in the world, contained dynamite for the orderly, hierarchical, social structure it was originally meant to support. The unintended consequence showed itself within two generations. Those who were abstemious, frugal and hardworking made a success in the world. They rose. And society, rather than the static and closed order in which, in Winthrop's words, "some must be rich some poor, some high and eminent in power and dignitie; others meane and in subjec-

cion," turned out to be dynamic, fluid and open.

If there is much of our national character implicit in Franklin's career, it is because, early in our history, he represents a response to the rapid social change that has remained about the only constant in American society. He was the self-made man, the jack-of-all-trades. He taught thirteen rules to sure success and purveyed do-it-yourself kits for those who, like himself, constituted a "rising" people. Franklin stands most clearly as an exemplary American because his life's story is a witness to the uncertainties about social status that have characterized our society, a society caught up in the constant process of change. The question, "Who was Benjamin Franklin?" is a critical question to ask of Franklin because it is the question to which Franklin himself is constantly seeking an answer. In a society in which there are no outward, easily discernible marks of social status, the question always is, as we put it in the title of reference works that are supposed to provide the answer, "Who's Who?"

Along with the uncertainties generated by rapid social mobility, there is another aspect to the difficulty we have in placing Franklin, an aspect that is more complex and harder to state, but just as important and equally characteristic. It takes us back again to the Puritans. In Puritan religious thought there was originally a dynamic equipoise between two opposite thrusts, the tension between an inward, mystical, personal experience of God's grace and the demands for an outward, sober, socially responsible ethic, the tension between faith and works, between the essence of religion and its outward show. Tremendous energy went into sustaining these polarities in the early years but, as the original piety waned, itself undermined by the worldly success that benefited from the doctrine of calling, the synthesis split in two and resulted in the eighteenth century in Jonathan Edwards and Benjamin Franklin, similar in so many ways, yet so radically unlike.

Franklin, making his own world as he makes his way through it, pragmatically rejects the old conundrum whether man does good works because he is saved, or is saved because he does good works. "Vicious actions are not hurtful because they are forbidden, but forbidden because they are hurtful," he decides, and then in an added phrase calmly throws out the God-centered universe of his forebears, "the nature of man alone considered."

Content with his success, blandly sure it must be in the design of Providence that printers hobnob with kings, Franklin simply passes by the problem of the relation between reality and appearance. In this world, appearance is sufficient. Humanely skeptical that the essence can ever be caught, Franklin decided to leave the question to be answered in the next world, if there proved to be one. For this world, a "tolerable character" was enough and he "valued it properly." The result was a common sense utilitarianism which sometimes verges toward sheer crassness. But it worked. For this world, what others think of you is what is important. If Franklin, viewed from the perspective of Max Weber and students of the Protestant ethic, can seem to be the representative, *par excellence,* of the character who internalizes the imperatives of his society and steers his own course unaided through the world, from a slightly different perspective he also turns out to be the other-directed character David Riesman has described, constantly attuned to the expectations of those around him, responding swiftly to the changing situations that demand he play different roles.

We admire, I think, the lusty good sense of the man who triumphs in the world that he accepts, yet at the same time we are uneasy with the man who wears so many masks that we are never sure who is there behind them. Yet it is this, this very difficulty of deciding whether we admire Franklin or suspect him, that makes his character an archetype for our national experience. There are great advantages to be had in belonging to a culture without clearly defined classes, without an establishment, but there is, along with the advantages, a certain strain, a necessary uneasiness. In an open and pluralistic society we have difficulty "placing" people, as we say. Think how often in our kind of society when we meet someone for the first time how our second or third question is apt to be, "What do you do?" Never, "Who are you?" The social role is enough, but in our more reflective moments we realize not so, and in our most reflective moments we realize it will never do for our own selves. We may be able to, but we do not want to go through life as a doctor, lawyer or Indian chief. We want to be ourselves, as we say. And at the beginning of our national experience, Benjamin Franklin not only puts the question that still troubles us in our kind of society, "Who's Who?" He also raises the question that lies at the heart of the trouble: "Who am I?"

8

SOCIAL CHANGE AND THE GROWTH OF PRE-REVOLUTIONARY URBAN RADICALISM

GARY B. NASH

Until recently, historians have viewed the political history of the American colonies as a single process in which a broadly elected lower house gradually eroded the prerogatives of the royal or proprietary governor and his elite council. The lower houses accomplished this political transformation through control of the colonial budget, and with it, the governor's salary. Since colonial governors required funds to pay for their programs and assembly approval in order to draw their salaries, they found it necessary to compromise and balance their royal instructions against the needs and desires of the colonial legislatures.

But this process of increasing autonomy and control gained by the colonial assemblies, while important, was not the only political transformation that took place in colonial America. Equally important was the political mobilization, in the eighteenth century, of the middling and lower ranks of colonial society. After 1700 the wealthy merchants, lawyers, and large landholders who controlled colonial politics faced a growing challenge from a group of rising young men who had made their fortunes in an expanding colonial economy. Excluded from the rarified social world of the colonial elites, as well as from the patronage they controlled, these political newcomers turned to the common men of colonial America for support.

Nowhere was this appeal to the common man more apparent than in the seaport cities of Boston, New York, and Philadelphia. There, in an era when the social structure was changing, ordinary carpenters, shoemakers, and shipbuilders, as well as common day laborers and mariners, responded to the appeals of popular politicians and gained for themselves a permanent voice in the administration of colonial affairs. I argue in this essay that it was the political mobilization of these urban artisans, shopkeepers, and laborers that created a truly democratic politics in America and set the stage for the American Revolution.

How does the process of popular politics in the seaport cities compare with the politics of the New England town, as discussed by Michael Zuckerman in Reading 6? Which do you think was more democratic, the New England town or the seaport city? What similarities and differences are there between popular mobilization in the northern seaports and in rural Virginia as discussed by Rhys Isaac in Reading 9?

Recent studies of the American Revolution have relied heavily on the role of ideas to explain the advent of the American rebellion against En-gland. The gist of the ideological interpretation of the Revolution is that colonists, inheriting a tradition of protest against arbitrary rule, became

Reprinted from Alfred F. Young, ed., *The American Revolution: Explorations in the History of American Radicalism* (DeKalb: Northern Illinois University Press, 1976), pp. 5–36, by permission of the publisher.

convinced in the years after 1763 that the English government meant to impose in America, as Bernard Bailyn writes, "not merely misgovernment and not merely insensitivity to the reality of life in the British overseas provinces but a deliberate design to destroy the constitutional safeguards of liberty, which only concerted resistance—violent resistance if necessary—could effectively oppose." It was this conspiracy against liberty that "above all else . . . propelled [the colonists] into Revolution."

An important corollary to this argument, which stresses the colonial defense of constitutional rights and liberties, is the notion that the material conditions of life in America were so generally favorable that social and economic factors deserve little consideration as a part of the impetus to revolution. "The outbreak of the Revolution," writes Bernard Bailyn, a leading proponent of the ideological school, "was not the result of social discontent, or of economic disturbances, or of rising misery, or of those mysterious social strains that seem to beguile the imaginations of historians straining to find a peculiar predispositions to upheaval." Nor, asserts Bailyn, was there a "transformation of mob behavior or of the lives of the 'inarticulate' in the pre-Revolutionary years that accounts for the disruption of Anglo-American politics." Another historian, whose focus is economic change and not ideas, writes that "whatever it might have been, the American Revolution was not a rising of impoverished masses— or merchants—in search of their share of the wealth. The 'predicament of poverty,' in Hannah Arendt's phrase, was absent from the American scene"—so much so that even though the "secular trend in the concentration of wealth created an increasing gulf between the rich and the poor over the years separating 1607 and 1775, the fact remains that not only were the rich getting richer but the poor were also, albeit at a slower rate."

One of the purposes of this essay is to challenge these widely accepted notions that the "predicament of poverty" was unknown in colonial America, that the conditions of everyday life among "the inarticulate" had not changed in ways that led toward a revolutionary predisposi-

tion, and that "social discontent," "economic disturbances," and "social strains" can generally be ignored in searching for the roots of the Revolution. I do not suggest that we replace an ideological construction with a mechanistic economic interpretation, but argue that a popular ideology, affected by rapidly changing economic conditions in American cities, dynamically interacted with the more abstract Whig ideology borrowed from England. These two ideologies had their primary appeal within different parts of the social structure, were derived from different sensibilities concerning social equity, and thus had somewhat different goals. The Whig ideology, about which we know a great deal through recent studies, was drawn from English sources, had its main appeal within upper levels of colonial society, was limited to a defense of constitutional rights and political liberties, and had little to say about changing social and economic conditions in America or the need for change in the future. The popular ideology, about which we know very little, also had deep roots in English culture, but it resonated most strongly within the middle and lower strata of society and went far beyond constitutional rights to a discussion of the proper distribution of wealth and power in the social system. It was this popular ideology that undergirded the politicization of the artisan and laboring classes in the cities and justified the dynamic role they assumed in the urban political process in the closing decades of the colonial period.

It is toward understanding this popular ideology and its role in the upsurge of revolutionary sentiment and action in the 1760s that this essay is devoted. Our focus will be on the three largest colonial cities—Boston, New York, and Philadelphia. Other areas, including the older, settled farming regions and backcountry, were also vitally important to the upwelling of revolutionary feeling in the fifteen years before 1776 and in the struggle that followed. But the northern cities were the first areas of revolutionary ferment, the communication centers where newspapers and pamphlets spread the revolutionary message, and the arenas of change in British North America where most of the trends overtaking colonial society in the eighteenth century were first and most intensely felt.

To understand how this popular ideology swelled into revolutionary commitment within the middle and lower ranks of colonial society, we must first comprehend how the material conditions of life were changing for city dwellers during the colonial period and how people at different levels of society were affected by these alterations. We cannot fathom this process by consulting the writings of merchants, lawyers, and upper-class politicians, because their business and political correspondence and the tracts they wrote tell us almost nothing about those below them in the social hierarchy. But buried in more obscure documents are glimpses of the lives of both ordinary and important people—shoemakers and tailors as well as lawyers and merchants. The story of changing conditions and how life in New York, Philadelphia, and Boston was experienced can be discerned, not with perfect clarity but in general form, from tax, poor relief, and probate records.

The most generally recognized alteration in eighteenth-century urban social structures is the long-range trend toward a less even distribution of wealth. Tax lists for Boston, Philadelphia, and New York, ranging over nearly a century prior to the Revolution, make this clear. By the early 1770s the top 5 percent of Boston's taxpayers controlled 49 percent of the taxable assets of the community, whereas they had held only 30 percent in 1687. In Philadelphia the top twentieth increased its share of wealth from 33 to 55 percent between 1693 and 1774. Those in the lower half of society, who in Boston in 1687 had commanded 9 percent of the taxable wealth, were left collectively with a mere 5 percent in 1771. In Philadelphia, those in the lower half of the wealth spectrum saw their share of wealth drop from 10.1 to 3.3 percent in the same period. It is now evident that the concentration of wealth had proceeded very far in the eighteenth-century cities.

Though city dwellers from the middle and lower ranks could not measure this redistribution of economic resources with statistical precision,

they could readily discern the general trend. No one could doubt that upper-class merchants were amassing fortunes when four-wheeled coaches, manned by liveried Negro slaves, appeared in Boston's crooked streets, or when urban mansions, lavishly furnished in imitation of the English aristocracy, rose in Philadelphia and New York. Colonial probate records reveal that personal estates of £5000 sterling were rare in the northern cities before 1730, but by 1750 the wealthiest town dwellers were frequently leaving assets of £20,000 sterling, exclusive of real estate, and sometimes fortunes of more than £50,000 sterling—equivalent in purchasing power to about 2.5 million dollars today. Wealth of this magnitude was not disguised in cities with populations ranging from about 16,000 in Boston to about 25,000 in New York and Philadelphia and with geographical expanses half as large as public university campuses today.

While urban growth produced a genuinely wealthy upper class, it simultaneously created a large class of impoverished city dwellers. All of the cities built almshouses in the 1730s in order to house under one roof as many of the growing number of poor as possible. This was the beginning of a long trend toward substituting confinement in workhouses and almshouses for the older familial system of direct payments to the poor at home. The new system was designed to reduce the cost of caring for a growing number of marginal persons—people who, after the 1730s, were no longer simply the aged, widowed, crippled, incurably ill, or orphaned members of society, but also the seasonally unemployed, war veterans, new immigrants, and migrants from inland areas seeking employment in the cities. These persons, whose numbers grew impressively in the 1750s and 1760s, were now expected to contribute to their own support through cloth weaving, shoemaking, and oakum picking in city workhouses.

Beginning in Boston in the 1740s and in New York and Philadelphia somewhat later, poverty scarred the lives of a growing part of the urban populations. Among its causes were periodic unemployment, rising prices that outstripped wage increases, and war taxes which fell with unusual severity on the lower classes. In Boston, where the Overseers of the Poor had expended only £25–35 sterling per thousand inhabitants in the 1720s and 1730s, per capita expenditures for the poor more than doubled in the 1740s and 1750s, and then doubled again in the last fifteen years of the colonial period. Poor relief rose similarly in Philadelphia and New York after 1750.

In the third quarter of the eighteenth century poverty struck even harder at Boston's population and then blighted the lives of the New York and Philadelphia laboring classes to a degree unparalleled in the first half of the century. In New York, the wartime boom of 1755–1760 was followed by postwar depression. High rents and unemployment brought hundreds of families to the edge of indigency. The incidence of poverty jumped more than fourfold between 1750 and 1775. By 1772 a total of 425 persons jostled for space in the city's almshouse, which had been built to accommodate about 100 indigents. In Philadelphia, in the decade before the Revolution, more than 900 persons each year were admitted to the city's institutions for the impoverished—the almshouse, workhouse, and Hospital for the Sick Poor. The data on poor relief leaves little room for doubt that the third quarter of the eighteenth century was an era of severe economic and social dislocation in the cities, and that by the end of the colonial period a large number of urban dwellers were without property, without opportunity, and, except for public aid, without the means of obtaining the necessities of life.

The economic changes that redistributed wealth, filled the almshouses to overflowing, and drove up poor rates, also hit hard at the lower part of the middle class in the generation before the Revolution. These people—master artisans rather than laborers, skilled shipwrights rather than merchant seamen, shopkeepers rather than peddlers—were financially humbled in substantial numbers in Boston beginning in the 1740s and in Philadelphia and New York a dozen years later.

In Boston, this crumbling of middle-class economic security can be traced in individual cases

through the probate records and in aggregate form in the declining number of "taxables." In that city, where the population remained nearly static, at about 15,500 from 1735 to the Revolution, the number of "rateable polls" declined from a high of more than 3,600 in 1735, when the city's economy was at its peak, to a low of about 2,500 around mid-century. By 1771, Boston's taxables still numbered less than 2,600. This decline of more than a thousand taxable adults was not caused by loss of population but by the sagging fortunes of more than 1,000 householders—almost one-third of the city's taxpaying population. Boston's selectmen made this clear in 1757 when they pointed out that "besides a great Number of Poor . . . who are either wholly or in part maintained by the Town, & so are exempt from being Taxed, there are many who are Rateable according to Law . . . who are yet in such poor Circumstances that Considering how little business there is to be done in Boston they can scarcely procure from day to day daily Bread for themselves & Families."

In Philadelphia, the decay of a substantial part of the "middling sort" similarly altered the urban scene, though the trend began later and did not proceed as far as in Boston. City tax collectors reported the names of each taxable inhabitant from whom they were unable to extract a tax, and the survival of their records allows for some precision in tracing this phenomenon. Taxpayers dropped from the rolls because of poverty represented less than 3 percent of the taxables in the period before 1740, but they increased to about 6 to 7 percent in the two decades beginning in 1740, and then to one in every ten taxpayers in the fifteen years before the Revolution.

The probate records of Boston and Philadelphia tell a similar tale of economic insecurity hovering over the middle ranges of urban society. Among these people in Boston, median wealth at death dropped sharply between 1685 and 1735 and then made a partial but uneven recovery as the Revolution approached. The average carpenter, baker, shopkeeper, shipwright, or tavernkeeper dying in Boston between 1735 and 1765 had less to show for a lifetime's work than his counterpart of a half century before. In Philadelphia, those in the lower ranges of the middle class also saw the value of their assets, accumulated over a lifetime's labor, slowly decline during the first half of the eighteenth century, though not so severely as in Boston. The startling conclusion that must be drawn from a study of nearly 4,500 Boston and Philadelphia inventories of estates at probate is that population growth and economic development in the colonial cities did not raise the standard of living and broaden opportunities for the vast majority of people, but instead conferred benefits primarily upon those at the top of the social pyramid. The long-range effect of growth was to erode the personal assets held at death by those in the lower 75 percent of Boston society and the lower 60 percent of Philadelphia society. Though many city dwellers had made spectacular individual ascents from the bottom, in the manner of Benjamin Franklin of Philadelphia or Isaac Sears of New York, the statistical chances of success for those beginning beneath the upper class were considerably less after the first quarter of the eighteenth century than before. The dominating fact of late colonial life for many middle-class as well as most lower-class city folk was not economic achievement but economic frustration.

Understanding that the cities were becoming centers of frustrated ambition, propertylessness, genuine distress for those in the lower strata, and stagnating fortunes for many in the middle class makes comprehensible much of the violence, protest, and impassioned rhetoric that occurred in the half-generation before the colonial challenge to British regulations began in 1764. Upper-class colonists typically condemned these verbal attacks and civil disorders as the work of the "rabble," the "mob," the "canaille," or individuals "of turbulent disposition." These labels were used to discredit crowd activity, and historians have only recently recognized that the "rabble" often included a broad range of city dwellers, from slaves and servants through laborers and seamen to artisans and shopkeepers—all of whom were directly or indirectly expressing grievances. Cutting across class lines, and often unified by economic conditions that struck at the welfare of both the lower and middle classes, these crowds began to play a larger role in a political process that grew more heated as the colonial period came to an end. This developing consciousness and political sophistication of ordinary city dwellers came rapidly to fruition in the early 1760s and thereafter played a major role in the advent of the Revolution.

Alienation and protest had been present in the northern cities, especially during periods of economic difficulty, since the early eighteenth century. In Boston, between 1709 and 1713, townspeople protested vigorously and then took extralegal action when Andrew Belcher, a wealthy merchant, refused to stop exporting grain during a bread shortage in the city. Belcher had grown fat on war contracts during Queen Anne's War, and when he chose to export grain to the Caribbean, at a handsome profit, rather than sell it for a smaller profit to hungry townspeople, his ships were attacked and his warehouses emptied by an angry crowd. Rank had no privileges, as even the lieutenant-governor was shot when he tried to intervene. Bostonians of meagre means learned that through concerted action, the powerless could become powerful, if only for the moment. Wealthy merchants who would not listen to pleas from the community could be forced through collective action to subordinate profits to the public need.

After the end of Queen Anne's War, in 1713, Boston was troubled by postwar recession and inflation, which cut into the wages of working people. Attempts to organize a land bank in order to increase the scarce circulating medium in Boston were opposed by wealthy men, many of them former war contractors. Gathering around the unpopular governor, Paul Dudley, these fiscal conservatives blamed the hard times on the extravagant habits of "the Ordinary sort" of people, who squandered their money on a "foolish fondness of Forreign Commodities & Fashions" and on too frequent tippling in the town's taverns. But such explanations did not deceive returning war veterans, the unemployed, or those caught in an inflationary squeeze. They protested openly against men who made their fortunes "by grinding the poor," as one writer expressed it, and who studied "how to oppress, cheat, and overreach their neighbours." "The Rich, Great, and Potent," stormed this angry spokesman, "with rapacious violence bear down all before them, who have not wealth, or strength to encounter or avoid their fury." Although the land bank movement failed in 1720, it was out of this defeat that the Boston Caucus, the political organization designed to mobilize the middle- and lower-class electorate in the decades to come, arose.

In Philadelphia, economic issues also set the mechanic and laborer against the rich as early as the 1720s. When a business recession brought unemployment and a severe shortage of specie (the only legal circulating medium), leading merchant-politicians argued that the problem was moral in nature. If the poor were unemployed or hungry, they had their own lack of industry and prudence to thank, wrote James Logan, a thriving merchant and land speculator. "The Sot, the Rambler, the Spendthrift, and the Slip Season," he charged, were at the heart of the slump. Schemes for reviving the economy with emissions of paper money were reckless attempts to cheat those who worked for their money instead of drinking their time away.

But, as in Boston, the majority of people were not fooled by such high-toned arguments. Angry tracts appeared on both sides of the debate concerning the causes and cure for recession. Those who favored paper money and called for restrictions on land speculators and monopolizers of the money market made an attack on wealth itself an important theme. Logan found bricks flying through his windows and a crowd threatening to level his house. Meanwhile, he looked on in disgust as Governor William Keith organized a political caucus, encouraged laboring men to participate in politics, and conducted a campaign aimed at discrediting Logan and other wealthy merchants. "It is neither the Great, the Rich, nor the Learned, that compose the Body of any People, and . . . civil Government ought carefully to protect the poor, laborious and industrious Part

of Mankind," Keith cautioned the Assembly in 1723. Logan, formerly respected as William Penn's chief proprietary officeholder, a member of council, a judge of the colony's highest court, and Pennsylvania's most educated man, now found himself reviled in widely distributed tracts as "Pedagogus Mathematicus"—an ambitious, ruthless elitist. He and his henchmen, cried the pamphleteers, deserved to be called "petty Tyrants of this Province," "Serpents in the Grass," "Rich Misers," "Phenomena of Aristocracy," "Infringers of our Priviledges," and "Understrappers of Government."

In a striking inversion of the conventional eighteenth-century thinking that only the rich and educated were equipped to hold high political offices, the Keithian faction urged the voters to recognize that "a mean Man, of small Interest, devoted to the faithful Discharge of his Trust and Duty to the Government" was far more to be valued than rich and learned men. For the rest of the decade the anti-Logan forces, organized into political clubs in Philadelphia, held sway at the annual elections and passed legislation to relieve the distress of the lower-class unemployed and middle-class debtors. Members of the Philadelphia elite, such as Logan and merchant Isaac Norris, hated the "new vile people [who] may be truly called a mob," and deplored Keith's "doctrine of reducing all to a level." But they could no longer manage politics from the top. The "moral economy of the crowd," as E. P. Thompson has called it—the people's sense that basic rules of equity in social relations had been breached—had intervened when the rich would do nothing to relieve suffering in a period of economic decline.

When an economic slump beset New York in the 1730s, causing unemployment and an increase in suits for debt, the reaction was much the same as in the other cities. The John Peter Zenger trial of this era is best remembered as a chapter in the history of the freedom of the press. But central to the campaign organized by Zenger's supporters were the indictment of the rich and the mobilization of the artisanry against them. A 1734 election tract reminded the New York electorate that the city's strength—and its future—

lay with the fortunes of "Shuttle" the weaver, "Plane" the joiner, "Drive" the carter, "Mortar" the mason, "Tar" the mariner, "Snip" the tailor, "Smallrent" the fairminded landlord, and "John Poor" the tenant. Pitted against them were "Gripe the Merchant, Squeeze the Shopkeeper, Spintext and Quible the Lawyer." In arguments reminiscent of those in Philadelphia a decade before, the Lewis Morris faction counseled the people that "A poor honest Man [is] preferable to a rich Knave." Only by electing men responsive to the needs of the whole community, the Morrisites advised, could New Yorkers arrest the forces that were impoverishing the artisan class while fattening the purses of merchants and moneylenders. The conservative clergy of the city advised working people to pray harder in difficult times, but the Morrisite pamphleteers urged the electorate to throw out of office those "people in Exalted Stations" who looked with disdain upon "those they call the Vulgar, the Mob, the herd of Mechanicks."

Attacks on wealth and concentrated power continued in New York through 1737. The opulent and educated of the city were exposed as self-interested and oppressive men, not the public-minded community servants that conventional political philosophy prescribed. Though the leaders of the Morris faction were themselves men of substantial wealth, and though they never advocated a truly popular form of politics, their attacks on the rich and their organization of artisan voters became imbedded in the structure and ideology of politics.

A decade later, political contention broke out again in New York City and attacks on the wealthy and well-born were revived. To some extent the political factionalism in the period from 1747 to 1755 represented a competition for power and profit between different elements of the elite. DeLanceys were pitted against Coldens, and Alexanders against Bayards, in a game where the stakes were control of land in neighboring New Jersey, the profits of the Iroquois fur trade, and the power of the assembly in opposition to the governor and his clique of officeholders. But as in earlier decades, the success of these intra-elite struggles depended upon gaining support from below. In appealing to the artisans and tradesmen, especially during periods of economic decline, bitter charges surfaced about the selfishness of wealthy men and the social inequities in society which they promoted. Cadwallader Colden's *Address to the Freeholders* in 1747 inveighed against the rich, who did not build their fortunes "by the honestest means" and who had no genuine concern for the "publick spirit." Colden attacked the wealthy, among whose ranks he figured importantly, as tax dodgers who indulged in wanton displays of wealth and gave little thought to the welfare of those below them. "The midling rank of mankind," argued Colden, was far more honest, dependable, sober, and public spirited "in all Countries," and it was therefore best to trust "our Liberty & Property" to them rather than to New York's "rich jolly or swaggering companions."

In Boston, resentment against the rich, focusing on specific economic grievances, continued to find voice in the middle third of the century. Moreover, since the forming of the caucus a generation before, well-coordinated street action channeled the wrath of townspeople against those who were thought to act against the interest of the commonality. In the 1730s an extended debate erupted on establishing a public market where prices and marketing conditions would be controlled. Many Bostonians in the lower and middle strata regarded a regulated public market as a device of merchants and fiscal conservatives to drive small retailers from the field and reap the profits of victualing Boston themselves. Though they lost their cause after a number of bitter debates and close votes at the town meeting in the mid-1730s, these humbler people, who probably included many without a vote, ultimately prevailed by demolishing the public market on Dock Square in 1737. The attack was accompanied by much "murmuring agt the Government & the rich people," lamented Benjamin Colman, an advocate of the regulated market and a member of the conservative faction. Worse yet, "none of the Rioters or Mutineers" could be discovered. Their support was so broad that they promised that any attempt to arrest or arraign the saboteurs would be met by "Five Hundred Men in Solemn League and Covenant," who would resist the sheriff and destroy any other markets erected by wealthy merchants. The timbers of the public market which fell before the night raiders in 1737 showed how widely held was the conviction that only this kind of civil disobedience would "deliver the poor oppressed and distressed People out of the Hands of the Rich and Mighty."

The Land Bank controversy from 1740 to 1742 further inflamed a wide segment of Boston society. Most of the colony, including Boston, favored a land bank which would relieve the economic distress of the period by issuing more paper money and thus continuing the inflationist policies of the last twenty years. In opposition stood a group of Boston merchants, who "had railed against the evils of paper money" for years and now "damned the Bank as merely a more invidious form of the soft money panacea typically favored by the province's poor and unsuccessful." One of their spokesman, William Douglass, reflected the elitist view by characterizing the dispute as a struggle between the "Idle & Extravagant who want to borrow money at any bad lay" and "our considerable Foreign Traders and rich Men."

Even though the inflationists swept the Massachusetts assembly elections of 1740 and 1741, they could not overcome the combined opposition of Governor Jonathan Belcher, a group of wealthy merchants, and officials in England. In the end, the Land Bank movement was thwarted. The defeat was not lightly accepted or quickly forgotten by debtors and Bostonians of modest means. Three years later, a committee of the Boston town meeting, which had consistently promoted inflated paper currency as a means of relief for Boston's numerous debtors, exploded with angry words at another deflationist proposal of the mercantile elite: "We cannot suppose, because in some extraordinary Times when a Party Spirit has run high there have been some Abuses of Our Liberties and Priviledges, that therefore We should in a Servile Manner give them all up. And have our Bread & Water measured out to Us by those Who Riot in Luxury & Wantonness on

Our Sweat & Toil and be told by them that we are too happy, because we are not reduced to Eat Grass with the Cattle."

The crowning blow to ordinary Bostonians came in 1748 when Thomas Hutchinson, the principal architect of the monetary policy favored by the wealthiest merchants, engineered a merciless devaluation of Massachusetts currency as a cure to the continuing inflation, which by now had reduced the value of paper money to a fraction of its face value. With many persons unemployed, with poverty afflicting hundreds of families, and with Hutchinson personifying the military contractors who had reaped fortunes from King George's War (1739–1747) while common people suffered, popular sentiment exploded. The newspapers carried a rancorous debate on the proposed devaluation, street fights broke out when the new policy was instituted, and Hutchinson was personally threatened on several occasions. An anonymous pamphleteer put into words the sentiment of many in the city who had watched the gap widen between rich and poor during hard times. "Poverty and Discontent appear in every Face, (except the Countenances of the Rich), and dwell upon every Tongue." A few men, fed by "Lust of Power, Lust of Fame, Lust of Money," had grown rich by supplying military expeditions during the last war and had now cornered the paper money market and manipulated the rates of exchange for English sterling to their own profit. "No Wonder such Men can build Ships, Houses, buy Farms, set up their Coaches, Chariots, live very splendidly, purchase Fame, Posts of Honour," railed the pamphleteer. But such "Birds of prey . . . are Enemies to all Communities—wherever they live."

The growing sentiment in the cities against the wealthy was nourished by the Great Awakening —the outbreak of religious enthusiasm throughout the colonies beginning in the late 1730s. Although this eruption of evangelical fervor is primarily identified as a rural phenomenon, it also had powerful effects in the cities, where fiery preachers such as George Whitefield and Gilbert Tennant had their greatest successes. We have no study as yet of the Great Awakening in the cities, but clues abound that one important reason for its urban appeal was the fact that the evangelists took as one of their primary targets the growth of wealth and extravagance, accompanied by a dwindling of social concern in colonial America. Nowhere was this manifested more noticeably than in the cities.

The urban dwellers who thronged to hear George Whitefield in Philadelphia in 1739 and 1741 and those who crowded the Common in Boston to hear Whitefield and the vituperative James Davenport in the early 1740s were overwhelmingly from the "lower orders," so far as we can tell. What accounts for their "awakening" is the evangelists' presentation of a personal religion where humble folk might find succor from debt, daily toil, sickness, and want, and might express deeply felt emotions in an equality of fellowship. At the same time, the revivalist preachers spread a radical message concerning established authority. City dwellers were urged to partake in mass revivals, where the social distance between clergyman and parishioner and among worshippers themselves was obliterated. They were exhorted to be skeptical toward dogma and to participate in ecclesiastical affairs rather than bow passively to established hierarchy.

Through the Great Awakening, doctrinal controversy and attacks on religious leaders became widely accepted in the 1740s. In Boston the itinerant preacher James Davenport hotly indicted the rich and powerful and advised ordinary people to break through the crust of tradition in order to right the wrongs of a decaying society. It was the spectre of unlearned artisans and laborers assuming authority in this manner that frightened many upper-class city dwellers and led them to charge the revivalists with preaching levelism and anarchy. "It is . . . an exceedingly difficult, gloomy time with us . . . ," wrote one conservative clergyman from Boston. "Such an enthusiastic, factious, censorious Spirit was never known here. . . . Every low-bred, illiterate Person can resolve Cases of Conscience and settle the most difficult Points of Divinity better than the most learned Divines."

Such charges were heard repeatedly during the Great Awakening, revealing the fears of those who trembled to see the "unthinking multitude" invested with a new dignity and importance. Nor could the passing of the Awakening reverse the tide, for this new sense of power remained a part of the social outlook of ordinary people. In fact, the radical transformation of religious feeling overflowed into civil affairs. The new feeling of autonomy and importance was bred in the churches, but now it was carried into the streets. Laboring people in the city learned "to identify the millenium with the establishment of governments which derived their power from the people, and which were free from the great disparities of wealth which characterized the old world."

The crescendo of urban protest and extralegal activity in the prerevolutionary decades cannot be separated from the condition of people's lives. Of course those who authored attacks on the growing concentration of wealth and power were rarely artisans or laborers; usually they were men who occupied the middle or upper echelons of society, and sometimes they were men who sought their own gain—installment in office, or the defeat of a competitor for government favors. But whatever their motives, their sharp criticisms of the changes in urban society were widely shared among humbler townspeople. It is impossible to say how much they shaped rather than reflected the views of those in the lower half of the social structure—urban dwellers whose opportunities and daily existence had been most adversely affected by the structural changes overtaking the colonial cities. But the willingness of broad segments of urban society to participate in attacks on narrowly concentrated wealth and power—both at the polls where the poor and propertyless were excluded, and in the streets where everyone, including women, apprentices, indentured servants, and slaves, could engage in action—should remind us that a rising tide of class antagonism and political consciousness, paralleling important economic changes, was a distinguishing feature of the cities at the end of the colonial period.

It is this organic link between the circumstances of people's lives and their political thought and action that has been overlooked by historians who concentrate on Whig ideology, which had its strongest appeal among the educated and well-to-do. The link had always been there, as detailed research into particular communities is beginning to show. But it became transparently clear in the late colonial period, even before England began demanding greater obedience and greater sacrifices in the colonies for the cause of the British Empire. The connection can be seen in New York in the 1760s, where the pleas of the impoverished against mercenary landlords were directly expressed in 1762, and where five years later the papers were pointing out that while the poor had vastly increased in recent years and while many families were selling their furniture at vendue to pay their rent, carriage owners in the city had grown from five to seventy. The link can also be seen in Philadelphia, where growing restlessness at unemployment, bulging almshouses, rising poor taxes, and soaring prices for food and firewood helped to politicize the electorate and drew unprecedented numbers of people to the polls in the last decade of the colonial period.

However, it was in Boston, where poverty had struck first, cut deepest, and lasted longest, that the connection between changing urban conditions and rising political radicalism is most obvious. That it preceded the post-1763 imperial debate, rather than flowing from it, becomes apparent in a close examination of politics in that city between 1760 and 1765.

The political factionalism of these years has usually been seen as a product of the accession of Francis Bernard to the governorship in 1760 and the subsequent appointment of Thomas Hutchinson to the chief justiceship of the colony over the claims of James Otis, Sr., who thought he had been promised the position. Hutchinson, already installed as lieutenant-governor, judge of probate, president of the provincial council, and captain of Castle William, now held high office in all three branches of government—executive, judicial, and legislative. The issues, as historians have portrayed them, were plural officeholding, prosecu-

tion of the colony's illegal traders under writs of assistance, and, ultimately, the right of England to fasten new imperial regulations on the colony. But running beneath the surface of these arguments, and almost entirely overlooked by historians, were issues that had far greater relevance to Boston's commonality.

For ordinary Bostonians, Thomas Hutchinson had long been regarded as a man who claimed to serve the community at large but devised policies which invariably benefitted the rich and hurt the poor. As far back as 1738, Hutchinson had disregarded instructions from the town meeting and pressed the General Court to pass deflationary measures which hurt the pocketbooks of common people, particularly those in debt. Hutchinson continued his hard money campaign in the 1740s. During the 1747 impressment riot, when an angry crowd took control of Boston and demanded the release of some fifty of the town's citizens seized for service in His Majesty's ships, Hutchinson lined up behind the governor in defense of law and order. Alongside other merchants who were chalking up handsome profits on war contracts issued by Governor William Shirley, Hutchinson now stood at the governor's side as his house was surrounded by a jeering, hostile crowd that battered the sheriff and then "swabb'd in the gutter" and locked in the town stocks a deputy sheriff who attempted to disperse them. Hutchinson and his future brother-in-law, Andrew Oliver, joined two other merchants in drafting a report condemning the impressment proceedings as a "Riotous Tumultuous Assembly" of "Foreign Seamen, Servants, Negroes, and Other Persons of Mean and Vile Condition."

One year later, Hutchinson became the designer and chief promoter of a plan for drastically devaluing Massachusetts currency. Enacted into law after bitter debate, the hard money plan was widely seen as a cause of the trade paralysis and economic recession that struck Boston in the early 1750s. Hutchinson's conservative fiscal measure was roundly attacked in the Boston press and specifically criticized for discriminating against the poor. Four months after the Hutchinson plan became law, Boston's voters turned him out of the House. Shortly thereafter, when his home mysteriously caught fire, a crowd gathered in the street, cursing Hutchinson and crying, "Let it burn!" A rump town meeting sardonically elected Hutchinson tax collector, a job which would take him out of his mansion and into the streets where he might personally see how laboring-class Bostonians were faring during hard times.

The animosity against Hutchinson continued during the next decade, because he aligned himself with a series of unpopular issues—the excise tax of 1754, the Albany Plan of the same year, and another devaluation scheme in 1761. More than anyone in Boston in the second third of the eighteenth century, Thomas Hutchinson stood in the common people's view as the archetype of the cold, grasping, ambitious, aristocratic merchant-politician who had lost touch with his humbler neighbors and cared little whether they prospered or failed.

Fanning the flames of rancor toward Hutchinson in the early 1760s was his leadership of a small group of conservative merchants and lawyers, known in the popular press as the "Junto." These men were known not only for fiscal conservatism but for their efforts to dismantle the town meeting system of government in Boston in order to enlarge their power while curbing that of the middle and lower classes. Most of them were friends of the new governor, Francis Bernard, enjoyed appointments in the provincial government, belonged to the Anglican church, and were related by blood or marriage. Among them were Hutchinson, Andrew and Peter Oliver, Eliakim Hutchinson, Charles Apthorp, Robert Auchmuty, Samuel Waterhouse, Charles Paxton, Thomas Flucker, John Erving, Jr., Edmund Trowbridge, and Chambers Russell.

The move to overthrow the town meeting in 1760 had deep roots. In 1715 and again in the early 1730s conservative merchants had argued that Boston should substitute a borough government for the town meeting. Under municipal incorporation, a system of town government widely used in England as well as in Philadelphia, appointed alderman would serve life terms and would elect the mayor. Under such a plan most municipal officers would be appointed rather than elected. The proposal was designed to limit popular participation in government and transfer control of the city to the elite, whose members argued that they would institute greater order and efficiency.

Both earlier attempts to scrap the town meeting had been staunchly attacked by pamphleteers, who warned that such "reforms" would give exorbitant power to men whose wealth and elevated social status were frail guarantees that they would act in the public interest. The gulf between the rulers and the ruled, between the rich and poor, would only increase, they prophesied, and the people would pay a fearful price for abdicating their political rights. Those who favored incorporation, argued a pamphleteer in 1715, despised "Mobb Town Meetings," where the rich, if they wished to participate, had to mingle with less elevated townspeople. They wished to substitute the rule of the few so that "the Great Men will no more have the Dissatisfaction of seeing their Poorer Neighbours stand up for equal Privilege with them." But neither in 1715 nor in the early 1730s could the elite push through their reorganization of town government.

The town meeting continued to rankle those who regarded laboring people as congenitally turbulent, incapable of understanding economic issues, and moved too much by passion and too little by reason to make wise political choices. Governor Shirley expressed this view most cogently after the demonstration against British impressment of Boston citizens in 1747: "What I think may be esteemed the principal cause of the Mobbish turn in this Town is its Constitution; by which the Management of it is devolv'd upon the populace assembled in their Town Meetings . . . where the meanest Inhabitants . . . by their constant Attendance there generally are the majority and outvote the Gentlemen, Merchants, Substantial Traders and all the better part of the Inhabitants; to whom it is irksome to attend." When so many workingmen, merchant seamen, and "low sort of people" could participate in town meetings, the governor lamented, what could be expected but "a factious and Mobbish Spirit" that kept educated and respectable people away?

In 1760, five months before Hutchinson's appointment as chief justice, the conservative "Junto" made another attempt to gain control of the town government. Realizing that common Bostonians could not be gulled into surrendering their political rights, the "Junto" plotted a strategy for swinging the May elections in Boston and sending to the General Court four representatives who would convince the House to pass a law for incorporating Boston. A "Combination of Twelve Strangers," who called themselves "The New and Grand Corcas," warned the populist *Boston Gazette,* were designing to "overthrow the ancient Constitution of our Town-Meeting, as being popular and mobbish; and to form a Committee to transact the whole Affairs of the Town for the future." In order to control the elections, the article continued, the "Junto" would attempt to keep "tradesmen, and those whom in Contempt they usually term the Low lived People," from voting. They would challenge their eligibility at the polls, attempt to buy their votes, and threaten them with arrest and loss of their jobs. As Samuel Adams later remarked, it was obvious that Hutchinson was bent on destroying the "Democratic part" of government. On the eve of the election, the "Committee of Tradesmen," working with the "old and true Corcas," used the press to urge Boston's working people to stand up to these threats. The artisans should "put on their Sabbath Cloathes . . . wash their Hands and faces that they may appear neat and cleanly," spurn the vote-buying tactics of the "Junto," and elect men who represented their interests.

A record number of voters turned out on 13 May 1760, as both factions courted the electorate. The result was indecisive. Royall Tyler, vociferously opposed by the Anglican "Junto," was re-elected. But Benjamin Prat and John Tyng, who during the preceding year had taken an unpopular stand on sending the province ship to England, lost their seats to two moderates, Samuel Welles and John Phillips, who were supported by the Hutchinsonians. The conservatives had succeeded to this extent in creating a "popular" issue and using it to rally the electorate against two of the Caucus's candidates. It was enough to hearten the Hutchinsonians, who now had reason to anticipate other electoral successes, and to galvanize the anti-Hutchinsonians into redoubling their efforts among Boston's electorate.

In the period immediately after the 1760 election, James Otis made his meteoric rise in the "popular" party in Boston, leading the fight to curb the growing power of the Hutchinsonian circle. The Otis-Hutchinson struggle has usually been interpreted as a fight over the regulation of trade and oligarchic officeholding, or, more recently, as the culmination of a long-standing interfamily competition. In both interpretations Otis appears as a sulphurous orator and writer (either brilliant or mad according to one's views), who molded laboring-class opinion, called the "mob" into action, and shaped its behavior. To a large extent, however, Otis was only reflecting the perceptions and interests of common Bostonians in his abusive attacks on the lieutenant-governor and his allies. For two years after the 1760 elections, which were dangerously indecisive from the viewpoint of the "popular" party, Otis filled the *Gazette* with vitriolic assaults on the Hutchinson clique, each fully answered in the conservative *Evening-Post.* Woven into Otis's offensive was the theme of resentment against wealth, narrowly concentrated political power, and arbitrary political actions which adversely affected Boston's ordinary people. But rather than seeing this campaign solely as an attempt to mobilize the artisans and laborers, we should also understand it as a reflection of opinion already formed within these groups. For years Boston's common people had shown their readiness to act against such oppression—in preventing the exportation of grain, in destroying the public market, and in harassing arbitrary officeholders. Otis, keenly aware of the declining fortunes and the resentment of ordinary townspeople, was mirroring as well as molding popular opinion.

In 1763 the Hutchinson circle made another attempt to strike at the town meeting system of politics, which was closely interwoven with the

Boston Caucus. Election messages in the *Evening-Post* urged the electorate to "keep the Public Good only in View" while burying "in everlasting Oblivion" old prejudices and animosities. But this much said, the paper ran a scathing "expose" of the Caucus, which read like the confessions of an ex-Communist. Allegedly written by a former member of the Caucus, it explained how Caucus leaders conducted all political affairs behind closed doors and in smoke-filled rooms. Then, "for form sake," the leaders "prepared a number of warm disputes . . . to entertain the lower sort; who are in an ecstasy to find the old Roman Patriots still surviving." All townspeople were invited to speak at these open meetings, it was claimed, but to oppose Caucus leaders was to earn their "eternal animosity" and end forever any chance of obtaining town office. Democracy, as practiced by the Caucus, was nothing but sham, mocked the *Evening-Post* writer.

The attempt to "expose" the Caucus as a dictatorial clique, with little genuine interest in the laboring classes, failed miserably. The Caucus responded by organizing its most successful roundup of voters in Boston's colonial history. On election day, 1,089 voters went to the poll, a number never to be exceeded even in the tumultuous years of the following decade. They drubbed the candidates favored by the Hutchinsonians. James Otis, the leading anti-Hutchinsonian, got the largest number of votes and was installed as moderator of the town meeting—a token of the confidence in which he was held for his open-handed attacks on Hutchinson.

The bitter Otis-Hutchinson fight of the early 1760s, carried on *before* English imperial policy became an issue in Massachusetts, revolved around a number of specific issues, including the replacement of William Bollan as provincial agent, the establishment of an Anglican mission in the shadow of Harvard College, the multiple offices held by Hutchinson and his relatives, the writs of assistance, and other problems. But more fundamentally, the struggle matched two incompatible conceptions of government and society. Developed during the controversies of preceding decades, these conceptions were spelled out in

an outpouring of political rhetoric in the early 1760s and in the crystallization of two distinct factions.

James Otis, Samuel Adams, Royall Tyler, Oxenbridge Thacher, and a host of other Bostonians, linked to the artisans and laborers through a network of neighborhood taverns, fire companies, and the Caucus, espoused a vision of politics that gave credence to laboring-class views and regarded as entirely legitimate the participation of artisans and even laborers in the political process. This was not a new conception of the rightful political economy, but a very old one. The leaders of this movement were merely following in the footsteps of earlier popular leaders—from John Noyes to Elisha Cooke to James Allen. The town meeting, open to almost all property owners in the city and responsive to the propertyless as well, was the foundation of this system. By no means narrowly based, the "popular" party included many of the city's merchants, shopkeepers, lawyers, doctors, clergymen, and other well-to-do men. They provided leadership and filled the most important elective offices—overseers of the poor, tax assessors, town selectmen, and delegates to the House of Representatives. Lesser people filled minor offices and voiced their opinions at the town meetings where they were numerically dominant.

For the conservative merchants and lawyers, led and personified by Thomas Hutchinson, the old system spelled only chaos. "Reform" for these men meant paring back the responsibilities of the town meeting, substituting appointive for elective officeholders, restricting the freedom of the press, and breaking down the virulent anti-Anglican prejudice that still characterized the popular party. Like their opponents, members of the "prerogative" party had suffered as Boston's economy stagnated after 1740. But they saw the best hope for reviving the economy in handing over the management of town government to the wealthy and well-born exclusively. To see Otis address the crowd and to witness "the Rage of Patriotism . . . spread so violently . . . thro' town and country, that there is scarce a cobler or porter but has turn'd mountebank in politicks and erected his stage near the printing-press" was their vision of hell.

Between 1761 and 1764 proponents of the "popular" and "prerogative" conceptions of politics engaged in a furious battle of billingsgate that filled the columns of the *Gazette* and *Evening-Post.* It is easy to be diverted by the extreme forms which the scurrility took. Charges of "Racoon," "stinking Skunk," "Pimp," "wild beast," "drunkard," and dozens of other choice titles were traded back and forth in verbal civil war. But more important than this stream of epithets was the deep-seated, class-tinged animosity which the polemical pieces exposed: hatred and suspicion of laboring people on the part of the Hutchinsonians; suspicion and hatred of the wealthy, Anglican, prerogative elite held by the common people.

Thus, Thomas Pownall, the popular governor from 1757 to 1760, was satirized by a conservative for confusing class lines by going aboard ships in Boston harbor to talk with "common people about ship-affairs" and mingling in the streets with the "dirtiest, most lubberly, mutinous, and despised part of the people." The anti-Hutchinsonians, on the other hand, urged Bostonians to oppose "The Leviathan in power [Hutchinson], or those other overgrown Animals, whose influence and importance is only in exact mathematical proportion to the weight of their purses." The Caucus, decried a Hutchinsonian, talked incessantly about the right "for every dabbler in politicks to say and print whatever his shallow understanding, or vicious passions may suggest, against the wisest and best men—a liberty for fools and madmen to spit and throw firebrands at those of the most respectable and most amiable character." In retort, Otis, speaking as a mechanic, poured out his resentment: "I am forced to get my living by the labour of my hand; and the sweat of my brow, as most of you are and obliged to go thro' good report and evil report, for bitter bread, earned under the frowns of some who have no natural or divine right to be above me, and entirely owe their grandeur and honor to grinding the faces of the poor, and other acts of ill gotten gain and power." In reply, the

conservatives charged anarchy: "The day is hastening, when some who are now, or, have lately been the darling idols of a dirty very dirty witless rabble commonly called the little vulgar, are to sink and go down with deserved infamy, to all posterity." This was doubtful, retorted a writer in the *Gazette:* the problem was that the rich were obsessed with money and "couldn't have the idea of riches without that of poverty. They must see others poor in order to form a notion of their own happiness." Thus, in what was once a flourishing town, "a few persons in power" attempted to monopolize politics, and promoted projects "for keeping the people poor in order to make them humble. . . ."

This reciprocal animosity and mistrust, suffusing the newspapers and pamphlets of the late colonial period, reveals the deeply rooted social tensions that Bostonians would carry into the revolutionary era. These tensions shaped the ways in which different social groups began to think about *internal* political goals once the conflict against *external* authority began. In the end, the Hutchinson faction, looking not to the future but staring into the distant past, faced an impossible task—to convince a broad electorate that the very men who had accumulated fortunes in an era when most had suffered were alone qualified to govern in the interest of the whole community. Lower- and middle-class Bostonians had heard fiscal conservatives and political elitists pronounce the same platitudes for half a century. Even now, a generation before James Madison formally enunciated an interest-group theory of politics, they understood that each group had its particular interest to promote and that aristocratic politicians who claimed to work for the commonweal were not to be trusted. Such men employed the catchwords of the traditional system of politics—"public good," "community," "harmony," and "public virtue"—to cloak their own ambitions for aggrandizing wealth and power. The growing inequalities of wealth in Boston, which could be readily seen in the overcrowded almshouse and flocks of outreliefers in contrast to the urban splendor of men like Hutchinson and Oliver, were proof enough of that.

Only by understanding the long animosity that the common people of Boston held for Thomas Hutchinson and his clique can sense be made of the extraordinary response to the Stamp Act in Boston in August 1765—the systematic destruction of the houses of Hutchinson and other wealthy and conservative Boston officials—and of the course of revolutionary politics in the city in the years that followed. It is possible, of course, to revert to the explanation of Peter Oliver, who, at the time, argued that "the People in general . . . were like the Mobility of all Countries, perfect Machines, wound up by any Hand who might first take the winch." In this view, the crowd was led by the nose by middle- and upper-class manipulators such as Otis and Samuel Adams, and used to further their own political ambitions. In this Newtonian formulation, the crowd could never be self-activating, for thought and planned action could have their source only in the minds of educated persons.

Such explanations, however, bear no relationship to the social realities in Boston at the time or to the long history of popular protest in the city. Again and again in the eighteenth century the Boston crowd had considered its interest, determined its enemies, and moved in a coordinated and discriminating way to gain its ends through street action. It was frequently supported in this by men higher up on the social scale—men who shielded the crowd leaders from subsequent attempts of the authorities to punish them. Thus, several socioeconomic groups, with interests that often coincided but sometimes diverged, found it profitable to coordinate their actions.

The attacks on Andrew Oliver's house on the evening of 14 August 1765, and on Hutchinson's house twelve days later, were entirely consistent with this pattern of politics. On the evening of 14 August, the crowd, led by the shoemaker Ebenezer MacIntosh, culminated a day of protest against the Stamp Act by reducing Oliver's mansion to a shambles. Accompanied by the sheriff, Hutchinson attempted to stop the property destruction. For his trouble, he was driven off with a hailstorm of stones. Less than two weeks later it was Hutchinson's turn. Forcing him and his

family to flee, the crowd smashed in the doors with axes, reduced the furniture to splinters, stripped the walls bare, chopped through inner partitions until the house was a hollow shell, destroyed the formal gardens behind the house, drank the contents of the wine cellar, and carried off every moveable object of value except some of Hutchinson's books and papers, which were left to scatter in the wind. Not a person in Boston, neither private citizen nor officer of the law, attempted to stop the crowd. Its members worked through the night with almost military precision to raze the building, spending three hours alone "at the cupola before they could get it down," according to Governor Bernard.

Historians agree that in destroying the Boston mansions of Oliver and Hutchinson, the crowd was demonstrating against the Stamp Act. Oliver had been appointed Stamp Collector, and Hutchinson, though he publicly expressed his view that the act was unwise, had vowed to use his authority as lieutenant-governor to see it executed. But in conducting probably the most ferocious attack on private property in the history of the English colonies, the crowd was demonstrating against far more than Parliamentary policy. Stamp collectors were intimidated and handled roughly in many other cities. But nowhere else did the crowd choose to destroy property on such a grand scale and with such exacting thoroughness. The full meaning of these attacks can be extracted only by understanding the long-standing animus against the Oliver-Hutchinson circle. Beyond intimidating British officialdom, the crowd was giving vent to years of hostility at the accumulation of wealth and power by the aristocratic, Hutchinson-led prerogative faction. Behind every swing of the ax and every hurled stone, behind every shattered plate and splintered mahogany chair lay the fury of a Bostonian who had read or heard the repeated references to the people as "rabble," and who had suffered economic hardship while others grew rich. The handsome furnishings in the houses of Hutchinson, Oliver, and others that fell before the "Rage-intoxicated rabble," as one young upper-class lawyer put it, provided psychological recompense for those Bostonians who had lost faith that opportunity or equitable relationships any longer prevailed in their city.

The political consciousness of the crowd and its use of the Stamp Act protests as an opportunity for an attack on wealth itself were remarked upon again and again in the aftermath of the August crowd actions. Fifteen houses were targeted for destruction on the night of 27 August, according to Governor Bernard, in what he thought had become "a War of Plunder, of general levelling and taking away the Distinction of rich and poor." "Everything that for years past, had been the cause of any unpopular discontent was revived," he explained; "and private resentments against persons in office worked themselves in, and endeavoured to exert themselves under the mask of the public cause." On the same day, the governor warned that unless "persons of property and consideration did not unite in support of government"—by which he meant that a way must be found to employ the militia or some kind of *posse comitatus* to control crowd actions —"anarchy and confusion" would continue in "an insurrection of the poor against the rich, those that want the necessities of life against those that have them." On 10 September, two weeks after the destruction of Hutchinson's house, another Boston merchant wrote that "the rich men in the town" were seized with apprehension and "were moveing their cash & valuable furniture, &c" to the homes of poorer friends who were above suspicion.

Seen in the context of three generations of social and economic change in Boston, and set against the drive for power of the Hutchinson-Oliver faction in Massachusetts, the Stamp Act riots provide a revealing example of the "moral economy of the crowd" in the early stages of the revolutionary movement. Members of the Boston "mob" needed no upper-class leaders to tell them about the economic stagnation of the late colonial period that had been affecting their lives and the structure of opportunity in the town. Nor did they need to destroy the homes of Oliver and Hutchinson in order to obtain the promise of these officeholders to hold the Stamp Act in abeyance. Instead, the crowd paid off some old debts and

served notice on those whom it regarded as enemies of its interests. It was the culminating event of an era of protest against wealth and oligarchic power that had been growing in all the cities. In addition, it demonstrated the fragility of the union between protesting city dwellers of the laboring classes and their more bourgeois partners, for in the uninhabited August attacks on property, the Boston crowd went much farther than Caucus leaders such as James Otis and Samuel Adams had reckoned or wished to countenance.

In the other cities the growing resentment of wealth, the rejection of an elitist conception of politics, and the articulation of artisan- and laboring-class interests also gained momentum after 1765. These were vital developments in the revolutionary period. Indeed, it was the extraordinary new vigor of urban laboring people in defining and pursuing their goals that raised the frightening spectre of a radicalized form of politics and a radically changed society in the minds of many upper-class city dwellers, who later abandoned the resistance movement against England that they had initially supported and led.

That no full-fledged proletarian radical ideology emerged in the decade before the Revolution should not surprise us, for this was a preindustrial society in which no proletariat yet existed. Instead, we can best understand the long movement of protest against concentrated wealth and power, building powerfully as social and economic conditions changed in the cities, as a reflection of the disillusionment of laborers, artisans, and many middle-class city dwellers against a system that no longer delivered equitable rewards to the industrious. "Is it equitable that 99, rather 999, should suffer for the Extravagance or Grandeur of one," asked a New Yorker in 1765, "especially when it is considered that Men frequently owe their Wealth to the impoverishment of their Neighbors?" Such thoughts, cutting across class lines, were gaining force among large parts of the urban population in the late colonial period. They were directed squarely at outmoded notions that only the idle and profligate could fail in America and that only the educated and wealthy were entitled to manage political affairs.

But the absence of clearly identifiable class consciousness and of organized proletarian radicalism does not mean that a radical ideology, nurtured within the matrix of preindustrial values and modes of thought, failed to emerge during the Revolution. Though this chapter in the history of the Revolution is largely unwritten, current scholarship is making it clear that the radicalization of thought in the cities, set in motion by economic and social change, advanced very rapidly once the barriers of traditional thought were broken down. A storm of demands, often accompanied by crowd action to insure their implementation, rose from the urban "tradesmen" and "mechanicks": for the end of closed assembly debates and the erection of public galleries in the legislative houses; for published roll-call votes which would indicate how faithfully elected legislators followed the wishes of their constituents; for open-air meetings where laboring men could help devise and implement public policy; for more equitable laying of taxes; for price controls instituted by and for the laboring classes to shield them from avaricious men of wealth; and for the election of mechanics and other ordinary people at all levels of government.

How rapidly politics and political ideology could be transformed, as colonists debated the issue of rebellion, is well illustrated by the case of Philadelphia. In one brief decade preceding the Revolution the artisanry and laboring poor of the city moved from a position of clear political inferiority to a position of political control. They took over the political machinery of the city, pushed through the most radical state constitution of the period, and articulated concepts of society and political economy that would have stunned their predecessors. By mid-1776, laborers, artisans, and small tradesmen, employing extralegal measures when electoral politics failed, were in clear command in Philadelphia. Working with middle-class leaders such as James Cannon, Timothy Matlack, Thomas Young, and Thomas Paine, they launched a full-scale attack on wealth and even on the right to acquire unlimited private property. By the summer of 1776 the militant

Privates Committee, which probably represented the poorest workers, became the foremost carrier of radical ideology in Pennsylvania. It urged the voters, in electing delegates for the constitutional convention, to shun "great and overgrown rich men [who] will be improper to be trusted, [for] they will be too apt to be framing distinctions in society, because they will reap the benefits of all such distinctions." Going even further, they drew up a bill of rights for consideration by the convention, which included the proposition that "an enormous proportion of property vested in a few individuals is dangerous to the rights, and destructive of the common happiness, of mankind; and therefore every free state hath a right by its laws to discourage the possession of such property." For four years, in an extremely fluid political scene, a radicalized artisanry shaped—and sometimes dominated—city and state politics, while setting forth the most fully articulated ideology of reform yet heard in America.

These calls for reform varied from city to city, depending on differing conditions, past politics, and the qualities of particular leaders. Not all the reforms were implemented, especially those that went to the heart of the structural problems in the economy. Pennsylvania, for example, did not adopt the radical limitation on property holding. But that we know from hindsight that the most radical challenges to the existing system were thwarted, or enjoyed only a short period of success, does not mean that they are not a vital part of the revolutionary story. At the time, the disaffected in the cities were questioning some of the most fundamental tenets of colonial thought. Ordinary people, in bold opposition to their superiors, to whom custom required that they defer, were creating power and suggesting solutions to problems affecting their daily lives. As other essays in this book explain, how far these calls for radical reform extended and the success they achieved are matters that historians have begun to investigate only lately. But this much is clear: even though many reforms were defeated or instituted briefly and then abandoned, political thought and behavior would never again be the same in America.

PART TWO
A
REVOLUTIONARY
PEOPLE

9

POLITICAL ENTHUSIASM, REVIVALISM, AND THE AMERICAN REVOLUTION

RHYS ISAAC

By the mid-eighteenth century questions of political and social authority were occupying the minds of all ranks of Americans. While the prosperous governing elites debated the nature of British parliamentary authority in the colonies, those of more humble station discussed the propriety of existing social arrangements. In rural communities where land scarcity meant that fathers could no longer offer the promise of propertied independence to their children, sons and daughters began to question the patriarchal control of their fathers and conceived children to force a marriage on their own terms. In towns and cities middling and laboring-class people joined in questioning the customary authority that the rural gentry and urban merchants had exercised. In the mobilization against Britain these people of lower status demanded a voice in their own affairs, which threatened the system of patronage and deference that had dominated social relations for generations.

In Virginia, as Rhys Isaac shows, popular questioning of elite control took a distinctive form. The system of deference in the Chesapeake region was expressed in a gentry-dominated culture of conviviality. Personal events, such as marriages and births, and public affairs, such as quarterly court sessions, were the scenes of drinking, gambling, dancing, horseracing, and general mirth. In the eighteenth century, however, another system of values began to challenge the domination of the elite-directed culture. This alternative culture was based upon a revival of religiosity among many of Virginia's commoners. Expressed in the growing number of Methodist and Baptist revivals that emphasized strict self-discipline and continence, this emerging culture directly challenged the worldliness of the dominant culture. As Isaac suggests, it was this evangelical culture that set the stage for popular support of the anti-British revolutionary movement as well as for a popular challenge to the power and authority of Virginia's planter elite. Finding themselves caught between the intransigence of British imperial policy and growing popular opposition, by the early 1770s most planter elites turned to the patriot cause in an attempt to reassert their hegemony over Virginia society.

How does the pattern of popular mobilization in pre-Revolutionary Virginia compare with that of rural New England described by John Shy in Reading 11? With the mobilization of the laboring classes in America's seaport cities discussed by Gary B. Nash in Reading 8?

Reprinted from *The Transformation of Virginia, 1740–1790* (Chapel Hill: The University of North Carolina Press, 1982), pp. 243–269, by permission of the publisher.

Revolutions, like the social life whose symbolic reorganization they express, have no clear-cut beginnings and endings. Yet the start of an irreversible chain reaction can now be recognized in the actions of that momentous Wednesday, June 1, 1774, when "the Honourable the Speaker, and as many Members of the late Assembly as were in Town, with the citizens of Williamsburg, assembled at the Courthouse." From that venue they moved "in Procession to the Church, where an excellent Sermon, well adapted to the . . . unhappy Disputes between Great Britain and her Colonies was preached."

A week before, the House of Burgesses had resolved to keep the first day of June (the date Parliament had set for the closing of the Boston port) as a day of "Fasting, Humiliation, and Prayer, devoutly to implore the Divine Interposition . . . that the Minds of his Majesty and his Parliament . . . may be inspired from above with Wisdom, Moderation, and Justice." The members were required to attend "in Order to proceed with the Speaker and the Mace to the Church," where the Reverend Mr. Price was appointed to read prayers, and the Reverend Mr. Gwatkin invited "to preach a Sermon suitable to the occasion." Mr. Gwatkin had returned an exquisitely Delphic answer to his invitation, informing the House that he could not comply—"on account of a disorder in his breast." But the governor, faced with such calculated dramatization of disapproval of His Majesty's Government, was more direct. He dissolved the Assembly immediately.

On the day after the dissolution eighty-nine of the burgesses had met in an assembly room near the capitol to subscribe solemnly to an "Association" for common action in the crisis. This public signing revived a form of action that would become an important ceremonial means of mobilizing the populace, and at the same time, a means of giving them a heightened sense that the basis of society lay in the consent of its members. By the time the Speaker led the procession of burgesses down Duke of Gloucester Street to Bruton Church, many of the members had gone back to their counties. These added their dignity to the little replications of the Williamsburg enactment

that took place in many of the parishes throughout the province. George Mason could not return to Fairfax County, but he sent instructions to his family there that reveal the striving of the gentry for dramaturgical effects. They were "to pay strict attention" to the fast, and his three eldest sons, with his two eldest daughters, were to "attend church in mourning."

A brief but anxious period of suspense followed. In the ten years that had passed since the Stamp Act crisis had called forth an astonishing demonstration of Virginia's potential for patriot mobilization, the commitment of the leading gentry—as revealed in formally drafted resolves and remonstrances—had not been matched by the overall performance of either the gentry at large or the common folk. The non-importation movement of 1769 had quickly weakened, and after attempts to revive it had failed, it had simply been allowed to die. It was therefore uncertain in the summer of 1774 whether the Old Dominion would respond vigorously to the new situation. The crisis, after all, arose from events in the remote city of Boston and pertained to acts of Parliament directed at Massachusetts alone. Philip Fithian, the New Jersey tutor, noted in his journal for May 31: "The lower Class of People here [northern Virginia] are in a tumult on account of Reports from Boston, many of them expect to be press'd & compell'd to go and fight the Britains."

It was imperative for the patriot gentry to communicate to the populace not only their fearful view of what awaited Virginians should they remain supine, but also the vision of the good life that inspired the struggle. At stake were "fortunes . . . liberties . . . and everything that is held most dear among men"—the heritage of "a brave, virtuous and free people." "Virtue," which was at the heart of patriot aspirations, was not just a moral quality or disposition; it was a program for the preservation and regeneration of society. The threatened British constitution was "the Gift of God . . . to relieve Virtue from every Restraint to its beneficent Operation, and to restrain Vice. . . . It elevates the Soul, by giving Consequence to every Individual, and enabling him to support that Consequence." It was to this vision that the patriot leaders thrilled.

Media and Messages of Anxiety

Three principal channels existed for conveying views of the crisis and guiding responses: the printed word; word of mouth (including oratory); and dramatic statement through concerted community action.

The newspaper treatment of the Burgesses' responses to the closing of the port of Boston reveals the workings of communications in this period. A small-print notice in Purdie and Dixon's *Virginia Gazette*, coming after news from London, Boston, New York, and Philadelphia, presented only a simple outline of the steps taken by the Burgesses and the governor. We might be inclined to suppose from the lack of headline emphasis that contemporaries did not attach great importance to these actions. Yet abundant evidence demonstrates an immediate and widespread sense of their momentousness. The rapid spread of shock throughout Virginia in the absence of newspaper publicity gives an indication of the customary relationship of the press to the total information system of the time. Printed reports authenticated news of local importance that was expected to circulate in fuller versions by word of mouth. The newspapers, with their small type, their long reports from the courts of Europe, and their polemical exchanges in learned literary style, were not directed to the general populace. The printed word was of the greatest importance in mobilizing opinion, but humble persons were expected to receive the more important messages through the mediation of leaders in society. The contents of the fine print would reach the plain folk through reading aloud and through conversations at courthouses, ordinaries, and other places of assembly. This oral dissemination incorporated news into the common stock of knowledge, opinion, and feeling.

It is difficult to form impressions of the spoken word from written texts. Little supports an attempt, since very few transcriptions, or even reports, of patriot speeches survive. It seems, indeed, from the character of the texts available that courthouse oratory was scarcely more effective than the newspaper as a medium for the communication of the gentry's sense of emergency to ordinary Virginians. (Patrick Henry's rhetoric was a conspicuous exception that will be discussed below.) The language and terms of Classical republicanism that underlay the literate gentry's conception of the struggle could not readily arouse a populace whose limited experience of higher culture was of the Bible rather than of the Classics. More effective than the imagery of Roman republicanism was the Anglo-Virginian sense of identity as a Protestant people.

The specter of the popish menace, long a part of Anglo-American folk culture, was raised afresh by Parliament's recent steps in the 1770s to establish the Roman Catholic church in the conquered French province of Quebec. In the *Virginia Gazette* a swinging ballad to a shanty tune categorized the king's advisers as "Papist Knaves" and asked defiantly whether "free born men" would be "rul'd by Popish law, Because they freedom claim." The words of a gentleman in Henrico County show the intensity of feeling on this issue in his community, where "the Idea of loosing civil or [and?] religious Liberty at one Stroke has raised such an enthusiastick spirit of Love of both as cannot be extinguished but with Life itself." He then emphatically declared that "there is no widdow among us who would not put the sword into the Hand of her only Son to fight [for] the Cause of God and our Country." The "Thoughts" of a writer in the newspaper reveal repellent ethnic stereotypes that reinforced the identification of oppression with popery:

Possessed of our inestimable Constitution, we may pour forth our Prayers and Thanksgivings to its Donor, with Peace, Purity, and Innocence. Let it be trifled away, and how shall we address him. . . . When legal redress of Injuries is denied, every Man becomes the Carver of his own Satisfaction. He infuses the Poison, he whets the Dagger; he does what the native Irish, the Portuguese, [and] the Neapolitans . . . have done before. . . . [Thus] our pure Religion must depart with our Liberty. It does not afford those Consolations the Horrours of our Conscience will require. We must involve ourselves in the Mazes of Superstition, and endeavour, by Penances, Absolutions, and a Thousand Mummeries, to quiet the Worm within, under a total Subversion of all the Principles of Reason and Understanding.

Liberty, virtue, and pure Protestant religion were all inextricably intertwined. Here lay nagging sources of anxiety that gave deep meaning to the play of emotions within the patriot movement. What if America—if Virginia—was already deficient in virtue? Corruption and the sinister designs of the overmighty in Great Britain could be readily discerned and denounced, but were there not signs that the same disorder was spreading to the colonies? This secular anxiety had a popular religious counterpart in the abhorrence with which converts to the evangelical culture suddenly viewed the ways of their society. The code of conduct prescribed in the non-importation association imposed upon upholders of the patriotic cause a similar set of forbearances to those obligatory for the adherents to "vital religion." Article eight of the association, adopted by the Continental Congress on October 20, 1774, and enforced in Virginia, engaged signatories to "discountenance and discourage every species of extravagance and dissipation, especially all horseracing, and all kinds of gaming, cockfighting, . . . and other expensive diversions and entertainments." In parts of Virginia the patriot committees took dancing to be forbidden, although it had not been specifically listed in the terms of the association.

The obligatory renunciation of important customary forms of social intercourse expressed a growing uneasiness at effete luxury among all ranks of free men. Concern over indebtedness not only vented itself in attacks on the Scots merchants but also highlighted misgivings about the way of life that the tobacco staple sustained in Virginia. Indebtedness, attributed in part to extravagant living, was seen to be more deeply responsible for the failure of craft industries to develop in Virginia. The absence of such industry—

and of the frugality and virtue that it was believed to promote—was in turn ascribed to the importation of African servile labor in place of "freemen and useful manufacturers." A ban on the importation of slaves was imposed by the second article of the Virginia association adopted in convention on August 6, 1774. A fervent petition had been addressed to the king from the Virginia House of Burgesses as early as April 1772, pleading for royal consent to legislation ending the importation of slaves because "it greatly retards the Settlement of the Colonies, with more useful Inhabitants." A patriotic writer suggested that the Privy Council's veto of this restrictive legislation arose from the conspiring ministry's determination that Virginia's love of liberty should continue to be undermined by their dependence on slaves. The author feared that the ministers "will therefore endeavour to increase amongst us the Number of those unhappy People."

Dramatized Ideology

Verbal pronouncements, whether in spoken or written addresses, did not emerge in Virginia in 1774 as the most effective means of alleviating widespread anxieties or seeking to realize aspirations. Rather, it was through participation in patterned forms of communal action that broad mobilization proceeded most effectively.

Since Parliament's measures for disciplining Massachusetts were the occasion of the crisis, dramatization of the plight of the Bostonians— and of Virginians' identification with them— played an important part in the activation of the patriot movement. Gentlemen like Landon Carter labored to fire sentiments of indignation and compassion in the hearts of the freeholders, developing ceremonies of concern that fixed attention on the victims of oppression. Subscription lists were opened, followed by the display of a solemn public promise by gentlemen who offered an example to the community, "subscribing" a generous donation to the cause. The celebration of this patriotic zeal was a powerful means of intensifying shared commitment.

The social process involved is clearly observable in a notice from Fredericksburg that "very liberal contributions have been made, in this place, for the relief of the poor in *Boston. Mr. Mann Page,* Junior, one of our Representatives, has taken uncommon pains to promote the subscriptions." An example of the community mobilization that the leaders were striving for is seen in the announcement late in July that "the county of Surry, from the highest to the lowest, are actuated with the warmest affection towards the suffering town of Boston . . . [and] that immediately after the meeting of freeholders and others, . . . upwards of 150 barrels of Indian corn and wheat were subscribed . . . for the benefit of those firm and intrepid sons of liberty, the Bostonians."

When the county community was gathered at the courthouse, the quest was above all for unanimity. This was especially evident in what a hostile observer called "the grand meetings for signing the association." In Princess Anne County, to take a well-documented example, the striving for solidarity evidently began overtly in July 1774 with a "meeting of a respectable body of Freeholders of the County at the Court-House, . . . for the purpose of choosing Deputies . . . and of entering into resolutions expressive of the sentiments of the County, in support of their just rights and privileges." One Mr. John Saunders alone "obstinately refused [to sign the resolves], though particularly solicited by some of the principal gentlemen then present." Subsequent events were to reveal the awkwardness that the county leaders felt at this open breach of solidarity. Perhaps for this reason the official minutes passed it over in silence, noting that "the above resolutions being unanimously agreed to, and signed . . . they then repaired to a place prepared for the occasion," where the freeholders drank a series of toasts expressive of unifying patriotic sentiments. Three weeks later, at the courthouse again, "the Provincial Association . . . was read, and offered to the people that they might express their approbation by signing it." Once more Mr. Saunders dissented publicly. Eventually the county committee published an account of his recalcitrance and declared him an enemy to the American cause.

The reports of these county meetings at the courthouse reveal the powerful communication made possible through the display of formal documents in a society where the written word was not yet commonplace. The first meeting ceremoniously adopted a set of resolutions embodied in a Latinate, literary draft that had been prepared in a gentleman's library. At the second meeting, three weeks later, the printed text of the provincial association, composed by some of the colony's most cosmopolitan gentlemen, was formally read aloud. This procedure was strongly calculated to reinforce the cultural dominance of the gentry. Later, when the copies of such papers were handed about, literary and dramaturgic modes of expression were spliced together as public signing in a communal context gave writing the character of emphatic gesture. Setting one's hand to a written bond was in itself an act of significance in this agrarian world.

The Princess Anne County committee's account of its tireless but unsuccessful efforts to persuade Mr. Saunders to adhere to the nonimportation agreement suggests the depth of the patriot yearning for communal unanimity. The ultimate publication of Saunders's name as an enemy to American liberty was a boundary-marking ceremony. Ostracism formally restored consensus by putting the offender outside the community. The patriot movement initially conceived of itself as a defensive mobilization to preserve a threatened constitutional status quo. Rituals of detestation were of great importance in defining the danger and amplifying the community's alarm at it.

More reassuring, however, were occasions when the denunciation of deviants was the preliminary, not to exclusion from the benefits of society, but to a public act of contrition on the part of the offender. The general fervor for the cause might, as in religious ritual, move the delinquents to purge their own guilt by confession. Thus "Silas Kirby, James Ingram . . . [and others] voluntarily appeared before [the Southampton County] committee, and acknowledged they had been guilty of violating the . . . association, by gaming . . . that it was an error they were unthinkingly led into, and are convinced of its evil tendency." The committee magnanimously declared that although these men had been guilty, "in consideration of their candid behaviour," they hoped that "the public will join . . . in considering the aforesaid persons as not inimical to American liberty."

Elaborate acts of contrition might be demanded, as in the case of Andrew Leckie, who had been present at the courthouse for "colonel EDMUND PENDLETON's address to the people of Caroline [County]." After "the resolutions of the association were . . . read to a company of people convened for the purpose of acceding to the association, and of raising contributions for the town of Boston," Leckie "was so unguarded and imprudent as to address [himself] to a negro boy who was present in this indecent manner: 'Piss, Jack, turn about, my boy, and sign.'" For this indelicate expression of contempt he was made to read before the committee and "a great concourse of people" on Caroline curt day, a full confession and a hearty avowal of friendship to the principles and measures of the patriots. His statement concluded with an open supplication "to regain the favour and good opinion of the public; an assurance of which would be the greatest consolation . . . under the insupportable weight of public censure and public hatred."

The rituals of detestation and the striving to bring deviants into conformity were, in some sense, negative celebrations of harmonious community. As popular passions were stirred up, the movement also elaborated a set of rituals whose tendency was to affirm the "virtue" of challenged Virginia society. The most direct of these rituals of affirmation were enactments of frugality and industry. These were of particular importance because they served as palliatives to nagging doubts about the moral soundness of Virginia society— anxieties over indebtedness (supposed to arise from luxurious extravagance) and over slavery (supposed to be the source of a debilitating indolence that exacerbated the same extravagance). Public declarations of frugality by wearing homespun also provided the patriot gentry with a means of setting an example to their inferiors while simultaneously narrowing social distance as signaled by richness of apparel. In a letter to George Mason discussing the 1769 non-importation proposal, George Washington expressed the view that it would be possible to check purchases "if the Gentlemen in their several Counties we'd be at some pains to explain matters to the people, & stimulate them to a cordial agreement." The more he considered the scheme, the more ardently he wished it success "because . . . there are private, as well as public advantages to result from it." By being "curtail'd in . . . living & enjoyments . . . the penurious Man . . . saves his money, & . . . saves his credit. . . . The extravagant & expensive man has the same good plea to retrench his Expenses. He is thereby furnished with a pretext to live within bounds. . . . And in respect to the poor & needy man, he is only left in the same situation he was found; better I might say, because as he judges from comparison, his condition is amended in Proportion as it approaches nearer to those above him." This statement, and its enactment in the wearing of homespun, epitomized the whig-republican ideal for society. Distinctions of rank based on material fortunes were to be subtly transformed into distinctions based on moral excellence.

But true virtue in the traditional social order of Virginia could not be "private" or individualistic. Ultimately it must contribute to, and draw from, a communal harmony that could most surely be restored and sustained by readiness to sacrifice oneself to the general good. The rallying to support Boston, the associations, the purge of unsound members, and the displays of frugality all contributed to the demonstration of the presence of such virtue in Virginia, but the most reassuring exhibitions were made through adaptations of that aspect of the constitution that was most dear to the patriots, namely elections.

In order to understand the dramaturgical potential of elections we have to divest ourselves of nearly all our current assumptions. Trials of strength between contending social classes and popular choice between rival programs were precisely the lines upon which it was believed elections should not be conducted. Polling, as we have seen, was a testing, face-to-face procedure in old Virginia, dominated entirely by the gentry, with the candidates confronting the voters over the table as the latter publicly declared their preferences. The true purpose was to enable the community to endow with authority those members whose manly virtue showed most clearly in their persons. An exhortation that reveals the idealizations that gave election procedures their meaning appeared in a paper signed "No Party Man," addressed to the freeholders of Accomack County in 1771. This broadside outlined the model that the patriots would seek to depict in action at the county courthouses. The voters should give their suffrages to gentlemen of "penetrating Judgment," who were able "to scan each Proposal, to view it in every Light . . . and, piercing into Futurity, behold even how remote Posterity may be thereby affected." The ideal representative should be able "to strip every Measure of that Disguise under Cover of which it may be artfully obtruded on his Mind, and penetrate through all the sinister Designs and secret Machinations of the Enemies of Freedom, the Slaves of Interest. . . . It is absolutely necessary that he be a Man of Probity . . . One who regards *Measures,* not *Men*" and who will follow his country's interest regardless of the effect of his course upon either his friends or his foes. To this end he must have "that Fortitude, or Strength of Mind, which enables a Man, in a good Cause to bear up against all Opposition, and meet the Frowns of Power unmoved."

Manly virtues were required not only of the representatives but also of the voters who were to select them. To begin with, the electors must be imbued with a strong sense of their exalted role: "It is your greatest Glory, . . . that you give Being to your Legislature, that from you they receive their political Existence. This renders an American Planter [i.e., farmer] superiour to the first Minister of an arbitrary Monarch, whose glittering Robes serve but to veil from vulgar Eyes the Chains of Slavery. Guard it then, as the most precious Pledge committed to you by the Deity. Let every Gentleman's true Merit determine his Place in the Scale of your Interest." Altogether it

was an inspiring vision, conjuring up a sturdy yeomanry who with dauntless honesty would by their virtuous trust elevate the wisest and sternest of the "Gentlemen" to give laws and "to meet the Frowns of Power unmoved."

Actual representations of this scenario, dramatically affirming the virtue that inspired the patriot cause, were staged in a series of unanimous elections at the commencement of the final crisis in 1774. A single example will convey how the vision could be translated into action. Rind's *Virginia Gazette* of July 14, 1774, reported:

> On Wednesday . . . came on the election of burgesses to represent the county of Prince George in the ensuing general assembly, when the people, sensible that their late representatives had discharged their duty to their country, in opposing those baneful, ministerial measures, which have been lately taken to enslave this continent, and highly applauding those sentiments of union among the colonies which occasioned the dissolution of the last assembly, unanimously agreed to re-elect RICHARD BLAND and PETER POYTHRESS, esquires, who were returned without a poll being taken.

This simple courthouse enactment—the election by acclamation of the representatives and the explanation of the reasons for according this honor—was highly effective in dramatizing to freeholders the awful menace of British power and the noble solidarity of Americans. A glow of virtue was combined with the exhilarating sense of brave defiance gestured on a world stage.

Virginia election customs provided another possibility for ideological statement. Demonstrations of the highest political virtues might be merged with the affirmation of frugality by the simple inversion of the time-honored custom of the candidates' treating the voters. On July 8, 1774, "a considerable number of the inhabitants of [Williamsburg] . . . met at the courthouse" to present an address to their representative, proposing that because they were

> greatly scandalized at the practice which has too much prevailed . . . of entertaining the electors (a practice which even its antiquity cannot sanctify)

and being desirous of setting a worthy example . . . for abolishing every appearance of venality (that only poison which can infect our happy constitution) and to give the fullest proof that it is to your singular merit alone you are indebted for the unbought suffrages of a free people . . . we earnestly request that you will not think of incurring any expence . . . , but that you will do us the honour to partake of an entertainment, which we shall direct to be provided for the occasion.

Five days later the freeholders met their representative, "attended by many respectable inhabitants, at the courthouse . . . to elect him again . . . , when he was immediately unanimously chosen." After the election the voters "conducted him to the Raleigh, where almost every inhabitant had met, a general invitation having been given by the generous electors, whose conduct . . . will be long remembered as a laudable . . . precedent, and highly worthy of every county . . . to adopt. Notwithstanding the festivity, and the pleasing, social intercourse, which here prevailed, harmony, decency, and decorum, were strictly maintained." It must be supposed that those who "directed" the "entertainment . . . to be provided" at the tavern were not the whole body of electors, but the men of substance among them. Treating thus continued to prove the liberality of genteel patrons, but their role could now be freed of "every appearance of venality." The prevailing "harmony, decency, and decorum" were signs of virtue diffused throughout the ranks of the free community.

The dramaturgical potential for celebrating the patriotism of local notables was even more fully realized in the feting of the heroes of Virginia and America at large. In these ceremonies they and their cause could be glorified in such a way that the heroes' own virtue and that of the people who identified with them were simultaneously affirmed. The sense of immediate participation in drama on a grand scale (already noted in the acclamation of the Prince George representatives) could thereby be intensified. The patriot leaders, of course, owed a great deal of their charisma to their own sense that they were engaged in a momentous struggle that would determine

the destiny of mankind. Peyton Randolph, Williamsburg's representative, Speaker of the House of Burgesses, and president of the Continental Congress, had certainly transcended local and provincial forms of authority, yet his manners and outlook epitomized him as a "liberal" Virginia gentleman in the traditional style—a clubman at ease with persons of all ranks. The persona ascribed to Randolph can be seen clearly in the report of a ceremony that took place on May 28, 1775:

Last Monday, about 10 o'clock, the WILLIAMSBURG TROOP OF HORSE left this city, well accoutred, in order to meet our good and worthy speaker on his return from the continental congress. Notwithstanding the inclemency of the weather, these hardy friends and supporters of American liberty pursued their journey with the utmost eagerness, whilst the most unfeigned joy diffused itself in every countenance.

For order, good discipline, and regularity, this company was greatly applauded. Ruffen's ferry was the place where they met the object of their wishes, whom, after giving three hearty cheers, they conducted until they arrived within two miles of the city, when they were joined by the COMPANY OF FOOT, who also gave three cheers, and shewed every other mark of decency and respect. The pleasing deportment of the speaker, on account of this peculiar honour done him, animated, in the highest degree, every person that attended; and on Tuesday, about 5 o'clock in the afternoon, the whole body arrived . . . surrounding the FATHER of his COUNTRY, whom they attended to his house, amidst repeated acclamations, and then respectfully retired.

In the feeling conveyed by the postures adopted (or believed by contemporaries to have been adopted) toward Peyton Randolph, we catch a vivid glimpse of the way in which the patriot movement momentarily evoked (or was intended by its leaders to evoke) the spirit of the traditional deferential social order. But as we see also in this account, men in arms were on the march. The struggle was unleashing forces that would not find their fullest expression in marks of "decency and respect."

A People Armed

The preceding accounts suggest that *tableaux vivants,* communicating more than words could do, worked to create a collective consciousness of belonging to a virtuous community unanimously roused in support of its dearest rights. The Anglo-American ideal of civic virtue was not, however, confined to frugality and political incorruptibility, for it enshrined martial valor at its heart. Military rituals provided opportunities for the self-presentation of the warrior that was expected to exist in every free man. Such displays ultimately had the greatest potential for stirring this aggressive, contentious people. During the initial phase of uncertainty in the summer of 1774, when the association was being promoted as a peaceful measure involving only "some inconveniences," warlike notes were not much sounded. By December 1774, however, the governor reported to the home authorities that every county was now "arming a Company of Men, whom they call an independent Company." Impressions of this new development can be gained from the record of a gathering at the Fairfax County courthouse on September 21, 1774. The proceedings reflect the valiant effort to produce a moral regeneration of the old order by the gentry's ostentatious assumption of public burdens. The minutes show that the gentlemen and freeholders who attended were "hoping to excite others by . . . Example." They formed themselves into "the Fairfax independent Company of Voluntiers," who would meet at times appointed for "learning & practising the military Exercise & Discipline; dress'd in a regular Uniform of Blue, turn'd up with Buff; with plain yellow metal Buttons, Buff Waist Coat & Breeches, & white Stockings" and furnished with a complete set of arms and equipment. Further, they would keep by them considerable stock of powder, lead, and flints. On the principle of noblesse oblige, the gentlemen (who alone could afford this dress and equipment) were setting an example of valiant patriotism.

By February 1775 a plan "for Embodying the People" was being circulated in Fairfax County, and a new conception of uniform marked the intrusion of the style of the backwoodsmen. The drive was now for a volunteer militia, "intended to consist of all the able-bodied Freemen from eighteen to fifty Years of Age." The enlistment of poorer men rendered the prescription of uniform impossible, but the proposal did call for those who could "procure Riphel Guns . . . to form a Company of Marksmen . . . distinguishing [their] Dress . . . by painted Hunting-Shirts and Indian Boots."

The aggressive assertion of plain countryfolk, as well as the excitement engendered by mustering for war, became manifest during the next phase of Virginia patriot mobilization, following the governor's seizure of the colony's store of gunpowder from the magazine in Williamsburg on April 21, 1775. It was the morning of Monday, April 24, when news of Lord Dunmore's coup reached Fredericksburg. "This being a day of meeting of the Independent Company," the assembled volunteers angrily considered the state of affairs and came "to a unanimous resolution, that a submission to so arbitrary an exertion of Government, may not only prejudice the common cause, by introducing a suspicion of a defection of this Colony from the noble pursuit, but will encourage the tools of despotism to commit further acts of violence." They informed the commanders of the companies in nearby counties that "this Company could but determine that a number of publick spirited gentlemen should embrace this opportunity of showing their zeal in the grand cause, by marching to *Williamsburgh.*" They declared that "to this end, they have determined to hold themselves in readiness to march from this place as Light-Horse, on *Saturday* morning; and, in the mean time, to submit the matter to . . . the neighbouring Counties."

The letters from Fredericksburg elicited immediate responses. The company in neighboring Prince William County was "called together . . . , and had the vote put, whether they would march to *Williamsburgh* . . . which was carried unanimously." Companies began to gather at Fredericksburg for a massive display of patriotism in warlike dress. The excitement, and the new tone that was becoming dominant, is conveyed in the words of a young gentleman volunteer, Michael Brown Wallace of Falmouth, who described for his brother's benefit how the governor's action "Occasioned . . . upwards of 1,000 men to assemble together at Fredericksburge among which was 600 good Rifle men." He was sure that "if we had continued there one or two days longer we should have had upwards of 10,-000 men [as] all the frontier Countys of Virginia were in motion." It seemed to Wallace that "Fredericksburge never was honour'd with so many brave hearty men since it was a Town[,] evry man Rich and poor with their hunting shirts Belts and Tomahawks fixed of[f] in the best manner." Disappointment plainly showed, however, in Wallace's concluding note that "thir was a Council of war held three days saturday sunday & monday[.] the third day in the evening we were all draw'd up in ranks and discharg'd on some promise of the governor's delivery of the Powder."

Patrick Henry, at the head of a body of men assembled at Hanover courthouse, was not so easily dismissed. He marched toward Williamsburg until some £330 was exacted from His Majesty's receiver general as reprisal for the confiscated powder. Henry was uneasy for an instant at the possible consequences of his conduct, but addresses from courthouses throughout the province revealed that the patriot movement was ready to go decisively into military action. He and his volunteers were congratulated upon showing "resentment" like true Virginians. When Henry soon after rode off to the Second Continental Congress, a succession of armed escorts proudly accompanied him on his journey. Ostensibly these were to protect him from arrest or insult; in fact, they were a defiant celebration of patriotism in martial array.

The new tone of the patriot movement—more popular and more belligerent—was sharply and dramatically signaled by the appearance of the men in hunting shirts. These "brave hearty men" had honored Fredericksburg with their presence in early May 1775. By June a Norfolk tory was writing home that Dunmore would only return to Williamsburg "provided the shirtmen are sent away." He explained that "these Shirt men, or Virginia uniform, are dressed with an Oznab[urg] Shirt over their Cloaths, a belt round them with a Tommyhawk or Scalping knife." The term had initially been applied by their enemies—"the damn'd shirtmen"—and was then adopted as a badge of pride. The revolution in cultural orientation that was taking place is most readily apparent in the contrast of the shirtmen's attire with the "Uniform of Blue, turn'd up with Buff . . . yellow metal Buttons, Buff Waist Coat and Breeches and white Stockings," appointed for the gentlemen of the Fairfax Independent Company. For all their intense provincial patriotism, the Virginia gentry had always boasted a strong church-and-king loyalty. Looking to the English metropolis for cultural values, they had tended to despise the "buckskin" of the backwoods. Now suddenly the riflemen from the west were the "heroes in huntingshirts," to whom even the most cosmopolitan gentlemen looked for protection. On July 19, 1775, a young Virginian recently returned from studies at Princeton wrote to a friend in Pennsylvania that "the strength of this Colony will lie chiefly in the rifle-men of the Upland Counties, of whom we shall have great numbers." That sentiment had become almost universal by this time. The intensity of the westward reorientation and a readiness among the gentry to identify with the woodsmen is indicated in a published recommendation to the burgesses that they attend the forthcoming Assembly in June 1775 wearing shirtmen's attire, "which best suits the times, as the cheapest, and the most martial." The advice was heeded, and "numbers of the Burgesses" did attend in the uniform of "Coarse linnen or Canvass over their Cloaths and a Tomahawk by their Sides."

Preparation for war was now the principal source of excitement for the patriot movement. The Classical Greco-Roman attitudes so characteristic of the early phases of resistance were being overlaid by more robust and popular styles. The two are blended in the correspondence of Colonel Adam Stephen, who had written in August 1774 that in the Virginia convention he "should expect to see the spirit of the Amphyctions shine, as . . . in their purest Times before Debauch'd with the Persian Gold." Later Stephen wrote that, having heard "that Lord North has declar'd that he has a Rod in piss for the Colony of Virginia," he wished he could see his lordship in America, for "in Spite of all the armies of Commissioners, Customs house officers and soldiers, I would make the meanest American I know piss upon him."

This last puts us in touch with the scatological ribaldry of the military camp. Although this form of communication appears little in the written records, it signifies the rude vigor of the male warrior fraternity that was more decorously manifested in the stirring resolves of the spring and summer of 1775. The "buckskins" and "Shirtmen" found solidarity not in Classical rhetoric but in forms of bravado, such as that which translated the old English "roast-beef" patriotism to a Virginia context. "Our peach-brandy fellows can never be beat," ran the line of a song. In this ethos the country squirearchy, many of whose members were schooled in boxing and quarter racing, could certainly hold their own; but social distance was inevitably reduced, while special advantages derived from cosmopolitan education were diminished and distinctions of rank were rendered less sharp. With the reduction in social distance, the momentary sense of a revived deferential order had passed. Gone was the celebrated unanimity that in 1774 had induced the freeholders of many counties to affirm the virtue of their communities. The spring elections of 1776 included "many . . . warm contests," and even that leading patriot, Colonel George Mason, was only "with great difficulty returned for Fairfax."

The shift from tableaus of constitutional loyalty and civic righteousness to the bustling scenes provided by the mustering of men in hunting shirts inevitably contributed to the increasing alienation of Virginians from the mother country. No account exists of popular ceremonies at the courthouses directed to the dramatic "killing" or dethroning of the king. Something of the persistence of old forms—and of the readiness to see them changed—is captured in a report of April 1776 from Gloucester County: "We hear . . . that

as the sheriff was opening the court . . . he was going to conclude with *God save the King,* when, just as he was about pronouncing the words a *five's ball,* struck by a soldier of the 7th regiment [playing handball], entered the window, and knocked him in the mouth, which prevented him from being guilty of so much impiety." Perhaps the impropriety of regicide enactments before an alternative locus of sovereignty had been declared, inhibited more deliberate performances.

In Williamsburg the official celebration of the formal decision of the Virginia convention for independence took place on May 15, 1776. In accordance with ancient Virginia custom, "some gentlemen made a handsome collection for the purpose of treating the soldiery." After a parade and salutes to *"The American independent states,"* to *"The Grand Congress of the United States,"* and to *"General Washington and victory to the American arms,"* refreshments were supplied "and the evening concluded with illuminations, and other demonstrations of joy." The newspaper account stated that everyone seemed "pleased that the domination of Great Britain was now at an end, so wickedly and tyrannically exercised for these twelve or thirteen years past." It had already declared that independence was "universally regarded as the only door which will lead to safety and prosperity." The complacent tone of the account suggests that whatever anguish Virginians had suffered over denying loyalties that they had once so strongly affirmed was short-lived.

New Evangelical Stirring

While the patriot cause was gaining momentum in 1774–1775, the Baptists' rate of advance was slowed. But another religious movement was spreading rapidly. Emissaries of the Anglican reformer John Wesley were gathering a great following in Virginia. The distinctive social and cultural meanings implicit in the Methodist upsurge are difficult to determine. Continuing the Great Awakening tradition, the Methodists met the same needs to which the Baptists had responded. Their rituals—extempore preaching and praying

—served in the same way to bring to crisis the feelings of many of the plain folk and to give ecstatic release from their sense of lost, guilty aloneness. "Class" meetings, watch nights, love feasts, and quarterly meetings likewise offered close, supportive fellowship and emotional sharing. On matters of conduct and style of life the same strict evangelical code of observances and forbearances was demanded and imposed by group discipline. Yet Methodism was much less intransigent on issues of authority, church, and society. It remained (until 1784) a movement for "vital religion" within the Church of England. While free use was made of enthusiastic lay preachers, and chapels were constructed for their meetings, the connection with the traditional establishment was formally maintained. Methodists continued to be dependent on clergymen ordained by an English bishop to conduct the communion services that were given great importance in the love feasts and quarterly meetings of the faithful. The ambivalence of Methodism—rejecting customary social morality but avoiding a break with established authority—was further complicated in Virginia between 1774 and 1784 by John Wesley's notoriety as a "tory" who had published a strong statement urging the colonials to submit to the rule of Parliament and the king's ministers. The Baptists had rallied their supporters to the patriot cause, sending preachers to the army camps, and in time raising bodies of fighting men from among their membership. The Methodists did none of these things, and some of their lay preachers even aroused the hostility of the newly constituted republican authorities by declaring themselves pacifists and refusing to be drafted into the American forces. Thus the rival new movement shared with the Baptists a rejection of traditional social values but was initially set apart from them by its refusal to break with the Established Church. Less radical in its organization of authority, Methodism, through its veiled pacifism, may nevertheless have served as a subconscious means of popular protest against gentry-led republicanism.

Methodism appealed primarily to the humble. The emotional release of the meetings was in sharp contrast to the ordered decorum of the services in the parish churches where the squires ruled. When Wesley's missionary Thomas Rankin came to Virginia in June 1776, he witnessed the climax in a surge of revivalistic piety that had been building up for some years.

Sunday, 30 . . . in the afternoon I preached again, from "I set before thee an open door, and none can shut it." I had gone through about two-thirds of my discourse, and was bringing the words home to the present—Now, when such power descended, that hundreds fell to the ground, and the house seemed to shake with the presence of God. The chapel was full of white and black, and many were without that could not get in. Look wherever we would, we saw nothing but . . . faces bathed in tears. . . . My voice was drowned amidst the groans and prayers of the congregation. I then sat down in the pulpit; and both Mr. Shadford and I were so filled with the divine presence, that we could only say, This is none other than the house of God! This is the gate of heaven! . . . Those who were happy in God themselves, were for bringing all their friends to him in their arms. This mighty effusion of the Spirit continued for above an hour; in which time many were awakened.

After such gatherings, "the multitudes that attended . . . returning home all alive to God, [would] spread the flame through their respective neighbourhoods, which ran from family to family." The intensity of the movement, reported Devereux Jarratt, was such that "scarce any conversation was to be heard . . . but concerning the things of God. . . . The unhappy disputes between England and her colonies, which just before had engrossed all our conversation, seemed now in most companies to be forgot, while things of far greater importance lay so near the heart."

The Methodist organization was centralized, with tiered structures of "classes," "societies," "circuits," and "conferences"; yet its hold on its members, and its impact therefore on local communities, was very similar to that of the Baptists. The close group of the "class" operated in much the same way as the independent "church meeting." Characteristically, candidates would be "awakened" to a sense of sin during a sermon, and then, while they attended both "classes" and preaching they would be guided through the desolate quest for a sense of total self-abnegation before God. The lonely experience of despair—the bleak sense that God's mercy could never reach the vile self—would be followed by a blissful release when "the Lord . . . spoke peace to their souls . . . [which] he usually did in one moment . . . so that all their griefs and anxieties vanished away, and they were filled with joy and peace in believing." Thus came the precious moment of ecstatic conversion.

Ample testimony exists as to the usual intensity of the sense of relief from guilt. Yet the experience was not in itself sufficient to confirm the convert in a radically new way of life, for it was almost invariably succeeded by doubt. Had God really extended His pardon and given the "present salvation" that came to true Christians? The "class" provided a social context in which this final anguish could be alleviated by the collective validation of each individual conversion. The self-discipline henceforth expected of the convert was reinforced through the shared commitment of the group. The stern evangelical code of forbearances was strictly maintained, asserting the distance intended to be set between the new way and customary laxity.

Aspects of the movement appear most clearly in Methodist preachers' journals and their published accounts of the working of the Holy Spirit. Preaching was the "ordinance" central to the movement and its cult of conversion. Under preaching, persons became awakened; by it, candidates were guided through the stages of conversion; and in its message the faith of the converts was periodically renewed. The text was always an introduction to the theme of rebirth, the need for "present" salvation. The preaching was undertaken without notes as the preachers sought a sense of inspiration in themselves and a response, or "liveliness," from the people. The phrases that recur again and again in the preachers' writings concerning their striving were pregnant in this time of political revolution—"had liberty," "had not as much liberty as at some other times." The

evangelicals' search was for a collective, emancipating sense of divine power.

Through extempore preaching in search of "liberty," the oral culture of the people was surfacing in a form of rebellion against the dominance of the literary culture of the gentry. In the eighteenth century the Bible was still generally conceived of as the highest arbiter of ultimate truth. Custody of this precious deposit was therefore required to be vested in those whose mastery of the ancient languages enabled them both to interpret Holy Writ soundly and to make informed judgments concerning the learned arguments that surrounded the many points of dispute. It has been seen how unlearned farmers' assumption of authority to expound the Scripture, if they felt moved by a "gift" of the Spirit, was interpreted by the gentry as an offense against the twin hierarchies of nature and society. The ironic term "New Light," by which the evangelicals were designated in common speech, suggests a general perception that what was at stake was the proper authority of ancient learning. The resurgence of oral culture in the calling of semiliterate men to preach extempore was a transitional ambiguous phase. At the same time that it engendered great outpourings of the spoken word, uncontrolled by scholastic conventions, it induced among preachers and hearers alike unprecedentedly intense reading, study, and searching of the Scriptures—often in private.

As with the Baptists so with the Methodists, a complex relationship can be discerned between their observances and the disturbed world into which they erupted. On the one hand their strict code of conduct symbolized order, and the close groups for the sharing and confirmation of religious experience functioned as effective popular agencies for discipline. On the other hand the individual loss of control and the collective confusion of the crowded revival meetings were both accorded sacred significance. The study of Scripture was intermediate—the quiet of close individual reading was preparation for the inspired outpourings of extempore preaching and exhorting. The popular evangelicals had instituted an inversion of customary relationships between religion and daily life. Where traditional conventions tended to assign compartmentalized times and places to religion—Sundays (and then the service hour only) at the churches—the New Lights strove to suffuse all aspects of living with reminders of God's wrath and of His saving grace. Where the liturgical services of the establishment had been short intervals of authoritative decorum in a rambunctious social world, the worship of the evangelicals was a tumultuous release from a social life upon which they sought to impose intense orderliness. Against the customary conviviality of proud contest and self-assertion was set solemn brotherhood commenced in denial of the flesh, confirmed in shared self-abnegation, and consecrated in an ecstatic release into joy through tears.

Patriots and New Lights

The spread of Methodism continued the expansion of evangelicalism at the same time that the crisis in the imperial disputes brought on the climax of patriot fervor. We should at least briefly review the similarities and differences between the contemporaneous movements. The gentry had long denounced the evangelical New Lights as a set of ignorant "enthusiasts," meaning fanatics. By 1775 the passionate involvement of gentlemen and their followers in the patriot movement had reached the pitch where it could aptly be designated by a critical participant as "political enthusiasm." Indeed the movements shared certain features. Most notable was the use of popular assemblies for arousing collective emotions and for intensifying the involvement of plain folk. Despite common characteristics, differences are also apparent.

The meetings of the patriot movement (typically to elect genteel delegates or to adopt resolutions cast in literary prose) were less participatory than those of the "vital religionists." Furthermore, they were less inclusive, since freeholders not from the gentry elite had a rather limited role, the landless white inhabitants were on the fringe only, and the blacks had no role at all. In the evangelical movement even the slaves participated vocally. A similar divergence is apparent in the leadership of the two movements. Patriot leaders were exclusively genteel, whereas many of the foremost evangelical preachers were self-taught men of humble origin. The prevailing tone of the meetings was again very different. We may contrast the preachers' strivings to achieve "liberty"—a state of ecstatic release—with such celebrations of order and deference as the feting of Peyton Randolph on his return from Congress.

But the most important distinction between the two movements lay in the relationship of each to the old way of life. Where evangelicalism began as a rejection and inversion of customary practices, the patriot movement initially tended toward a revitalization of ancient forms of community. The mobilization to defy Parliament—the meetings at courthouses, the elections, the committees and their resolutions—coincided with, and for a short-lived moment reinforced, the traditional structures of local authority. The independent companies were a barely popularized form of the old militia, while the ceremonies of the toasts and the feting were but adaptations of customary conviviality. With aggressions for the moment turned outward, all of these forms featured and intensified the style and values of pride and self-assertion that evangelicalism so sternly condemned. The political enthusiasts experienced no equivalent of the isolated anguish of the awakened who were awaiting conversion.

Fundamental shifts in values and organization that occur outside and against existing structures are highly subversive of established authority. The spread of concern for vital religion challenged the hegemony of the gentry; the patriot leaders, on the contrary, vigorously reasserted the cultural dominance of the elite. A view of the diametrically opposed social tendencies of the two movements raises the question of whether the patriot ideology did not gain in appeal among the Virginia gentry partly because it served as a defensive response to the open rejection of deference that was increasingly manifested in the spread of evangelicalism.

The concurrent taxation and toleration crises of the 1760s and 1770s had confronted the cultural and political elite of Virginia's mobile and expanding society with a dilemma that was inherent in their dependent situation. The gentry, having an image of themselves drawn from English models, had found themselves trapped between the nether millstone of popular disaffection and the upper millstone of imperial determination to keep the colonial ruling groups in a subordinate position. Lacking the means to bargain effectively with the authorities at the center of the empire, the greater part of the elites in all Britain's long-standing continental American colonies felt impelled to unite themselves with popular forces in their own communities to defy Westminster. In Virginia, a society that had begun to be riven by bitter internal discord found itself for the moment tightly bound in an enthusiastically accepted whig-patriot consensus under its traditional leaders. Only a tiny number of individuals were drawn in the opposite direction, to unite themselves with king, ministry, and Parliament. These Virginia tories were so isolated as to be ineffectual.*

Resonances

A deep-lying connection between popular evangelicalism and patriot republicanism can be more certainly established if we consider certain shared orientations. Viewed as social forms and as cultural expressions, the contrast and opposition between the values of the evangelicals and the patriots is striking, but both seem to have met a general need for relief from collective anxiety and perceived disorder. The two ideologies struck common chords. Certainly both called for posi-

*Here the proposed model of the patriot rebellion as a social process seeks to go beneath the programs and forms of communication detailed in this chapter, to discover possible sources of emotional appeal—reasons why the gentry were so susceptible to the passions aroused by the movement of resistance to Parliament. Such an interpretation of collective psychology is necessarily more speculative than the study of statements and public enactments and must here be referred not to particular texts but to large configurations such as the undermining of gentry hegemony implicit in the rise of popular evangelicalism that is the major theme of this book. The interpretation of the Virginia patriot movement offered here is aligned with others that stress the importance of the Great Awakening as a crisis of authority that prepared the way for the Revolution among both colonial elites and lower orders.

tive individual acts of affirmation as the basis for a new moral order. The patriots attested their participation in revitalized community by signing self-denying "Associations." The evangelicals did so by bringing to meeting the humble testimony of hearts regenerated by God's grace.

The resonances between the two movements can be sensed in the popular appeal of the man most universally celebrated in the troubled Virginia of his day. What was the secret of Patrick Henry's success? Full treatment of this question would be inappropriate here, but an answer may be briefly suggested. As it happens, Patrick Henry's surviving writings are few and give no clue to his powers, for he was a master of the *spoken word*—the spoken word in a form that did not derive, as did the Latinate oratory of his nearest rival, Richard Henry Lee, from the language of writing. His genius lay instead in the exploitation of the possibilities of the oral culture of his society. For this reason Henry could scarcely have prepared drafts of his speeches. The departure of his performances from the conventions of literary culture made even note-taking by others inappropriate. What has been passed on to us in writing, however, are vivid accounts of the impressions created by his rhetoric.

It is clear that when, some two or three decades after the patriot mobilization, Edmund Randolph wrote the history of his own times, he felt as though he was still in the presence of Patrick Henry's oratory. The memoirist, trained in letters, could not retain the verbal content of even the greatest of the speeches, but the manner of delivery and the thematic traits of Henry's performances had been indelibly impressed upon the young listener's memory. Randolph's constant recurrence to the subject indicates his virtual obsession with the conflict between Henry's style and that of his colleagues in the leadership of Virginia. Henry annihilated the Classical rules of rhetoric to which, as a gentleman, he should have adhered. Despite "an irregularity in his language, a certain homespun pronunciation," Henry entered public life "regardless of that criticism which was profusely bestowed on his language, pronunciation, and gesture," for he soon discovered that "a pronunciation which might disgust in a drawing room may yet find access to the hearts of a popular assembly."

In his memory Randolph followed the orator through a powerful performance: "In Henry's exordium there was a simplicity and even carelessness. . . . A formal division of his intended discourse he never made." The ardent young patriot would fix his eyes "upon the moderator of the assembly addressed without straying in quest of applause." In this way "he contrived to be the focus to which every person present was directed, . . ." and so "transfused into the breast[s] of others the earnestness depicted in his own features, which ever forbade a doubt of sincerity." The memoir then drops the most revealing clue concerning the effectiveness of Henry's mode of oratory: "His was the only monotony which I ever heard reconcilable with true eloquence." Here was a form of sermonic chant, intended primarily to arouse moral fervor. Most of the remaining traits fall into place around this core:

> [The] chief note was melodious, but the sameness was diversified by a mixture of sensations which a dramatic versatility of action and of countenance produced. His pauses, which for their length might sometimes be feared to dispel the attention, riveted it the more by raising the expectation. . . . His style . . . was vehement, without transporting him beyond the power of self-command. . . . His figures of speech . . . were often borrowed from the Scriptures. The prototypes of others were the sublime scenes and objects of nature. . . . His lightning consisted in quick successive flashes, which rested only to alarm the more.

Henry had brought into the politics of the gentry world an adaptation of that popular oral form, the extempore sermon, that had been setting different parts of Virginia ablaze ever since the coming of the New Side Presbyterians in the 1740s. The success of this mode of oratory with the assemblies of country squires on whose reported impressions Henry's popularity must largely have rested, is striking evidence of fundamental cultural continuities between "gentle" and "simple" folk in the Virginia countryside. Living closely integrated in rural society, the squires could respond fervently to this style of oratory when it was introduced in the service of their own cause rather than in direct condemnation of their life-style.

Throughout his career Patrick Henry remained firmly attached to the world of the gentry. His mastery of the convivial style of that world is suggested by some of the earliest recollections of him as an excellent performer on the "violin," whose "passion was music, dancing and pleasantry." Henry never made the dramatic renunciations characteristic of evangelical converts, but his personal conduct developed with sensitivity to the popular moral concerns of the time and achieved a harmony above the clashing discords of the old traditional culture and the new evangelical counterculture. The great patriot always retained the easy affability of the gentleman, yet he adopted a sober manner of dress and became deeply preoccupied with fostering Christian virtue in his society. Supremely, what enabled Patrick Henry to tower above his generation—in its general estimation—was his ability to communicate in popular style the passion for a world reshaped in truly moral order that lay at the heart of both the religious revolution of the evangelicals and the political revolution of the patriots.

10

BLACK FREEDOM STRUGGLES ON THE EVE OF WHITE INDEPENDENCE

PETER H. WOOD

Historians of the American Revolution have generally focused their attention on the growing antagonism that characterized Anglo-American relations after 1760. For most of these historians it was English encroachments upon traditional colonial freedoms and prerogatives that sparked the revolutionary movement. More recently, however, some historians have begun to reassess this traditional interpretation of the revolution. Viewing it as more than an imperial crisis, these historians have turned their attention to the social tensions that drove the colonists toward revolution.

One of the most deep-seated of these tensions was that which existed between white master and black slave. By the time of the revolution nearly a half-million Africans had been brought into the North American colonies against their will. From the beginning these slaves fought their condition in whatever ways they found available. Some chose extreme forms of resistance such as suicide, rebellion, and the poisoning of their masters while others utilized more subtle forms of resistance such as breaking work tools, establishing familial bonds, and developing an autonomous Afro-American culture to sustain them in the travails of bondage.

In this essay, Peter Wood recounts one of the most dramatic and successful forms of slave resistance in American history. As the colonies moved closer toward revolution in the 1760s and 1770s, southern slaveholders grew increasingly concerned about the potential slave insurrection that such a war would bring. The presence of British troops near the plantations, they reasoned, would provide an unparalleled opportunity for slaves to escape, or worse to rise up against their masters. When, in 1775, Governor Dunmore of Virginia offered freedom to any slave (or servant) who deserted his master and crossed British lines, the fears of the southern planters were confirmed. As Wood shows, thousands of slaves chose to declare their independence in this way and to mount what was America's greatest slave rebellion.

Wood suggests that the British offer of freedom to American slaves drove southern planters to support the revolutionary cause. Do you think that changes in southern popular culture, such as those discussed by Rhys Isaac in Reading 9, played a part in their decision? What similarities and differences do you see in the struggle for independence by American slaves and by "Long Bill" Scott in Reading 11?

In February 1774 20-year-old Phillis Wheatley, the African-born slave-turned-author living in Boston, shared with another non-white, the In-dian minister Samson Occum, her belief that "in every human Breast, God had implanted a Principle, which we call love of freedom; it is impa-

Reprinted from *Southern Exposure* No. 8 (1984): 10–16, with the permission of Peter H. Wood and *Southern Exposure*.

tient of Oppression, and pants for Deliverence; and by the leave of our modern Egyptians I will assert, that the same Principle lives in us." Among roughly half a million Afro-Americans living in the thirteen colonies, few were in a position to record their feelings so clearly for posterity. But for nearly a decade thousands of blacks, particularly in the southern colonies, had been feeling and demonstrating a growing impatience with the "modern Egyptians" who held such sway over their lives.

On the eve of white Independence, blacks constituted a larger portion of the population of America than they would at any subsequent time. Nine of every ten Afro-Americans lived in the South, primarily in the coastal areas that produced tobacco, rice, and indigo, and nearly all were ensnared in the dominant labor system of hereditary race slavery. Since the adoption of that coercive institution in England's mainland provinces more than a century earlier, acts of individual resistance had been commonplace, and occasionally groups of enslaved colonists had risked more organized rebellion efforts. As historian Herbert Aptheker suggested more than 40 years ago, the plots came in waves, and these cycles of increased resistance continued intermittently in different forms until the end of the slave regime almost a century later.

Often these surges occurred during periods when the white community was distracted by external affairs or divided by internal controversy. So it is not entirely surprising to discover that just such a wave gradually built momentum during the years of colonial disquiet following the Stamp Act controversy of 1765 and crested a decade later in the eventful months before the Declaration of Independence. Yet scholars of black history, often studying a single colony or state, and historians of the American Revolution, traditionally preoccupied with the splits emerging in the white populace during these years, have never acknowledged the swell of hope and discontent that rippled through the slave communities between 1765 and 1776.

This wave of rebellious activity deserves attention, for it touched every major slave colony, and it was closely related to—and influential upon—the political unrest that gripped many white subjects in these years. Indeed, the familiar story of "Tories" and "Whigs" squaring off in a two-sided struggle drastically oversimplifies the tensions of the time. Besides the merchants and planters who directed the emerging "patriot" cause and the English functionaries and "loyalist" sympathizers who opposed them, other groups had equally large stakes in the turbulent course of events.

Near the beginning of this century the "progressive" historians stressed that the American Revolution actually involved two struggles. One was the first successful anti-colonial movement against European imperialism—the battle for independence from Britain. But this contest for "home rule," led by the colonial merchant-planter elite, was entwined with another contest along social class lines over "who should rule at home." The latter revolution was for the most part unsuccessful, and postwar "consensus" historians have done their best to downplay its importance and even deny its existence altogether. But in the past decade scholars have taken a renewed look at these domestic struggles, coinciding with the better-known independence movement, and they are finding them to have been more complicated, varied, and significant than even the progressive historians had understood.

In the 1760s, after England's triumph in the French and Indian War, longstanding power relationships came under new strains in Britain's American colonies. Tensions between provincial leaders and imperial officials were only one element in a web with many interlacing strands. Urban workers, backcountry farmers, and Indian nations living beyond the frontier all applied pressure on occasion to protect their interests and exert their influence in an increasingly volatile political situation.

No group had less formal power, or a larger potential interest in the unraveling of established social relationships, than Afro-Americans confined on southern plantations. Though virtually powerless under the prevailing system of law, these enslaved blacks still represented a crucial force in the overall political equation, for their numbers were great, their situation seemed desperate, and their detachment from the niceties of the imperial debate was considerable. Attentive leaders in the black communities, like their Native American and white working-class counterparts, realized they represented key constituencies that could conceivably sway events in one direction or another with results that would be of lasting consequence to themselves and others.

Phase I: Groundswell

In the 1760s thousands of Africans were being sold every year into "Babylonian Captivity" in the American colonies. But these "saltwater" slaves from across the Atlantic found themselves surrounded by a far greater number of "country-born" blacks whose heritage already blended African and European elements. The first phase of the pre-Revolutionary wave of resistance, which began in the mid-1760s and stretched to the emergence of armed violence between whites at Concord Bridge in April 1775, inevitably reflected and built upon this emerging Afro-American culture.

For example, among an increasingly Christian slave population, itinerant preaching developed rapidly and incurred mounting planter resentment. Jupiter, a tall man in his middle thirties also known as Gibb, who belonged to George Noble of Prince George County, Virginia, bore the scars of previous whippings when detained in Sussex County in 1767. Arrested with his mother and brother, he was whipped again "for stirring up the Negroes to an insurrection, being a great New light preacher." Soon such preaching was outlawed by whites in Virginia and elsewhere as a political liability. In 1772, slaveholders on the Committee for Religion of the Virginia House of Burgesses drafted a Toleration Bill intended to define the limits of dissenting worship among Baptists, who frequently included blacks in their meetings. The law not only prohibited slaves from attending church without their master's permission; it also forbade any night services.

In music, black songs often became political and threatening to authorities, much as *reg-*

gae can be today. By the mid-1770s we find reports of slaves playing the African gourd-guitar and singing "in a very satirical stile and manner" about the treatment they had received. Stories of secret night meetings involving "deep and solemn" deliberations by "private committees" raised anxiety among whites. So did the frequency of slave runaways and their suspected motives. In 1773, shortly after word reached Virginia that slavery had been ruled illegal in England in the Somerset Case, a planter stated he had lost a slave couple who were heading for England "where they imagine they will be free (a Notion now too prevalent among the Negroes, greatly to the Vexation and Prejudice of their Masters)." By the following summer the news had reached the Virginia backcountry, where Bacchus absconded from Augusta County and set out "to board a vessel for Great Britain . . . from the knowledge he had of the late determination of Somerset's Case."

Occasionally, especially in the coastal towns where the divisions among whites were most apparent, groups of blacks moved openly to exploit these rifts to their own advantage, often using tactics drawn from the white independence struggle. In the fall of 1765 Christopher Gadsden's white Sons of Liberty took to the streets of Charleston to protest the Stamp Act, chanting "Liberty, Liberty" and carrying a British flag with the word spelled across it. During the New Year holiday, according to Henry Laurens, Charleston blacks began "crying out 'Liberty' " on their own, and the whites "all were Soldiers in Arms for more than a Week," while "patrols were riding day and night" throughout the province.

Such occurrences did not escape the notice of British officials formulating contingency plans; they realized that thousands of discontented slave workers made the southern colonies highly vulnerable. "The great Disproportion, there is between White men and Negroes in South Carolina," an agent reminded the Lords of Trade in 1770, renders the colony "less formidable to a foreign or an Indian Enemy, in Case of Hostilities." Conversely, they knew armed and loyal blacks could be a major asset. In 1771 the English governor of West Florida prepared an assessment of Spanish strength at New Orleans, noting that their forces included "upwards of four thousand Negroes upon whom they have great dependence being all used to Muskets and the Woods."

In 1772 Virginia's Governor Dunmore summarized these perceptions when he described conditions in the southern tidewater region. "At present," he said, "the Negroes are double the number of white people in this colony, which by natural increase, and the great addition of new imported ones every year is sufficient to alarm not only this colony but all the Colonies of America." Dunmore, who would give further attention to this subject in the years ahead, observed that in case of war, the white colonists, "with great reason, trembled at the facility that an enemy would find in procuring Such a body of men, attached by no tye to their Masters or to the Country." Indeed, he added, "it is natural to Suppose that their Condition must inspire them with an aversion to both, and therefore are ready to join the first that would encourage them to revenge themselves by which means a conquest of this Country would inevitably be effected in a very Short time."

Dunmore's planter opposition also sought to assess the relative strength and restiveness of the slave population and speculated about Britain's willingness to exploit it. "If America & Britain should come to a hostile rupture I am afraid an Insurrection among the slaves may and will be promoted," wrote young James Madison, beginning his political career as a member of the Committee on Public Safety for Orange County. In a letter to printer William Bradford in Philadelphia late in 1774, he reported: "In one of our Counties lately a few of those unhappy wretches met together and chose a leader who was to conduct them when the English troops should arrive— which they foolishly thought would be very soon and that by revolting to them they should be rewarded with their freedom. Their intentions were soon discovered and the proper precautions taken to prevent the Infection. It is prudent," Madison reminded the printer, that "such at-

tempts should be concealed as well as suppressed."

Six weeks later Bradford replied, "Your fear with regard to an insurrection being excited among the slaves seems too well founded." The Philadelphian informed Madison that "A letter from a Gentleman in England was read yesterday in the Coffee-house, which mentioned the design of [the] administration to pass an act (in case of rupture) declaring ['] all Slaves & Servants free that would take arms against the Americans.' By this," Bradford concluded, "you see such a scheme is thought on and talked of; but I cannot believe the Spirit of the English would ever allow them publically to adopt so slavish a way of Conquering."

As the prospects for insurrectionary acts improved and the anxiety of white patriots grew, the frequency and harshness of punishments increased, and the rate of slave executions seems to have risen. "The most significant exceptions to the rule of moderacy," writes historian Pauline Maier, "lay with those accused of inciting slave insurrections in the South." In October 1773, a North Carolina slave charged with murder was burned at the stake by the sheriff of Granville County. The next fall, two Georgia blacks accused of arson and poisoning were burned alive on the Savannah Common, and in December several more slaves were "taken and burnt" for leading an uprising in nearby St. Andrew's Parish that killed four whites and wounded others.

Significantly, some white colonists, through a blend of religious scruples, ideological consistency, and strategic necessity, reacted to these mounting tensions with thoughts other than harsh reprisal. Weeks after the murders and executions in St. Andrew's Parish, Georgia, for example, a group of Scottish parishioners met at Darien. On January 12, 1775, they adopted a resolution that slavery was an "unnatural practice . . . founded in injustice and cruelty, and highly dangerous to our liberties, (as well as lives), debasing part of our fellow-creatures below men, and corrupting the virtues and morals of the rest." Slavery's existence, they asserted, "is laying the basis of that liberty we contend for . . . upon a very wrong foundation," and they pledged to work for the manumission of Georgia slaves.

Another immigrant expressed similar sentiments. On March 8, 1775, Thomas Paine, using the pen name "Humanus," published his first article, three months after reaching Philadelphia. His essay in the *Pennsylvania Journal* was entitled "African Slavery in America," and it pointed out that blacks had been "industrious farmers" who "lived quietly" in Africa before "Europeans debauched them with liquors" and brought them to the New World. Paine reminded white colonists that because they had "enslaved multitudes, and shed much innocent blood in doing it," the Lord might balance the scales by allowing England to enslave them. To avoid such retribution and give greater consistency to the patriot cause, "Humanus" urged the abolition of slavery and suggested (in terms which resurfaced later in the year) that freed Negroes be given land in the West to support themselves, where they might "form useful settlements on the frontiers. Thus they may become interested in the public welfare, and assist in promoting it; instead of being dangerous as now they are, should any enemy promise them a better condition."

Phase II: Resistance and Reprisals

During the spring of 1775, even as Paine wrote, the interlocking struggles of Tories, Patriots and blacks intensified. In this second phase, as talk of rebellion grew, the issue of who controlled supplies of powder and shot took on central importance, and Loyalists charged white radicals with spreading rumors of slave unrest. "In the beginning of 1775," Thomas Knox Gordon of South Carolina recalled, "the Malecontents being very anxious to have some plausible pretence for arming with great industry propogated a Report that the Negroes were meditating an Insurrection."

Patriots, in turn, claimed authorities were prepared to enlist black strength if necessary to quell white dissent. The Committee of Safety for New Bern, North Carolina, announced in a circular letter that "there is much reason to fear, in these Times of General Tumult and Confusion, that the Slaves may be instigated and encouraged by our inveterate Enemies to an Insurrection, which in our present defenseless State might have the most dreadful Consequences." The Committee advised "Detachments to patrol and search the Negro Houses, and . . . to seize all Arms and Ammunition found in their Possession."

Black activists sought to capitalize on white divisions in their plans for freedom fully as much as white factions tried to implicate half a million blacks in their political designs. Whatever the schemes of Patriot and Tory leaders during 1775, local slave leaders were attentive and active participants rather than ignorant and passive objects. Consider a report from backcountry New York that was being publicized and discussed as far away as Virginia by mid-March. In Ulster County one Johannes Schoonmaker caught part of a conversation between two of his slaves, discussing the powder needed and support available to carry out a plot which included burning houses and executing slave-owning families as they tried to escape. This organized liberation plan involved blacks from the villages of Kingston, Hurly, Keysereck, and Marbletown, and the twenty persons who were taken into custody had considerable powder and shot in their possession. In addition, rumor had it that these Negroes were to be joined in their freedom struggle by five or six hundred Indians.

Because we have studied both slavery and the Revolution on a colony-by-colony basis, we have failed to appreciate the full extent of the black freedom struggle in the summer of 1775. In every southern colony, from Maryland to Georgia, slaves threatened armed revolt. Their local leaders engaged in desperate high-stakes calculations as to when to assert themselves and gain liberation with the help of outside forces. In this they were perhaps not unlike the Jews and other resistance fighters who awaited allied aid during World War II; premature action in each instance was suicidal. Enough weapons were confiscated during the year so that even if one makes room for frame-ups, the extent of the wave is still considerable when we look at each colony in turn.

In Virginia in mid-April, Governor Dunmore

ordered the barrels of gunpowder in the Williamsburg magazine removed to a ship under cover of night. The local mayor immediately submitted a petition claiming that widespread rumors of a slave revolt made internal security a crucial matter, and news reached the capital of irate citizens coming from the west to reclaim the powder by force. Word spread that Dunmore was fortifying the Governor's Palace and had issued arms to his servants; a physician testified that the governor swore to him "by the living God that he would declare Freedom to the slaves and reduce the City of *Williamsburg* to Ashes" if disorder continued. Hearing this, several blacks presented themselves at the Palace to offer their services but were turned away. On April 29, a special supplement of the *Virginia Gazette* reported that two Negroes had been sentenced to death in nearby Norfolk "for being concerned in a conspiracy to raise an insurrection in that town."

Word of Lord Dunmore's threat quickly reached Thomas Gage, the British general serving as Governor of Massachusetts. "We hear," he wrote in mid-May, "that a Declaration his Lordship has made, of proclaiming all the Negroes free, who should join him, has Startled the Insurgents." And on June 12, 1775, a week before the disastrous engagement at Bunker Hill which was to cost him his command, Gage wrote to his friend Lord Barrington, "You will have heard of the boldness of the rebels, in surprising Ticonderoga; and making excursions to the frontiers of Montreal; but I hope such hostilities, will justify General Carleton in raising all the Canadians and Indians in his power to attack them in his turn." Steeling the Secretary of War for such tactics, Gage continued, "You may be tender of using Indians, but the rebels have shown us the example, and brought all they could down upon us here. Things are come to that crisis, that we must avail ourselves of every resource, even to raise the Negro[e]s, in our cause."

Two weeks later Dunmore himself observed regarding Virginia's planter elite: "My declaration that I would arm and set free such Slaves as should assist me if I was attacked has stirred up fears in them which cannot easily subside." The *Virginia Gazette* proclaimed that the governor planned "to take the field as generalissimo at the head of the Africans." James Madison, like other planter rebels versed in classical literature, realized that slavery constituted their Achilles' heel; "if we should be subdued," he wrote, "we shall fall like Achilles by the hand of one that knows the secret." Weeks later Dunmore was at work on a secret plan with John Connelly of Fort Pitt to add the threat of an Indian attack on the backcountry to the prospect of slave insurrections.

In Maryland in late April planters pressured Governor Robert Eden into issuing arms and ammunition to guard against rumored insurrections, though the governor feared their acts "were only going to accelerate the evil they dreaded from their servants and slaves." In May John Simmons, a wheelwright in Dorchester County, refused to attend militia muster, saying "he understood that the gentlemen were intending to make us all fight for their land and Negroes, and then said damn them (meaning the gentlemen) if I had a few more white people to join me I could get all the Negroes in the county to back us, and they would do more good in the night than the white people could do in the day." According to James Mullineux, Simmons told him "that if all gentlemen were killed we should have the best of the land to tend and besides could get money enough while they were about it as they have got all the money in their hands." Mullineux told the grand jury "that the said Simmons appeared to be in earnest and desirous that the negroes should get the better of the white people." Simmons was later tarred, feathered, and banished on the accusation of fomenting a slave insurrection.

In August a Maryland minister—a strict believer in the "outside agitator" creed—protested that "the governor of Virginia, the captains of the men of war, and mariners, have been tampering with our Negroes; and have held nightly meetings with them; and all for the glorious purpose of enticing them to cut their masters' throats while they are asleep. Gracious God!" he exclaimed, "that men noble by birth and fortune should descend to such ignoble base servility." By fall the Dorchester County Committee of Inspection reported, "The insolence of the Negroes in this county is come to such a height, that we are under a necessity of disarming them which we affected on Saturday last. We took about eighty guns, some bayonets, swords, etc."

In North Carolina the black freedom struggle during the summer of 1775 was even more intense. "Every man is in arms and the patroles going thro' all the town, and searching every Negro's house, to see they are all at home by nine at night," wrote Janet Schaw, an English visitor to Wilmington. "My hypothesis is," she said, "that the Negroes will revolt." Her view was confirmed when a massive uprising in the Tar River area of northeastern North Carolina was revealed just before it was to begin, on the night of July 8. Scores of blacks were rounded up and brought before Pitt County's Committee of Safety, which "Ordered several to be severely whipt and sentenced several to receive 80 lashes each [and] to have [their] Ears crapd [cropped,] which was executed in the presence of the Committee and a great number of spectators."

Colonel John Simpson reported that, "in disarming the negroes we found considerable ammunition" and added: "We keep taking up, examining and scourging more or less every day." According to Simpson, "from whichever part of the County they come they all confess nearly the same thing, vizt that they were one and all on the night of the 8th inst to fall on and destroy the family where they lived, then to proceed from House to House (Burning as they went) until they arrived in the Back Country where they were to be received with open arms by a number of Persons there appointed and armed by [the] Government for their Protection, and as a further reward they were to be settled in a free government of their own."

In South Carolina, meanwhile, the impending arrival of a new royal governor fueled mounting speculation among both blacks and whites. Josiah Smith, Jr. wrote that "our Province at present is in a ticklish Situation, on account of our numerous Domesticks, who have been deluded by some villanous Persons into the notion of being all set free" on the arrival of the new governor, Lord

William Campbell. According to the Charleston merchant, this rumor "is their common Talk throughout the Province, and has occasioned impertinent behaviour in many of them, insomuch that our Provincial Congress now sitting hath voted the immediate raising of Two Thousand Men Horse and food, to keep those mistaken creatures in awe, as well as to oppose any Troops that may be sent among us with coercive Orders."

When Campbell arrived he found the story circulating that the "Ministry had in agitation not only to bring down the Indians on the Inhabitants of this province, but also to instigate, and encourage an insurrection amongst the Slaves. It was also reported, and universally believed," Campbell stated, "that to effect this plan, 14,000 Stand of Arms were actually on board the Scorpion, the Sloop of War I came out in. Words, I am told, cannot express the flame that this occasion'd amongst all ranks and degrees, the cruelty and savage barbarity of the scheme was the conversation of all Companies." A free black pilot named Thomas Jeremiah was jailed on charges of being in contact with the British Navy and seeking to distribute arms. Black witnesses for the prosecution testified Jeremiah had alerted them to the impending war and informed them that it could well mean freedom for blacks. Jeremiah was publicly hanged and burned in Charleston on the afternoon of August 18.

The situation in Georgia was scarcely different, as John Adams learned through a discussion with several other delegates to the Continental Congress in Philadelphia. "In the evening," Adams wrote on September 24, "two gentlemen from Georgia, came into my room [and] gave a melancholy account of the State of Georgia and South Carolina. They say that if one thousand regular troops should land in Georgia, and their commander be provided with arms and clothes enough, and proclaim freedom to all the negroes who would join his camp, twenty thousand negroes would join it from the two Provinces in a fortnight." The New Englander continued, "They say their only security is this; that all the king's friends, and tools of government, have large plantations and property in negroes; so that the slaves of the Tories would be lost, as well as those of the Whigs."

Adams included in his diary entry the observation, no doubt shared by the two Georgia slave-owners, that "The negroes have a wonderful art of communicating intelligence among themselves; it will run several hundreds of miles in a week or fortnight." Such an acknowledgment of the effective oral network that kept blacks informed is rare indeed among the print-oriented leaders of the anti-colonial independence movement. But such a grapevine clearly existed, and it would be stretched and strengthened in the months ahead, as the triangular freedom struggle entered a third and climactic phase.

Phase III: The Dream Deferred

In Virginia Governor Dunmore, who had retreated from Williamsburg to the safety of a British ship, was preparing to use the desperate card he had threatened to play, and perhaps should have played, six months earlier. When his marines raided a printing office in Norfolk in September, they were joined by cheering blacks. During October he continued to conduct raids and to remove slaves to British naval vessels via small sloops and cutters as he had been doing for months. "Lord Dunmore," charged the Committee of Safety in Williamsburg on October 21, "not contented with . . . inciting an insurrection of our slaves, hath lately, in conjunction with the officers of the navy, proceeded to commence hostilities against his Majesty's peaceable subjects in the town and neighborhood of Norfolk; captivated many, and seized the property of others, particularly slaves, who are detained from the owners." "Lord Dunmore sails up and down the river," a Norfolk resident wrote to London the following week; "where he finds a defenseless place he lands, plunders the plantation and carries off the negroes."

Edmund Pendleton estimated in early November that perhaps fewer than one hundred slaves had taken refuge with Dunmore, but the situation changed drastically on November 14 when the governor's forces won a skirmish at Kemp's Landing. Dunmore capitalized on this small victory in two ways. First, he sent off John Connelly toward Detroit with secret orders approved by Gage to return to Virginia with Indian troops, seize Alexandria, and await forces from the coast. Secondly, Dunmore used the occasion to publish the less-than-sweeping proclamation he had drawn up the week before, emancipating any servants or slaves of the opposition faction who would come serve in his army. It read in part, "I do hereby further declare all indented servants, negroes, and others (appertaining to Rebels) free, that are able and willing to bear arms, they joining his Majesty's Troops, as soon as may be, for the more speedily reducing this Colony to a proper sense of their duty."

Connelly was soon captured, but the proclamation had its intended effect. "Letters mention that slaves flock to him in abundance," Pendleton wrote to Richard Henry Lee at the end of the month, "but I hope it magnified." Landon Carter also hoped it was not true. When fourteen enslaved workers on his plantation responded to Dunmore's call, he had a dream that they came back, looking "most wretchedly meager and wan," and pleaded for his assistance. "Whoever considers well the meaning of the word Rebel," stated a white resident of Williamsburg, "will discover that the author of the Proclamation is now himself in actual rebellion, having armed our slaves against us and having excited them to an insurrection." He added, in a line reminiscent of Patrick Henry, "there is a treason against the State, for which such men as Lord *Dunmore,* and even Kings, have lost their heads."

Since it ultimately failed from both the British and the black vantage points, there is a tendency to minimize the combined initiative of the months following November 15. But at the time, these events in Virginia had enormous potential significance for blacks and whites alike. On December 14, a Philadelphia newspaper related that a gentlewoman walking near Christ Church had been "insulted" by a Negro, who remained near the wall on the narrow sidewalk, refusing to step off into the muddy street as expected. When she reprimanded him, he replied, according to the report, "Stay, you d—d white bitch, till Lord Dunmore and his black regiment come, and then we will see who is to take the wall."

That same day George Washington urged Congress "to Dispossess Lord Dunmore of his hold in Virginia" as soon as possible. In repeated letters the planter-general stressed that "the fate of America a good deal depends on his being obliged to evacuate Norfolk this winter." Washington spelled out his fears to Richard Henry Lee on December 26: "If my dear Sir, that man is not crushed before spring, he will become the most formidable enemy America has; his strength will increase as a snow ball by rolling; and faster, if some expedient cannot be hit upon to convince the slaves and servants of the impotency of his designs."

Reports from the Chesapeake southward after Dunmore's proclamation are suggestive of the events surrounding Lincoln's emancipation order. With the prospect of freedom at hand, flight became the logical form of rebellion, and along the coast hundreds took direct action despite terrible odds. The newspapers told of "boatloads of slaves" seeking out British ships, not always successfully. Seven men and two women from Maryland "who had been endeavouring to get to Norfolk in an open boat" were apprehended near Point Comfort. Three blacks who boarded a Virginia boat that they mistakenly took to be a British vessel were only "undeceived" after they had openly "declared their resolution to spend the last drop of *their blood* in Lord *Dunmore's* service." Though perhaps more than a thousand reached Dunmore's ships safely, an outbreak of smallpox among the refugees the next spring reduced their numbers and discouraged others from following. If it had "not been for this horrid disorder," he wrote, "I should have had two thousand blacks; with whom I should have had no doubt of penetrating into the heart of this Colony."

News that black freedom had been sanctioned in Virginia must have reached South Carolina by early December. On Sullivan's Island at the mouth of Charleston harbor, fugitives hopeful of escaping slavery were gathering near the "pest

house,' the small structure beside the water supervised by a black named Robinson and used to quarantine the sick off of incoming ships from Africa and the Caribbean. From here, some runaways had already joined the British fleet and begun to participate in raiding parties to liberate their comrades. On December 5, Captain Jacob Milligan of the sloop *Hetty* reached Charleston with a cargo of rum and sugar, but not before he had been seized and searched by Captain Tollemache of the *H.M.S. Scorpion.* The next day Milligan informed the Council of Safety "that there were considerable number of slaves upon Sullivan's Island, and that he learnt huts were building for them in the woods."

The next day the Council of Safety promptly ordered Colonel William Moultrie to dispatch a force of 200 men to Sullivan's Island that night "to seize and apprehend a number of negroes, who are said to have deserted to the enemy." According to Josiah Smith Jr., Moultrie moved against the encampment at night with a force of 50 or 60 men and "early in the Morning sett Fire to the Pest house, took some Negroes and Sailors Prisoners, killed 50 of the former that would not be taken, and unfortunately lost near 20 that were unseen by them till taken off the Beach by the Men [of] Warrs Boats." When a local citizen spoke with officers of the *Scorpion* several days later, he reported that Captain Tollemache "did not deny having some of our negroes on board, but said they came as freemen, and demanding protection; that he could have had near five hundred, who had offered. . . ."

Within weeks similar conditions prevailed in Georgia. On March 13, Stephen Bull wrote to Henry Laurens from Savannah to report that two hundred enslaved workers had deserted (nearly fifty from Arthur Middleton's plantation alone) and were on Tybee Island, apparently in contact with the British ships frequenting the coast. The next day, at the end of a dictated letter to Colonel Laurens, Bull added an extraordinary handwritten note regarding a matter of utmost secrecy. "The matter is this: It is far better for the public and the owners, if the deserted negroes . . ., who are on Tybee Island, be shot, if they cannot be taken, [even] if the public is obliged to pay for them; for if they are carried away, and converted into money, which is the sinew of war, it will only enable an enemy to fight us with our own money and property." Since members of the local Council of Safety were "timid" to agree to such a brutal mission, Bull sought authorization from his own home colony of South Carolina for dispatching a party of Indian allies to capture or kill the runaways. He told Laurens that "all who cannot be taken, had better be shot by the Creek Indians, as it, perhaps, may deter other negroes from deserting, and will establish a hatred or aversion between the Indians and negroes."

Laurens, as the president of South Carolina's revolutionary Council of Safety, had already dealt with such a situation in the search-and-destroy mission to Sullivan's Island. So he chose his words discreetly in responding to Bull's request for permission to act. "Now for the grand we may say awful business contained in your letter," he responded on March 16; "it is an awful business notwithstanding it has the sanction of the Law, to put even fugitives and Rebellious Slaves to death—the prospect is horrible." But then, without hesitation, he continued, "We think the Council of Safety in Georgia ought to give that encouragement which is necessary to induce proper persons to seize and if nothing else will do to destroy all those Rebellious Negroes upon Tybee Island or wherever they may be found." Apparently Bull left Savannah before this letter arrived and received word of it while on his way back to Charleston. "Could I have heard from you but twelve hours sooner," he wrote Laurens, "I should not have left Savannah as soon as I have done, as there is one piece of service which I wanted to have put into execution, which I did not think myself properly authorised to do." The fate of the two hundred "fugitives and Rebellious Slaves" on Tybee Island remains unknown.

A great deal had changed in the year since Tom Paine had advocated emancipation and western resettlement. The British had coopted these ideas and used them to their own advantage, capitalizing on slave aspirations for freedom and tipping black hopes decidedly toward the loyalist position with the carrot of emancipation. When Dunmore's proclamation gave public substance to this stance, the planter elite viewed the threat to their property as a compelling argument for independence, just as their grandchildren would more than four score years later. Patriot opinion had solidified around the notion that the freedom struggles of enslaved Africans were a liability rather than an asset. When Paine's *Common Sense* first appeared on January 9, 1776, it spoke of the British as barbarous and hellish alligators and of Indians and blacks as brutal and destructive enemies.

Preoccupied with imperial misrule and prejudiced from the start against members of another class and different race, it was impossible for colonial leaders to acknowledge accurately (or perhaps even to perceive) the nature of the struggle for liberation which was being waged passionately around them. When this struggle was diverted, postponed, crushed in its early stages—as is the way with most such difficult liberation movements—they could hardly sense the full weight of the despair or measure the full extent of the contradictions. Rather than elaborate upon the difficult triangular struggle, acknowledging the shifts and compromises of their own course and the strength of the opposition from below as well as from abroad, they instead adopted the hypocritical view that outside agitators had been at work, unsuccessfully, among passive and anonymous victims of enslavement.

By relying upon their persuasive and partisan words, we have been largely blinded for two centuries to a major factor in the turmoil leading up to the Revolution. Hemmed in by our categories of color, we have failed to recognize a significant chapter in the story of worker and artisan political unrest. We have underestimated the complexity and importance of this little-known wave of struggle within the crosscurrents of revolution. It concerned nothing less than the proper boundaries of American freedom.

11

HEARTS AND MINDS IN THE AMERICAN REVOLUTION: THE CASE OF "LONG BILL" SCOTT

JOHN SHY

All successful revolutions have relied upon the active participation of common people who chose to interrupt the rhythms of their everyday existence in order to risk their lives in the cause of basic social and political transformation. The American Revolution, too, depended upon the commitment of farmers, artisans, and laborers to the revolutionary cause. Yet, though anti-British sentiments were widespread among the common people of the American colonies, the mobilization of such persons required men and women who could focus popular resentments and organize effective resistance to Britain. After 1775, as colonial protests against British colonial policy moved into actual armed resistance, these local leaders became increasingly important to the revolutionary movement. Without these leaders who were close to the hearts and minds of their constituents there would have been no revolution.

In this essay, John Shy traces the career of one of these local leaders, William Scott, of Peterborough, New Hampshire. Like his fellow townsmen, Scott was not much inclined toward revolution. Yet in the course of the war he served in four campaigns against the British and escaped capture on three different occasions. What, asks Shy, motivated people like Scott and his townspeople to commit themselves to the revolutionary cause?

The answer, for Shy, lay in the nature of the local militia and the pinched conditions of northern New England life. While the rocky soil, heavily forested terrain, and short growing season of northern New England had never been kind to colonial farmers, early settlers in the region had been able to make an adequate, if not luxurious, life for themselves as tillers of the soil. But by the last quarter of the eighteenth century the grandchildren of the original settlers faced a different prospect. As families increased in size during the eighteenth century and the available land was taken up by succeeding generations of farmers, the rural economy of northern and eastern New England began to stagnate. No longer could a farmer's son depend on an inheritance which would allow him to establish his family's independence. It was the opportunity to escape from these straitened conditions and to achieve some degree of advancement in the world that led men like "Long Bill" Scott to join the revolutionary cause.

How do the reasons for Scott's revolutionary commitment compare with those of the common people of Isaac's Virginia or Nash's seaport cities in Readings 8 and

Reprinted from John Parker and Carol Urness, eds., *The American Revolution: A Heritage of Change* (Minneapolis: James Ford Bell Library, University of Minnesota, 1975), with permission of the publisher.

9? What role did religion and popular ideologies, such as those discussed by Isaac and Nash, have in the revolutionary mobilization?

Armed force, and nothing else, decided the outcome of the American Revolution. Without armed force mobilized on a decisive scale, there would be today no subject for discussion. Deprived even of its name, the "Revolution" would shrink to a mere rebellion—an interesting episode, but like dozens of others in the modern history of Western societies. Crude, obvious, and unappealing as this truism may be, it is still true; without war to sustain it, the Declaration of Independence would be a forgotten, abortive manifesto. Writing about an earlier revolutionary war, Thomas Hobbes rammed home the point when he said that "covenants without swords are but words."

But the cynicism of Hobbes can too easily mask a second, equally important truism, perhaps best expressed a century later by David Hume. "As force is always on the side of the governed," Hume wrote, "the governors have nothing to support them but opinion." For all their peculiar aggressiveness, even human beings do not kill and risk death for no reason. Beneath the raw irrationality of violence lies motive—some psychic web spun from logic, belief, perception, and emotion that draws people to commit terrible acts and to hazard everything they possess. Perhaps Hume's view—that persuasion, not force itself, must ultimately govern, because no ruling minority can control a truly aroused majority—has lost some of its validity in our own time, when technology vastly multiplies the amount of force that a few people can wield, but it certainly held good for the eighteenth century, when even the best weapons were still relatively primitive and widely available. If Hobbes—like all his fellow cynics down through history—is right in believing that public opinion is a fairly fragile flower which can seldom survive the hot wind of violence, Hume reminds us that no one, not even a soldier, uses force without somehow being moved to do so.

John Adams put his finger on this matter of motivation when he said that the real Ameri-can Revolution, the revolution that estranged American hearts from old British loyalties and readied American minds to use (and to withstand) massive violence, was over before the war began. But Adams also opined that a third of the American people supported the Revolutionary cause, another third remained more or less loyal to Britain, and that the rest were neutral or apathetic. Clearly, Adams conceded that not all hearts and minds had been permanently affected in the same way. Many British observers thought that the real American Revolutionaries were the religious Dissenters, Congregationalists and Presbyterians who had always been secretly disloyal to the Crown because they rejected the whole Anglican Establishment, whose head was the king; and that these Revolutionaries persuaded poor Irishmen, who poured into the American colonies in great numbers during the middle third of the eighteenth century, to do most of the dirty business of actual fighting. American Whigs, on the other hand, generally assumed that all decent, sane people supported the Revolution, and that those who did not could be categorized as timid, vicious, corrupt, or deluded. Each of these opinions contains a measure of truth, but they seem to contradict one another, and they do not carry us very far toward understanding.

Like these stock opinions, we have two standard images of the popular response to the Revolutionary War. One is of whole towns springing to arms as Paul Revere carried his warning to them in the spring of 1775. The other is of a tiny, frozen, naked band of men at Valley Forge, all that are left when everyone else went home in the winter of 1778. Which is the true picture? Both, evidently. But that answer is of no use at all when we ask whether the Revolution succeeded only by the persistence of a very small group of people, the intervention of France, and great good luck; or whether the Revolution was—or became—unbeatable because the mass of the population simply would not give up the struggle, and the British simply could not muster the force and the resolution to kill them all or break their will or sit on all or even any large proportion of them. This problem posed by the motivation for violence breaks down into more specific questions: Who actually took up arms and why? How strong was the motivation to serve, and to keep serving in spite of defeat and other adversities? What was the intricate interplay and feedback between attitude and behavior, events and attitude? Did people get war weary and discouraged, or did they become adamant toward British efforts to coerce them? If we could answer these questions with confidence, not only would we know why the rebels won and the government lost, but we would also know important things about the American society that emerged from seven years of armed conflict. Differing answers to these questions lay at the root of what had divided Charles Lee and George Washington.

The essential difficulty in answering these questions lies less in the lack of evidence than in the nature of the subject. Violence, with all its ramifications, remains a great mystery for students of human life, while the deeper motivational sources of human behavior—particularly collective behavior under conditions of stress—are almost equally mysterious. When these two mysteries come together, as they do in wars and revolutions, then the historian faces a problem full of traps and snares for the unwary, a problem that challenges his ability to know *anything* about the past. A certain humility is obviously in order. If any of us are tempted not to be humble, we might recall how recently intelligent, well-informed American leaders spoke glibly about winning the "hearts and minds" of another few million people caught up by war and revolution [in Vietnam]. That, then, is the subject: the hearts and minds of Americans whose willingness to engage in violence, two centuries ago, fundamentally changed the course of history.

A suitably humble approach to these difficult questions lies at hand in a book written by Peter Oliver, who watched the Revolution explode in Boston. Oliver descended from some of the oldest

families of Massachusetts Bay, he was a distinguished merchant and public official, and he became a bitter Tory. His book, *The Origin and Progress of the American Rebellion, . . .* is a fascinatingly unsympathetic version of the Revolution, and in it Oliver makes an attempt to answer some of our questions. Using the device, more fully developed by S. L. A. Marshall during the Second World War, of the after-action interview, Oliver asked a wounded American lieutenant, who had been captured at Bunker Hill, how he had come to be a rebel. The American officer allegedly replied as follows:

> The case was this Sir! I lived in a Country Town; I was a Shoemaker, & got my Living by my Labor. When this Rebellion came on, I saw some of my Neighbors get into Commission, who were no better than myself. I was very ambitious, & did not like to see those Men above me. I was asked to enlist, as a private Soldier. My Ambition was too great for so low a Rank; I offered to enlist upon having a Lieutenants Commission; which was granted. I imagined my self now in a way of Promotion: if I was killed in Battle, there would an end of me, but if my Captain was killed, I should rise in Rank, & should still have a Chance to rise higher. These Sir! were the only Motives of my entering into the Service; for as to the Dispute between great Britain & the Colonies, I know nothing of it; neither am I capable of judging whether it is right or wrong.

Those who have read U.S. Government publications of the 1960's will find this POW interrogation familiar; during the Vietnam War, the State and Defense Departments published many like it, and more than one Vietcong or North Vietnamese prisoner is said to have spoken in the accents of the wounded American lieutenant so long ago.

Now the lieutenant was not a figment of Oliver's embittered imagination. His name is given by Oliver as Scott, and American records show that Lieutenant William Scott, of Colonel Paul Sargent's regiment, was indeed wounded and captured at Bunker Hill. Scott turns out, upon investigation, to have been an interesting character. Perhaps the first thing to be said about him is that nothing in the record of his life down to 1775 contradicts anything in Oliver's account of the interview. Scott came from Peterborough, New Hampshire, a town settled in the 1730s by Irish Presbyterians. Scott's father had served in the famous Rogers' Rangers during the French and Indian War. At the news of the outbreak of fighting in 1775, a cousin who kept the store in Peterborough recruited a company of local men to fight the British. Apparently the cousin tried to enlist our William Scott—known to his neighbors as "Long Bill," thus distinguishing him from the cousin, "Short Bill." But "Long Bill"—our Bill—seems to have declined serving as a private, and insisted on being a lieutenant if cousin "Short Bill" was going to be a captain. "Short Bill" agreed. So far the stories as told by Oliver and as revealed in the New Hampshire records check perfectly. Nor is there any reason to think that "Long Bill" had a deeper understanding of the causes of the Revolution than appear in Oliver's version of the interview.

What Peter Oliver never knew was the subsequent life history of this battered yokel, whose view of the American rebellion seemed so pitifully naïve. When the British evacuated Boston, they took Scott and other American prisoners to Halifax, Nova Scotia. There, after more than a year in captivity, Scott somehow managed to escape, to find a boat, and to make his way back to the American army just in time for the fighting around New York City in 1776. Captured again in November, when Fort Washington and its garrison fell to a surprise British assault, Scott escaped almost immediately, this time by swimming the Hudson River at night—according to a newspaper account—with his sword tied around his neck and his watch pinned to his hat. He returned to New Hampshire during the winter of 1777 to recruit a company of his own; there, he enlisted his two eldest sons for three years or the duration of the war. Stationed in the Boston area, he marched against Burgoyne's invading army from Canada, and led a detachment that cut off the last retreat just before the surrender near Saratoga. Scott later took part in the fighting around Newport, Rhode Island. But when his light infantry company was ordered to Virginia under Lafayette in early 1781, to counter the raiding expedition led by Benedict Arnold, Scott's health broke down; long marches and hot weather would make the old Bunker Hill wounds ache, and he was permitted to resign from the army. After only a few months of recuperation, however, he seems to have grown restless, for we find him during the last year of the war serving as a volunteer on a navy frigate.

What would Scott have said if Oliver had been able to interview him again, after the war? We can only guess. Probably he would have told Oliver that his oldest son had died in the army, not gloriously, but of camp fever, after six years of service. Scott might have said that in 1777 he had sold his Peterborough farm in order to meet expenses, but that the note which he took in exchange turned into a scrap of paper when the dollar of 1777 became worth less than two cents by 1780. He might also have said that another farm, in Groton, Massachusetts, slipped away from him, along with a down payment that he had made on it, when his military pay depreciated rapidly to a fraction of its nominal value. He might not have been willing to admit that when his wife died he simply turned their younger children over to his surviving elder son, and then set off to beg a pension or a job from the government. Almost certainly he would not have told Oliver that when the son—himself sick, his corn crop killed by a late frost, and saddled with three little brothers and sisters—begged his father for help, our hero told him, should all else fail, to hand the children over to the selectmen of Peterborough—in short, to put them on welfare.

In 1792, "Long Bill" Scott once more made the newspapers: he rescued eight people from drowning when their small boat capsized in New York Harbor. But heroism did not pay very well. At last, in 1794, Secretary of War Henry Knox made Scott deputy storekeeper at West Point; and a year later General Benjamin Lincoln took Scott with him to the Ohio country, where they were to negotiate with the Indians and survey the land opened up by Anthony Wayne's victory at Fallen Timbers. At last he had a respectable job, and even a small pension for his nine wounds; but Lincoln's group caught something called "lake fever" while surveying on the Black River, near Sandusky. Scott, ill himself, guided part of the group back to Fort Stanwix, New York, then returned for the others. It was his last heroic act. A few days after his second trip, he died, on September 16, 1796.

Anecdotes, even good ones like the touching saga of "Long Bill" Scott, do not make history. But neither can a subject like ours be treated in terms of what Jesse Lemisch has referred to as the lives of Great White Men—Washington, Adams, Jefferson, Hamilton, and the handful like them. Scott's life, in itself, may tell us little about how armed force and public opinion were mobilized in the Revolution; yet the story of his life leads us directly—and at the level of ordinary people—toward crucial features of the process.

Peterborough, New Hampshire, in 1775 had a population of 549. Town, state, and federal records show that about 170 men were credited to Peterborough as performing some military service during the Revolution. In other words, almost every adult male, at one time or another, carried a gun in the war. But of these 170 participants, less than a third performed extensive service; that is, service ranging from over a year up to the whole eight years of the war. And only a fraction of these—less than two dozen—served as long as Bill Scott. In Scott we are not seeing a typical participant, but one of a small "hard core" of revolutionary fighters—the men who stayed in the army for more than a few months or a single campaign. As we look down the list of long-service soldiers from Peterborough, they seem indeed to be untypical people. A few, like Scott and his cousin "Short Bill" and James Taggart and Josiah Munroe, became officers or at least sergeants, and thereby acquired status and perhaps some personal satisfaction from their prolonged military service. But most of the hard core remained privates, and they were an unusually poor, obscure group of men, even by the rustic standards of Peterborough. Many—like John Alexander, Robert Cunningham, William Ducannon, Joseph Henderson, Richard Richard-

son, John Wallace, and Thomas Williamson—were recruited from outside the town, from among men who never really lived in Peterborough. Whether they lived *anywhere*—in the strict legal sense—is a question. Two men—Zaccheus Brooks and John Miller—are simply noted as "transients." At least two—James Hackley and Randall McAllister—were deserters from the British army. At least two others—Samuel Weir and Titus Wilson—were black men, Wilson dying as a prisoner of war. A few, like Michael Silk, simply appear, join the army, then vanish without a documentary trace. Many more reveal themselves as near the bottom of the socioeconomic ladder: Hackley, Benjamin Allds, Isaac Mitchell, Ebenezer Perkins, Amos Spofford, Jonathan Wheelock, and Charles White were legal paupers after the Revolution, Joseph Henderson was a landless day-laborer, Samuel Spear was jailed for debt, and John Miller was mentally deranged.

We can look at the whole Peterborough contingent in another way, in terms of those in it who were, or later became, prominent or at least solid citizens of the town. With a few exceptions, like "Short Bill" Scott and "Long Bill"'s son John, who survived frost-killed corn and a parcel of unwanted siblings to become a selectman and a leader of the town, these prominent men and solid citizens had served in the war for only short periods—a few months in 1775, a month or two in the Burgoyne emergency of 1777, maybe a month in Rhode Island or a month late in the war to bolster the key garrison of West Point. The pattern is clear, and it is a pattern that reappears wherever the surviving evidence has permitted a similar kind of inquiry. Lynn, Massachusetts; Berks County, Pennsylvania; Colonel Smallwood's recruits from Maryland in 1782; several regiments of the Massachusetts Line; a sampling of pension applicants from Virginia—all show that the hard core of Continental soldiers, the Bill Scotts who could not wangle commissions, the soldiers at Valley Forge, the men who shouldered the heaviest military burden, were something *less* than average colonial Americans. As a group, they were poorer, more marginal, less well anchored in the society. Perhaps we should not be surprised; it is easy to imagine men like these actually being attracted by the relative affluence, comfort, security, prestige, and even the chance for satisfying human relationships offered by the Continental army. Revolutionary America may have been a middle-class society, happier and more prosperous than any other in its time, but it contained a large and growing number of fairly poor people, and many of them did much of the actual fighting and suffering between 1775 and 1783: A very old story.

The large proportion of men, from Peterborough and other communities, who served only briefly might thus seem far less important to our subject than the disadvantaged minority who did such a large part of the heavy work of revolution. This militarily less active majority were of course the militiamen. One could compile a large volume of pithy observations, beginning with a few dozen from Washington himself, in which the military value of the militia was called into question. The nub of the critique was that these part-time soldiers were untrained, undisciplined, undependable, and very expensive, consuming pay, rations, clothing, and weapons at a great rate in return for short periods of active service. By the end of the war, the tendency of many Continental officers, like Colonel Alexander Hamilton, to disparage openly the military performance of the militia was exacerbating already strained relations between State and Continental authorities. And indeed there were a number of cases in which the failure of militia to arrive in time, to stand under fire, or to remain when they were needed, either contributed to American difficulties or prevented the exploitation of American success. But the Revolutionary role of the men from Peterborough and elsewhere who did *not* serve as did Bill Scott, but whose active military service was rather a sometime thing, is easily misunderstood and underestimated if we look at it only in terms of traditional military strategy and set-piece battles.

To understand the Revolutionary militia and its role, we must go back to the year before the outbreak of fighting at Lexington and Concord.

Each colony, except Pennsylvania, had traditionally required every free white adult male, with a few minor occupational exceptions, to be inscribed in a militia unit, and to take part in training several times a year. These militia units seldom achieved any degree of military proficiency, nor were they expected to serve as actual fighting formations. Their real function might be described as a hybrid of draft board and modern reserve unit—a modicum of military training combined with a mechanism to find and enlist individuals when they were needed. But the colonial militia did not simply slide smoothly into the Revolution. Militia officers, even where they were elected, held royal commissions, and a significant number of them were not enthusiastic about rebellion. Purging and restructuring the militia was an important step toward revolution, one that deserves more attention than it has had.

When the news reached America that Parliament would take a very hard line in response to the Boston Tea Party, and in particular had passed a law that could destroy, economically and politically, the town of Boston, the reaction in the colonies was stronger and more nearly unanimous than at any time since the Stamp Act. No one could defend the Boston Port Act; it was an unprecedented, draconian law, the possible consequences of which seemed staggering. Radicals, like Samuel Adams, demanded an immediate and complete break in commercial relations with the rest of the Empire. Boycotts had worked effectively in the past, and they were an obvious response to the British hard line. More moderate leaders, however, dreaded a hasty confrontation that might quickly escalate beyond their control, and they used democratic theory to argue that nothing ought to be done without a full and proper consultation of the popular will. Like the boycott, the consultative congress had a respectable pedigree, and the moderates won the argument. When Congress met in September 1774 there were general expectations in both Britain and America that it would cool and seek to compromise the situation.

Exactly what happened to disappoint those expectations is even now not wholly clear; our own sense that Congress was heading straight toward revolution and independence distorts a complex moment in history, when uncertainty about both ends and means deeply troubled the minds of most decision-makers. Congress had hardly convened when it heard that the British had bombarded Boston. For a few days men from different colonies, normally suspicious of one another, were swept together by a wave of common fear and apprehension. Though the report was quickly proved false, these hours of mutual panic seem to have altered the emotional economy of the Congress. Soon afterward it passed without any serious dissent a resolution in favor of the long-advocated boycott, to be known as the Association. Local committees were to gather signatures for the Association, and were to take necessary steps to enforce its provisions. The Association was the vital link in transforming the colonial militia into a revolutionary organization.

For more than a year, a tenuous line of authority ran directly from the Continental Congress to the grass roots of American society. The traditional, intermediate levels of government, if they did not cooperate fully, were by-passed. Committees formed everywhere to enforce the Association, and sympathetic men volunteered to assist in its enforcement. In some places, like Peterborough, the same men who were enrolled in the militia became the strong right arm of the local committee; reluctant militia officers were ignored because, after all, not the militia as such but a voluntary association of militia members was taking the action. In other places, like parts of the Hudson valley and Long Island, reluctance was so widespread that men opposed to the Association actually tried to take over the committee system in order to kill it; when meetings were called to form the new armed organization of Associators, loyal militiamen packed the meetings and re-elected the old, royally commissioned lieutenants and captains. But even where the Association encountered heavy opposition, it effectively dissolved the old military structure and created a new one based on consent, and whose chief purpose was to engineer consent, by force if necessary. The new Revolutionary militia might

look very much like the old colonial militia, but it was, in its origins, less a draft board and a reserve training unit than a police force and an instrument of political surveillance. Although the boycott could be defended to moderate men as a constitutional, non-violent technique, its implementation had radical consequences. Adoption by Congress gave it a legitimacy and a unity that it could have gained in no other way. Ordinary men were forced to make public choices, and thus to identify themselves with one side or the other. Not until the Declaration of Independence clarified the hazy status of the traditional levels of government did the local committees, acting through the new militia, relinquish some of their truly revolutionary power.

It is difficult to overestimate the importance of what happened in 1775 to engage mass participation on the side of the Revolution. The new militia, which repeatedly denied that it was in rebellion and proclaimed its loyalty to the Crown, enforced a boycott intended to make Britain back down; Britain did not back down, but the attempt drew virtually everyone into the realm of politics. Enlistment, training, and occasional emergencies were the means whereby dissenters were identified, isolated, and dealt with. Where the new militia had trouble getting organized, there Revolutionary activists could see that forceful intervention from outside might be needed. Connecticut units moved into the New York City area; Virginia troops moved into the Delmarva Peninsula; in Pennsylvania, men from Reading and Lancaster marched into Bucks County. Once established, the militia became the infrastructure of revolutionary government. It controlled its community, whether through indoctrination or intimidation; it provided on short notice large numbers of armed men for brief periods of emergency service; and it found and persuaded, drafted or bribed, the smaller number of men needed each year to keep the Continental army alive. After the first months of the war, popular enthusiasm and spontaneity could not have sustained the struggle; only a pervasive armed organization, in which almost everyone took some part, kept people constantly, year after year, at the hard task of revolution. While Scott and his sons, the indigent, the blacks, and the otherwise socially expendable men fought the British, James and Samuel Cunningham, Henry Ferguson, John Gray, William McNee, Benjamin Mitchell, Robert Morison, Alexander and William Robbe, Robert Swan, Robert Wilson, and four or five men named Smith—all militiamen, but whose combined active service hardly equalled that of "Long Bill" Scott alone—ran Peterborough, expelling a few Tories, scraping up enough recruits for the Continental army to meet the town's quota every spring, taking time out to help John Stark destroy the Germans at the battle of Bennington.

The mention of Tories brings us, briefly, to the last aspect of our subject . . . Peterborough had little trouble with Tories; the most sensational case occurred when the Presbyterian minister, the Rev. John Morrison, who had been having difficulties with his congregation, deserted his post as chaplain to the Peterborough troops and entered British lines at Boston in June 1775. But an informed estimate is that a half million Americans can be counted as loyal to Britain. Looking at the absence of serious Loyalism in Peterborough, we might conclude that Scotch-Irish Presbyterians almost never were Tories. That, however, would be an error of fact, and we are impelled to seek further for an explanation. What appears as we look at places like Peterborough, where Tories are hardly visible, and at other places where Toryism was rampant, is a pattern —not so much an ethnic, religious, or ideological pattern, but a pattern of raw power. Wherever the British and their allies were strong enough to penetrate in force—along the seacoast, in the Hudson, Mohawk, and lower Delaware valleys, in Georgia, the Carolinas, and the transappalachian West—there Toryism flourished. But geographically less exposed areas, if population density made self-defense feasible—most of New England, the Pennsylvania hinterland, and piedmont Virginia—where the enemy hardly appeared or not at all, there Tories either ran away, kept quiet, even serving in the rebel armies, or occasionally took a brave but hopeless stand against Revolutionary committees and their gunmen. After the war, of course, men remembered their parts in the successful Revolution in ways that make it difficult for the historian to reconstruct accurately the relationship between what they thought and what they did.

The view here presented of how armed force and public opinion were mobilized may seem a bit cynical—a reversion to Thomas Hobbes. True, it gives little weight to ideology, to perceptions and principles, to grievances and aspirations, to the more admirable side of the emergent American character. Perhaps that is a weakness; perhaps I have failed to grasp what really drove Bill Scott. But what strikes me most forcibly in studying this part of the Revolution is how much in essential agreement almost all Americans were in 1774, both in their views of British measures and in their feelings about them. What then is puzzling, and thus needs explaining, is why so many of these people behaved in anomalous and in different ways. Why did so many, who did not intend a civil war or political independence, get so inextricably involved in the organization and use of armed force? Why did relatively few do most of the actual fighting? Why was a dissenting fifth of the population so politically and militarily impotent, so little able to affect the outcome of the struggle? Answers to these questions cannot be found in the life of one obscure man, or in the history of one backwoods town. But microscopic study does emphasize certain features of the American Revolution: the political structuring of resistance to Britain, the play of social and economic factors in carrying on that resistance by armed force, and the brutally direct effects on behavior, if not on opinions, of military power.

12

SHAYS' REBELLION AND THE CONSTITUTION

DAVID P. SZATMARY

Like all wars, the American revolution was an expensive undertaking. Fortifications had to be built, ordance produced, ships built, soldiers and sailors paid, and food and shelter provided for the Continental Army. Paying for these burdensome expenses was a point of considerable controversy during the revolution as the Continental Congress sought to fund the growing war debt. By the end of the war, in 1783, each of the states, as well as the national government, owed enormous war debts. In Massachusetts, long a bulwark of fiscal conservatism, the legislature sought to retire its war debt as quickly as possible by increasing tax rates and by taxing previously untaxed goods. This post-Revolutionary taxation fell with particular force upon the many small farmers of rural Massachusetts. At first hundreds, and then thousands, of farmers faced foreclosure, imprisonment for debt, and even servitude when they could not pay increased state taxes.

As state officials turned a deaf ear to the plight of western farmers, these men began to take matters into their own hands by closing the courts which were the instruments of their dispossession. When state officials mobilized the militia against them, these farmers organized themselves into a popular army of opposition and fought for social justice. The resulting conflict, known as Shays' Rebellion, began in 1787 and lasted for 18 months before its supporters were finally defeated in late 1788.

As David P. Szatmary points out in this essay, Shays' Rebellion had an impact far beyond the borders of Massachusetts. The spectacle of an armed popular uprising in one of the new nation's most influential states not only served as an impetus for similar tax revolts in other states, but also drove many supporters of limited federal powers, what Szatmary calls "localists," to support the Constitution of 1788 and the increased powers which it gave to the national government.

Do you think there was a connection between Shays' Rebellion and the political violence of the 1790s, discussed by John R. Howe in Reading 14? Which of the two visions of the Constitution, discussed by Drew R. McCoy in Reading 13, do you think the farmers and political leaders of Massachusetts supported? The human dimension of the crisis that post-Revolutionary farmers faced can be found below in Paul Johnson's story of Mayo Greenleaf Patch in Reading 15.

The uprising of New England farmers in 1786 and 1787 has a historic significance much deeper than that of a regional chronicle. For it is clear that Shays' Rebellion played an integral part in the genesis and formation of the United States Constitution adopted at Philadelphia in September 1787. The crisis atmosphere engendered by agrarian discontent strengthened the resolve of

Reprinted from *Shays' Rebellion: The Making of an Agrarian Insurrection* by David P. Szatmary (Amherst: University of Massachusetts Press); copyright © 1980 by the University of Massachusetts Press.

the nationalists and shocked some reluctant localists into an acceptance of a stronger national government, thereby uniting divergent political elements of commercial society in the country at large.

Besides affecting the formation of the Constitution, the Shaysite troubles influenced the ratification debates in New England, and especially in Massachusetts. The ratification contest generally pitted backcountry Antifederalists against merchants, professionals, and urban artisans. Following the pattern of Shaysite resistance to government, Massachusetts antifederalism represented an attempt to save a subsistence-oriented way of life from the penetrating edge of a commercial society. As Van Beck Hall has argued, "the debate over the Constitution, instead of raising the curtain on new divisions that would exist in a new political era, actually climaxed the political struggles of the earlier period." In both the formation of the Constitution at Philadelphia and the ratification debates in Massachusetts, then, Shays' Rebellion assumed an important role.

During the 1780s, most state leaders had been oriented toward a commercial society. New England legislators usually gained their livelihoods through merchant or professional enterprises. In the middle states, lawyers such as James Wilson of Pennsylvania and New Jersey's William Paterson along with such wholesalers as Philadelphia merchants George Clymer and Thomas Mifflin exercised leadership. A few merchants in and around Charleston, South Carolina, lawyers such as North Carolina's William Davie and John Rutledge of South Carolina, and such plantation owners as Pierce Butler, Charles Pinckney, and Richard Dobbs Spaight of the Carolinas held the reins in the southern states. Together, merchants, professionals, and planters dominated the political life of the United States.

Despite common ties to a commercial society, American leaders disagreed over the political system. For most leaders of the Confederation and many coastal wholesalers, a strong national government seemed imperative. Some prominent Confederation officials, headed by Secretary at War Henry Knox and congressional leader James Madison of Virginia, consistently pushed for a more powerful national government. In March 1785, Knox advocated a new government established "upon more national principles," probably sensing the impotence of the weak Confederation from his position of national power. According to Rhode Island representative and Baptist minister James Manning, almost "every member of Congress" similarly pointed "to a crisis within the Federal government" and demanded a more centralized political system.

Some New England merchants joined Confederation officials in endorsing a stronger national government. Feeling the damaging consequences of a depressed postwar economy, they blamed losses upon an inefficient Confederation and cried out for a more powerful central government. In late 1785, New Hampshire wholesaler John Sparhawk demanded a strengthened "union of the United States by delegating ample powers to Congress." Many Boston merchants echoed Sparhawk's plea. According to Massachusetts political leader Nathan Dane, "the restrictions laid by the British on our trade" along with the subsequent credit crisis in New England created a "disposition especially among mercantile men, to lodge a power somewhere in the Union." In 1785, pressure laid upon the Massachusetts legislature by coastal merchants produced a resolution "to propose to the several states a convention of delegates for the express purpose of a *general revision of the Confederation.*" As Confederation delegate Rufus King observed on June 11, 1786, "the merchants through all the states are of one mind, and in favor of a national system."

In September 1786, both Confederation officials and merchants pressed for an implementation of the nationalist plan at a general economic convention in Annapolis. Led by Alexander Hamilton, they focused upon the "delicate and critical" economic situation of the United States and cautioned fellow leaders about possible financial collapse and resulting anarchy unless the states quickly instituted measures for a more vigorous national government. "If we do not control events we shall be miserably controlled by them," warned Massachusetts lawyer Theodore Sedgwick.

Despite the obvious economic problems facing the United States in late 1786, many state officials rejected the nationalist arguments. Having gained influence and prestige through positions in the state governments and recognizing the possible dangers that a stronger national government posed to their state-based power, they ignored the nationalist-inspired Annapolis meeting. Connecticut, Maryland, South Carolina, and Georgia snubbed it, while Massachusetts, New Hampshire, Rhode Island, and North Carolina waited until the last moment. In consequence, the delegates from the latter states arrived after the convention had adjourned. Because only Virginia, Delaware, Pennsylvania, New Jersey, and New York were represented, the delegates at Annapolis decided not "to proceed on the business of their mission, under the circumstances of so partial and defective a representation." They then recommended another convention to be held at Philadelphia in May 1787 and disbanded on September 14, 1786. Although some historians have contended that the delegates went home prematurely to secretly further the nationalist cause, nationalist Rufus King privately expressed disappointment over the failure at Annapolis:

> Foreign nations had been notified of this convention, the friends to a good government through these states looked at it with anxiety and hope; the history of it will not be more agreeable to the former, than it must be seriously harmful to the latter.

In the time between the abortive Annapolis meeting and the proposed Philadelphia convention, nationalist resolve intensified, and some localists accepted the necessity for a stronger national government. The resulting union of American leaders originated at least in part from the domestic upheavals taking place in 1786 and 1787. To the nationalists, Shays' Rebellion reflected the overall inadequacy of a political system dominated by semisovereign states. Prolonged domestic conflict in Massachusetts, one of the most respected and influential states in the

Confederation, disclosed the vulnerability of individual states in the loose-knit union. For nationalist-minded leaders such as George Washington, no "stronger evidence" could be given "of the want of energy in our governments than these disorders." At the same time, the Massachusetts insurrection brought into full relief the impotence of the federal government. Even though "Congress have been much alarmed at the prospect of the insurgents," wrote Confederation delegate John Stevens of New Jersey, it possessed few means to arm troops against the rebels. Confronted with such debility, nationalists such as Foreign Secretary John Jay felt that "the inefficiency of the Federal government becomes more and more manifest."

The New England rebellion also convinced some state-oriented leaders of the need for a more powerful national government. For many localists, Shaysite activity came as a shock. "The commotions in Massachusetts daily become more alarming," exclaimed planter William Blount of North Carolina in late 1786. "The disturbances in Massachusetts Bay have been considerable, and absolutely threaten the most serious consequences," agreed Virginia planter William Grayson that November. "How it will end, God only knows; the present prospects are, no doubt, extremely alarming."

Much of the localist fear of the disturbances stemmed from the perceived goals of the Shaysites and the supposed effects that a successful insurrection might have upon commercial relations. Along with New England merchants and professionals, officials in the middle and southern states feared that the insurgents sought a general redistribution of property. Frightened Pennsylvania merchant and legislator Charles Pettit thought that the Shaysites envisioned "a total abolition of all debts both public and private and even a general distribution of property." Events in Massachusetts likewise convinced South Carolina slaveholder Edward Rutledge that the rebels would "stop little short of a distribution of property—I speak of a general distribution." Such an event, cautioned Rutledge, would destroy commercial exchange and lead to economic anarchy.

Pockets of backcountry resistance to debt and tax collection in the middle and southern states caused added concern among American leaders. In Maryland on June 8, 1786, "a tumultuary assemblage of the people" rushed into the Charles County courthouse and closed the court. Like the Massachusetts rebels, the insurgents demanded a suspension of debt suits and an adjournment of the court until the Maryland Assembly issued paper money. Just after the Charles County court incident, yeomen in Harford and Calvert counties organized public boycotts against government sales of debtor property. In Cecil County, farmers circulated unsigned handbills that threatened state officers with violence in the event of government seizure of property for unpaid taxes. By early 1787, widespread agrarian protests had created fear among state leaders. Alexander Hamilton, engaged in some Maryland debt suits, felt that the disturbances portended a general movement against "every well wisher to the Constitution, laws, and peace of their country." Governor William Smallwood likewise condemned "riotous and tumultuous" proceedings and dreaded further "violence and outrages" against the Maryland government.

Officials in South Carolina confronted similar protests. During May of 1785, sheriffs and deputies were "threatened in the execution of their duty; and at length the people in the district of Camden grew outrageous." They "planted out centinels to intercept the sheriffs, and put the laws at defiance." In one incident, Colonel Hezekiah Mayham "being served by the sheriff with a writ obliged him to eat it on the spot." The next month, farmers assaulted the Camden courthouse in a demonstration against debt collections, successfully blocked the consideration of debt suits, and sent the judges scurrying home. Yeomen also struck out against debt collections in other South Carolina districts, preventing debtor courts "by tumultuous and riotous proceedings from determining actions for debt." Although partially calming farmers with the Pine Barrens Act and a £100,000 emission of paper money, South Carolina officials nonetheless feared future attacks upon debtor courts. If the legislature allowed "creditors to sue debtors," warned Judge Aedanus Burke, "the people would not suffer it." Not even "5,000 troops, the best in America or Europe, could enforce obedience to the Common Pleas." About the same time, Governor William Moultrie informed the assembly that "confusion and anarchy" still threatened the state.

New Jersey officials also faced outbreaks of rural violence. As early as January 1785, wrote minister Joseph Lewis, "a spirit of rebellion caught hold of the greatest part of the community" around Morristown. Farmers refused to pay taxes and blocked attempts by sheriffs to auction debtor property. In one case, yeomen in Mendham armed themselves with clubs and forcibly stopped the sale of "some property at vendue" that a constable had "distrained for taxes." A year later, brothers John, Ralph, Jacob, and Abraham Schenck planned an attack upon the Hunterdon County debtor court. Driven by "the madness of poverty" and angered by debt prosecutions, they surrounded the building and "began to nail up the courthourse." In July 1786 Jersey farmers assaulted the Elizabethtown debtor court, planted a stake in the ground, and impaled an effigy of Governor William Livingston on the pole.

Yeomen in Virginia similarly protested against debt collections. In March and April 1787, they complained of their heavy load of debts and taxes, seeking relief through peaceful protest. Some husbandmen formed associations and boycotted property sold at auction. Others flooded the legislature with petitions for paper money and tender laws, hoping the measures would alleviate the credit crisis in Virginia. Rebuked by the state assembly, some yeomen, wrote John Dawson to James Madison, began "following the example of the insurgents in Massachusetts and preventing the courts proceeding to business." On the eve of the May court session, the King William County courthouse "with all the records of the county, was burnt down." In late August, over 300 yeomen stormed the Greenbrier County court, successfully stopping its proceedings. And in Amelia County, "disorderly people of desperate circumstances" obstructed the county debtor court session. Throughout the state in 1787, Madison reported, Virginia officials watched the "prisons and courthouses and clerk's offices willfully burnt." Backcountry resistance to debt collections caused concern among some Virginia leaders. "The friends to American honor and happiness," wrote Richard Henry Lee from Philadelphia in September, "here all join in lamenting the riots and mobbish proceedings in Virginia." Planter Archibald Stuart, closer to the outbreaks of violence than Lee, "trembled with the apprehensions of a rebellion."

The same fear of domestic insurrection seized Pennsylvania leaders. On November 29, 1786, 200 yeomen, "about twenty armed with guns, and the rest with clubs, marched into York, and by force attempted to rescue some goods and chattels that had been executed for taxes." On January 25, 1787, the same husbandmen staged another attack, assembling "at the house of Justice Sherman, where a public sale of some cattle seized for taxes was to have been held, and effecting a rescue of them." Although they satisfied many farmers with an issue of paper money, Pennsylvania leaders feared trouble. To Pennsylvania official Michael Hahn, the York incidents appeared "epidemic, the infection of which has spread itself from the eastward and therefore ought to be cautiously as well as spiritedly treated." The "wild fire" of the Massachusetts rebellion, agreed Lutheran minister Henry Melchior Muhlenberg, "may cause a conflagration in the rest of the independent states because combustible materials, both physical and moral, are heaped up here." While state leaders in Rhode Island, North Carolina, New York, and Georgia avoided trouble by issuing paper money, other state elites, including those in Pennsylvania, felt the anger of discontented farmers.

Fearing continued domestic turmoil, many state leaders oriented to the Confederation began to accept the idea of a stronger national government. Massachusetts, the state most plagued by domestic unrest, saw the need in late 1786. According to Henry Knox, the uprising "wrought prodigious changes in the minds of men in that state respecting the powers of government—

everybody says they must be strengthened and that unless this shall be effected, there is no security for liberty and property." Shays' Rebellion taught Connecticut Lieutenant Governor Oliver Wolcott, formerly a staunch localist, the same lesson. The Massachusetts uprising pointed to "such radical defects in our general system as will, unless soon remedied, produce unhappy convulsions." The "authority or rather the influence of Congress and the system connected with it, I consider at about an end," Wolcott wrote to his son on February 18, 1787. To Pierce Butler, a South Carolina planter and lawyer, a strengthened national government also seemed to be "the only thing at this critical moment that can rescue the states from civil discord."

By contributing to a change in the outlook of some localists, rural outbursts in New England and throughout the country may have made a general convention in Philadelphia possible. Backcountry violence did not *cause* the May 1787 meeting—in fact, the assembly had been planned before the most extreme Shaysite activity had occurred—but domestic unrest helped to ensure in certain quarters a favorable reaction toward the meeting. Developing at a critical juncture in time, the rebellion convinced the elites of sovereign states that the proposed gathering at Philadelphia must take place.

George Washington believed that the Shaysite disturbances so shocked localists, "that most of the legislatures have appointed and the rest will appoint delegates to meet at Philadelphia." The revolutionary war hero attributed his own presence at the Constitutional Convention in May to the Massachusetts troubles. Fellow Virginian Edward Carrington likewise considered the "tendency to anarchy" in Massachusetts a major reason that the convention was well attended. From his perspective, it jarred into action state leaders "who had consigned themselves to an eve of rest." James Madison saw a similar connection between Shays' Rebellion and the formation of the Philadelphia convention. To the Virginian, the insurrection seemed "distressing beyond measure to the zealous friends of the Revolution." It furnished "new proofs of the necessity of such a vigor in the general government as will be able to restore health to any diseased part of the Federal body." "To bring about such an amendment of the Federal Constitution," wrote Madison, state leaders pinned their hopes on the convention "to be held in May next in Philadelphia." The actions of state assemblies confirmed Madison's observation. Of the twelve states represented at the gathering—the pro-agrarian Rhode Island refused to send delegates—eight appointed delegates from October 16, 1786, to February 28, 1787, during the most threatening stages of Shays' Rebellion.

As well as helping to guarantee good attendance, fears over agrarian uprising affected decisions made at the federal convention. North and South, delegates sought to block paper money and tender laws, two measures tied to backcountry discontent and insurrection. Connecticut lawyer Oliver Ellsworth "thought this a favorable moment to shut and bar the door against paper money" and tender laws. "The mischiefs of the various experiments which had been made, were now fresh in the public mind and had excited the disgust of all the respectable part of America." To guard against the two measures, convention members proposed that no state shall "coin money, emit bills of credit, making anything but gold and silver coin a tender in payment of debts." By this decision, observed Benjamin Rush, the delegates gave America the "advantage of a future exemption from paper money and tender laws."

State leaders also framed provisions to guard against future domestic unrest. According to some prominent Americans, the Shaysite turmoil had hurt the prospects of merchants engaged in international trade. "Shutting up the courts of *justice*," contended a group of Boston wholesalers and lawyers, "loudly proclaims to our foreign creditors their *total insecurity*." British merchants, they warned, eventually would withdraw all credit and would completely cut commercial ties with their American counterparts due to fears of property loss at the hands of the rebels. Perceiving a similar link between the Shaysite

troubles and commercial stagnation in 1786, George Washington felt "the commotions among the Eastern people have sunk our national character much below par," bringing American "Credit to the brink of a precipice." Washington may have accurately described the situation. As early as November 1786, a London journal instructed "all our traders not to have any trans-Atlantic dealings, except for ready money" due to the "flames of civil war" bursting forth in New England.

Making a connection between domestic turmoil and commercial decline, most state leaders agreed upon the urgent need for some coercive measures to suppress future insurgency. "A certain portion of military force is absolutely necessary in large communities. Massachusetts is now feeling the necessity," Alexander Hamilton told the Philadelphia convention on June 18, 1787. Virginia planter George Mason expressed the same sentiments a month later. "If the General Government should have no right to suppress rebellions against particular states, it will be in a bad situation indeed," he told fellow delegates. "As rebellions against itself originate in and against individual states, it must remain a passive spectator of its own subversion."

To suppress future rural rebellions and slave insurrections, state officials recommended two types of military force. Some delegates at Philadelphia pushed for national control of the militia. George Mason "introduced the subject of regulating the militia. He thought such power necessary to be given to the General Government." Since "the states neglect their militia now," agreed James Madison, "the discipline of the militia is evidently a *National* concern, and ought to be provided for in the *National* Constitution." He warned that "without such a power to suppress insurrections, our liberties might be destroyed by domestic faction." Other delegates suggested a national army to put down uprisings. In times of widespread domestic upheaval, Pinckney of South Carolina had "but a scanty faith in the militia. There must also be a real military force. This alone can effectively answer the purpose. The United States have been making an experiment without it, and we see the consequences in their rapid approaches to anarchy." "The apprehension of the national force will have a salutary effect in preventing insurrections," added merchant-speculator John Langdon of New Hampshire.

State leaders in Philadelphia provided for both types of military force in the proposed Constitution. They conferred upon the proposed Congress powers "for calling forth the militia to execute the laws of the Union, suppress insurrections and repel invasions; to provide for organizing, arming, and disciplining the militia, and for governing such part of them as may be employed in service of the United States." Although they did not create a standing army, the nationalists additionally provided Congress with the ability "to raise and support armies" for a maximum of two years.

After giving military powers to the proposed national government, the delegates assured the states of protection against domestic discord. According to the provisions of the so-called guarantee clause, the national government would give each state protection "on application of the legislature, or of the Executive (when the legislature cannot be convened) against domestic violence." "The object," noted Pennsylvania lawyer James Wilson who himself had been the target of a Philadelphia crowd in 1779, "is merely to secure the states against dangerous commotions, insurrections, and rebellions." Shays' Rebellion may have motivated Wilson's support of the clause. "I believe it is generally not known on what a perilous tenure we held our freedom and independence" during the Massachusetts troubles, he explained. "The flames of internal insurrection were ready to burst out in every quarter . . . and from one end to the other of the continent, we walked in ashes concealing fire beneath our feet." Instructed by experience gleaned during the Shaysite uprising, delegates at Philadelphia such as James Wilson passed the guarantee clause. In addition, they agreed upon a suspension of the writ of habeas corpus "in cases of rebellion" and, to discourage rebels from hiding in bordering states as the Shaysites had done after February 1787, the delegates proposed that:

A person charged in any state with treason, felony, or other crime, who shall flee from justice, and be found in another state, shall on demand of the executive authority of the state from which he fled, be delivered up.

Although not dominating the Philadelphia debates, concern with domestic unrest proved important to many decisions made at the convention.

Framed at least partly in response to mercantile fear of rural insurrection, the proposed Constitution gained support from the commercial interest and met stiff opposition from the yeomanry in Massachusetts. According to Henry Knox, "the new Constitution is received with great joy by all the commercial part of the community. The people of Boston are in raptures with it as it is." Besides the "commercial part of the state," added Knox, "all the men of considerable property, the clergy, the lawyers, including the judges of the court, and all the officers of the late army" advocated the "most vigorous government." Among the ranks of the Massachusetts nationalists stood former governor James Bowdoin, Governor John Hancock, "three judges of the supreme court—fifteen members of the Senate, twenty from among the most respectable clergy —ten, or twelve of the first characters of the bar —Judges of Probate, High Sheriffs of Counties, and many other respectable people, merchants, etc.," including wholesalers William Phillips, Caleb Davis, John Coffin Jones, Thomas Russell, and Tristram Dalton.

In contrast, Massachusetts Antifederalism gained its impetus from the rural areas. "The *whole opposition,* in this commonwealth, is *that cursed spirit of insurgency* that prevailed last year," contended Henry Jackson who sat in the gallery of the Massachusetts state house during the debates. Jackson's friend Henry Knox likewise ascribed resistance to the Constitution "to the late insurgents, and all those who abetted their designs." Although somewhat overrating the influence of Shaysism and downplaying the importance of Maine farmers and the pacifist whalers of Nantucket in the Antifederalist cause,

Knox and Jackson nevertheless captured the Shaysite orientation of the opponents to the Constitution. Direction of the Antifederalists fell to twenty-nine former insurgents, among them Phanuel Bishop of Rehoboth and a few farmers from Maine.

Of the few merchants and professionals opposing the Constitution, most offered only lukewarm resistance to the proposed government. Antifederalist merchant Elbridge Gerry of Marblehead, for example, accepted the basic tenets of the Constitution. On October 18, 1787, he told legislative leaders Samuel Adams and James Warren that he believed the federal plan had "great merit and by proper amendments, may be adapted to the 'exigencies of government,'" pledging "to support that which is finally adopted." Two years later, the Marblehead merchant admitted to his overall approval of the Constitution. "I was never for rejecting the Constitution, but for suspending the ratification until it could be amended," he explained to his friend John Wendall. Lawyer James Sullivan similarly accepted the general premises of the new government, objecting merely to specific provisions. "I have this day seen the report of the Convention and cannot express the heartfelt satisfaction I have from it," he wrote on September 23, 1787. "I am more than pleased, having only one doubt, which is, whether the object of the judicial power is well defined." By mildly criticizing the Constitution, merchants and lawyers such as Gerry and Sullivan stood out conspicuously among the mercantile elite, but they provided little leadership to the rural-based Antifederalist movement.

The objections to the proposed Constitution revealed the rural orientation of most Massachusetts Antifederalists. To Antifederalists such as "Cornelius," the new government laid the foundation "for throwing the whole power of the federal government into the hands of those who are in the mercantile interest; and for the landed, which is the greatest interest of this country, to lie unrepresented, forlorn, and without hope." Some Antifederalists believed that the mercantile elite would seize power through the proposed national military force. With national military

power, argued farmer Amos Singletary of Sutton, "lawyers and men of learning, and monied men" expected to "get all the power and all the money into their own hands, and then they will swallow up all us little folks, like the great Leviathan," degrading independent farmers to tenants or wage laborers. Fearing such a fate for Massachusetts farmers, Phanuel Bishop warned delegates at the ratification convention that "the liberties of the yeomanry are at an end." Antifederalists such as farmer Samuel Nasson consequently urged fellow representatives to "show to the world that you will not submit to tyranny" by defeating the Constitution.

The showdown between the commercial and the agrarian interests came on February 6, 1788. As convention president John Hancock took the roll call, a vast majority of seaboard delegates joined hands with representatives from inland market towns such as Worcester, Stockbridge, and Springfield in approving the document. Of the towns with Shaysite sympathies, ninety voted against the Constitution, and a mere seven supported the plan. The rest of the opposition centered in other Maine and western Massachusetts farming communities. After the ballots had been tabulated, Hancock announced the results. The Constitution had passed by a slim margin of 187 to 168.

The victory of the nationalists arose from a variety of factors. Holding the ratification assembly in Boston undoubtedly gave the mercantile group an undue influence over convention proceedings and made possible the superior organization of the commercial interest. The coastal site of the convention also imposed a significant financial burden upon some inland towns for transportation costs, prohibiting about fifty Antifederalist towns from sending delegates. The pronationalist outlook of most newspapers in Massachusetts furthered the nationalist cause while the addition of amendments during the final days of the session probably coaxed a few yeomen into the nationalist ranks. A last-minute endorsement of the Constitution by a supposedly bedridden Governor Hancock similarly helped the nationalists. According to Boston merchant Caleb Gibbs, if

Hancock had not "appeared in convention, it was more than probable that *important* question would have been lost." Moreover, five states had already ratified the document by the time of the Massachusetts contest, lending legitimacy to nationalist arguments. Coupled with the fears generated by Shays' Rebellion, these factors united the mercantile interest against the Shaysites and their sympathizers who opposed the Constitution.

Shays' Rebellion, then, marked an important point in the social development of the United States, as evidenced by the reaction of the dominant commercial elite to it on the regional and national levels. As George Washington wrote to George Richards Minot after the publication of Minot's *History of the Insurrections in Massachusetts* in 1788, "the series of events which followed from the conclusion of the War, forms a link of no ordinary magnitude, in the chain of the American Annals. That portion of domestic History, which you have selected for your narrative deserved particularly to be discussed."

13

TWO VISIONS OF THE CONSTITUTION

DREW R. McCOY

The men who met in 1787 to consider how best to reform the national government were of a variety of minds. Northerners, southerners, from cities and the countryside, these men represented the diverging interests that marked early America. Yet, whatever their differences, these men shared a common concern: as leaders of the world's newest republic, how could they prevent the inevitable slide into decline and despotism that marked the history of all previous republics? To these men, schooled in the classical doctrine that republics required a virtuous people who could put self-interest aside, the competing interests of class, region, and party were sure signs of decay and impending doom. How then could they act to prevent these social divisions from developing in America?

As Drew R. McCoy demonstrates, the men of 1787 offered two answers. Following Benjamin Franklin, many saw the large expanses of land in the West as a safety valve, a way of offering every American a plot of land that would guarantee his family's independence. With every American a small-holder of property, there would be no large accumulations of wealth to challenge the virtuous government of the republic, and every citizen would have a stake, and interest, in society.

A different and more modern view was offered by Alexander Hamilton, who thought the entire Whig conception of government, upon which so much of contemporary thought rested, misconceived. Instead, Hamilton envisioned America as a great commercial and industrial empire on the model of Great Britain. For him the creation of classes and competing interests was both inevitable and ultimately desirable. Much like modern-day conservatives, Hamilton saw capitalists as the creators of national wealth and sought to link the state with these men of wealth, thus augmenting their power and influence in society and ensuring American economic development. In this way Hamilton hoped to move America away from the agrarian republic of Franklin and Jefferson and make it into a modern industrial state. As McCoy shows, it was ultimately these two notions of national development that competed at the Constitutional Convention of 1787–1788.

Compare these competing notions of national development as expressed in the debate over the Constitution with the political violence of the 1790s, discussed by John R. Howe in Reading 14. Do these two visions help explain the intensity of rhetoric and personal feeling of the postratification decade?

While speaking in January 1811 in defense of the constitutionality of the Bank of the United States, a Virginia congressman rhetorically asked his colleagues if the authors of the Constitution had not wisely anticipated the irrepressible consequences of social development in America:

Is it in the least probable that the men selected for their wisdom, perfectly acquainted with the progress of man in every age; who foresaw the changes which the state of society must undergo in this country from the increase of population, commerce, and the arts, could act so absurdly, as to prescribe a certain set of means to carry on the operations of a Government intended not only for the present but for future generations?

No doubt the framers would have been pleased with this assessment of their prescience. By the summer of 1787 most of them were acutely aware that America was maturing rapidly and that the future promised the development of an even more complex and sophisticated society. Not all of them found it easy to confront the implications of this promise, but very few refused to accept its inevitability. Even those who had not lost faith in Franklin's original vision of a youthful republic recognized more clearly than ever that they could hope only to forestall for as long as possible the unavoidable ramifications of social development.

"Civilization and corruption have generally been found," noted one of the more pessimistic American observers in 1785, "to advance with equal steps." Ultimately, the United States would become as corrupt as the most advanced areas of Europe; yet it was undoubtedly within the power of its citizens to place this "sad catastrophe at a distance." Perhaps more than any other prominent American of the 1780s, James Madison thought precisely in these terms. Like most supporters of the new Constitution, this astute young Virginian believed that a reorganization of American government was the necessary prerequisite to the establishment of a republican political economy. Madison later discovered, however, that not all of his Federalist colleagues shared his particular conception of a republican America; some of them, he was appalled to learn, even thought in terms of deliberately promoting what he thought it necessary to forestall. Different men were developing quite different solutions to the persistent problem of adapting the traditional republican impulse to modern commercial America. Although the ideological flux of the

1780s created the basis for the Federalist consensus of 1787, it also assured future controversy about the precise meaning of American republicanism and the role of the new federal government in securing it.

Madison's initial post-war vision of a republican America was quite similar in its general outline to Franklin's, for above all Madison thought in terms of developing across space rather than through time. Westward expansion was central to Madison's outlook, but equally important were his commitments to the principles of commercial liberalism and to the promise of a new, more open international commercial order. The dynamics of the Virginian's vision were straightforward. If Americans could continue to resort to virgin lands while opening adequate foreign markets for their produce, the United States would remain a nation of industrious farmers who marketed their surpluses abroad and purchased the "finer" manufactures they desired in return. Household industry would be relied upon to supply the coarser manufactures that were necessary to prevent a dangerously unfavorable balance of trade. Like Adam Smith, Madison believed this brand of social "development" proper because it comported with natural law. America could remain young and virtuous, while offering both a haven for the landless poor of Europe and a bountiful market for the advanced manufacturers that a fully peopled Europe was forced to produce. Indeed, Madison's commitment to westward expansion and "free trade" put him in the mainstream of republican thought at the end of the war.

Like most Americans, however, Madison always realized that the viability of landed expansion in America was contingent on the ability of new settlers to get their surpluses to market. If frontier farmers had no way of marketing what they produced, there was little incentive to emigrate to the West at all. A non-existent or inaccessible market would turn those who did settle the frontier into lethargic subsistence farmers instead of industrious republicans. This perception of the importance of commerce to the settlement of the frontier had always carried serious implications for the character of American society. If the men and women who emigrated to the West were not properly tied to a commercial nexus, various commentators had long suggested, they would degenerate into a socially and politically dangerous form of savagery. Expressions of this concern often accompanied appeals for the construction of "internal improvements"—roads and canals—that would rescue the fringes of American settlement from this danger by integrating them into a commercial economy. As early as 1770, for example, Pennsylvanians anxious to promote a canal in their state had typically cited the "complicated and numerous" mischiefs that arose from the isolation of their western settlements. "It is from hence," one writer asserted, "that many of the distant back inhabitants are become uncivilized, and little better than barbarians.—They are lazy, licentious, and lawless—and, instead of being useful members of society, are become seditious, and dangerous to the community." Once these settlers were drawn into the civilizing orbit of commerce, however, a dramatic transformation in their character would occur: "The uncivilized will, by a communication with the civilized, lose their ignorance and barbarism. They will learn industry from the industrious, virtue from the virtuous, loyalty from the loyal; and thereby become useful members of society, and good subjects." Most important, they would be molded into productive citizens: "Render it practicable for them to gain by their industry, and they will be industrious, and, by their industry, add to the surplus of our foreign exportation." This matter of civilizing the West had seemed particularly pressing before the Revolution to eastern Pennsylvanians who were disturbed by the chronic political turmoil on their frontier, but the content and wide-ranging implications of their concern were of continuing relevance to all American republicans who worried about the character of their landed expansion.

As America looked westward in the 1780s, control of the Mississippi River to its mouth became an essential goal of national policy, for this river was the necessary avenue to foreign markets

for those who were settling the immediate frontier. This concern drew the United States into an inevitable confrontation with the Spanish, who in early 1784 formally denied Americans the right to navigate the Mississippi and to deposit their goods at New Orleans. The problem of gaining uncontested American control of the Mississippi River arose from disputes over the boundary settlements of the peace treaties that ended the Revolution and would not be fully resolved until the Louisiana Purchase of 1803. During the initial decade of independence, control of the Mississippi posed an especially disturbing dilemma for Madison and other American republicans.

Madison was both outraged and perplexed by the unexpected display of Spanish arrogance, and he insisted that it was not in the interests of either Spain or the United States to deny Americans use of the Mississippi. Writing to Jefferson in the summer of 1784, Madison argued that American settlement of the backcountry, which only a free use of the Mississippi could promote, would benefit all European nations who traded with the United States by delaying the establishment of competitive American manufactures for many years and by increasing the consumption of foreign manufactures. If Americans were kept profitably occupied in agriculture, in other words, there would be no "supernumerary hands" to produce manufactures who might compete with foreign producers for the American market. In a passage that reflected many of the traditional assumptions of eighteenth-century political economy, Madison sketched two possible scenarios for American development:

The vacant land of the U.S. lying on the waters of the Mississippi is perhaps equal in extent to the land actually settled. If no check be given to emigrations from the latter to the former, they will probably keep pace at least with the increase of people, till the population of both become nearly equal. For 20 or 25 years we shall consequently have few internal manufactures in proportion to our numbers as at present, and at the end of that period our imported manufactures will be doubled. . . . Reverse the case and suppose the use of the Miss. denied to us, and the consequence is that many of our supernumerary hands who in the former case would [be] husbandmen on the waters of the Missipi will on this other supposition be manufacturers on this [side] of the Atlantic: and even those who may not be discouraged from seating the vacant lands will be obliged by the want of vent for the produce of the soil and of the means of purchasing foreign manufactures, to manufacture in a great measure for themselves.

The thrust of Madison's analysis was clear; in order to remain predominatly agricultural, America needed to combine landed and commercial expansion. If, on the contrary, Americans were denied access to export markets for their produce, a fundamental reorientation of their political economy in the direction of increased manufacturing was inevitable.

The diplomatic crisis in the West neatly fused the issues of western expansion and foreign trade, but Madison's concern with the latter issue extended far beyond the question of the Mississippi River. By the mid-1780s the commercial crisis afflicting the United States was wreaking havoc in virtually all areas of the country. This commercial problem, according to Madison, spawned the political and moral chaos that threatened the republican character of America. "Most of our political evils," he wrote in March 1786, "may be traced up to our commercial ones, as most of our moral may to our political." Like most Americans, Madison was particularly concerned with the restrictions Britain placed on American trade with its West Indian islands. Many Americans argued that the interest of every state was involved with this trade and, in a broader sense, that American commerce as a whole was dependent on it, since without a prosperous intercourse with these islands the balance of American trade with Great Britain would inevitably be unfavorable. "Access to the West Indies," as Jefferson put it in 1785, "is indispensably necessary to us." Several ways existed to improve the unfavorable balance of American trade, including the exercise of self-restraint on the part of those citizens who overindulged in their consumption of foreign lux-

uries. The key for Madison, however, was to liberate American trade from the shackles of British mercantilism. Above all, the United States had to break down the barriers that confined its commerce to "artificial" channels and denied it full access to "natural" markets like those in the West Indies.

By 1786 many Americans had decided that a policy of commercial retaliation against restrictions on their trade was mandatory. Few of them, however, could match Madison's faith in the efficacy of such a policy. His confidence in the ability of the United States to coerce Britain and other foreign countries into lowering barriers to American commerce was predicated on several key assumptions, the primary belief being that a young, virile society had natural advantages in its intercourse with older, fully peopled, more complex societies. Due to its highly advanced, luxury-ridden condition, for instance, Britain depended on foreign demand to employ its surplus inhabitants. "It is universally agreed," wrote one American of England, "that no country is more dependent on foreign demand, for the superfluous produce of art and industry;—and that the luxury and extravagance of her inhabitants, have already advanced to the ultimate point of abuse, and cannot be so increased, as to augment the home consumption, in proportion to the decrease that will take place on a diminution of foreign trade." The prosperity of the British economy was thus contingent on access to the rich American market. Should the United States ever restrict this market for British manufactures in retaliation for restraints on its export trade, the "manufacturing poor" in England would be thrown out of work and perhaps even starve. Such were the pitfalls, Franklin and Madison would have reminded the British, of a mercantilist political economy geared to the exportation of finer manufactures and luxuries.

By 1786 Madison thought it obvious that the implementation of an effective commercial policy, as well as the resolution of the crisis in the West, required a national government stronger than the Continental Congress. In a broader sense, this reorganization of the American political system was necessary to create the basis for a republican political economy. Madison feared, as did many other members of the American elite, that the disorder and unrest of the 1780s signified the decay of industry, diligence, frugality, and other republican character traits among the American people. The task at hand was to form a national political economy capable of permitting and encouraging Americans to engage industriously in virtue-sustaining occupations. To Madison this task entailed the creation of a central political authority able to reverse the dangerous trends of the decade and to stave off, for as long as possible, the advance of America into a more complicated and dangerous stage of social development. Because social conditions in the United States encouraged such reflection, Madison entered the constitutional convention in the spring of 1787 having already given much serious thought to the problems of poverty and unemployment in advanced, densely populated societies.

Of particular interest in this regard is an exchange of letters between Madison and Jefferson in late 1785 and early 1786. Writing from France, Jefferson pondered the plight of the laboring and idle poor of Europe. He blamed their wretchedness on an unequal division of property and entrenched feudal privilege, then further observed that "whenever there is in any country, uncultivated lands and unemployed poor, it is clear that the laws of property have been so far extended as to violate natural right." The earth had been given as a common stock for all men to labor and live on, and "if, for the encouragement of industry we allow it to be appropriated, we must take care that other employment be furnished to those excluded from the appropriation." Jefferson extended this analysis of the situation in France to his native land. Although it was "too soon yet in our country to say that every man who cannot find employment but who can find uncultivated land, shall be at liberty to cultivate it, paying a moderate rent," it was "not too soon to provide by every possible means that as few as possible shall be without a little portion of land." Indeed, Jefferson's sobering contact with the landless poor in Europe made him all the more anxious to prevent the development of a similar class in America.

Madison agreed that Jefferson's reflections formed "a valuable lesson to the Legislators of every Country, and particularly of a new one." However, in assessing the causes of the comparative comfort of the people in the United States, at least for the present, he asserted that more was involved than the absence of entrenched feudal privileges. "Our limited population," Madison argued, "has probably as large a share in producing this effect as the political advantages which distinguish us." "A certain degree of misery," he stated, as a general rule "seems inseparable from a high degree of populousness." This rule had profoundly disturbing implications for Madison, because it meant that even if a nation's land was equitably distributed and its laws thoroughly liberal and republican, a large population in itself might still create dangerous social problems. "No problem in political economy has appeared to me more puzzling," he wrote,

> than that which relates to the most proper distribution of the inhabitants of a Country fully peopled. Let the lands be shared among them ever so wisely, and let them be supplied with labourers ever so plentifully; as there must be a great surplus of subsistence, there will also remain a great surplus of inhabitants, a greater by far than will be employed in cloathing both themselves and those who feed them, and in administering to both, every other necessary and even comfort of life. What is to be done with this surplus? Hitherto we have seen them distributed into manufacturers of superfluities, idle proprietors of productive funds, domestics, soldiers, merchants, mariners, and a few other less numerous classes. All these classes not withstanding have been found insufficient to absorb the redundant members of a populous society.

Madison thus wrestled with the familiar problem of securing viable and sufficient sources of employment for the landless human surplus characteristic of the highly developed, old countries of Europe. He was struck, furthermore, by a depressing irony. Referring to the "manufacturers of superfluities, idle proprietors of productive funds, domestics, soldiers, merchants, mariners," and the like, he observed that "a reduction of most of those classes enters into the very reform which appears so necessary and desirable." The equal, more republican division of landed property that Jefferson espoused, he explained, would inevitably lead to "a greater simplicity of manners, consequently a less consumption of manufactured superfluities, and a less proportion of idle proprietors and domestics," while a "juster government" would also occasion "less need of soldiers either for defence against dangers from without, or disturbances from within." Republican reforms thus eventually compounded rather than ameliorated the problem, since they closed off the customary avenues of escape for an idle, surplus population. For this reason, Madison implied, the dilemma in a "fully-peopled" republic would ironically be even worse than in a corrupt, luxury-ridden society.

As always, Madison had one eye on the American future. During the constitutional convention, Charles Pinckney of South Carolina chastised his countrymen for considering themselves "the inhabitants of an old instead of a new country," and Madison's response to this charge is revealing. Pinckney made the traditional argument for America's youthfulness by pointing to the West: "In a new Country, possessing immense tracts of uncultivated lands, where every temptation is offered to emigration and where industry must be rewarded with competency, there will be few poor, and few dependent." Indeed, Pinckney concluded, "that vast extent of unpeopled territory which opens to the frugal and industrious a sure road to competency and independence will effectually prevent for a considerable time the increase of the poor or discontented, and be the means of preserving that equality of condition which so eminently distinguishes us."

Madison was not convinced by Pinckney's analysis of American society. "In all civilized Countries," he observed, "the people fall into different classes havg. a real or supposed difference of interests." In addition to creditors and debtors, farmers, merchants, and manufacturers, there "will be particularly the distinction of rich and poor." Madison agreed with Pinckney that America had neither the hereditary distinctions of rank nor the horrendous extremes of wealth and poverty that characterized Europe, but he quickly added that "we cannot however be regarded even at this time, as one homogeneous mass, in which every thing that affects a part will affect in the same manner the whole." Indeed, America was already a fairly complex, stratified society. "The man who is possessed of wealth, who lolls on his sofa or rolls in his carriage," Madison was reported to have argued, "cannot judge of the wants or feelings of the day laborer." And when Madison looked at the inevitable ramifications of continued population growth in America, he became even more pessimistic. "In framing a system which we wish to last for ages, we shd. not lose sight of the changes which ages will produce. An increase of population will of necessity increase the proportion of those who will labour under all the hardships of life, and secretly sigh for a more equal distribution of its blessings." When in time such men would outnumber "those who are placed above the feelings of indigence," there would be a serious danger of social upheaval and of radical attacks on property. Referring to the Shays uprising in Massachusetts, Madison remarked that although "no agrarian attempts have yet been made in this Country, . . . symptoms of a leveling spirit . . . have sufficiently appeared in a certain quarters to give notice of the future danger."

Madison returned to this general theme again and again during the course of the convention. "In future times," he predicted of the United States, "a great majority of the people will not only be without landed, but any other sort of property." As the population of America increased, its political economy would inevitably become more complex. Although the relative proportion between the commercial and manufacturing classes and the agricultural was yet small, Madison contended that it would daily increase. "We see in the populous Countries in Europe now," he declared, "what we shall be hereafter." And in the Virginia ratifying convention of 1788, Madison hinted strongly that the day when "population becomes so great as to compel us to recur to manufactures" lay not very far in the future: "At the expiration of twenty-five years hence, I conceive that in every part of the United States, there will be as great a population as there is now in the settled parts. We see already, that in the most populous parts of the Union, and where there is but a medium, manufactures are beginning to be established."

The profound impact of the economic and social dislocations of the 1780s on Madison's vision of America is perhaps best revealed in his correspondence with John Brown in 1788 concerning a constitution for the prospective state of Kentucky. Madison argued strongly that property be made a qualification for suffrage, and that there be a dual suffrage for the upper and lower houses of the legislature in order to protect both "the rights of persons" and "the rights of property." His reasoning here was that both the indigent and the rich, who invariably formed classes in any civilized society, had each to be given its proper share in government. Madison reminded Brown that although the specific need to protect property rights had not been given much attention at the commencement of the Revolution, subsequent experience had demonstrated the naiveté of the assumption that the United States was a peculiarly undifferentiated society in which "the rights of property" and "the rights of persons" were synonymous.

> In the existing state of American population, and American property[,] the two classes of rights were so little discriminated [at the commencement of the Revolution] that a provision for the rights of persons was supposed to include of itself those of property, and it was natural to infer from the tendency of republican laws, that these different interests would be more and more identified. Experience and investigation have however produced more correct ideas on this subject. It is now observed that in all populous countries, the smaller part only can be interested in preserving the rights of property. It must be foreseen that America, and Kentucky itself will by degrees arrive at this state of Society; that

in some parts of the Union a very great advance is already made towards it.

Prudence thus demanded that the Kentucky constitution, as well as the United States Constitution, allow for the changes that the future would inevitably bring.

While Madison always worried about the political implications of these future developments, he never really resolved his underlying dilemma: once the inevitable pressure of population increase had created large numbers of propertyless indigents in America, what would sustain the republican character of the United States? At the core of republicanism was an intense concern with the autonomy or "independence" of the individual, and particularly with the material or economic basis for that autonomy. Since the abject dependence of the landless or laboring poor rendered them vulnerable to bribery, corruption, and factious dissension, a society with large numbers of these dependents was hardly suited to the republican form. Although Madison evinced a fatalistic acceptance of the future as he envisioned it, always urging that the new Constitution be so drawn that it could accommodate these social changes, he seemed unable to escape the traditional fear that all republics, including the one in America, were necessarily short-lived. It was wise to anticipate and provide for future changes; it was even wiser to forestall their development for as long as possible. Madison's republic was in a race against time.

The new Constitution promised to create a government equal to the task of forestalling, if not of preventing, these adverse developments. A stronger national government with the power to raise revenue and regulate commerce would ideally be capable of resolving the foreign policy problems that threatened to prematurely age the country. Such a government could pave the way for westward expansion by dealing forcefully with threatening foreign powers like Spain, but even more important, it could fulfill the commercial promise of the Revolution by forcing the dismantling of the restrictive mercantilist systems that obstructed the marketing of American agricultural surpluses. As Oliver Ellsworth of Connecticut argued in defense of the Constitution, American farmers suffered because American merchants were "shut out from nine-tenths of the ports in the world" and forced to sell at low prices in the "few foreign ports" that were open to them. Addressing the farmers of America, he asserted that "you are oppressed for the want of power which can protect commerce, encourage business, and create a ready demand for the productions of your farms." Thomas Jefferson, writing in early 1789, agreed that the American system should be to "pursue agriculture, and open all the foreign markets possible to our produce."

Continued westward expansion would ease the impact of a rapidly increasing population in the United States, and the opening of foreign markets for American produce would further ensure that Americans not be forced into occupations detrimental to the republican character of their society. It could be hoped, then, that Madison's human "surplus" in America might continue to produce "necessaries" required by foreigners for as long as possible rather than be forced by adverse circumstances like those of the 1780s to become manufacturers of superfluities, idle properietors of productive funds, soldiers, or the like. In short, the exportation of American agricultural surpluses appeared to offer a tentative republican solution to the "problem in political economy" that had so puzzled the young Virginia. America needed open markets as well as open space to make republicanism work. Perhaps a government strong enough to encourage the proper form of westward expansion and to force free trade could answer the dilemma of population growth in an agricultural and republican nation—at least for the foreseeable future.

One of Madison's closest allies in the struggle to ratify the Constitution was a brilliant lawyer from New York, Alexander Hamilton, who several years earlier in *The Continentalist* had warned his countrymen against their obsession with classical republicanism. In many respects Hamilton was an anomaly; perhaps more than any of his countrymen, he had succeeded in discarding the traditional republican heritage that had so heavily influenced the Revolutionary mind. He was particularly receptive in this regard to the writings of David Hume as they applied both to political economy and to constitutional thought. Indeed, it seems clear that Hamilton's introduction to many of Hume's works during the course of the Revolution had greatly influenced the development of his social and political outlook. He came to accept the commercialization of society is not only inevitable but fundamentally salutary as well, and he never doubted that the real disposition of human nature was toward luxury and away from classical virtue. Such a condition, he concluded, made traditional or classical republicanism hopelessly irrelevant to the American experience. Any talk either of Spartan equality and virtuous agrarianism, or of fear of commercial corruption, was nothing more than sententious cant that evaded the necessary realities of life in modern commercial society. In this connection, his reaction to Pinckney's speech in the constitutional convention was even more incisive than Madison's. "It was certainly ture," Hamilton remarked, "that nothing like an equality of property existed: that an inequality would exist as long as liberty existed, and that it would unavoidably result from that very liberty itself." The "difference of property" in America was already great, and "commerce and industry" would inevitably increase it still further.

Hamilton's commitment to constitutional revision long predated the convention of 1787. He subscribed to the formula for reform that Robert Morris and other nationalists had established at the end of the war, a formula that integrated constitutional change with the funding of the Revolutionary debt and a vigorous program of economic expansion tied to the consolidation and mobilization of mercantile capital. Hamilton envisioned America not as a virtuous agrarian republic, but as a powerful, economically advanced modern state much like Great Britain—a state that would stand squarely on the worldly foundations of "corruption" that Bernard Mandeville had spoken of in *The Fable of the Bees.* Thus Hamilton's vision of the future was not clouded by the traditional republican fears that continued to plague Madison and much of agrarian America. He simply accepted social inequality, propertyless dependence, and virtually unbridled avarice as the necessary and inevitable concomitants of a powerful and prosperous modern society. In one sense, Madision was still caught between the conflicting claims of classical republicanism and modern commercial society, struggling to define and implement a viable synthesis that was relevant to the American experience. Hamilton had stepped confidently and unequivocally into modernity.

On a very general but significant level, therefore, Hamilton supported the new Constitution for reasons quite different from Madison's. He did not intend to use the new government as a means of promoting the conditions that would stabilize America at a predominantly agricultural state of development; he wanted instead to use that new government to push the United States as rapidly as possible into a higher stage of development, for he interpreted this change as progress, not decay. Unlike Madison, in other words, Hamilton had an unabashedly positive sense of development through time. As his famous economic reports of the next decade revealed, he looked forward to the establishment of advanced, highly capitalized manufacturers in the United States and did everything he could within the constraints of his fiscal system to promote them. An anonymous pamphleteer caught the spirit of Hamilton's vision in 1789 when, after praising England as "the most opulent and powerful nation in Europe," he urged the new national government to give every possible encouragement to large-scale manufactures, the hallmark of British greatness. To men of this stripe, England offered a positive rather than a negative model for American development. Both Madison and Hamilton had abandoned the idea of perpetual youth for the republic; both accepted the inevitability of social complexity and the futility of the purely classical vision. Nevertheless, they brought very different attitudes and expectations to bear on their incipient careers as national political leaders.

The new American government thus began its operations in April 1789 in an ideological environment that can best be described as confused and transitional. The dislocations of the 1780s had raised complex questions and problems about the nature of American society and its republican potential. Caught between ancient and modern ways of thinking, most Americans came to realize that there could be no simple formula for a republican America. Perhaps no better evidence of the recognition of this new complexity can be found than in two premiums offered by the *American Museum* in 1789. The first was for "the best essay on the proper policy to be pursued in America, with respect to manufactures—and on the extent to which they may be carried, so as to avoid, on the one hand, the poverty attendant on an injurious balance of trade—and, on the other, the vices—the misery —and the obstruction of population, arising from assembling multitudes of workmen together in large cities or towns." The second premium was for "the best essay on the influence of luxury upon morals—and the most proper mode, consistent with republican freedom, to restrain the pomp and extravagance of ambitious or vain individuals."

These premiums reflected an ideological universe in flux. No single individual, however, could possibly have done more to draw and harden the lines of ideological combat among Americans than Alexander Hamilton who, as the first secretary of the Treasury, quickly seized the policymaking initiative in the new federal government.

14

REPUBLICAN THOUGHT AND THE POLITICAL VIOLENCE OF THE 1790s

JOHN R. HOWE

By 1790 Anti-Federalism was moribund as a political movement, and most Americans, Federalists and Anti-Federalists alike, accepted the Constitution of 1788 as the foundation of national government. But the Federalist victory did not end factional strife. During the 1790s Anti-Federalist leaders worked tirelessly to build an opposition movement to counter the Federalist sweep of local, state, and national offices.

One crucial aspect of the struggle to build such an opposition movement in the new nation was the battle for men's minds (women would not become part of the political nation for another 130 years). As John Howe describes it, the ideological battle between Federalists and their opponents was characterized by a violence of language and a desperation of thought almost unique in American history. In explaining the unusually vitriolic contests of the 1790s, Howe turns to the notion of republicanism, which dominated American political thought during the eighteenth and early nineteenth centuries.

Republicanism was a theory of the nature and operation of those governments that derived their authority from the will of the people rather than from the hereditary power of a monarch or aristocracy. Republics, the theory held, were fragile creations constantly threatened by human frailties, of which the most dangerous was the corrupting nature of power. Popularly-based republics thus required an unusual degree of vigilance on the part of its citizens to keep those who held power in check. Seen through the lens of republicanism, the splenetic politics of the 1790s takes on a more understandable dimension: both Federalists and their opponents viewed each other, not as mere political opponents, but as caterpillars gnawing at the very substance of history's newest republic.

To what extent can the upheavals of the 1790s be explained by the apocalyptic visions of republican political theory? How important was the theory of republicanism to the farmers who revolted against ruinous taxes and threats of foreclosure in Shays' Rebellion, discussed in Reading 12? How far down the social scale did the idea of republicanism travel?

One of the characteristics of the 1790s that strikes the attention even upon first glance and demands explanation is the peculiarly violent character of American political life during these years.

Throughout our history, politics had not been a notably calm or gentlemanly affair. One need only recall some of the contests of the Jacksonian period, the Populist tactics of the late nineteenth

Reprinted from *American Quarterly,* 19 (Summer 1967), 147–165. Copyright 1967, Trustees of the University of Pennsylvania. Reprinted with permission of the author and *American Quarterly.*

century, the demagogy of Huey Long, or the rough and tumble of Joe McCarthy to realize this. But evidence abounds that the last decade of the eighteenth century constituted a time of peculiar emotion and intensity.

Indication of this is on every hand; for example, in the physical violence, both actual and threatened, which appeared with disturbing regularity. Note the forceful resistance within the several states to the authority of the central government. In Pennsylvania, the flash-point of civil disturbance seemed particularly low, as the Whiskey Rebellion and John Fries' brief rising attest. Or recall the high emotions generated first by such domestic measures as Hamilton's financial program and reinforced by the complex of issues, both foreign and domestic, revolving around the French Revolution and the near-war with France: the Alien and Sedition Acts and the Provisional Army, designed in substantial measure to rid the Federalists of effective political opposition at home; the bands of Jeffersonian militia, formed in the various states and cities from Baltimore to Boston, armed and openly drilling, preparing to stand against the Federalist army. During the critical days of 1798 and 1799, mobs roamed the streets of Philadelphia inspiring the President of the United States (as John Adams later recalled) to smuggle arms into his home secretly through the back streets.

Events of this sort, however, constituted neither the only nor indeed the most impressive form of violence displayed during the decade. Even more pervasive and ominous was the intensity of spirit and attitude displayed on every hand—and in no place more emphatically than in the political rhetoric of the time. Throughout American political life—in the public press, in speeches, sermons, the private correspondence of individuals—there ran a spirit of intolerance and fearfulness that seems quite amazing. Foreign travelers commented frequently upon it. "The violence of opinion," noted one Frenchman, the "disgraceful and hateful appellations . . . mutually given by the individuals of the parties to each other" were indeed remarkable. Party spirit, he concluded,

"infects the most respectable, as well as the meanest of men."

Men in the midst of the political controversy noted the same thing. "You and I have formerly seen warm debates and high political passions," observed Jefferson to Edward Rutledge in 1797. "But gentlemen of different politics would then speak to each other, and separate the business of the Senate from that of society. It is not so now. Men who have been intimate all their lives, cross the streets to avoid meeting, and turn their heads another way, lest they should be obliged to touch their hats. This may do for young men for whom passion is an enjoyment," Jefferson concluded. "But it is afflicting to peaceable minds." Virtually every political figure at some time or another expressed disgust at the abuse to which he was subjected. "I have no very ardent desire to be the butt of party malevolence," complained John Adams to his wife. "Having tasted of that cup, I find it bitter, nauseous, and unwholesome."

Further evidence of the ferocity and passion of political attitudes abounds: in the editorializing of William Cobbett, Benjamin Bache, and Philip Freneau; in the acidulous writings of Thomas Paine; in John Quincy Adams' *Publicola* articles. Perhaps most remarkable were the verbal attacks on the venerable Washington which mid-decade brought. In Virginia, men drank the toast: "A speedy Death to General Washington"; and one anti-Federalist propagandist (probably Pennsylvania's John Beckley) composed a series of articles with the express purpose of proving Washington a common thief. Few men (perhaps with the exception of William Cobbett) could surpass Thomas Paine for sheer ferocity of language. Attend to his public comment on Washington's retirement in 1796: "As to you, sir, treacherous in private friendship, and a hypocrite in public life; the world would be puzzled to decide, whether you are an apostate or an imposter; whether you have abandoned good principles, or whether you ever had any."

As one reads the political literature of the time, much of it seems odd and amusing, contrived and exaggerated, heavily larded with satire. But the satire contained venom; it appears amusing to us largely because our own rhetoric of abuse is simply different.

All in all, then, this seems a quite remarkable phenomenon, this brutality both of expression and behavior that marked American political life with such force during these years. Involved were more than disagreements over matters of public policy—though these were real enough. For the political battles of the 1790s were grounded upon a complete distrust of the motives and integrity, the honesty and intentions of one's political opponents. Men were quick to attribute to their enemies the darkest of purposes. Jefferson acknowledged in 1792 his grim distrust of Hamilton. "That I have utterly, in my private conversations, disapproved of the system of the Secretary of the Treasury," he told Washington, "I acknowledge and avow; and this was not merely a speculative difference. His system flowed from principles adverse to liberty, and was calculated to undermine and demolish the republic, by creating an influence of his department over the members of the legislature." James Madison was even more suspicious of Federalist intentions than was Jefferson. And Federalists were quick to find patterns of French Jacobinism in the Republican opposition at home. "I often think that the Jacobin faction will get the administration of our government into their hands ere long," worried Stephen Higginson; "foreign intriguers will unite with the disaffected and disappointed, with Seekers after places, with ambitious popular Demagogues, and the vicious and corrupt of every class; and the combined influence of all these . . . will prove too much for the feeble efforts of the other Citizens." Similarly, John Quincy Adams warned in 1798 that "the antifederalism and servile devotion to a foreign power still prevalent in the style of some of our newspapers is a fact that true Americans deplore. The proposal for establishing a Directory in America, like that of France, is no new thing."

By the middle of the decade, American political life had reached the point where no genuine debate, no real dialogue was possible for there no longer existed the toleration of differences which debate requires. Instead there had developed an emotional and psychological climate in which stereotypes stood in the place of reality. In the eyes of Jeffersonians, Federalists became monarchists or aristocrats bent upon destroying America's republican experiment. And Jeffersonians became in Federalist minds social levelers and anarchists, proponents of mob rule. As Joseph Charles has observed, men believed that the primary danger during these years arose not from foreign invaders but from within, from "former comrades-in-arms or fellow legislators." Over the entire decade there hung an ominous sense of crisis, of continuing emergency, of life lived at a turning point when fateful decisions were being made and enemies were poised to do the ultimate evil. "I think the present moment a very critical One with our Country," warned Stephen Higginson, "more so than any one that has passed. . . ."

In sum, American political life during much of the 1790s was gross and distorted, characterized by heated exaggeration and haunted by conspiratorial fantasy. Events were viewed in apocalyptic terms with the very survival of republican liberty riding in the balance. Perhaps most remarkably of all, individuals who had not so long before cooperated closely in the struggle against England and even in the creation of a firmer continental government now found themselves mortal enemies, the bases of their earlier trust somehow worn away.

Now the violent temper of American political life during the 1790s has often been noted by political scientists and historians; indeed, one can scarcely write about these years without remarking upon it. But almost without exception, students of the period have assumed the phenomenon as given and not gone much beyond its description. Professor Marshall Smelser has made the most sustained effort at explanation. The key to an understanding of the decade he finds in differences of political and social principle, and in state and sectional rivalries. Similar explanations are implicit in most other treatments of the period.

This argument is certainly to the point, for very real differences of principle and belief did distinguish Federalists from Jeffersonians. As I shall argue more fully in a moment, matters of social and political ideology were of paramount importance to Americans of the late eighteenth century; and this generation divided sharply in its basic definition of social and political life—particularly over the degree of equality and the proper balance between liberty and authority believed desirable. Certainly any explanation of political behavior during the 1790s must take these differences closely into account; nothing in this paper is intended to deny their importance.

I should like, however, to suggest a different approach to the problem; one which emphasizes not the points of opposition between Federalists and Jeffersonians but the peculiar pattern of attitudes and beliefs which most Americans, both Federalists and Jeffersonians, shared—that is, the dominant republican ideology of the time.

Historians have recently claimed that the American people throughout their history have been profoundly nonideological; that they are now and were equally so during the revolutionary era. Daniel Boorstin is at present perhaps the most articulate spokesman of this point of view. The American Revolution, he argues, was a "revolution without dogma." The revolutionary years "did not produce in America a single important treatise on political theory." In fact, during the latter part of the eighteenth century, "a political theory failed to be born." Indeed, Professor Boorstin insists, the revolutionary generation had no "need" for system-building, for their protests were simply "an affirmation of the tradition of British institutions." Missing was any "nationalist philosophy"; the American revolutionaries "were singularly free from most of the philosophical baggage of modern nationalism." In sum, "the American Revolution was in a very special way conceived as both a vindication of the British past and an affirmation of an American future. The British past was contained in ancient and living institutions rather than in doctrines; and the American future was never to be contained in a theory. The Revolution was thus a prudential decision taken by men of principle rather than the affirmation of a theory. What British institutions meant did not need to be articulated; what America might mean was still to be discovered."

Now this understanding of the revolutionary experience raises numerous difficulties. For one thing, the Revolution involved quite rash, even presumptuous, decisions. More importantly, the revolutionary generation was profoundly dogmatic, was deeply fascinated with political ideology—the ideology of republicanism. This was a generation of Americans which, perhaps more than any other, viewed the world about them very much through the lens of political ideology, and which found meaning in their own experience largely as republican theory explained it to them. This point emerges clearly enough from examination of early revolutionary tracts written during the 1760s and 1770s, the debates over the new constitutions constructed within the several states, argumentation over the proposed federal constitution, and the political wrangling of the 1790s. Recent studies of the Revolution's political ideology argue much the same point.

The revolutionary break with England and the task of constructing new governments made the American people consciously, indeed self-consciously, republican in loyalty and belief. However lightly royal authority may have rested on the colonies prior to the Revolution, they had then been fully loyal to the idea of monarchy. The English constitutional system they had regarded as the wisest and most benevolent ever devised by man.

With independence, however, they turned their backs willfully not only upon the Crown but upon the whole conception of monarchical government and became aggressively, even compulsively, republican in orientation. Bernard Bailyn is quite right in suggesting that the break with England forced the American people to sit down and systematically explore political principles for the first time in at least half a century, to come to grips intellectually with the political systems which they had already developed, and to decide where their newly embraced republicanism would carry them in the future. Indeed, the whole revolutionary era may be most profitably viewed as a continuing effort by the American people to decide what for them republicanism was to mean.

Republicanism, one quickly finds, is no easy concept to define. Certainly as used within the United States during the late eighteenth century the term remained supple and elusive. Most Americans agreed that republicanism implied an absence of monarchy and English-like aristocracy, and the establishment of governments directly upon the authority and will of the people. But beyond this, concerning the details of republican political forms, agreement vanished. The concept of republicanism was obviously subject to a variety of readings when individuals as diverse as Alexander Hamilton and Thomas Jefferson, John Adams and John Taylor could each claim allegiance to it.

If the men of this generation differed, however, over the specifics of republican theory, most of them shared a common body of assumptions about republican political society—the problems involved in its establishment and the prerequisites for its maintenance and survival—assumptions which together constituted what I would identify as a distinctive world-view, a republican set-of-mind encompassing certain patterns of thought common to both Federalists and Jeffersonians.

One of the fundamental elements of this republican world-view, indeed the most important element for the purposes of this paper, was a widespread belief in the essential frailty and impermanence of republican governments. This notion was founded jointly on the historical assumption that republics had never lasted for long at any time in the past and on the psychological premise that the moral prerequisites of a republican order were difficult if not impossible to maintain.

The men of the revolutionary generation were quite aware that history offered little promise of the success of their republican experiments. From their study of examples both ancient and modern, they knew that the life-span of most republics had been limited. Unlike the English republican theorists of the seventeenth century, they were impressed not with the possibilities of establishing permanent republican orders but with the diffi-

culties of maintaining them at all. Nowhere outside of the United States, with the exception of certain Swiss cantons and scattered European principalities, did republican government prevail by the time of the American Revolution. Of this single, brute historical fact the revolutionary generation was profoundly aware.

For one thing, republics had proved vulnerable historically to hostile threats from the outside, both direct military attack and more subtle forms of influence and subversion. The reasons for this were understood to be several. Republican government, at least by American definition, was described as limited government, carefully restricted in its powers and duties. Republican political society was characterized by a broad permissiveness, by the free play of individual liberty, by the absence of any powerful, dominating central authority; in short, by the minimizing of power (that is, the capacity of some individuals to coerce and control others). Thus, republican governments proved particularly susceptible to outright attack (for by definition there should be no standing army, no military machine ready to discourage external foes) and to manipulation by outside powers (the people, after all, could be easily reached and their sensibilities played upon).

To be sure, certain circumstances rendered the United States less vulnerable in this regard than other republics had been: their isolated geographical location, the people's sense of identity with and loyalty to their governments and their willingness to stand in their governments' defense. (The recent struggle against England had demonstrated this.) But still the problem remained, as John Jay took pains to point out in the first numbers of *The Federalist*. In numbers two through five, he warned vigorously against the dangers the American states faced from inadequate coordination of their relations with the outside world. The difficulties experienced under the Articles of Confederation, of course, he offered as evidence. Safety against foreign domination, he explained, depended on the states, "placing and continuing themselves in such a situation as not to *invite* hostility or insult. . . ." Nations, he reminded, make war "whenever they have a prospect of getting any thing from it." And such prospects were increased when a people seemed either incapable or unwilling to stand firmly in their own defense. Sensing the continuing suspicion of centralized government, Jay urged upon his readers the importance of learning from past experience and providing their central government with powers adequate to its own preservation. "Let us not forget," he concluded, "how much more easy it is to receive foreign fleets into our ports, and foreign armies into our country, than it is to persuade or compel them to depart." In the late eighteenth century, the American republic stood virtually alone in an overwhelmingly nonrepublican world; in a world, in fact, dominated by monarchies and aristocracies to which the very concept of republicanism was anathema. And the burden of this loneliness was keenly felt.

More importantly, republican governments were deemed frail because of their tendency toward internal decay. If there was one thing upon which virtually the entire revolutionary generation could agree, it was the belief that republican governments were closely dependent upon a broad distribution of virtue among the people. Virtue was one of those marvelously vague yet crucially important concepts that dotted late-eighteenth-century moral and political thought. As used within the United States, it signified the personal virtues of industry, honesty, frugality and so forth. But more importantly, it meant as well a certain disinterestedness, a sense of public responsibility, a willingness to sacrifice personal interest if need be to the public good. Montesquieu had identified virtue as the animating spirit of republican societies; and the American people fully agreed. "The foundation of every government," explained John Adams, "is some principle or passion in the minds of the people." The informing principle of republican government was virtue. "The only foundation of a free constitution," Adams repeated, "is pure virtue. . . ." To Mercy Warren, he made the same point: "public Virtue is the only Foundation of Republics." There had to be among the people a positive passion for the public good, superior to all private passions. In short, "the only reputable Principle and Doctrine must be that all things must give Way to the public."

Countless Americans echoed Adams' refrain. The problem was that virtue constituted a frail reed upon which to lean. For while men were capable of virtuous behavior, they were also and more often creatures of passion, capable of the most selfish and malicious actions. Americans liked to believe themselves more virtuous than other people, and American behavior during the active years of the revolutionary struggle had convinced many of them of this. The revolution had made extraordinary demands upon their public spiritedness, and they had proved themselves more than adequate to the test. The revolutionary trials had constituted a "furnace of affliction," John Adams believed, testing and refining the American character. The sucess of the struggle against England had demonstrated virtue's strength among the American people.

By the 1790s, however, the revolutionary crisis was over and it was widely believed that after a period of exhausting moral discipline, men were reverting to their more normal selfish, ambitious and extravagant ways. Evidence was on every hand. The greatest dissolvants of virtue, both private and public, were commonly recognized to be wealth and luxury, for these excited the selfish passions, set men into jealous competition with each other and dimmed their sense of obligation to the larger society. As Thomas Paine remarked in *Common Sense,* "commerce diminishes the spirit both of patriotism and military defence. And history informs us, that the bravest achievements were always accomplished in the non-age of a nation. . . ." "Youth is the seed-time of good habits," he repeated, "as well in nations as in individuals." After an extended period of economic dislocation, brought on by the break with the empire and the war with England, the late 1780s and 1790s witnessed an impressive economic recovery. And this returned prosperity raised powerful questions about American virtue.

Throughout the revolutionary era, gloomy observers had wondered if American virtue would prove lasting. "The most virtuous states have become vicious," warned Theophilous Parsons. "The morals of all people, in all ages, have been shockingly corrupted. . . . Shall we alone boast an exemption from the general fate of mankind? Are our private and political virtues to be transmitted untainted from generation to generation, through a course of ages?" Parsons and others had thought it doubtful. The dilemma was compounded by the belief that once begun, the erosion of virtue spiraled downward out of control. When the people grow lax, John Adams had explained, "their deceivers, betrayers, and destroyers press upon them so fast, that there is no resisting afterwards." Designing men forced their attack relentlessly. "The people grow less steady, spirited, and virtuous, the seekers more numerous and more corrupt, and every day increases the circles of their dependents and expectants, until virtue, integrity, public spirit, simplicity, and frugality, become the objects of ridicule and scorn, and vanity, luxury, foppery, selfishness, meanness, and downright venality swallow up the whole society." Though written during an earlier year, this reflected the moral and political logic of an entire generation and was the logic of moral and political crisis.

America's economic recovery raised a further problem. Another postulate of republican theory, deriving most clearly from Harrington, declared that republican governments were suitable only for societies which enjoyed a broad distribution of property. "Power follows property," ran the maxim; and republican government presumed the broad distribution of political power among the people. The problem arose from the fact that as wealth increased, its tendency was to consolidate in the hands of a few, thus threatening both the economic and political bases of republicanism. John Taylor in his *Enquiry into the Principles and Tendency of Certain Public Measures* (1794) made precisely these points. "It is evident that exorbitant wealth constitutes the substance and danger of aristocracy," he wrote. "Money in a state of civilization is power. . . . A democratic republic is endangered by an immense disproportion in wealth." J. F. Mercer of Maryland warned the federal Congress of the same thing. "A love

and veneration of equality is the vital principle of free Governments," he declared. "It dies when the general wealth is thrown into a few hands." Both Taylor and Mercer found this insidious tendency at work during the 1790s. Indeed Taylor's whole book was aimed directly at Hamilton's financial program and what Taylor conceived to be its effect in promoting the growth of a monied aristocracy. Mercer's comments were uttered in the context of a sustained attack upon Hamiltonian "stock-jobbers." Not only Jeffersonians were disturbed about the matter, however; for by the 1790s, John Adams was warning vigorously against the social and political dangers posed by a growing aristocracy of wealth.

One further element in the dominant republican ideology of these years contributed to the sense of vulnerability with which it seemed to be enveloped. This involved the problem of faction. Few notions were more widely held by the revolutionary generation than the belief that "faction," the internal splintering of society into selfish and competing political groups, was the chief enemy of republican political society. Republican government, as we have seen, depended essentially upon virtue's broad distribution among the people. Faction was virtue's opposite; instead of an overriding concern for the general good, faction presumed the "sacrifice of every national Interest and honour, to private and party Objects." The disruptive effects of faction increased as a society developed, as wealth increased, as the people became more numerous and their interests more disparate. Gradually, differences of interest hardened into political divisions, with parties contesting against each other for power. Voters were organized and elections manipulated, thus destroying both their political independence and integrity. Permanent party organizations took root, organizations which cared more for their own survival than for the society as a whole. In their resulting struggle, passions were further aroused, internal divisions deepened and ultimately civil conflict was brought on. Such was the deadly spiral into which republican governments too often fell.

Because of republicanism's vulnerability to

faction, republican governments were widely believed suitable only for small geographic areas with essentially homogeneous populations. Even during the 1770s and 1780s, when the various states had set about constructing their own republican systems, fears had been voiced that some of them (New York and Virginia were frequently mentioned) were too large and diverse. The problem was infinitely compounded when talk began of a continental republic encompassing thousands of square miles, sharply opposed economic interests and radically different ways of life. To attempt a republican government of such dimensions was to fly in the face both of accepted republican theory and the clearest lessons of historical experience. This, of course, is what the anti-federalists repeatedly argued. "The idea of an uncompounded republik," remarked one incredulous observer, "on an average of one thousand miles in length, and eight hundred in breadth, and containing six millions of white inhabitants all reduced to the same standard of morals, of habits, and of laws, is in itself an absurdity, and contrary to the whole experience of mankind." The argument had a powerful effect upon the whole course of constitutional debate, as is evidenced by the efforts of Madison and Hamilton in *The Federalist* to answer it.

As the decade of the 1790s progressed, the dangers of faction grew ever more compelling. Acknowledging the political divisions which had sharpened during his second administration, Washington spoke directly to the problem in his Farewell Address, issuing a warning which echoed the fears of the whole society. The latter half of the 1790s witnessed further intensification of the struggle between Federalists and Jeffersonians, bringing ever closer what seemed to many the ultimate danger: a division of the nation into two powerful political parties locked in deadly struggle with each other. In such a setting, it was easy to believe that the familiar pattern of republican collapse was threatening once more.

Again, republican governments were believed frail because liberty, which was peculiarly their product, was under constant attack from power. In this notion lay one of the basic political conceptualizations of the republican generation. History was seen as comprising a continuing struggle between liberty and tyranny, between liberty and power. In this contest, power was the aggressive element, threatening relentlessly through the medium of ambitious and misguided men to encroach upon and narrow liberty's domain. The antagonism between the two was believed inevitable and endless, for by definition they stood unalterably opposed: liberty signifying law or right, the freedom of individuals to determine their own destiny, and power specifying dominion, force, the compulsion of some men by others. The whole course of recorded history displayed the ceaseless antagonism between the two, and America was not to escape the dilemma. "A fondness for power," Alexander Hamilton had declared knowingly, "is implanted in most men, and it is natural to abuse it when acquired." With this belief, most Americans concurred. As Cecelia Kenyon has shown, the anti-federalists of 1787–88 were especially fearful of power's effects upon human nature. But the federalists shared their fears. The reality of this self-interested drive for power, as Professor Kenyon has shown, was "an attitude deeply imbedded and widely dispersed in the political consciousness of the age."

The dilemma posed by power's continuing encroachment upon liberty's domain provided what Edmund Morgan has identified as "the great intellectual challenge" of the revolutionary era: that is, how to devise ways of checking the inevitable operation of depravity in men who sought and wielded power. The devices most widely, indeed almost universally invoked to achieve this goal were the separation and balance of powers within government. The hope was that in these ways power could be kept under proper restraint by the prevention of its fatal accumulation in the hands of any single individual or group of men.

And yet problems immediately arose, for the American people were by no means in agreement concerning who or what was to be separated from or balanced against each other. Was the proper thing to separate executive, legislative and judicial powers? Or was the more important aim to balance the "constituted bodies" of society against each other: the rich versus the poor, the "aristocracy" versus the "democracy"? Throughout the revolutionary era, there remained substantial disagreement over what the notions of separation and balance really involved.

Moreover, given power's restless and unrelenting character, it was hard to believe that any system of separation or balance could prove permanent. The only hope for liberty's preservation lay in posing power against itself, in setting at balance men's self-interests. And yet given the dynamic character of power's advance, it seemed unlikely that any system of counterpoise could be permanently maintained. This, indeed, was one of the most powerful arguments that critics of the balanced government, such as John Taylor, developed.

A still further consideration contributing to the prevailing belief in the frailty of republican government, one which underlay and informed the notions of virtue and power which we have already examined, involved the revolutionary generation's understanding of the cyclical character of history. In this view, history consisted of the gradual rise and fall of successive empires, each for a period dominating the world and then giving way to another. Over the centuries, there had taken place a constant ebb and flow of ascendant nations, each rising to preeminence and then, after a period of supremacy, entering an era of decline and ultimately giving way to another. This process was often described in terms of a biological analogy; that is, political societies were believed to pursue a natural cycle of infancy, youth, maturity, old age and death. Every nation had unavoidably to pass through the full revolution. Governor James Bowdoin of Massachusetts described with particular clarity the law of cyclical development to which most Americans adhered. "It is very pleasing and instructive," Bowdoin declared,

> to recur back to the early ages of mankind, and trace the progressive state of nations and empires, from infancy to maturity, to old age and dissolution:—to observe their origin, their growth and improvement . . . to observe the progress of the arts

among them . . . to observe the rise and gradual advancement of civilization, of science, of wealth, elegance, and politeness, until they had obtained the summit of their greatness:—to observe at this period the principle of mortality, produced by affluence and luxury, beginning to operate in them . . . and finally terminating in their dissolution. . . . In fine—to observe, after this catastrophe, a new face of things; new kingdoms and empires rising upon the ruins of the old; all of them to undergo like changes, and to suffer a similar dissolution.

Not only did empires wax and wane, but every phase in their life cycle of growth, maturity and decline could be traced out in the character and behavior of their people. David Tappan, Hollis Professor of Divinity at Harvard, explained how this was true. In the early stages of development, he observed, nations were inhabited by men "industrious and frugal, simple in their manners, just and kind in their intercourse, active and hardy, united and brave." Gradually, the practice of such virtues brought the people to a state of manly vigor. They matured and became flourishing in wealth and population, arts and arms. Once they reached a certain point, however, their manners began to change. Prosperity infected their morals, leading them into "pride and avarice, luxury and dissipation, idleness and sensuality, and too often into . . . impiety." These and kindred vices hastened their ruin. A direct correlation existed, then, between national character and the stages of empire.

This cyclical theory of empire provided a perspective within which the events of the 1790s could be viewed, a way of reading their hidden—and ominous—meaning. For if it implied that in contrast to Europe, America was still young—an "Infant Country" it was frequently called—and on the ascent, it implied as well that eventually America must mature and enter its period of decline. And if this cyclical conception of moral and political change allowed success in the revolutionary contest to be interpreted as evidence of youthful virtue, it demanded that the moral decay, personal extravagance and internal bickering of the 1790s be accepted as indication that the American empire had reached its summit and begun its decline far more quickly than anticipated.

Few people, to be sure, jumped immediately to such a gloomy conclusion. The exhilaration of the Revolution continued to work its hopeful effects upon this generation of men. Even the most pessimistic individuals projected America's demise vaguely into the future; some refused to accept the theory's implications at all. Yet the logic of the argument could not be entirely escaped. At the least, it encouraged people to examine with minute care evidences of public and private morality and to search out patterns of significance in them. The doctrine, moreover, had a certain manic quality about it. During moments of hopefulness and success, it acted as a multiplier to expand the future's promise. And yet when the society became troubled, when virtue seemed to fade, when internal divisions deepened and the sense of common purpose receded, the cyclical doctrine could work just as powerfully in the opposite direction to enhance the sense of crisis. For the logic of the doctrine was clear: a nation's position in its cycle could be clearly perceived in the behavior of its people. And the downward slide, once begun, could not be reversed.

Finally, this sense of the instability of republican government was heightened still further by the American people's understanding of the critical importance of the historical moment through which they were passing. Few generations of Americans have so self-consciously lived an historical epic as did these men of the late eighteenth century. Virtually every important action they took over a span of more than three decades seemed a turning point of great significance: their defense of basic liberties against England, the declaration of national independence, the establishment of republican governments in the several states, the creation of a new national constitution. This sense of historic grandeur carried into the 1790s. As the first administrative agents of the national government, they found themselves setting precedent with every decision made, every act taken: laying the bases of both foreign and domestic policy, determining by their decisions how the new government would function in prac-

tice, how popular or elitist it would be, what powers it would possess and what would be retained by the states. "Many things which appear of little importance in themselves and at the beginning," explained Washington, "may have great and durable consequences from their having been established at the commencement of a new general government. It will be much easier," he continued, "to commence the administration, upon a well adjusted system, built on tenable grounds, than to correct errors or alter inconveniences after they shall have been confirmed by habits." Only with this in mind does the intensity of emotion generated by the debate over the use of titles or over President Washington's levees become understandable.

In effect, the American people were carrying further during the 1790s a process upon which they had been embarked for several decades: that is, of defining what republicanism within the United States should in fact mean. Every decision they made loomed as fundamentally important. Their opportunity, they firmly believed, would come but once, and if mishandled could not be recovered. Given the cycle of empire, never again would the American be so competent for the task of understanding or defending liberty. The insidious pressures of power, the perpetual tendency of virtue to decay, the relentless historical cycle of nations promised that.

Their moment, then, was historically unique. "How few of the human race," noted John Adams in wonder, "have ever enjoyed the opportunity of making an election of government, more than of air, soil, or climate for themselves or their children." Throughout history, other peoples had suffered under governments imposed by accident or the wiles of ambitious men. Americans, however, now faced the prospect of modeling their governments anew, "of deliberating upon, and choosing the forms of government under which they should live." To blunder in the face of such opportunity would be to compound their disaster.

Moreover, they firmly believed that upon the success of their venture hung the fate of republicanism not only for America but the entire world. "Let us remember that we form a government for millions not yet in existence," reminded one anxious soul. "I have not the act of divination. In the course of four or five hundred years, I do not know how it will work." "I consider the successful administration of the general Government as an object of almost infinite consequence to the present and future happiness of the citizens of the United States," acknowledged Washington.

And yet the success of this momentous undertaking was by no means assured. As late as the 1790s, the American people were painfully aware that theirs was still a political society in process of change; that their political institutions were new, lacking the habit of regularity which only long establishment could provide; that their republican faith was still undergoing definition. The whole venture, as witnesses repeatedly pointed out, remained very much an "experiment." They were embarked directly upon the task of "determining the national character"; of "fixing our national character," as one Jeffersonian remarked, and "determining whether republicanism or aristocracy [the Federalists would say democracy]" would prevail. The society remained malleable, its understanding of "true" republican principles not yet firmly developed, the design of its social and political institutions still unclear.

In sum, the Americans of this generation found themselves living on a balance, at a moment in history given to few men, when decisions they made would determine the whole future of mankind. Surely their reading of their own historic importance was overdrawn; but it seemed not in the least so to them. And altogether it posed at once an exhilarating and yet terrifying responsibility.

These, then, are some of the attitudes, some of the peculiar understandings which informed this republican generation. It was, I submit, a peculiarly volatile and crisis-ridden ideology, one with little resilience, little margin for error, little tradition of success behind it, and one that was vulnerable both psychologically and historically. Within this context, politics was a deadly business, with little room for optimism or leniency, little reason to expect the best rather than suspect the worst of one's political enemies. And in the end, this republican set of mind goes far to make understandable the disturbing violence of American political life during the 1790s.

15

THE MODERNIZATION OF MAYO GREENLEAF PATCH: LAND, FAMILY, AND MIGRATION IN NEW ENGLAND, 1766–1818

PAUL E. JOHNSON

The agrarian history of late eighteenth- and early nineteenth-century New England is the story of too many people and too little land. By the time of Mayo Greenleaf Patch's birth in 1766, many New England farmers faced the problem of Mayo's father. New England soil had always been thin, rocky, and forested so that early settlers had to expend much of their time clearing rather than cultivating the land. Moreover, the northern latitude of the region meant long, cold winters and a short growing season. The founders of New England had solved these problems by granting large tracts of land, often 200–300 acres at a time, to each immigrant who agreed to farm it. These settlers in turn produced large families in order to provide the labor necessary to bring the land into cultivation.

Large families and generous land grants had their own limitations, however, and by the third or fourth generation following settlement New England farmers found themselves facing a crisis. Unlike England, where primogeniture was the rule, New Englanders practiced partible inheritance. As each generation divided and subdivided the family land to accommodate its children, the size of each farm shrank accordingly. By the mid-eighteenth century many farm families faced the prospect of being unable to provide for the succeeding generation. Thus developed a floating population of New Englanders who moved westward in search of the land that they could not claim at home or headed for the maritime towns, wandering from place to place in search of work or some opportunity of establishing themselves in a permanent community. The story of Mayo Greenleaf Patch and his family recounts the story of one such migration.

The New England town was an encompassing institution, and it was not easy for people such as Mayo Patch to pull up ancient roots and move elsewhere. The earlier essay by Michael Zuckerman (Reading 6) gives an idea of the cohesiveness of the New England communities from which Patch and people like him migrated. Does Patch's story help to explain some part of "Long Bill" Scott's revolutionary commitment, as described by John Shy in Reading 11?

This is the story of Mayo Greenleaf Patch and Abigail McIntire Patch, ordinary people who helped write a decisive chapter in American history: they were among the first New Englanders to abandon farming and take up factory labor. They did so because rural society had no room for them, and their history is a tale of progressive exclusion from an agrarian world governed by

Reprinted from *The New England Quarterly*, 55(1982), 488–516. Copyright *The New England Quarterly*, 1982. Used with permission of the author and publisher.

family, kinship, and inherited land. Mayo Greenleaf Patch was the youngest son of a man who owned a small farm. He inherited nothing, and in his early and middle years he improvised a living at the edges of the family economy. He grew up with an uncle and brother, combined farming and shoemaking with dependence on his wife's family in the 1790s, recruited a half-sister into schemes against his in-laws' property, then lived briefly off an inheritance from a distant relative. Finally, having used up his exploitable kin connections, he left the countryside and moved to a mill town in which his wife and children could support the family.

That is how Greenleaf and Abigail Patch made the journey from farm to factory. But they experienced their troubles most intimately as members of a family; their story can be comprehended only as family history. Greenleaf Patch was a failed patriarch. His marriage to Abigail McIntire began with an early pregnancy, was punctuated by indebtedness and frequent moves, and ended in alcoholism and a divorce. Along the way, a previously submissive Abigail began making decisions for the family, decisions that were shaped by an economic situation in which she but not her husband found work and by her midlife conversion into a Baptist church.

The outlines of the Patch family history are familiar, for recent scholarship on New England in the century following 1750 centers on its principal themes: the crisis of the rural social order in the eighteenth century, the beginnings of commercial and industrial society in the nineteenth, and transformations in personal and family life that occurred in transit betweeen the two. The Patches shared even the particulars of their story—disinheritance, premarital pregnancy, alcoholism, transiency, indebtedness, divorce, female religious conversion—with many of their neighbors. In short, Abigail and Greenleaf Patch lived at the center of a decisive social transformation and experienced many of its defining events.

The story of the Patches throws light on the process whereby farmers in post-Revolutionary New England became "available" for work outside of agriculture. That light, however, is dim and oblique, and we must confront two qualifications at the outset. First, the Patches were obscure people who left incomplete traces of their lives. Neither Greenleaf nor Abigail kept a diary or wrote an autobiography, their names never appeared in newspapers, and no one bothered to save their mail. Apart from one rambling and inaccurate family reminiscence, their story must be reconstructed from distant, impersonal, and fragmentary sources: wills and deeds, church records, tax lists, censuses, the minutes of town governments, court records, and histories of the towns in which they lived and the shoe and textile industries in which they worked. The results are not perfect. The broad outlines of the story can be drawn with confidence, and a few episodes emerge in fine-grained detail. But some crucial points must rest on controlled inference, others on inferences that are a little less controlled, still others on outright guesswork. Scholars who demand certainty should stay away from people like Greenleaf and Abigail Patch. But historians of ordinary individuals must learn to work with the evidence that they left behind. In part, this essay is an exploration of the possibilities and limits of such evidence.

A second qualification concerns the problem of generalizing from a single case. It must be stated strongly that the Patches were not typical. No one really is. The Patches, moreover, can claim uniqueness, for they were the parents of Sam Patch, a millworker who earned national notoriety in the 1820s as a professional daredevil. The younger Patch's life was an elaborate exercise in self-destruction, and we might question the normality of the household in which he grew up. Indeed the history of the Patch family is shot through with brutality and eccentricity and with a consistent sadness that is all its own. The Patches were not typical but marginal, and that is the point: it was persons who were marginal to rural society who sought jobs outside of agriculture. The number of such persons grew rapidly in post-Revolutionary New England. This is the story of two of them.

New England men of Greenleaf Patch's generation grew up confronting two uncomfortable facts. The first was the immense value that their culture placed on the ownership of land. Freehold tenure conferred not only economic security but personal and moral independence, the ability to support and govern a family, political rights, and the respect of one's neighbors and oneself. New Englanders trusted the man who owned land; they feared and despised the man who did not. The second fact was that in the late eighteenth century increasing numbers of men owned no land. Greenleaf Patch was among them.

Like nearly everyone else in Revolutionary Massachusetts, Patch was descended from yeoman stock. His family had come to Salem in 1636, and they operated a farm in nearby Wenham for more than a century. The Patches were church members and farm owners, and their men served regularly in the militia and in town offices. Greenleaf's father, grandfather, and great-grandfather all served terms as selectmen of Wenham; his great-grandfather was that community's representative to the Massachusetts General Court; his older brother was a militiaman who fought on the first day of the American Revolution.

The Patches commanded respect among their neighbors, but in the eighteenth century their future was uncertain. Like thousands of New England families, they owned small farms and had many children; by mid-century it was clear that young Patch men would not inherit the material standards enjoyed by their fathers. The farm on which Greenleaf Patch was born was an artifact of that problem. His father, Timothy Patch, Jr., had inherited a house, an eighteen-acre farm, and eleven acres of outlying meadow and woodland upon his own father's death in 1751. Next door, Timothy's younger brother Samuel farmed the remaining nine acres of what had been their father's homestead. The father had known that neither Timothy nor Samuel could make a farm of what he had, and he required that they share resources. His will granted Timothy access to a shop and cider mill that lay on Samuel's land and drew the boundary between the two farms through the only barn on the property. It was the end of the line: further subdivision would make both farms unworkable.

Timothy Patch's situation was precarious, and he made it worse by overextending himself, both as a landholder and as a father. Timothy was forty-three years old when he inherited his farm, and he was busy buying pieces of woodland, upland, and meadow all over Wenham. Evidently he speculated in marginal land and/or shifted from farming to livestock raising. He financed his schemes on credit, and he bought on a fairly large scale. By the early 1760s Timothy Patch held title to 114 acres, nearly all of it in small plots of poor land.

Timothy Patch may have engaged in speculation in order to provide for an impossibly large number of heirs. Timothy was the father of ten children when he inherited his farm. In succeeding years he was widowed, remarried, and sired two more daughters and a son. In all, he fathered ten children who survived to adulthood. The youngest was a son born in 1766. Timothy named him Mayo Greenleaf.

Greenleaf Patch's life began badly: his father went bankrupt in the year of his birth. Timothy had transferred the house and farm to his two oldest sons in the early 1760s, possibly to keep the property out of the hands of creditors. Then, in 1766, the creditors began making trouble. In September Timothy relinquished twenty acres of his outlying land to satisfy a debt. By March 1767, having lost five court cases and sold all of his remaining land to pay debts and court costs, he was preparing to leave Wenham. Timothy's first two sons stayed on, but both left Wenham before their deaths, and none of the other children established households in the community. After a century as substantial farmers and local leaders, the Patch family abandoned their hometown.

Greenleaf Patch was taken from his home village as an infant, and his family's wanderings after that can be traced only through his father's appearances in court. By 1770 the family had moved a few miles north and west to Andover, where Timothy was sued by yet another creditor. Nine years later Timothy Patch was in Danvers, where he went to court seven times in three years.

The court cases suggest that the family experienced drastic ups and downs. Some cases involved substantial amounts of money, but in the last, Timothy was accused of stealing firewood. He then left Danvers and moved to Nottingham West, New Hampshire. There Timothy seems to have recouped his fortunes once again, for in 1782 he was a gambler-investor in an American Revolutionary privateer.

That is all we know about the Patch family during the childhood of Mayo Greenleaf Patch. About the childhood itself we know nothing. Doubtless Greenleaf shared his parents' frequent moves and their bouts of good and bad luck, and from his subsequent behavior we might conclude that he inherited his father's penchant for economic adventurism. He may also have spent parts of his childhood and youth in other households. Since he later named his own children after relatives in Wenham, he probably lived there in the families of his brother and uncle. We know also that during his youth he learned how to make shoes, and since his first independent appearance in the record came when he was twenty-one, we might guess that he served a formal, live-in apprenticeship. Even these points, however, rest on speculation. Only this is certain: Greenleaf Patch was the tenth and youngest child of a family that broke and scattered in the year of his birth, and he entered adulthood alone and without visible resources.

In 1787 Mayo Greenleaf Patch appeared in the Second (North) Parish of Reading, Massachusetts—fifteen miles due north of Boston. He was twenty-one years old and unmarried, and he owned almost nothing. He had no relatives in Reading; indeed no one named Patch had ever lived in that town. In a world where property was inherited and where kinfolk were essential social and economic assets, young Greenleaf Patch inherited nothing and lived alone.

Greenleaf's prospects in 1787 were not promising. But he soon took steps to improve them. In July 1788 he married Abigail McIntire in Reading. He was twenty-two years old; she was seventeen and pregnant. This early marriage is most easily explained as an unfortunate accident. But from the viewpoint of Greenleaf Patch it was not unfortunate at all, for it put him into a family that possessed resources that his own family had lost. For the next twelve years, Patch's livelihood and ambitions would center on the McIntires and their land.

The McIntires were Scots, descendants of highlanders who had been exiled to Maine after the Battle of Dunbar. Some had walked south, and Philip McIntire was among those who pioneered the North Parish in the 1650s. By the 1780s McIntire households were scattered throughout the parish. Archelaus McIntire, Abigail's father, headed the most prosperous of those households. Archelaus had been the eldest son of a man who died without a will, and he inherited the family farm intact. He added to the farm and by 1791 owned ninety-seven acres in Reading and patches of meadowland in two neighboring townships, a flock of seventeen sheep as well as cattle and oxen and other animals, and personal property that indicates comfort and material decency if not wealth. Of 122 taxable estates in the North Parish in 1792, Archelaus McIntire's ranked twenty-third.

In 1788 Archelaus McIntire learned that his youngest daughter was pregnant and would marry Mayo Greenleaf Patch. No doubt he was angry, but he had seen such things before. One in three Massachusetts women of Abigail's generation was pregnant on her wedding day, a statistic to which the McIntires had contributed amply. Archelaus himself had been born three months after his parents' marriage in 1729. One of his older daughters had conceived a child at the age of fourteen, and his only son would marry a pregnant lover in 1795.

Faced with yet another early pregnancy, Archelaus McIntire determined to make the best of a bad situation. In the winter of 1789/90, he built a shoemaker's shop and a small house for Greenleaf Patch and granted him use of the land on which they sat. At a stroke, Patch was endowed with family connections and economic independence.

Greenleaf Patch took his place among the

farmer-shoemakers of northeastern Massachusetts in 1790. The region had been exporting shoes since before the Revolution, for it possessed the prerequisites of cottage industry in abundance: it was poor and overcrowded and had access to markets through Boston and the port towns of Essex County. With the Revolution and the protection of footwear under the first national tariffs, with the expansion of the maritime economy of which the shoe trade was a part, and with the continuing growth of rural poverty, thousands of farm families turned to the making of shoes in the 1790s.

Their workshops were not entrepreneurial ventures. Neither, if we listen to the complaints of merchants and skilled artisans about "slop work" coming out of the countryside, were they likely sources of craft traditions or occupational pride. The trade was simply the means by which farmers on small plots of worn-out land maintained their independence.

The journal of Isaac Weston, a Reading shoemaker during the 1790s, suggests something of the cottage shoemaker's way of life. Weston was first and last a farmer. He spent his time worrying about the weather, working his farm, repairing his house and outbuildings, and trading farm labor with his neighbors and relatives. His tasks accomplished, he went hunting with his brothers-in-law, took frequent fishing trips to the coast at Lynn, and made an endless round of social calls in the neighborhood. The little shop at the back of Weston's house supplemented his earnings, and he spent extended periods of time in it only during the winter months. With his bags of finished shoes, he made regular trips to Boston, often in company with other Reading shoemakers. The larger merchants did not yet dominate the trade in country shoes, and Weston and his neighbors went from buyer to buyer bargaining as a group and came home with enough money to purchase leather, pay debts and taxes, and subsist for another year as farmers.

Isaac Weston's workshop enabled him to survive as an independent proprietor. At the same time, it fostered relations of neighborly cooperation with other men. He was the head of a self-supporting household and an equal participant in neighborhood affairs; in eighteenth-century Massachusetts, those criteria constituted the definition of manhood. Mayo Greenleaf Patch received that status as a wedding present.

Greenleaf and Abigail occupied the new house and shop early in 1790, and their tax listings over the next few years reveal a rise from poverty to self-sufficiency with perhaps a little extra. In 1790, for the first time, Greenleaf paid the tax on a small piece of land. Two years later he ranked fifty-sixth among the 122 taxpayers in the North Parish. Patch was not getting rich, but he enjoyed a secure place in the economy of his neighborhood. That alone was a remarkable achievement for a young stranger who had come to town with almost nothing.

With marriage and proprietorship came authority over a complex and growing household. Few rural shoemakers in the 1790s worked alone; they hired outside help and put their wives and children to work binding shoes. Isaac Weston brought in apprentices and journeymen, and Greenleaf Patch seems to have done the same. In 1790 the Patch family included Greenleaf and Abigail and their infant daughter, along with a boy under the age of sixteen and an unidentified adult male. In 1792 Patch paid the tax on two polls, suggesting that again the household included an adult male dependent. It seems clear that Greenleaf hired outsiders and (assuming Abigail helped) regularly headed a family work team that numbered at least four persons.

During the same years, Patch won the respect of the McIntires and their neighbors. When Archelaus McIntire died in 1791, his will named Patch executor of the estate. Greenleaf spent considerable effort, including two successful appearances in court, ordering his father-in-law's affairs. In 1794 he witnessed a land transaction involving his brother-in-law, again indicating that he was a trusted member of the McIntire family. That trust was shared by the neighbors. In 1793 the town built a schoolhouse near the Patch home, and in 1794 and 1795 the parish paid Greenleaf Patch for boarding the schoolmistress and for escorting her home at the end of the term. Those were duties that could only have gone to a trusted neighbor who ran an orderly house.

Greenleaf Patch's marriage to Abigail McIntire rescued him from the shiftless and uncertain life that had been dealt to him at birth. In 1787 he was a propertyless wanderer. By the early 1790s, he was the head of a growing family, a useful member of the McIntire clan, and a familiar and trusted neighbor. Greenleaf Patch had found a home. But his gains were precarious, for they rested on the use of land that belonged not to him but to his father-in-law. When Archelaus died, the title to the McIntire properties fell to his nineteen-year-old son, Archelaus, Jr. Young Archelaus was bound out to a guardian, and Patch, as executor of the estate, began to prey openly on the resources of Abigail's family. In succeeding years bad luck and moral failings would cost him everything that he had gained.

With Archelaus McIntire dead and his son living with a guardian, the household that the senior Archelaus had headed shrank to two women: his widow and his daughter Deborah. The widow described herself as an invalid, and there may have been something wrong with Deborah as well. In the will that he wrote in 1791, Archelaus ordered that his heir take care of Deborah. His son would repeat that order ten years later, when Deborah, still unmarried and still living at home, was thirty-five years old. Shortly after the death of Archelaus McIntire (and shortly before Patch was to inventory the estate), the widow complained to authorities that "considerable of my household goods & furniture have been given to my children" and begged that she be spared "whatever household furniture that may be left which is but a bare sufficiency to keep household." At that time two of her four daughters were dead, a third lived with her, and her only son was under the care of a guardian. The "children" could have been none other than Greenleaf and Abigail Patch, whose personal property taxes mysteriously doubled between 1791 and 1792. Greenleaf Patch had entered a house occupied by helpless women and walked off with the furniture.

Patch followed this with a second and more treacherous assault on the McIntires and their resources. In November 1793 Archelaus McIntire, Jr. came of age and assumed control of the estate. Greenleaf's use of McIntire land no longer rested on his relationship with his father-in-law or his role as executor but on the whim of Archelaus, Jr. Patch took steps that would tie him closely to young Archelaus and his land. Those steps involved a woman named Nancy Barker, who moved into Reading sometime in 1795. Mrs. Barker had been widowed twice, the second time, apparently, by a Haverhill shoemaker who left her with his tools and scraps of leather, a few valueless sticks of furniture, and two small children. Nancy Barker, it turns out, was the half-sister of Mayo Greenleaf Patch.

In November 1795 Nancy Barker married Archelaus McIntire, Jr. She was thirty-one years old. He had turned twenty-three the previous day, and his marriage was not a matter of choice: Nancy was four months pregnant. Archelaus and Nancy were an unlikely couple, and we must ask how the match came about. Archelaus had grown up with three older sisters and no brothers; his attraction and/or vulnerability to a woman nearly nine years his senior is not altogether mysterious. Nancy, of course, had sensible reasons for being attracted to Archelaus. She was a destitute widow with two children, and he was young, unmarried, and the owner of substantial property. Finally, Greenleaf Patch, who was the only known link between the two, had a vital interest in creating ties between his family and his in-law's land. It would be plausible—indeed it seems inescapable—to conclude that Nancy Barker, in collusion with her half-brother, had seduced young Archelaus McIntire and forced a marriage.

Of course, that may be nothing more than perverse speculation. Nancy and Archelaus may simply have fallen in love, started a baby, and married. Whatever role Greenleaf Patch played in the affair may have added to his esteem among the McIntires and in the community. That line of reasoning, however, must confront an unhappy fact: in 1795 the neighbors and the McIntires began to dislike Mayo Greenleaf Patch.

The first sign of trouble came in the fall of 1795, when town officials stepped into a boundary dispute between Patch and Deacon John Swain. Massachusetts towns encouraged neighbors to settle arguments among themselves. In all three parishes of Reading in the 1790s, only three disagreements over boundaries came before the town government, and one of those was settled informally. Thus Greenleaf Patch was party to half of Reading's mediated boundary disputes in the 1790s. The list of conflicts grew: after 1795 the schoolmistress was moved out of the Patch household; in 1797 Patch complained that he had been overtaxed (another rare occurrence), demanded a reassessment, and was reimbursed. Then he started going to court. In 1798 Greenleaf Patch sued Thomas Tuttle for nonpayment of a debt and was awarded nearly $100 when Tuttle failed to appear. A few months earlier, Patch had been hauled into court by William Herrick, a carpenter who claimed that Patch owed him $480. Patch denied the charge and hired a lawyer; the court found in his favor, but Herrick appealed the case, and a higher court awarded him $100.52. Six years later, Patch's lawyer was still trying to collect his fee.

There is also a question about land. In the dispute with John Swain, the description of Patch's farm matches none of the properties described in McIntire deeds. We know that Patch no longer occupied McIntire land in 1798, and town records identified him as the "tenant" of his disputed farm in 1795. Perhaps as early as 1795, Patch had been evicted from McIntire land.

Finally, there is clear evidence that the authorities had stopped trusting Mayo Greenleaf Patch. Nancy Barker McIntire died in 1798 at the age of thirty-four. Archelaus remarried a year later, then died suddenly in 1801. His estate—two houses and the ninety-seven-acre farm, sixty acres of upland and meadow in Reading, and fifteen acres in the neighboring town of Lynnfield —was willed to his two children by Nancy Barker. Archelaus's second wife sold her right of dower and left town, and the property fell to girls who were four and five years of age. Their guard-

ian would have use of the land for many years. By this time Greenleaf and Abigail Patch had moved away, but surely authorities knew their whereabouts and that they were the orphans' closest living relatives. Yet the officials passed them over and appointed a farmer from Reading as legal guardian. The court, doubtless with the advice of the neighbors, had decided against placing Greenleaf Patch in a position of trust. For Patch it was a costly decision. It finally cut him off from property that he had occupied and plotted against for many years.

Each of these facts and inferences says little by itself, but together they form an unmistakable pattern: from the date of his marriage through the mid-1790s, Greenleaf Patch accumulated resources and participated in the collective life of Abigail's family and neighborhood; from 1795 onward he entered the record only when he was fighting the neighbors or being shunned by the family. The promising family man of the early 1790s was a contentious and morally bankrupt outcast by 1798.

Late in 1799 or early in 1800 Greenleaf and Abigail and their four children left Reading and resettled in Danvers, a community of farmer-shoemakers on the outskirts of Salem. We cannot know why they selected that town, but their best connection with the place came through Abigail. Danvers was her mother's birthplace, and she had an aunt and uncle, five first cousins, and innumerable distant relatives in the town. Indeed Abigail's father had owned land in Danvers. In 1785 Archelaus McIntire, Sr. had seized seven acres from John Felton, one of his in-laws, in payment of a debt. Archelaus, Jr. sold the land back to the Feltons in 1794 but did not record the transaction until 1799. Perhaps he made an arrangement whereby the Patches had use of the land. (Doubtless Archelaus was glad to be rid of Greenleaf Patch, but he may have felt some responsibility for his sister.)

Danvers was another shoemaking town, and the Patches probably rented a farm and made shoes. In 1800 the household included Greenleaf and Abigail, their children, and no one else, suggesting that they were no longer able to hire help. But this, like everything else about the family's career in Danvers, rests on inference. We know only that they were in Danvers and that they stayed three years.

Late in 1802 Greenleaf Patch received a final reprieve, again through family channels. His half-brother Job Davis (his mother's son by her first marriage) died in the fishing port of Marblehead and left Patch one-fifth of his estate. The full property included a butcher's shop at the edge of town, an unfinished new house, and what was described as a "mansion house" that needed repairs. The property, however, was mortgaged to the merchants William and Benjamin T. Reid. The survivors of Job Davis inherited the mortgage along with the estate.

The other heirs sold to the Reids without a struggle, but Greenleaf Patch, whether from demented ambition or lack of alternatives, moved his family to Marblehead early in 1803. He finished the new house and moved into it, reopened the butcher's shop, and ran up debts. Some of the debts were old. Patch owed Ebenezer Goodale of Danvers $54. He also owed Porter Sawyer of Reading $92 and paid a part of it by laboring at 75¢ a day. Then there were debts incurred in Marblehead: $70 to the widow Sarah Dolebar; a few dollars for building materials and furnishings bought from the Reids; $50 to a farmer named Benjamin Burnham; $33 to Zachariah King of Danvers; $35 to Joseph Holt of Reading; another $35 to Caleb Totman of Hampshire County. Finally, there was the original mortgage held by the Reids.

Patch's renewed dreams of independence collapsed under the weight of his debts. In March 1803 a creditor repossessed the property up to a value of $150, and a few weeks before Christmas of the same year the sheriff seized the new house. In the following spring, Patch missed a mortgage payment, and the Reids took him to court, seized the remaining property, and sold it at auction. Still, Patch retained the right to reclaim the property by paying his debts. The story ends early in 1805, when the Reids bought Greenleaf Patch's right of redemption for $60. Patch had struggled

with the Marblehead property for two years, and all had come to nothing.

With this final failure, the Patches exhausted the family connections on which they had subsisted since their marriage. The long stay in Reading and the moves to Danvers and Marblehead were all determined by the availability of relatives and their resources. In 1807 the Patches resettled in Pawtucket, Rhode Island, the pioneer textile milling town in the United States. It was the climactic event in their history: it marked their passage out of the family economy and into the labor market.

When the family arrived in Pawtucket early in 1807, they found four textile mills surrounding the waterfall at the center of town. The mills were small and limited to the spinning of yarn, and much of the work was done by outworkers. Children picked and cleaned raw cotton in their homes, then sent it to the mills to be carded by other children. The cotton next went to the spinning rooms, where, with the help of water-driven machinery, a few skilled men, and still more children, it was turned into yarn. Millers put the yarn out to women, many of them widows with children, who wove it into cloth. There was thus plenty of work for Abigail and her older children, and it was they who supported the family in Pawtucket. Samuel, the second son, spent his childhood in the mills, and his sisters probably did the same. It is likely that Abigail worked as a weaver; certainly the wool produced on her father's farm suggests that she knew something about that trade.

That leaves only the father. Pawtucket was booming in 1807, and if Greenleaf Patch were willing and physically able, he could have found work. We know, however, that he did not work in that town. He drank, he stole the money earned by his wife and children, and he threatened them frequently with violence. Then, in 1812, he abandoned them. Abigail waited six years and divorced him in 1818. She recounted Greenleaf's drinking and his threats and his refusal to work, then revealed what for her was the determining blow: Greenleaf Patch had drifted back to Massachusetts and had been caught passing counterfeit money. In February 1817 he entered the Massachusetts State Prison at Charlestown. He was released the following August. Patch was fifty-two years old, and that is the last we hear of him.

In a society that located virtue and respectability in the yeoman freeholder, Mayo Greenleaf Patch never owned land. We have seen some public consequences of that fact: his lifelong inability to attain material independence, the troubled relations with in-laws, neighbors, creditors, and legal authorities that resulted when he tried, and the personal and moral disintegration that accompanied unending economic distress.

Now we turn to private troubles, and here the story centers on Abigail McIntire Patch. Recent studies of late eighteenth- and early nineteenth-century family life have documented a decline of patriarchal authority, the creation of a separate and female-dominated domestic sphere, an increase in female religiosity, and, bound up with all three, the elevation of women's status and power within the home. Most of these studies center on middle- and upper-class women, and we are left to wonder whether the conclusions can be extended to women further down the social scale. In the case of Abigail Patch, they can: her story begins with patriarchy and ends with female control. In grotesque miniature, the history of the Patches is a story of the feminization of family life.

Abigail grew up in a family that, judged from available evidence, was ruled by her father. Archelaus McIntire owned a respected family name and a farm that he had inherited from his father and that he would pass on to his son; he was the steward of the family's past and future as well as its present provider. As a McIntire, he conferred status on every member of his household. As a voter he spoke for the family in town affairs; as a father and church member he led the family in daily prayers; and as a proprietor he made decisions about the allocation of family resources, handled relations with outsiders, and performed much of the heavy work.

Archelaus McIntire's wife and daughters were subordinate members of his household. He had married Abigail Felton of Danvers and had brought her to a town where she lived apart from her own family but surrounded by his; her status in Reading derived from her husband's family and not from her own. On the farm, she and her daughters spent long days cooking and cleaning, gardening, tending and milking cows, making cloth and clothing, and caring for the younger children—work that took place in and near the house and not on the farm. That work was essential, but New England men assumed that it would be done and attached no special importance to it. The notion of a separate and cherished domestic sphere was slow to catch on in the countryside, and if we may judge from the spending patterns of the McIntires, it played no role in their house. Archelaus McIntire spent his money on implements of work and male sociability—horses, wagons, well-made cider barrels, a rifle—and not on the china, tea sets, and feather beds that were appearing in the towns and among the rural well-to-do. The McIntires owned a solid table and a Bible and a few other books, and there was a clock and a set of glassware as well. But the most valuable item of furniture in the house was Archelaus's desk. Insofar as the McIntires found time for quiet evenings at home, they probably spent them listening to the father read his Bible (the mother was illiterate) or keeping quiet while he figured his accounts.

As the fourth and youngest of Archelaus McIntire's daughters, Abigail had doubtless traded work and quiet subordination for security, for the status that went with being a female McIntire, perhaps even for peace and affection in the home. As she set up housekeeping with Mayo Greenleaf Patch, she doubtless did not expect things to change. Years later Abigail recalled that in taking a husband she wanted not a partner but "a friend and protector." For her part, Abigail spoke of her "duties" and claimed to have been an "attentive and affectionate wife." It was the arrangement that she had learned as a child: husbands protected their wives and supported them, wives worked and were attentive to their husbands' needs and wishes. All available evidence suggests that those rules governed the Patch household during the years in Reading.

Abigail and Greenleaf Patch maintained neither the way of life nor the standard of living necessary for the creation of a private sphere in which Abigail could have exercised independent authority. The house was small and there was little money, and the household regularly included persons from outside the immediate family. Greenleaf's apprentices and journeymen were in and out of the house constantly. For two summers the Patches boarded the schoolmistress, and Nancy Barker may have stayed with Greenleaf and Abigail before her marriage. With these persons present in hit-and-miss records, we may assume that outsiders were normal members of the Patch household.

At work, rural shoemakers maintained a rigid division of labor based on sex and age, and Greenleaf's authority was pervasive. Abigail's kitchen, if indeed it was a separate room, was a busy place. There she bound shoes as a semiskilled and subordinate member of her husband's work team, cared for the children (she gave birth five times between 1789 and 1799), did the cooking, cleaning, and laundry for a large household, and stared across the table at apprentices and journeymen who symbolized her own drudgery and her husband's authority at the same time. As Abigail Patch endured her hectic and exhausting days, she may have dreamed of wallpapered parlors and privacy and quiet nights by the fire with her husband. But she must have known that such things were for others and not for her. They had played little role in her father's house, and they were totally absent from her own.

Greenleaf Patch seems to have taken his authority as head of the household seriously. Available evidence suggests that he consistently made family decisions—not just the economic choices that were indisputably his to make but decisions that shaped the texture and meaning of life within the family.

Take the naming of the children. Greenleaf Patch was separated from his own family and dependent on McIntire resources, so when children came along we would expect him and Abi-

gail to have honored McIntire relatives. That is not what happened. The first Patch child was a daughter born in 1789. The baby was named Molly, after a daughter of Greenleaf's brother Isaac. A son came two years later, and the Patches named him Greenleaf. Another daughter, born in 1794, was given the name Nabby, after another of Isaac Patch's daughters. A second son, born in 1798, was named for Greenleaf's uncle Samuel. That child died, and a son born the following year (the daredevil Sam Patch) received the same name. The last child was born in 1803 and was named for Greenleaf's brother Isaac. None of the six children was named for Abigail or a member of her family. Instead, all of the names came from the little world in Wenham— uncle Samuel's nine-acre farm, the shared barn and outbuildings, and the eighteen acres operated by brother Isaac—in which Greenleaf Patch presumably spent much of his childhood.

Religion is a second and more important sphere in which Patch seems to have made choices for the family. Abigail McIntire had grown up in a religious household. Her father had joined the North Parish Congregational Church a few days after the birth of his first child in 1762. Her mother had followed two months later, and the couple baptized each of their five children. The children in their turn became churchgoers. Abigail's sisters Mary and Mehitable joined churches, and her brother Archelaus, Jr. expressed a strong interest in religion as well. Among Abigail's parents and siblings, only the questionable Deborah left no religious traces.

Religious traditions in the Patch family were not as strong. Greenleaf's father and his first wife joined the Congregational church at Wenham during the sixth year of their marriage in 1736, but the family's ties to religion weakened after that. Timothy Patch, Jr. did not baptize any of his thirteen children, either the ten presented him by his first wife or the three born to Thomasine Greenleaf Davis, the nonchurchgoing widow whom he married in 1759. None of Greenleaf's brothers or sisters became full members of the church, and only his oldest brother Andrew owned the covenant, thus placing his family under the government of the church.

Among the Wenham Patches, however, there remained pockets of religiosity, and they centered, perhaps significantly, in the homes of Greenleaf's brother Isaac and his uncle Samuel. Uncle Samuel was a communicant of the church, and although Isaac had no formal religious ties, he married a woman who owned the covenant. The churchgoing tradition that Greenleaf Patch carried into marriage was thus ambiguous, but it almost certainly was weaker than that carried by his wife. And from his actions as an adult, we may assume that Greenleaf was not a man who would have been drawn to the religious life.

As Greenleaf and Abigail married and had children, the question of religion could not have been overlooked. The family lived near the church in which Abigail had been baptized and in which her family and her old friends spent Sunday mornings. As the wife of Greenleaf Patch, Abigail had three options: she could lead her husband into church; she could, as many women did, join the church without her husband and take the children with her; finally, she could break with the church and spend Sundays with an irreligious husband. The first two choices would assert Abigail's authority and independent rights within the family. The third would be a capitulation, and it would have painful results. It would cut her off from the religious community in which she had been born, and it would remove her young family from religious influence.

The Patches lived in Reading for twelve years and had five children there. Neither Greenleaf nor Abigail joined the church, and none of the babies was baptized. We cannot retrieve the actions and feelings that produced these facts, but this much is certain: in the crucial area of religious practice, the Patch family bore the stamp of Greenleaf Patch and not of Abigail McIntire. When Greenleaf and Abigail named a baby or chose whether to join a church or baptize a child, the decisions extended his family's history and not hers.

Abigail Patch accepted her husband's dominance in family affairs throughout the years in Reading, years in which he played, however ineptly and dishonestly, his role as "friend and protector." With his final separation from the rural economy and his humiliating failure in Marblehead, he abdicated that role. In Marblehead Abigail began to impose her will upon domestic decisions. The result, within a few years, would be a full-scale female takeover of the family.

In 1803 the sixth—and, perhaps significantly, the last—Patch child was baptized at Second Congregational Church in Marblehead. And in 1807, shortly after the move to Rhode Island, Abigail and her oldest daughter joined the First Baptist Church in Pawtucket. At that date Abigail was thirty-seven years old, had been married nineteen years, and had five living children. Her daughter Molly was eighteen years old and unmarried. Neither followed the customs of the McIntire or Patch families, where women who joined churches did so within a few years after marriage. Abigail and Molly Patch presented themselves for baptism in 1807 not because they had reached predictable points in their life cycles but because they had experienced religion and had decided to join a church.

At the same time (here was feminization with a vengeance) Abigail's daughters dropped their given names and evolved new ones drawn from their mother's and not their father's side of the family. The oldest daughter joined the church not as Molly but as Polly Patch. Two years later the same woman married under the name Mary Patch. Abigail's oldest sister, who had died in the year that Abigail married Greenleaf, had been named Mary. The second Patch daughter, Nabby, joined the Baptist church in 1811. At that time she was calling herself Abby Patch. By 1829 she was known as Abigail. The daughters of Abigail Patch, it seems, were affiliating with their mother and severing symbolic ties with their father. It should be noted that the father remained in the house while they did so.

In Pawtucket Abigail built a new family life that centered on her church and her female relatives. That life constituted a rejection not only of male dominance but of men. For five years Abigail worked and took the children to church while her husband drank, stole her money, and issued sullen threats. He ran off in 1812, and by 1820 Abigail, now officially head of the household, had rented a house and was taking in boarders. Over the next few years the Patch sons left home: Samuel for New Jersey, Isaac for the Northwest, Greenleaf for parts unknown. Abigail's younger daughter married and moved to Pittsburgh. Among the Patch children only Mary (Molly, Polly) stayed in Pawtucket. In 1825 Mary was caught committing adultery. Her husband left town, and Mary began calling herself a widow. Abigail closed the boardinghouse and moved into a little house on Main Street with Mary and her children sometime before 1830. She and her daughter and granddaughters would live in that house for the next quarter-century.

The neighbors remembered Abigail Patch as a quiet, steady little woman who attended the Baptist church. She did so with all of the Patch women. Mary had joined with her in 1807, and each of Mary's daughters followed in their turn: Mary and Sarah Anne in 1829, Emily in 1841. First Baptist was a grim and overwhelmingly female Calvinist church, subsidized and governed by the owners of Pawtucket's mills. The Articles of Faith insisted that most of humankind was hopelessly damned, that God chose only a few for eternal life and had in fact chosen them before the beginning of time, "and that in the flesh dwelleth no good thing." It was not a cheerful message. But it struck home among the Patch women.

Apart from the church, the women spent their time in the house on Main Street. Abigail bought the house in 1842—the first land that the Patches owned—and her granddaughters Mary and Emily taught school in the front room for many years. The household was self-supporting, and its membership was made up of women whose relations with men were either troubled or nonexistent. Abigail never remarried. We cannot know what preceded and surrounded the instance of adultery and the breakup of Mary's marriage, but she too remained single for the rest of her life. Sarah Anne Jones, one of the granddaughters,

was thirty-six years old and unmarried when called before a church committee in 1853. Although she married a man named Kelley during the investigation, she was excommunicated "because she has given this church reason to believe she is licentious." Sarah Anne's sisters, the schoolteachers Mary and Emily, were spinsters all their lives. The lives of Abigail Patch and her daughter Mary Jones had been blighted by bad relations with men; the women whom they raised either avoided men or got into trouble when they did not. Abigail Patch lived on Main Street with the other women until 1854, when she died at the age of eighty-four.

We know little of what went on in that house. The women lived quietly, and former pupils remembered Abigail's granddaughters with affection. But beyond the schoolroom, in rooms inhabited only by the Patch women, there was a cloistered world. Within that world, Abigail and her daughter Mary reconstructed not only themselves but the history of their family.

Pawtucket celebrated its Cotton Centennial in 1890, and a Providence newspaperman decided to write about the millworker-hero Sam Patch. He asked Emily Jones, one of Abigail's aged granddaughters, about the Patch family history. Emily had been born after 1810, and her knowledge of the family's past was limited to what she had picked up from her mother and grandmother. Her response to the reporter demonstrated the selective amnesia with which any family remembers its history, but in this case the fabrications were sadly revealing.

Miss Jones told the newspaperman that her oldest uncle, Greenleaf Patch, Jr., had gone off to Salem and become a lawyer. That is demonstrably untrue. No one named Greenleaf Patch has ever been licensed to practice law in Massachusetts. About her uncle Sam Patch, Emily said: in the 1820s he operated a spinning mill of his own north of Pawtucket, but failed when his partner ran off with the funds; it was only then that he moved to New Jersey and became a daredevil. That too is a fabrication. What we know about Sam Patch is that he was an alcoholic with powerful suicidal drives, and that he succeeded in killing himself at the age of thirty. Miss Jones remembered that her youngest uncle, Isaac, moved to Illinois and became a farmer. That was true: in 1850 Isaac Patch was farming and raising a family near Peoria. It seems that Abigail Patch and Mary Patch Jones idealized the first two Patch sons by giving them successes and/or ambitions that they did not have. The third son was born in 1803 and grew up in a household dominated by Abigail and not by her dissipated husband; he became a family man. By inventing a similar ordinariness for the older sons, Abigail may have erased some of the history created by Mayo Greenleaf Patch.

Emily's memory of her grandfather provokes similar suspicions. We know that Greenleaf Patch lived in Pawtucket until 1812. But Miss Jones remembered that her grandfather had been a farmer in Massachusetts, and that he died before Abigail brought her family to Rhode Island. Greenleaf Patch, it seems, was absent from Abigail's house in more ways than one.

16

CHANGING CUSTOMS OF
CHILDBIRTH IN AMERICA, 1760–1825

CATHERINE M. SCHOLTEN

The life course of women in early America was largely marked by the experiences of marriage, childbearing, the maintenance of house and family, and death. Of these experiences, the most intimate and important was childbirth. Late eighteenth- and early nineteenth-century women typically married in their early twenties and, lacking reliable contraception, were pregnant during 8 to 12 of the following 20 years. As Catherine Scholten suggests, these were years of considerable apprehension and fear. Not only could the average woman expect to deliver at least one stillborn child, but the prospect was great that she herself might die in childbirth.

Before the late eighteenth century women of all ranks relied, as they had for generations, on the ministrations, advice, and comfort of midwives. These women, who learned their trade through practice and experience rather than formal education, followed a woman's pregnancy, delivered her baby, and watched over her postpartum recovery. Perhaps as important, the midwife, along with female relatives and neighbors, gave emotional and psychological support during the difficult hours of labor.

Beginning in the 1770s, however, a new practitioner entered the birthing room and sought to displace the age-old practice of midwifery. This interloper was the male physician who, as Scholten shows, brought with him modern medical knowledge and a new attitude toward the pain of childbirth. By the 1820s the new ways of the male physician had displaced the old practices of the midwife, and his new knowledge and procedures became institutionalized as the science of obstetrics.

While the male physician reduced the pain of childbirth and contributed to a decline in infant mortality, was something lost in the transit of birthing from female to male supervision?

In October 1799, as Sally Downing of Philadelphia labored to give birth to her sixth child, her mother, Elizabeth Drinker, watched her suffer "in great distress." Finally, on the third day of fruitless labor, Sally's physician, William Shippen, Jr., announced that "the child must be brought forward." Elizabeth Drinker wrote in her diary that, happily, Sally delivered naturally, although Dr. Shippen had said that "he thought

he should have had occasion for instruments" and clapped his hand on his side, so that the forceps rattled in his pocket.

Elizabeth Drinker's account of her daughter's delivery is one of the few descriptions by an eighteenth-century American woman of a commonplace aspect of women's lives—childbirth. It is of special interest to social historians because it records the participation of a man in the

Reprinted from *The William and Mary Quarterly,* 34 (1977), 426–45, with the permission of Dr. Paul Scholten and Pauline Scholten.

capacity of physician. Shippen was a prominent member of the first generation of American doctors trained in obstetrics and, commencing in 1763, the first to maintain a regular practice attending women in childbirth. Until that time midwives managed almost all deliveries, but with Shippen male physicians began to supplant the midwives.

The changing social customs and medical management of childbirth from 1760 to 1825 are the subjects of this article. By analyzing the rituals of childbirth it will describe the emergence of new patterns in private and professional life. It shows that, beginning among well-to-do women in Philadelphia, New York, and Boston, childbirth became less a communal experience and more a private event confined within the intimate family. In consequence of new perceptions of urban life and of women, as well as of the development of medical science, birth became increasingly regarded as a medical problem to be managed by physicians. For when Shippen, fresh from medical studies in London, announced his intention to practice midwifery in Philadelphia in 1763, he was proposing to enter a field considered the legitimate province of women. Childbearing had been viewed as the inevitable, even the divinely ordained, occasion of suffering for women; childbirth was an event shared by the female community; and delivery was supervised by a midwife.

During the colonial period childbearing occupied a central portion of the lives of women between their twentieth and fortieth years. Six to eight pregnancies were typical, and pregnant women were commonly described as "breeding" and "teeming." Such was women's natural lot; though theologians attributed dignity to carrying the "living soul" of a child and saluted mothers in their congregations with "Blessed are you among women," they also depicted the pains of childbirth as the appropriate special curse of "the Travailing Daughters of Eve." Two American tracts written specifically for lying-in women dwelt on the divinely ordained hazards of childbirth and advised a hearty course of meditation

on death, "such as their pregnant condition must reasonably awaken them to."

Cotton Mather's pamphlet, *Elizabeth in Her Holy Retirement,* which he distributed to midwives to give to the women they cared for, described pregnancy as a virtually lethal condition. "For ought you know," it warned, "your Death has entered into you, you may have conceived that which determines but about Nine Months more at the most, for you to live in the World." Pregnancy was thus intended to inspire piety. John Oliver, author of *A Present for Teeming American Women,* similarly reminded expectant mothers that prayer was necessary because their dangers were many. He noted that women preparing for lying-in "get linnen and other necessaries for the child, a nurse, a midwife, entertainment for the women that are called to the labour, a warm convenient chamber, and etc." However, "all these may be miserable comforters," argued Oliver, for "they may perchance need no other linnen shortly than a Winding Sheet, and have no other chamber but a grave, no neighbors but worms." Oliver counseled women to "arm themselves with patience" as well as prayer, and "abate somewhat those dreadful groans and cries which do so much to discourage their friends and relatives who hear them."

Surely women did not need to be reminded of the risks of childbirth. The fears of Mary Clap, wife of Thomas Clap, president of Yale College, surface even through the ritual phrases of the elegy written by her husband after her death in childbirth at the age of twenty-four. Thomas remembered that before each of her six lyings-in his wife had asked him to pray with her that God would continue their lives together. Elizabeth Drinker probably echoed the sentiments of most women when she reflected, "I have often thought that women who live to get over the time of Child-bearing, if other things are favourable to them, experience more comfort and satisfaction than at any other period of their lives."

Facing the hazards of childbirth, women depended on the community of their sex for companionship and medical assistance. Women who had moved away at marriage frequently returned to their parents' home for the delivery, either because they had no neighbors or because they preferred the care of their mothers to that of their in-laws. Other women summoned mothers, aunts, and sisters on both sides of the family, as well as female friends, when birth was imminent. Above all, they relied on the experience of midwives to guide them through labor.

Women monopolized the practice of midwifery in America, as in Europe, through the middle of the eighteenth century. As the recognized experts in the conduct of childbirth, they advised the mother-to-be if troubles arose during pregnancy, supervised the activities of lying-in, and used their skills to assure safe delivery. Until educated male physicians began to practice obstetrics, midwives enjoyed some status in the medical profession, enhanced by their legal responsibilities in the communities they served.

English civil authorities required midwives to take oaths in order to be licensed but imposed no official test of their skills. The oaths indicate that midwives had responsibilities which were serious enough to warrant supervision. They swore not to allow any infant to be baptized outside the Church of England, and promised to help both rich and poor, to report the true parentage of a child, and to abstain from performing abortions. Oath-breaking midwives could be excommunicated or fined.

Some American midwives learned their art in Europe, where midwifery was almost exclusively the professional province of women. Though barber surgeons and physicians increasingly asserted their interest in midwifery during the seventeenth century, midwives and patients resisted the intruders. The midwives' levels of skill varied. Some acquired their medical education in the same way as many surgeons and physicians, by apprenticeship; some read manuals by more learned midwives and physicians; and after 1739, when the first British lying-in hospital was founded, a few were taught by the physicians who directed such hospitals. But more often than not, women undertook midwifery equipped only with folk knowledge and the experience of their own pregnancies.

Disparity of skills also existed among American midwives. Experienced midwives practiced alongside women who were, one physician observed, "as ignorant of their business as the women they deliver." By the end of the eighteenth century physicians thought that the "greater part" of the midwives in America took up the occupation by accident, "having first been *catched,* as they express it, with a woman in labour." The more diligent sought help from books, probably popular medical manuals such as *Aristotle's Master Piece.*

American midwives conducted their practice free, on the whole, from governmental supervision and control. Only two colonies appear to have enacted regulatory statutes, and it does not seem that these were rigorously enforced. In the seventeenth century Massachusetts and New York required midwives, together with surgeons and physicians, not to act contrary to the accepted rules of their art. More specifically, in 1716 the common council of New York City prescribed a licensing oath for midwives, which was similar to the oaths of England, though without the provision on baptism. The oath included an injunction—significant for the theme of this article—that midwives not "open any matter Appertaining to your Office in the presence of any Man unless Nessessity or Great Urgent Cause to Constrain you to do so." This oath, which was regularly re-enacted until 1763, suggests the common restriction of midwifery to women, excluding male physicians or barber surgeons, who, in any case, were few and usually ill trained. There are records of male midwives in New York, Philadelphia, Charleston, and Annapolis after 1740, but only one, a Dr. Spencer of Philadelphia, had London training in midwifery, and it was said of another that "he attended very few natural labors."

Though their duties were not as well defined by law, American midwives served the community in ways similar to those of their British counterparts. In addition to assisting at childbed, they testified in court in cases of bastardy, verified birthdates, and examined female prisoners who pleaded pregnancy to escape punishment. Some colonials also observed the English custom of having the midwife attend the baptism and burial of infants. Samuel Sewall reported that Elizabeth Weeden brought his son John to church for christening in 1677, and at the funeral of little Henry in 1685 "Midwife Weeden and Nurse Hill carried the Corps by turns."

The inclusion of the midwife in these ceremonies of birth and death shows how women's relationships with their midwives went beyond mere respect for the latters' skill. Women with gynecologic problems would freely tell a midwife things "that they had rather die than discover to the Doctor." Grateful patients eulogized midwives. The acknowledgment of the services of one Boston midwife, recorded on her tombstone, has inspired comment since 1761. The stone informs the curious that Mrs. Phillips was "born in Westminister in Great Britain, and Commission'd by John Laud, Bishop of London in ye Year 1718 to ye Office of a Midwife," came to "this Country" in 1719, and "by ye Blessing of God has brought into this world above 3000 Children."

We may picture Mrs. Phillips's professional milieu as a small room, lit and warmed by a large fire, and crowded by a gathering of family and friends. In daytime, during the early stages of labor, children might be present, and while labor proceeded female friends dropped in to offer encouragement and help; securing refreshments for such visitors was a part of the preparation for childbirth, especially among the well-to-do families with which we are concerned. Men did not usually remain at the bedside. They might be summoned in to pray, but as delivery approached they waited elsewhere with the children and with women who were "not able to endure" the tension in the room.

During the final stages of labor the midwife took full charge, assisted by other women. As much as possible, midwives managed deliveries by letting nature do the work; they caught the child, tied the umbilical cord, and if necessary fetched the afterbirth. In complicated cases they might turn the child and deliver it feet first, but if this failed, the fetus had to be destroyed. In all circumstances the midwife's chief duty was to comfort the woman in labor while they both waited on nature, and this task she could, as a woman, fulfill with social ease. Under the midwife's direction the woman in labor was liberally fortified with hard liquor or mulled wine. From time to time the midwife examined her cervix to gauge the progress of labor and encouraged her to walk about until the pains became too strong. There was no standard posture for giving birth, but apparently few women lay flat in bed. Some squatted on a midwife's stool, a low chair with an open seat. Others knelt on a pallet, sat on another woman's lap, or stood supported by two friends.

Friends were "welcome companions," according to one manual for midwives, because they enabled the woman in labor "to bear her pains to more advantage," and "their cheerful conversation supports her spirits and inspires her with confidence." Elizabeth Drinker endeavored to talk her daughter into better spirits by telling her that as she was thirty-nine "this might possibly be the last trial of this sort." Some women attempted to cheer the mother-to-be by assuring her that her labor was easy compared to others they had seen, or provoked laughter by making bawdy jokes.

For some attendants, a delivery could be a wrenching experience. Elizabeth Drinker relived her own difficult deliveries when her daughters suffered their labors, and on one such occasion she noted with irony, "This day is 38 years since I was in agonies bringing her into this world of troubles: she told me with tears that this was her birthday." For others the experience of assisting the labors of friends was a reminder of their sex. Sarah Eve, an unmarried twenty-two-year-old, attended the labor of a friend in 1772 and carried the tidings of birth to the waiting father. "None but those that were like anxious could be sensible of a joy like theirs," she wrote in her journal that night. "Oh! Eve! Adam's wife I mean—who could forget her today?"

After delivery, the mother was covered up snugly and confined to her bed, ideally for three to four weeks. For fear of catching cold she was not allowed to put her feet on the floor and was constantly supplied with hot drinks. Family members relieved her of household duties. Restless women, and those who could not afford weeks of idleness, got up in a week or less, but not without occasioning censure.

The social and medical hold of midwives on childbirth loosened during the half century after 1770, as male physicians assumed the practice of midwifery among urban women of social rank. Initially, physicians entered the field as trained practitioners who could help women in difficult labors through the use of instruments, but ultimately they presided over normal deliveries as well. The presence of male physicians in the lying-in chamber signaled a general change in attitudes toward childbirth, including a modification of the dictum that women had to suffer. At the same time, because medical training was restricted to men, women lost their position as assistants at childbirth, and an event traditionally managed by a community of women became an experience shared primarily by a woman and her doctor.

William Shippen, the first American physician to establish a steady practice of midwifery, quietly overcame resistance to the presence of a man in the lying-in room. Casper Wistar's *Eulogies on Dr. Shippen,* published in 1809, states that when Shippen began in 1763, male practitioners were resorted to only in a crisis. "This was altogether the effect of prejudice," Wistar remarked, adding that "by Shippen this prejudice was so done away, that in the course of ten years he became very fully employed." A few figures testify to the trend. The Philadelphia city directory in 1815 listed twenty-one women as midwives, and twenty-three men as practitioners of midwifery. In 1819 it listed only thirteen female midwives, while the number of men had risen to forty-two; and by 1824 only six female midwives remained in the directory. "Prejudice" similarly dissolved in Boston, where in 1781 the physicians advertised that they expected immediate payment for their services in midwifery; by 1820 midwifery in Boston was almost "entirely confined" to physicians. By 1826 Dr. William Dewees, professor of midwifery at the University of Pennsylvania and the outstanding American obstetrician of the

early nineteenth century, could preface his textbook on midwifery with an injunction to every American medical student to study the subject because "everyone almost" must practice it. He wrote that "a change of manners within a few years" had "resulted in almost exclusive employment of the male practitioner."

Dewees's statement must be qualified because the "almost exclusive" use of men actually meant almost exclusive use among upper- and middle-class urban women. Female midwives continued throughout the nineteenth century to serve both the mass of women in cities and women in the country who were "without advantage of regular practitioners." During the initial years of their practice physicians shared obstetrical cases with midwives. On occasion Philadelphia women summoned Shippen together with their midwives, and Dewees reports that when he began to practice in the 1790s he depended on midwives to call him when instruments were needed. It is clear, however, that by the 1820s Dewees and his colleagues had established their own practice independent of midwives.

On one level the change was a direct consequence of the fact that after 1750 growing numbers of American men traveled to Europe for medical education. Young men with paternal means, like Shippen, spent three to four years studying medicine, including midwifery, with leading physicians inthe hospitals of London and the classrooms of Edinburgh. When they returned to the colonies they brought back not only a superior set of skills but also British ideas about hospitals, medical schools, and professional standards.

In the latter part of the eighteenth century advanced medical training became available in North America. At the time of Shippen's return in 1762 there was only one hospital in the colonies, the Pennsylvania Hospital, built ten years earlier to care for the sick poor. Shippen and his London-educated colleagues saw that the hospital could be used for the clinical training of physicians, as in Europe. Within three years the Philadelphia doctors, led by John Morgan, established formal, systematic instruction at a school of medicine, supplemented by clinical work in the hospital. Morgan maintained that the growth of the colonies "called aloud" for a medical school "to increase the number of those who exercise the profession of medicine and surgery." Dr. Samuel Bard successfully addressed the same argument to the citizens of New York in 1768.

In addition to promoting medical schools, Morgan and Bard defined the proper practitioner of medicine as a man learned in a science. To languages and liberal arts their ideal physician added anatomy, material medicine, botany, chemistry, and clinical experience. He was highly conscious not only of his duty to preserve "the life and health of mankind," but also of his professional status, and this new emphasis on professionalism extended to midwifery.

The trustees of the first American medical schools recognized midwifery as a branch of medical science. From its founding in 1768, Kings College in New York devoted one professorship solely to midwifery, and the University of Pennsylvania elected Shippen professor of anatomy, surgery, and midwifery in 1791. By 1807 five reputable American medical schools provided courses in midwifery. In the early years of the nineteenth century some professors of midwifery began to call themselves obstetricians or professors of obstetrics, a scientific-sounding title free of the feminine connotations of the word midwife. Though not compulsory for all medical students, the new field was considered worthy of detailed study along the paths pioneered by English physicians.

Dr. William Smellie contributed more to the development of obstetrics than any other eighteenth-century physician. His influence was established by his teaching career in London from 1741 to 1758, and by his treatise on midwifery, first published in 1752. Through precise measurement and observation Smellie discovered the mechanics of parturition. He found that the child's head turned throughout delivery, adapting the widest part to the widest diameter of the pelvic canal. Accordingly, he defined maneuvers for manipulating an improperly presented child. He also recognized that obstetrical forceps, generally known for only twenty years when he wrote in 1754, should be used to rectify the position of an infant wedged in the mouth of the cervix, in preference to the "common method" of simply jerking the child out. He perfected the design of the forceps and taught its proper use, so that physicians could save both mother and child in difficult deliveries, instead of being forced to dismember the infant with hooks.

To Smellie and the men who learned from him, the time seemed ripe to apply science to a field hitherto built on ignorance and supported by prejudice. Smellie commented on the novelty of scientific interest in midwifery. "We ought to be ashamed of ourselves," he admonished the readers of his *Treatise,* "for the little improvement we have made in so many centuries." Only recently have "we established a better method of delivering in laborious and preternatural cases." Smellie's countryman Dr. Charles White reflected in his text on midwifery in 1793 that "the bringing of the art of midwifery to perfection upon scientific and medical principles seems to have been reserved for the present generation."

Some American physicians shared this sense of the new "Importance of the Obstetrick Art." Midwifery was not a "trifling" matter to be left to the uneducated, Thomas Jones of the College of Medicine of Maryland wrote in 1812. Broadly defined as the care of "all the indispositions incident to women from the commencement of pregnancy to the termination of lactation," it ranked among the most important branches of medicine. "With the cultivation of this branch of science," women could now "reasonably look to men for safety in the perilous conditions" of childbirth.

Jones maintained, as did other physicians, that the conditions of modern urban life produced a special need for scientific aid in childbirth. Both rich and poor women in large cities presented troublesome cases to the physician. Pelvic deformities, abortions, and tedious labors Jones considered common among wealthy urban women because of their indolent habits and confining fashionable dress, and among the poor because of inadequate diet and long hours of work indoors. There was, he believed, a greater need for "well informed obstetrick practitioners in large cities than in country places."

Although it cannot be established that there was an increase in difficult parturitions among urban women, social as well as medical reasons account for the innovations in the practice of midwifery in such cities as Boston, Philadelphia, and New York. Physicians received their medical education in cities, and cities offered the best opportunities to acquire patients and live comfortably. Urban families of some means could afford the $12 to $15 minimum fee which Boston physicians demanded for midwife services in 1806. Obstetrics was found to be a good way to establish a successful general practice. The man who conducted himself well in the lying-in room won the gratitude and confidence of his patient and her family, and they naturally called him to serve in other medical emergencies. It was midwifery, concluded Dr. Walter Channing of Boston, that ensured doctors "the permanency and security of all their other business."

The possibility of summoning a physician, who could perhaps insure a safer and faster delivery, opened first to urban women. The dramatic rescue of one mother and child given up by a midwife could be enough to convince a neighborhood of women of a physician's value and secure him their practice. Doctors asserted that women increasingly hired physicians because they became convinced "that the well instructed physician is best calculated to avert danger and surmount difficulties." Certainly by 1795 the women of the Drinker family believed that none but a physician should order medicine for a woman in childbed, and had no doubts that Dr. Shippen or his colleague Dr. Nicholas Way was the best help that they could summon.

Although she accepted a male physician as midwife, Elizabeth Drinker still had reservations about the use of instruments to facilitate childbirth and was relieved when Shippen did not have to use forceps on her daughter. Other women feared to call a physician because they assumed that any instruments he used would destroy the child. However, once the capabilities of obstetrical forceps became known, some women may

have turned to them by choice in hope of faster deliveries. Such hope stimulated a medical fashion. By about 1820 Dewees and Bard felt it necessary to condemn nervous young doctors for resorting unnecessarily to forceps.

The formal education of American physicians and the development of midwifery as a science, the desire of women for the best help in childbirth, the utility of midwifery as a means of building a physician's practice, and, ultimately, the gigantic social changes labeled urbanization explain why physicians assumed the ordinary practice of midwifery among well-to-do urban women in the late eighteenth and early nineteenth centuries. This development provides insight into the changing condition of women in American society.

The development of obstetrics signified a partial rejection of the assumption that women had to suffer in childbirth and implied a new social appreciation of women, as admonitions to women for forbearance under the pain of labor turned to the desire to relieve their pain. Thus did Dr. Thomas Denman explain his life's work: "The law of a religion founded on principles of active benevolence, feelings of humanity, common interests of society, and special tenderness for women" demanded that men search for a method by which women might be conducted safely through childbirth. In his doctoral dissertation in 1812 one American medical student drew a distinction between childbirth in primitive societies and his own. In the former, "women are generally looked on by their rugged lords as unworthy of any particular attention," and death or injury in childbirth is "not deemed a matter of any importance." Well-instructed assistants to women in childbirth were one sign of the value placed on women in civilized societies.

The desire to relieve women in childbirth also signified a more liberal interpretation of scripture. At the University of Pennsylvania in 1804, Peter Miller, a medical student, modified the theological dictum that women must bear in sorrow. The anxieties of pregnancy and the anguish caused by the death of so many infants constituted sorrow enough for women, argued Miller. They did not need to be subjected to bodily pain as well. Reiterating this argument, Dewees bluntly asked, "Why should the female alone incur the penalty of God?" To relieve the pain of labor Dewees and his fellows analyzed the anatomy and physiology of childbirth and defined techniques for the use of instruments.

If the development of obstetrics suggests the rise of a "special tenderness for women" on the part of men, it also meant that women's participation in medical practice was diminished and disparaged. A few American physicians instructed midwives or wrote manuals for them, but these efforts were private and sporadic, and had ceased by 1820. The increasing professionalization of medicine, in the minds of the physicians who formed medical associations that set the standards of the field, left little room for female midwives, who lacked the prescribed measure of scientific training and professional identity.

William Shippen initially invited midwives as well as medical students to attend his private courses in midwifery. His advertisement in the *Pennsylvania Gazette* in January 1765 related his experience assisting women in the country in difficult labors, "most of which was made so by the unskillful old women about them," and announced that he "thought it his duty to immediately begin" courses in midwifery "in order to instruct those women who have virtue enough to own their ignorance and apply for instructions, as well as those young gentlemen now engaged in the study of that useful and necessary branch of surgery." Shippen taught these private lessons until after the Revolution, when he lectured only to the students at the University of Pennsylvania, who, of course, were male.

At the turn of the century Dr. Valentine Seaman conducted the only other known formal instruction of midwives. He was distressed by the ignorance of many midwives, yet convinced that midwives ought to manage childbirth because, unlike physicians, they had time to wait out lingering labors, and, as women, they could deal easily with female patients. Seaman offered his private lectures and demonstrations at the New York Almshouse lying-in ward, and in 1800 published them as the *Midwives Monitor and Mothers Mirror.* A handful of other men wrote texts at least nominally directed to midwives between 1800 and 1810; some of these, like Seaman's, discussed the use of instruments. In 1817 Dr. Thomas Ewell proposed that midwives be trained at a national school of midwifery in Washington, D.C., to be supported by a collection taken up by ministers. There is no evidence that Ewell's scheme, presented in his medical manual, *Letters to Ladies,* ever gained a hearing.

Seaman and Ewell, and other authors of midwives' manuals, presumed that if women mastered some of the fundamentals of obstetrics they would be desirable assistants in ordinary midwifery cases. In 1820 Dr. Channing of Boston went further in his pamphlet, *Remarks on the Employment of Females as Practitioners of Midwifery,* in which he maintained that no one could thoroughly understand the management of labor who did not understand "thoroughly the profession of medicine as a whole." Channing's principle would have totally excluded women from midwifery, because no one favored professional medical education for women. It was generally assumed that they could not easily master the necessary languages, mathematics, and chemistry, or withstand the trials of dissecting room and hospital. Channing added that women's moral character disqualified them for medical practice: "Their feelings of sympathy are too powerful for the cool exercise of judgement" in medical emergencies, he wrote; "they do not have the power of action, nor the active power of mind which is essential to the practice of the surgeon."

Denied formal medical training, midwives of the early nineteenth century could not claim any other professional or legal status. Unlike Great Britain, the United States had no extensive record of licensing laws or oaths defining the practice of midwifery. Nor were there any vocal groups of midwives who, conscious of their tradition of practice or associated with lying-in hospitals, were able to defend themselves against competition from physicians. American midwives ceased practice among women of social rank with few words uttered in their defense.

The victory of the physicians produced its own problems. The doctor's sex affected the relationships between women and their attendants in childbirth, and transformed the atmosphere of the lying-in room. In his advice to his male students Dewees acknowledged that summoning a man to assist at childbed "cost females a severe struggle." Other doctors knew that even the ordinary gynecologic services of a physician occasioned embarrassment and violated woman's "natural delicacy of feeling," and that every sensitive woman felt "deeply humil[i]ated" at the least bodily exposure. Doctors recognized an almost universal repugnance on the part of women to male assistance in time of labor. Because of "whim or false delicacy" women often refused to call a man until their condition had become critical. It is unlikely that physicians exaggerated these observations, although there is little testimony from women themselves about their childbed experience in the early nineteenth century.

The uneasiness of women who were treated by men was sometimes shared by their husbands. In 1772 the *Virginia Gazette* printed a denunciation of male midwifery as immoral. The author, probably an Englishman, attributed many cases of adultery in England to the custom of employing men at deliveries. Even in labor a woman had intervals of ease, and these, he thought, were the moments when the doctor infringed on the privileges of the husband. It would be a matter of utmost indifference to him "whether my wife had spent the night in a bagnio, or an hour of the forenoon locked up with a man midwife in her dressing room." Such arguments were frequently and seriously raised in England during the eighteenth century. They may seem ludicrous, but at least one American man of Dr. Ewell's acquaintance suffered emotional conflict over hiring a male midwife. He sent for a physician to help his wife in her labor, yet "very solemnly he declared to the doctor, he would demolish him if he touched or looked at his wife."

Physicians dealt with the embarrassment of patients and the suspicion of husbands by observing the drawing-room behavior of "well-bred gentlemen." Dewees told his students to "endeavor, by well chosen conversation, to divert your patient's mind from the purpose of your visit." All questions of a delicate nature were to be communicated through a third party, perhaps the only other person in the room, either a nurse or an elderly friend or relative. The professional man was advised "never to seem to know anything about the parts of generation, further than that there is an orifice near the rectum leading to an os."

Physicians did not perform vaginal examinations unless it was absolutely important to do so, and they often had to cajole women into permitting an examination at all. Nothing could be more shocking to a woman, Shippen lectured his students, "than for a young man the moment he enters the Chamber to ask for Pomatum and proceed to examine the uterus." Doctors waited until a labor pain clutched their patients and then suggested an examination by calling it "taking a pain." During examination and delivery the patient lay completely covered in her bed, a posture more modest, if less comfortable, than squatting on a pallet or a birth stool. The light in the room was dimmed by closing the shutters during the day and covering the lamps at night. If a physician used forceps, he had to manipulate them under the covers, using his free hand as a guide. On this point doctors who read Thomas Denman's *Obstetrical Remembrancer* were reminded that "Degorges, one of the best obstetricians of his time, was blind."

The crowd of supportive friends and family disappeared with the arrival of the doctor. The physician guarded against "too many attendants; where there are women, they must talk." The presence of other women might increase the doctor's nervousness, and they certainly did not help the woman in labor. Medical men interpreted women's talk of other experiences with childbirth as mere gossip "of all the dangerous and difficult labours they ever heard any story about in their lives," which ought to be stopped lest it disturb the patient. Especially distracting were the bawdy stories visitors told, expecting the physician to laugh, too. Medical professors recommended "grave deportment," warning that levity would "hurt your patient or yourself in her esteem." Far from providing the consolation of a friend, the physician was often a stranger who needed to "get a little acquainted" with his patient. One medical text went so far as to coach him in a series of conversational ice breakers about children and the weather.

Etiquette and prudery in the lying-in chamber affected medical care. Physicians were frustrated by their inability to examine their patients thoroughly, for they knew full well that learning midwifery from a book was "like learning shipbuilding without touching timber." Examinations were inadequate, and the dangers of manipulating instruments without benefit of sight were tremendous. Dewees cautioned his students to take great care before pulling the forceps that "no part of the mother is included in the locking of the blades. This accident is frequent." Accidental mutilation of infants was also reported, as the navel string had to be cut under the covers. Lecturers passed on the story of the incautious doctor who included the penis of an infant within the blades of his scissors.

In view of such dangers, the conflict between social values and medical practice is striking. The expansion of medical knowledge brought men and women face to face with social taboos in family life. They had to ask themselves the question, Who should watch a woman give birth? For centuries the answer had unhesitatingly been female relatives and friends, and the midwife. The science of obstetrics, developing in the eighteenth century, changed the answer. Though women might socially be the most acceptable assistants at a delivery, men were potentially more useful.

In consequence of the attendance of male physicians, by 1825, for some American women, childbirth was ceasing to be an open ceremony. Though birth still took place at home, and though friends and relatives still lent a helping hand, visiting women no longer dominated the activities in the lying-in room. Birth became increasingly a private affair conducted in a quiet, darkened room. The physician limited visitors because they hindered proper medical care, but the process of birth was also concealed because it embarrassed both patient and physician.

Between 1760 and 1825 childbirth was thus transformed from an open affair to a restricted one. As one consequence of the development of obstetrics as a legitimate branch of medicine, male physicians began replacing midwives. They began to reduce childbirth to a scientifically managed event and deprived it of its folk aspects. Strengthened by the professionalization of their field, these physicians also responded to the hopes of women in Philadelphia, New York, and Boston for safe delivery. Although they helped some pregnant women, they hurt midwives, who were shut out of an area of medicine that had been traditionally their domain. All these innovations took place in the large urban centers in response to distinctly urban phenomena. They reflected the increasing privatization of family life, and they foreshadowed mid-nineteenth-century attitudes toward childbirth, mother, and woman.

17

TECUMSEH, THE SHAWNEE PROPHET, AND AMERICAN HISTORY

R. DAVID EDMUNDS

The close of the Revolutionary War meant many things to Americans. To some it conferred a guarantee of freedom, to others a return to the peacefulness of everyday life, and to yet others an opportunity to establish a life of independence beyond the Appalachian mountains. But for Native Americans the defeat of the British meant the removal of their last defense against expanding American settlements full of farmers hungry for their land. Even before the war ended in 1783, settlers poured into Indian land in the middle South and Ohio River valley. There they met tribes that, cut off from a reliable supply of arms and trade goods, had difficulty preventing these incursions on their ancestral land. Moreover, in the eyes of these advancing Americans, who had gained vast military experience during the Revolution, Indians were enemies, having sided with the British during the Revolution in hope of receiving royal protection for their lands.

As tribes were pushed west, small pockets of resistance began to develop. Settler outposts were raided, outlying settlements attacked, farmers and livestock killed. But these remained isolated incidents and offered little prospect for sustained resistance to white incursions. It was against this background that two extraordinary Indian leaders of America emerged. Tenskwatawa and Tecumseh, Shawnee brothers, learned of the rapacity of American land hunger at an early age and from the dishonor of displacement dreamed of an Indian nation as strong and vigorous as the 13 colonies which had just won their independence. In different ways they both worked for nothing less than the revitalization of Native American culture and the securing of an independent nation for all Native Americans. Their quest is the subject of this essay by R. David Edmunds, who offers us a different view of the better-known Tecumseh than is generally found in history books.

Do you find any similarities in the values and motivations of Tecumseh and white Revolutionary leaders portrayed in history books? What does Paul Johnson's account of Mayo Greenleaf Patch in Reading 15 tell us about the sort of person the post-Revolutionary settler might be? How does Tecumseh's resistance compare with Mary Young's account of "The Trail of Tears" in Reading 18?

High upon a granite pedestal overlooking "the Yard" at the United States Naval Academy at Annapolis stands a bronze statue of an Indian warrior. Midshipmen passing in and out of Bancroft Hall traditionally salute the statue before taking examinations in the hope that the renowned warrior's medicine will assist them during their tests. Most midshipmen, if asked whom the statue represents, will reply that it is a replica of Tecumseh, the famous war chief of the Shawnees. In reality, however, the statue was never intended to be Tecumseh. It represents Tamenend, a chief among the Delawares.

The midshipmen's incorrect identification of the bronze figure is not surprising, for Americans have long regarded Tecumseh as one of their foremost Indian heroes. He is one of the few militant Indian leaders who was almost universally praised by his white contemporaries. During the War of 1812 both British and American officers spoke highly of the Shawnee, and since his death his image has grown accordingly. Eulogized by historians, Tecumseh has achieved an almost legendary status. His biographers have presented an Indian of superhuman qualities; and Alvin M. Josephy, in his volume *The Patriot Chiefs,* entitles his chapter on the Shawnee as "Tecumseh: The Greatest Indian."

If the white observers and historians have been laudatory in their description of Tecumseh, they have been universal in their condemnation of his brother, Tenskwatawa, the Shawnee Prophet. Both British and American leaders denounced the holy man as a "pretender" and a "coward," and historians have enlarged upon such qualities to present an image of a charlatan who manipulated the tribesmen for his own purposes. While Tecumseh's political and military movement is pictured as logical and praiseworthy, the Prophet represents the darker side of Indian life. A religious fanatic, Tenskwatawa is presented as riding his brother's coattails to a position of minor prominence.

Unquestionably, the Shawnee brothers emerged to positions of leadership during a period of great stress for Native Americans. Although the Treaty of Greenville supposedly had drawn a line between Indian and American lands in Ohio, the treaty was ignored. Frontier settlement continued to advance north from the Ohio valley, threatening the remaining Indian land base in the region. Meanwhile, white hunters repeatedly trespassed onto Indian lands to hunt

game needed by the tribesmen, and by the first decade of the nineteenth century game was becoming scarce. The fur trade declined in a similar manner, and after 1800 many warriors were hard pressed to provide for their families. Not surprisingly, the Indians retaliated by stealing settlers' livestock, and the resulting clashes produced casualties on both sides. Obviously, both Indians and whites suffered, but losses were much larger among the natives. Governor William Henry Harrison of Indiana admitted that "a great many of the Inhabitants of the Fronteers *(sic)* consider the murdering of the Indians in the highest degree meritorious," while Governor Arthur St. Clair of the Northwest Territory reported that "the number of those unhappy people (the Indians) who have been killed since the peace at Greenville . . . is great enough to give serious alarm for the consequences."

Much of the Indian-white conflict was triggered by alcohol. Frustrated over their declining political and economic status, beleaguered tribesmen drowned their sorrows in frontier whiskey. Although illegal, alcohol was in plentiful supply, and brawls resulting from the Bacchanalia spread social chaos throughout the Indian villages. Once-proud warriors quarreled among themselves or abused their kinsmen, while others retreated into drunken stupors. Some Shawnees, weakened by their dissipation, fell victims to influenza, smallpox, and other diseases. Others sat passively in their lodges, bewildered by the changes swirling around them. Meanwhile, the clans—traditional kinship systems designed to regulate and provide cohesiveness among the separate Shawnee villages—were unable to cope with the multitude of problems besetting the tribe.

Overwhelmed by the chaos within their villages, the Shawnees pondered the causes. Although many tribesmen realized that the majority of their problems emanated from outside sources such as loss of lands, economic deterioration, injustice, and alcohol, others suspected darker elements and probed inward, examining the fabric of tribal society. Predictably, traditional Shawnees concluded that much of their trouble resulted from witchcraft, for the fear of witches and their evil power permeated Shawnee culture, and neighboring tribes believed the Shawnees to have a particular affinity for sorcery and the supernatural.

The basis for such fear lay deep in tribal tradition. The Shawnees believed that in the dim past, when they first crossed the Great Water in search of their homeland, they had been opposed by a huge water serpent who represented the evil powers in the universe. Although their warriors had killed the serpent, witches had saved part of its body, which still held a potent and malevolent power. Contained in medicine bundles, this evil had been passed down through the ages and was used by witches to spread disorder throughout the tribe.

The balance between order and chaos formed a focal point for Shawnee cosmology. The Shawnees believed they were a people chosen by the great power in the universe—"the Master of Life"—to occupy the center of the earth and bring harmony to the world. For their assistance, the Master of Life provided the Shawnees with a sacred bundle possessing powerful medicine that could be used for good. He also gave the tribe a series of laws regulating their personal conduct. If the Shawnees cherished the bundle, and used its medicine properly, and if they followed the sacred laws, they would prosper and their world would be orderly. But if witches gained the ascendancy, or if the Shawnees relinquished the ways of their fathers, their lives would be full of turmoil. In the years following the Treaty of Greenville, many traditional Shawnees believed that the witches had gained the upper hand.

Not surprisingly, many associated the Americans with these forces of evil. The Shawnees believed that the sea was the home of the Great Serpent—the embodiment of disorder. Their forefathers had always warned that pale-skinned invaders might emerge from the water to disrupt the harmony of the Shawnee homeland. Since the Americans had first appeared on the eastern seashore, many tribesmen were certain the invaders were the children of the Serpent, intent upon the Indians' downfall. In 1803 Shawnees at Fort

Wayne informed Indian agents that their ancestors had stood on the eastern seashore, watching as a strange ship came over the horizon.

> At first they took it to be a great bird, but they soon found it to be a monstrous canoe filled with the very people who had got the knowledge which belonged to the Shawnees. After these white people had landed, they were not content with having the knowledge which belonged to the Shawnees, but they usurped their lands also.—But these things will soon end. The Master of Life is about to restore to the Shawnees their knowledge and their rights and he will trample the Long Knives under his feet.

And even Black Hoof, a government chief committed to the American cause, admitted, "The white people has spoiled us. They have been our ruin."

Yet the same chaos that threatened the tribesmen also produced a man who promised them deliverance. Known as Lalawethika ("The Noisemaker" or "Loud Mouth"), the man had been born in 1775 on the Mad River in eastern Ohio. Prior to Lalawethika's birth, his father had been killed by the Americans and his mother had abandoned him when he was only four years old. Raised by a sister, his childhood had been overshadowed by two older brothers, Chiksika and Tecumseh. Lalawethika never excelled as a hunter or a warrior, and during his adolescence he became an alcoholic. Following the Treaty of Greenville he lived in a small village headed by Tecumseh, where he unsuccessfully aspired to the status of shaman. But in April 1805 this alcoholic ne'er-do-well experienced a vision that changed his life and propelled him to the forefront of Indian leadership.

While lighting his pipe from the fire in his lodge, Lalawethika collapsed, falling into a coma so deep his wife and neighbors believed him to be dead. As his wife began her mourning song he astonished his family by first stirring, then regaining consciousness. Visibly shaken, he informed the gathered onlookers that indeed he had died and had visited heaven, where the Master of Life had shown him both an Indian paradise and a hell where eternal fires lay in wait for sinful tribesmen. Alcoholics like himself suffered the most, for molten lead was poured down their throats until flames shot out their nostrils. Amidst much trembling, Lalawethika vowed to renounce his former ways and never again drink the white man's whiskey. No longer would he be known as Lalawethika. Henceforward he would be called Tenskwatawa—"The Open Door"—a name symbolizing his new role as a holy man destined to lead his people down the narrow road to paradise.

In the following months Tenskwatawa experienced other visions and enlarged upon his doctrine of Indian deliverance. Much of his teachings addressed the decline of traditional moral values among the Shawnees and other tribes. Tenskwatawa claimed he "was particularly appointed to that office by the Great Spirit" and that his "sole object was to reclaim the Indians from bad habits and to cause them to live in peace with all mankind." While he continued to denounce whiskey as "poison and accursed," he also condemned the violence that permeated tribal society. He urged warriors to treat each other as brothers, to stop their quarreling, and to refrain from striking their wives and children. Husbands and wives should remain faithful to each other, and marriages should be monogamous. Shawnee warriors currently married to more than one woman "might keep them," but such marriages displeased the Master of Life.

Convinced that his forefathers had enjoyed a happier existence, the new Shawnee Prophet attempted to revitalize some facets of traditional tribal culture. Indeed, much of Tenskwatawa's teaching was nativistic in both tone and content. He asked his followers to return to the communal life of the past and to renounce all desire to accumulate property as individuals. Those tribesmen who hoarded their possessions were doomed, but others who shared with their kinsmen, "when they die are happy; and when they arrive in the land of the dead, will find their wigwams furnished with everything they had on earth." He also instructed them to use only the food, implements, and dress of their fathers.

Pork, beef, and mutton were unclean, and the tribesmen were instructed to eat only the game they killed in the forests. Neither were the Indians to eat bread, but only corn, beans, and other crops raised by their ancestors. Stone or wood implements should replace metal tools, and although guns could be used for self-defense, the warriors were to hunt with bows and arrows. With the exception of weapons, all items of American manufacture were to be discarded. In a similar manner, the Indians were to dress in skin or leather clothing and were ordered to shave their heads, leaving only the scalp lock of their forefathers. False gods should be forgotten, but the tribesmen should pray to the Master of Life, asking that he return fish to the streams and game to the forest. To assist his disciples, Tenskwatawa provided them with sacred "prayer sticks." The sticks were inscribed with pictographs illustrating certain spirits who would help the tribesmen in their supplications. If the Shawnees were faithful and their hearts pure, the Master of Life would restore order, the earth would be fruitful, and they would prosper.

While Tenskwatawa attempted to revitalize some part of Shawnee culture, he condemned others. He warned that many of the traditional dances and ceremonies no longer had any meaning and offered new ones in their place. He also instructed his followers to throw away their personal medicine bundles, which he claimed had been powerful in the past, but no longer possessed the potency needed to protect the Shawnees from the new dangers that threatened them. Tenskwatawa alone spoke for the Master of Life, and only those tribesmen who subscribed to the new faith would ever know happiness. But his disciples would be rewarded above all men, for they alone would eventually "find your children or your friends that have long been dead restored to life."

If the Prophet condemned some of the old religious practices, he was particularly suspicious of those tribesmen who held religious beliefs differing from his own. At best those shamans or medicine men who opposed his doctrine were misguided fools. At worst they were witches, in league with the Great Serpent to spread disorder among the tribes. And the Prophet did not limit his accusations to religious leaders. For the holy man, religion and politics were the same. He had been chosen by the Master of Life to end the chaos in the Shawnee world. All those who opposed him also opposed the Master of Life. Therefore, he was particularly suspicious of tribesmen who were becoming acculturated or who had been converted to Christianity. Such men also were suspect of witchcraft. Unless they repented, they too should be destroyed.

Tenskwatawa's distrust of those Indians who adhered to American values reflected his general condemnation of the Long Knives. He informed his followers that the Master of Life had made the British, French, and Spanish, but the Americans were the children of the Great Serpent. In his visions Tenskwatawa had seen the Americans take the form of a great crab that crawled from the sea, and the Master of Life had told him, "They grew from the scum of the great water when it was troubled by the Evil Spirit. And the froth was driven into the woods by a strong east wind. They are numerous, but I hate them. They are unjust. They have taken away your lands, which were not made for them." Only if the Indians rejected the Americans would order ever be restored to the Shawnee world. The Prophet instructed his people to cease all contact with the Long Knives. If they met an American in the forest, they might speak to him from a distance, but they should avoid touching him or shaking his hand. They were also forbidden to trade Indian foods to their white neighbors, for these provisions were the special gifts of the Master of Life, to be used by his children, not the spawn of the Serpent. Tenskwatawa instructed his disciples to cut their ties with frontier merchants, and "because they (the Americans) have cheated you," the Indians were to pay "no more than half their credits." Moreover, Indian women married to American men should return to their tribes, and the children of such unions were to be left with their fathers.

The new faith soon spread to other tribes, who like the Shawnees were unable to adjust to the great changes sweeping around them. By the autumn of 1805 warriors from the Delawares and Wyandots were traveling to Greenville, Ohio, where the Prophet had established a new village. There Tenskwatawa converted the visitors, then sent them back to proselytize their home villages. The Delawares proved particularly susceptible to the new religion, and during the late winter of 1806 they accused about one dozen of their tribesmen of witchcraft. In March 1806 the Prophet journeyed to the Delaware villages, where he examined the captives, exonerating some, but condemning others. The Delawares eventually burned four of their kinsmen before the witch-hunt terminated. Predictably, all those burned were converted Christians whose acculturation made them more suspicious.

The witch-hunt among the Delawares frightened Moravian missionaries associated with the tribe and brought a storm of protest from government officials. During the spring of 1806 Harrison wrote to the Delawares denouncing the Prophet and asking, "If he is really a prophet, ask him to cause the sun to stand still—the moon to alter its course—the rivers to cease to flow—or the dead to rise from their graves. If he does these things, you may believe that he has been sent from God."

Ironically, Harrison's challenge played into Tenskwatawa's hands. In the spring of 1806 several astronomers had traveled through Indiana and Illinois locating observation stations to study an eclipse of the sun scheduled to occur on June 16. Although Harrison either ignored or forgot about the event, the Prophet remembered. Among the Shawnees such an eclipse was known as a "Black Sun," an event surrounded with dread and portending future warfare. Accepting Harrison's challenge, in early June Tenskwatawa surprised even his closest followers by promising to darken the sun. On June 16, while his disciples and skeptics both assembled in his village, the Prophet remained secluded in his lodge throughout most of the morning, but as the noon sun faded into an eerie twilight he stepped forth exclaiming, "Did I not speak the truth? See the sun is dark!" He then assured his audience that he would restore the sun's former radiance, and as the eclipse ended even those tribesmen who still remembered him as Lalawethika, the drunken loudmouth, now were convinced of his medicine.

Following the eclipse, the Prophet's influence spread rapidly. During the summer of 1806 Kickapoos from the Wabash visited his village, were converted, and by the following summer their towns in eastern and central Illinois had become seedbeds for the new religion. Early in 1807 large numbers of Potawatomis and Ottawas from the Lake Michigan region traveled to Greenville and then carried the new faith back to the western Great Lakes. One of the Ottawas, Le Magouis, or "the Trout," became a special envoy for Tenskwatawa and journeyed into upper Michigan where he taught the Prophet's doctrines to the Chippewas. The results were phenomenal. At Chequamegon Bay hundreds of Chippewas gathered opposite Madeline Island to "dance the dances and sing the songs" of the new deliverance. Subscribing to the Prophet's instructions, they threw their medicine bags into Lake Superior and made plans to visit the holy man in Ohio. In the following months so many tribesmen were enroute to the Prophet's village that white traders found most of the Chippewa towns along the southern shores of Lake Michigan deserted. The Menominees, Sacs, and Winnebagos also were swept up in the religious frenzy, and during the summer of 1807 they trekked to Greenville in large numbers.

Unable to comprehend the religious nature of the movement, American officials at first believed that Tenskwatawa was only a figurehead controlled by more traditional chiefs among the Shawnees. During 1807 several groups of American agents arrived at the Prophet's village to investigate the character of the new movement. After meeting with Tenskwatawa, most of the envoys agreed that the holy man was the dominant Indian leader in the village. Moreover, the Prophet was able to persuade them that his religion posed no threat to the government. But Harrison and other officials refused to admit that the movement was an indigenous uprising, resulting from desperate conditions among the Indians. Instead, they charged that the Prophet was actually a British agent, intent upon raising the tribes against the United States.

Yet the British were as mystified about Tenskwatawa as were the Americans. During the summer of 1807 British agents were active among the Indians of Michigan and Wisconsin, but they remained suspicious of the Prophet. Although they invited the Shawnee to visit them in Canada, he refused. In response, William Claus, Deputy Superintendent of Indian Affairs for Upper Canada, warned other Indians to avoid him, speculating that the holy man might be working for the French.

The large numbers of Indians who journeyed to Tenskwatawa's village enhanced his prestige, but they also alarmed white settlers in Ohio. Moreover, the influx of tribesmen exhausted Tenskwatawa's food supply, and he was hard pressed to feed his followers. In November 1807 the Potawatomis suggested that he withdraw from Greenville and establish a new village on the Tippecanoe River in Indiana. The new site would be much less exposed to white influence and was located in a region where game was more plentiful. Therefore, in April 1808 the Prophet and his followers abandoned Ohio and moved to Prophetstown.

The withdrawal to Indiana temporarily removed Tenskwatawa from white scrutiny, but his logistical problems continued. Since Prophetstown was located further west, it was more accessible to potential converts, and during 1808 and 1809 Indians flocked to the new village in numbers surpassing those who had visited him at Greenville. Although the villagers planted fields of corn and scoured the surrounding countryside for game, they could not feed the multitude. To obtain additional food, the Prophet brazenly turned to the Americans. In June 1808 he sent a delegation of warriors to Harrison assuring the governor of his peaceful intentions and asking for provisions. The Indians were so persuasive that Harrison sent food to Prophetstown and invited Tenskwatawa to meet with him in Vincennes. Two months later, in August 1808, the Prophet and his retinue arrived at Vincennes and spent two weeks conferring with Harrison. The governor was astonished at "the considerable talent of art and address" with which Tenskwatawa mesmerized his followers. Moreover, the holy man's pleas of friendship toward the United States were so convincing that Harrison provided him with additional stores of food and gunpowder and reported to his superiors that his earlier assessments of the Shawnee were in error, for "the influence which the Prophet has acquired will prove advantageous rather than otherwise to the United States."

Tenskwatawa was also able to hoodwink John Johnston, the Indian agent at Fort Wayne. In May 1809 he met with Johnston, and although the agent previously had expressed misgivings about the Prophet's motives, Tenskwatawa assured him of his friendship. The Shawnee spent four days, denying "in the most solemn manner, having any views inimical to (the Americans') peace and welfare." Indeed, when the conference ended, Johnston, like Harrison, exonerated the holy man from all charges and reported, "I have taken much pains and have not been able to find that there existed any grounds for the alarm."

But the facade of friendship was too fragile to last. Although the Prophet feigned goodwill toward the government, he could not control his followers, many of whom were less devious in their relations with the United States. As Indian depredations spread along the Wabash Valley, Harrison became convinced of the Shawnee's duplicity. During the summer of 1809 Tenskwatawa again visited with the governor in Vincennes, but this time Harrison was less hospitable. Tenskwatawa's protestations of friendship had little impact, and Harrison informed the War Department that his suspicions of the Prophet "have been strengthened rather than diminished in every interview I have had with him since his arrival." Moreover, by the summer of 1809 Harrison was making preparations for the Treaty of Fort Wayne, and he assumed that such a transaction would terminate any pretense of amity between the government and the holy man.

Harrison was correct. The Treaty of Fort Wayne, signed in September 1809, ceded over three million acres in Indiana and Illinois to the United States. Negotiated by friendly chiefs among the Miamis, Delawares, and Potawatomis, the treaty was adamantly opposed by Tenskwatawa. In response, he redoubled his efforts to win new disciples. Messengers were sent to the Ottawas and Potawatomis, and many Wyandots who earlier had shunned the new faith now were converted to the Prophet's teachings. Once again Harrison received reports that the Indians were burning witches, and friendly chiefs among the Miamis and Piankashaws complained that warriors long faithful to the government now were flocking to Prophetstown.

Concerned over the new upsurge in the Prophet's influence, Harrison sent informers to the Tippecanoe and invited Tenskwatawa to again meet with him in Vincennes, but the holy man refused. He also ignored an invitation by the governor to travel to Washington and meet with the president. Instead, he informed Harrison that the recent treaty was illegal and threatened to kill all those chiefs who had signed it. He also vowed that the lands would never be settled by white men and warned Harrison to keep American settlement south of the mouth of the Vermillion River.

The Treaty of Fort Wayne ended any pretense of cooperation between Tenskwatawa and the government. By 1810 the lines were drawn. Tenskwatawa and his movement were unequivocally opposed to American expansion, and in the years following the treaty the anti-American sentiment was both transformed and intensified.

Tecumseh's role in the formation of this movement was entirely a secondary one. He subscribed to the new faith and lived with the Prophet at Greenville, where he assisted his brother in meeting the delegations of both Indian and white visitors. Tecumseh sometimes spoke in council upon such occasions, but no more so than Blue Jacket, Roundhead, or other Indians prominent in the village. In 1807 he accompanied a group of tribesmen who met with Governor Thomas Kirker of Ohio, but in this instance he spoke in defense of his brother, convincing the governor that the

Prophet and his movement were no threat to peace. Although primary materials from this period are full of references to the Prophet, almost none mention Tecumseh. Most accounts of Tecumseh's activities during these years are from the "reminiscences" of American observers recorded decades later.

Indeed, Tecumseh did not challenge the Prophet's position of leadership until 1810, two years after the move to Prophetstown and five years after the religious movement's beginnings. During 1808 Indians continued to flock to Prophetstown to see the holy man, not his brother; and in that year it was the Prophet, not Tecumseh, who met with Harrison at Vincennes. In the summer of 1808 Tecumseh did visit Malden seeking supplies for the Indians at Prophetstown, but he made no claims to leadership; and British accounts of the visit, which are quite specific in listing other Indians' names, refer to him only as "the Prophet's brother," not as Tecumseh, a chief among the Shawnees.

The springboard to Tecumseh's emergence was the Treaty of Fort Wayne. From Tecumseh's perspective it was obvious that the religious emphasis of his brother could no longer protect the remaining Indian land base. During the summer of 1809 he visited a few Indian villages in Illinois, but after the treaty Tecumseh took a new initiative and began to travel widely, emphasizing a political and military solution to the Indians' problems. The tribesmen should still adhere to the new religion, but they should abandon their old chiefs who remained friendly to the Americans. Instead, all warriors should politically unite under Tecumseh, for in his own words, "I am the head of them all. . . . I am alone the acknowledged chief of all the Indians."

Therefore, for two years—in 1810 and 1811—Tecumseh traveled extensively among the Indians of the West. During these years he met twice with Harrison, who reported to his superiors that Tecumseh now had emerged as "really the efficient man—the Moses of the family." In this period Tecumseh slowly eclipsed the Prophet's position of leadership, but ironically as the character of the Indian movement changed, its appeal to the tribesmen declined. In 1810 and 1811 parties of warriors recruited by Tecumseh temporarily joined the village at Prophetstown, but their numbers never approached the multitude of Indians who earlier had flocked to the Prophet. And although the Prophet no longer dominated the movement, he continued to exercise considerable influence. For example, his ability to convince his followers that they could easily obtain a victory over the Americans contributed to their ill-fated attack upon Harrison's forces at the Battle of the Tippecanoe in 1811. Obviously, after the battle the Prophet's influence was broken, and Tecumseh remained the dominant leader of the battered movement. But Tecumseh's preeminence was of short duration, for he was killed less than two years later, on October 5, 1813, at the Battle of the Thames.

It is evident, therefore, that the Prophet, not Tecumseh, was the most important figure in the emergence of the Indian movement prior to the War of 1812. Tecumseh used the widespread religious base earlier established by his brother as the foundation for his unsuccessful attempt to unite the tribes politically and militarily. Although the Prophet has been pictured as either a charlatan or a religious fanatic whose teachings seem quite bizarre, such an appraisal reflects an ethnocentric bias. He certainly seemed logical to the Indians, and for several years he exercised a widespread influence throughout the Old Northwest. In retrospect, such a phenomenon is not surprising. In times of oppression native American peoples have often turned to a religious deliverance. The Shawnee Prophet fits into a historical pattern exemplified by the Delaware Prophet, Handsome Lake, Wovoka and the Ghost Dance, and many others. Indeed, Tecumseh's emphasis upon political and military unification was much less typical than the Prophet's messianic nativism.

Why then has Tecumseh emerged as "the Greatest Indian"? The answer is obvious. If white Americans could design an "ideal Indian," they would have designed Tecumseh. His concepts of political and military unification under a centralized leadership appealed to whites because it was what *they* would have done. His solution had much less appeal to native Americans who had little tradition of either centralized leadership or of pan-Indian confederacies in response to American expansion. White Americans also praised Tecumseh's intervention in behalf of prisoners, but such intervention reflected European concepts of warfare more than those practiced by native Americans. Much of traditional Indian warfare was based upon vendetta, and prisoners expected the worst. Indeed, captured warriors took pride in their ability to withstand torture and laugh in the faces of their captors.

White Americans have championed Tecumseh because he, more than any other Indian, exemplifies the American or European concept of the "noble savage": brave, honest, a true "prince of the forest"—natural man at his best. Since his death, his American and British contemporaries and later historians have continued to embellish his memory with qualities and exploits that have added to his image. Many of the attributes and incidents were apocryphal (for example, his reputed love affair with the white woman, Rebecca Galloway, or the assertion that his skin was of a lighter hue than other Indians), but they only strengthened what Americans wanted to believe and have been incorporated into his biographies. Even his death added to the romantic appeal of the man. He fell, fighting to the last, in the Battle of the Thames—the red Armageddon. And his body was not among the dead on the field, but buried mysteriously by his followers in the forest. In contrast, the poor Prophet survived the war, was exiled in Canada, returned to the United States, was removed to the West, and in 1836 died an inglorious death in Kansas.

This reassessment does not mean that Tecumseh was not a remarkable man. Indeed, he was a brave and farsighted leader who sacrificed his life for his people. But the real Tecumseh stands on his own merits. He does not need the romantic embellishments of ethnocentric historians. Tragically, the Tecumseh who has emerged from the pages of history is, in many respects, a "white man's Indian."

PART THREE
AN
EXPANDING
PEOPLE

18

THE CHEROKEE NATION:
MIRROR OF THE REPUBLIC

MARY YOUNG

At the turn of the nineteenth century the United States contained fewer than 4 million men, women, and children. Little more than a generation later, in 1830, that population stood at 13 million, more than a fourfold increase. With the existence of this rapidly growing population there was little question of American remaining a nation pinned to the Atlantic coastline; as it had since the eighteenth century, westward expansion became an American way of life.

Both northern settlers, seeking western land for their small farms, and southern slaveowners, eager to expand cotton cultivation into the West, faced a formidable obstacle in the numerous Native American tribes occupying that land. Through treaty, purchase, and military force these settlers fought, usually successfully, to push the tribes westward, away from developing American settlements. One of the most notorious cases of this dispossession involved the forced "removal" of the Cherokee Nation from its homelands in Georgia, North Carolina, Tennessee, and Alabama and its resettlement on arid land in present-day Oklahoma.

This forced resettlement, known as the "Trail of Tears," was ill-planned, haphazard, and unmindful of the health and well-being of the Cherokees themselves. Not only did the Cherokee suffer the loss of their ancestral homelands and the humiliation of defeat and resettlement, but in addition they suffered from exposure to the heat, cold, and diseases that marked a journey hundreds would never see to its conclusion.

In this essay, Mary Young draws attention to the interaction of white American and Cherokee society. From the time of the American Revolution, Cherokee tribal leaders had urged their kinsmen to adopt the ways of white Americans in order to preserve their ancestral lands. By the second decade of the nineteenth century the Cherokee had almost completely abandoned traditional tribal practices and adopted Euro-American notions of property, law, and productive relations in the desperate hope that they could stem the tide of encroaching white settlers. Thus, as Young points out, the removals of 1837–1838 were the culmination of a long-term program designed to dispossess the Cherokee, not only of their land, but of their cultural autonomy as well.

What are the similarities and differences between Indian-white relations in the nineteenth-century South and those in seventeenth-century New England, portrayed by William Cronon in Reading 4? Do you think that Tecumseh's failure to form a united Indian nation, as detailed by R. David Edmunds in Reading 17, influenced the government's decision to remove the Cherokee?

Reprinted from the *American Quarterly* 33 (1981): 502–524. Copyright 1981, Trustees of the University of Pennsylvania. Reprinted with the permission of the author and *American Quarterly*.

In the early nineteenth century, the United States government through its own agents and through federally subsidized missionaries undertook an ambitious and comprehensive effort to change the economy, institutions, and culture of the Cherokee Indian Nation. By 1830, substantial change had occurred. The Cherokee had schools, churches, plantations, slaves, and a written language, newspaper, and constitution. At precisely that point, President Andrew Jackson encouraged the state of Georgia to extend its jurisdiction over the most populous part of the Cherokee Nation. By both action and inaction, the federal executive abetted thousands of trespassers who violated both United States treaties guaranteeing protection of Cherokee borders and a Supreme Court decision upholding treaty guarantees against the sovereign pretensions of the state of Georgia. The president and his War Department fostered a small faction of the tribe who, in 1835, signed the Treaty of New Echota, ceding Cherokee holdings in Georgia, North Carolina, Tennessee, and Alabama, and promising to remove the Cherokee people to present-day Oklahoma. The vast majority of the tribe rejected the Treaty, whose signers possessed no authority under the Cherokee constitution. In 1838, volunteer militia under federal command expelled approximately 16,000 Cherokee from their lands. They rode, walked, sickened, and died along the Trail of Tears to the Cherokee Nation West. After those who survived had settled in the West, earlier migrants or "Old Settlers," those who had participated in the Treaty of New Echota, and the new arrivals from the Cherokee Nation East struggled violently over who should control the government of the still "civilized" but deeply divided Nation.

As often as their story has been told, the Cherokee experiment in building and defending a modern Nation still evokes varied and conflicting interpretations. How "civilized"—or acculturated—were the Cherokee of the 1830s? Did the transformation of their social and political institutions represent "progress" in the sense of more effective defense of traditional values or the discovery of more effective ways of coping with change, or did it represent primarily the exploitation of a tradition-oriented majority by a white-oriented, white-parented planter elite? Should one view the Treaty Party as traitors or as far-sighted patriots? Scholars do not agree. The character and the fate of Cherokee "civilization" were political questions in the 1820s and 1830s, and federal officials, Georgia governors, Protestant missionaries, and Cherokee chiefs did not agree, either.

To their own and later generations, the Cherokee of the 1820s and 1830s symbolized the "civilized" tribes. If the effort to remodel Native American culture after the collective self-image of Jackson's generation worked anywhere, it worked among the Cherokee. In the familial metaphor presidents so often employed, the Cherokee were the White Father's "red children of the forest." If among these precocious children the experiment of civilization failed, where might it succeed? If, as Jackson's opponents believed, Cherokee improvement demonstrated the improvability of all Native Americans, and if the president's policy of Indian removal fatally damaged that progressive Nation, then the Cherokee migrants' Trail of Tears symbolized the tragic destruction by the United States of its own cherished work.

The young Republic's experiment in self-reproduction succeeded, in retrospect, better than either its authors or its beneficiaries could comfortably acknowledge. Like "children" in one sense, the Cherokee mirrored their various parental models in images too accurate, in some particulars, for child or parent to perceive. At the same time, the Cherokee grew into themselves, not mere replications of their "parents." The American society that shaped and conditioned Cherokee efforts to remodel themselves was involved in its own processes of growth, change, differentiation, and conflict. In perceiving, manipulating, and distorting the Cherokee Nation, the *soi-disant* parent society reproduced no ideal model, but multiple and refracted images of its own internal conflicts.

In the early nineteenth century, church and state collaborated to present the Cherokee with a unitary vision of republican, Christian, capitalist civilization. Their model American lived under written laws framed by chosen representatives and enforced by impartial public authority. Law protected property, and industrious males strove to increase their property by honest labor at the plow, the forge, or the mill, while industrious females kept the family clothed, and the home neatly groomed and governed. All worshipped a stern, transcendent, but benevolent God Whose Will was known through His written Word.

To achieve this model of civilization, presidents, federal agents, and federally subsidized missionaries ceaselessly recommended that the Cherokee abandon clan revenge for written law enforced by elected public authorities, paying particular attention to laws governing the descent of property. They recommended that the Cherokee allot their lands—held in common—to individual, male family heads; that men rather than women take major responsibility for farming; that these potential patriarchs use the plow and fence their fields. Women should abandon agriculture in favor of the wheel and the loom, so that their husbands need not hunt an ever-diminishing supply of game to trade for civilized clothing. Children, meanwhile, should be at school, learning to spin and weave, if female; or plow and reap, if male. Both sexes should discover how to count their money and read understandingly in the New Testament. Thus might sloth give way to industry; and magic, superstition, heathen dance, and conjuring, to reason, reflection, and revealed religion. Thus might American natives become model Americans.

As subjects, rather than objects, of cultural change, the Cherokee exercised a wider range of choice than any of their mentors intended to offer them. They perceived not only idealized self-images, but day-to-day habits and behavior; not only agents and missionaries but soldiers, planters, traders, and horse-thieves. According to position, disposition, and opportunity, various persons and parties in the tribe watched, listened, selected, and improved themselves in quite different ways.

Were the Cherokee 'civilized" in 1808? in 1817? in 1830? This question carried heavy political import for all parties, since the extent of Cherokee "improvement" was widely regarded as a measure of their qualifications for keeping their lands. Overtly, the tribal leaders accepted the definitions of "civilization" their improvers gave them. They offered censuses of their wealth, descriptions of their dress, housing, furniture, tableware, and work habits; copies of their constitutions and laws; and enumerations of their Christian converts, to prove that if not equal—that is to say, identical—to white people, they tended rapidly toward equality. John Ridge and Elias Boudinott, among the brightest of their anglicized young men, traveled among pious audiences in the northeastern states advertising the similarities between good society in New Echota and good society in New Haven or Baltimore.

Since the practical disadvantages of civil amalgamation under conditions of legal inequality and racial prejudice proved abundantly obvious, tribal leaders adopted the familial metaphor and took care to explain that their Nation as a whole was still in its "infancy," unready for full integration with a white population under a white-controlled government. The same elite made no secret, however, that they thought *themselves* adults, and they identified their own grown-ups status with the sovereign respectability of their independent Nation. When the white "parents" found these Cherokee grownups unwilling to sell their land and remove, they assaulted the Nation.

Faced with brutal trespass aided and abetted by the government pledged to protect their rights, the Cherokee elite brought their own varieties of selective perception to bear on the "parents." If the United States was indeed a republic of laws, were not Cherokee treaties sacred? Could not the American legal system shield Cherokee rights? Principal Chief John Ross believed inflexibly that such was the case. If the United States exemplified a Christian commonwealth, would not the good people of the country rush to the aid of the beleaguered and the oppressed? So tribal officials like John Ross, John Ridge, and Elias Boudinott believed—even more naively and firmly than their Christian champions in politics, Edward

Everett, Theodore Freylinghuysen, and Jeremiah Evarts.

Or, had the United States become, in truth, a nation of thieves and hypocrites—or squatters and rapists and drunkards specializing in felonious assault? When the Cherokee of the 1830s abandoned their hope of assistance from the Christian public—that is, when the Christian public abandoned them—John Ridge and Elias Boudinott finally rejected hope for equitable treatment and adopted this wilder image of Americans as their own, and signed a treaty agreeing to remove themselves beyond the reach of their wild white neighbors.

All these honorable men saw rightly, but partially. Both white and Cherokee society proved more complex and less predictable than most parties cared to allow. The process of change in Cherokee society created a Nation unique in its own ways, but in its very complexity more nearly like that of the United States than either red or white fully acknowledged.

Naturally enough, the Cherokee found numerous models among the planters who were their near neighbors. Most of the presidents who paternally recommended civilization to the southern Indians were themselves planter-aristocrats. George Washington, the "noblest Roman" among the Americans of his time, owned a plantation and slaves. So did John Ross, Richard Taylor, Major Ridge, John Ridge, and scores of others among the Cherokee upper class. The tribal elite themselves appreciated the fact that the habit some red planters developed of hiring white farm laborers provoked other farmers to intrude without invitation. How much of the extensive agricultural improvement attributed to Cherokee industry derived from the efforts of black and white laborers cannot be determined with cliometric exactitude. But from the mid-1820s, between five and ten percent of the eastern Cherokee Nation consisted of black slaves.

Andrew Jackson's portraits reflect his sometimes Roman, sometimes Napoleonic image. Many Cherokee respected the Old General as a fellow warrior. Jackson, a gentleman planter, had

also owned a store, raced horses, and gambled. John Ross's brother Lewis, one of the wealthiest Scotsmen in the Nation, earned his money in trade. After their removal to the vicinity of Fort Gibson in the Cherokee Nation West, the Cherokee joined the soldiers in gambling and horseracing. Frequently they got drunk with their fellow gamblers, and their delegation in Washington vainly petitioned for the removal of the fort as a temperance measure.

Apart from making their report on July 4, the framers of the Cherokee constitution of 1827 made much not only of their independence, but also of the similarity between their constitution and that of the United States. In truth, their constitution more nearly resembled those of some southern states than that of the federal union. The Cherokee constitution of 1827 gave their legislature the privilege of electing the executive, the Principal Chief; their later constitution of 1839 provided for the chief's popular election. In this evolutionary pattern, they followed Georgia.

The Cherokee constitution required officeholders to believe in a Supreme Being and a future state of rewards and punishments. Several states did so too, while not even the elastic clause placed that burden of belief on Thomas Jefferson or Andrew Jackson. Like most states, the Cherokee disfranchised those of African descent. Like all state constitutions of the period, theirs, departing from ancient Cherokee tradition, confined political privileges to males. The Cherokee legal code, like the codes of other slaveholder states, progressively reduced the right of slaves to own property, learn to read, move about, and assemble. The social disorganization incident on removal, and the roving gangs of black Seminole and Creek desperadoes in the Nation West, provoked the Nation to intensify the rigors of its slave code, though missionaries testified that the tribal government enforced restrictions on slaves even less reliably than it carried out other laws.

As in other southern states, notably Georgia, the planter-merchant class proved more active politically than other elements of the population and the law reflected their cultural and economic interests as well as the accommodation of those interests to the interests of other classes. Laws provided for the collection of debts, protected property and regulated its descent, handed out licenses and franchises, fixed fees for ferries and turnpikes, and enabled citizens to borrow from the national treasury. More Whiggish than his fellows, John Ross would have had his government establish a national bank.

Cherokee "aristocrats" democratized their government by progressively increasing the number of salaried offices available to the aspiring. Their anger in the face of losing office and valuable saline privileges at the government's disposal helps explain the tenacity with which, in the early 1840s, the Old Settlers Party of the Cherokee West resisted the takeover of their government by the more numerous migrants from the Cherokee Nation East.

Respectable state governments of the antebellum period concerned themselves with cultural improvement, especially education. In the range of their concern for culture, the Cherokee elite reflected the New England model more strongly than the Georgian, though a "progressive" Georgian like Wilson Lumpkin might have denied the difference. After the missionary school at Brainard got underway, the Cherokee National Council provided it with a Board of Visitors. In the 1840s, when their treasury permitted such expenditure, the Nation established a public school system. In this establishment they were ahead of their neighbors in Arkansas, who did not enjoy the luxury of federal annuity payments. Presbyterians, Baptists, and Methodists in the 1840s vied for control of the Nation's schools, while the pagan Cherokee poor, like the Irish and other minority voters of Massachusetts, complained that the expensive institutions mainly served the children of the Prostestant elite.

In subsidizing a national newspaper with avowedly educational and propagandistic objectives, the Cherokee State went beyond even New England's mandate. More than most contemporary governments, the Cherokee accepted cultural improvement as a public obligation. The leaders of the new Nation had obvious reasons for identifying their hegemony with cultural progress. Since their government, unlike others, depended on federal annuities and missionary subsidies rather than on taxation, they found less reason than the gentlemen planters of Georgia to identify respectability with economy in government. Cherokee criminal law, which relied on fines and physical punishments rather than penitential incarceration, resembled the codes of such less progressive states as Tennessee and North Carolina. Probably, however, the Cherokee modeled their penalties initially on the practice of federal army units stationed near them. Courts-martial at the garrison of Southwest Point in the early nineteenth century regularly handed out up to one hundred lashes for theft, as did the Cherokee. North Carolina's maximum was thirty-nine.

Since the Cherokee state represented a population quite different from Georgia's, North Carolina's, or the army's, its constitution and laws reflect both compromise among elements of the tribe and cultural differences between white and Cherokee. The United States viewed the introduction of written law enforced by public authority as a response to its "civilization" program. So, in part, it was. But the laws and constitutions of the Cherokee reflect as well the striving of mixed-bloods for political ascendency, their compromises with those whose tastes and ambitions were more traditional than their own, and the motive that unified nearly all Cherokee, especially the traditionalists—keeping their country.

The first written laws punished theft. Clearly they benefited those who had the most worth stealing, and reflected both growing national wealth and increasing differentiation between richer and poorer. Yet most families owned pigs, black cattle, horses, or sheep. Losing one's only horse could prove much more damaging than parting with the best seven out of ten. To treat horse theft, as William McLoughlin has done, as a kind of patriotic resistance movement may well be just, but one should not overlook the fact that what the laws sought to prevent was theft by Cherokee from Cherokee. Delinquency may, as McLoughlin points out, have provided a few of the poor with an alternative career, but one can hardly believe their Cherokee victims applauded it.

The law of oblivion for murders (1810) redefined murder to exclude accidental homicide and to include fratricide. The notion of agreeing upon mutual forgiveness, or "oblivion," putting an end to a cycle of revenge, was thoroughly traditional, though the law modified the traditional definitions of murder entailed in the system of clan revenge. Yet we must notice that not until the emigration crisis of 1828, when the federal government hired western Cherokee to go among their relatives in the East persuading them to sell their improvements to the United States and emigrate West, did Cherokee law explicitly penalize the crime of murder. Until that time, no written command prevented clans from continuing to work revenge.

Cherokee property law remained notably more egalitarian than comparable legislation among whites. The tribe defined land as the common property of all. Improvements belonged to those who made them, purchased them, or inherited them. No one might settle within a quarter mile of another's improvement without his or her permission. Though the Council modified tradition by providing for the inheritance of a father's property by his children, mothers enjoyed entire control over improvements they made or personal property they acquired. Any white husband who mistreated his Cherokee wife might face a fine and forfeiture.

Cherokee creditors could satisfy themselves out of a delinquent debtor's property—provided, however, the debtor retained his home, farm, horse, saddle, some corn, a cow and a calf, and a pig or so. Otherwise, the tribal custom of hospitality might place too large a burden on the debtor's kin or neighbors.

Laws such as those prohibiting theft benefited all ranks. The poor had unimpeded access to the means of production. The wealthy could add to their estates as much land as their slaves could till. Cherokee observers emphasized how much this departure from bourgeois custom benefited the common citizen. Unfriendly white critics alleged that free land made the rich richer and the poor careless.

In deference to those who resented missionary influence, the constitution of 1827 disqualified ministers of the gospel from holding office in Council. In deference to ministers of the gospel, the constitution explained that such persons had better things to do. John Huss, "The Spirit," a preacher of uncommon talent who achieved Presbyterian ordination for a sermon that had to be interpreted from his Cherokee, did not serve on the Council. More appropriately, he became Chief Justice of the Supreme Court. The Council mandated in the 1827 constitution was an elective body created by enacted law. It nonetheless had evolved from less formal Councils that had been called on an *ad hoc* basis at least since the eighteenth century. Traditional full-blood leaders expected—and were expected—to exercise influence by winning election to council. They had no such expectation of the Supreme Court, an institution created *de novo* in the 1820s. The 1839 constitution, formed by emigrés in the Cherokee Nation West, contained no prohibition against ministerial councillors. Young Wolf, a Methodist licentiate, served on the National Council and credited himself with persuading that body not to prohibit intermarriage with whites. Young Wolf had a wife of German descent.

In deference to missionary opinion, the National Council prohibited polygamy—first for whites, then for everyone. Unlike other Cherokee laws, this one prescribed no penalty for violators.

Such legislation reflects a generation of political conflict and compromise. The mixed-blood elite's usefulness in doing public business with the United States gave it an advantage; the fortunate politicians improved their advantage tactfully and most of them proved loyal partisans of the Nation they strove to unify.

Charles Renatus Hicks, a literate Moravian convert, established his role as adviser to old chief Pathkiller during the first decade of the nineteenth century. At the same time, Pathkiller himself emerged as principal spokesman for his people, while his competitors took their ambitions to

Arkansas. Chief Doublehead's treachery in the treaty negotiations of 1806, the tradition of bribery as a method of negotiation, and conflicts over the leasing of ferries, sawmills, and the distribution of tribal annuities all contributed to the creation, in 1809, of a committee composed largely of mixed-bloods. The committee took charge of the annuity and asked for it in cash. Charles Renatus Hicks became national treasurer. Shortly after forming the committee, the mixed-bloods co-opted several more traditional leaders to membership.

Andrew Jackson's successful maneuvering of the 1816 treaty negotiations and the War Department's enthusiasm for general removal provoked the tribe to formulate its first written constitution. Several leading women, who had refrained from interfering directly in negotiations with the whites (since white gentlemen did not bring their women with them), presented the Council of fifty-four towns at Amohoee in April, 1817, with an address on the crisis. For the sake of their children and grandchildren, the Council must prevent further cessions. The land, the women explained, belonged to all "who worked at the mother's side." The Council responded with a document that conferred on the committee exclusive responsibility for conducting treaty negotiations and gave the National Council power to veto the committee's actions. By formally centralizing responsibility, the Towns defeated the United States' favorite tactic—ignoring chiefs who seemed stubborn and conferring sovereign power to sell on those who proved compliant.

The committee and Council functioned together as a legislative body as well. As their laws reflected increasing missionary influence, traditional leaders grew restive. Pathkiller and Charles Renatus Hicks both died in 1827, and thus raised the question of who might succeed them. White Path, who had recently suffered expulsion from the Council, tried to foment a rebellion against the establishment of a new constitution that would formalize methods of electing the Council and the Principal Chiefs. According to white observers, few influential men of any party joined White Path. In any case, the constitutional

party met with the dissidents and all agreed to harmonize their differences. White Path again won election to the Council, which continued for many years to reflect strong full-blood representation.

As compromise and accommodation marked the tribe's political rearrangements, variety and relative tolerance distinguished their cultural and economic development. By 1830, the Presbyterians had converted, churched, and disciplined perhaps 200 of the approximately 18,000 eastern Cherokee—though as in the neighboring states, congregations usually outnumbered church members. Moravians also established small congregations. The more permissive and egalitarian Methodists, in the Cherokee Nation as elsewhere, rapidly outdistanced the Presbyterians, acquiring a society membership of approximately 800. Baptists in the Nation East concentrated their efforts on the Cherokee of North Carolina, whom they supplied with preaching and literature in the native language, vocational instruction, exhortations to temperance, and such remarkably effective political leadership that General John Wool, charged with assembling migrants for removal, expelled Reverend Evan Jones from North Carolina. Afterward, the War Department tried, unsuccessfully, to keep Jones out of the Cherokee Nation West. In the 1850s, Evan Jones and his son John provided active leadership for the traditionalist Keetowuh Party in Cherokee national politics.

The Baptist and Methodist emphasis on lay preaching, emotional piety, and song probably accounts as much for their long-run dominance of Cherokee christendom as does their relative doctrinal elasticity. Presbyterians noted that the Baptist practice of baptism by total immersion corresponded to the curing ceremonies of native "conjurors," and that Methodists treated conjuring as a branch of medicine rather than as a species of idolatry. Not even all Presbyterians insisted on making conjuring a matter of church discipline.

Though the Presbyterian missionaries of the American Board clearly regarded themselves as upholding more rigorous doctrinal standards than did the Baptists or Methodists, even Presbyterianism could embrace the special spirit of the Cherokee community. When John Huss preached his ordination sermon, he took for a text Matthew 7: 13–14: "Enter ye at the strait gate: for wide *is* the gate, and broad the way, that leadeth to destruction, and many there be which go in thereat: Because strait *is* the gate, and narrow is the way, which leadeth unto life, and few there be that find it." The sentiment of his text, especially the concluding lines, expresses perfectly the Presbyterian experience among the Cherokee. But in expounding the text, Huss stressed the evils of drink, a matter on which Matthew keeps silent, and the importance of avoiding quarrels. Matthew does bless the peacemaker; he also reports another kind of statement: "I come not to bring peace, but the sword." Huss chose from Matthew a sermon on the harmony ethic, and he chose his sins, like his theme, from Cherokee experience rather than from the letter of the Gospel.

When any church attacked traditional practices—ballplaying, conjuring, or lively and prolonged ceremonial dancing—it succeeded in relocating some celebrations and in making them disreputable among some of the "respectable" class. A Presbyterian Female Society expelled members for attending ball-plays. Yet those who preferred the traditional ways continued to follow them, and politicians who sought votes patronized ball-plays and dances. Not until the 1850s did the tribe fracture into enduring political factions along cultural lines. Pagans and Christians of the 1820s and 1830s could still be neighbors, accommodating their inevitable contentions as they arose.

The westward migration of several thousand Cherokee between the 1790s and the general removal of 1838–1839 almost certainly contributed to the geographic segregation of the traditional from the progressive. Many of those who first went West voluntarily resented the accommodation tribal leaders were offering to federal diplomats; others took the trip to escape the land of the Bible and the Cherokee police, or Light Horse Cavalry. Opportunities for hunting both bison

and Osages beckoned; and fur traders followed the hunters. By the 1820s, though, both missionaries and police had arrived in Arkansas. The fur trade of the western Cherokee attracted merchants; the broad acres along the river beckoned slaveholding planters. In the 1820s, Arkansas, like the Cherokee portion of North Carolina, had its full-blood villages and its towns where English predominated, as well as bilingual settlements. Missionaries and temperance societies met more active resistance in the West than in the eastern Nation. Laws there were fewer and the hunting better, but the virus of cultural change thrived in Arkansas as well as Georgia. After the 1838 migration, people tended to settle near neighbors they found culturally congenial, though no wholesale segregation of the churched from the unchurched came to prevail.

Most significantly, cultural variations among the Cherokee in the 1830s reflected the choices of those who varied, and while most mixed-bloods got richer than most full-bloods, cultural conservatism did not necessarily follow racial lines, nor did it entail poverty for those who continued in the old ways. Cherokee law established new and violent sanctions against theft and slave delinquency; however, in most other respects the experiment in "civilization" broadened, rather than constricted, the people's range of choice as to how they would live.

In 1830, some Cherokee wore frock coats, pantaloons, stiff collars, and top hats. Other males wore pantaloons, a blanket, a turban, and ear-bobs. Old men still wore deerskin hunting shirts, leggings, and moccasins.

When the troops came to Georgia and North Carolina in 1838, Chief John Ross's traditionalist followers suffered extensive material loss. Many refused to register their claims with any agents but Ross's. The Principal Chief's agents recorded claims for an extensive array of goods, both real and personal. George Beamer, of Hanging Dog Creek, left behind him a fourteen-foot square log house, "skelped down inside," having a "cabbin" roof, a loft, and two doors; a nearly finished fourteen-foot square round log house, never occupied; a "Potatoe or hot house," also fourteen-feet square, well-finished; a new house, fifteen by thirteen, "skelped down inside and ready for covering"; a twelve-acre upland field, another eight acres of cleared land, three-quarters of it bottom land; eight acres fenced and not cleared, thirteen peach trees, and an apple tree. Tahlaltuskee of Chutoogatah Town, Georgia, left among his possessions a twelve-foot square sugar camp with a shed roof, and one hundred troughs. Standing Wolf, of Cheohee, North Carolina, left cabins much like George Beamer's, and three ten-foot square covered rail hog pens, a sheep pen, five well-fenced fields totaling twenty-two acres, twenty small peach trees, and ten small apple trees. He also took leave of a nine-by-fifteen fish trap and "1 Canoe, very strong 30 feet long and 2 feet wide." Will, Standing Wolf's more modest neighbor, left simply a board "camp," seven apple trees and a one and one-half acre field. Buck, of Stekoa Town, North Carolina, left a fourteen-foot-square round-log loom house among his several cabins; his neighbor, Cullesawee, left a blacksmith shop.

Similar "savages" left behind them barrows, breeding sows, chickens, ducks, geese, guinea hens, wash pots, skillets, teacups and saucers, teaspoons, pewter dishes, plows, plow gears, chains, axes, augers, chisels, planes, wheels and looms, tomahawks, cane sifters, ox yokes, currycombs, weeding hoes, mattocks, a man's plaid cloak, an umbrella, a large looking glass, scissors, andirons, door locks, featherbeds, counterpanes, deerskins, rifles, frying pans, churns, saddles, horse collars, "Delph ware valued $6," good fur hats, silver bands, bows and arrows, beaver traps, blow-guns, "2 callico frocks," log chains, fish hooks, and "4 empty barrels."

Such claims derived from the districts where federal appraisers generally recorded comparatively small improvements; where a few round log cabins, with stick and clay chimneys, a hot house, and a dozen acres of land with a few fruit trees put their owner in the middle class; where a few elderly men and women still owned claims to an acre or two in town fields; where the most impressively equipped "improvement" was Evan Jones's Baptist missionary establishment in the Valley.

To the south and west of the hillbilly Cherokee, the solid yeomanry built hewed-log cabins, with hinged doors and shutters, and stone chimneys, roundlog kitchens, corncribs and stables; they cultivated more land and generally did without hothouses.

At the upper end of the social scale, twenty men in the Cherokee Nation registered claims for real property exceeding ten thousand dollars assessed valuation. The very wealthy included "Rich Joe Vann," who was worth just under thirty thousand dollars; Lewis Ross, Major Ridge, John Ridge, John Ross, John Martin, Michael Hildebrand, Alexander McCoy, Joseph Crutchfield, Edward Gunter, John Gunter, Jr., Joseph Lynch, and the heirs of John Walker, Jr. At one time or another, all the men listed played active roles in Cherokee politics. None earned his living exclusively from planting, though all but one had one or several large plantations. Stores, taverns, mills, and ferries accounted for their exceptional wealth. Their way of life nonetheless reflected the plantation culture of the upland South. Their hewed-log, frame, or brick houses, painted and "well-finished throughout," boasted multiple windows, piazzas, and an occasional portico. Their numerous outbuildings included large kitchens with multiple brick fireplaces, great stables and barns, fields ranging into the hundreds of acres, "Negro houses," orchards, and sometimes ornamental trees and gardens.

Full-blooded Major Ridge, whose hospitality the Treaty Party councils frequently enjoyed, was the only member of the elite who owned a hothouse. In a hothouse, one could keep warm in winter, store potatoes, or sweat oneself out in ritual purification. Major Ridge owned plenty of fireplaces and storehouses; in 1832 he received Presbyterian baptism. But the sometime Speaker of the National Council also hosted councils and Green Corn Festivals, and probably catered to the tastes of his guests.

The coincidence of political and economic elites that this list reflects appears hardly accidental. The National Council regulated ferries, traders, the sale of liquor, and the admission of millers and other artisans into the Nation. The way to wealth might be paved with legislation; certainly its protection repaid attention to politics. This aspect of the Cherokee elite's activity also resembles—perhaps in exaggerated form, since the community was comparatively small—the style to which the gentlemen planter of Georgia also aspired.

A simple skeptic might regard the patriotism of this elite, and their work of nation-building, as the outward sign of inward avarice. So Andrew Jackson believed. When the elite fractured into pro-Treaty and anti-Treaty factions, each attributed mere avarice to the other. The men and women who left behind their canoes, blow-guns, Delft, pewter, and fishtraps believed otherwise. Andrew Jackson thought the plain Indian merely deluded, but he may have been wrong.

Sovereign independence protected Cherokee control over roads, ferries, taverns, plantations, and artisans. National legislation tended increasingly to render that control exclusive; to restrict individual Cherokee rights to hire white agricultural labor, to award franchises for roads and ferries to mixed-blood politicians who required no white partners, rather than to old chiefs who did; and to place discriminatory taxes on traders who were not Cherokee citizens—though the United States nullified the discrimination. Such exclusiveness infuriated good citizens in Georgia. They complained that it was not white intruders the Cherokee minded, just white intruders without Indian bosses. When Georgia established counties in the Nation and set up the Guard, one of the Guard's first acts was to break down the Turnpike gates at John Martin's ferry.

The Cherokee Nation West, however, offered broad fields for slaves to work, opportunities in trade, roads, ferries, and even salines. And the United States from 1828 on offered ample compensation for eastern improvements that had to be abandoned. Many wealthy people took advantage of such opportunities between 1828 and 1838.

Contrary to the maxim that "dukes don't emigrate," in the period 1828–1838, it was mainly "dukes" who did. By 1828, the "poorer" Cherokee usually stayed behind. When they faced eviction, they migrated as far as the Carolina hills. John Ross's insistence on getting a fair price for the gold mines argues that he had as keen a sense for economic values as Governor Lumpkin of Georgia. But John Ross as a planter and merchant could find riches enough in the West—in the 1840s and 1850s he did. Perhaps he "merely" craved power, as his enemies ceaselessly supposed. But missionary Daniel S. Butrick, who "itinerated" more miles in the Cherokee Nation than almost any other white man living there, thought Ross more nearly a "captive" to his constituency than they to him. If he craved power, the only way he could satisfy the craving was to serve the deepest interest his people thought they had—keeping their country. Several hundred of these "deluded" people risked starvation or death from exposure to elude the troops who came to take them from their mountains. General John E. Wool, detailed to occupy the Cherokee Nation prior to removal, offered blankets and rations to the destitute. In February, 1837, he reported, " . . . those in the mountains of North Carolina during the summer past, preferred living upon the roots and sap of trees rather than receive provisions from the United States and thousands, I have been informed, had no other food for weeks. Many have said they will die before they leave the country."

In the summer of 1838, thousands left their homes literally at the point of bayonet, herded like swine into camps and onto steamboats from which hundreds still managed to escape. Probably, they revered John Ross and supported his government not because he "deluded" them, but because he did everything in his power to keep their country.

If twenty-twenty hindsight defines John Ross as a patriot who did what he could to defend traditional Cherokee territory, were men such as John Ridge, Major Ridge, and Elias Boudinott, who drew up the Treaty of Echota, traitors? By Cherokee law, they had committed treason. The written law that defined selling the country without consent of the National Council as a capital crime specified that the criminal be convicted in court. If the accused failed to appear for trial, he became an outlaw—anyone's target. But in 1835 no Cherokee courts could operate in Georgia, where the Treaty Party leaders lived. Georgia, which sought to supplant Cherokee jurisdiction with state law, made the exercise of office under the Cherokee constitution a penitentiary offense. State authorities prohibited the arrest of the signers in Georgia, and the Georgia Guard and federal troops occupied the Cherokee Nation. The signers could not be tried. Perhaps more important, John Ross, a stickler for legalisms, did not recognize the New Echota agreement as a treaty: no treaty, no crime.

Instead, the treason of the Treaty Party was handled in terms of an older tradition of clan revenge. If missionary testimony can be credited, members of the clans to which John Ridge, Major Ridge, and Elias Boudinott belonged agreed among themselves to kill these leading members of the Treaty Party, and carried out their intentions in the Cherokee Nation West in June, 1839. At that time, the party opposed to the Treaty, recent emigrants, did not recognize any official public authority as finally established in the Nation West. The anti-Treaty relatives of the signers apparently fell back on the "unwritten law," which the written law avowedly recorded, and on the older tradition of clan revenge. According to that older system, members of one's own clan might agree to kill a clansman so that no other person of his clan need suffer for his guilt. Had everyone accepted the older tradition, the murder of the Ridges and Boudinott by members of their own clan would have ended the conflict, since these men would not have been subject to revenge for killing their own. Since by 1839, traditional definitions of clan relations existed side by side with Anglo-American kinship and legal systems, to say nothing of different norms governing the treatment of murder and revenge, blood feuds could not be limited so simply. In the Cherokee Nation West, they increased and multiplied. The revenge motif persisted; the customs and assumptions that had limited its range did not.

Whatever the legal norms involved, the Ridge-Boudinott faction did sell their country in defiance of national authorities and several mem-

bers of the faction profited personally from the transaction. Georgia authorities protected their property and federal agents appraised it generously. Did they sell out for profit?

Anyone who had wanted to sell out for profit without hazarding assassination could have done so at any time after August, 1831, by appealing to federal emigration agent Benjamin Franklin Currey for an appraisal, and enrolling for emigration at United States' expense. Currey's anxiety to enroll prominent emigrants profited many planters who foresook the hazards of politics in Georgia and pursued the opportunity to preempt plantation sites in Oklahoma.

The Ridges and Boudinott, who stayed until a treaty was signed and ratified, saw themselves as men who understood the real Cherokee condition as John Ross did not. They had many reasons for believing that they saw correctly. In late adolescence, John and Elias had studied at the missionary boarding school in Cornwall, Connecticut. They married the white daughters of school employees. The managers of the school disavowed their action, the women's relatives accused the young ladies of endangering the missionary cause out of mere lust, and pious citizens of Cornwall tolled the church bell as they burned pictures of Elias Boudinott and Harriet Gould, his wife, on the village green. Though both the Prudential Committee of the American Board of Commissioners for Foreign Missions and the missionaries to the Cherokee defended the two scholars, Ridge and Boudinott undoubtedly acquired an understanding of racism that light-skinned Lewis Ross, who married a white relative of Cherokee agent Return J. Meigs, and light-skinned John Ross, who joined a Masonic Lodge in Jasper, Tennessee, never appreciated.

While John Ross sent his children to preparatory school in Lawrenceville, Pennsylvania, and spent his winters in Washington, the dark-skinned men of the treaty party and their mixed-blood children spent their days mainly among Georgians. Repeatedly, John Ridge tried to persuade John Ross that the Cherokee's condition had become intolerable. It is clear that by 1832, both John Ridge and Elias Boudinott had concluded that removal was inevitable and that delaying the inevitable might destroy both the wealth and, more important, the moral fiber of the nation. By November, 1834, their party concluded that with "all the unrelenting prejudices against our language and color in full force, we must believe that the scheme of *amalgamation* with our oppressors is too horrid for a serious contemplation. . . . Without law in the States, we are not more favored than the poor African. . . ."

They hoped to persuade John Ross to make a treaty; in 1833 and again in 1835 they expected him to do so. But John Ross retained control of the press and the Council, refused to permit discussion, appeared willing to accept even state citizenship rather than leave the gold mines, and treated Ridge and Boudinott as traitors long before they had in fact become so. In the winter of 1835, after John Ross agreed to act with the Treaty Party and then went off to Washington without dealing with the only man authorized to make a treaty on behalf of the United States, Elias Boudinott signed the treaty he hoped might save his people from being overrun by Georgians. His missionary mentors disapproved his action; yet they had taught its rationale. The virtuous and the enlightened have a duty to do what they can for the good of the people, even when the people fail to understand what is good for them.

After John Ross and his delegation in Washington refused to accept the New Echota Treaty and failed to negotiate an alternative to it, John Ridge signed that treaty too. Had no one signed a treaty, Georgians promised within the year to take possession with all necessary force of everything the Cherokee still owned in that state. John Ross was of course perfectly correct, in the long run, in his belief that if the Cherokee could not sustain their legal rights in Georgia, they would in the end sustain them nowhere. Yet if, as John Ridge had come to believe, the United States was "utterly corrupt," her practice belying her principles, one might as well buy time, and temporarily, asylum. This the Treaty Party did. They also made permanent a factional split that lasted longer than the Cherokee Nation West managed

to persist as a territorial entity. John Ross seemed no better able than Andrew Jackson to entertain the notion of a loyal opposition. By sending the Nation down the Trail of Tears, Jackson, Ridge, and Boudinott made certain that no other Cherokee would develop such notions either.

In the 1850s, the slavery issue divided the Cherokee Nation, and the "full-bloods" identified themselves as a party, rather than a persuasion. But the factional division that originally rent the Nation, the division that persisted, the struggle whose bitterness destroyed the reputability of compromise, did not result from cultural change, or from the mundane malignity of self-interested Cherokee politicians. Political oppression—the sustained cooperative effort of the United States and the sovereign state of Georgia to destroy first the unity and then the existence of the Cherokee Nation East—created that faction.

An alternate reading of antebellum Cherokee politics might, however, cast a different light on the impact of federal policy on tribal unity and national reintegration. The model of constitutional government so deliberately fostered by Meigs and his missionary allies offered not only an opportunity for the political ascendancy of a white-oriented elite, but also a means for reestablishing and maintaining at least some kind of political order in a society that was rapidly becoming more differentiated and stratified, more diverse in its social and spiritual values, than the "traditional society" pictured by the informants who spoke to John Howard Payne and James Mooney, or by twentieth-century scholars such as Fred Gearing and John Philip Reid.

Ironically, the omnipresence of common enemies—the Treaty commissioners, the emigration agents, Andrew Jackson, and the messengers from his War Department—probably did much to maintain such political unity and relative social harmony as the Cherokee enjoyed in the generation between 1810 and 1840. Whatever importance one may attach to outbreaks of antimissionary sentiment, or to White Path's abortive "rebellion" of 1827, it seems clear that the Cherokee could not devote themselves wholeheartedly to factional disputes over cultural alternatives until the late 1840s and 1850s, when they experienced a degree of relief from Washington's recurrent threat to take their land away from them.

The Cherokee Nation's reputation as a model Christian Indian republic proves well deserved. Cherokee men, women, and children learned well the lessons of literacy, the artisan skills, and the governmental techniques their agents and missionaries taught them. More gradually, many Cherokee became converted Christians—or perhaps they converted Christianity, as they converted other features of the model, to their own special needs. Yet the Cherokee Nation mirrored not only the ideal images their mentors sought to foster, but the competitive, contentious, and exploitive human relationships their masters so cunningly, if half-consciously, modeled for them as well.

19

CLASS AND RACE IN THE ORIGINS OF THE MASS-CIRCULATION PRESS

ALEXANDER SAXTON

The growth of factories in the first half of the nineteenth century was the most visible aspect of American industrialization. The creation of large three- and four-story buildings housing hundreds of operatives who worked to the rhythm of steam- or water-driven machinery presented a striking contrast to the predominantly rural scale and pace of American life.

But while the factory system has long been the hallmark of America's transformation from an agrarian to an industrial nation, the most important industrial changes took place not in the factory, but in the small artisan shops that dominated the American economy. As late as 1850, for example, Philadelphia, one of America's industrial centers, counted fewer than a third of its work force employed in shops with more than 20 workers.

In these shops skilled craftsmen, who had learned their trades through long years of apprenticeship and journeyman training, controlled the shop's daily output, product quality, and the rhythm of work itself following long-established craft rules and customs. Beginning in the early nineteenth century, however, growing numbers of merchants and master craftsmen began to view the slow pace of craft production as a hindrance in their quest to supply large quantities of cheap manufactured goods to the rapidly expanding West and South. Breaking craft skills into simple, easily learned tasks and hiring unskilled workers to perform them, these early manufacturers undercut the craft system and placed all aspects of production under their control.

It was this decomposition of the craft system that formed the backdrop for the rise of the mass-circulation press. Published by artisan printers, these newspapers played a major role in forging artisan discontent into a powerful, class-conscious labor movement. But ironically, as Alexander Saxton reveals in this essay, the need for expensive equipment to maintain the low cost of production drove the popular press from the hands of their artisan founders into those of the industrial capitalists they opposed.

How do the ideas of class consciousness disseminated in the press compare with the "Free Labor" ideology of the Republican Party (Reading 23)? How do you think the various members of the "industrial order," discussed by Jonathan Prude in Reading 21, would have responded to the message of the popular press?

In the America of 1828, daily newspapers in the United States belonged to and served the upper-class coalition that had dominated politics throughout the era of national independence and constitution making. Aimed at an urban male readership of commercial and professional men, the daily press transmitted political polemics, public statements, documents, and commercial and foreign news deemed by the editors significant to American men of affairs. Advertising cards, unchanged month after month, offered a memento of local enterprise nearly as fixed as the brass plates that marked the places of business. Dailies in the 1820s carried little general news; neither humor nor sex except in the form of political invective; no sports, high crimes only occasionally, no regular theater notices, and no items of family interest or of special appeal to women or children. Fiercely competitive within these narrow limits, the editors, who were of upper-class status, or aspired thereto, stood ready with cane and dueling pistol to act out the self-image of the *grande bourgeoisie.*

The number of papers and their circulation reflected these affinities. In 1830 there were sixty-five dailies in the United States with an average circulation of twelve hundred. They sold for six cents a copy; but since there were no newsstands and no vendors, a prospective purchaser had to seek out a book store or find his way to the newspaper office. Spoken of as "blanket sheets" by their detractors (35 × 24 inches, they unfolded to a 4-foot width), such papers obviously were intended to be spread out on the library table at home, or across the counting house desk. Most circulation was by subscription and subscriptions cost ten dollars a year, the equivalent of a week's wages for a skilled journeyman.

Daily news, then, at the beginning of the Jackson administration remained a luxury of the urban wealthy. Within the next twenty years the spread of the penny press expanded both the numbers and class base of newspaper readership. In 1840 there were 138 dailies, in 1850, 254. Average daily circulation rose from twelve hundred in 1830 to just under three thousand in 1850. New York City alone had fourteen dailies in 1850 with a combined circulation running well over 150 thousand. This amounted to one newspaper a day for every 4.5 inhabitants, in contrast to one for every 16 twenty years earlier. Democratization of newspaper reading sprang from the same sources as did the upsurge of the Jacksonian co-

alition, paralleled, and initially reinforced it. Just as political revolt against class deference opened the era of mass politics, so the cultural transformation of the 1830s and 1840s swept the nation into the age of mass media. While the Jacksonian coalition was both urban and rural, its most radical egalitarian tendencies flowed from the artisan culture of the cities and entered the Democracy through the Workingman's movement. The first wave of penny dailies duplicated this sequence. Their appearance coincided with the formation of the Democratic party. Their territory comprised the cities of the Atlantic seaboard. Initiated by artisan printers, they propagated an urban artisan ideology that was rationalist and secular in tone, democratic in politics, expansionist in aspiration, and ferociously white egalitarian in its identification. Pioneers of the new press included influential veterans of the Workingmen's parties of the late 1820s whose grudging adherence to the Democratic coalition mirrored the suspicious separatism that had characterized the relationship of Workingmen to Jacksonians.

The first successful penny daily, the New York *Sun,* was founded in September 1833 by a twenty-three year old journeyman printer, Benjamin Day. Day might have been the model for Mark Twain's Connecticut Yankee. A New England artisan of Protestant Anglo-American old stock, proud of his common school education, combining vast enthusiasm for money and machinery with an egalitarian contempt for the higher learning of colleges and universities, Day typified the pioneers of the penny dailies, and for this reason his career is worth following in some detail. The son of a West Springfield, Massachusetts, hatter, Day apprenticed on the Springfield *Republican* when it was still a weekly edited by Samuel Bowles, Senior. Drawn like other young artisans to the metropolis, Day hired out on the New York *Evening Post* and soon opened his own job shop. The Workingmen's movement was just beginning. Many of its activists were young printers, their lives centered around shops like Day's, who poured their energies into short-lived little journals, radical in the radical republican tradition of Ethan Allen and Tom Paine. When Robert Dale Owen and Frances Wright came east from Indiana in 1829, these young artisans grouped around the *Free Enquirer,* first issued from the New York shop of George Henry Evans, a journeyman printer six years older than Day. As Day typified the New England connection of artisan radicalism, Evans embodied its origins in old England. Born to parents of the lesser gentry (his father had been a commissioned officer in the British army), Evans grew up in central New York state where his parents settled, and served his apprenticeship at Ithaca. His journeyman's wander years he spent in small town printing offices of the Burned-Over District.

The upsurge of Workingmen's activity during the summer and fall of 1829 thrust Evans, Owen, and their associates into political leadership. Wright, concentrating on her course of lectures, remained somewhat in the background, but supported the collective endeavor by urging *Free Inquirer* readers to form associations for the "Protection of Industry and for the Promotion of National Education." Robert Dale Owen summarized the purposes of this organization in a paraphrase of the Apostles' Creed:

> I believe in a National System of Equal, Republican, Protective Practical Education . . . the only redeemer of our suffering country from the equal curses of chilling poverty and corrupting riches, of gnawing want and destroying debauchery, of blind ignorance and unprincipled intrigue. By this creed I will live. . . .

In 1829 and 1830 members of the New York association functioned as a radical caucus inside the Workingmen's Party.

Meanwhile Wright's flamboyant reputation exposed the entire movement to conservative attack, especially in the blanket press, which referred to the associations for National Education as "Fanny Wright societies." Typical of the multitiered invective directed against her involvement with radical artisans were the following lines from a "doleful ditty" published in the *Courier and Enquirer:*

> Oh Fanny Wright—sweet Fanny Wright
>   We ne'er shall see her more:
> She's gone to take another freight
>   To Hayti's happy shore . . .

Wright actually was leaving for a visit to Europe; the reference to Haiti called up a trip she had made the preceding autumn to provide personal escort for several slaves from the ill-fated Nashoba commune, who were to be set free in the Haitian Republic. The ditty continued:

> Farewell ye young mechanics
>   Ye lusty men and true;
> All—one and all—both great and small,
>   My heart is warm for you.
>
>   . . .
>
> Ye are the bone and sinew
>   The marrow of this land;
> And yet ye are but blockheads
>   Who cannot understand.
>
> So I have come to teach you. . . .

When it became obvious that the *Free Enquirer,* with its commitment to anticlericalism and shocking the bourgeoisie, was by no means the most effective vehicle for mass mobilization, Evans at the end of October, 1829, began the *Workingmen's Advocate.* Generally regarded as the nation's second labor paper (the *Mechanic's Free Press* of Philadelphia preceded it in 1828), the *Workingmen's Advocate* served for the next fifteen years under varying formats as a major voice of artisan radicalism.

Soon after the first issue of the *Advocate* the New York Workingmen's ticket demonstrated impressive strength in the November election. The party at once came under redoubled attack from the established press, while at the same time agents of the old political apparatus began to infiltrate, seeking (successfully, as it turned out) to break up and co-opt its constituency. Leaders of the Workingmen now recognized their need for a mass circulation daily and apparently took steps to meet the need. The *Free Enquirer* hinted at such a possibility. The *Workingmen's Advocate* predicted that a "new daily paper" would soon be launched by printers of the city's leading blanket sheet, the *Courier and Enquirer,* who found its politics intolerable. In mid-December the *Workingmen's Advocate* carried a formal announcement that the *Daily Sentinel,* devoted to the interests of "mechanics and workingmen," was to begin publication in January. Yearly subscriptions at eight dollars were to be somewhat cheaper than those of the blanket press, advertising rates "proportionately low."

Benjamin Day was involved in these events, probably at the periphery. Frederic Hudson, a contemporary who became managing editor of the *Sun*'s major rival, the New York *Herald,* described Day as having been associated with the *Free Enquirer.* While doubtless invidious, this must have been partially accurate. Prepublication announcements of the *Sentinel* listed Day as one of six directors. The six described themselves in the first issue of the *Sentinel* as "all practical printers . . . [who] have, in common with their fellow laborers in every branch of industry, participated largely in the distress which pervades the producing classes of this community." Among the other five were P.C. Montgomery Andrews who served in 1830 as Fourth Ward Secretary for the Workingmen's Party and was elected to its General Executive Committee; William J. Stanley, a member of the Workingmen's Fourth Ward Vigilance Committee; and Willoughby Lynde, journeyman and master, and esteemed member of the New York Typographical Association. The *Workingmen's Advocate* characterized the *Sentinel* as in "our cause" and both the *Advocate* and the *Free Enquirer* boosted it enthusiastically. Frances Wright, according to her biographer, William Waterman, loaned one thousand dollars to help capitalize the new daily. Nonetheless the first issue, scheduled for January 15, did not come off the press until one month later. Through this period Day's name continued to appear as director, although he dropped out during the second month of publication. By that time it must have been obvious that the *Sentinel* was a dying cause. The party itself was disintegrating into factionalism and the *Sentinel*—unlike the *Workingmen's Advocate*—had failed to

establish an independent base of readership. Evans, who joined the board of directors in June 1830, tried to rescue it but succeeded only in taking the wreckage in tow by combining the *Sentinel* with his own narrowly focused but more solidly supported (and much less expensive) labor weekly.

The notion of a mass circulation daily based on New York City's working class must have been intensely discussed by directors of the *Sentinel.* Within three years of its demise, Day launched the *Sun,* and soon afterwards William J. Stanley and Willoughby Lynde, with a third partner, Billings Hayward, also an active member of the New York Typographical Association, founded the New York *Transcript.* Whereas the *Sentinel,* retaining the general style of upper-class dailies, and with only a modest reduction in price, had relied on the shift from conservative to radical politics to win readers, Day and the Stanley group experimented with massive changes in format, price, and distribution, as well as content. The new papers measured 8.5 × 11 inches in contrast to the 24 × 35 inches of the blanket sheets. Selling for a penny a copy, they priced subscriptions at three dollars a year instead of six cents or ten dollars. For circulation, however, they relied not on subscriptions but on a system (borrowed from the London press) of selling bundles of one hundred at two thirds of a cent per copy to news vendors who then fanned out into preassigned districts of the city.

To radical politics, Day—and the *Transcript* partners as well—gave scant visibility. What remained of 120 column inches after four columns had been sold to advertisers was divided amongst financial items (everybody followed the ups and downs of bank notes in the 1830s), shipping, humor and anecdotes, local news, and crime, much of it clipped from out-of-town papers. Yet the *Sun* and *Transcript* both covered the city police court, again borrowing from British precedents. Day engaged with one of his printers to report police court proceedings every morning before the regular shopwork. Since these reports brought forward primarily the city's brawlers, burglars, pimps, alcoholics, and prostitutes, they furnished local news par excellence: crime, violence, humor, and sex in a single package. The *Transcript* equalled the *Sun* in this respect and also dabbled occasionally in sports reporting. Both papers were successful. They outstripped the sixpenny press, increased their sales of advertising, and brought in handsome profits. Success bred competition. Scores of penny dailies entered the field between 1834 and the depression of 1837. Some lasted only a few weeks; most of the rest collapsed during the depression; one, James Gordon Bennett's New York *Herald* (1835), lived to become a giant.

However, it was the spread of daily papers to other cities, rather than their proliferation, which had the most lasting consequences for the industry. Arunah Shepherdson Abell, born in 1806 of an old stock Protestant family in East Providence, Rhode Island, apprenticed on the Providence *Patriot,* a Jeffersonian weekly, moved as journeyman printer to Boston, and soon afterwards to New York. Employed by Benjamin Day on the *Sun,* he made the acquaintance of two other printers, Azariah H. Simmons and William M. Swain. Born in Onondaga, New York, in 1809, Swain had apprenticed in Utica and worked as a journeyman in Albany and Philadelphia before coming to the New York *Sun,* where, by the time of Abell's arrival, he was printing foreman at twelve dollars a week. The three men talked about starting their own paper, decided New York was overcrowded, and signed a partnership agreement to produce a penny daily in Philadelphia. The result was the Philadelphia *Public Ledger,* first issued on March 25, 1836. Abell, retaining his share in the *Ledger,* moved south to Baltimore, then the nation's second largest city, to found the Baltimore *Sun* in 1837. Both papers imitated the New York *Sun* and *Transcript,* and throve as spectacularly. In Boston, where earlier efforts at penny dailies had failed, George Roberts, following the New York model, put the *Daily Times* into the mass circulation orbit in 1836.

The penny dailies so far referred to—three in New York, one each in Philadelphia, Baltimore, and Boston—were, with one exception (the Balti-more *Sun,* May 1837), solidly established before the panic of 1837. With the exception of the New York *Transcript,* all survived the depression to continue as circulation leaders into the booming fifties. These were the major papers in what I have described as the first wave of the mass circulation press. They institutionalized working-class readership in the great cities of the Central Atlantic seaboard. They created methods and models, applied existing technology and promoted new. They demonstrated the sorts of relationships that must prevail between publisher and readers, readers and advertisers, if mass circulation was to be achieved. In this sense they staked out the boundaries within which second, and ongoing, waves of daily newspapers would be obliged to operate.

Circulation figures have been notoriously unreliable, especially for the first half of the nineteenth century, when they were based largely on claims of the publishers themselves. Nonetheless they offer an index to scale of magnitude. In the summer of 1833, New York's eleven dailies shared a total circulation of about twenty-six thousand. The *Sun,* opening in September with an issue of less than a thousand, equalled its largest competitor (the *Courier and Enquirer,* 4,500) before the end of the year and passed ten thousand in 1834. The *Transcript* went to nine thousand in its first year and by 1836 was running neck and neck with the *Sun* at about twenty thousand. Frederick Hudson wrote that the New York *Herald* reached seven thousand within a few weeks of its first appearance in 1835. The *Herald* held close to the *Sun* for the next twenty years, finally passing it in the late 1850s to become the most widely circulated daily in the United States. Their combined circulation by that time exceeded 125 thousand. Rates of increase in other large cities were no less dramatic. The Baltimore *Sun,* despite the depression of 1837, reached twelve thousand in its first year and went to thirty thousand in the 1850s. The Philadelphia *Public Ledger* climbed to twenty thousand, fell off in the depression, but by the end of the 1840s had passed forty thousand. The Boston *Daily Times* reached twenty thousand in the late 1830s.

Growth rate for the second wave, which, after

the depression of 1837, carried mass journalism to medium cities of the hinterland and new cities in the West, probably exceeded that for the first wave, and for the first time brought Whig editors like Horace Greeley and Henry Raymond into the mass circulation field. In 1850, when the ratio of daily newspaper issue to New York City population was 1 to 4.5, it stood at 1 to 3.8 for "urban places" (more than eight thousand inhabitants) nationally. Ten years later the corresponding ratios were 1 to 3.9 for the city and 1 to 3.4 for "urban places." During that decade New York City's population had increased by sixty-nine percent, that of "urban places" by seventy-five percent. Horace Greeley estimated that a city of fifteen thousand could support a daily paper, while cities of twenty thousand were likely to have competitive dailies.

Expansion of readership involved more than aggressive distribution and attractive packaging. It rested on the technology of printing and paper making. In both cases technologies imported from Europe were adapted to meet American needs and potentials. Paper making shifted from handicraft to factory production, becoming increasingly mechanized and steam-powered after 1815. By 1829 American paper mills, most of them in Pennsylvania, New York, and New England (the largest was in Springfield, Massachusetts), employed over ten thousand people and turned out a product valued annually at seven million dollars. Newspapers in America spent about half a million dollars a year on newsprint. Search for cheaper methods and materials led to two breakthroughs prior to the Civil War: application of chlorine to processing rags and then in the 1850s substitution of wood pulp for rags. Largely as a result of these innovations, newsprint fell from 16 cents a pound in 1830 to 8.3 cents in 1860.

When Benjamin Day started the New York *Sun* he used a hand-cranked flatbed capable of two hundred copies an hour. Success led him to acquire a press recently marketed by a New York manufacturer, Robert Hoe, modeled on the British Napier press. This also was a hand-cranked flatbed, but the application of paper to the type by means of rotating cylinders made possible an output of two thousand copies an hour. The *Sun,* however, was now approaching a circulation of twenty thousand. " . . . the difficulty of striking off the large edition . . . in the time usually allowed to daily newspapers was very great," Day recalled twenty years later. "In 1835 I introduced steam power . . . but even this great aid to the speed of the Napier machines did not keep up with the increasing circulation of the *Sun.* . . . " A next logical step toward high-speed printing —transfer of the type from the flatbed to the rotating cylinders—bogged down for more than a decade in mechanical difficulties of locking the type to the curved cylinder face. Robert Hoe eventually solved these problems in a press built for the Philadelphia *Public Ledger* in 1846. By the mid-fifties Hoe presses operated at twenty thousand impressions per hour. Such machines required twenty mechanics in attendance, together with their "carry-off boys." Big city dailies were likely to use several. The New York *Herald,* for example, invested in five.

While the secondary literature is packed with statistics on circulation, it contains only meager information as to costs, profits, and capitalization. This reflects the fact that newspaper publishers, eager to boast of circulation, were likely to be reticent about financial matters. Clearly, however, the technology of mass journalism was expensive and costs rose as technology became more complex. In 1836 Day had bought two Napier-type Hoe presses for seven thousand dollars, exclusive of the cost of converting to steam power. Six years later, James Gordon Bennett valued the physical plant of the New York *Herald* (a six-story building together with "10 presses, types, newsboats, etc.") at 55 thousand dollars. When Henry Raymond launched the New York *Times* in 1851 he paid twenty thousand dollars for a steam-driven Hoe press similar to the one built for the Philadelphia *Ledger.* Charles Dana in 1850 estimated that while five to ten thousand dollars might have sufficed to start a daily ten years earlier, 100 thousand dollars at least was needed in 1850. Thus it was obvious that the threshold of investment was rising at an accelerating rate. Open briefly to artisan printers before the depression of 1837, the mass circulation field increasingly shut them out, in part as a result of their own successful application of technology.

"Capital! Bless you, I hadn't any capital," Day recalled of the beginnings of the *Sun.* "I had no capital except my job office. . . ." Day's recollection accorded with the Jacksonian ethic. His job office together with a journeyman's mastery of the craft were acceptable forms of capital since they accrued from his own labor. Reinforced by success of the *Sun,* they gave him access to other capital that enabled him to invest in steam-powered presses. *Other* capital probably took the form of credit from paper wholesalers and manufacturers of printing equipment. Whatever the details of financing, Day's investments added to the fixed charges of the enterprise. The larger the circulation, the greater the irreducible costs. Aside from printers and reporters, the *Sun* now carried engineers, firemen, mechanics, bookkeepers, and salesmen on its payroll. Entire outfits of type wore out every few months. Such costs were irreducible because mass circulation was the source of financial success. Unfortunately for Day, however, circulation, although necessary to success, by no means ensured it. Expanding circulation generated a diminishing portion of gross revenue. What produced revenue was advertising, which varied directly with circulation, but varied also with the cycle of boom and depression that characterized capitalist growth in the nineteenth century. Advertising revenues dropped off in 1837; in 1838 Day sold the *Sun* to his brother-in-law, Moses Beach, for forty thousand dollars.

Beach, like Day, was a Connecticut Yankee. Born to an old stock New Haven family, Beach apprenticed in a cabinet shop, shifted to paper manufacturing, and invented a rag cutter used in paper mills. Moving to New York, he joined Day as head of the mechanical department, then as partner. Perhaps because of their relation by marriage Day may have sold the *Sun* to Beach at a generous price; or for the same reason, perhaps, Beach paid more than Day (in 1838) could have gotten on the open market. I incline to the latter.

However that may be, Day, still a young man, dropped out of the penny daily field, whereas Beach rose with the *Sun* to wealth and prominence. Whether or not the *Sun* could have survived without the modest infusion of capital Beach apparently brought, we know that most dailies launched before the depression failed before 1840. Among them was the *Sun*'s chief rival of the early years, the New York *Transcript,* which despite William Stanley's struggle to keep it alive, went under in 1839. The Philadelphia *Ledger* appears to have been hard pressed during the depression. So was the Boston *Times.* Its founder, George Roberts, after losing control of his paper for three years, finally raised enough capital to reclaim the property in 1840. At that time Roberts announced a news-pooling arrangement with a New York daily, probably the *Sun.* In 1845 Moses S. Beach, son of the New York *Sun*'s owner, and Benjamin Day's nephew, became Roberts's partner on the Boston *Times.* Later that same year, Beach returned to New York to take over management of the *Sun* as his father prepared for retirement.

Of the ten men listed as publishers of first wave penny dailies, biographical clues show that eight began as artisans—seven printers and one cabinet maker—and that two were New Yorkers at least by 1829; five came of old stock New England or upper New York state background. Three of the ten (Day, Lynde, and Stanley) experienced direct involvement in the New York Workingmen's movement; five others (Swain, Simmons, Abell, Beach, and Hayward) entered the penny daily field as a result of association with Day, Lynde, or Stanley; while one (Roberts) seems to have survived in that field partly through linkages to the New York *Sun* and the Beach family. Roberts, apparently not a printer himself, often worked in tandem with owners of job shops. The last of the ten first wave publishers was something of a maverick. Neither a New Yorker nor a Yankee, and never an artisan, James Gordon Bennett, founder of the *Herald,* was born in Scotland of middle-class Catholic parentage. Migrating to America in 1819, he worked as a reporter on the Charleston (South Carolina) *Courier* and later as

Washington correspondent for the grandest of New York's blanket sheets, the *Courier and Enquirer.* Yet like the others, Bennett was a wage earner, and in 1836 he was unemployed and nearly broke. Speaking in the same egalitarian vein as Day, he claimed he had started the *Herald* with only five hundred dollars.

Men such as these—on the basis of their journeyman's and editorial skills—might have had access to working credit, scarcely to large capital. One reason for the affinity of their newspapers to Workingmen's and Jacksonian politics was the anger many of these editors felt at seeing upper-class dailies like the *Courier and Enquirer* subsidized by bank loans, especially from the Second Bank of the United States, while they themselves were starving for capital. Given the favorable coincidence of technology, flush times, and politics in the early thirties, these artisan editors created the mass circulation press; men of their economic and social status would not have that opportunity again. This did not mean that artisan editors ceased to play a role in American political and intellectual history; but that their sphere would be limited to small circulation newspapers in western towns (Mark Twain and Dan DeQuille at Virginia City, for example) or to the radical and labor press (Henry George, George Swinton, and a host of others).

Majors among mass circulation dailies launched after the depression of 1837 were as likely to be Whig as Democratic. Horace Greeley, founder of the New York *Tribune* in 1841, came of old New England stock like many founders of the first wave, and like them began his career as a journeyman printer; yet with respect to capitalization and credit his sponsorship by the New York state Whig apparatus gave him entry to a different world. Henry Raymond, who launched the New York *Times* in 1851, had few if any links to the artisan tradition. Born in Lima, New York, graduate of the University of Vermont, his class background was that of editors of the old sixpenny press. Leaving Greeley, who was too radical for him, he went to the *Courier and Enquirer,* not as a printer but as an editor; and when he set up his own paper he enjoyed the backing

of a group of investors who subscribed 100 thousand dollars not after, but before, the first issue of the *Times* came off the press.

The transition from Day's hand cranked flatbed to the 100 thousand-dollar capitalization of the *Times* suggests that within that span of less than twenty years two lines of development already several centuries old converged briefly and separated. Since the first application of modern technology to written words there has been a continuing trend to reduce the unit cost for delivery of words to consumers; and a trend toward higher price of entry into the field. By comparison to the monk who transcribed manuscripts by hand, the Gutenberg press marked the beginning of mass communications. It expanded readership at the cost of a fixed investment in technology as prerequisite to entry. At one end of this sequence lay minimal price of entry and prohibitive unit cost; at the other, a unit cost curve approaching zero and an investment curve rising almost vertically: mass illiteracy at one end, oligopolistic or monopolized control of communication at the other. Differing value ascriptions would define the optimal relationship between these two curves in different terms. Egalitarianism certainly would seek to combine low unit cost with minimal cost of entry. For the United States such an optimum must have occurred sometime in the first half of the nineteenth century—say, during the twenty years from 1833 to 1853. To Jacksonians at the time this may have seemed a happy coincidence. Viewed retrospectively, it appears not as coincidence but as one of several necessary conditions for the era of mass politics and the party system. It made possible while it lasted something like a free market in ideological commodities that corresponded to the Jacksonian ideal type for the economy as a whole.

So far I have touched on content of the Jacksonian press to the extent only of suggesting that certain political and ideological directions were implicit in the technology and economics of mass journalism. Penny dailies of the first wave—in contrast to the heavily political focus of their immediate predecessor, the New York *Sentinel—*

gave politics low visibility. Much of their limited news space was devoted to crime and sex. It has sometimes been proposed that journalistic sensationalism served to divert mass readership from political issues. What is usually overlooked in this connection is that sensation was not politically neutral. With respect to crime and sex—closely linked because sex entered the press mainly in the form of reports on prostitution and crimes of passion—news stories worked at three interrelated levels. They shocked and excited; they conveyed conventional admonitions about the perils of liquor and moral profligacy; and they criticized corruption or bias of law enforcement while simultaneously exposing the hypocrisies of the upper class. Long before Stephen Crane, Maggie and her supporting cast were playing out their sad dramas in the penny press.

Scholars of journalism generally agree that crime reporting like that of New York's famous Robinson-Jewett murder trial boosted circulation of the new dailies. Doubtless it did. Yet it is also important to understand how such material was presented. On the acquittal of Robinson—an upper-class young man accused of murdering a prostitute—the New York *Sun* commented that "an opinion is prevalent and openly expressed that any man may commit murder, who has $1500 to give to Messers Hoffman, Price and Maxwell." The Ogden Hoffman here referred to was a successful New York lawyer and leading Whig. The *Transcript* agreed with the *Sun*. So did the editor of the Philadelphia *Public Ledger* who added: "We believe it too, and we think that no calm observer of the whole trial would believe otherwise." This probably was directed at Bennett of the *Herald* who had unexpectedly supported the defense, charging that Robinson had been set up as a scapegoat by higher-ups in order to forestall exposure of wealthy aristocrats who patronized the house where Jewett was murdered. The *Transcript* editors, and doubtless Benjamin Day as well, regarded Bennett as a traitor because the effect of his assertion of Robinson's innocence was to exonerate Hoffman and the presiding judge of any accusation of class bias. In fact Bennett seems to have been

hated by most of his contemporaries on both sides of the political spectrum. The point here is that although the *Herald* broke ranks on the question of Robinson's guilt, it followed the other penny dailies in the tactic of turning traditional morality against its upper-class sponsors. In this sense nonpolitical news became politicized because it tended to unmask hypocrisies in the dominant culture.

Characteristic of penny press editors of the first wave was their identification with wage earner interests. Reporting on labor trials, they often expressed indignation against courts that convicted workingmen for trade union activities and against judges who meted out severe sentences. Following the New York conviction of twenty-five journeyman tailors for combination to obtain higher rates, the Philadelphia *Ledger* quoted with approval an assertion that

the whole aristocracy of this city [New York] have [sic] been arrayed against the journeyman tailors, for the purpose of frightening the mechanics and workingmen of this country. During this trial we have every reason to believe that justice has been kept as far out of sight as possible . . . [by men who] set themselves up as the lawful organs of keeping one class as the mere slaves of the other.

The editor of the *Ledger* had no need to remind his readers that the judge who sentenced the twenty-five journeyman tailors was the same who presided over the acquittal of Robinson. Not all penny dailies spoke as clearly as the *Ledger, Sun,* and *Transcript* in denouncing conspiracy prosecutions against trade unionists. The *Herald* was ambivalent on the question, while the Boston *Times* endorsed such prosecutions. Perhaps significantly, it was only these two among the six first wave dailies that were published by men of other than artisan background; Roberts of the Boston *Times* later acknowledged, in a different connection, that he expected the political views of his readers to be at odds with his own.

Early penny dailies frequently advocated higher wages and shorter hours. "There can be no doubt," the New York *Sun* declared, "that owners of factories obtain more real benefit from ten hours work of hale, hearty and willing hands, than twelve hours from sickly and puny persons. Confinement wears out the constitution." The Philadelphia *Ledger* hoped that striking mechanics at the Brooklyn Navy Yard would "be able to stand out long enough to bring their oppressors to terms. The laborer has been curtailed of his just dues long enough." Both papers championed the cause of seamstresses and women factory workers. In 1834 the *Sun,* featuring accounts of a "Turn Out at Lowell" by women mill hands, reprinted in full their manifesto, "Union is Power," which declared that none should go back to work "unless our wages are continued as they have been," and until "they receive us all as one." The *Ledger* praised the *Sun* for "taking up the glove" in defense of underpaid seamstresses, whose situation it described as even worse in Philadelphia than New York, and urged the "Sewing Sisterhood" to organize into "societies" for enforcement of a "scale of adequate prices." Endorsing a call for statewide organization of "Mechanics and their Apprentices" in 1841, the *Sun* predicted that "the mighty influence which this numerous class is destined to exert," would work towards "the lasting good of our State and Nation."

"Since the *Sun* began to shine upon the citizens of New York," Benjamin Day wrote, recalling the early years of his paper,

> there has been a great and decided change in the condition of the laboring classes and the mechanics. Now every individual, from the rich aristocrat who lolls in his carriage to the humble laborer who wields a broom in the streets, read [sic] the *Sun;* . . . Already can we perceive a change in the mass of the people. They think, talk and act in concert. They understand their own interest, and feel that they have numbers and strength to pursue it with success. . . .

Penny daily editors saw themselves as fellow soldiers of justice and progress, embattled against reactionary interests represented by the sixpenny press. In a burlesque report of a newspaper pub-

lishers' convention in 1833, the *Sun* defined the attributes of the common enemy:

> "Who is that schoolmaster looking little fellow, out there by the window, with a psalm book in his vest pocket?" [inquires one of the delegates.] "O, he edits a mammoth sheet, also in Wall Street and always opposes 'turn-outs' among the mechanics."

"Mammoth" here referred of course not to circulation but to paper size; the specific target of the satire being the New York *Journal of Commerce,* founded by the Tappan brothers, wealthy merchants, advocates of temperance, sabbatarianism, and antislavery. The Philadelphia *Public Ledger* from its first appearance linked itself to the *Sun* and the *Transcript.* What newspapers first rallied public opinion against class bias in the courts?, the *Ledger* asked its readers. "Not those dull papers who have the arrogance to call themselves 'respectable' . . . but the penny press: the *Sun* and *Transcript* there—and [the] *Ledger* in Philadelphia. . . ." The Baltimore *Sun,* placing itself among "the independent, the industrious penny press" which had "gained the ear of the before neglected mass," claimed for penny daily editors collectively "this victory of laborious effort over indolence, inactivity, luxurious ease, and disregard of the moral and intellectual welfare of the great mass of the people, by those who cared only for the welfare, and catered only to the intellectual appetite of the few. . . ."

A common misapprehension with respect to mass circulation dailies of the Jacksonian era is that they were politically nonpartisan. Certainly the editors themselves contributed to this illusion with their denials of party affiliation. What they meant was that they were not subsidized by parties or candidates, hence not in the condition of subserviency they charged against their sixpenny adversaries. The New York *Sentinel,* doubtless one of the most adamantly partisan sheets of its era, already had perfected this stance by 1830. "The hydra-headed monster PARTY SPIRIT" at the behest of "wealth and aristocracy" controlled the "public press," according to the *Sentinel,* by keeping it in "a state of subsidy." Six years later the Boston *Times* reported that Virginia voters must be in a "quandary" since two papers, Whig and Democratic, had published contradictory accounts of an election result: "both tell the truth—political editors never lie, you know—."

When penny daily editors described their counterparts of the sixpenny press as creatures of "party trammels," "loathesome and pestilent fungi," they acted in the context of a belief that parties, prior to the overthrow of John Quincy Adams, had been dominated by upper-class elites. Were not Adams and Jackson men equally offspring of National Republicanism? Day and many of his printer colleagues had once hoped for an independent party of artisans and producers; failing this, they conceded that Democrats more often than Whigs spoke for what the Workingmen had put forward; but they never lost their suspicion that Democratic leaders might revert to the politics of deference and consequently never felt secure with party commitments.

The Whig editor, Horace Greeley, by contrast, seems to have felt no inhibitions with respect to party connection. Of the origins of the New York *Tribune* in 1841 Greeley later recalled that he had been "incited to this enterprise by several Whig friends who deemed a cheap daily, addressed . . . to the laboring class" urgently needed; especially so, Greeley added, because New York's mass circulation dailies, the *Sun* and the *Herald,* "were in decided, though unavowed, and therefore more effective, affiliation with the Democratic party." Greeley's assessment was undoubtedly accurate. While generally avoiding endorsements of candidates or electoral tickets, penny editors in the first wave nonetheless managed to come down on the Democratic side of most issues controverted between the major parties during the 1830s and 1840s. They supported Jackson's crusade against the Second Bank of the United States. Bennett, according to biographers, had quit his prestigious post as Washington correspondent for the New York *Courier and Enquirer* when the owner of that paper accepted loans from the Bank and decided to oppose Jackson in the bank war. After failing

to woo subsidies from the New York Regency for a Jacksonian organ in Philadelphia, Bennett made his plunge with the *Herald,* imitating patterns of format, distribution, and "nonpartisanship" already tried out by the *Sun* and the *Transcript.* He then outpaced the rather stodgy editorial skills of these artisan predecessors with a sequence of brilliantly populist articles exposing alleged collusion between blanket press editors and bankers in manipulation of the money market.

Penny dailies of the first wave were likely to stress issues that had come to prominence during the Workingmen's movement, such as imprisonment for debt and the inequities of the militia system. They condemned contracting of prison labor as detrimental to working people. They tended to be sympathetic to recent immigrants, including Catholics. The New York *Sun* was even willing to exempt Catholics from school taxes in order not to penalize their preferences for parochial schools. Here again the *Herald* and the *Sun,* briefly, followed divergent tracks. Bennett, who had sublimated his Catholic education into a militantly anticlerical republicanism, committed his paper in its early days to ferocious attacks against the papist hierarchy (in opposition to normal Democratic strategy) and systematically portrayed Protestant clergy as hypocrites and whited sepulchres. After about 1840, perhaps because of an advertising boycott in which the *Sun* joined the blanket press against him, he soft-pedaled such themes and for the most part made common cause with the orthodox Democracy of Polk and Pierce—and the *Sun.*

A sampling of the first wave penny press on selected partisan divisions shows consistent expressions of concurrence with the Democratic side and few disagreements with that side. Thus the *Sun* and the *Ledger* advocated cheaper lands in the West and opposed distribution of federal land sale revenues to the states. Both papers argued against protective tariff, although not with great fervor. The *Sun* and the Boston *Times* applauded President Tyler after he broke with Whig leaders in Congress. The *Sun* and the *Ledger* favored James Fenimore Cooper in his celebrated

controversy with Whig editors over the battle of
Lake Erie. By and large Whigs in public life were
likely to be handled more roughly than Demo-
crats—as in the contrasting treatment of John
Quincy Adams, William Seward, and Joshua
Giddings on one hand, and Ely Moore, Robert
Dale Owen, Lewis Cass, and James K. Polk on
the other.

The most spectacular display of solidarity by
these mass circulation dailies was on the issue
that united them most closely to the Jacksonian
party: territorial expansion. They pushed for Indian removal, supported the government in the
Second Seminole War, and rejoiced at Texan independence. The Philadelphia *Public Ledger* in
its second day of existence urged the acquisition
of Texas by purchase and soon afterwards blasted
those who remained "chill" to the "Texian"
cause as lacking "all the lofty and noble impulses
of the human bosom." In May, 1836, the
Ledger carried a poem on "The Fall of the
Alamo" that ended with the following stanza:

> Ne'er did the gory pyre of fame
> Send forth a brighter, purer flame
>   Than from the victims rose—
> While round in hecatombs did lay
> The savage slaves who fell that day—
> And ne'er on glory's funeral pyre
> Did purer offering feed the fire,
>   Than Santa Anna's foes.

Sympathy with American settlers in Texas,
however, might not quite justify unleashing war
against a sister republic, especially in view of the
complications Texas as a slave state would introduce into the balance of national politics. Like
other Democrats of the North and Central Atlantic regions, first wave penny daily editors hung
fire on this issue. The New York *Sun* in 1837
welcomed recognition of Texan independence but
wanted no steps toward annexation. The *Transcript* took a similar position. The *Ledger* also
opposed annexation, mainly on antislavery
grounds. Subsequently the *Sun* cautioned against
permitting recruitment of military companies for
Texas on American soil, yet approved emigration

since what the migrants did after they got to
Texas was their own business. By 1844 such scruples had largely been set at rest. The New York
Herald and Boston *Times* supported Polk. The
New York *Sun,* Philadelphia *Public Ledger,* and
the Baltimore *Sun,* as usual, made no endorsements; but all three probably agreed with the
Ledger's assessment of the election of Polk and
Dallas as a return to "political moderation" and
national unity. These papers welcomed annexation and supported the war that followed, celebrating battle by battle the advances of the
American army into Mexico. More than any
other newspapers, the *Suns* of New York and
Baltimore, the *Herald,* and the *Public Ledger*
stretched technology to its limits in providing
detailed and rapid coverage of the war. The Boston *Times* sailed enthusiastically in their wake.
Special steamers, pony express couriers, new
trains, and telegraph—previously used mainly for
promotional stunts—now became standard fare.

Underpinning these positions was a line of
thought first developed in the *Sentinel* and *Workingmen's Advocate* by the printer and former
Workingmen's leader, George Henry Evans, that
western land offered the solution for social and
economic problems of eastern cities. In the midst
of the depression of 1837, the New York *Sun,*
pointing to the "rich teeming soil and vitality
waiting only for the hand of industry," counseled
"western emigration" as the "means of securing
welfare and safety against such revulsions. . . .
The angel of relief and independent prosperity
presented herself to our mind's eye, and admonished us to beckon toward her the suffering excess
of population." In 1845 the *Sun* had joined the
campaign for a transcontinental railroad by way
of the South Pass to Oregon. Not long before the
outbreak of war, quoting Oliver Goldsmith, "Ill
fares that land, to hastening ills a prey/Where
wealth accumulates and men decay," the *Sun*
advocated release of public lands at the lowest
possible prices as homesteads for actual settlers.
The Philadelphia *Public Ledger* at the end of
1848—after Guadalupe Hidalgo and after the
great upsurge of European revolutions—declared
that the "mission" of the United States was to

extend "political Christianity" across the continent "under federal democracy." Then "civil liberty founded upon equality" and upon the duty of each to "do as he would be done by" would spread by power of example to all continents, thus filling out "the prophecy 'one Lord, one Gospel.' " The nation, in order to carry out this mission, must learn the lessons of history. History's greatest lessons, according to the editors of the *Public Ledger,* related to land distribution. Peace and prosperity always had accompanied wide land tenure, whereas nations that permitted monopolization of land perished by internal dissension or foreign conquest. "History gives solemn warning against landed monopoly. Let us profit by them." The *Ledger*'s historical essay bore the title, "Land! Land!"

Territorial expansion in alliance with the slaveholding South necessarily rested upon assertions of racial superiority. First wave penny dailies—and Democratically oriented mass circulation papers that followed them—methodically propagated such assertions. Indians, as in Jackson's Indian Removal message of 1830, were always bloody savages blocking the path of civilization. Conflicts with Indians typically were summarized under such headlines as, "More Indian Outrages in Florida." When the army in 1836 brought artillery against the mud fortifications of "Powell town" where Indians were entrenched "in great force," the Philadelphia *Public Ledger* hoped the next dispatches would tell of their being "totally routed and Dade and his gallant associates finally avenged." In reference to rumored conflict between settlers in western Illinois and Indians led by Black Hawk, the New York *Sun* speculated editorially that Black Hawk would soon be defeated and captured; upon which, having washed the blood of white scalps from his hands, he would be fetched to New York in coach and four to be petted and kissed by "the civilized ladies of our city." On his previous visit, the editor recalled, a young lady of society had presented Black Hawk with a turban, and throwing her arms around him, "impressed a kiss on the murderous cheek of the sunburnt savage."

When the *Sun* in 1837 printed a western trapper's account of having been treated kindly and honestly by members of a Crow village in the Black Hills, the editor added: "Trust to their honesty and they will steal the hair off your head." The Philadelphia *Public Ledger,* quoting an Ohio editor, presumably Whig, who had expressed admiration for the Florida Seminoles and a hope that they might "never be conquered," set forth its own position:

> In all ages patriotism has been classified among the first of virtues, and treason among the basest of crimes; and to express a hope that these savages may never be conquered, is, in our view, nothing less than moral treason.

More closely than any other segment of American culture in the 1830s and 1840s, that of urban artisans remained linked to radical republicanism of the Age of Reason. Since the Enlightenment had stressed the one-ness of humanity and sought historical explanations through geography and environment for racial differentiation, one would expect to find some ambivalence regarding assertions of white racial superiority in mass circulation dailies of the first wave. The *Sentinel,* predecessor of these dailies, had in fact displayed just such ambivalence in treating the Cherokee-Georgia controversy. On one hand, according to the *Sentinel,* Georgia was wrong to defy the United States Supreme Court; state power ought to defer to national authority; and the Indians should not be transported against their will. On the other hand, Georgia Indians were the catspaws of missionaries—"drones who are growing fat upon their substance"; the missionaries themselves mere agents "of the party in favor of ecclesiastical encroachments on the freedom of our institutions." Thus radical republican anticlericalism came down on the side of Georgia and against the Cherokee. The *Sentinel* at that time was pushing the presidential candidacy of Colonel Richard M. Johnson, "hero of Kentucky," slayer "of the pretended Prophet, Tecumseh," and champion of the "rights of conscience" who, by leading the fight in Congress against Sunday mail closures, had prevented " 'the Christian party in politics' " from "effecting a junction of the power of Church and State." When Colonel Johnson slipped from the contest, the *Sentinel,* in a shift that adumbrated later politics of first wave penny dailies, transferred its endorsement to Andrew Jackson. Traces of similar ambiguity with respect to Indians surfaced occasionally in the Boston *Times* and New York *Transcript.* Yet for the most part first wave editors of the penny press were content, as had been those of the *Sentinel,* to adopt and elaborate racist justifications for westward expansion without demur.

No such total acquiescence applied to justifications of African slavery. Here the republican tradition, exemplified for artisan editors by Frances Wright and Robert Dale Owen, bucked strongly against the onset of racist apologetics for slavery. What resulted was a division of conscience within the first wave of penny dailies, despite their prevailing Jacksonian orientation. The New York *Transcript* oscillated between angry hostility toward antislavery agitators and a commitment to defend their freedom of speech. Early issues of the New York *Sun,* coinciding with the beginnings of abolitionist organization, contained scatterings of antislavery material. Thus in March, 1834, a news item announced that the secretary of the American Anti-Slavery Society would lecture at the Chatham Street Chapel on the "Cruelty and Injustice of Slavery as it Exists in the United States." Only a few days later came an anecdote of a "Captain Strickland" who hated "these New York niggers." The Captain had gone down to Five Points where "two big greasy niggers" jostled him. When he knocked one down, others set on him; and the Captain, not wanting to hurt any of them too badly, knocked them all down carefully one by one. Benjamin Day later explained that he and George Wisner, the journeyman printer who became his police court reporter and, briefly, partner, disagreed.

> We split on politics. You see, I was rather Democratic in my notions; Wisner, whenever he got a chance, was always sticking in his damned little

Abolitionist articles. We quarreled . . . [I] kept the paper, paying him $5,000 for his share.

Racial attitudes characteristic of the *Sun* after Wisner's departure are suggested by a dialect piece, "Cuffee's Lecture on Phrenology," that occupied two front page columns in the summer of 1834, an early example of a genre later to become standard repertory for blackface minstrelsy. Day's successor and brother-in-law, Moses Beach, displayed approximately the same views on race as Day. Under Beach's direction, the *Sun* applauded the American Colonization Society on the ground that it offered to Afro-Americans a challenge comparable to that of westward migration for Anglo-American pioneers. If American blacks failed to respond to that challenge by departing for Africa, it would "go far to prove all their enemies allege of their inherent aptitude for a servile condition." The *Sun* regularly denounced John Quincy Adams and charged Joshua Giddings with rendering "aid and comfort to Britain" when he introduced a resolution in Congress commending the black slaves who had seized control of the American brig *Creole* and taken it to a British port. Warning that Giddings advocated slave insurrection, the *Sun* likened him to "Robespierre, Brissot and Marat," who "set themselves up as champions of the freedom of speech and of the negroes, and led the way to deeds of blood, the history of which will appall the world throughout all time to come."

The *Herald* as usual outdid the *Sun.* Bennett, who had learned newspaper business in South Carolina, remained loyal to the slaveholding South until after the outbreak of the Civil War. Bennett liked to use racist invective to affect a belligerently egalitarian style. Thus he would refer to the *Sun*—the competitor upon which his own paper largely had been modeled—as that "decrepit, dying penny paper, owned and controlled by a set of woolly-headed and thick-lipped Negroes;" or, "our highly respected, dirty, sneaking, drivelling contemporary nigger paper." The *Sun*'s second owner and publisher, the Connecticut Yankee Moses Beach, became "a pale-faced nigger from the banks of the Senegal." Beach shared distinguished company, since Bennett wrote of the earlier Moses that he had fled Egypt "with all the second hand clothes he could lay his hands upon . . . [and] according to the best biblical critics, was the first white man who married a Negro woman, and thus gave a sanction to amalgamation and abolition."

Despite such tokens of hostility, the *Sun* and *Herald* represented a dominant trend among first wave dailies. These papers diverged tactically with respect to Texas and they were later divided —as was the Democratic party itself—by the complexities of extending slavery and black population into the West. Yet the disagreements did not necessarily differentiate the editors in terms of their racial concepts. When the *Ledger* in the spring of 1836 proposed as a solution to the sharpening Texas controversy that the federal government buy Texas and terminate slavery there, its editors offered the following justification:

> We believe the best course would be to exclude colored population, bond or free. This would save Texas from the curse of slavery; and from that greater curse, a free negro population, and save the neighboring states from the curse of its being a receptacle of runaway negroes.

Anticipating the Wilmot Proviso by ten years, the *Ledger* doubtless helped to fashion a political climate that made the proviso viable in Pennsylvania.

The mass circulation press, then, pioneered by artisan printers who had been politicized during the Workingmen's movement of the late 1820s, came into existence as a nearly identical twin to the urban artisan wing of the Democracy. Its rapidly expanding readership created the urban constituency first of the Democratic party, subsequently for the party system in its entirety. Scattered but consistent evidence regarding the early penny dailies points to the following conclusions. They were by no means politically neutral. Through editorials and news stories and through reportage of such seemingly class-neutral subjects as crime and sex, they transmitted egalitarian messages about class and social values. Despite formal disavowals of partisanship, major dailies of the first wave, as well as others in waves that followed, propagated elements of the Jacksonian legitimizing synthesis, including its structural keystone, the concept of white egalitarianism.

Mass circulation dailies, although originating in conjunction with the rise of the Democratic party, were not inherently limited to that party's purposes. By bringing forward artisan editors, the low costs of entering the mass circulation field during the 1830s resolved a dichotomy, characteristic of the old blanket press, between the interests and class identity of owner-publishers on one hand and working printers on the other. Technological innovation, spurred by mass circulation, then escalated costs of entry. The result was to reestablish the earlier internal dichotomy; and at the same time to open a new and more formidable gap between owner-publishers and mass readership. Egalitarian rhetoric, which for the artisan editors had served as a weapon against an established oligarchy, would become for their successors a means of obscuring newly developing class separations.

20

RELIGIOUS LIFE IN THE SLAVE COMMUNITY

ALBERT J. RABOTEAU

In the 1730s and 1740s the northern colonies experienced a series of religious revivals that became known collectively as the Great Awakening. One of the most important aspects of the Great Awakening was the attempt by preachers, many of them laymen, to reach out and spread the gospel to those in the lower ranks of society. As the Great Awakening spread from the North to the South after midcentury, this message of popular redemption was carried to the most oppressed of colonial peoples: the slaves.

In the beginning southern slaveholders welcomed the revivalists, seeing in the conservative aspects of Protestantism a means to augment their control over their slaves. But as many slave owners quickly learned, revivalism was a double-edged sword. While Protestantism could communicate a message of otherworldliness and reconciliation with one's lot in life, it could also transmit a powerful message of redemption and deliverance from oppression. In spite of slaveholder attempts to suppress the redemptive side of Protestantism, many southern revivalists preached the full gospel to slaves, including in their sermons tales of Moses, Daniel, and other biblical leaders who sought the liberation of their people. As slaves listened to the preachings of these revivalists, they began to construct their own interpretation of Christian religion, drawing parallels between their plight and that of the Israelites whom Moses led out of their Egyptian captivity. By the nineteenth century, as Albert J. Raboteau points out, religion was a fundamental source of resistance, moral example, and psychological comfort for enslaved Americans.

How does the slave religion of the nineteenth century compare with the popular religion of eighteenth-century Virginia as discussed by Rhys Isaac in Reading 9? What are the similarities and differences between the slaveowners' and the temperance reformers' use of religion as a means of social control?

By the eve of the Civil War, Christianity had pervaded the slave community. The vast majority of slaves were American-born, and the cultural and linguistic barriers which had impeded the evangelization of earlier generations of African-born slaves were generally no longer a problem. The widespread opposition of the planters to the catechizing of slaves had been largely dissipated by the efforts of the churches and missionaries of the South. Not all slaves were Christian, nor were all those who accepted Christianity members of a church, but the doctrines, symbols, and vision of life preached by Christianity were familiar to most. During the closing decades of the antebellum period the so-called invisible institution of slave Christianity came to maturity. The religious life of slaves in the late antebellum period is well documented by sources from the slaves themselves.

At first glance it seems strange to refer to the

religion of the slaves as an invisible institution, for independent black churches with slave members did exist in the South before emancipation. In racially mixed churches it was not uncommon for slaves to outnumber masters in attendance at Sunday services. But the religious experience of the slaves was by no means fully contained in the visible structures of the institutional church. From the abundant testimony of fugitive and freed slaves it is clear that the slave community had an extensive religious life of its own, hidden from the eyes of the master. In the secrecy of the quarters or the seclusion of the brush arbors ("hush harbors") the slaves made Christianity truly their own.

The religion of the slaves was both institutional and noninstitutional, visible and invisible, formally organized and spontaneously adapted. Regular Sunday worship in the local church was paralleled by illicit, or at least informal, prayer meetings on weeknights in the slave cabins. Preachers licensed by the church and hired by the master were supplemented by slave preachers licensed only by the spirit. Texts from the Bible which most slaves could not read were explicated by verses from the spirituals. Slaves forbidden by masters to attend church or, in some cases, even to pray risked floggings to attend secret gatherings to worship God.

His own experience of the "invisible institution" was recalled by former slave Wash Wilson:

> When de niggers go round singin' 'Steal Away to Jesus,' dat mean dere gwine be a 'ligious meetin' dat night. De masters . . . didn't like dem 'ligious meetin's, so us natcherly slips off at night, down in de bottoms or somewhere. Sometimes us sing and pray all night.

Into that all-night singing and praying the slaves poured the sufferings and needs of their days. Like "Steal Away" and the rest of the spirituals, Christianity was fitted by the slave community to its own particular experience. At the same time the symbols, myths, and values of Judeo-Christian tradition helped form the slave community's image of itself.

"Steal Away"

Slaves frequently were moved to hold their own religious meetings out of disgust for the vitiated Gospel preached by their masters' preachers. Sermons urging slaves to be obedient and docile were repeated ad nauseam. The type of sermon to which he and other slaves were constantly subjected was paraphrased by Frank Roberson:

> You slaves will go to heaven if you are good, but don't ever think that you will be close to your mistress and master. No! No! there will be a wall between you; but there will be holes in it that will permit you to look out and see your mistress when she passes by. If you want to sit behind this wall, you must do the language of the text "Obey your masters."

Another former slave, Charlie Van Dyke, bitterly complained: "Church was what they called it but all that preacher talked about was for us slaves to obey our masters and not to lie and steal. Nothing about Jesus, was ever said and the overseer stood there to see the preacher talked as he wanted him to talk." Consequently, even a black preacher "would get up and repeat everything that the white preacher had said, because he was afraid to say anything different."

For more authentic Christian preaching the slaves had to turn elsewhere. Lucretia Alexander explained what slaves did when they grew tired of the white folks' preacher:

> The preacher came and . . . He'd just say, 'Serve your masters. Don't steal your master's turkey. Don't steal your master's chickens. Don't steal your master's hawgs. Don't steal your master's meat. Do whatsomever your master tells you to do.' Same old thing all the time. My father would have church in dwelling houses and they had to whisper. . . . Sometimes they would have church at his house. That would be when they would want a real meetin' with some real preachin'. . . . They used to sing their songs in a whisper and pray in a whisper. That was a prayer-meeting from house to house once or twice —once or twice a week.

Slaves faced severe punishment if caught attending secret prayer meetings. Moses Grandy reported that his brother-in-law Isaac, a slave preacher, "was flogged, and his back pickled" for preaching at a clandestine service in the woods. His listeners were flogged and "forced to tell who else was there." Grandy claimed that slaves were often flogged "if they are found singing or praying at home." Gus Clark reported: "My Boss didn' 'low us to go to church, er to pray er sing. Iffen he ketched us prayin' er singin' he whupped us. . . . He didn' care fer nothin' 'cept farmin.' " According to another ex-slave, "the white folks would come in when the colored people would have prayer meeting, and whip every one of them. Most of them thought that when colored people were praying it was against them. For they would catch them praying for God to lift things out of their way and the white folks would *lift them.*" Henry Bibb was threatened with five hundred lashes on the naked back for attending a prayer meeting conducted by slaves on a neighboring plantation, because he had no permission to do so. The master who threatened Bibb with this punishment was, incidentally, a deacon of the local Baptist church. Charlotte Martin asserted that "her oldest brother was whipped to death for taking part in one of the religious ceremonies." Despite the danger, slaves continued to hold their own religious gatherings because, as Grandy stated, "they like their own meetings better." There the slaves could pray and sing as they desired. They were willing to risk threats of floggings at the hands of their earthly masters in order to worship their "Divine Master" as they saw fit.

Slaves devised several techniques to avoid detection of their meetings. One practice was to meet in secluded places—woods, gullies, ravines, and thickets (aptly called "hush harbors"). Kalvin Woods remembered preaching to other slaves and singing and praying while huddled behind quilts and rags, which had been thoroughly wetted "to keep the sound of their voices from penetrating the air" and then hung up "in the form of a little room," or tabernacle. On one Louisiana plantation, when "the slaves would steal away into the woods at night and hold services," they "would form a circle on their knees around the speaker who would also be on his knees. He would bend forward and speak into or over a vessel of water to drown the sound. If anyone became animated and cried out, the others would quickly stop the noise by placing their hands over the offender's mouth." When slaves got "happy an' shout[ed]" in their cabins, "couldn't nobody hyar 'em," according to George Young, "'caze dey didn't make no fuss on de dirt flo," but just in case, "one stan' in de do' an' watch." The most common device for preserving secrecy was an iron pot or kettle turned upside down to catch the sound. The pot was usually placed in the middle of the cabin floor or at the doorstep, then slightly propped up to hold the sound of the praying and singing from escaping. A variation was to pray or sing softly "with heads together around" the "kettle to deaden the sound." Clara Young recalled, "When dark come, de men folks would hang up a wash pot, bottom upwards, in de little brush church house us had, so's it would catch de noise and de overseer wouldn't hear us singin' and shoutin'." According to one account, slaves used the overturned pot to cover the sound of more worldly amusements too: "They would have dances sometimes and turn a pot upside down right in front of the door. They said that would keep the sound from going outside."

Whether the pots were strictly functional or also served some symbolic purpose is not clear. The symbolic element is suggested by Patsy Hyde, former slave in Tennessee, who claimed that slaves "would tek dere ole iron cookin' pots en turn dem upside down on de groun' neah dere cabins ter keep dere white folks fun herein' w'at dey waz sayin'. Dey claimed dat hit showed dat Gawd waz wid dem." The origin of this custom also remains unclear. When asked about the custom, one ex-slave replied, "I don't know where they learned to do that. I kinda think the lord put them things in their minds to do for themselves, just like he helps us Christians in other ways. Don't you think so?" One theory has been advanced which explains the slaves' use of the pot as a remnant of African custom. Sidney Mintz

has offered an interesting suggestion: "One is entitled to wonder whether a washtub that 'catches'
sound, rather than producing it, may not represent some kind of religious symbolic inversion on
the part of a religious group—particularly since
the suppression of drumming by the masters was
a common feature of Afro-American history."
He explains further: this is perhaps "a case in
which some original symbolic or instrumental
commitment has outlived its original circumstantial significance. Rather than disappearing however, that commitment is somehow transmitted
and preserved." Whatever the origin of this folk
custom, the widespread belief among slaves was
that the pots worked. The need for secrecy even
dictated that children keep quiet about what went
on in the slave quarters. "My master used to ask
us children," recalled one former slave, " 'Do
your folks pray at night?' We said 'No' cause our
folks had told us what to say. But the Lord have
mercy, there was plenty of that going on. They'd
pray, 'Lord, deliver us from under bondage.' "

Looking back at these secret and risky religious gatherings, an ex-slave declared, "Meetings
back there meant more than they do now. Then
everybody's heart was in tune, and when they
called on God they made heaven ring. It was
more than just Sunday meeting and then no god-
liness for a week. They would steal off to the fields
and in the thickets and there . . . they called on
God out of heavy hearts." Truly communal,
these meetings, as Hannah Lowery noted, needed
no preacher because "everyone was so anxious to
have a word to say that a preacher did not have
a chance. All of them would sing and pray." A
description of a secret prayer meeting was recorded by Peter Randolph, who was a slave in
Prince George County, Virginia, until he was
freed in 1847:

> Not being allowed to hold meetings on the planta-
> tion, the slaves assemble in the swamp, out of reach
> of the patrols. They have an understanding among
> themselves as to the time and place of getting to-
> gether. This is often done by the first one arriving
> breaking boughs from the trees, and bending them
> in the direction of the selected spot. Arrangements

are then made for conducting the exercises. They
first ask each other how they feel, the state of their
minds, etc. The male members then select a certain
space, in separate groups, for the division of the
meeting. Preaching . . . by the brethren, then praying and singing all around, until they generally feel
quite happy. The speaker usually commences by
calling himself unworthy, and talks very slowly,
until feeling the spirit, he grows excited, and in a
short time, there fall to the ground twenty or thirty
men and women under its influence . . .

Randolph went on to elucidate the importance of
these gatherings for the life of the slave community:

> The slave forgets all his sufferings, except to remind
> others of the trials during the past week, exclaim-
> ing: 'Thank God, I shall not live here always!' Then
> they pass from one to another, shaking hands, and
> bidding each other farewell. . . . As they separate,
> they sing a parting hymn of praise.

Prayer, preaching, song, communal support, and
especially "feeling the spirit" refreshed the slaves
and consoled them in their times of distress. By
imagining their lives in the context of a different
future they gained hope in the present.

The contrast between present pain and future
relief formed the matter of slave prayer and song.
From his memory of slavery, Anderson Edwards
cited a song which starkly combined suffering
and hope.

> We prayed a lot to be free and the Lord done heered
> us. We didn't have no song books and the Lord
> done give us our songs and when we sing them at
> night it jus' whispering so nobody hear us. One
> went like this:

> My knee bones am aching,
> My body's rackin' with pain,
> I 'lieve I'm a chile of God,
> And this ain't my home,
> 'Cause Heaven's my aim.

Slaves sought consolation in the future, but they
also found it in the present. Exhausted from a
day of work that stretched from "day clean" to

after sundown, the slaves sometimes found tangible relief in prayer, as Richard Caruthers attested: "Us niggers used to have a prayin' ground down in the hollow and sometime we come out of the field . . . scorchin' and burnin' up with nothin' to eat, and we wants to ask the good Lawd to have mercy. . . . We takes a pine torch . . . and goes down in the hollow to pray. Some gits so joyous they starts to holler loud and we has to stop up they mouth. I see niggers git so full of the Lawd and so happy they draps unconscious."

Freedom was frequently the object of prayer. According to Laura Ambromson, "Some believed they'd git freedom and others didn't. They had places they met and prayed for freedom." Others were certain it would come. "I've heard them pray for freedom," declared another former slave. "I thought it was foolishness then, but the old time folks always felt they was to be free. It must have been something 'vealed unto 'em." Mingo White remembered: "Somehow or yuther us had a instinct dat we was goin' to be free," and "when de day's wuk was done de slaves would be foun' . . . in dere cabins prayin' for de Lawd to free dem lack he did chillun of Is'ael." Andrew Moss revealed that his mother would retreat to her private praying ground, "a ole twisted thick-rooted muscadine bush," where she prayed for the deliverance of the slaves. George Womble, former slave from Georgia, recalled that "slaves would go to the woods at night where they sang and prayed" and some used to say, "I know that some day we'll be free and if we die before that time our children will live to see it." The father of Jacob Stroyer, before his family went to bed, would pray that "the time which he predicted would come, that is, the time of freedom when . . . the children would be [their] own masters and mistresses." Forbidden to pray for liberation, slaves stole away at night and prayed inside "cane thickets . . . for deliverance."

Secrecy was characteristic of only part of the slave community's religious life. Many slaveholders granted their slaves permission to attend church, and some openly encouraged religious meetings among the slaves. Baptisms, marriages, and funerals were allowed to slaves on some plantations with whites observing and occasionally participating. Annual revival meetings were social occasions for blacks as well as for whites. Masters were known to enjoy the singing, praying, and preaching of their slaves. Nevertheless, at the core of the slaves' religion was a private place, represented by the cabin room, the overturned pot, the prayin' ground, and the "hush harbor." This place the slave kept his own. For no matter how religious the master might be, the slave knew that the master's religion did not countenance prayers for his slaves' freedom in this world.

The Seasons of Religious Life

The religious format varied from plantation to plantation for the slaves. Former slave John Brown depicted two extremes:

> Sunday was a great day around the plantation. The fields was forgotten, the light chores was hurried through, and everybody got ready for the church meeting. It was out of the doors, in the yard . . . Master John's wife would start the meeting with a prayer and then would come the singing—the old timey songs. But the white folks on the next plantation would lick their slaves for trying to do like we did. No praying there, and no singing.

Some masters did not allow their slaves to go to church and ridiculed the notion of religion for slaves because they refused to believe that Negroes had souls. Others forbade their slaves to attend church because, as an ex-slave explained, "White folks 'fraid the niggers git to thinkin' they was free, if they had churches 'n things." Refusal to grant a slave permission to participate in religious meetings was also a means of punishment or a result of capricious malice on the part of the master or overseer. On the other hand, many slave owners did permit—some even required—their slaves to worship on the Sabbath, either at the local church or at meetings conducted on the plantation by white ministers or slave preachers. On those plantations where slaves enjoyed religious privileges the slave community was able to openly celebrate the religious side of its folk culture. The Reverend Greene gave a detailed description of religion in the quarters to interviewers from Fisk University:

> At night, especially in the summertime, after everybody had eaten supper, it was a common thing for us to sit outside. The old folks would get together and talk until bedtime. Sometimes somebody would start humming an old hymn, and then the next-door neighbor would pick it up. In this way it would finally get around to every house, and then the music started. Soon everybody would be gathered together, and such singing! It wouldn't be long before some of the slaves got happy and started to shouting. . . .

A similar picture of evening prayer meetings was rendered by Robert Anderson:

> We would gather out in the open on summer nights, gather around a big bonfire, to keep the mosquitoes away, and listen to our preachers preach sometimes half the night. There would be singing and testifying and shouting. Usually when we had these meetings there would be people there from other plantations, and sometimes there would be white visitors who would stand on the outside of the circle and listen to our services.

Sunday prayer meetings in the quarters could, if allowed to, last all day. The emotional power of these meetings left a deep impression on Mose Hursey, who many years later vividly recalled them:

> On Sundays they had meetin', sometimes at our house, sometimes at 'nother house. . . . They'd preach and pray and sing—shout, too. I heard them git up with a powerful force of the spirit, clappin' they hands and walkin' round the place. They'd shout, 'I got the glory. I got that old time 'ligion in my heart.' I seen some powerful 'figurations of the spirit in them days.

Nor were white visitors to the slave meetings immune to their emotional impact. Despite her criticism that a prayer she heard offered at one

meeting was meaningless, Mary Boykin Chesnut admitted she was deeply moved nonetheless:

> Jim Nelson, the driver . . . was asked to lead in prayer. He became wildly excited, on his knees, facing us with his eyes shut. He clapped his hands at the end of every sentence, and his voice rose to the pitch of a shrill shriek, yet was strangely clear and musical, occasionally in a plaintive minor key that went to your heart. Sometimes it rang out like a trumpet. I wept bitterly. . . . The Negroes sobbed and shouted and swayed backward and forward, some with aprons to their eyes, most of them clapping their hands and responding in shrill tones: 'Yes, God!' 'Jesus!' 'Savior!' 'Bless de Lord, amen,' etc. It was a little too exciting for me I would very much have liked to shout, too. Jim Nelson when he rose from his knees trembled and shook as one in a palsy, and from his eyes you could see the ecstasy had not left him yet. He could not stand at all, and sank back on his bench.

Some whites found the slaves' ways of worship humorous; many others went "to hear the colored ones sing and praise God," as John Thompson observed, "and were often much affected by their simple but earnest devotion."

In the evenings, after work, while religious slaves met to pray, sing, and shout, other sounds also rang out in the slave cabins. Apparently, the traditional conflict between sacred and secular music in Afro-American culture was alive even then, as the antecedents of gospel and blues clashed in the quarters. Harry Smith's recollection could only hint at the riot of sound:

> After eating, often preaching and prayer meetings by some of the old folks in some of the cabins and in others fiddles would ring out. It was a scene never to be forgotten, as the old christians sing and pray until four in the morning, while at the other cabins many would be patting, singing and dancing.

To the religious slaves, fiddling, dancing, and secular music were the devil's work. According to John Thompson, when a master on one plantation wished to halt a revival among his slaves he shrewdly hired a slave named Martin who was a talented fiddler. Thompson reported that the plan succeeded: "what the whip failed to accomplish, the fiddle completed, for it is no easy matter to drive a soul from God by cruelty, when it may easily be drawn away by worldly pleasures." The backsliding was temporary, however, since Martin left with his fiddle when his term of hire expired and the revival of Christianity sprang up anew. The only form of "dancing" allowed to the converted was the movement which occurred in prayer meetings under the influence of the holy spirit, as in the ring shout.

Morally sanctioned enjoyments were to be found at Sunday church service and revival meetings which were occasions for socializing, news gathering, and picnicking as well as for prayer. Robert Anderson acknowledged that "I always liked to go to church for I always found some of the colored folks from the other plantations that I could visit with for a little while before church started." Another former slave recalled, "The young folks would ride in wagons to and from church and have a big time singing songs n' things." For most field hands Sunday was a holiday when they could wear their better clothes to church, "the onliest place off the farm we ever went," recalled one. Olmsted observed a Sabbath worship service in which the slaves were more neatly dressed than the poor whites present. Some slaveholders took pride in showing how well "their people" dressed at Sunday service. Slaves themselves were fond of dressing up on Sunday and, if allowed to earn a little money, would add to their Sunday wardrobe. For example, Tom Singleton, former slave from Georgia, recalled that as a slave he was allowed to hire out his time at night to cut wood and fix fences for neighboring whites. "With the money they paid me," he admitted, "I bought Sunday shoes and a Sunday coat, because I was a Nigger what always did like to look good on Sunday." The pleasure of dressing up no doubt added to the specialness of the day and expressed in small measure the slaves' sense of proper dignity, of that value which they called "being quality folks." "Looking good" at Sabbath and revival services also had a special purpose for the younger slaves, since these were potential occasions for courting.

Another opportunity for asserting one's dignity came when the collection plate was passed. It was not unusual for slaves to add their contributions from money they had earned selling the produce of their own garden patches.

When slaves from neighboring plantations were allowed to congregate for worship, visiting and fellowship added an almost festive dimension to the service. Julia Francis Daniels, a slave on a Georgia plantation remembered: "We'd ask niggers from other farms and I used to say, 'I like meetin' jus' as good as I like a party.'" Camp meetings were also "big times." "When de crops was laid by and most of de hardest wuk of de year done up, den was camp meetin' time, 'long in de last of July and sometimes in August," reminisced Robert Shepherd. "Det was when us had de biggest times of all. Dey had great big long tables and jus' everything good t'eat." According to Charlie Aarons: "there would be camp meetings held and the slaves from all the surrounding plantations would attend, going . . . in these large wagons . . . They then would have a jolly time along the way, singing and calling to one another, and making friends."

Sundays and revival meetings were not the only respites from work anticipated by the slaves. Christmas was the most festive holiday of all. Generally, the slaves received three to six days off to celebrate the Christmas season and were permitted to visit family and friends on neighboring plantations. On Christmas day it was customary for slaves to greet the master's family with cries of "Christmas gift, Christmas gift," to which the whites were obliged to respond with a small gift, perhaps tobacco for the men, ribbons for the women, ginger cakes for the children, and some special tokens for favorite slaves. Drams of whiskey, bowls of eggnog and other spirits were freely distributed, and a special Christmas supper was prepared for the quarters as well as for the big house. The slaves dressed in the best clothes they could gather in anticipation of the supper and the visiting and merrymaking which followed. Then, as now, Christmas was more a holiday than a holy day. Feasting, drinking, and dancing were the order of the day and must have sorely tempted the more religious slaves. As Adeline Jackson recalled, "Everything lively at Christmas time, dances wid fiddlers, pattin' and stick rattlin', but when I jined de church, I quit dancin'," She allowed that the fiddlers, dancers and patters were "all nothin' but sinners, I wuz too, but we sho' had a good time." Christmas season did give the religious slave time to hold prayer meetings, to preach and to pray. Yet "many of the strict members of the church who did not dance," Jacob Stroyer asserted, "would be forced to do it to please their masters." At any rate, slaves whether religious or not looked forward to Christmas as an all-too-short break from plantation routine. With the arrival of New Year's the celebration ended, and another year of work faced the slaves.

Of course, many slaves cared not at all about church, revival meetings, or prayer services, would not go if they could, and resented being forced to attend. Nonreligious slaves spent Sundays in hunting, fishing, marble shooting, storytelling, or simply resting when allowed. Not all slaves appreciated the opportunity to attend church. "On Sunday after workin' hard all de week dey would lay down to sleep and be so tired; soon ez yo' sleep, de overseer would come an' wake you up an' make you go to church," complained Margrett Nickerson. Some reprobate and ingenious slaves even rationalized a way to dance on the Sabbath: "The cabins were mostly made of logs and there were large cracks in them" through which the sunlight filtered, "so on Sunday mornings when they were dancing and did not want to stop" they filled "up the cracks with old rags. The idea was that it would not be Sunday inside if they kept the sun out, and thus they would not desecrate the Sabbath." Sunday also served as market day for those slaves who were allotted individual plots to produce vegetables or poultry for their own use.

The camp meeting had its nonreligious attractions. John Anderson, who courted his wife, Maria, at a camp meeting, remarked: "Many slaves who have no religion, go to camp meetings that they may be merry, for there is much whiskey sold at these gatherings, and the people drink

and play at cards while others attend to religion." While some slaves were allowed holidays to attend camp meetings, other took advantage of the time to enjoy "dances, raffles, cock-fights, foot-races, and other amusements . . ."

Although religious slaves enjoyed the fellowship and excitement of church services and revival meetings, their enjoyment was marred by the shadow of white control. When they attended church, slaves often felt inhibited by the presence of whites, so they preferred to worship at a separate service by themselves. As Sarah Fitzpatrick, a slave in Alabama, explained:

> "Niggers" commence ta wanna go to church by de'selves, even ef dey had ta meet in de white church. So white fo'ks have deir service in de mornin' an' "Niggers" have deirs in de evenin', a'ter dey clean up, wash de dishes, an' look a'ter ever'thing. . . . Ya' see "Niggers" lack ta shout a whole lot an' wid de white fo'ks al' round 'em, dey couldn't shout jes' lack dey want to.

Slaves assembled separately at the camp meetings, as one white observer explained, so they could enjoy the "freedom in speaking, singing, shouting, and praying they could not enjoy in the prescence of their masters." This freedom of expression was circumscribed, however, by the attendance of some whites at slave church services to ensure that nothing occurred which could be construed as subversive of the system. Moreover, to attend separate services, slaves needed written passes from their masters which stated the time when the slave had to return home. A slave who stayed too late at meeting risked a beating from the "padderollers" [patrols] or his master. The slaves' enjoyment of religious "privileges" was diminished by those masters who forced them to attend prayer service whether they wanted to or not. Sometimes moments of religious celebration were interrupted by the cruel realities of slavery. James Smith related one such incident which took place at a revival he attended. A slave named Nancy Merrill was converted; the next day of the meeting someone came to the church door seeking the new convert. It was a "slave trader, who had bought her during the day from her mistress! As soon as she went to the door, he seized and bound her, and then took her off to her cabin home to get her two boys he had bought also." That this was not an isolated incident is suggested by Moses Roper, who accompanied his slave-trading master to "many such meetings," where there was "a fruitful season for the drover" who caried on a profitable traffic with the slave owners attending the revival. Roper claimed this was a practice "common to Baptists and Methodists." Nevertheless, Sunday services, Christmas seasons, annual revival meetings, and especially the slaves' own evening prayer meetings in the quarters were times of refreshment and renewal amid the routine toil of the slave life.

Religion not only added some moments of brightness to the day-to-day life of the slave community, but it also provided special rituals to mark the important events of life by means of baptisms, weddings, and funerals. Baptism, the central Christian symbol of spiritual death, rebirth, and initiation was a memborable occasion for the slaves. Accompanied by song, shouting, and ecstatic behavior, baptism—especially for Baptists—was perhaps the most dramatic ritual in the slave's religious life. "De biggest meetin' house crowds was when dey had baptizin'," noted a former Georgia slave. "Dey dammed up de crick on Sadday so as it would be deep enough on Sunday . . . At dem baptizin's dere was all sorts of shoutin', and dey would sing *Roll, Jordan, Roll, De Livin' Waters,* and *Lord, I'se Comin' Home.*" Dressed in white robes and attended by the "brothers and sisters," the candidates proceeded "amidst singing and praises" to the local pond or creek, symbol of the river Jordan, where, according to Baptist practice, each was "ducked" by the preacher. Sometimes the newly regenerate came up from the baptismal waters shouting for joy at being made new in the Lord. Presbyterians, Methodists, and Episcopalians did not go down to the waters of baptism to be "ducked," but were "sprinkled" instead. Though less dramatically stated, the symbolism

of death and rebirth still pertained: "Except a man be born again, he cannot see the kingdom of God" (John 3:3). For the newly baptized a major change had occurred, an event which they believed transformed them and which they would remember for the rest of their lives. Recollecting the baptism of his mother, Isaiah Jeffries has left a description which conveys something of the excitement and the sense of new beginning which "baptizings" brought to many slaves:

> When I got to be a big boy, my Ma got religion at de Camp meeting at El-Bethel. She shouted and sung fer three days, going all over de plantation and de neighboring ones, inviting her friends to come to see her baptized and shouting and praying fer dem. She went around to all de people dat she had done wrong and begged dere forgiveness. She sent fer dem dat had wronged her, and told dem dat she was born again and a new woman, and dat she would forgive dem. She wanted everybody dat was not saved to go up wid her. . . . My Ma took me wid her to see her baptized, and I was so happy dat I sung and shouted wid her. All de niggers joined in singing.

Occasionally, especially after revivals, there would occur mass baptisms of large numbers of slaves. The manager of one Florida plantation, for example, wrote the owner, "There was forty one 41 of your Negroes Baptised Last Sunday in the Canall above the Bridge . . . the largest Negroe meeting I ever saw . . ." The excitement of "baptizings" attracted slaves from all around. Charlie Hudson claimed "if there was a baptizing inside of ten miles around from where us lived, us didn't miss it. Us knowed how to walk and went to git the pleasure."

The wedding ceremony was meant to solemnize and publicly announce the union, in love, of two individuals—and here lay the terrible irony —which was to last for life, a union which God had made and no man was to break asunder. For slave weddings, no matter what form they took, could not escape the threat inherent in slavery, a threat which contradicted the very notion of Christian marriage: the constant possibility of separation by sale. Unrecognized by law, the most stable slave marriages were all too fragile in their dependence upon the will of the slaveholder. As Lunsford Lane noted of his own marriage, "In May, 1828, I was bound as fast in wedlock as a slave can be. God may at any time sunder that band in a freeman; either master may do the same at pleasure in a slave." Despite this contingency the unions of slave couples were celebrated by wedding ceremonials of some kind on many plantations. The most frequent method of marrying two slaves was the custom of jumping the broomstick. One of several variations of the ritual was described by William Davis: "Dey lays de brooms on de floor and de woman put her broom front de man and he put he broom front de woman. Dey face one 'nother and step 'cross de brooms at de same time to each other and takes hold of hands and dat marry dem." Another variation was to hold the broomstick a foot off the ground and then require the bride and groom one after the other to jump over it backwards. William Wells Brown asserted that "this custom had as binding force with negroes, as if they had been joined by a clergyman; the difference being the one was not so high-toned as the other. Yet, it must be admitted that the blacks always preferred being married by a clergyman."

Some slave weddings were performed according to Christian ritual by ministers, either white or black. Minerva Davis proudly stated that when her parents married, their master "had a white preacher to read out of a book to them. They didn't jump over no broom . . ." There were slaves, particularly favorite or prominent ones—cooks, butlers, maids—who were treated to elaborate weddings by the white folks. A mistress of a Louisiana plantation, Priscilla Bond, described a wedding of this type in her diary:

> Had a wedding here tonight. Two of the servants got married. . . . The bride looked quite nice dressed in white. I made her turban of white swiss pink tarlatan and orange blossoms. They were married at the gallery. The moon shone beautifully. They afterwards adjourned to the 'hospital' where they enjoyed a 'ball'. . . . The groom had on a suite of black,

white gloves and tall beaver. The bride was dressed in white swiss, pink trimmings and white gloves. The bridesmaid and groom's man were dressed to correspond.

At the opposite pole, there were slaveholders, who merely told their slaves they were married without further ado. Occasionally the broomstick ceremony was combined with the regular marriage rite at the slaves' request so that "they felt more married."

"The slaves . . . in regard to marriage . . . try to make it as near lawful as they can," commented escaped slave John Warren. After emancipation some slaves felt the desire to regularize already long-standing marriages. Bongy Jackson enjoyed the rare privilege of attending her parents' wedding: "During slavery, us niggers just jumped the broom wit' the master's consent. After the Cibil War, soon's they got a little piece of money they got a preacher and had a real wedding.' My ma dressed like a bride an' all, an' she done already had nine children by my pa. All us kids was there an' we sure had a fine time." With or without preacher or license, some slaves viewed marriage as permanent and formed lasting relationships. James Curry and his wife were refused permission to marry, and even though they dared not risk any ceremony, they knew they were married and that their marriage was binding, Curry insisted, because "God married us." Others, "since they had no law to bind them to one woman . . . could have as many as they pleased by mutual agreement," observed Jacob Stroyer. The slaves held "different opinions about plurality of wives as have the most educated and refined among the whites."

Like weddings, funeral services for slaves required permission, which was not always given. When Samuel Andrew's father died, his body "was driven in an ox-cart to a hole that had been dug, put in it and covered up"; his wife and children were not allowed "to stop work to attend the funeral." On the other hand, Isaam Morgan recalled that on his plantation "De slaves had dere own special graveyard an' us'd make de coffins raght on de place dar. When someone died, he was taken in a ox cart to de grave, wid all de slaves a-walkin' 'long behine de cart singin' de spirituals." Frequently slave funerals were held at night, when work stoppage was no problem. According to witnesses, these night funerals were impressive, solemn, and eerie ceremonies. The procession from the quarters to the grave site lit by pine-knot torches, the "wild" mournful strains of the hymns, the prayers of the slave preacher, the graves marked with posts and, as in Africa, decorated with the broken belongings of the deceased, all formed a dramatic backdrop for the slave community's farewell to one of its members. Mixed with the sadness was consolation. For some the deceased had returned home to Guinea, for others to heaven, "where bondage is never known." When permission could be obtained, fellows from neighboring farms attended, and when it couldn't they might steal away to pay last respects.

It was not unusual for the funeral sermon to be separated from the burial by several days, weeks, and even months. Sometimes several funerals were preached at once. Charles Raymond, a white minister, noticed that slave funerals were usually preached on Sundays and explained that "there was no immediate chronological connection between the death and the funeral; and no necessary allusions in the sermon to the life, death, or virtues of the departed." Former slave Paul Smith testified "Later on dey had de funeral sermon preached in church, maybe six months atter de buryin'. De white folkses had all deir funeral sermons preached at de time of buryin'." John Dixon Long, commenting on this time lag between burial and funeral observances, noted that "unless the funeral is preached," whether the deceased was sinner or saint, "there is no peace of mind to his friends." It is difficult to say whether this practice reflected an African system of multiple funerals or was simply a necessity dictated by the uncertainty of permission and the lack of time available to the slaves to attend such services.

Funerals were the last in a cycle of ceremonies during the life of a slave. Sunday worship, prayer meetings, revivals, Christmas, "baptizing," weddings, funerals, all came and went, alternating like the seasons of the year, from day to day, from week to week, from month to month, in the life of the plantation. To the slaves these services and celebrations were special times, counteracting the monotony of life in slavery. Furthermore, the slaves asserted repeatedly in these seasons of celebration that their lives were special, their lives had dignity, their lives had meaning beyond the definitions set by slavery. In their meetings slaves enjoyed fellowship, exchanged mutual consolation, and gave voice to individual concerns. And here, too, some slaves found the place to exercise their talents for leadership.

Slave Preachers

Presiding over slave baptisms, funerals, and weddings was the slave preacher, leader of the slaves' religious life and an influential figure in the slave community. Usually illiterate, the slave preacher often had native wit and unusual eloquence. Licensed or unlicensed, with or without permission, preachers held prayer meetings, preached and ministered in a very difficult situation. Carefully watched and viewed with suspicion, the preacher had to straddle the conflict between the demands of conscience and the orders of the masters. As one former slave put it, "Back there they were harder on preachers than they were on anybody else. They thought preachers were ruining the colored people." Anderson Edwards reflected on the difficulty he experienced as a slave preacher in Texas:

> I been preachin' the Gospel and farmin' since slavery time. . . . When I starts preachin' I couldn't read or write and had to preach what massa told me and he say tell them niggers iffen they obeys the massa they goes to Heaven, but I knowed there's something better for them, but daren't tell them 'cept on the sly. That I done lots. I tell 'em iffen they keeps prayin' the Lord will set 'em free.

The slave preacher who verged too close on a gospel of equality within earshot of whites was in trouble. Sarah Ford told how "one day Uncle

Lew preachin' and he say, 'De Lawd made everyone to come in unity and on de level, both white and black.' When Massa Charles hears 'bout it, he don't like it none, and de next mornin' old Uncle Jake git Uncle Lew and put him out in de field with de rest." Henry Clay Bruce retold the story of an old preacher named Uncle Tom Ewing, "who was praying on one occasion, after the close of his sermon, in the church near Jacob Vennable's place . . . The old fellow got warmed up, and used the words 'Free indeed, free from work, free from the white folks, free from everything.' After the meeting closed, Jacob Vennable, who sat in front of the pulpit, took Tom to task and threatened to have his license revoked if he ever used such language in public." Bruce concluded: "I heard Uncle Tom preach and pray many times after the above described occurrence, but never heard him use the words quoted above." Uncle Lew and Uncle Tom got off light; Rev. R. S. Sorrick, a slave preacher in Washington County, Maryland, was placed in prison in 1841 for three months and eight days "for preaching the gospel to my colored brethren."

By comparison with other slaves, some preachers were privileged characters. One former slave, from Alabama, remarked that "Nigger preachers in dem times wuz mighty-nigh free." Amanda McCray declared that the preacher on her plantation, though a slave, was exempt from hard manual labor. Conscious of his own importance, he went about "all dressed up" in frock coat and "store bought shoes." As long as he didn't interfere with other slaves' work he was allowed to hold services whenever he wished, and frequently he traveled to neighboring places to conduct prayer meetings. It was from the preacher, this relatively mobile and privileged slave, that the rest "first heard of the Civil War." During the war he offered whispered prayers for the success of the Union Army. Another former slave recalled: "I saw a preacher in Mississippi carry on a revival and he had persuaded the white man's son to go, and he professed and they would let him have meetings any time, 'cause that white man's son professed under him." James L. Smith reported that he was able to exercise a busy ministry while still a slave:

> I had a meeting appointed at a freedwoman's house . . . I left home about seven o'clock on Saturday evening, and arrived there about ten; we immediately commenced the meeting and continued it till about daylight . . . After breakfast we went two miles further, and held another meeting till late in the afternoon, then closed and started for home reaching there some time during the night. I was very much fatigued . . . so much so that I was not able to work the next day.

Most slave preachers were hampered by illiteracy in a religion that placed such importance on the written word of the Bible. White folks would sometimes read a biblical verse for the preacher, and he would proceed to preach from it to his fellow slaves. William Pease, a fugitive from slavery in Tennessee, complained that the minister on his plantation, the slave driver, was "as ignorant as the rest of the slaves . . . knew nothing at all of the book and did not know enough to preach." There were slave preachers, however, who learned on the sly the rudiments of reading. After a friend had taught him the alphabet, Peter Randolph taught himself to read the Bible while in slavery. London, the head cooper on Frances Kemble's plantation, had secretly "obtained some little knowledge of reading, and was able to read "prayers and the Bible to his fellow-slaves." When asked how he learned to read, London replied evasively, "Well missis me learn . . . me try . . . me 'spose Heaven help me." Sam Johnson, slave preacher on a South Carolina plantation, learned to read from his master's young son. The boy's parents had forbidden him to drink tea or coffee which he liked. Sam, who was also the butler, supplied him with both in exchange for reading and writing lessons, from which he learned enough to be able to read the Bible.

Yet illiteracy did not necessarily prevent eloquent preaching. As one former slave claimed, "My grandfather was a preacher and didn't know A from B. He could preach." And Louis Fowler remembered that the slave "preacherman" back on the Georgia plantation "am not educated, but can he preach a pow'ful sermon. O Lawd! He am inspire from de Lawd and he preached from his heartfelt." Clara Young testified about the power of the slave preacher:

> De preacher I liked de best was named Mathew Ewing. He was a comely nigger, black as night, and he sure could read out of his hand. He never learned no real readin' and writin' but he sure knowed his Bible and would hold his hand out and make like he was readin' and preach de purtiest preachin' you ever heard.

Several observers noted that slaves preferred their own preachers. Anthony Dawson exclaimed: "Mostly we had white preachers, but when we had a black preacher that was heaven!" A white minister remarked in 1863 that "the 'colored brethren' are so much preferred *as preachers*. When in the pulpit there is a wonderful sympathy between the speaker and his audience. . . . This sympathetic influence seems the result of a . . . peculiar experience. None but a negro can so preach as fully to arouse, excite, and transport the negro."

Vivid imagery and dramatic delivery were characteristic of the slave preacher's sermons. Speaking of their abilities in general, a white traveler observed somewhat critically, "they acquire a remarkable memory of words, phrases, and forms; a curious sort of poetic talent is developed, and a habit is obtained of rhapsodizing and exciting furious emotions . . ." David Macrae, another traveler, who listened to ex-slave preachers shortly after the Civil War, acknowledged: "Some of the most vivid reproductions of Scripture narrative I have ever listened to were from the lips of such men, who might with proper training have been orators." Missionaries to the freedmen were frequently amazed at the wisdom and eloquence of the black preachers recently released from slavery. "What wonderful preachers these blacks are!" exclaimed one correspondent from Georgia to the editor of the *American Missionary*:

I listened to a remarkable sermon or talk a few evenings since. The preacher spoke of the need of atonement for sin. "Bullocks c'dn't do it, heifers c'dn't do it, de blood of doves c'dn't do it—but up in heaven, for thousan and thousan of years, the Son was saying to the Father, 'Put up a soul, put up a soul. Prepare me a body, an I will go an meet Justice on Calvary's brow!" He was so dramatic. In describing the crucifixion he said: "I see the sun when she turned herself black. I see the stars a fallin from the sky, and them old Herods comin out of their graves and goin about the city, an they knew 'twas the Lord of Glory."

George Hepworth, a war correspondent, was similarly impressed by a slave he heard preach behind the Union lines:

> The moment I looked at him, I saw that he was no common man. He had a full forehead, a tall commanding figure. . . . I remember, too, some of his phrases: they were very beautiful, and were epic in grandeur. He spoke of *'the rugged wood of the cross,'* whereto the Saviour was nailed; and, after describing that scene with as much power as I have ever known an orator to exhibit, he reached the climax, when he pictured the earthquake which rent the veil of the temple, with this extremely beautiful expression: 'And, my friends, *the earth was unable to endure the tremendous sacrilege, and trembled.'* He held his rude audience with most perfect control; subdued them, excited them, and, in fact, did what he pleased with them."

Attempting to analyze the preaching of Uncle Robert, a slave in Beaufort, North Carolina, a white missionary noted, "In his sermons there is often a clearness of statement, an earnestness of address, a sublimity and splendor of imagery, together with a deep pathos, which give his public addresses great power." As a result, "Many who affect to despise the negro, want to hear Uncle Robert when it is announced that he is to preach." A. M. French, writing of the "Colored Ambassadors" at Port Royal, touched upon the reasons which the slave preachers themselves gave for their authority:

The real spiritual benefit of these poor Colored people, instrumentally, seems to have been mostly derived from a sort of local preachers, Colored, and mostly slaves, but of deep spiritual experience, sound sense, and capacity to state Scripture facts, narratives, and doctrines, far better than most, who feed upon commentaries. True, the most of them could not read, still, some of them line hymns from memory with great accuracy, and fervor, and repeat Scripture most appropriately, and correctly. Their teaching shows clearly that it is God in the soul, that makes the religious teacher. One is amazed at their correctness and power. They say: "God tell me 'you go teach de people what I tell you; I shall prosper you; I teach you in de heart.' "

The style of the folk sermon, shared by black and white evangelicals, was built on a formulaic structure based on phrases, verses, and whole passages the preacher knew by heart. Characterized by repetition, parallelisms, dramatic use of voice and gesture, and a whole range of oratorical devices, the sermon began with normal conversational prose, then built to a rhythmic cadence, regularly marked by the exclamations of the congregation, and climaxed in a tonal chant accompanied by shouting, singing, and ecstatic behavior. The preacher, who needed considerable skill to master this art, acknowledged not his own craft but, rather, the power of the spirit which struck him and "set him on fire." The dynamic pattern of call and response between preacher and people was vital to the progression of the sermon, and unless the spirit roused the congregation to move and shout, the sermon was essentially unsuccessful.

A highly visible figure in the community, the preacher occupied a position of esteem and authority and undoubtedly developed a reputation which could form the basis for folk tales. The prestige of the role attracted some characters to the ministry who furnished the prototypes of the rascal jackleg preacher. Perhaps the genre of black-preacher tales began during slavery. For some the call to preach might have been a call to status and privilege, but for the majority it was the command of God to spread the Gospel. One

former slave explained his calling in simple and eloquent words which epitomized the ideal of the preacher's vocation:

> Yer see I am a preacher. De Lord call me once when I was workin'. . . . He call me and told me, in imagination, you know, that he wanted me to preach. I told him I didn't know enough—that I was ig'nant, and the folks would laugh at me. But he drew me on and I prayed. I prayed out in the woods, and every time I tried to get up from my knees He would draw me down again. An' at last a great light came down sudden to me, a light as big as the moon, an' struck me hard on the head and on each shoulder and on the bress, here and here and here . . . And den same time warm was in around my heart, and I felt that the Book was there. An' my tongue was untied, and I preached ever since and is not afraid. I can't read de Book, but I has it here, I has de text, and de meanin', and I speaks as well as I can, and de congregation takes what the Lord gives me.

The preacher was not the only figure of religious influence in the quarters. The conjurer was the preacher's chief rival for authority of a supernatural kind. Witches possessed a negative kind of power to frighten. Elder slaves, who had earned respect because of their wisdom or vision acted as spiritual mentors to their fellows. Frederick Douglass, for example, as a boy frequently sought the counsel of Uncle Charles Lawson, whom he called his spiritual father and "chief instructor in religious matters." Lawson taught Douglass "that the Lord had great work for me to do. . . . When I would tell him, 'I am a slave, and a slave for life, how can I do anything?' he would quietly answer, 'The *Lord* can make you free . . .' " Sinda, an elderly slave woman on Frances Kemble's plantation, exerted considerable religious influence among the slaves as a prophetess until she damaged her credibility by predicting an imminent end to the world. On the Sea Islands in 1864 Laura Towne encountered Maum Katie "an old African woman, who remembers worshipping her own gods in Africa." Over a century old, she was a " 'spiritual mother,' a fortune-teller or, rather, prophetess, and a woman of tremendous influence over her spiritual children." The "watchman" was also an important religious leader on the plantation. His duties included advising on spiritual matters, opening and leading prayer meetings, counseling "mourners," sinners seeking conversion, and generally setting Christian example for the slaves.

Much discussion has focused on the question, Were the slave preachers a force for accommodation to the *status quo* or a force for the exercise of slave autonomy? On the one hand, the slave preacher was criticized by former slaves as the "mouthpiece of the masters." On the other hand, some slave preachers preached and spoke of free-dom in secret. The weight of slave testimony suggests that the slaves knew and understood the restrictions under which the slave preacher labored, and that they accepted his authority not because it came from the master but because it came from God. They respected him because he was the messenger of the Gospel, one who preached the word of God with power and authority, indeed with a power which sometimes humbled white folk and frequently uplifted slaves. For a black man and a slave to stand and preach with eloquence, skill, and wisdom was in itself a sign of ability and talent which slavery's restrictiveness could frustrate but never completely stifle.

21

THE NEW INDUSTRIAL ORDER

JONATHAN PRUDE

In the first half of the nineteenth century the northern United States experienced profound social and economic changes. At the time of Jefferson's election in 1800, America was a predominantly rural society of small farmers and urban artisans, but by the end of the Civil War the northern United States had become a rapidly developing industrial society.

This process of economic and social change began in the last decade of the eighteenth century when, following English models, American merchants began to construct small textile mills along the many rivers of the northern states. Encouraged by Jefferson's Embargo of 1807–1808 and the War of 1812, both of which eliminated British competition for American-made goods, textile production became the mainstay of the domestic industrial economy.

At the same time that textile factories were being established, America's domestic economy was changing in another way as well. In the cities, nascent capitalists were building manufactories and hiring workers to perform tasks that in the past had been done by independent craftsmen in their own shops. As increasing numbers of artisan crafts were taken out of the control of individual craftsmen themselves, a whole artisanal way of life, marked by independence and economic sufficiency, was replaced by a wage-earning life of social dependence and economic impoverishment.

While the impact of industrialization was most apparent in the case of the urban artisan, the industrial revolution of the nineteenth century affected every American. In this essay, Jonathan Prude describes these changes as they occurred among three crucial groups in American society. Directing his attention to rural southern Massachusetts, Prude follows the path of economic change among the small farmers, shopkeepers, and factory workers who made up a majority of American society in the nineteenth century.

How do you think each of the groups discussed in this essay would have responded to the ideology of the Republican Party, as discussed by Eric Foner in Reading 23? How do you think the factory operatives of Massachusetts would have responded to the class-conscious message of the mass-circulation press, as discussed by Alexander Saxton in Reading 19?

The economic structure of Dudley and Oxford [Massachusetts] during the generation after 1810 had three broad characteristics. First, the increased, but still significantly limited, commercial involvement of agriculture. Second, the dramatic expansion of small-business establishments; and

From Jonathan Prude, *The Coming of Industrial Order: Town and Factory Life in Rural Massachusetts, 1810–1860* (Cambridge: Cambridge University Press, 1983), pp. 100–132.
Reprinted with the permission of the publisher.

third, the appearance of manufactories along the streams of the two communities. Together with the emergence of investors to sponsor the new shops, stores, and textile mills, and the alterations in local occupational patterns produced by post-1810 ventures, it was farming, small-business activities, and textile manufacturing that determined the basic economic format of Dudley and Oxford between 1810 and the early 1830s.

In a sense, the three strands were complementary. Local agricultural patterns, for example, both reflected and supported the spread of non-agricultural enterprises to at least some degree; and shops and factories, for their part, often provided mutual technical and commercial encouragement. But there were significant distinctions among the organizational regimens—the basic internal orderings—of the three economic sectors. And to understand what local residents faced in this period, it becomes important to identify these distinctions: to specify precisely how yeomen governed—or, as it turned out, failed to govern—their daily affairs; how nontextile businesses were administered; and how cotton and woolen manufactories orchestrated their machines and workers.

The ordering of life and labor inside the mill villages requires particularly detailed treatment. It was by far the most complex disciplinary structure—involving dense, sometimes conflicting interweavings of new ideologies and practices—and it impinged directly upon the largest single group of local wage laborers. But taken as a whole, the populations of Dudley and Oxford confronted the order of agricultural and nontextile labor as well. And in the final analysis, it was the blend—and contrast—of regiments ramifying through all three economic spheres that shaped the experience of local residents in the decades after 1810. A key factor conditioning farm life in these years was the lack of adequate labor. As already remarked, the average yeoman's effort to improve a larger proportion of his homestead with a fixed, or even diminishing, roster of children and servants represented a wearisome burden. The pressures behind this burden—the reasons that youngsters permanently quit their farming homes

and that agricultural laborers required increasingly high wages—have already been explored. But how did the shortage—or expense—of farming labor affect those remaining on the homestead?

In the first place, it added new shadows to relations between parents and their offspring, for the rising number of permanent youthful departures had cultural as well as economic dimensions. On the one hand, these departures almost certainly strengthened the belief among sons and daughters (even while they remained on the farm) that they could and should ultimately seek independence. Even if (as was probably often the case) departing children launched into ventures with their parents' blessing and assistance, the children themselves may well have experienced an unprecedentedly vivid sense of autonomy. "The weight," observes one student of youthful culture in this era, "was increasingly on the side of independence."

For their part, parents seem to have responded to the wave of departures with growing frustration and worry. Anxiety about the integrity of domestic life had been part of American discourse, both public and private, since the earliest colonial days. But beginning in the 1820s, mounting steadily in the 1830s and 1840s, pressures on the family seem to have become sufficiently disruptive to generate a new structure of feeling about rural life: a sustained wondering among rural parents—by turns nostalgic and angry—about whether they could get the job of farming done and whether, even if they could, farming as they had known it was not in serious jeopardy. For even if it was economically rational for a given yeoman's children to leave, was not the basic continuity of husbandry threatened by the flight of "every farmer's son and daughter"? And even if children turned to nonagricultural ventures with the approval of their parents, could not these same parents still accuse their sons of turning into "dandies" (into "Tom, my Twattle") when these young men decided that "it was ungentlemanly to know how to handle a hoe or a pitchfork"? Could not these parents complain that, with so few daughters willing to "join the mother in her domestic duties," young women were growing up "so little informed . . . , they can hardly cook a potato"? And could not these parents also fear for the viability of their own farming ventures? "Why thus alone at your ploughing, Mr. Thrifty?" asked the *Old Farmer's Almanack* in one of its famous cautionary dialogues:

> O, sir, my boys have all left me and turned shoe-peggers. I was in hopes to keep at least one of them to help carry on the farm; but they have all five gone . . . If this is the way things are going on, our farms must soon run up to bushes.

Yeomen in Dudley and Oxford could not have avoided this mounting sense of vulnerability. Nor could they have offset their concern with hired laborers. It was not only that such workers were scarce and thus expensive but also that relations between farmers and servants showed increased strain. If trends evident in other communities held up in Dudley and Oxford, local farmers using agricultural workers could afford to hire them only by the season rather than by the year as formerly. And this, in turn, meant that such workers were less frequently treated as full members of the farming household. Contemporary reports held that even skilled reapers were refused permission "to sit at table with the family." And testimony was growing that farm laborers, for their part, no longer felt any shared interest with their yeoman-employers. Instead, laborers were said to display a "plebian envy of those above them"; and they "do not consider themselves bound for any length of time, and occasionally absent themselves for a day or two without giving notice of their intention." With employers, as with children, there was the sense of a domestic chemistry turning increasingly sour: "So you see," intoned the *Almanack*'s bitter-sad summary in the early 1840s,

> that it will not do to trust altogether to servants, though you may think them all trustworthy. Slam! Slam! go the green blinds, amidst the storm, in the absence of the owner; but what care servants about

this? . . . Was the master at home, eyes, ears, and feet would all be in full employment. But, suppose now, in these modern times, so famous for *quid pro quo,* your servant has as many eyes as Argus, sleeping with two only at once—would he heed or care for this rattle and ruin? Not unless there is a special provision for it in the bargain; for good old fashions are done away.

But in the end, any shifts in social relationships on local homesteads were more than offset by the continuities of farming life. To balance scarce labor, for example, yeoman households throughout the region retained the custom of aiding one another during busy planting and harvest seasons. Despite the rapid transiency through these two communities, nearly one-fifth of all farming households in Dudley and Oxford may still have had relatives of some sort living in the vicinity; and together with neighboring friends and acquaintances, those kinsmen would have provided a safety net of willing workers. Nor should the altered dynamics between parents and children be exaggerated, for the fact remains that children often *did* move on with parental advice and consent. And there exist, in any case, too many examples of widely scattered relatives maintaining contact with one another to assume that family bonds crumbled beneath the comings and goings of rural Yankees.

But the most concrete continuities lay in the actual processes of husbandry, in the ordering of daily agricultural work. The evidence here must again be culled from across the region. But the indications are that agricultural commercialization had by no means proceeded far enough in the early nineteenth century to force wholesale revision in the routines of Yankee farming. On the contrary, yeomen like those in Dudley and Oxford evinced almost glacial reluctance to alter the substance of their daily labors.

Their inertia is the more notable because the period witnessed repeated efforts to alter farming technology and technique. New machines—cast-iron ploughs, horse-drawn cultivators (for corn), and hay rakes—were introduced, and a deluge of new agricultural journals advised an entire curriculum of new methods. The basic seasonal rhythms of Yankee farming were not challenged. But yeomen were called upon to use more manure, to adopt soil-saving crop rotations, to confine homesteads to the acreage they could entirely cultivate every year, and generally to adopt rigidly systematic methods of "general management." "A farmer needs more drilling in this business," announced *The Young Farmer's Manual* in a passage that neatly captured the zeal of antebellum farming reformers, "than a general does in military tactics to be able to manage an army of soldiers."

But even the most enthusiastic missionaries of change found Yankee husbandmen to be slow converts. New tools were not totally ignored, and fertilizer and English hay evidently did gain broader favor. But the revised hardware never won more than spotty acceptance, and apart from a trend toward eliminating summer fallows, there was little systematic crop rotation. Moreover, judging from the steady complaints of reformers and data from Dudley and Oxford, most New England farmers maintained or raised productivity by "improving" more acres within their homesteads rather than by limiting homesteads to just those fields and meadows they could continuously exploit.

Why this resistance to change? In part it was probably simply an intuitive hostility toward the unfamiliar. But a recent analysis concludes that Yankee stolidness in the early antebellum era also arose because innovations "intruded upon a system of production which represented a rough balance between the various resources applied within each farm unit." New England farmers might shift more heavily toward the market, might cultivate more land per farm, might demonstrate more concern over soil fertility, and might even (as they did in Oxford in 1812) organize agricultural societies to promote these trends. But to go further would have disrupted the "form of balanced operations" yeomen had achieved. New technologies were thus rejected, not out of "rural idiocy," but because using them would have produced surpluses beyond levels they could sell or consume, or because (especially

in the case of hay rakes) they would have required unreasonable allocations of scarce labor resources to smooth out rocky New England fields. And so with crop rotations: The investment of capital and labor called for was frequently beyond Yankee husbandmen or involved an expanded production of crops (like wheat) that were already produced in large and cheap supply beyond the Hudson River.

In sum, reforms were often impractical. But it was also the case that even feasible innovations implied an outlay of resources that made sense only if farmers were committed to the market and only if they were willing to adopt the long-term perspective of businessmen. In fact, farmers had by no means wholeheartedly adopted this position.

It was, to reiterate, a question of balance. If New England yeomen placed greater stress on marketable goods during the 1820s and 1830s, and if they were drifting increasingly into nonagricultural enterprises, the tilt to commerce still did not necessitate a thorough acceptance of market priorities. Most farmers still mixed their quest for gain with a commitment to immediate "family needs." In Dudley and Oxford (as already noted) it was probably often to satisfy such "needs" that farmers undertook business ventures or helped sons and daughters move in this direction. Within the context of farming itself, the persisting stress on household priorities was demonstrated in the continued cultivation of foodstuffs for domestic consumption. And it may even explain why local husbandmen resisted smaller landholdings: For it might have been believed that preserving farms of some size would increase the possibility of passing on land to heirs. That debts and youthful migrations often eviscerated this hope would not have weakened its fervor. Indeed, considering northeastern farmers generally, the abiding importance of family priorities underlay antipathy toward many elements of the reform program. Unwilling to accept gain as their exclusive goal, farmers saw little reason to reject "the customary practices of an area."

Not surprisingly, such recalcitrance met strong criticism from agricultural writers of the period. The stubborn Yankee husbandman was reduced virtually to a stock character and ridiculed repeatedly as a man "who condemns new things because they are new; who dislikes to see them attempted, and likes to see them fail." In communities like Dudley and Oxford attacks on yeoman conservatism often also led to observations that farms represented the cultural antithesis of textile mills. Factories, after all, were easily taken to represent the very culmination of "general management" and commercialization. Pursuing an argument initiated by profactory writers in the late eighteenth century, agricultural reformers hailed antebellum manufactories as crucial instruments in forwarding the market's leavening influence on the hinterland. The capacity of mills to provide a "ready home market" for farm goods, it was said, was the "impelling and most efficient cause of Agricultural employment" in New England. If, therefore, farmers were seen as consistently rejecting an innovative and profit-hungry outlook on life, they could scarcely avoid also being viewed as rejecting the entire influence of textile factories. Thus the stereotyped contrast: "For within the hum of a single textile mill," a Connecticut pamphlet concluded as late as 1850, "there is more . . . skill and science applied to practical art and labor than in a township of farms."

But this was to put the matter pejoratively. Husbandmen who resisted full-tilt commercialization, and the scattering of writers sympathetic to them, could describe their stance very differently: as evidence that farming yielded a prosperity "money cannot purchase, and money cannot measure . . . [,] a competency for the evening of life, . . . a mind unencumbered from the vexatious caprices of trade and speculation."

Indeed, judging from the town-factory controversies that would ultimately erupt in Dudley and Oxford, yeomen in these communities may well have taken a further step. Precisely because manufactories were so frequently linked to "bookfarming," there is reason to suppose yeomen who resisted the latter may have come to regard the former with particular alarm. Surveying what was befalling them as the nineteenth

century advanced, farmers of this stripe would have found little difficulty in judging factories as the source of several long-term, profound, and painful dislocations. Such husbandmen, after all, would hardly have failed to notice that their children were not simply leaving but frequently "posting off" to mills, or that the commercialization encouraged by mills often yielded more debt than prosperity. It was credible, in brief, for Yankee farmers to hold textile factories in some measure responsible for the changes pounding their lives. Sharpened and rendered more immediate by other challenges the mills would in time appear to pose—in particular, challenges to community notions of governance and social hierarchy—a general, brooding sense of grievance among yeomen of Dudley and Oxford could easily have contributed to the friction slowly emerging between the two townships and their mills.

The daily operations of small, nonagricultural enterprises in these communities are, if anything, even more difficult to uncover than labor routines on local homesteads. But sufficient clues do exist to suggest that, like farms, many nontextile businesses clung to established conventions.

In their work rhythms, for example, rural stores apparently still permitted late morning breaks for toddies, and many handicraft enterprises evidently retained similarly discontinuous schedules. Thus it is certain that Oxford's scythe-making shop shut down completely five months every year. It is not certain, but it is likely, that employees in local boot and shoe shops also cut down work in certain seasons and (following patterns persisting in this trade) may well have taken off occasional days throughout the year to undertake other jobs or just to fish. And if examples from other communities provide any example, much the same irregularity probably obtained in the smaller one- and two-man workshops. Even the region's mythically reliable blacksmith "Seth Steady," whose "hammer is heard at the dawn of the day, and [whose] fire blazes in his shop during the evenings," worked at his trade only from September to March. The entirely unmythical Nailer Tom outside Providence labored year round and even aimed toward six-day weeks; but he still frequently took to the road on many afternoons to settle accounts or to fetch supplies or (in the summer) to work "among the Hay."

The most continuous and rigorously specified labor schedule outside local textile manufactories was probably found in Thomas Chatman's textile machine works. There, if comparable enterprises of the period are indicative, employees faced twelve- and fourteen-hour days and may even have found their attendance checked by "time-keepers." But such arrangements were exceptional in Dudley and Oxford in this period, for work outside factory villages generally proceeded far more sporadically. Indeed, after 1810 as before, payments for labor were typically not linked to time at all but continued to be doled out by the task.

Nor, for the most part, had the division of labor advanced very far. Again there were exceptions. It has already been suggested that local boot and shoe works may well have embraced enough division of labor to cast some employees as overseers and distribute certain jobs to outlying households. Chatman's machine works also may have used overseers and (again drawing on nonlocal data) may have divided its shop operations into several departments: a blacksmithy, possibly a foundry, pattern and drafting rooms, the machine room for tooling parts of each apparatus the shop produced, and an assembly area. It is likely too that within the machine room labor was broken into further discrete steps, each distributed to different clusters of employees.

But this was not the overall pattern. The relatively small size of most nontextile operations meant that jobs were commonly undertaken entirely by a single individual or shared equally among a few people. In fact, even Chatman's enterprise probably embraced practices that blunted the impact of divided work processes. Machine shops during the 1820s and 1830s typically used the "inside contracting" system under which individual skilled machinists "contracted" for specific jobs, hired whatever help they needed, signed for appropriate tools and materials, and were paid (either by the piece or the day) at the

job's completion. By permitting substantial autonomy to each contracting machinist, the arrangement tended to curtail the overseers' authority and prevent machine making from collapsing into a progression of minutely defined rote jobs performed entirely by unskilled operatives. In important ways, the machines Thomas Chatman produced thus likely stood as handicrafted creations.

But what of machinery used in nontextile establishments; how far had the technology of their daily activities advanced? It would appear not very far: It was the general absence of mechanically elaborate hardware, it may be recalled, that helped reduce the cost (and thus facilitated the growth) of these ventures.

Once more the exceptions deserve notice. At least three trip-hammers, one of them waterpowered, were used in Oxford (in one instance to manufacture scythes) during this period. By 1814, moreover, Rufus Moore had purchased for his small nail-making shop a rather extraordinary machine that automatically "*cut* and *headed* [nails] at the same time." Some dexterity was needed to run this apparatus, but a contemporary description of a similar mechanism in Newark reveals that the "machine's feeder" had little control over either the pace or substance of his labors:

> The human portion of the machine holds in his hands a staff or stick, one end of which rests in a prop behind him for the sake of steadiness, and upon the other end is a clamp with which the plate is held. As the action of the cutter is not reciprocal, it is necessary that the plate should be turned at each cut; and as the machine moves rather rapidly, this is a delicate operation which the feeder only acquires after considerable practice . . .
>
> When the plate is cut up the feeder throws his clamp over a spur which projects from the side of the machine, pries it open, throws the remnant aside to be reheated with the rest of the scraps, seizes another plate with a pair of pincers, fixes it in his clamp, and goes on as before.
>
> The machines are gauged to cut different-sized nails, and their speed decreases in the same ratio as the size of the nail increases. Thus the machine

which cuts a "twenty-penny" moves at about one-eighth the speed of another which is cutting "eight-pennies."

But such machines were scarcely the norm outside local mill compounds. Despite their probable divisions of labor, the boot and shoe shops of Dudley and Oxford would have possessed only hand-powered tools. And Chatman's machine shop was probably equipped with no more than "very primitive" technologies: treadle-run lathes, cold chisels, hammers, and files.

Work schedules, division of labor, technologies—these are all obvious aspects of the regimen informing nontextile businesses after 1810. But equally important is the way motivations of nonfactory proprietors were confirmed and reflected in the actual ordering of local stores and workshops.

With at least some involvement in nonlocal market dealings, a few of these establishments were evidently touched, to at least some degree, by desire for financial success pure and simple. There are indications that after 1810 businesses increasingly began suing to collect debts rather than permitting credit to extend indefinitely. Then too, the steps probably taken by the cordwaining and textile machine shops to introduce supervision, division of labor, and (in the machine shop) timekeeping suggest that proprietors of these ventures were intent on increasing productivity and reducing costs. The owners and managers of these particular enterprises may have ranked, in fact, among the most profit-conscious local businessmen outside those involved in the daily operation of cotton and woolen manufactories.

Even storekeepers occasionally tilted in this direction, with several managing to link themselves directly to the energies and ambitions of waterpowered textile operations. The General Store Craggins and Andrews ran in Oxford was not a factory store in the sense of standing in a mill village. But their account books (laid out in the latest double-entry bookkeeping style) indicate that, besides selling goods and "sundries," the two proprietors were by the early 1820s run-

ning a power-weaving shed employing a dozen women. And although William Law's store in Dudley did not trade only with millworkers, it was the conduit (again by the early 1820s) through which operatives of a local manufactory received their wages.

Yet this increased emphasis on profit proceeded only to a point. If debts more frequently led to judicial wrangles, it was equally true that credit remained widespread and interest-free. Moreover, the apparent absence of organizational and technological innovations in most nontextile ventures—indeed, the apparent limits to changes even in shoe and machine shops—suggests that individuals connected to these enterprises (employees if not always employers) had not entirely forsaken customary notions of how and why work should be done. Nor had barter disappeared. Although money was used more frequently after 1810, most purchases (even in stores associated with textile production) were paid with labor or in kind: currencies that promoted exchanges of goods and services more easily than systematic calculations and accumulations of gain. And finally, the way proprietors exploited local resources signaled the persisting strength of customary attitudes. Nontextile millers and triphammer operators, for example, clung to notions of communal good, at least to the extent of sharing local streams with minimal fuss or friction.

The core rationale of nonmanufactory ventures thus embraced considerable variety. Indeed, some enterprises actually may have simultaneously retained and rejected earlier mores. On balance, however, the routines of most small businesses in this period expressed the same restrained commercial ambitions characterizing local stores and workshops before 1810. This hesitancy to adopt new motivations would not as easily or as necessarily have connoted the antifactory animus attributable to agricultural conservatism. For in the debates that swirled about in these years, farmers found it easier—and judged it more necessary—than merchants or blacksmiths to perceive mills as threatening. Yet, in the final analysis, the policies and practices typical of most local nontextile projects during the second and third decades of the nineteenth century confirmed a perspective closer to the yeoman's quest for success that "money cannot measure" than to the sustained profit seeking that fueled local manufactories.

Profit, of course, had always been the goal of New England textile factories. From the 1790s up through later antebellum decades, manufactories operated to make money. Not all of them succeeded, of course. Slater's ventures (both before and after his arrival in southern Massachusetts) demonstrably did well; and the large works at Waltham reportedly registered returns of more than 20 percent during the 1820s. But many country establishments brought no more than 5 or 6 percent on investments, and numerous bankruptcies followed every economic downturn. Whatever fortune actually fell its way, however, each mill at least sought a favorable balance of trade.

Thus factories like those in Dudley and Oxford diverged from prevailing rural conventions. It was not just that these enterprises boasted payrolls larger than other local businesses, or that they routinely used machines matched in complexity only by Rufus Moore's nail-making apparatus, or that they employed a division of labor that certainly equaled, and probably surpassed, the most thoroughly subdivided work arrangements outside factory walls—it was not just all this but also that local manufactories pursued market priorities with a single-minded enthusiasm unmatched by most nontextile businesses. If, for example, factories in Dudley and Oxford occasionally paid wages and accepted payments in goods and if they constantly complained about the scarcity of money, they also tended to stipulate "no barter" as soon as possible. And although these mills (like others throughout the region) routinely extended six to eight months' credit to customers, they also frequently awarded discounts of up to 4 percent for prompt payments —an arrangement that effectively levied interest on postponed reimbursements. Of all local businesses, moreover, manufactories were perhaps the readiest to sue over debts. They were certainly

the readiest to build unprecedentedly large dams across local waterways, even though (unlike the stream harnessed by the Green Mill) the brooks and rivers thus blocked off were often needed by other Dudley and Oxford residents. And if, despite all such efforts, smaller Yankee mills on the average still earned little more than farms, this fact produced unrelieved concern among factory masters. There was no effort to celebrate mills as havens from "vexatious caprices of trade and speculation." Low profit margins in manufactories yielded only complaints about the price of technology or demands for governmental subsidies and tariffs or calls for improved efficiency.

And yet, despite its obvious centrality, profit did not dominate the way owners and enthusiasts of textile factories justified the construction of cotton and woolen mills in the generation after 1810. Now it is true (in ways detailed presently) that these men implicitly intended their rhetoric to encourage attitudes and performances compatible with business success. But it is the explicit, formal message of their slogans that must first be examined, and here a rather different brief for manufactories emerges. Exploring the order of life and labor in antebellum textile factories— including factories in Dudley and Oxford—starts with this different brief, this ideology, generated in the early nineteenth century to explain and defend these new institutions.

To some degree, it was an ideology built upon the effort defenders of Yankee mills had always made to describe factories as more than self-serving. The early arguments that manufactories could fuel overall American economic prosperity —arguments initiated by Alexander Hamilton and Tench Coxe and invoked by Slater in the 1790s—did not disappear. Factory ideologies continued to insist (increasingly in chorus with agricultural reformers) that mills provided useful markets for farmers; and such propositions offered continuing points of departure for profactory statements. But as the 1800s wore on, economic defenses of mills were increasingly alloyed with themes of social reform.

There were precursors of the trend. As early as

1785 profactory writers in England had praised Jedediah Strutt's factories, and particularly his Sunday schools, as effective weapons against the "Tide of Immorality" supposedly washing through England's working poor. "In that first generation of industrialization," a recent student of English institutional discipline has concluded, "factories could still be justified not simply as technical achievements, but as moral ones as well." Even across the Atlantic, the United Company of Philadelphia had maintained in 1785 that waterpowered mills would bring "a general and laudable spirit of industry" to their employees; and of course Hamilton had spoken early on of factories providing Americans with "independence." But in the United States such rationales appear at first only sporadically. It was during the years after 1810, and continuing up through roughly the mid-1840s, that supporters of Yankee manufactories began consistently suggesting that mills showed "regard to the welfare of their operatives" and that consequently "Hundreds" of mill employees were being "reclaimed, civilized, Christianized."

How did mills perform this ethical magic? First, it was said, by providing employment that was more "regular"—and thus more conducive to anchored, responsible social interaction—than seasonal or occasional labor. "A steady employer," Harriet Martineau pronounced approvingly during her tour of American mills, "has it in his power to do more for the morals of the society about him than the clergy themselves." But factories supplemented their uplifting efficacy by also imposing particular disciplines on their hands: "prudent and effectual regulations against disorderly and immoral behaviour." "Rules and regulations" varied from mill to mill. But, generally speaking, Yankee factories of this period—including family mills like those in Dudley and Oxford—demanded that during working hours operatives display the traits of punctuality, temperance, "industriousness," "steadiness," and obedience to mill authorities. Adopting (though probably few realized it) the materialist psychology advanced originally by John Locke and later by (among others) David Hartley and Benjamin

Rush, antebellum factory spokesmen maintained that people were malleable and hence that steady applications of mill discipline would "improve" employees.

It can scarcely be ignored that the notion of effecting reform through discipline linked manufactories to several other institutions emerging in this period. It created similarities between factories and the new schools spreading throughout the North, for example, as well as with the penitentiaries, poorhouses, and insane asylums that began appearing in antebellum America. Like mills, these expanded facilities for students and deviants were frequently described by advocates as efforts to "correct" social ills through "regular" routines. The endemic transiency of postrevolutionary America, the restless lurching from job to job, the fissures opening up in families—all this (the argument ran) had eroded "external restraints" that had once "repressed the passions of men"; lacking such "restraints," citizens of the young Republic were sinking beneath rising tides of crime, insanity, and poverty. If America was to survive, "internal and moral restraints" had to be substituted. Thus, along with their other instructional duties, schools were commonly charged with using institutional regimens to implant the values—indeed, the compulsions—of good behavior. For students who failed to heed the lesson and subsequently—inevitably, it was supposed—succumbed to social pathology, the new asylums were to employ tireless routines to reintroduce stability into their inmates' psyches and so instill habits requisite for life on the outside.

This was the context within which mill masters implemented factory discipline in the years after 1810. Of course, other employers of the era administered their ventures amid the same cultural clues and anxieties. But because of their complexity and because of their need to synchronize large labor forces, manufactories were particularly likely to adopt regimens paralleling strictures in schools and asylums. And they were thus particularly likely to find themselves described in terms of such institutions. The British immigrant Samuel Ogden was using a figure of speech soon to become commonplace when he announced in 1815 that "a cotton factory is a school for the improvement of ingenuity and industry."

This is not to suggest that all operatives accepted the factory order as educational or therapeutic, for they assuredly did not. Many mill-workers in the generation after 1810 found reasons and methods to resist their employers' regimen. Indeed, the tugs back and forth between managers and operatives over work discipline, and the compromises that consequently developed, represent a crucial unfolding motif in the antebellum history of textile factories. Nor would it be correct to suppose that mill masters modeled all their policies around contemporary reform programs. Aiming primarily toward business success, daily practices of manufactories like those in Dudley and Oxford were actually becoming steadily less compatible with the ameliorative project proclaimed by their ideology. The point is rather that mill masters, managers, operatives, and northerners generally were all familiar with the idea of the factory-as-asylum. It was an important part of the meaning that mills had begun trailing across Yankee society by the second and third decades of the nineteenth century. And it was thus an important element in the way these establishments came to be experienced in New England.

But a distinction has to be made between the ideologies of Waltham-style and family mills. Although proprietors of both genres adopted the rhetoric of uplift, those supporting the larger ventures could also drift into more conservative formulations. Because these factories aimed to hire mainly "well-educated" young women from middling and "virtuous rural homes," the Waltham regimen was often depicted more as *maintaining* than improving their operatives' moral character. It was to *protect* their workers that these factories imposed tight supervision over the girls' boardinghouses, implemented curfews, and made church attendance mandatory. And it was their putative success in returning their employees to the countryside with "unsullied reputation" that permitted boardinghouse mills to boast that they would never harbor the degradation rumored to fill England's factory centers.

Some family-mill owners took issue with this vision, claiming that "mammoth Waltham establishment[s]" replicated, by their very size, the worst features of Old World industrialization. But there was a more pervasive and important ideological distinction: Small rural mills consistently clung to their claim of effecting improvement. Even though their operatives were by no means uniformly poor, factories such as those in Dudley and Oxford never wavered from the claim that they "combatted . . . vice, ignorance, and poverty." In fact, they dared not waver. For given the close connection between "vice, ignorance, and poverty," once masters of family mills acknowledged hiring any poor workers, they willy-nilly faced charges of fostering "contagion." Grafted deeply into Anglo-American social thought of the eighteenth and early nineteenth centuries, the notion of contagion linked moral decay and physical disease as aspects of a common deformity and concluded that immorality, like sickness, could spread rapidly among tightly clustered gatherings of the "vicious, improvident, and indigent." Country-mill owners who recruited poor employees into their closed workplaces might thus be guilty of serious "abuse" unless they used discipline to "change the current of vice from its filthy and offensive channel." An obvious implication was that only "prudent and effectual regulations" separated family mills from pesthouses.

And there were further implications as well. If poor people required institutional tutelage, and if poor operatives often came from the countryside, was not rural life itself flawed? The answer was inescapably affirmative—and here country mill proprietors and their supporters extended the distinction agricultural reformers posited between backward farms and efficient factories. Here, in fact, was the entrepreneurs' ideological counterattack against antifactory suspicions likely circulating among husbandmen. Without factories to buy goods, provide employment, and organize "moral and religious instruction," it was suggested, the hinterland would descend into "wretchedness." Samuel Slater himself described a rural landscape devoid of mills as characterized by "universal bankruptcy and poverty; the utter extinction of the arts of civilized life; in fine, a retrograde movement of the whole community to ignorance, weakness, and barbarism." By the 1820s and 1830s, the order of country mills was thus moored to a rationale that dismissed the basic worth of country life.

Such were the rather stern conclusions following from an ideological commitment to uplift. Against this grim tone, however, must be set the more friendly, or at least more familiar, connotations of the rubric commonly invoked to summarize the order of rural factories. Striving to specify both the authority and responsibility of this regimen, aiming to emphasize its ameliorative and altruistic impulse, owners and supporters of country mills took to calling these factories "paternalistic." It was a powerfully evocative term, an efficient and effective label for the perspective industrial ideologues sought to advance. Domestic concepts and themes were much in mind during antebellum decades, after all, for the family was widely perceived as a frontline social mechanism in the battle for good behavior, a structure whose supposed unraveling was a key reason asylums had become necessary. Waltham-style factories and specifically their minutely monitored boardinghouses occasionally carried the label. But because smaller rural mills could claim the direct personal involvement of "fatherly" proprietors, paternalism seems to have achieved particular currency in early nineteenth century discussions of New England's smaller textile ventures.

Thus Dexter Ballow of Mendon "with his sleeves rolled up, and his working suit on . . . watched over the welfare of his help with parental solicitude." And thus Samuel Slater maintained "a strict, though mild and paternal scrutiny of the conduct of the workpeople" and "a kindly and paternal interest" in their "welfare." Indeed, it was just this "interest" (so the celebratory commentaries continued) that permitted small Yankee mills to remain just as distinct as Waltham-style establishments from England's "corrupt" factory communities. Certainly the example Slater set in his "care and efforts, extending

through forty years," went far to explain "the superior condition of the manufacturing villages of Rhode Island and the adjoining districts in moral and social respects as compared with that of most manufacturing villages of Great Britain."

Paternalism, of course, also inserted an obvious paradox into the ideology of factory order. For here were manufactories—establishments far larger than the shops and stores still typical of the Yankee hinterland—emerging as the only ventures self-consciously wrapping themselves in a rhetoric of personal, managerial involvement with each employee's "welfare." Here were business ventures that flatly contradicted the conventional rural emphasis on "family need," calmly describing themselves as households writ-large and brimming with fatherly concern.

None of this, however, has prevented paternalism from achieving a permanent place in discussions of New England textile factories. As late as 1874, long after Samuel Slater's death, a local historian described the North, South, and East villages as resembling "one large and well-conducted family, where the head is not only respected, but regarded with attachment and pride, as the patriarch and father." Even more significantly, modern scholars looking back to Yankee mills of the early nineteenth century have commonly employed the notion of paternalism. They have used the term both pejoratively (to describe an overly intrusive managerial presence) and approvingly. But in either case the concept itself is entrenched within the historiography of early antebellum New England manufactories.

Probing the ideology of factory order is the point of departure for understanding that order. But the way Yankees experienced textile mills in this period was also shaped by how management used this ideology for its own ends. If the formal apologias surrounding manufactories help identify an important cultural resonance of antebellum cotton and woolen factories, equally important are the self-serving advantages mill masters implicitly sought to win through their apologias.

Put simply, factory masters in tended their ideology to promote behavior leading to profit as well as reform. Claims of concerned "interest" and "parental solicitude," for example, were aimed toward calming suspicions stirred up within and around antebellum manufactories. Then too, the diligence, sobriety, and punctuality employers sought to instill in their "reclaimed" workers were obviously also the traits of a highly productive labor force. But perhaps the clearest expression of this pragmatic manipulation of ideology lies in the way managers justified their dealings with families inside the mill villages. Because, ironically enough, arguments pivoting around assertions of paternalism were used to legitimize the intrusions factories made into the households under their jurisdiction.

The relationship between family mills and the families they hired was complex. On the one hand, these factories took steps to preserve—even bolster—customary domestic patterns among their hands. Thus (judging from East Village and Dudley Woolen Manufacturing Company data) local factories not only provided cottages so that family members could live together; they also went out of their way to retain family workers during economic depressions. In both good and bad times, moreover, the bookkeeping iconography of these mills reveals further efforts to acknowledge conventional household relationships and hierarchies: by listing coresiding operatives together, whatever their job assignments, in the Time Books; by transferring wages earned by younger children directly to their parents; and by always paying fathers at higher rates than any of their operative offspring.

Such policies helped assure the viability of families inside local factory compounds. But it would be fundamentally incorrect to construe the operatives' domestic life as entirely determined by factory priorities. However strongly antebellum reformers may have *wished* families would instill "internal restraints," disaffections emerging among local operatives in the years after 1810 make it highly unlikely that parents of Dudley and Oxford factory workers systematically cooperated with management to produce "steady" young laborers. There are, in fact, reasons to suppose that millworking families main-

tained their strength *despite* the factory order. Factory policies supporting the integrity of operative families were only part of the picture.

In the first place, mills did not prevent children above 14 from receiving their own wages or occasionally even taking up lodgings separate from their parents and siblings. Nor did managers prevent operatives in later teen years from mimicking nonfactory youths of comparable age in leaving to seek employment opportunities—for both extended and brief periods—many miles from their parents. But of greater significance was willingness of local mills to intrude directly on operative families. Occasionally managers specified precise billeting arrangements: In 1829, for example, the East Village permitted Mary Kingsbury to live in the compound "on condition" that her unemployed father "does not remain." Much more regularly, and hence much more consequentially, factory administrators took pains to prevent families from working together. Siblings might tend adjacent machines. But a close scrutiny of job assignments inside four local factories suggests that at least until the late 1830s managers systematically separated parents and children during the working day.

Probably the mills feared that adults placed near their offspring would challenge the overseers, or if overseers themselves, that they would cause friction by favoring their own youngsters. Coupled with contemporary prejudices against wage-earning mothers, such concerns would explain the exclusion of married women from local factory payrolls during the generation after 1810. Fathers were never totally barred, but those with berths inside the mills were segregated from their children. Even the relationship between mule spinners and their young piecers was purged of kinship: Despite sporadic references to spinners "find[ing their] own piecers," most local mule operators evidently let management select these assistants before 1840, and most boys serving as piecers thus ended up tying threads for nonrelatives. As time passed, moreover, it became increasingly difficult for children to find their fathers anywhere inside the mills. An emerging pattern of awarding skilled "male" jobs to unmarried men (promoted from below or recruited from outside) forced growing numbers of male household heads to remain idle, accept outdoor jobs, or leave the factory villages to seek work elsewhere. In the East Village, the proportion of families with fathers working somewhere inside the Green or Union mills fell from nearly three-quarters in 1817 to just over one-third in 1830.

The work-time separation of children and parents must have affected domestic relations. Far more than the broad, gradually accumulating pressures acting on parent–child relations of farming families, management's intrusions forcefully and directly challenged received notions of parental authority and responsibility. The operatives preserved their families. But in settings where parents controlled neither the work nor the discipline their children faced during working hours, where both parents and children were subjected to the same overriding managerial control —in such settings parental prestige could only suffer. And this is where claims of paternalism proved so useful. Owners and admirers of country mills like those in Dudley and Oxford asserted that factories could legitimately undermine patriarchy among operatives because they themselves were acting in loco parentis. When pressed to defend their stance more precisely, factory masters sometimes pointed to schools, arguing that mill families "delegated" parental authority to managers just as Yankee households surrendered authority to teachers. More often mills simply stressed their "regard" for workers. But in either case, it seems clear that rather than signaling continuity between operative families and the factory regimen, managerial assertions of "interest" and paternalism were invoked to justify managerial interventions between parents and youngsters.

Did any of this work? Did self-interested protestations that factories "showed regard" soften antagonisms toward these establishments? Did grounding labor discipline in moral uplift produce industrious operatives? Did stressing paternalism reduce concern about the domestic disruptions attending factory employment? To some extent, the ideology probably did all this. In Dudley and Oxford the halo of arguments surrounding manufactories by the 1820s and 1830s almost certainly provided at least some counterweight to the suspicions stirred up by factory villages. It quite possibly helped draw some Yankees into millwork (those entering factory jobs out of choice, for example), and it may well have encouraged these recruits to work diligently and without complaint during their stints.

But the suspicions were at most modified, not eradicated. Despite the mill masters' ideology, local operatives and townspeople still felt a strong —even growing—ambivalence toward the mills. Indeed, what requires notice at this point is that the ideology itself could generate alarm. A vision of paternalistic factory villages might strike sympathetic commentators as idyllic, as a conception underscoring the progressive potential of textile mills. But to those who viewed factory villages less as arenas for social therapy and more as merely places to live and work, the notion could have different implications.

It could, for example, make mill villages appear curiously anachronistic. Even while factory enclaves were introducing an architectural scale, social order, and demographic density that stood out dramatically in the postrevolutionary Yankee countryside, there is a sense in which their description as a "large and well-conducted family" could provoke nostalgic memories. By emphasizing the close-knit quality of mill life, by stressing how factory hands operated under the authority of a few officials, the paternalistic motif signaled ways in which manufactories more closely paralleled the more centralized and consistently hierarchical society of seventeenth and early eighteenth century rural New England than the fluid, physically dispersed, and lightly governed townships of the late eighteenth and early nineteenth centuries. Invoking paternalism, in other words, could make mill villages seem like throwbacks to an earlier age.

But the ideology could also make mills seem dangerous—and here was the final paradox of paternalistic rhetoric. Yankees might express concern about rising social instability and weakened family bonds. But Yankees who heard mill managers repeatedly stress their "paternal scrutiny" of textile hands could also worry that manufactories harbored conflations of executive power inappropriate in a nation dedicated to "liberty." This latter concern arose because, in the final analysis, paternalistic slogans surrounding factory order collided head on with another perspective: the widespread desire for a society peopled by citizens living in rough equality and independence and the correspondingly widespread fear of overweening authority. They confronted, in sum, the "republican" ideology that had fueled the Revolution and that remained deeply influential during the early antebellum era. From a republican viewpoint, fatherly mill masters could seem like "monarch[s]," and to all the other complaints about manufactories could be added the charge that they were run like "tyrannies."

So it was that the immigrant industrial apologist Samuel Ogden had acknowledged as early as 1815 that Americans often opposed textile factories because they believed operatives were "subjected to tyrannical rule." So too, by the late 1820s a Providence newspaper assumed that managers ruled "their mills with a rod of iron" and then raised the portentous suspicion that mill masters might "step out into the community with the same air . . . What is this but tyranny[?]" And a few years later, also in Providence, there appeared an extraordinary poem by "Sui Generis: Alias Thomas Man." Of thin literary merit, the work is nonetheless notable for its unflagging catalogue of factory-induced ills. Among them:

> For liberty our fathers fought
> Which with their blood they dearly bought,
> The Fact'ry system sets at nought. . . .
> Great Britain's curse is now our own,
> Enough to damn a King and Throne.

By the late 1820s and through the 1830s, concern about "tyranny" penetrated criticisms issued against both Waltham- and family-style factories. Because of their more obviously personal proprietary approach, however, owners of country mills were especially vulnerable to the charge, often (as it turned out) from people living in townships surrounding or lying near manufactories. In Dudley and Oxford specifically, "tyranny"—raised in various forms and contexts—would prove a highly explosive issue.

Such was the character—and uncertain efficacy—of attempts to use ideology to aid rural mills. But there is a final perspective on claims of proprietary "regard" and "paternal interest" that needs to be considered. Management's slogans have to be placed within the context of routine mill operations. For it turns out, at least in the manufactories of Dudley and Oxford, that notions of factory paternalism were not simply used by self-interested mill masters; paternalism was also *limited* by structural constraints and long-term policies that dictated the flow of daily factory life. Understanding the regimen of local manufactories requires specifying these constraints and policies. And it requires exploring how they imposed limits on the ideology antebellum factory supporters so loudly proclaimed.

The fundamental constraint was the market. The iron pressure to maintain profit margins and stave off losses cut across any pledge of "regard" or "interest." Despite management's commitment to provide "steady" employment, for example, full-time operatives (especially those unattached to families) were, as noted earlier, routinely laid off during slumps. Moreover, as the number of Yankee mills continued to increase during the 1820s and 1830s and as competition among them intensified, factories moved to confine their pay scales—in both good and bad times—under formal guildelines designed to control production costs. Although mill masters in Dudley and Oxford might occasionally act out proprietary largesse with cash "presents" to favorite workers, the East Village had determined by 1837 that the "average price of all the labor of every description should not be more than 35 to 37½ cents per yard."

It was this same growing competitiveness, and the effort it produced to increase efficiency, that explains why local mills revised their use of ad hoc hands. Several tasks, for example, became more seasonal. Up through the 1830s men were still hired from surrounding townships to join with the brothers and fathers of operatives in tending crops, driving wagons, and digging ditches for the mills. But to cut costs, local factories began reducing such hands. By the late 1820s, Slater, for one, was mimicking Yankee farmers and jettisoning his agricultural laborers as quickly as possible in the fall. "As soon as Captain Starr [supervisor of outdoor labor] can spare some of those high priced farmers," Slater wrote to his East Village agent in August 1828, "do have some of them dismissed." And again a month later: "I hope Capt. Starr has before this dismissed Mr. Kemp and several others off the Farm."

Skilled ad hoc workers faced a different kind of pruning. Rather than continuing to distribute occasional jobs among several local artisans, factories found it more efficient to recruit a single carpenter or blacksmith into the mill compound, employ him full time, place him under close supervision and a regimen of precise instructions, and pay him by the month or year (instead of by the job). Thus the Dudley Woolen Manufacturing Company had its own blacksmith shop as early as 1824. For its part, Slater's South Village shifted Asa Wood from sporadic to full-time carpentry in 1828, and the East Village orchestrated the same change for blacksmith Stephen Harwood in 1832.

But the most dramatic transformation, affecting the largest group of employees, occurred among outworkers. Again, the basic issue was management's desire, fueled by market pressures, to increase efficiency. Proprietors of cotton mills, it is true, had vented impatience with outlying pickers and weavers even before perpetual textile production had reached southern Massachusetts. Working for the most part whenever and for as long as they wished, aiming to supplement, rather than maintain, household incomes, such employees had never labored as reliably or as carefully as some proprietors had wished. "A part of this day's cotton," Slater had moaned as early as 1791, "appear as if the mice had been in it as it is picked all to pieces." Indeed, even outworking journeymen weavers had faced criticisms for being tardy or careless or for following the "almost traditional" practice among English weavers of stealing portions of the cloth they produced. But it was after 1810, against the background of rising competition, that rural cotton factories began consistently pushing for greater efficiency. And they pushed especially hard after 1814, for at that point clothes produced by outwork began meeting stiff rivalry from cheap, coarse fabrics turned out by the power looms of Waltham-style factories.

Judging from East Village records, local mills responded to all these pressures promptly and forcefully. Beginning virtually with the opening of the Green Mill, Slater ordered "poor picking" returned "to Pick Over." Beginning around 1816, he cut the piece rates of his weavers (to reduce costs) and limited their output exclusively to the plaids and checked goods that were beyond the capacity of early power looms. What was equally important, he sought to impose tighter discipline. After 1816, outlying weavers who took more than eight weeks to work up a web or who turned in faulty cloth faced probation or even expulsion from the network: "In future . . . examine closely as to weaving, and have good weaving or none from S. Sears and family"; "No more weaving [for E. Sprague's family] . . . under any conditions."

These goadings had effect. Slater's outworking weavers were returning their cloth far more promptly by the mid-1820s than ten years earlier; and (undoubtedly motivated in part by the lower piece rates) they also, as a group, turned out 10 to 15 percent more cloth per work stint. Yet it was not enough. For even after the new standards and schedules were implemented, all outworkers continued to set their own daily work pace; and most of them—all but journeymen—continued to view their employment as simply a stopgap. So long as it retained these basic structural features, outwork could never achieve the efficient productivity mill masters demanded.

So outwork was replaced. In 1818 the East Village exchanged its outlying pickers for picking machines (probably available since 1807) operated by full-time factory employees. In 1823, impressed by the experiments in power-loom "weave shops" already running in Oxford, and evidently possessing the necessary liquid capital, Slater began introducing waterpowered looms into the Green Mill. His discovery that unit production costs were lower with the new technology, combined with a sudden infusion of inexpensive British handwoven cloths in 1825–6, hardened his resolve. In 1828 Slater summarily dismissed the several hundred handloom weavers then on his books and bequeathed his production of cotton cloth entirely to young women tending power looms inside the East Village. Because they labored only part time, the majority of outworkers thus laid off probably did not suffer too seriously from their dismissals—certainly they did not experience the catastrophic immiserization of contemporary British handloom weavers. But journeymen weavers must have faced considerable economic disruption, and all outworkers had regarded their East Village wages as at least useful supplementary income. Slater's decision to terminate his picking and weaving networks was thus scarcely congruent with his putative "regard" for employees.

Non-Slater cotton manufactories in Dudley and Oxford probably eliminated outworkers at about the same time as the East Village. But significantly, several local proprietors, including Slater, also went further. The same logic leading them to dismiss outlying pickers and cotton weavers also led owners of woolen mills to dismiss the skilled handloom weavers living and working inside these enclaves. Although less sharply buffeted by competing Waltham and British cloths than cotton establishments, woolen factories felt sufficient pressure to cut weaving piece rates in the 1820s. Then too, because of their skill, woolen weavers occasionally evinced an independence—and once, amid a protest over falling piece rates, even a militancy—that must have worried local factory managers. Attracted by the greater control implicit in hiring semi-skilled operatives to tend power looms, and (again) finding that machine weaving offered substantial savings in unit labor costs, Slater had shifted much of his cloth production in the South

Village to water-driven looms by 1830. And so with other factories: The Dudley Woolen Manufacturing Company had begun considering these machines in 1824 (because "it will make the weaving come [i.e., cost] very low indeed"), and by the end of the decade this mill too was depending largely on power looms.

Woolen handloom weavers, in sum, discovered they were not exceptional. In the context of uncertain sales and rising competition, these skilled employees found that for them, as for other hands, management's "regard" was constrained by management's need to get and keep profits.

But the limits of management's "regard" were also revealed by steps not taken. Unlike Waltham-style mills—with their scrupulously monitored boardinghouses and tight supervision of operatives' leisure time—local mills made little consistent effort to extend their order into the operatives' nonworking hours.

Consider, for example, the relatively laissez-faire attitude taken toward the period of each day in which workers were in their quarters or went shopping. Judging from the Slater mills and the Dudley Woolen Manufacturing Company, the relative isolation of the factory villages encouraged most full-time operatives to use company residences and company stores. But it was never required that employees live within the mill villages, and it was only sporadically required (in the South Village, for example) that they buy provisions from company retail facilities. Mills did appoint individuals (often widows) to administer their boardinghouses, but if Dudley and Oxford factories followed the pattern typical of other rural mills in this period, such officials exerted little control over employee behavior. "Trouble at the boardinghouse," complained the agent at a small Exeter, Massachusetts, factory in 1831, because "the girls in one chamber frightened the girls in the other at 12 o'clock at night." As for family cottages, except for occasional—and undoubtedly disturbing—interventions to stop particular kinsmen from coresiding, these residences apparently received no supervision at all.

Given the received wisdom that factory life would improve operatives, it is perhaps even more noteworthy that local mills failed to initiate strenuous campaigns to educate their hands. It is true that several proprietors did attempt to establish schools within their compounds: Their motivation appears to have been largely financial, and their efforts in any case met heated resistance in Dudley and Oxford town meetings. But what needs to be stressed here is that no matter where schools were located, factory masters (again judging from the Slater mills and the Dudley Woolen Manufacturing Company) never required children to attend classes. Quite the opposite: Eager to retain youngsters on their payrolls, factory masters obliged parents to petition for the "privelege" of dispatching millworking offspring to school. So Abel Dudley's two daughters received the "privelege of going to school 2 months each —one at a time—and [their brother] Amos is to work at 4/wk when they are out." But Abel Dudley was exceptional. Most operative households needed the wages their children earned, and most local mill children were thus innocent of formal education. In the East Village, only six families requested schooling (for a total of ten children) between 1827 and 1836.

Upon close examination, even the millowners' commitment to "devine instruction" appears tempered. Dudley and Oxford as a whole during this period witnessed abundant religious interest: At least four revivals crackled across the two communities between 1810 and the mid-1830s. Moreover, Congregationalists, Baptists, and Universalists in one or the other of the two townships had all gathered sufficient support in these years to build new meetinghouses, as did a new group, the Methodists, who began meeting in Dudley during the 1820s. Now, there is evidence that millowners sympathized with all these developments. In a general sense, after all, entrepreneurs and philosophies of the textile industry had always sought to link characteristics of good hands —punctuality, sobriety, "industriousness," "steadiness"—with received Protestant morality. This had been Strutt's goal in fashioning Sunday schools in Derbyshire, and the theme had per-

sisted in America, providing useful theological ballast to arguments highlighting factory uplift. Dudley and Oxford factory masters were thus entirely in character when (as local chronicles reveal) they supported local churches and (in part through Slater's efforts) helped introduce the Sunday school to southern Massachusetts.

But the nature of their support needs careful definition. In the first place, the contribution in time and money made by millowners was no greater than investments made by proprietors of nontextile enterprises. Gristmillers, blacksmiths, and (above all) storekeepers were equally generous to local religious institutions and campaigns.

In the second place, the religious bequests made by millowners were remarkably diffuse. As a group, local textile proprietors supported Congregationalists, Baptists, Universalists, and Methodists. Indeed, such ecumenicalism was displayed even by individual millowners: by members of the Slater family, for example. Born an Anglican, married to a Quaker, Slater's religious activities in Pawtucket soon moved beyond his early Sunday school to include participation in Baptist, Episcopal, and Catholic churches; in southern Massachusetts, his son George supported (at one time or another during his career) Baptists, Methodists, and Congregationalists. It followed from their scattered theological involvement that, although some local churches received substantial backing from millowners, no church was supported exclusively by factory proprietors. It followed too that factory proprietors did not regard any one sect as the exclusive vehicle of their religious ambitions.

But equally significant was the restraint of their ambitions, particularly as they related to operatives. Local mill masters do not appear to have systematically planted churches inside their villages: The Methodist chapel in which George Slater took interest, for example, went up "near" the East Village and even then only in 1833. The evidence also suggests that factory masters urged, rather than required, employees to attend church (or Sunday school). The Slaters—both father and sons—were undoubtedly pleased that some employees (including overseers) did attend the

Methodist chapel, just as proprietors of Dudley's village factory (later Slater's North Village) were undoubtedly pleased to see a Baptist society start meeting in a loft of their mill in 1814. But the indications are that only a fraction of the textile labor force in either Dudley or Oxford ever committed itself to regular churchgoing.

And it is likely that those who did attend went as much to please themselves as their employers. In the fellowship of church meetings and revivals, in the harsh but clear message (especially available from Baptists and Methodists) that sin was always present in life and could only be overcome through effort and discipline—in all this, operatives may have found solace. But churchgoing did not offer only anesthesia. Scattered through the records are hints that, in the end, workers would use religion to galvanize their mounting, restless grievances against management. Rather than something received passively from patriarchal employers, religion should be understood as something operatives took for themselves—when they wished and largely for their own purposes.

Taken together, the force of economic pressures and the limited involvement in nonworking hours comprised two significant limits on management's protestations of "paternal interest." The automatic, impersonal discipline imposed by "perpetual" technology comprised another.

The machines in Dudley and Oxford mills up through the early 1830s bore close resemblance to those constructed in the earliest American manufactories. The waterpowered picking and weaving technologies that local cotton factories adopted along the way were, of course, new. And the spinning mule that Samuel Slater's brother John had helped introduce into Smithfield was employed in local enterprises at least by 1820. But overall, despite some modifications, the carding, roving, and throstle (water-frame) spinning machines used in the cotton factories of Dudley and Oxford were not qualitatively different from technologies used in the first Yankee textile manufactories. Nor did local woolen works vary appreciably from their prototypes. Again, there was the shift to power looms; and although they appar-

ently always used residential pickers, woolen manufactories may also have started performing this process mechanically by the 1830s. But carding engines remained essentially unaltered, and the only shift in woolen spinning was to place more semiautomatic "jacks" alongside the jennies.

The relatively fixed inventory of machines did not mean that all operatives inside mill buildings tended waterpowered mechanisms. Work in factory machine shops was probably performed with hand tools; mule spinning and (in the woolen mills) jenny spinning both remained hand-powered throughout the period; and roughly half the operation of woolen jacks continued under the spinners' manual control. Moreover, certain preparatory processes necessary for power-loom weaving remained largely or wholly free of mechanization. The application (dressing) of a starch solution (sizing) to harden warp threads was accomplished with warping and dressing frames, but preparation of the sizing was a difficult, hand-operated procedure, and the dressing operation as a whole ranked among the most highly skilled—and well-paid—jobs in local factories. "Drawing-in" threads through the tackles and harness of power looms was a semiskilled job (usually reserved for women), which was also performed entirely without mechanical aid. Finally, although the gigging (raising the nap) and shearing of woolen cloths may have benefited from water-driven machines, key finishing processes like dying and bleaching persisted as tasks performed mainly by hand in both cotton and woolen mills.

Yet all this was exceptional. Most operatives —perhaps 60 to 70 percent—laboring within the mills worked on machines powered by the energy of falling water. And the mechanically dictated work rhythms of such "perpetual" machines represented an inescapable, continuous, and anonymous pressure that intervened between workers and any human supervisors—even the watchful, circulating room overseers.

In some cases the work pace thus dictated was steady, as in the task of feeding "laps" of cotton to the carding engines. More often, tending machines involved irregular bursts of activity. This might take the form of collecting processed material from a machine: "doffing" full bobbins on spinning frames and replacing them with empty ones. Or it might involve the kind of work performed by power-loom weavers and throstle spinners: gazing at spindles and shuttles pounding before them in order to be ready—at any moment —to reach in and tie off (piece) threads broken during the weaving and spinning processes. This latter task is also what "piecing" for mule spinners entailed. The young boys assigned this job had to attach threads broken during "the few instants" when the mule, having advanced forward along its tracks, was pushed back to its frame. As a result, although mules were not waterpowered in this period, the "lively little piecers" were, effectively, another group subjected to mechanically governed work rhythms. Indeed, because of the distribution of jobs by age and sex in the local mills, most operatives under machine discipline were either children, like piecers, or young women, like weavers and spinners, which in turn created a curious irony deep in the daily chemistry of mill operations. Given the assumptions of adult male dominance implicit in management's paternalistic rhetoric, factory supervisors undoubtedly assumed that women and youngsters would be particularly receptive to claims of patriarchal authority; but women and youngsters were precisely the operatives at least partially buffered from such claims by the more immediate drumbeat of demands issuing from their machines.

This does not mean that machine discipline was necessarily experienced as harsh. Child operatives (the doffers for example) were often able to play between chores. And the fact that operating machines like power looms and water frames required little physical strength often led contemporaries—even workers themselves—to conclude that machine tending was easy. Labor requiring constant attention and repetitive motion (instead of obvious exertion) was so novel that the strain it produced was not immediately understood. So it was that millworkers complained of swollen feet from standing so many hours and of listlessness from (they supposed) overeating and insufficient exercise. But even into the late 1840s the work itself was judged "not laborious"; "not half so hard," wrote one woman, "as . . . attending the dairy, washing, cleaning house, and cooking."

Nonetheless, machine discipline did intervene between employees and management's supposedly personal and paternal authority—and it intervened more emphatically as years went by. Because another consequence of increasing competition among Yankee mills was a decision by factory masters to increase output by expanding the number and speed of machines assigned to operatives. In the East Village between 1817 and 1835, the number of water frames per spinner doubled (from two to four). In the same village between the mid-1820s and the mid-1830s, the output per power loom jumped two and a half times, and the output per spinning mule climbed by just under 40 percent.

The final limitation on management's relationship with the hands, and particularly on the personal proprietary relationship conjured up by invocations of "paternalistic interest," was the bureaucratic dimension of early antebellum mills.

This took three forms. There was, first, the hierarchical chain of command already remarked: the division of authority under which the most frequent and direct dealings with employees was in practice left mainly to officials below owners and agents. There was, second, the complex bookkeeping apparatus common even among smaller family mills. Monitoring the operation of such enterprises—recording and balancing out sales, costs, orders, production levels, and shipments of raw materials and finished goods—required an interlocking array of Time Books, Day Books, Ledgers, and Blotters far more elaborate than records typically generated in Dudley and Oxford by either the town governments or nontextile business ventures. One result of factory paper work, however, was that information shaping management's outlook—and particularly data disclosing the growing competitive necessity for increased efficiency—was unavailable to mill operatives. The arrival and implications of

a major market downturn were obvious. But beyond such dramatic episodes, proprietors were
motivated by pressures that remained largely
opaque to their hands. And the hands, consequentially, may well have felt distanced from
their employers, may well have found it difficult
to believe that they labored in common cause
with those paying their wages.

The most significant bureaucratic aspect of the
factory order, however, was its webbing of established bylaws and procedures. No full listing of
"rules and regulations" has survived from Dudley and Oxford mills. But drawing on comparable
manufactories of the period, local prescriptions
were probably both written and unwritten, probably focused mainly on work-time activities, and
probably ranged from stipulations concerning
how work was to be done (how, as opposed to
when, threads should be pieced) to specifying
that operatives evince a punctual, respectful, and
sober demeanor on the job.

Not all directives were always enforced. It
was, in fact, precisely amid these "rules and regulations" that managers and employees would develop many significant compromises in the regimens of local factories. Still, the rules in principle
dictated the norms of mill labor. What is just as
significant, they dictated norms that, again in
principle, were fixed—and hence impervious to
nuances of personal relationships. Even the non-
machine discipline of factory rooms—even the
discipline implemented by overseers—was more
likely to derive from established codes of behavior than from personal understandings between
supervisors and hands. As a result, although certain strictures (like prohibitions against tardi-
ness) were freighted with moral "interest," management's rules inevitably introduced an element
of formality between employers and employees.

"Rules and regulations" ran like stiff girders
all through the order of local mills, but they are
especially obvious in management's treatment of
time. It was not, after all, the number of working
hours that was novel in early manufactories: It
was customary for rural Yankees during harvest
seasons to labor as long as operatives. Nor, as
demonstrated by their willingness to yoke factory

ideology to received religious values, did millowners break new moral ground by emphasizing
punctuality. What was striking about textile factories—from Strutt's establishment up through
the mills of antebellum New England—was the
metronomic inflexibility of their work schedule.

After 1810, as before, Yankee factories aimed
to run seventy-two hours per week. They generally operated "from the time it is light enough to
work," which meant their precise starting-up
times changed with the seasons. Moreover, because clocks were still rare in the hinterland, and
because "boys [who] rung the Bell" to wake mill-
village residents rose themselves at slightly different hours from day to day, the moment of starting
up could vary even within a single week. But once
under way, rural factories planned to run twelve
hours a day (continuously except for breaks at
seven o'clock for breakfast and twelve-thirty for
"dinner") six days a week every week of the year.
The only days off management accepted were
Sundays and whichever of the two or three re-
gionally celebrated annual holidays happened to
fall on week days in a given year. Work by candle-
light during winter months thus continued to be
the norm, and during such periods the New England custom of commencing sabbath observances Saturday at dusk obviously went by the
board. Logistical and mechanical difficulties
might force unexpected pauses, of course, but
only the conventional postrevolutionary holidays
of Thanksgiving, the Fourth of July, and April's
Fast Day were accepted as scheduled interruptions. In Dudley and Oxford it is likely that the
only nontextile venture to essay the rigid operating timetable typically sought by local manufactories was Thomas Chatman's machine shop.

The inflexibility of factory schedules pressed
all the more heavily on operatives because mills
made strenuous efforts to evaluate (though again
not necessarily to require) their workers' obedience. Like pre-1810 factories, New England mills
in the second and third decades of the nineteenth
century generally measured labor by time. In
Dudley and Oxford most millworkers from the
outset received wages calculated by the number
of days or, more exactly, the fraction of days they

put in. Even wages designated at weekly or monthly rates were actually tallied up in units of twelve-hour working days. As a result, supervisors naturally desired to reckon their employees' attendance with great care. Indeed, even workers paid by the piece (mule spinners and after 1830 many power-loom weavers as well) had their daily presence noted down in minute units. Transcribed (in coded shorthand) into Time Books, attendance in the Dudley Woolen Manufacturing Company was recorded to the nearest three hours in the 1820s—almost certainly a more accurate standard than that used for nontextile employees (save for some highway workers and, again, possibly the men in Chatman's employ). The Slater books were equally precise before 1817. Thereafter—as yet one more emblem of Slater's mounting stringency—the unit became the nearest ninety minutes.

Thus the different faces presented by the regimen of local textile mills: On the one hand, the factory order put forward a credo of personal managerial "regard"; on the other hand, it was, in practice, a self-serving regimen, limited in scope and bounded—in some respects increasingly bounded—by technology, bureaucracy, and the vicissitudes of the market.

For all its internal divisions, however, the factory order was clearly distinct from organizational patterns informing most other economic activities. Indeed, it is tempting to see a linear progression among the different regimens operating in Dudley and Oxford. From the altered but still essentially semicommercial outlook and traditional organization of local farms and most small businesses, to the more intensely commercial ambitions and more elaborate administrative structure and technology that likely characterized a few of the larger nontextile enterprises, to the waterpowered machines, complex divisions of authority and labor, and (in practice) the thoroughly profit-centered goals of cotton and woolen mills—all this might seem to suggest a straight line of development.

But it must be remembered that these regimens coexisted. In many ways the changes emerging during the second and third decades of the nineteenth century—even the dramatic novelties introduced by manufactories—developed out of mores and pressures already extant in 1810. Yet there was no consistent, pervasive evolution of local economic institutions. If custom could lead to entirely new kinds of ventures, it could also encourage the retention of patterns in agricultural and business activities that were distinct from—even hostile to—innovations embraced by textile mills. The coming of industrial order in Dudley and Oxford between 1810 and the early 1830s represented not an irresistible advance down a single track but the pressing forward of several institutional structures and strategies.

It was within this complex pattern, this milieu embracing both change and hesitancy to change, that local residents—in different ways, for different reasons, and according to their own varying perspectives and goals—would fashion their responses.

22

MEN'S AND WOMEN'S WORK
ON THE OVERLAND TRAIL

JOHN M. FARAGHER

The years between 1820 and 1860 witnessed the development of an intensive campaign to define the proper place of women in American society. Sponsored initially by established male religious leaders, the impulse to create a distinctive "woman's sphere" spread rapidly throughout America. This campaign depicted the home as a realm of special virtue as well as a domestic haven against an increasingly competitive and commercial world. Known as the "Cult of True Womanhood," this domestic ideology attributed to women a vital function in maintaining republican virtue during the threatening period of industrialization and urbanization.

If the domestic realm was to be a temple of virtue in a changing America, women were charged with becoming its priestesses. To accomplish this, the "Cult of True Womanhood" prescribed a series of characteristics that women, as guardians of the home and domestic virtue, must cultivate. Of these characteristics the most important were religious piety, moral purity, submissiveness to men, and the maintenance of the home as place of comfort and moral education. One result of the widespread acceptance of this domestic ideology was the development of rigidly separated men's and women's spheres in nineteenth-century America, each with a well-defined set of tasks and functions.

Could such an ideology survive the transcontinental trek to the Oregon Territory, which thousands of pioneers undertook in the mid-nineteenth century? In this essay John Faragher examines the diaries of women who made the long journey across the American wilderness. Pioneer women, he finds, lived in even greater isolation from the world of men than they had in the homes they left behind. The rigors of migration, it seems, only added to the mutual isolation of American men and women.

How does the domestic sphere of these migrating women compare with that of Mayo Greenleaf Patch's wife and daughters, as discussed by Paul Johnson in Reading 15? Do you see any similarities between the separation of women's and men's work on the Oregon Trail and in the New England industrial villages, described by Jonathan Prude in Reading 21?

The routines of farm life and the sexual division of farm labor were translated smoothly into the work of the trail. By contrast, in all-male parties the assignments of trail duty were a source of conflict. As Noah Brooks remembered,

From John M. Faragher, *Women and Men on the Overland Trail* (New Haven: Yale University Press, 1979). Reprinted by permission of the publisher.

At the onset none knew who should drive the oxen, who should do the cooking, or whose ingenuity would be taxed to mend broken wagons or tattered clothing. Gradually, and not altogether without grumbling and objection each man filled his own proper place. . . . Indeed, the division of labor in a party of emigrants was a prolific cause of quarrel. . . . We saw not a little fighting in the camps of others who sometimes jogged along the trail in our company, and these bloody fisticuffs were invariably the outcome of disputes over the divisions of labor.

Likewise Rebecca Ketcham, traveling without family in a volunteer party of men and couples, noted after almost two months on the trail and considerable shifting of jobs, "I believe the day's work is pretty regularly laid out now."

For family parties this division of labor was more easily accomplished; it was assumed that men would drive the oxen and mend the wagons, that women would cook and sew. We might expect that the extraordinary conditions of the trip would have disturbed the standard patterns, but as both men and women recorded in the diaries, journals, and reminiscences of the emigration, from the preparations for the journey right through to arrival on the Pacific Coast, responsibilities were apportioned in strict adherence to the traditional sexual division.

As far as the preparations were concerned, the first necessity was raising the cash for the outfit. The first task, then, was men's: the sale of the farm property. Although a cash sale might not realize the farm's full value, demand for midwestern farm property was high enough that nearly all emigrants were able to sell their farms without much difficulty. William Thompson, a boy of ten in 1852, remembered years later that "in February a gentleman came to our house and after dinner he and my father rode over the plantation. The next morning they rode over to Bollivar, the county seat. Returning in the evening my father announced that the plantation was sold." In nearly all accounts women are absent from this process. Frequently men sold the farm equipment and household effects as well. Since very little could be taken, the object was to liquidate the

property and accumulate all the cash possible. Reverend Neill Johnson spent several weeks circulating among his Mount Pleasant, Iowa, parishioners collecting outstanding debts to supplement his stake. Men then had to procure the necessary provisions from town. If after purchasing the necessary supplies there was a little cash to spare, they might convert it to cattle or sheep to drive to the coast; this was an investment they determined would pay off handsomely at inflated Pacific prices. At any rate most men wanted good, fresh yokes of oxen to pull the wagons. After lengthy haggling over prices and numerous trips to town, there were wagons to build or modify, running gear to make ready, storage boxes to construct, and oxen to break to wagon load and yoke.

January, February, and March were normally quiet months on the farm, but now they bristled with activity as family members readied themselves for the move. As Mary Ellen Todd remembered,

> After we decided to go to Oregon we found there were many things to be thought about and done in order to prepare for such a journey. As time went on I noticed that father was not taking his customary five or ten minutes just before mealtime for reading his favorite books; and I did not get my lessens quite so regularly, nor commit so much of Bobby Burns or other poets. . . . Sometimes father and mother were calling to me at the very same time. I heard, first, "Mary Ellen, bring me the saw, or the hammer, or take this to mother," or "Help the baby down, or take this little bucket and get some water"; again from mother, "Mary Ellen, won't you finish this churning while I get my soap to boiling: we'll need a lot of soap you know; also I must finish spinning all those rolls that we have been carding, as we just must take with us plenty of yarn."

Soapmaking was an important preparatory task. A family of four required at least ten pounds of washing and body soap for the trip. It was, however, clothing manufacture that most preoccupied women in those days of preparation. The family needed appropriate clothing for the strenuous work of six long months, during which time there would be no chance for manufacture and only incidental opportunities for mending. Weight limitations, of course, required that clothing like everything else be restricted to a minimum, and some clothes, already made, could be packed. Nonetheless, a great deal of the family's clothing had to be made especially for the trip. The standard wardrobe included two or three changes for each person. Men needed cotton or linen shirts, gathered at the waist by a broad leather belt, coarse and roomy fustian or linsey-woolsey pantaloons, heavy stockings, certainly an overcoat of jean or fustian and perhaps an India rubber poncho, and rough cowhide boots. Women required two or three dresses, usually of dark gingham, calico, or heavy wool, with perhaps one or two petticoats of linen, aprons and shoulder kerchiefs, a warm shawl, and perhaps a coat. Like men, women wore cowhide boots. Many women also packed in at least one good dress, often a feminine heirloom. Children over six or seven dressed like their parents; a small child might be fitted in a simple chemise, called a wannis. To protect themselves from the sun, it was necessary for all to wear something on their heads. Men donned floppy, big-brimmed felt hats, or wheat-straw hats to match those the children made for themselves; women wore the inevitable sunbonnets, made from heavy calico stretched over wire frames.

Spinning, weaving, and sewing, regularly accomplished bit by bit throughout the year, now in the final weeks before departure had to be compressed: six months' work in two. During all of February and March 1852, the women of the Thompson family

were busy spinning and weaving. Every article of wearing apparel must be made at home. "Store clothes" were out of the question in those days. Wool must be carded and spun into thread for Aunt Ann's old wooden loom. The cloth was then fashioned into garments for clothing to last a year after we should reach our goal far out on the Pacific shores. The crank of the old wooden loom was almost ceaseless. Merrily the shuttle sang to an ac-

companiment of a camp meeting melody. Neighbors also volunteered their services in weaving and fashioning garments for the family. All was bustle and hurry.

The home-manufactured clothing for women and children was frequently inadequate for the volatile weather on the trail. Thunderstorms along the Platte drenched the emigrants, and on the mountain plateaus and passes the summer could turn suddenly cold, with unexpected night freezes. Men nearly always had coats, but women and children were generally underdressed in their shawls and jackets. "The great and sudden change of the temperature connected with the heavy fall of rain last night, completely drenching everything exposed to it," Edwin Bryant noted on June 1, 1846, "is exceedingly distressing to the women and children, who generally are thinly clothed and unprepared to resist the efforts of exposure and atmospheric eccentricities."

Clothing accounted for most but not all of the preparatory sewing. Wagon covers and tents too were made by the women. For sleeping each person would require at least two blankets, and sometimes this meant additional weaving. Blankets were the only protection from the summer night's chill for most of the emigrants, unless one counts the cover afforded by the bottom side of a wagon. About a third of the families, however, took tents in which the young or female children and old folks slept. Husband and wife most commonly enjoyed the privacy of the wagon, where, if they were lucky, they slept on a feather mattress laid atop the provisions. "William and I have slept in the light wagon lately, as Ma came into the tent, and we preferred a place to ourselves. But it's very crowded in the wagon, and I have to lay baby across our heads. But we'll still try to make it answer." Infants invariably slept with their mothers.

In addition to sewing, women had to make careful plans for the family's diet. The weight limitations demanded simple meals, but wives tried to add variety by including some home-produced foods in the wagon larder. Virginia Ivins spent her winter evenings "putting up such preserves, pickles and other delicacies as could be kept to become most acceptable when afterwards compelled to partake of cold meals as we often were throughout our trip." Allene Taylor's mother and aunt "baked as much as they could that would keep well. Mother made a large fruit cake and it was to be a surprise to the men folks after we had gone on the journey for some time. I can remember I was in a hurry to have them surprised." From the large quantity of staples, women had to measure out daily portions; a few days of overabundant cooking at the first of the trip would be balanced by days of scarcity at the end. So women practiced cooking with camp staples before they were actually on the road, trying to perfect the amounts. As Louise Rahm wrote in her diary two days before they packed the wagons, she set up a campfire, "was browning coffee and got dinner for the men just to see how it would go."

Husbands built a "grub box" and attached it to the end or the side of the wagon; wives filled it with their cooking utensils. "In ours," Helen Carpenter entered in her diary, "there is a Dutch oven, a camp kettle, frying pan, and coffee pot—these with some tin plates, tin cups, tin spoons, knives and forks; a rolling-pin, bread pan, milk can and a smoothing iron, constitute my entire kitchen furniture." Add a small coffee mill and a length of chain on which to hang the pots, and this could well be the average kitchen inventory for a traveling family. The well-appointed farm wife, even on the frontier, certainly had accumulated many more implements than this in her kitchen. Caroline Kirkland, in her contemporary view of frontier farm life, for example, found that even backwoods women displayed their china tea sets proudly on their hewn-log tables. Leaving items like this behind must have been a disappointment. "But for my part," Margaret Frink wrote in her first days out, "I was satisfied to do as other immigrants did, and if it was the fashion to drink out of tin, I was quite content to do so."

Packing was the final and perhaps most difficult job, for here was finally revealed how little families could take. Husbands and wives worked together packing and deciding what could and could not be taken. Filling the few pounds of space left after the food, arms, kitchen utensils, bedding, clothing, and tools had been packed was a matter of contention between men and women. Wives argued for household items and furniture; husbands might want a few pounds of trade goods to placate begging Indians. A temporary compromise was generally negotiated which allowed women to pack some of their precious household possessions at the risk of overloading. "Along the sides were long boxes like window gardens where were kept sewing materials and various odds and ends dear to the housewife's heart," Virginia Ivins recalled. Charles True wrote home the first day out that "in the hind end of the wagon are what things Elizabeth could not possibly give up." And Frances Peabody remembered that "although my father often said that many necessities could be found in Denver, my mother clung to familiar things." The couple finally agreed to tie her rocking chair on the back of the wagon, and Frances, years later, could still recall her mother "sitting in that chair in the midst of the endless plains when we stopped for the night."

On the trail, men's work was narrowed to one principal task—getting the wagons and the family safely through to the coast. Thus men were concerned almost exclusively with transportation: the care of wagons and stock, driving and droving, leadership and protection of the family and party. On a normal day of travel the men of each family were up between four and five in the morning to cut out their oxen from the herd and drive them to the wagon for yoking and hitching. The wagon and running gear had to be thoroughly checked over. After breakfast the wagons pulled out, often in single file, but frequently drivers spread themselves out to avoid the choking dust thrown up by the hooves and wheels to the front. Normally a man drove each wagon. Since many parties had some additional loose stock, some men herded and drove the stock to the rear of the line. A good morning march began by seven and continued until the noon hour, when drivers pulled up, unhitched their oxen, set the stock to grazing, and settled down for the midday meal the women produced. After an hour or so for lunch and rest, the men hitched up the oxen again and picked up the line of march.

Driving and droving were strenuous and demanding occupations. Some men drove their wagons while sitting on the wagon perch, but most drove by walking alongside the oxen; a few men owned horses they rode along the trail, but most walked. "Of course riding was out of the question. We had one horse, but he was reserved for emergencies, and nobody but a shirk would think of crawling into a wagon, loaded down as it was with the necessities of life, unless sickness made it impossible for him to walk." Walking the fifteen or so miles of trail each day was, in the best of conditions, enough to tire any man. Conditions, of course, were not always the best. Soaring midday summer temperatures on the shadeless plains sapped the strength. The mornings, on the other hand, especially in the high plains and mountains, were sometimes frigid. " 'Tis dredful cold," Agnes Stewart scratched early on May 17, 1853, "Oh, the wind goes to a person's heart. I will shiver to death. I feel for the men gathering the cattle and yoking them up. It was so cold for them, and no warm breakfast." Driving, and especially herding the cattle, meant eating large portions of dust. "It has been immensely disagreeable for the drivers today for a Northwest wind drove the dust in clouds into their faces, as they walk besides their teams. Am glad that I am not an ox driver." The sun and wind decreed another common fate, painful chapped skin. "I feel well except my lips, they have been sore ever since I left Council Bluffs; but one half of the Emigrants share the same fate, something I had never heard of before."

The most common obstacles were the rivers. By the 1850s many crossings were served by ferries, and as long as the emigrants could afford the toll, the only inconvenience was the wait. At other times and places, however, oxen and wagons had to be driven down steep embankments and across the flow, and the danger of quicksand

bogs or rapid currents that could sweep away goods, stock, or men lurked in even the shallowest of streams. Consequently men took the greatest care at crossings. Women and children frequently shuttled over on horseback or raft. Sometimes men labored to build rude bridges or ferries for the wagons. Most often they double- or triple-teamed the oxen and drew each wagon across. At any rate, it was slow, frustrating, demanding work. Along the road wagons could always break down; axles especially were prone to snap with all the jolting. Only a lucky man did not have to jerry-rig or abandon a wagon along the road.

By the late afternoon the normal demands of most days had so tired the men that sleep could not be resisted. "A drowsiness has fallen apparently on men and beast; teamsters fall asleep on their perches and even when walking by their teams, and the words of command are now addressed to the slowly creeping oxen in the soft tenor of women or the piping trebel of children, while the snores of the teamsters make a droning accompaniment." "It is with the greatest effort we can keep awake. Even Mr. Gray sometimes nods with the lines in his hands," Rebecca Ketcham wrote in her journal. "We can all, as soon as we stop, lie down on the grass or anywhere and be asleep in less than no time almost."

In the evenings the stock sometimes had to be driven a distance for grazing. "The men of the company divided into two bands. The elderly ones were detailed to stay with the wagons; keeping one or two horses with them while the others, taking with them the other horses, drove the cattle up the creek valley, searching for food." After a hard day's drive in 1853, George Belshaw and some other men from his party "took the Cattle and Horses about one mile to feed and watched them all night. I fealt well but it is hard fateage loosing so much rest and Driving the teams through the Day and to manage so large a company and get them along as fast as I can."

Belshaw was, as he noted, captain of his train. For those men in the advance guard there was added responsibility. George complained in a letter to his brother, Henry, "They have elected me captain. I have taken them across one stream and it keeps me very busy all the time to pick the camping places for them and attend to everything, besides, and lead them along, as you know some of them are very slow so I have to urge them up. I do not get to bed until ten or eleven, and have to be up at daylight. I have my hand full, but you know I will persevere for a better climate."

Guard duty was another responsibility that fell to men. The duty rotated, two or three men splitting the night's watch, protecting the stock from wolves or Indians, preventing a sudden stampede. Guard duty was probably the most hated male chore but one—chasing lost stock. A slipshod night's watch could halt a party for days as the men roamed the prairie, often unsuccessfully, in search of the stock. Men measured their success in units of forward progress: the mileage they calculated and noted in their daily journals. A setback of days because of lost stock was, in these terms, a frustrating failure.

There was a distinctive dialectic to men's work on the trail. The heads of household had overall responsibility for movement. It was men who had made the decision to move, it was men who determined the route, direction, and speed of travel, it was men who would make the sometimes fateful decisions to turn back or move on, it was men upon whom fell the burden of repairing faulty or broken equipment. In short, it was men who provided the leadership for the emigration: men would take the credit, and they had to accept the blame. This responsibility bore heavily upon husbands and fathers as they led their wives and children into hardships they had not fully anticipated. There is, of course, no way to measure their burden; we can be sure, however, that it took its toll of energy, vitality, and good humor.

The physical work of men was organized so as to provide compensations for this heavy burden of responsibility. While the wagons were rolling, men worked at peak capacity. Time and again in men's accounts of their trips, they took spiteful aim at the few shirking able-bodied males who dared to hitch a ride on one of the wagons. A man worked the trail from the time the oxen were yoked in the morning until they were herded in

the evening; a person who did not work at this full capacity and with this constancy was simply not a man. But when the wagons were parked once more, the oxen and cattle set out to graze, and the guard was posted, men were off duty. There were occasional jobs to be done, of course, and men were still in command, to be sure, but in the evening they acted out their responsibilities at a leisurely pace, intermingling work with the pleasures of food, relaxation, and company. Men bore final responsibility, but they enjoyed a rhythm of long periods of hard work punctuated by periods of rest.

Women's trail work was structured around the men's: women were the working support of the trail's labor system. In the first instance, women enjoyed little overall responsibility for the direction or outcome of the emigration. They were not called upon to participate in making the critical decisions; indeed, a wife had probably played almost no role in the decision to emigrate in the first place. The lack of overall responsibility, however, was accompanied by a demanding work schedule that made adult women the most fully and materially responsible members of the family. The men's work schedule required that a woman tend to the needs of her family when the wheels stopped turning for the day. The need to work did not disappear when the men went off duty; work merely changed its character. Randall Hewitt put it most bluntly: "Having ladies do the 'housework' everything went along smoothly." Amelia Knight confirmed this view from a distinctively feminine perspective. Her husband was upset at having lost three hired hands who had decided to pack through alone; Amelia saw it differently. As she confided in her diary, "I am pleased, as . . . I shall have three less to wait on."

On the other hand, in contrast to men, women were not at liberty to relax while their opposite numbers worked. After all, who could relax while bumping and jogging along in a wagon? More to the point, during the hours of travel women were either working or on call, available to lend a hand, do a critical job, or take over for an ailing male. When the overriding principle of the trail was to "keep moving," could an able body simply stand by? Women's work, then, was a reflex of men's: a rhythm of long hours on call to substitute and supplement the work of men, punctuated by shorter periods of intense activity.

First we shall look at work that belonged distinctively to women. They regularly began the trail day by getting up around four, an hour to half an hour before the men, to stoke the fire and put up kettles of water to begin breakfast. If there was a cow along, wives milked her before breakfast. James Clyman arose early one morning to write in his journal as the women prepared breakfast and noted that other than the breakfast bustle there was no other activity "except Sleeping which is performed by the male part of the camp to the greatest perfection." By the time coffee had been boiled, bacon fried, beans warmed, and bread baked, all of which required a good hour's work, the men had arisen to hear the report from the last guard, brought in the oxen, and were ready for their meal.

Cooking in the open was a new experience for most women. As Lodisa Frizzell wrote, "it goes so much 'agin the grane' at first." "Eliza soon discovered that cooking over a campfire was far different from cooking on a stove or a range." "Two forked sticks were driven into the ground, a pole laid across, and the kettle swung upon it." Pots were continually falling into the fire, and families soon became accustomed to ashen crust on their food. In the absence of tables, all preparation was on the ground. This "requires me to stoop considerably. All our work here requires stooping. Not having tables, chairs or anything it is very hard on the back." The weather rarely cooperated, especially in the early morning. "Everything was soaked with water and dry wood so scarce that our women could scarcely make coffee or fry meat." "Rainy this morning; very disagreeable getting breakfast," Cecelia Adams complained in her dairy, and she noted a few weeks later that she "could not raise enough fire to cook breakfast." James Clyman, ever an admiring observer of women, committed to his journal the story of "one young lady which showed herself worthy of the bravest undaunted pioneer

of west, for after having kneaded her dough she watched and nursed the fire and held an umbrella over the fire and her skillet with the greatest composure for near 2 hours."

After breakfast the women washed the tinware, stowed away the cooking equipment and food, and packed up while the men readied the wagons. After several hours on the road there was a brief stop at noon. Then, while the men relaxed, the women brought out the lunch, usually prepared the night before, and the party enjoyed a cold meal and a few minutes of rest. After the women had again packed up their gear, the wagons pushed off once more for the remainder of the afternoon.

By evening everyone was ready for camp. After one particularly rough day of moving their wagons across a cold stream, the Burns party moved into camp. "Our campfire was soon burning brightly and in a few minutes we sat down to a nice warm supper prepared by Mrs. W. P. Burns, which was eaten with relish." For men, the evening was the reward for a hard day's labor; for women, who prepared the reward, unpacking the wagons was the prelude to four or five hours of sustained work. Rebecca Ketcham lamented these relentless demands: "To ride on horseback, rain or shine, tired or sick, or whatever might be the matter, then as soon as we get into camp, go to work!"

The fire had to be kindled and water brought to camp. If the travelers were lucky, the camp was close by a spring. The fear of mosquitoes, unhealthy vapors, or hidden Indians, however, kept them away from the covered, low-lying river bottoms, so water had to be hauled, usually by women. Collecting fuel for the fire was also women's work. Presumably if wood had had to be chopped, men would have done it, but there being no trees, women cooked with sagebrush, cottonwood twigs, or buffalo chips, which they gathered. James Reed, writing in his diary, noted that "the women and children are now out gathering 'Buffalo Chips' to burn in order to do the cooking." Some women complained about having to handle and cook with dried dung, but necessity, of course, prevailed. Because there was frequently not enough kindling in the vicinity of camp for both the evening and morning fires, women collected chips as they traveled. "We always had a sack of them hanging on the side of the wagon on the plains. We used to average about ten miles a day and I believe that I ran an extra five miles trying to gather feed for our toothless ox or buffalo chips for our evening fire."

Despite the primitive surroundings, women continued to practice midwestern culinary arts. Judging from the diary notations of menus, women worked mightily to overcome the limit imposed by hauling weights. In addition to the basics—cooking bacon, beans, and coffee—women milked, made butter and cheese, boiled and mashed potatoes, made gravies, stewed dried fruit, made bread, biscuits, pies, and cakes, puddings of bread, rice, or cracker, and even prepared preserves and jellies from wild berries and fruit gathered along the way. The cooking continued past the dinner hour and into the late evening as food for the next day's breakfast and lunch was prepared: "Everybody is in bed but Agnes and myself i believe and we would be there to but we have wait til the apples are stewed enough."

Camp was just like home in one respect—there was plenty of housework. After dinner the beds had to be made up, wagons cleaned out, and provisions taken out to air to prevent mildew. There were always clothes to mend or socks to knit. "I visited the tents of our fellow-travelers and found the ladies busily employed, as if sitting by the fireside which they had so recently left. . . . Mrs West, a lady of seventy, and her daughter Mrs Campbell, were knitting."

Except for rinsing out a few garments in the evening, however, the family washing piled up; women waited for a day when the wagons might stop over near an ample supply of water. Washing "was not done always on Monday to the annoyance of our excellent housekeepers who at home had been accustomed to thus honoring 'blue Monday.'" The wagons made frequent, unavoidable stops for one reason or another, and women invariably used these occasions to wash. "Came to a creek so high we could not cross, camped, the women to washing and the men to examining their provisions." "It is agreed to stay in this camp until tomorrow to rest the cattle. Water and grass are both fine. The women are going to wash. It is the best chance we have had for a long time, wood and water are plenty and convenient." "One of the company broke the axletree of his wagon, then camped, the women washed." "Still at Bridger. Here we have a good time for washing, which we women deem a great privilege." For parties that had agreed to "rest" on Sundays, the day was turned to washing, but under the pressures of time few parties could observe the Sabbath strictly. If there had been no occasion to stop over for two or three weeks, women demanded a chance to wash; or, as George Belshaw put it, "the women ruled and would wash." In most parties women spent a full day washing about every two weeks.

Washing began early. "The banks of the small rivulet was lined at an early hour after breakfast with fires, kettles, washtubs, and piles of unwashed linen, showing conclusively that a general lustration was to be performed by the female portion of our party." If there was fuel to spare, water was heated, but generally women had to be content to suds their harsh soap in hard, cold water. A day of sun, wind, soap, and water could be a painful combination. "Camilia and I both burnt our arms very badly while washing. They were red and swollen and painful as though scalded with boiling water. Our hands are blacker than any farmer's, and I do not see that there is any way of preventing it, for everything has to be done in the wind and sun."

With all this, there were the children to be watched, although the burden of other responsibilities made child care a relatively low priority. Notes on children are rare in the accounts of men and women, and when they do appear, children are the accompaniment to other work. "In getting up a steep bank after we had forded a stream I had to carry a heavy stone to block the wheels . . . , and carry and pull along the children at the same time." "Descending the mountain, which was steep and difficult, the men having to steady the wagons down while we women carried and led our children." At most times children fended for themselves, the older boys working with the men, the older girls appointed as nursemaids to the younger ones. The ultimate responsibility, however, resided with the mothers.

In parties with more than one able-bodied woman, women divided up their responsibilities just as the men did. Women would commonly take turns cooking. However, as Helen Carpenter complained to her diary, even with help from sisters and children

> the plain fact of the matter is *we have no time for sociability.* From the time we get up in the morning, until we are on the road, it is hurry scurry to get breakfast and put away the things that necessarily had to be pulled out last night—while under way there is no room in the wagon for a visitor, nooning is barely enough to eat a cold bite—and at night all the cooking utensils and provisions are to be gotten about the camp fire and cooking enough done to last until the next night.
>
> Although there is not much to cook, the difficulty and inconvenience of doing it, amounts to a great deal—so by the time one has squatted around the fire and cooked bread and bacon, and made several dozen trips to and from the wagon—washed the dishes (with no place to drain them) and gotten things ready for an early breakfast, some of the others already have their night caps on—at any rate its time to go to bed.
>
> In respect to women's work the days are all very much the same. . . . Some women have very little help about the camp, being obliged to get the wood and water (as far as possible), make camp fires, unpack at night and pack up in the morning—and if they are Missourians they have the milking to do, if they are fortunate enough to have cows.
>
> I am lucky in having a Yankee for a husband, so I am well waited on.

Most women, of course, were from Missouri and its midwestern environs and had the worst of it by Mrs. Carpenter's description.

Indeed, despite Mrs. Carpenter's disclaimer for Yankee men, men assisted in only the most unusual of circumstances. In some parties men did the cooking during storms and very bad weather. And most husbands, like Jessy Thornton, took over when their wives fell sick; Thornton only asked that Nancy "not scold me for my blunders." There were other instances where husband and wife both hired into a party to do the cooking, or where women were relieved of cooking when a man hired on as trail cook.

Men, however, made inept domestic helpers. The experience of single men again places the family experience in perspective.

> "How do you like it overland?"
> His mother she will say;
> "All right, except for cooking,
> Then the devil is to pay.
>
> For some won't cook, and others can't,
> And then it's curse and damn;
> The coffee pot's begun to leak,
> So has the frying pan.

John A. Johnson was one of the many who followed his heart to the goldfields in 1849, leaving his wife Almire and their children behind. In a rich series of letters written home, he discussed among many other things the cooking arrangements in his party of five men. "It would no doubt be interesting to hear how we manage matters in camp as to cooking, etc.," he wrote. "All of us seem to understand cooking as well as our wives and are anxious to try their hands." A few weeks later he added: "We have, as I said before, several excellent cooks in our company. Some crack on making one thing and some another and really we get along very well in this respect. Today each mess made a pot-pie; I had the honor of officiating at our mess; it was good of course."

Perhaps inspired by his success at Sunday dinner, his confidence was building; a week later he wrote that

> yesterday our mess . . . proposed that if I would act as cook on the road I would be relieved from every other kind of work and further that I need not stand guard at night. I said *I would do it* and it was unanimously agreed to; so that I need not harness or touch a mule, or do any other work on the road, save preparing the food, which to me, you know,

will not be burdensome as I have a rather natural taste for that kind of work and they all think so. . . . The beauty of my berth is that I can walk, ride in the wagon or on a mule all day as I please and after supper go to bed and *sleep all night* while others have to watch or stand guard two hours every other night and are consequently exposed to danger if there be any dangers at any time for Indians.

A friend of the family traveling with the male party wrote to Johnson's wife as if to address her suspicions about her husband's newfound capacity for the wifely role: "He is decidedly the best cook in the camp. He goes about it rather awkwardly but really I don't think his wife can beat him at making bread."

Johnson's tenure as trail cook was all too predictable. A week later he wrote home again: "I have given up the office of chief cook and take my turn with the rest and my portion of other duties. I had rather do so as it is more slavish work than I had anticipated and by far the hardest post to occupy. I found I was working all the time during our halts while others were at least a portion of the time resting. I could not get time to write a letter or a note—as for guarding, my turn will not come oftener than once in two and perhaps three nights and then only two hours at a time with some eight or ten others."

Where families, not single men, made up the parties, women were only too glad to replace men at the campfire. Men's clumsiness with domestic details was an object of feminine scorn. "Mr Gray does most of the cooking," Rebecca Ketcham noted, "and it is most amusing to see some of his operations." Lucy Cooke traveled all the way to Salt Lake with a hired male cook but went on to California the next season without male domestic assistance: "It's so nice to have women folks manage the cooking; things look so much sweeter." "We are in a camp tonight with a small company of emigrants among whom are several ladies," Frances Sawyer wrote. "These, like myself, were engaged in helping to cook supper, and I have no doubt, but that they all enjoyed it heartily as I did." She was, undoubtedly, correct. Camp

housework was "more slavish" than even experienced farm women might have expected. It was "by far the hardest post to occupy" but accepted by women, nonetheless, as their responsibility.

What about the work women did during the hours of travel? The picture that emerges from men's and women's accounts is fuzzy and indistinct, reflecting a confusion as to what was normative in the actual situations that developed out on the trail. Men were supposed to be the drivers of the wagons and stock, and clearly the leaders of the march; women were to enjoy the privilege of riding in the wagons. Both men and women agreed on this division of labor, and during the early weeks on the trail most people conformed to this ideal. Certainly men rarely rode the wagons, and women frequently did. This distinction between riding and walking was so basic that it came close to a role-defining division between the sexes.

> Mrs. Ridgley said that her back ached riding all day in a wagon that jolted you to pieces every time you hit a stone. She didn't see how that poor woman in the wagon in back of the deacon's could get along, with a cross baby. And if one was a man one wouldn't have to sit cramped up all day and every day.
>
> In mild defense of his sex Mr Ridgley would reply that it wasn't exactly easy to walk halfway across the continent alongside of a team of oxen with a yoke of steers in the center that you had to keep watching continually. At which his good wife would smile a little wearily. *She* knew who had the hardest part of the bargain, etc.

If there was a formulaic quality to this conjugal debate it was because this behavior was taken to be standard for men and women. Essentially the haggling was about the respective virtues of the sexes themselves.

In fact, this was not the full picture. Women walked too, and many women walked most of the time. We have already noted women gathering fuel as they walked. As the emigrants matured with the march, they could see how every extra pound lessened the distance a team could haul, so "the women would walk to lighten the load" and even "would push to help the poor teams up the hills." There is cause for believing that by the time the journey was well under way women walked as a matter of course. The difference remained that women could ride when they tired of the walk, while men could not. When they did choose to ride, women busied themselves with mending or knitting.

When teamsters fell sick or were otherwise incapacitated, women, of course, substituted. Emergencies—stranded wagons, prairie fires, Indian scares—also called on women to carry out male duties. This is not surprising. More unexpected, perhaps, is that many women took a regular turn at driving both the wagons and the stock. As we have seen, men only rarely took over the women's work. Women, however, regularly performed certain details of what were men's responsibilities. "Mrs Burnett and myself drove and slept alternately during the day," Peter Burnett recalled. "I drive a great deal now, as I am very fond of handling the lines," Frances Sawyer wrote in her journal. In their diary accounts women were more likely than men to note women's work with the stock; fewer than a fifth of the men's diaries mention women driving, compared to a full third of the women's. Yet women themselves seemed a bit reluctant to admit this discrepancy in the conventional division of labor. "The two-horse spring wagon was our bed room and was driven by the Major," Margaret Haun wrote, and then added "and in good stretches of the road by myself." Susan Angell declared that their mule-drawn wagon was "driven by my husband"—certainly a clear statement, except that later, in passing, she added the important qualifier that she "took turns in driving the mule teams during each day." These women stated the normative as if it were the actual situation; the truth only came out in elaboration. Their values prevented them from writing simply, "My husband and I drove the wagon." These indications suggest that the work of women during the traveling hours violated normative standards of work.

There was, of course, a social life in the camps. Young people frequently got together for singing and sometimes dancing around the campfires. "The young ones of our party are all assembled around a blazing fire, from which sounds of mirth and hilarity come floating on the evening breeze." Special occasions, like the Fourth of July or a stopover at Fort Laramie or Fort Bridger, might generate an evening of merrymaking. But women were mostly just too busy for evening entertainments. If they were able to end their domestic duties a little early, women too gathered around the campfires, but mostly in feminine groups. "High teas were not popular but tatting, knitting, crochetting, exchanging recepts for cooking beans or dried apples or swapping food for the sake of variety kept us in practice of feminine occupations and diversions." For their part, the menfolk spent their evening hour "lolling and smoking their pipes and guessing, or maybe betting, how many miles we had covered during the day."

Quite simply, women had little extra time, although men found time for a variety of leisure activities. Fishing and swimming were common at the rivers and occasional ponds. Randall Hewitt remembered men producing "greasy, well-thumbed packs of cards," and games of euchre, old sledge, and pinochle were "something for amusement constantly."

The most popular male pastime, however, was hunting. Nearly every man hunted whenever he could. When the wagons stopped for a wash day, men would hunt. "We shall not move today. The women will wash and the men will hunt," John Zeiber wrote in his diary. The captain's order for the day in one 1844 train was "a rest for the cattle, wash day for the women, and a day to hunt for the men." Although captains' orders in general soon fell out of favor, the priorities remained the same. Moreover, despite expert advice as to the folly of stopping the march for a hunt, men who otherwise stressed the importance of continual movement above all else would stop their wagons, saddle all available mounts, and head out for the kill at the slightest sign of a distant buffalo herd. When the cry "Buffalo!" was raised, excitement pulsed from one man to the next;

Minto's captain, "General" Cornelius Gilliam, "called loudly for his hourse. . . . He slung himself into the saddle, and turning his face to the train called in a raised voice, 'You boys with the teams camp where there is wood and water, and you that can get horses and guns mount and follow me.' He did not speak to any particular officer, and in the ardor of the hunter seemed to have forgotten the responsibility of the general." When the buffalo appeared, many men left their responsibilities behind with the women. As her party moved across buffalo country, Cecelia Adams noted in her diary that "our boys are on the chase most of the time."

Men had this opportunity for play, and play it was. The amount of usable food produced by these masculine sorties was dismally low. Edward Parrish recorded that his comrades had killed buffalo enough for 40,000 pounds of meat but left nearly all for the birds; the hunters had neither the time, the equipment, nor the inclination for butchering. "God forgive us for such waste and save us from such ignorance," Parrish pled. Burnette offered sound advice: "When you reach the country of buffalo, never stop your wagons to hunt, as you will eat up more provisions than you will save." Hunting could not, then, be justified as a working activity. Nor did very many men seem to feel, as Parrish did, that it required such a justification. Most simply felt as George Belshaw: "Fine sport was this for all the Boys."

There was no comparable play activity for women outside of their working time. Hunting was but a glaring example of the contrasting ways in which men and women employed their time on the trail. Men worked within a pattern of activity/inactivity geared for functional efficiency; periods of maximum exertion were matched by periods of rest and relaxation. This pattern was in literal accord with the principal function of the trip; indeed, men could and did see themselves as the motive force itself, since it was principally men's labor that drove the wagons. In addition, men had the prerogative of leadership, including the option of stopping the train. Women's work, on the other hand, was at the mercy of the march and its male leadership. Unable to rest during the long hours on the road, often called upon to lend a crucial hand during the day, women finally shifted into high gear in the evenings, precisely when the men and the wagons lay still.

Hunting well illustrates a second characteristic distinction between the work of the sexes. In their roles as leaders of the march, men had to work together with other men. As we have seen, cooperation, whether in trains or informally, was at a premium for the length of the march. It was during the moving hours that cooperation was most in demand: agreeing and holding to the line and pace of the march, agreeing to a camping time and place, assisting one another in the difficult stretches. Men were the representatives of the parties and families, and security was dependent upon their ability to communicate and cooperate. Collective games, storytelling, singing and dancing—all shaped mainly by the male participants—were important ways of building and sustaining social cooperation. Hunting together was another important way. The buffalo hunters returning from their successful (albeit wasteful) foray, Minto remembers, "made a jolly party going back to camp, as the man who led the way, walking beside his mule, Joseph Watt, started us singing"—an archetypal scene of male camaraderie. Women's work confined wives to the family circle. There was little chance, as Helen Carpenter said, to visit while traveling, and in the evening women were all but bound to the domestic fires.

These distinctions could ordinarily be contained by family dynamics habituated to the everyday differences between men's and women's work. Women, as we have seen, were used to working beyond the boundaries of "sun to sun." There was a difference on the trail, however, which produced some significant conflict. On their simple farms, men and women were engaged in common work with an internal character. Here on the trail the work of men and women diverged: men fixed exclusively on outward goals —the stock, grass and water, mileage, the destination, future planning—compatible with their working goals. Women, because of the repetitive features of their work, found it more difficult to achieve this outward perspective.

Phoebe Judson articulated this divergence of the sexes:

> During the week our men had been very busily employed. . . . Saturday night found them very tired and much in need of physical rest, so they lolled around in the tents and on their blankets spread on the grass, or under the wagons out of the sunshine, seeming to realize that the "Sabbath was made for man." But the women, who had only been anxious spectators of their arduous work, . . . not being weary in body, could not fully appreciate physical rest, and were rendered more uneasy by the continual passing of emigrant trains all day long. . . . To me, much of the day was spent in meditating over the past and in forebodings for the future.

Reams of testimony could be marshaled to demonstrate the physical exhaustion of women, so we can only assume that Mrs. Judson's memory was faulty. The anxiety she remembered feeling, however, was real enough and pervaded nearly every woman's account of her experience. The immediate source of this anxiety was the divergent goals and work patterns of men and women on the trail. On a deeper level, however, these divergences themselves were part and parcel of significant cultural distinctions between men and women. The conflict between sexual styles we see revealed in the analysis of the division of labor found more fundamental expression on the level of values, beliefs, expectations, and emotions.

23

FREE LABOR: THE REPUBLICANS AND NORTHERN SOCIETY

ERIC FONER

From the Constitutional Convention of 1787 until the 1850s American politicians labored to suppress what was the greatest threat to national unity: controversy over the institution of slavery. In 1788 political leaders adopted the Three-Fifths Compromise, which allowed southern slaveholders to count a portion of their slaves in determining representation in the House of Representatives, thus forestalling a stalemate that would have made adoption of the Constitution impossible. Again in 1820 Congress engineered the Missouri Compromise, which admitted Maine as a free state to counterbalance Missouri's petition for admission as a slave state. But by the early 1850s industrialization in the North, and the growth there of a powerful abolitionist movement, brought increasing friction between the slave and free states. In the aftermath of "bleeding Kansas," where opponents and supporters of slavery in that western territory fought each other in pitched military campaigns, the national political parties, Democrats and Whigs, split into northern and southern wings and the "second party system" disintegrated. As the Democrats and Whigs made last-ditch efforts in the early 1850s to reknit their parties, remnants of both parties, along with men who considered themselves independents, joined to form the Republican party. Running on a platform of "Free Soil, Free Labor, Free Men," the Republicans elected Abraham Lincoln president in 1860, only a few short years after the formation of the party.

In this essay Eric Foner seeks to explain the sudden rise of the Republican party and the reasons for its immense popularity. In doing this he turns to the free-labor ideology, which party leaders used to cement their coalition. Foner argues that it was the wide appeal of their free-labor ideology which drew men of different social positions together and insured the Republican victory.

How does the Republicanism of the 1850s compare with the republicanism of the 1790s discussed by John R. Howe in Reading 14? How does Foner's view of the Republican ideology compare with that discussed by Don E. Fehrenbacher in Reading 25?

On May 26, 1860, one of the Republican party's leading orators, Carl Schurz of Wisconsin, addressed a Milwaukee audience which had gathered to endorse the nomination of Abraham Lincoln. "The Republicans," Schurz declared, "stand before the country, not only as the anti-slavery party, but emphatically as the party of free labor." Two weeks later, Richard Yates, the gubernatorial candidate in Illinois, spoke at a similar rally in Springfield. "The great idea and basis of the Republican party, as I understand it," he proclaimed, "is free labor. . . . To make labor honorable is the object and aim of the Republican party." Such statements, which were reiterated countless times by Republican orators in the 1850's, were more than mere election-year appeals for the votes of laboring men. For the concept of "free labor" lay at the heart of the Republican ideology, and expressed a coherent social outlook, a model of the good society. Political anti-slavery was not merely a negative doctrine, an attack on southern slavery and the society built upon it; it was an affirmation of the superiority of the social system of the North—a dynamic, expanding capitalist society, whose achievements and destiny were almost wholly the result of the dignity and opportunities which it offered the average laboring man.

The dignity of labor was a constant theme of ante-bellum northern culture and politics. Tocqueville noted that in America, "not only work itself, but work specifically to gain money," was considered honorable, and twenty years later, the New York editor Horace Greeley took note of "the usual Fourth-of-July declamation in behalf of the dignity of labor, the nobleness of labor." It was a common idea in both economic treatises and political pronouncements that labor was the source of all value. Lincoln declared in 1859 that "Labor is prior to, and independent of capital . . . in fact, capital is the fruit of labor," and the New York *Tribune* observed that "nothing is more common" than this "style of assertion." Republican orators insisted that labor could take the credit for the North's rapid economic development. Said William Evarts in 1856, "Labor, gentlemen, we of the free States acknowledge to be the source of all our wealth, of all our progress, of all our dignity and value." In a party which saw divisions on political and economic matters between radicals and conservatives, between former Whigs and former Democrats, the glorification of labor provided a much-needed theme of unity. Representatives of all these segments included paeans to free labor in their speeches; even the crusty old conservative Tom Corwin delivered "a eu-

logy on labor and laboring men" in an 1858 speech.

Belief in the dignity of labor was not, of course, confined to the Republican party or to the ante-bellum years; it has been part of American culture from the very beginning. In large part, it can be traced to the fact that most Americans came from a Protestant background, in which the nobility of labor was an article of faith. One does not need to accept in its entirety Max Weber's association of the "Protestant ethic" with the rise of capitalism in Europe to believe that there is much validity in Weber's insight that the concept of "calling" provided the psychological underpinning for capitalist values. Weber pointed out that in Calvinist theology each man had an occupation or calling to which he was divinely appointed. To achieve success in this calling would serve the glory of God, and also provide visible evidence that an individual was among the few predestined to enter heaven. The pursuit of wealth thus became a way of serving God on earth, and labor, which had been imposed on fallen man as a curse, was transmuted into a religious value, a Christian duty. And the moral qualities which would ensure success in one's calling—honesty, frugality, diligence, punctuality, and sobriety—became religious obligations. Weber described the Protestant outlook on life as "worldly asceticism," since idleness, waste of time, and conspicuous display or expenditure for personal enjoyment were incompatible with its basic values.

There was more to the Republican idea of free labor, however, than the essentials of the Protestant ethic, to which, presumably, the South had also been exposed, for the relation of that ethic to the idea of social mobility was highly ambiguous. On the one hand, the drive to work zealously in one's calling, the capital accumulation which resulted from frugality, and the stress on economic success as a sign of divine approval, all implied that men would work for an achievement of wealth and advancement in their chosen professions. But if one's calling were divinely ordained, the implication might be that a man should be content with the same occupation for his entire life, although he should strive to grow rich in it. In a static economy, therefore, the concept of "a calling" may be associated with the idea of an hierarchical social order, with more or less fixed classes. But Republicans rejected this image of society. Their outlook was grounded in the Protestant ethic, but in its emphasis on social mobility and economic growth, it reflected an adaptation of that ethic to the dynamic, expansive, capitalist society of the ante-bellum North.

Contemporaries and historians agree that the average American of the ante-bellum years was driven by an inordinate desire to improve his condition in life, and by boundless confidence that he could do so. Economic success was the standard by which men judged their social importance, and many observers were struck by the concentration on work, with the aim of material advancement, which characterized Americans. Tocqueville made the following observation during Jackson's presidency: "The first thing that strikes one in the United States is the innumerable crowd of those striving to escape from their original social condition." On the eve of the Civil War, the Cincinnati *Gazette* reported that things had not changed. "Of all the multitude of young men engaged in various employments of this city," it declared, "there is probably not one who does not desire, and even confidently expect, to become rich, and that at an early day." The universal desire for social advancement gave American life an aspect of almost frenetic motion and activity, as men moved from place to place, and occupation to occupation in search of wealth. Even ministers, reported the Cincinnati *Gazette,* "resign the most interesting fields of labor to get higher salaries." The competitive character of northern society was aptly summed up by Lincoln, when he spoke of the "race of life" in the 1850s.

The foremost example of the quest for a better life was the steady stream of settlers who abandoned eastern homes to seek their fortunes in the West. The westward movement reached new heights in the mid-1850s, and it was not primarily the poor who migrated westward, but middle class "business-like farmers," who sold their farms to migrate, or who left the eastern farms of their fathers. "These emigrants," said a leading Republican newspaper of Ohio, "are not needy adventurers, fleeing from the pinchings of penury. They are substantial farmers." Those without means who came to the West were interested in obtaining their own farms as quickly as possible, because to the American of the nineteenth century land was not the bucolic ideal of the precapitalist world, but another means for economic advancement. Tocqueville noted that the small farmer of the West was really a landed businessman, an entrepreneur who was prepared to sell his farm and move on, if he could get a good price. What Horace Greeley called "the nomadic tendency" of Americans contributed to the rapid expansion of the western frontier. "The men who are building up the villages of last year's origin on the incipient Railroads of Iowa," said the New York editor, "were last year doing the like in Illinois, and three years since in Ohio." The acquisitive instincts of western settlers were described by Kinsley Bingham, the first Republican governor of Michigan: "Like most new States, ours has been settled by an active, energetic and enterprising class of men, who are desirous of accumulating property rapidly."

The Republican idea of free labor was a product of this expanding, enterprising, competitive society. It is important to recognize that in ante-bellum America, the word "labor" had a meaning far broader than its modern one. Andrew Jackson, for example, defined as "the producing classes" all those whose work was directly involved in the production of goods—farmers, planters, laborers, mechanics, and small businessmen. Only those who profited from the work of others, or whose occupations were largely financial or promotional, such as speculators, bankers, and lawyers, were excluded from this definition. Daniel Webster took a similarly all-embracing view. In his famous speech of March 7, 1850, Webster asked, "Why, who are the laboring people of the North? They are the whole North. They are the people who till their own farms with their own hands; freeholders, educated men, independent men." And the Republican definition, as it emerged in the 1850's, proved equally broad. Some Republicans did exclude commercial enterprise from their idea of labor—the Springfield *Republican,* for example, suggested that three-quarters of the traders in the country should go into some field of "productive labor." In general, however, Republicans would agree with Horace Greeley that labor included "useful doing in any capacity or vocation." They thus drew no distinction between a "laboring class" and what we could call the middle class. With Webster, they considered the farmer, the small businessman, and the independent craftsmen, all as "laborers."

If the Republicans saw "labor" as substantially different from the modern-day notion of the "working class," it was partly because the line between capitalist and worker was to a large extent blurred in the ante-bellum northern economy, which centered on the independent farm and small shop. Moreover, for the Republicans, social mobility was an essential part of northern society. The ante-bellum Republicans praised the virtues of the enterprising life, and viewed social mobility as the glory of northern society. "Our paupers to-day, thanks to free labor, are our yeomen and merchants of tomorrow," said the New York *Times.* Lincoln asserted in 1859 that "advancement, improvement in condition—is the order of things in a society of equals," and he denounced southern insinuations that northern wage earners were "fatally fixed in that condition for life." The opportunity for social advancement, in the Republican view, was what set Americans apart from their European forebears. As one Iowa Republican put it:

> What is it that makes the great mass of American citizens so much more enterprising and intelligent than the laboring classes in Europe? It is the stimulant held out to them by the character of our institutions. The door is thrown open to all, and even the poorest and humblest in the land, may, by industry and application, attain a position which will entitle him to the respect and confidence of his fellow-men.

Many Republican leaders bore witness in their own careers to how far men could rise from hum-

ble beginnings. Lincoln's own experience, of course, was the classic example, and during the 1860 campaign Republican orators repeatedly referred to him as "the child of labor," who had proved how "honest industry and toil" were rewarded in the North. Other Republican leaders like the former indentured servant Henry Wilson, the "bobbin boy" Nathaniel P. Banks, and the ex-laborer Hannibal Hamlin also made much of their modest beginnings in campaign speeches.

In the free labor outlook, the objective of social mobility was not great wealth, but the middle-class goal of economic independence. For Republicans, "free labor" meant labor with economic choices, with the opportunity to quit the wage-earning class. A man who remained all his life dependent on wages for his livelihood appeared almost as unfree as the southern slave. There was nothing wrong, of course, with working for wages for a time, if the aim were to acquire enough money to start one's own farm or business. Zachariah Chandler described in the Senate the cycle of labor which he felt characterized northern society: "A young man goes out to service—to labor, if you please to call it so—for compensation until he acquires money enough to buy a farm . . . and soon he becomes himself the employer of labor." Similarly, a correspondent of the New York *Tribune* wrote in 1854, "Do you say to me, hire some of the thousands and thousands of emigrants coming to the West. Sir, I cannot do it. They come West to labor for themselves, not for me; and instead of laboring for others, they want others to labor for them." The aspirations of the free labor ideology were thus thoroughly middle-class, for the successful laborer was one who achieved self-employment, and owned his own capital—a business, farm, or shop.

The key figure in the Republicans' social outlook was thus the small independent entrepreneur. "Under every form of government having the benefits of civilization," said Congressman Timothy Jenkins of New York, "there is a middle class, neither rich nor poor, in which is concentrated the chief enterprise of the country." Charles Francis Adams agreed that the "middling class . . . equally far removed from the temptations of great wealth and of extreme destitution," provided the surest defense of democratic principles. In a nation as heavily agricultural as the ante-bellum United States, it is not surprising that the yeoman received the greatest praise. "The middling classes who own the soil, and work it with their own hands," declared Thaddeus Stevens, "are the main support of every free government." But the exponents of the development of manufacturers also looked to the small capitalist, not the very wealthy, as the agents of economic progress. "The manufacturing industry of this country," said Representative Samuel Blair of Pennsylvania, "must look to men of moderate means for its development—the men of enterprise being, as a class, in such circumstances." In their glorification of the middle class and of economic independence, the Republicans were accurately reflecting the aspirations of northern society. As Carl Schurz later recalled of his first impressions of the United States, "I saw what I might call the middle-class culture in process of formation."

The Republicans' glorification of northern labor might have led them to a radical political appeal, in which the rights of workingmen were defended against the prerogatives of the rich and propertied. And there was a substantial body of Republicans—the former Democrats—who came from a political tradition which viewed the interests of capitalists and laborers as being in earnest conflict. As Marvin Meyers points out, the political rhetoric of Jacksonian Democrats involved a series of sharp social antagonisms. They insisted that there existed real class differences between rich and poor, capital and labor, and consciously strove to give their party an anti-wealth persuasion. Democrats traditionally opposed measures like the protective tariff, which they viewed as government aid to the capitalist class, and paper money, which they claimed, robbed the laborer of a portion of his wages by depreciating in value.

Behind the radical rhetoric of the Jacksonians, however, lay a basically middle-class perception of the social order. They believed that the social opportunity inherent in northern society would enable most laborers to achieve ownership of capital, and they were also convinced that the growth of the northern economy would lead to an increasing equalization in the distribution of wealth, rather than merely adding to the holdings of the rich. The primary aim of the Jacksonians was not to redistribute the property of the rich, but to open the avenues of social advancement to all laborers. Several historians have pointed out that, despite their disagreements over such matters of economic policy as tariffs and banks, Democrats and Whigs did not differ on such basic assumptions as the value of economic individualism, the rights of property, and other capitalist virtues. Nor should Jacksonian rhetoric be confused with a lack of enthusiasm for the economic development which most northerners saw as an essential part of social progress. Democrats insisted that their economic policies of free trade and destruction of economic privilege would allow free play to natural economic forces, and actually speed up economic advancement. Salmon P. Chase, for example, condemned the government's aid to the Collins Steamship Line in the 1850's, by arguing that if a real economic necessity existed, steam lines would be established by private enterprise, whether the government subsidized them or not. Similarly, Democratic free-traders like William Cullen Bryant argued that competition with foreign producers would stimulate the growth and progress of American firms, while protection would only encourage sluggishness. Democrats who entered the Republican party in the 1850's thus shared the Whig commitment to the nation's economic growth, even while they differed on the specific economic policies that would facilitate it.

Most Republicans, of course, were former Whigs, and they accepted the economic outlook, expressed by Carey and propagated in the pages of the New York *Tribune,* that there existed no real conflict between the interests of different social classes. Since all classes would benefit from economic expansion, this argument went, all had a stake in the national prosperity. "The interests of the capitalist and the laborer," Carey wrote, "are . . . in perfect harmony with each other, as each derives advantage from every measure that tends to facilitate the growth of capital." During the 1850's, Carey served as a consultant to Greeley on economic matters, and the *Tribune*—the North's "sectional oracle"—reflected his views. Other Republican papers, like the Springfield *Republican,* also stressed the "perfect and equal mutual dependence" which existed between capital and labor. Republicans consistently deplored attempts of labor spokesmen to arouse hostility against the capitalist class. "We are not of the number of those who would array one class of society in hostility to another," the Cincinnati *Gazette* announced during the social dislocations caused by the Panic of 1857. Greeley agreed that "Jacobin ravings in the Park or elsewhere, against the Rich, or the Banks," could in no way alleviate "the distress of the poor." The conservatism implicit in the harmony of interests outlook was reflected in Lincoln's remarks to a delegation of workingmen during the Civil War. Condemning those who advocated a "war on property, or the owners of property," the President insisted that as the fruit of labor, property was desirable; it was "a positive good in the world." That some had wealth merely demonstrated that others could achieve wealth, and the prospect encouraged individual enterprise. "Let not him who is houseless," Lincoln told the workingmen, "pull down the house of another; but let him labor diligently and build one for himself, thus by example assuring that his own shall be safe from violence when built." In other words, the interests of labor and capital were identical, because equality of opportunity in American society generated a social mobility which assured that today's laborer would be tomorrow's capitalist.

The most striking example of the Whig-Republican doctrine of the harmony of interests was the idea, developed in the 1840's and expanded in the next decade, that the protective tariff was designed primarily to advance the interests of labor. Led by Greeley and Webster, Whig spokesmen developed the argument that the tariff was really intended to protect American work-ingmen against the competition of cheap foreign labor. Unless the tariff was used to increase the prices of foreign manufactures before they entered the American market, according to this argument, the only way for American businessmen to compete would be to depress their wage payments to the low European levels. Republican spokesmen for protection almost uniformly made this their major argument in the pre-war decade. "Mr. Chairman," declared a Pennsylvania Congressman as he opened a tariff speech in 1860, "I rise to advocate the rights of labor." Republicans also argued that the development of American industry, fostered by protection, would aid all sectors of the economy, by providing an expanding market for farm produce. Greeley insisted that a country without a home market for agriculture "can rarely boast a substantial, intelligent and virtuous yeomanry. . . . It may have wealthy Capitalists and Merchants, but never a numerous Middle Class."

In spite of their faith in the harmony of interests and their commitment to economic progress and social mobility, there was a certain suspicion of wealth within the Republican party. To some extent this was a natural reaction on the part of those who witnessed the reluctance of what Greeley called the "wealthy, timid, and mercantile classes" to support anti-slavery. It was well known that in the major cities of the East the wealthiest citizens placed the preservation of the Union (and of their markets and business connections in the South) above agitation of the slavery question. In Massachusetts, Conscience Whig leaders like Sumner, Wilson, and others had long condemned the political alliance between "the lords of the loom and the lords of the lash"—the cotton manufacturers and merchants of Massachusetts and the southern planters. Even the sedate Springfield *Republican* complained that "property . . . has frequently stood in the way of very necessary reforms, and has thus brought itself into contempt." Like their Boston counterparts, New York merchants were notorious for their close economic, political, and personal ties with the South. "Our greatest obstacle," one Republican wrote William Seward in 1856, "is the respectable fashionable well to do class," and the New York *Tribune* spoke of the "plain tendency to a union between the slave capitalists of the South and the moneyed capitalists of the North." During the 1856 campaign, Republicans throughout the North found themselves in difficulty when the wealthiest businessmen refused to contribute money to the party's coffers.

But Republican attacks on "the money capitalists" had deeper roots than political antagonisms. Many Republicans, of both Democratic and Whig antecedents, were deeply suspicious of corporations and of economic concentration. Israel Washburn, a leading Maine Republican, expressed a common fear when he warned of the danger "that the money-power will be too much centralized—that the lands and property of the country, in the course of time may come to be held or controlled by a comparatively small number of people." To some Republicans the growth of corporations was a harbinger of just such a development. Amasa Walker, the Massachusetts economist who left the Democratic party to join the Free Soilers and Republicans, insisted at the Massachusetts Constitutional Convention of 1853 that "this system of corporations is nothing more nor less than a moneyed feudalism. . . . It concentrates masses of wealth, it places immense power in a few hands. . . ." Walker's objections to corporations reflected the traditional economic anxieties of the small farmer and independent artisan:

> Corporations change the relation of man to wealth. When a man has his property in his own hands, and manages it himself, he is responsible for the manner in which he does it. . . . But when the management of property is put into the hands of corporations, the many delegate the power of managing it to the few. . . . It aggregates power, of course, and necessarily all the property of the Commonwealth, included in these corporations, must be put into the hands of a few men. . . . Hence, the agent of a factory, or a corporation of any kind, has absolute control over all persons connected with that corporation.

At the same convention, the Whig William Schouler, who was soon to become a leading Republican editor, indicated that he felt corporations were merely devices enabling businessmen to escape responsibility for paying their debts. The Republicans' distrust of corporations typified the ante-bellum American outlook. In an economy in which most mills and factories were still owned by individuals or by unchartered joint-stock companies or partnerships, the corporate form was generally confined to enterprises like banks and transportation companies, which serviced the public at large. Indeed, most were quasi-public in nature.

"The middle class," wrote the Catholic social critic Orestes Brownson, "is always a firm champion of equality when it concerns humbling a class above it, but it is its inveterate foe when it concerns elevating a class below it." Brownson's statement can be taken as a critique of the free labor ideology. For while it is true that the Republicans insisted on opening the opportunity for social advancement to all wage earners, it must be borne in mind that as true disciples of the Protestant ethic, they attributed an individual's success or failure in the North's "race of life" to his own abilities or shortcomings. Given the equality of opportunity which the Republicans believed existed in northern society, it followed that economic success was, as Horace Greeley argued, a reflection of the fact that a man had respected the injunctions to frugality, diligent work, and sobriety of the Protestant ethic.

In the North, one Republican declared in 1854, "every man holds his fortune in his own right arm; and his position in society, in life, is to be tested by his own individual character." This belief explains the fact that for all their glorification of labor, Republicans looked down upon those who labored for wages all their lives. "It is not the fault of the system," if a man did not rise above the position of wage earner, Lincoln explained, "but because of either a dependent nature which prefers it, or improvidence, folly, or singular misfortune." Poverty, or even the failure to advance economically, were thus individual, not social failures, the consequence of poor personal habits—laziness, extravagance, and the like. Greeley believed that "chance or 'luck,' " had "little to do with men's prosperous or adverse fortunes," and he complained that too many men blamed banks, tariffs, and hard times for their personal failures, while in reality the fault was "their own extravagance and needless ostentation." The Springfield *Republican* summed up this outlook when it declared in 1858 that there could be "no oppression of the laborer here which it is not in his power to remedy, or which does not come from his own inefficiency and lack of enterprise."

The free labor attitude toward the poor was made doubly clear in the aftermath of the Panic of 1857, when northern cities were struck by widespread unemployment and labor unrest. Demonstrations of the poor—"never before witnessed in the towns of the abundant West"—occurred all too frequently. As they were to do many times subsequently, Republicans blamed the Panic not on impersonal economic forces, but on the individual shortcomings of Americans, particularly their speculation in land and stocks which had reached "mania" proportions in the years preceding the crash, and on generally extravagant living. The Cincinnati *Gazette* defined the basic economic problem as an overexpansion of the credit system, rooted in too many "great speculations." But speculation was only one aspect of the problem of general extravagance. "We have been living too fast," complained the *Gazette.* "Individuals, families, have been eagerly trying to outdo each other in dress, furniture, style and luxury." The Chicago *Press and Tribune* likewise blamed "ruinous extravagance" and "luxurious living" for the economic troubles, and both papers urged a return to "republican simplicity," and the frugal, industrious ways of the Protestant ethic.

This kind of advice infused the Republican answer to the problems of the poor in the difficult winters of the late 1850's. Republican papers throughout the North urged the unemployed to tighten their belts and retrench their expenditures. The Chicago *Press and Tribune* went so far as to say that drunkenness and laziness accounted for nine-tenths of the pauperism in the West, and

that the only remedy was "a little wholesome hunger and a salutary fit of chattering by reason of excessive cold." Some Republicans did favor emergency public works to employ those unavoidably out of work, but they tended to oppose public charity, on the grounds that this led to dependence and rendered the recipients unwilling to work in the future. And when the poor took to the streets demanding bread and work, Republicans reacted with shock and indignation. The *National Era,* one of the most radical Republican journals on the slavery question, declared that the noisiest demonstrators were those who were poor because of their own faults. "We do not believe," said the *Era,* "that the noisy meetings in our Eastern cities, pretending to be composed of working men, represent the real feelings of the working classes. . . . Their style of proceedings and spirit have a flavor of communism about them; they suggest a foreign origin." The reaction of Republicans to the poverty of the late 1850's revealed the basic deficiency of their middle-class free labor outlook. Even as they demanded equal opportunity for social advancement for all laborers, they also subscribed to an ideology which told them that an almost perfect opportunity for social mobility existed. They could therefore say with Senator Harlan of Iowa that their object was to place the laborer "on a platform of equality—let him labor in the same sphere, with the same chances for success and promotion—let the contest be exactly equal between him and others—and if, in the conflict of mind with mind, he should sink beneath the billow, let him perish."

Of course, the ideology of mobility was never quite so simple that it condemned out of hand all who failed to achieve success. As Stephan Thernstrom has pointed out, many nineteenth-century Americans recognized that environmental and social factors could hinder a man's social advancement. Republicans like Lincoln and Greeley had a genuine compassion for the plight of the poor, and were sincerely interested in their advancement. They recognized that not all the poverty in the nation's urban centers could be blamed on the character deficiencies of the poor. Thaddeus Stevens, for instance, insisted that it was wrong to blame the unemployed for their plight, for "almost all of them would rather work even at moderate wages, if they could find employment, than to go from house to house and beg."

Yet even the most sympathetic Republicans clung to the free labor ideology, and their prescriptions for the ills of society reflected this. Greeley, for example, used the New York *Tribune* to expose the shocking working conditions in many New York City shops, and, unlike many other Republicans, supported a legislative limit on hours of labor. He even believed that the government had the responsibility to guarantee work for all who wanted it. However, his belief in the harmony of interests made him unable to view laborers as a distinct class with its own interests—rather, they were merely nascent capitalists, whose aim was to acquire capital and achieve economic independence. He therefore strenuously opposed self-conscious working-class actions like strikes, though he agreed that laborers could join unions to peacefully petition for higher wages. But shutting down their employers' businesses, and preventing other laborers from working struck Greeley as intolerable. Strikes were a form of "industrial war," the antithesis of the labor-capital co-operation which Greeley desired. If a worker found his wages inadequate, Greeley wrote, he should not "stand idle" by striking, but should take another job or move to the West. And while Greeley recognized the social barriers to economic advancement in the cities, he also believed that it was primarily in the lowest class "that we encounter intemperance, licentiousness, gambling," and other vices.

Other Republicans shared Greeley's outlook. Those Republicans, like Lincoln, who endorsed the right to strike, usually meant that laborers should be free to leave their jobs and take others, rather than that they should shut down the establishments of their employers. The Boston *Atlas and Daily Bee* declared strikes "fundamentally wrong," and the Cincinnati *Gazette,* in criticizing a western railroad strike, observed, "We are not speaking of *leaving* work—that all men have the right to do; but of combining to interrupt and arrest the machinery. The first is a plain, individ-

ual right. The last is a conspiracy against the interest, and even the safety of the public." And many Republicans opposed legal limits on working hours, on the grounds that, as Samuel Gridley Howe put it, "It emasculates people to be protected in this way. Let them be used to protecting themselves."

The basic Republican answer to the problem of urban poverty was neither charity, public works, nor strikes, but westward migration of the poor, aided by a homestead act. The safety-valve conception of the public lands, popularized half a century later by Frederick Jackson Turner, was accepted as a reality by ante-bellum Republicans. Nascent labor organizations and workingmen's parties had made free land a political issue in the 1830's, by urging it as a panacea for the ills of eastern urban society. Their simple argument—that encouraging the westward movement of eastern workingmen would reduce labor competition in the East and thereby raise wages, provided one basis for the homestead arguments of the 1840's and 1850's. This was the aspect of the plan which attracted Horace Greeley, who became the homestead's leading propagandist. "The public lands," he wrote, "are the great regulator of the relocations of Labor and Capital, the safety valve of our industrial and social engine," and he never wavered in the advice he offered to New York's poor and unemployed: "go straight into the country—go at once!" Greeley also stressed the economic benefits which would accrue to the entire country from the rapid settlement of the West, but the primary aim of his homestead policy was to reduce the excess laboring population of the East. Under his editorship, the New York *Tribune* carried the word of the great opportunities for labor in the West far and wide, and the demand there, not only for farmers, but for skilled craftsmen, artisans, and laborers of all kinds.

It is well known how the homestead issue became increasingly sectional in the 1850's. Republicans believed that the settlement of the western territories by free farmers would prove an effective barrier against the extension of slavery, and this made some eastern anti-slavery men, who feared that free land might set off a migration which would depopulate their states, willing to accept the homestead idea. For the same reason, southerners increasingly opposed any plan for giving free land to settlers. The Republican platform of 1860 gave the homestead plan a ringing endorsement, in a plank which Greeley said he "fixed exactly to my own liking" on the platform committee. The homestead plan played a key role in the Republicans' free labor outlook, for in their view, the measure was essential to keeping open the geographical and social mobility which was the hallmark of northern society. Free land, said Richard Yates, would aid "the poor but industrious laborer," in his search for economic advancement, and the *National Era* agreed that the policy would offer "an equal chance to the poor of all states. . . ." The Panic of 1857 gave a great impetus to the Republicans' support for the homestead idea. They blamed the large-scale urban unemployment on the difficulty workers had in securing land. Too many men, said the Cincinnati *Gazette,* had "crowded into the cities," while there was an "abundance of land to be possessed" further west. Some Republicans saw for the first time the specter of a permanent population of urban poor. "In many of the free states," said Illinois' Orville H. Browning, "population is already pressing hard upon production and subsistence, and new homes must be provided, or the evils of an overcrowded country encountered." Such overcrowding would effectively bar eastern workers from sharing in the economic mobility which was the heritage of free laborers.

As an expression of the free labor mentality, the homestead idea was defended in middle-class, capitalistic terms. "The friends of land reform," George Julian assured Congress, "claim no right to interfere with the laws of property of the several States, or the vested interests of their citizens. They advocate no *leveling* policy, designed to strip the rich of their possessions." Richard Yates agreed that "the measure is not agrarian [that is, socialistic]. It does not take your property and give it to me. . . . It does not bring down the high, but it raises the low." What the homestead policy did propose to do was to aid the poor in achieving

economic independence, to raise them into the middle class. If the policy of free land were adopted, said Greeley's *Tribune,* every citizen would have the essential economic alternative "of working for others or for himself." The homestead policy would transform the dependent poor of the cities into prosperous yeomen. "It would," said Schuyler Colfax, "by giving them independent freeholds, incite them . . . to rear families in habits of industry and frugality, which form the real elements of national greatness and power." And Congressman Owen Lovejoy summed up all these arguments with another whose spirit must have been congenial to all Republicans. The homestead measure, he declared, "will greatly increase the number of those who belong to what is called the middle class."

In the eyes of the Republicans, northern society exemplified the best aspects of the free labor ideology. The ideal of equal opportunity for social mobility and economic independence seemed to them to be not dreams but living realities. Lincoln declared that the majority of northerners were neither capitalists nor employees—rather, they worked for themselves in shops and farms, "taking the whole product to themselves, and asking no favors of capital on the one hand, nor of hirelings and slaves on the other." To southerners who compared northern laborers with their own slaves, Lincoln insisted that the North had no class who "are always to remain laborers." "The man who labored for another last year," he insisted, "this year labors for himself, and next year he will hire others to labor for him." To Republicans, northern society was the model of what Henry Wilson called "a progressive, permanent, Christian civilization," and Republican speeches contained abundant praise of their social order. Republicans admitted that in the cities—which were carried by the Democrats anyway—there was poverty, intemperance, and ignorance, but the Republican areas of the North represented the best of middle-class America. "Sir," said a Connecticut Congressman, "a majority of the citizens of my State occupy that happy social position which is a medium between a wealthy aristocracy on the one hand, and a poverty, which is generally wedded to ignorance, on the other." And Henry Wilson extolled the social order of Massachusetts, where laborers were "more elevated than can be found in any other portion of the globe," and where "our soil is divided into small estates," not large plantations.

The same ideal social order characterized the free states of the West, according to Republican leaders of that section. In rural Ohio, said Congressman Philemon Bliss, "the farmer works his own farm; the mechanic labors in his own shop, and the merchant sells his own goods. True, labor is there sold, but mainly as a temporary expedient to enable the laborer to acquire a small capital. . . ." According to Senator James Doolittle, four-fifths of the population of Wisconsin were economically independent. The superiority, indeed, the all but perfect character of northern society, was graphically depicted by Carl Schurz:

> Cast your eyes over that great beehive called the free States. See by the railroad and telegraph wire every village, almost every backwoods cottage, drawn within the immediate reach of progressive civilization . . . look upon our society, where by popular education and continual change of condition the dividing lines between the ranks and classes are almost obliterated; look upon our system of public instruction, which places even the lowliest child of the people upon the high road of progressive civilization.

How accurate was the Republican picture of northern society? On visiting the United States in the 1820's, the German economist Friedrich List was impressed by the fact that "the best work on Political Economy which one can read in that modern land is actual life." The Republicans' concept of free labor was obviously a reflection of their experiences in the economic and social life of the North, particularly the Republican North, whose heartland had a predominantly agricultural population, with small towns and independent farmers. The idea that labor created all value, and that all men could aspire to economic

independence, were products of the age of independent craftsmen and yeomen, and up to the Civil War, the northern economy could still be described in these terms. It is true that the industrial sector of the economy was expanding rapidly, especially in the 1850's, and that by 1860, the United States had achieved an industrial status second only to Great Britain's. In New England and some of the middle states the rise of the factory system and large-scale production gave a glimpse of the industrial nation which was to emerge later in the century. But on the eve of the war, large factories and great corporations were the exception, not the rule, even in New England. In the West, manufacturing establishments were widely dispersed, located near raw materials such as flour and lumber, and servicing local markets. The typical enterprise employed only a few workmen and only a small amount of capital, and was owned by an individual or partnership. Throughout the North, manufacturing firms had an average of only ten workmen each, and, as Bernard Mandel points out, even in New England the expansion of so important an industry as boot and shoe production in the 1850's and 1860's was due largely to the establishment of many new small plants, not the expansion of old ones.

On the other hand, the Republican image of northern society was already outdated in some respects. The decade of the 1850's, according to George R. Taylor, witnessed "the emergence of the wage earner"—a permanent working class, yet in 1859, Lincoln could state that the wage system "does not embrace more than one-eighth of the labor system of the country." Census statistics for the pre-war period are notoriously inaccurate, but Lincoln's statement was surely in error. David Montgomery estimates that almost 60 per cent of the American labor force was employed in some way, not economically independent, in 1860. And, particularly in the large eastern cities, where large-scale immigration was increasing class stratification and holding down the real wages of all workers, the prospect for rising to self-employment was already receding. Nor did the homestead act provide the safety-valve which Republicans claimed. Many studies have shown that it was eastern farmers, not wage earners from the crowded cities, who were able to take advantage of the offer of free land. Moreover, the 1850's saw the widespread introduction of agricultural machinery in the West, resulting in increased production, but raising the costs of farming and making it more difficult for farm laborers to enter the ranks of independent yeomen. Western farmers were already faced with a loss of their economic independence, as they came to rely on banks for credit. Lincoln could say, "I scarcely ever knew a mammoth farm to sustain itself," but the age of large-scale mechanized farming was fast approaching.

We know today, of course, that in spite of the wide acceptance of the ideology of social mobility, the years after 1860 saw a steady diminution of the prospects for a worker or farm laborer to achieve economic independence. This does not mean that industrialization and mechanized agriculture ended social mobility—on the contrary, the evidence is that they expanded it. But the mobility of the age of the independent producer, whose aspiration was economic self-sufficiency, was superseded by the mobility of industrial society, in which workers could look forward to a rising standard of living, but not self-employment. On the eve of the Civil War, however, these developments still lay largely in the future. If economic mobility was contracting in northern cities, the old social opportunity was at least close enough in time to lend plausibility to the free labor ideology. And in the rural and small-town North, the Republican picture of northern society corresponded to a large degree with reality. The two decades before the Civil War witnessed a substantial improvement in the level of living of western farmers, the result of the transportation revolution and the rise of eastern markets for their products. Farm tenancy was increasing, but the number of northern farmers was still double that of farm laborers and tenants. The factory system was expanding, undermining the economic independence of the small craftsman and artisan, but western industry was still concentrated in small towns and in small-scale enterprises. And according to Douglass North, the

small towns and villages of the Republican heartland "showed every sign of vigorous expansion."

In what Stuart Bruchey has termed "an essentially fluid society," with "broadly egalitarian economic opportunity," the free labor outlook had a strong cultural authenticity. A well-organized, persistent person could expect to achieve economic success, and a skilled wage earner could reasonably look forward to the day he acquired enough capital to start a small business of his own. The free labor ideology became inadequate, of course, when applied to the permanent wage earners and unemployed of ante-bellum northern society, but increasing numbers of these were Irish immigrants who, Republicans believed, lacked the qualities of discipline and sobriety essential for social advancement. When Republicans extolled the virtues of free labor, they were merely reflecting the experiences of millions of men who had "made it" and millions of others who had a realistic hope of doing so.

When Republicans spoke of their party's basic constituency, it was these successful middle-class northerners they had in mind. Charles Francis Adams declared that the party was composed of "the industrious farmers and mechanics, the independent men in comfortable circumstances in all the various walks of life," while the Democrats drew their support from the very rich and "the most degraded or the least intelligent of the population of the cities." Similarly, Seward, when visiting Great Britain, was struck by the parallel between British and American voting patterns. "All artisans and manufacturers are republicans—all their employees (speaking in general terms) are conservative. How like the United States." (Seward's statement again reminds us that when Republicans referred to themselves as a party of "free labor," they meant that their supporters were primarily middle class, not "employees.") Republicans also insisted that there was a high correlation between education, religion, and hard work—the values of the Protestant ethic—and Republican votes. "Where free schools are regarded as a nuisance," declared the Chicago *Democratic Press* after Buchanan's defeat of Frémont, "where religion is least honored, and lazy unthrift is the rule, there Buchanan has received his strongest support." And an Iowa Republican, comparing the election returns with census data on education, concluded that wherever free schools were most common, the Democrats were in the minority. The image which Republicans had of their party was vividly summarized by the Springfield *Republican:*

Who form the strength of this party? Precisely those who would most likely be expected to—the great middling-interest class. The highest class, aristocratically associated and affiliated, timid, afraid of change, . . . and the lowest class . . . those are the forces arrayed against Republicanism as a whole. . . . Those who work with their hands, who live and act independently, who hold the stakes of home and family, of farm and workshop, of education and freedom—these as a mass are enrolled in the Republican ranks. They form the very heart of the nation, as opposed to the two extremes of aristocracy and ignorance. . . .

Although a great deal of work needs to be done before the social basis of the ante-bellum political parties can be established with precision, it is safe to say that the Republicans were weakest in the large cities and strong in the North's rural areas and small towns. A Pennsylvania Congressman described his district—"the most intensely Republican one of the State"—as follows:

We find it densely populated, mainly with a rural people. Thickly planted, each on its own few acres we behold the unpretentious, but neat and comfortable dwellings of free laboring farmers, with as many tradesmen, manufacturers, and mechanics, mostly located in the villages, as the wants of the region require.

But although Republicans celebrated the rural virtues, they left more than a little room for those "tradesmen, manufacturers, and mechanics . . . located in the villages." They recognized that economic development was bound to result in an increase in the urban population, and that a growing nation needed artisans, craftsmen, and capitalists as much as farmers. John Bigelow of the New York *Evening Post* pointed out at the height of the Panic of 1857 that it was preposterous to urge the poor to go from urban centers to the country, because there were as many opportunities for social advancement in industry and commercial towns as on the farm. Indeed, Bigelow predicted that the independent yeoman would rapidly lose ground to the large-scale capitalist farmer, and he urged the urban poor to stick to "mechanic arts," rather than going into agriculture.

Few Republicans were as pessimistic as Bigelow about the prospects for the family farm, but most were firm advocates of economic development. As Leo Marx points out, Americans eagerly embraced the new technology of their expanding capitalist economy, and the western states cried out for railroads and industry. "Industry," said the Indianapolis *Journal,* "is as essential to the development of a virtuous community as education," and the Chicago *Press and Tribune* declared that the western economy was too dependent on agriculture, and needed manufactures for a balanced economic order. Many western Republicans who supported a protective tariff in the late 1850's had just this view in mind. One Iowa Congressman said he favored protection because he wanted to see the abundant water power of his state "applied to mechanical use. I want to see manufactures spring up there . . . [and] machinery be put up and set in motion throughout every beautiful valley of the State."

Republicans therefore accepted the growth of industry as one part of the nation's economic development, and in the 1850's they took a broad view of the power of the federal government to aid in economic growth, supporting such measures as the tariff, homesteads, and internal improvements. But they also believed that industrial development should take place within the context of the society with which they were familiar, and they emphatically rejected the idea that industrialization and the rise of great cities and large factories necessarily went hand in hand. The idea that the North could remain a society of family farms and small towns, while still experiencing the benefits of industrialization, was put forward most clearly by Henry C. Carey, the Pennsylvania economist. Carey insisted that industrialization would lead to an increase, not a decline, in economic opportunity for the laborer, for it would create a balanced, diversified economy in which many different enterprises competed for the services of labor and thus drove wages upward. Carey's advocacy of the protective tariff was based on precisely this premise—that the growth of industry was essential to the betterment of the worker, for "where all are farmers, there can be no competition for the purchase of labor." His ideal was a decentralized economy, centered on the small town, in which artisans, farmers, and small factories all served the needs of a small regional economy. One of his associates, a Pennsylvania Congressman, explained that the aim of protection was not to build up large-scale industries, but to "locate communities around an industrial point." Carey believed that the producer and the consumer should exist side by side, and that long-range transportation—either of western food to the East, or of manufactured goods from Europe or from the East westward—was in large degree a waste of labor and money. "The *nearer* the grist-mill is to the farm," he wrote, "the less will be the labor required for converting wheat into flour, . . . the *nearer* [the farmer] can bring the hatter, the shoemaker, and the tailor, the maker of ploughs and harrows, the less will be the loss in labor in exchanging his wheat for their commodities."

Carey shared the farmer's suspicion of the nation's great commercial centers, which, he wrote, profited from the labor of others, "while producing nothing themselves." He envisioned a society of "little towns and cities," each a local center of manufacturing, serving the surrounding countryside, and providing a market for its industrial produce. The economy of New England approximated his idea most closely, although he and other Republicans were disturbed by the increasing concentration of industry there. One of his economic disciples wrote that he would like to see the large amount of machinery concentrated in the city of Lowell "divided among twenty or thirty little towns."

Of course, Carey's ideas were in a sense romantic, for at the same time that he extolled the virtues of the "little towns and cities" of the North and urged a regional, locally oriented economy, the nation was moving toward an increasingly centralized industrialism and a national market. Yet in Carey's writings we can see the optimism and self-confidence of northern society. For his image for the nation's future involved no fundamental social reorganization—it was basically an extension of the northern present as he saw it. Tocqueville had observed that Americans had a "lively faith in human perfectibility," and that they thought of society as "a body progressing," rather than as a static structure. But in the Republican conception of progress, the North would retain the social order of the 1850's, while making the distribution of income even more equitable, and social mobility even more accessible, through continuing economic development.

The contradictions and ambiguities of the free labor ideology, the tension between its conservative aspects and its stress on equality of opportunity and an open society, reflected the world view of the northern middle class. If the social outlook of the Republican party was in many ways conservative, it was not because it defended privilege but because Republicans were satisfied with the economic and social order they perceived in the North. In post-war years, the same cult of the self-made man and of economic success would come to be a justification of every action and privilege of the business class, but in the antebellum world of the Republicans, the promise of economic advancement implied not the rise of big business but the guarantee of mobility to the laborer. Many Republicans insisted that equality of rights and opportunities was a cardinal principle of their party; Seward, for example, stressed that the Republicans stood for "one idea . . . the idea of equality—the equality of all men before human tribunals and human laws." And Lincoln summarized the egalitarian aspects of the free labor outlook when he declared, "In due time the weights should be lifted from the shoulders of all men . . . *all* should have an equal chance."

To the self-confident society of the North, economic development, increasing social mobility, and the spread of democratic institutions were all interrelated parts of nineteenth century "progress." Each step in the progress of civilization, said Henry Carey, voicing his characteristic optimism, "is marked by a tendency to equality of physical and intellectual condition, and to the general ownership of wealth." Horace Greeley predicted that the age which had witnessed the invention of railroads, telegraphs, and other marvels could not depart "without having effected or witnessed a vast change for the better, alike in the moral and the physical condition of mankind." The important point was that material and moral developments were but two sides of the same coin. "Good roads and bridges," wrote the New York *Tribune,* "are as necessary an ingredient to the spread of intelligence, social intercourse, and improvement in population, as schools and churches." An Indiana Republican Congressman declared on the eve of the Civil War that throughout the world, manufactures and commerce were "the missionaries of freedom," and William Henry Seward agreed that "popular government follows in the track of the steam-engine and the telegraph." It was but a short step, and one which Republicans took almost unanimously, to the view that for a society as for individuals, economic progress was a measure of moral worth. As Henry Adams later recalled, he was taught in his youth that "bad roads meant bad morals." On this basis, northern society was eminently successful. But when Republicans turned their gaze southward, they encountered a society that seemed to violate all the cherished values of the free labor ideology, and seemed to pose a threat to the very survival of what Republicans called their "free-labor civilization."

24

"GREASERS" IN THE DIGGINGS: CALIFORNIANS AND SONORANS UNDER ATTACK

LEONARD M. PITT

The American victory in the Mexican War of 1846–1848 brought to the United States those territories which were to become Texas, Arizona, New Mexico, and California. The American victory also raised the question of the status of the Mexican and native-born inhabitants of these territories. Were they to retain their lands? Were they to have the same rights as citizens of the United States? Nowhere was this question more sharply posed than in California where descendents of the Spanish conquistadores had been living for three centuries. These native-born Californios composed the elite of Spanish California, owning huge haciendas and holding the reins of power in the territory. With the end of the Mexican War there was little sign that the power of the Californios would be significantly diminished.

Then, in the same year that the war ended, gold was discovered in the Sierra Nevada. As news of the unprecedented scale of the discovery and the ease with which it could be mined reached the outside world, thousands of Americans, Mexicans, and Europeans flocked to the California "Mother Lode" in search of quick fortunes. As Leonard Pitt shows in this essay, the California gold rush brought forth some of the worst of American traits. From the beginning American miners ignored the Californios' hereditary claims to the land and through intimidation and force drove them from the gold fields. They offered the same treatment to Mexican and European prospectors who dared to encroach upon "their" claims. This rampant nativism of the early years did not diminish once statehood was declared in 1850; instead, prejudicial laws were written onto the books by a legislature in which only white Americans were represented. It was only when groups defined as "outsiders" began to offer armed resistance to these attacks that more moderate forces prevailed in early California.

Do you find any parallels in the racial attitudes expressed in the California gold rush and those displayed in the Cherokee removals described by Mary Young in Reading 18?

Why did the Spaniards and Mexicans fail to discover gold before 1848? What would have happened to them had they done so? These are two of the "iffiest" questions in all of California history.

The Mexicans had, in fact, discovered minor deposits of gold in southern California more than a decade prior to the historic Coloma discovery, but they did miss the big find in the Sierra. The causes of their oversight include a fear of Indian attack in the interior and a decision to hug the coast for protection; no population pressure ever

From Leonard M. Pitt, *The Californios: A Social History of the Spanish-speaking Californians, 1846–1890* (Berkeley: University of California Press, 1966), pp. 48–68. © 1966 The Regents of the University of California, used by permission of the University of California Press.

drove them inward. The Spanish tradition of looking for signs of *oro* among the Indians, as in Hernán Cortés' conquest of the Aztecs, also played a role, although a negative one, for the California Indians did not manipulate gold. Another cause may have been that the contentment of rancho life after 1834 had sapped the rancheros' energy necessary to explore new territory. Or perhaps the trouble was, simply, bad luck: Captain Gabriel Moraga's forty-six expeditions before 1820 had brought him near, if not directly atop, the Mother Lode, yet no gleam caught his eye. The Spanish Americans generally did not want for daring as explorers or for skill as miners; centuries of experience in both had equipped them ideally for the fateful discovery they somehow failed to make.

As to what might have been their history had they chanced upon the Sierra gold, the possibilities are numerous. They range from the attainment of genuine cultural maturity and political independence to an even more crushing defeat than the one they received after 1849. Perhaps California would have become one of the most populous and heavily defended places in the Spanish Empire or in the Mexican Republic. The Californios might have had genuine Mexican military support in a war with the Yankees, and thus also a better treaty settlement. Conquest by a European power would not have been entirely out of the question either. The answer, of course, depends upon *when* one supposes the gold to have been discovered: the earlier the better for the Californios, from the standpoint of the growth of Yankee expansionism in the 1840's. One suspects, however, that Manifest Destiny somehow was bound to triumph along the Pacific Coast and eventually convert California into a Yankee province.

The Californios themselves scarcely ever engaged in such ruminations, for they were not a people to pine over lost opportunities and were faced with realities that gave them enough food for thought. The discovery of gold in 1848 made an enormous impact on them—the greatest in their brief experience: it brought them riches, for one thing; it threw them together with other

Latin Americans, for another; and, most important, it opened them to full-scale Yankee penetration and conquest.

As news of the discovery spread in 1848, Californios speedily converged on the Sierra from all directions and, in a sense, made up for lost time. The experience of the Angeleños was typical. With Don Antonio Coronel taking on the function of patrón, the thirty Californios, Sonorans, and Indian servants had good luck from the outset. They immediately enticed some mountain tribesmen to accept baubles in exchange for gold nuggets and, after spying out the Indians' trove and plying them with more trinkets, they obtained their digging labor into the bargain. In one day Antonio himself ended up with 45 ounces of gold; Dolores Sepúlveda found a 12-ounce nugget; and Señor Valdez discovered a boulder buried only 3 feet down which had once blocked the flow of an ancient alluvial stream and produced a towelful of nuggets in a short time. He sold his claim to Lorenzo Soto, who took out a whopping 52 pounds of gold in eight days and then sold it to Señor Machado, who also became rich. Even a Sonoran servant became fabulously wealthy overnight.

In all, about 1,300 native Californians mined gold in 1848, the year of the bonanzas. If they had missed the opportunity to discover Sierra gold in the past, they did not do so now; nearness to the placers gave them the head start on the thousands of prospectors still getting their wits together for the voyage halfway around the world. The Californios had additional advantages in knowing precisely where and how to find gold and in gladly pooling their resources and dividing their labor. As a result, the organized Californians, though less numerous than the 4,000 individualistic Yankees in the mines that year, probably extracted as much gold as they. Coronel, a struggling Mexican schoolteacher, had pocketed enough gold to become a prominent landowner, viticulturist, and community leader. He and many other Californios resolved to make a second expedition the next year. They dismissed the news that a few Californios had been harried from their claims by fist-swinging Oregon Yankees, who refused to acknowledge that the Treaty of Guadalupe Hidalgo granted some Mexicans full citizenship: in 1848 "everything ended peacefully."

In the year that followed, the story changed drastically. Coronel's return trip to the mines began badly, with a near-fatal brawl in a Sonoma saloon. One day he and *compadre* Juan Padilla were waiting for the wet January weather to clear, when a former Bear Flagger began to bully Padilla for having served as Bernardo García's henchman in the wartime atrocity against Cowie and Fowler. Padilla insisted that the charge was a lie, and the American replied with an assault. After a severe beating, Padilla lay in an upstairs room, hovering near death for several weeks, while below his accuser continued to threaten his life. Only Coronel's good reputation and the intercession of friendly Americans restrained the former Bear Flagger.

After nursing his friend back to life, Coronel returned to the Sierra. He fell in among Chileans, Mexicans, and Germans doing well at dry diggings until confronted with posters declaring that foreigners had no right to be there and must leave the mines at once; resistance would be met by force. Although this threat never materialized, excitement mounted. In a nearby camp, a Mexican gambler's tent had been raided, and some Yankees accused five foreigners of stealing 5 pounds of gold. Coronel's associates doubled the accusation against at least one apparently honorable man and raised 5 pounds of gold to offer as ransom. Coronel conferred with a Yankee delegation and gave them the gold. The delegates then retired to consider the offer but never reemerged from the drunken and agitated crowd, which by then numbered into the hundreds. The money did no good; all five prisoners were convicted and flogged at once, and two of them, a Frenchman and a Chilean, were charged with a previous murder and robbery. Guilty or not, the pair scarcely understood enough of the proceedings to reply to the accusations. When Coronel next saw them they were standing in a cart, lashed together back to back and pinned with a note warning away defenders such as might come from Coronel's

camp. A horse then jolted the cart from under the men, and California had witnessed its first lynching. That incident resulted, Coronel thought, from a declining gold supply and the Yankees' increasing jealousy of successful Spanish Americans.

As quickly as possible Don Antonio led his group away from the newly named "Hangtown," and resettled in the remote northern mines. But even there a hundred gringos appeared with the gruff announcement that the entire riverbed belonged exclusively to Americans who would tolerate no foreigners. Furious, some of Coronel's people who had reached the limit of their endurance planned armed resistance, even at the cost of their lives, but Coronel held back and sadly announced, "For me gold mining is finished."

By July many other Californios had cause to echo Coronel's words. As the only true native-born citizens they did have a legitimate place in the mines, yet they knew no way to convince 100,000 hostile strangers of this truth. Fisticuffs or hand combat simply was not the Californians' style. Consequently, one of them carried into the field of combat a safe-conduct pass, signed by the army's secretary of state, which certified him as a bona fide citizen deserving of every right and privilege, of every lawful aid and protection. What good the pass did is not recorded, but the attacks mounted. For most Californios, the best answer was to go home and stay there: "Don't go to the mines on any account," one *paisano* advised another. Out of pride, which prevented them from being converted into aliens by Yankee rogues and upstarts, few Californians ventured back into the maelstrom after 1849.

Musing over the gold rush from a safe distance, the Californians once more concluded that outsiders were, by and large, despicable. Mariano Vallejo said of the forty-niners without sparing any nationality, "The good ones were few and the wicked many." Hugo Reid ticked off the list of troublemakers:

> . . . vagabonds from every quarter of the globe. Scoundrels from nowhere, rascals from Oregon, pickpockets from New York, accomplished gentle-

men from Europe, interlopers from Lima and Chile, Mexican thieves, gamblers of no particular spot, and assassins manufactured in Hell for the expressed purpose of converting highways and biways into theatres of blood; then, last but not least, Judge Lynch with his thousand arms, thousand sightless eyes, and five-hundred lying tongues.

The Californians now simply reverted to their customary circular logic, which held that evil came from outsiders, that outsiders were mostly evil, and that evil mothered evil. In no other way could they explain the ugly behavior of so many people, especially Americanos.

After a century of slow population growth, during which the arrival of twenty-five cholos or fifty Americans seemed a momentous occasion, suddenly and without warning California faced one of the swiftest, largest, and most varied folk migrations of all time. More newcomers now arrived each day in California than had formerly come in a decade. Briefly told, the story of the Californians in the gold rush is their encounter with 100,000 newcomers in the single year of 1849—80,000 Yankees, 8,000 Mexicans, 5,000 South Americans, and several thousand miscellaneous Europeans—and with numbers that swelled to a quarter million by 1852. Even assuming the goodwill of every last one of these strangers, they outnumbered the Californians ten and fifteen times over and reduced them to feelings of insignificance.

It is the destiny of ethnic groups in the United States to be thrown together with people of "their own kind" whom they neither know nor particularly like—perhaps even despise. This was the lot of the Californios in 1849, with the massive migration of Latin Americans. It was bad enough that by 1850 the Mexican cholos outnumbered the 15,000 Californios; even worse, angry Yankees simply refused to recognize any real distinctions between Latin Americans. Whether from California, Chile, Peru, or Mexico, whether residents of twenty years' standing or immigrants of one week, all the Spanish-speaking were lumped together as "interlopers" and "greasers." In this

molding, the Californians, who had always kept aloof from cholos and earlier had won some grudging respect from the Yankees, lost most heavily. Their reputation as a people more heroic, handsome, and civilized than other "Spaniards" now dissolved. Their proximity to the greasers between 1849 and 1852 put them in actual jeopardy of their lives. In essence then, the Latin-American immigrants were a sort of catalyst whose presence caused the sudden and permanent dissolution of the social elements.

The biggest waves of Latin Americans came from Chile and northern Mexico. The Chileans excelled in baking and bricklaying and other skills and thus found themselves in especially great demand in California. They settled down at the foot of San Francisco's Telegraph Hill, in a place called "Little Chile," or went into the mines to dig, until expelled by the Yankees.

Even more prominent and numerous were the northern Mexicans. Distinguishable from other Latin Americans by their billowy white pantaloons, broad sandals, and sombreros, the "Sonoranians" or "Sonorans," as the Yankees called them, first entered the Sierra late in 1848, after either trudging across the Colorado deserts or sailing via Mazatlán. Some had sojourned in California earlier; in 1842, well before the advent of James Marshall, a Sonoran had discovered gold near San Fernando Mission. More visibly mestizo, less consciously Spanish than the Californians, they seemed "primitive" by local standards. Apache raiders kept them from their own mines and pastures, so that the Sonorans pounced on the California discovery as a panacea. The northern Mexican patróns themselves encouraged the migration of the peons by sponsoring expeditions of twenty or thirty underlings at a time, giving them full upkeep in return for half of their gold findings in California. The migration included so broad a spectrum of the population of Sonora and Sinaloa and was so large and continuous throughout 1850, that it compelled the governors of northern Mexico to admonish repeatedly about the dangers of life on gringo soil.

The Sonorans came on swiftly, heedless of any warnings, knowing that they had vital services to offer California—as prospectors and hired hands, as supply merchants and mule skinners, also as monte gamblers and prostitutes. The leading merchants of Altar and Horcasitas, Sonoran towns near the international boundary, stripped their shelves in the spring of 1849, loaded up every available pack animal, and scurried for the mines. There they sold everything they had brought, dug some gold, and shortly left their followers to return to Sonora for new stock or for quick investment in Mexican securities—much of this accomplished before most of the Yankee Argonauts had even arrived.

Sonorans gravitated mainly toward the San Joaquin River tributaries, called the "southern mines" or "dry diggings," especially near a spot named in their honor, Sonora. Here they introduced Yankees to many of the rudimentary mining techniques that typified the early gold rush era. Sonorans somehow could probe the topsoil with knives and bring up nuggets, or work the *batea* (pan) to great advantage. Where water was scarce and quartz plentiful, as in the southern mines, they had the endurance to sit for hours and winnow dirt in their serapes, sometimes using their own gargantuan breath if the wind died down. They could also improvise the *arastra* (mill), consisting of a mule harnessed to a long spoke treading in a circle and grinding ore under a heavy, flat boulder. Others eventually caught on to those techniques and machines and later surpassed them, but the Sonorans' sixth sense for finding gold and their willingness to endure physical hardship gave them great advantages. Talent made them conspicuously "lucky" —and, therefore,—subject to attack by jealous Yankees.

Although the Californios quietly withdrew from the Sierra and left the field to the Mexicans and the Yankees, the scene in the mines deserved their closest attention. For, the mines became the staging ground for widespread attacks on their ranchos and pueblos, the rehearsal place for broad-scale assaults on the Spanish-speaking.

The problem of precisely how to react to the remaining "Spaniards" made the Yankees squirm. They shifted from violence to legislation, from legislation to litigation, and back again to violence. Some wished to exploit, others to expel, and still others to control the Latin Americans. On occasion, some Yankees even proposed allowing them completely free access to the mines.

It would have given small comfort to Coronel, Vallejo, Reid, and other Californios to learn that good and decent men had inspired the purge trials of the winter and spring of 1849. Yet, in truth, a great deal of antiforeigner agitation originated from the most reputable new citizens—army officers, lawyers, merchants, clergy, and public officials. It is a fact that the first organized and officially sanctioned outburst against Spanish Americans came from three hundred "white-collar" Yankees. While stranded in Panama in January, 1849, on their way to San Francisco, they heard distressing rumors that "foreign plunderers" from all over the Pacific littoral had already siphoned off $4 million worth of gold in California; how much remained for "true citizens" thus was problematic. On a slight provocation, the Yankees called a public meeting to deal sternly with the interlopers. No less a dignitary than the justice of the Oregon Territory presided over the gathering, and in the background hovered General Persifor F. Smith, traveling to Monterey to take charge of the army. Smith drafted a circular declaring that, in California, he would "consider everyone who is not a citizen of the United States, who enters upon public land and digs for gold as a trespasser." This declaration won him three hundred vows of support.

The miners, who twice confronted Coronel with the charge that "foreigners" had "no right" to dig gold, were simply enforcing Smith's hastily improvised "doctrine of trespass." In April, vigilantes at Sutter's Mill drove away masses of Chileans, Mexicans, and Peruvians; and during a similar purge along the Sacramento River on the Fourth of July lives were lost, property was destroyed, and foreigners' goods were sold at auction. More than a thousand victims, mainly Chileans, came pouring down into San Francisco shortly afterward, many of them embarking for home. "General Smith is blamed by everyone as the sole cause of the outrage."

Smith beat a hasty retreat when he discovered that the consequences of the plunderers' activities had been grossly overrated: gold was still plentiful, and most of the dust already exported from California had found its way into the hands of American supply merchants. His successor, Brigadier General Bennett Riley, rode through the mines trying to undo some of the damage caused by the doctrine of trespass by telling Americans that technically all diggers were guests on government land, and that thereafter none should be denied access to its bounty.

Resentment against the "greasers" mounted, however, a product of deep and abiding feelings of nationalism, racism, and despair over the debasement of free labor. The nationalism was partly a hangover from the war. Some men imagined seeing whole battalions, armed to the teeth . . . moving through the heart of Mexico . . . gotten up by the great capitalists and friends of Santa Anna . . . rising in one solid mass whose cry is 'California's recovery or death!' " Yankee veterans unhappy in the diggings and nostalgic for army comradery saw in the coming of the "greasers" the pretext for a "muss," whether for mayhem or for merriment. Northern Europeans—the Irish in particular—and Australians became implacable foes of the Spanish Americans, more so perhaps than many native-born citizens of the United States. The notorious San Francisco gang, the "Hounds," for example, which was staffed by former New York Volunteers and Australians, took particular delight in attacking the Chileans who came to San Francisco after fleeing enemies in the mountains.

The forty-niner's xenophobia also stemmed from fear of unfair economic competition. Back home, one could normally see who became rich, how rich, and by what means; a community could use institutional means to regulate the process and keep it fair. But on the periphery of civilization, controls broke down: men sometimes prospered by unfair means; the population upsurge, the ceaseless shuffling of men from camp to camp, and their scrambling for the top of the social

ladder defied control by ordinary methods. Thus the forty-niner improvised new devices, even vigilante justice.

Fear of economic competition had some basis in reality. Sonoran peddlers marched into the mines and sold 10,000 pack mules in three years, thereby depressing the prices of mules (from $500 to $150 a head in a matter of weeks) and of freight rates (from $75 to $7 per hundredweight in two months). This reversal of fortunes evoked no complaint from the Yankee miners, who could buy onions, potatoes, and other supplies all the more cheaply and had come to associate Mexican mule bells with savory cooking odors and a few cheap comforts of life; but it brought, in 1850, a pained outcry from Stockton entrepreneurs, who sought mass expulsion of their business rivals. Moreover, when the Mexicans set to work as peons in the employ of their patróns, they did make themselves the target of the prospectors. Miners who began muttering against the Mexicans and plotting violence felt keenly conscious that the Spanish Americans were cheapening the value of labor.

The treatment of immigrant Spanish Americans in the mines hinged also on the slavery question. They came into California precisely when the Yankees felt most irritated on this score and could see most clearly the parallels between Negroes and their masters, on the one hand, and peon and patróns, on the other. Yankee prospectors ejected from the mines with equal vigor any combination of bondsmen and masters. In July a prominent Texan, Thomas Jefferson Green, and his slaves were unceremoniously tossed out of Rose Bar on the Yuba River. The prospectors put into effect a local code prohibiting the mining operations of all master-servant teams, whatever their relationship. Three months later this provision cost the life of a Chilean and led to the ear cropping and whipping of Chileans and Mexicans who tried to oppose it.

With California's entry into the Union as a free state, the plight of the Spanish Americans in the mines worsened momentarily. Their protagonists proclaimed that, if slaves were prohibited from the mines, then so should be the "refuse population from Chile, Peru and Mexico and other parts of the world [who are] . . . as bad as any of the free negroes of the North, or the worst slaves of the South." The apparent inconsistency in immigration policy annoyed both the friends and the enemies of slavery. In the first California legislature, nativists freely categorized the Pacific immigrants as a race whose morality and intelligence stood "but one degree above the beasts of the field." The State Assembly, in no uncertain terms (by a vote of twenty-two to two), asked Congress to bar from the mines all persons of foreign birth, *even* naturalized citizens.

This extreme nativism soon brought about its own backlash. A fraction of the entrepreneurs in the mines began to worry less about the alleged dangers of unlimited immigration or of competition from "foreign capitalists" and more about the "disgregated, fractioned, broken up" techniques of mining; more about the possibilities of investing capital and hiring Mexican laborers, and less about expelling the interlopers. Usually outshouted at public meetings and outvoted in the legislature, this Yankee faction nonetheless had on its side the logic of economy and the ear of a few outspoken politicians who began a campaign to exploit, rather than exclude, aliens.

Advocates of this new position were most numerous and effective in the southern mines. There, the Sonorans evicted from the northern placers late in 1849 found relative safety, hiring themselves out to Yankees who maintained loaded pistols, "cool eyes . . . [and] steady nerves" against possible opposition by other Yankees. The Yankee patróns especially appreciated the Sonorans' skill and willingness to work for a daily wage of a dollar in food and a fraction of gold. "Greasers" worked speedily, when prompted, although work itself—and riches or savings—bored them, and gambling, drinking, dancing, and indolence cut down their work time. The argument ran as follows: The American, "with all his impatience of control, his impetuous temperament, his ambitions and yearning will . . . [never] be content to deny himself the pleasure of civilized life in the states for the sake of $4.00 to $3.00 per day, to develop the resources of the dry

diggings"; the Mexican, on the other hand, is "milder in spirit, more contented to endure more willing to suffer, more weak spirited, if you please," but for those very reasons he is the man for the job. Although a mere "hewer of wood and drawer of water," he would unlock California's wealth much as the Negro had done in the South. American freight shippers at the same time learned that the Mexican *arrieros* (mule skinners) were the most reliable of hired hands—skillful, proud of their work, and sure to get the pack train through the worst blizzard, over the toughest mountain trail. A genuine paternal fondness sometimes linked the arriero and his new Yankee patrón.

Yankee tradesmen of the southern mines came to see the Spanish Americans as particularly good customers. It occurred to them that, in contrast with the stingy Yankee who saved his money and sent it home, the Latin American invariably wanted to take home goods, not money; he spent all he had. Just as the Spaniard's eccentric work habits could be turned to the operator's profit, so could his spendthrift tendencies be turned to the advantage of the merchant. General Riley discovered that "Americans, by their superior intelligence and shrewdness in business, generally contrived to turn to their own benefit the earnings of Mexicans, Chileans and Peruvians."

The tension between Yankee and Latin-American miners climaxed in the Foreign Miners' Tax Law of 1850, one of the most original if benighted laws ever passed in a California legislature.

Thomas Jefferson Green, its author, boasted that he personally could "maintain a better stomach at the killing of a Mexican" than at the crushing of a body louse. A Texan, he had come to this opinion in a Mexican prison while brooding over the failure of a filibustering expedition. After a harrowing escape from the prison, Green published an account of his exploits, together with a tirade against all things Mexican (and Negro) and a proposal that the United States swallow up all of Mexico. He had come to California in the hope of using slaves to plant cotton, although the episode at the Yuba River smashed that idea completely. Because he had served in three Southern legislatures, however, and had a good reputation among Southerners, he easily won election as state senator from Sacramento.

Green had legendary powers of persuasion, even over men who disliked his social ideals. It was he who always gained adjournment of the California Senate to "more comfortable surroundings"—namely, his own bar—and thus earned his colleagues the sobriquet, "Legislature of the Thousand Drinks." In his tax bill—a kind of personal rejoinder to the men who had expelled him from Rose Bar for attempting to use Negro bondsmen—he proposed to issue mining permits to foreigners at a cost of $20 monthly (he later reduced it to $16). This tax, he thought, would bolster the bankrupt state treasury by $200,000 each month and would also encourage Yankee operators to buy licenses for their operatives, and to employ them "at a fair rate . . . until the labor is performed according to contract." The law would delight Americans no end and discourage mob action, or what Green grandly called "the interruption of the stronger power which is in the people." This possibility so neatly wrapped up all the nagging problems of labor competition, foreign monopolies, taxation, bondage, immigration, and mob violence that the Assembly passed it nineteen to four and the Senate seven to four; the latter house, by a vote of eleven to two, also gave Green a special commendation for originating so "splendid" a plan.

Although later condemned as an intemperate and malicious act, "conceived in drink and brought forth in jollity," the Foreign Miners' Tax Law actually had quite sober intentions. Its main difficulty was that instead of flatly trying to either exploit, expel, or give free rein to the foreign-born, it tried to straddle the issue. It promised something for everybody: the prospector would be able to evict all "unprotected" aliens, the operator would be able to undercut the "agents of foreign bankers" who sponsored immigration, the government would receive money to pay its bills (among them, the expense vouchers of the legislature), the collectors would make a commission of $3 on each permit sold, and the immigrants themselves could claim the protection of the law if they paid their tax. On the face of it, one could hardly have asked for a more equitable solution.

Yet the Foreign Miners' Tax Law hardly worked that way at all. In Tuolumne County, where most of the potential taxpayers were entrenched, the impost caused outright defiance. Printed posters immediately denounced the tax and implored its intended victims to "put a bridle in the mouths of that horde who call themselves citizens of the United States, thereby profaning that country." Two French radicals, schooled in the Revolution of 1848, engineered a rebellion and for its success needed the cooperation of the Mexicans. Although the Mexicans were gun-shy, they nevertheless went to tell the Yankees what was on the mind of all non-Yankees. An impressive array of 4,000 "aliens"—mostly Mexicans—congregated on the outskirts of Sonora on Sunday, May 19, to consider proper action against the law, which was to take effect the next day. To the collector's face the delegation flatly declared that the foreign-born might pay $3 or even $5 monthly, but not $20—a token sum for protection against rowdies, but not an entire fortune monthly. When the collector held his ground and demanded the full amount, most foreigners fled the town. One remaining Mexican threatened the sheriff, or so it seemed to the bystander who killed him with a bowie knife. Local officials prohibited merchants from selling supplies to any foreign miners and spread an alarm to nearby camps to call up reinforcements for the forthcoming "war" at the county seat.

One hundred and fifty war veterans promptly stopped work at Mormon Gulch, selected a captain, put on the remains of their uniforms, and, with regimental colors high, marched to Sonora for action. Sonora received them warmly with fulsome speeches, food, and free liquor. By nightfall the town seethed with inevitable rumors of Mexican incendiarism, assassination, and massacre. Officers posted pickets, stored weapons, and briefed the men for the next day's action. Sonora was under martial law.

Next morning, into the diggings marched four

hundred Americans—a moving "engine of terror"—heading for Columbia Camp, the foreigners' headquarters. They collected tax money from a few affluent aliens and chased the rest away, with a warning to vacate the mines. One trooper recalls seeing "men, women and children—all packed up and moving, bag and baggage. Tents were being pulled down, houses and hovels gutted of their contents; mules, horses and jackasses were being hastily packed, while crowds were already in full retreat." The posse finally arrested the two "hot-headed Frenchmen. . . . of the red republican order," who started everything, fined them $5 for "treason," and dismissed them. Thus ended the "muss." The men liquored up for the road, hoisted the Stars and Stripes to the top of a pine tree, fired off a salute, and headed for home. Next day, about five hundred French and German forty-eighters stormed into Sonora shouting revolutionary slogans and vowing to liberate the Frenchmen. Upon hearing that the pair had been freed, the would-be liberators dispersed sheepishly.

Sonora had just about recovered from the excitement of this "French Revolution" when a new attack broke over the heads of the Spanish-speaking. A series of robberies and violent deaths came to light near town in which the victims were Yankees and the murder weapons *riatas;* this made it easy to blame "foreigners of Spanish-American origin." Next, a Sonoran and his three Yaqui Indian retainers were caught burning two bodies and would have been lynched, but for the timely intervention of the justice of the peace and the sheriff, who remanded the prisoners to the district court. On the morning of the court trial (July 15), the Mormon Gulch veterans again descended on Sonora in military order and spoiling for action. Informed that the prisoners might be hirelings of a "notorious Mexican chief" at Green Flat, they marched there, rounded up practically every male in sight, herded them back to Sonora, and literally corralled them for safekeeping overnight. In the morning, the justice of the peace investigated the "caze of murther against 110 Greasers . . . captured by 80 brave Americans," but, having determined that the Mexicans were

innocent newcomers, he let them go. After a momentary riot scene in the courtroom, the Sonoran, on bended knees, convinced the jury that he and his Indians had killed no one but had accidentally discovered the bodies and were trying to dispose of them according to Yaqui burial custom. The crowd dispersed grudgingly.

Unhappily, another gruesome death, uncovered the very next day, again made Sonora the prey of every rumor incriminating Latin Americans. Since all previous measures had failed to stop the atrocities, it was proposed to cleanse the hillsides thoroughly of every Spanish American with the least tinge of "evil." The present emergency demanded that "all Mexicans should suffer for a few." The "better element" of Yankees in the southern mines, who normally recoiled from drastic measures, now feared that their territory was fast acquiring the reputation of a bandit refuge, which was bad for business, and felt impelled to join the broadside attack. Outshouting one dissenting voice, a large public meeting in Sonora voted to force all foreigners to deposit their arms with Americans and apply for permits of good conduct. All Latin Americans, except "respectable characters," were given fifteen days in which to depart. The Mormon Gulch veterans set to work enforcing these dicta with gusto.

The screening plan to expel the "obnoxious" Spanish Americans worked well. It reduced the danger of *bandido* attack and frightened off economic rivals. Between May and August, from five to fifteen thousand foreign-born diggers scattered from the southern mines. Mexicans went elsewhere looking for surcease of trouble but were dogged everywhere; eventually, they came streaming out of the Sierra, some showing signs of "pinching want." Even those who paid the extortionate $20 found that it bought very little protection, for if the collector neglected his monthly rounds their certificates lapsed, and if the Americans of one county refused to honor permits bought in another, the Spanish-speaking had little recourse but to leave. They knew that they alone of all foreign miners were being subjected to the tax: when they taunted the collectors to tax Irishmen, Frenchmen, and other Europeans they received no satisfactory reply. Masqueraders posing as collectors came into Mexican camps, solemnly tore up valid permits, and demanded money for new ones; when rebuffed, they auctioned off the victim's dirt and installed in his claim a "loyal citizen." One imposter carried off his charade so well at Don Pedro's Bar that he convinced a posse to help him chase away forty peons and their patrón and killed two Mexicans in the action, before his identity was uncovered.

Even when seeking an escape from California, Mexicans found the Americans lying in wait for them. On the Colorado River, a United States Army lieutenant had express orders "to make all Sonorans passing out of California with gold, pay a duty . . . and for my trouble, to put the whole of it in my pocket." A troop of California militiamen blandly confiscated from homebound Sonorans more than a hundred "stolen" mules and horses, ignoring the brand marks, proving ownership and compelling the Mexicans to walk 300 miles, including 100 miles across desert.

In the preceding year misunderstanding, fear, and hatred had created an atmosphere so hostile to "Sonorans" as to sanction fraud and murder. Nonetheless, the argument for both protecting and exploiting the foreign miners once more gathered strength. The earliest and most effective counterattack against prejudice was made by the San Francisco Vigilance Committee of 1849, which summarily expelled the "Hounds" from town and made amends to the Chileans who had been tormented by them. Thereafter many individuals took up the cause, speaking in behalf of civil law or laissez-faire competition or on grounds of simple revulsion against mob violence. Among those spokesmen were judges, editors, lawyers, a sheriff, a brigadier general, merchants, mine operators, and the French consul. Several sympathetic collectors ceased selling permits. Even the state attorney general disliked the tax so thoroughly that he refused to defend the collector prosecuted in the California Supreme Court and ignored the governor's threat to prosecute him for dereliction of duty.

Xenophobia had injured its perpetrators as

well as its victims. As Mexicans fled the southern mines in 1850, the profits of Yankee merchants plunged alarmingly. Eight-dollar crowbars in one afternoon dropped to fifty cents; a plot of land worth several thousand dollars went begging "for a few bits." Out of sheer dollars-and-cents self-interest, if nothing else, businessmen collected money, hired a lawyer to sue the local collector, and circulated a mass petition asking the governor to lower the impost to $5; all but one merchant signed the document. In July and August, after the second wave of expulsions caused retail losses as high as $10,000 a day in three southern counties, merchants who had helped expel the "evil characters" during the bandit scare became aware that *all* Mexicans were fleeing, not merely the undesirables. A crowd gathered at Georgetown, down the road from Sonora, and went on record as denouncing antiforeigner vigilantes and as supporting civil law. As a result the Stockton *Times* reported that the screening plan enforced at Mormon Gulch and elsewhere was "speedily held in contempt."

These forces had planned to persuade the governor to reduce the tax, the legislature to repeal it, or, best of all, the courts to nullify it. In the state Supreme Court they pleaded that it infringed the exclusive right of the federal government to govern federal lands and abridged the protection granted to aliens by the state constitution and by two treaties with Mexico. Neither of these arguments, however, swayed the high tribunal, which advanced a philosophy of states' rights in all matters relating to the federal government. Two Southern attorneys convinced the court that a state (1) could rightfully tax federal lands, unless specifically prohibited from doing so, and (2) had police powers to defend itself against undesirables. The court, in effect, agreed with the author of the tax act, Green, who had grandly declared that congressional inaction on the California mines had thrown the state back onto "universal laws . . . higher, greater, and stronger than the written constitution." Gratuitously, the court added that even had the law violated a treaty—which had not been demonstrated—it might still be valid, for state laws could take precedence over treaties. Thus, the Spanish Americans had unknowingly become the victims of the imponderable and pervasive sectional controversies of the day.

Notwithstanding its new judicial seal of approval, the tax was a practical failure, as even its original supporters admitted. The Mexican was not the Negro slave; California was not Texas. The governor, aware that the tax was reaping more resentment than revenue, cut the rate to $20 for four months. Even after this corrective, however, the state obtained only $30,000 instead of an expected $2,400,000. The collector in a county that had 15,000 potential taxpayers, sold only 525 permits and was so harassed on his job that he resigned. By 1851 Stockton's leading citizens had developed such loathing for the tax—"a law for the killing of children to get their fat"—that they decided to rally the entire county and lobby in the state capital to obtain its repeal. This they accomplished early in 1851.

The tax had failed to make the state wealthy, to prevent mob action, and to convert immigrants into hirelings as promised. It had eliminated the Latin Americans already in California and curtailed new immigration, a result that did not altogether fill the original bill. Now, having pushed the tax aside, the boosters of the foreign miners hoped to summon them back and make amends. The Yankees had a sudden vision that with the law gone, tens of thousands of Latin Americans would come flooding out of Mexico and Chile and the California towns and wash up into the southern mines, thus opening a new era in gold mining.

That dream failed to materialize, however, since the Spanish Americans by now mistrusted the Yankees and suspected that gold was giving out. They withdrew to Los Angeles and other villages or returned home, informing their countrymen of the dangers of venturing forth into California. Of course, small parties of Spanish Americans continued to enter the diggings, rummaging about on their own hook and staying alert to the possibility of trouble. The one lone Mexi-

can patrón who dared bring in peons in 1852 stood out so conspicuously that he became the center of an international incident. His case made the complete circuit to Mexico City, Washington, and back to California. The district attorney investigated it for the United States Secretary of War, who determined that, although the crowd of Americans who stopped the Mexican was "wholly unprincipled and deserving of punishment," Mexican nationals should seek reparations in the state courts, since the federal government took no responsibility for riots. Thereafter, no patrón was courageous or indiscreet enough to enter the mines, and the Yankee triumph over "foreign capitalists" and "slaves" was complete.

In the long view of California history, the Mexican miners represent merely a link in a long chain of migrants who reach across the "Spanish borderland." They unwittingly followed the trail blazed by the Spanish soldier Juan Bautista Anza and used later by Mexican cholos and colonists. They foreshadowed the coming of the "wetbacks" and the braceros in the twentieth century. As ever, the Mexicans met with mixed success in California, often defeat. They did find some gold, but had to fight for every ounce. That they escaped Yankee bondage was perhaps the most fortunate thing that happened to them.

The migration of the Mexican forty-niners affected the Californios in two ways: for one thing, it put the Yankees in an ugly frame of mind toward all the Spanish-speaking, including the native-born; for another, it sent the newcomers into the established old communities of California, where they fused imperceptibly with those born there. This tended to break down the old and somewhat artificial distinction between "native Californians" and "Mexicans." The fusion went on continuously thereafter.

The Mexican newcomers had, however, one major advantage over their California-born brethren; whereas they could ultimately evade the gringo enemy by returning home, the Californios, attacked on their own soil, could not.

25

A NEW LOOK AT THE GREAT DEBATES OF 1858

DON E. FEHRENBACHER

By the end of the 1850s the American political system was in crisis with both national parties, the Democrats and the Whigs, internally divided over the issue of slavery. Should slavery be abolished throughout the United States as many northerners advocated? Should it be allowed to continue and to expand into new western territories as many southerners thought? Or should it be allowed to continue in the Old South but be prohibited in the West? These were the questions that agitated the nation in this crucial decade and split the second-party system into sectional fragments.

It was against this backdrop of sectional antagonism that the famous Lincoln-Douglas debates took place in 1858. As Don E. Fehrenbacher points out in this essay, while the debates are usually seen as part of Lincoln's march to the White House, the debates themselves focused less on the two protagonists, Stephen Douglas and Abraham Lincoln, than on the positions of the Democratic and Republican parties regarding slavery. The great debates of the nineteenth century thus indicated the political system's increasing inability to accommodate the sectional conflicts that had punctuated American politics since the early nineteenth century. The real importance of the debates was not that they served as a rehearsal for Lincoln's future presidency, but that they symbolized the political deadlock of the 1850s and prefigured the coming of the Civil War.

How does Fehrenbacher's account of the Republican party's position on the slavery issue compare with that of Eric Foner in Reading 23? How does Fehrenbacher's depiction of the Republican party ideology compare with that of Foner? Do you think Foner would treat the Lincoln-Douglas debates differently?

"The great battle of the next Presidential election is now being fought in Illinois," said the Richmond *Enquirer* on August 10, 1858. This was shortly after the seven debates between Lincoln and Douglas had been announced, but eleven days before their first encounter at Ottawa. The editorial writer, unaware of the hidden prophecy in his statement, was thinking only of Douglas and the latter's enormous stake in the senatorial contest. Already facing bitter opposition from the South, the Little Giant could scarcely hope to obtain the Democratic presidential nomination if he were defeated for re-election in Illinois. On the Republican side, meanwhile, Seward appeared to have a commanding lead over other potential candidates, among whom no one had yet thought to include Lincoln.

The full significance and the irony of the Lincoln-Douglas debates was not revealed until 1860, when Fortune whimsically bestowed her generous consolation prize upon the man who had been denied the senatorship. Lincoln's elec-

Reprinted from *Prelude to Greatness: Lincoln in the 1850's* by Don E. Fehrenbacher with the permission of the publisher, Stanford University Press. © 1962 by the Board of Trustees of the Leland Stanford Junior University.

tion to the presidency rounded off the history of his dramatic rivalry with Douglas—and at the same time seriously distorted it; for the debates, although held in 1858, have been interpreted and evaluated in the light of what happened two years later. In retrospect, the tall form of Lincoln dominates the scene; Douglas, originally the star of the show, is relegated to second billing; and the hard-fought battle for a Senate seat shrinks to the proportions of a dress rehearsal. Historiography thus inverts history and makes yesterday the determinant of the day before.

The primary significance of the Lincoln-Douglas contest must indeed be sought in its consequences, but with due precaution, always, against the *post hoc* traps and other hazards that are scattered over the ground of inquiry. The House Divided speech, for example, undoubtedly contributed to Lincoln's emergence as a presidential contender; yet there is not the slightest evidence that any objective beyond the senatorship was in his mind when he drafted it. Retrospection runs riot in the assertion of Henry C. Whitney (quoted with approval by Beveridge) that "while . . . his political friends were training him for the Senate he was coaching himself for the Presidency, two years thereafter." The tendency to explain motives by consulting results, and to mistake mere sequence for cause and effect, has cast a veil of legend over a well-documented historical event. Despite all that has been written about the Lincoln-Douglas campaign of 1858, certain aspects of this familiar story can still be examined with profit.

The seven formal debates beginning on August 21 and ending on October 15 provided the ceremonial framework for a campaign that would have been unique and exciting even without them. The spectacle of a stump contest between two avowed candidates for the United States Senate—one of them already the central figure in national politics—could not fail to attract wide attention all across the country. Very often, however, the out-of-state interest was haphazard and spasmodic. Newspapers, with a few exceptions, were still limited to four pages, and local politics

had first claim upon their meager space, not to mention such events as the laying of the Atlantic cable, the championship prize fight between John Morrisey and John Heenan, the burning of the famous Crystal Palace in New York, and the dispatch of the first overland mail to California. Some editors printed frequent reports on the campaign in Illinois, while others completely ignored it. The total effect was a fragmentary national coverage which nevertheless greatly exceeded that given most state elections.

Southerners showed little interest in Lincoln as an individual. He fitted the odious stereotype of a black Republican, and nothing else mattered. It was Douglas whom the slaveholders watched intently, knowing that they would soon have to reckon with his bid for leadership of the Democratic party. The question debated extensively by Southern newspapers as the campaign in Illinois progressed was whether the South would suffer more from the re-election of a powerful renegade or from the triumph of a Republican nonentity. Many editors insisted that Douglas should be beaten whatever the cost. Others argued that in spite of his defection on the Lecompton issue he was still preferable to Lincoln. A third group washed its hands of the Illinois contest, agreeing with the Jackson *Mississippian* that the South could have no choice between a "pair of depraved, blustering, mischievous, lowdown demagogues."

Elsewhere in the nation, there was greater curiosity about Lincoln. "You are like Byron, who woke up one morning and found himself famous," wrote Charles H. Ray on July 27 from his old home in Chenango County, New York. "I have found hundreds of anxious enquirers burning to know all about the newly raised-up opponent of Douglas—his age, profession, personal appearance and qualities, etc." Lincoln, as he proved himself a match for his formidable adversary, won increasing admiration from Eastern Republicans, although Greeley and the other editors who had supported Douglas remained aloof and almost neutral. Interest in the campaign became more pronounced as one traveled westward, and Illinois itself seemed like bedlam to many visitors. There, the newspaper accounts were unusually full and fiercely partisan. The decision of the Chicago *Times* and the Chicago *Press and Tribune* to print complete stenographic reports of the seven debates constituted a landmark in political journalism. It was also something new to have a corps of paid correspondents trailing the two candidates wherever they went.

The historic contest between Lincoln and Douglas actually began in Chicago on July 9, 1858, when an uproarious celebration welcomed the latter home from Washington. That evening, with Lincoln by invitation sitting near him, the Little Giant addressed a huge crowd from the balcony of the Tremont House. The speech, besides lifting the morale of local Democrats, had two other significant effects. In it, Douglas renewed his quarrel with the Buchanan administration at the very moment when a truce was being arranged. He also undertook an extensive refutation of the House Divided speech, thereby publicly recognizing Lincoln as his rival for the senatorship. Lincoln spoke in reply from the same balcony twenty-four hours later. Then Douglas, traveling southward, delivered speeches at Bloomington July 16 and at Springfield in the afternoon of July 17. He again centered much of his fire upon the House Divided address, but now added a rejoinder to Lincoln's remarks at Chicago. Lincoln, having heard Douglas at Bloomington, responded at Springfield in the evening of the 17th.

And so, before any formal arrangements were made, a brisk running debate had been launched, as much on Douglas's initiative as on Lincoln's. Left to his own devices, Lincoln might have been satisfied to continue in just this manner. "My recent experience shows," he wrote later in the summer, "that speaking at the same place the next day after D[ouglas] is the very thing—it is, in fact, a concluding speech on him." Some Republicans were afraid, however, that Lincoln would lose face if he kept on following Douglas about the state, especially since Democratic newspapers had begun to jeer at the strategy. The obvious solution was a series of joint discussions in which the two men would appear as equals. An

editorial in the Chicago *Press and Tribune* broached the subject on July 22: "We have a suggestion to make . . . Let Mr. Douglas and Mr. Lincoln agree to canvass the State together, in the usual western style. . . . If Mr. Douglas shall refuse to be a party to such arrangement, it will be because he is a coward." Lincoln, who had just arrived in Chicago for talks with party leaders, was quickly persuaded. On the 24th, he wrote to Douglas proposing that they "divide time, and address the same audiences during the present canvass."

It is inaccurate to say, as so many historians do, that the Little Giant "accepted" this challenge. Lincoln's plan, if agreed to, would have meant at least fifty debates, an exhausting thing even to contemplate. Douglas dared not respond with an outright refusal, but he had no intention of going through the entire campaign yoked to Lincoln. Explaining that his speaking schedule precluded such a comprehensive arrangement, he offered instead to "accommodate" his rival by meeting him seven times. Lincoln, with some unseemly grumbling about the terms, accepted this wholesale revision of his original proposal. Republican papers in the state left no doubt that they considered the challenge declined. The *Press and Tribune* exclaimed: "The little dodger shirks, and backs out, except at half a dozen places which he himself selects." In Springfield, the *State Journal* maintained that about one hundred debates ought to have been scheduled, and that Douglas, by his "inglorious retreat from a public discussion," had stamped himself as only "seven hundredths of a candidate for the Senate."

For the most part, then, each man went his own way, and the debates, although they were the dramatic high points of the campaign, represented only a small fraction of its total oratory. Lincoln, according to his own count, made a total of sixty-three speeches. Most of them were at scheduled meetings and averaged about two hours in length. Douglas, who followed an even more strenuous schedule, later asserted that he had delivered "just one hundred and thirty speeches" during the senatorial contest, but he was apparently including all his impromptu responses to welcoming addresses, serenades, and other demonstrations. In addition, the political battle was waged by the hundreds of lesser candidates who took their turns on the stump, by volunteer orators from within and without the state, by newspaper editors and their reporters, and by the countless enthusiasts of all ages and both sexes who contributed to the pageantry of the campaign by making banners, decorating halls and platforms, organizing parades, playing in bands, preparing feasts, firing cannon, and filling the air with their cheers.

Both Lincoln and Douglas concentrated their efforts in the middle of the state, where the contest would be won and lost. Yet together they covered nearly ten thousand miles in about a hundred days, traveling by train, river boat, and carriage, enduring intense heat and sudden rain storms, snatching food and sleep at odd hours, riding in processions, waving, smiling, shaking hands, conferring with swarms of local party leaders, and making hasty notes for the next speech that was always in the offing. So killing was the pace that, as Paul M. Angle says, "it would not have been surprising had both men broken under the strain." Lincoln's voice stood up better than that of his opponent, which dwindled almost to a whisper near the end of the canvass, but neither warrior seems to have missed a single scheduled engagement.

Even stripped of all its folklore, the Lincoln-Douglas campaign was a remarkable chapter in American political history, full of homespun vivacity and colorful incident, revealing the youthful exuberance of a still youthful nation. "The prairies are on fire," wrote the correspondent of a New York newspaper. "It is astonishing how deep an interest in politics this people take." In every community favored with a visit from one or both of the senatorial candidates, there were weeks of preparation, spurred by a fierce resolve to outdo the enemy in numbers, noise, and display. Clouds of dust, raised by wagons approaching from all points of the compass, ushered in the great day. At eight o'clock in the morning of the Ottawa debate, we are told, "the streets and avenues leading from the country were so enveloped

with dust that the town resembled a vast smoke house." The din of the gathering crowd was usually swelled by band music, booming cannon, and the cries of peddlers hawking their wares. Adults mingled to gossip, children to romp, and great quantities of food, brought from home or served at long tables by a local committee, fortified the multitude against its long wait. As the hour appointed for the festivities drew near, there was often a rush to secure positions close to the speaker's stand. Bolder spirits sometimes swarmed upon the platform itself and, like true squatters, rebuffed all efforts to dislodge them. Then, when the speakers and other dignitaries arrived, they had to fight "a hand-to-hand conflict for even the meagerest . . . standing room."

Despite the wearisome length of most such meetings, the audiences were generally attentive and responsive, but not always courteous. The stump speaker, no matter how well he pleased his partisans, usually had to contend with a certain amount of heckling from the opposition. At Freeport, where Douglas was in unfriendly territory, his repeated use of the phrase "Black Republicans" brought so many roars of anger from the crowd that he finally exclaimed: "I wish to remind you that while Mr. Lincoln was speaking there was not a Democrat vulgar and black-guard enough to interrupt him." When he spoke at Joliet a few days later, the Little Giant was pestered with interruptions not only from Republicans in his audience but from the abolitionist congressman, Owen Lovejoy, who had seated himself uninvited on the speaker's platform.

Democrats welcomed Lincoln to Rushville on October 20 by flying a black flag from the top of the courthouse steeple. While he was speaking, a gang of boys climbed into the steeple and tried to drown out his voice with cheers for Douglas. And several ladies looking down on the stand from upper rooms in the courthouse annoyed him with laughter and offensive remarks until he stopped his speech and asked them to be silent. Entering the Mississippi town of Dallas City on October 23, Lincoln found the main street decorated with a huge banner which pictured a Negro and bore the single word "Equality." Here again, his address was punctuated with hostile interruptions. Neither Rushville nor Dallas had been included in Douglas's itinerary, and so the local Democrats could show their mettle only in such counterattacks against the enemy invasion.

At Sullivan, on the other hand, both candidates were scheduled to speak the same day (September 20), and a general brawl almost ensued when parading Republicans descended in force upon the Douglas meeting. From Sullivan, Douglas moved on to Danville and there received the campaign's most eloquent token of disrespect when the carriage waiting for him at the station was smeared with "loathsome dirt," or, as another reporter put it, "in a manner unmentionable."

The extreme bias of most contemporary observers makes it impossible to determine whether one of the two candidates was appreciably superior to the other as a campaigner. Each man was a conquering hero in the newspapers of his own party and a pitiful failure in the opposition press. His audiences were large and spirited or small and listless, his arguments were wonderfully persuasive or wretchedly futile, depending upon the political allegiance of the sheet in which they were described. Lincoln's awkward appearance drew much ridicule. His gestures, said the Chicago *Times,* seemed "positively painful," like those of a man "suffering from an attack brought on by an imprudent indulgence in unripe fruit." Douglas was equally vulnerable because of the characteristic vehemence with which he spoke, and Republican editors, knowing his convivial habits, did not hesitate to suggest that much of his fierceness came out of a bottle. At Ottawa, according to the *Press and Tribune,* the face of the Little Giant was "livid with passion"; he resembled "a wild beast in looks and gesture, and a maniac in language and argument."

Lincoln had the underdog's advantage. For him, as the election was to prove, there could be moral victory in a stand-off with his illustrious rival. Furthermore, Lincoln surpassed Douglas as an orator. His ear was better tuned to the rhythms and subtleties of language. He used words more consciously and with greater versatility, passing easily from wit to sarcasm, from homely analogy to solemn eloquence. Deliberation and revision improved his style, whereas Douglas, for whom speech was but a mode of action, needed the thrust of spontaneity and often became dull with preparation. Neither a storyteller nor a phrasemaker, and seldom very original in his thought or expression, Douglas is among the least quoted of major American statesmen. Yet in debate he was a formidable antagonist, and the anti-Lecompton Douglas of 1858, fighting enemies on two fronts, was an especially attractive figure. Printed speeches reveal the man's alertness, fluency, and intelligence, but not his enormous vitality, not the dynamic quality of his platform presence. The truth seems to be that these two adversaries, so different in appearance and temperament, were exceedingly well matched, each having his peculiar sources of strength. There is perhaps no better estimate of their achievement than the one written by an editor in Portland, Maine: "Without regard to politics the contest in Illinois is taking magnificent proportions. Douglas and Lincoln are both giants, and the way they discuss political questions before immense crowds of people is an admirable illustration of the workings of our institutions."

It has been the fashion at times to belittle the actual content of the Lincoln-Douglas debates. They are, admittedly, burdened with tiresome repetition and trivial dispute. Douglas jabbed repeatedly at his opponent's stand on the Mexican War. Lincoln took full advantage of an honest mistake which Douglas made at Ottawa when he quoted a set of Republican resolutions and attributed them to the wrong convention. More than half of the time at the Charleston meeting was occupied with a tedious rehashing of Douglas's part in framing the Toombs bill, an enabling act for Kansas passed by the Senate in 1856. Yet the worst faults of the debates derive from the circumstances of their presentation, which did not encourage compactness, strict relevancy, or logical progression. Intended for the ears of clamorous partisans in seven separate meetings, not for the eyes of one reader, these twenty-one hours of oratory deserve to be judged by their superior passages, rather than by the average level of the discussion.

From the text of the seven debates it appears that Lincoln expected the argument to be somewhat different in each new encounter, whereas Douglas had the skeleton of a set speech which he intended to use, with suitable variations, at every meeting. The Little Giant's primary purpose, besides defending his own political record, was to persuade uncommitted moderates that Lincoln's views were those of a dangerous radical. The house-divided doctrine therefore continued to be his point of departure. Lincoln, he declared, was not only preaching sectional warfare, but advocating an oppressive uniformity that would be repugnant alike to the principle of state sovereignty and to the cultural diversity which had made America great. The nation *could* endure half slave and half free, Douglas insisted, if each state and territory were allowed to regulate its own domestic institutions in accordance with local needs and customs.

The moderate platform adopted by Illinois Republicans in 1858 was less vulnerable than the House Divided speech, and Douglas consequently paid little attention to it. Instead, he endeavored to identify his rival with the more radical Republicanism of 1854, at which time, he charged, Lincoln had joined Trumbull in a plot to "abolitionize" the Whig and Democratic parties of the state. Douglas found the true spirit of the Republican movement most starkly revealed in the militant antislavery resolutions that emanated from many northern counties during the Kansas-Nebraska excitement. Such resolutions, besides demanding the exclusion of slavery from the territories, usually called for repeal of the Fugitive Slave Law, abolition of slavery in the District of Columbia, and various other assaults upon the outer defenses of slave society. The seven questions that Douglas reeled off at Ottawa were designed to measure the extent of Lincoln's concurrence with these aggressive proposals and to expose the inherent radicalism of his sympathies.

Another weapon upon which Douglas relied was the exploitation of race prejudice. He scornfully rejected Lincoln's contention that the philosophy of the Declaration of Independence embraced Negroes as well as white men. If this belief ever won general acceptance, he warned, an inferior race, utterly incapable of self-government, would be elevated to a position of absolute equality, and the nation would experience all the degradation and misery that had accompanied racial amalgamation in the countries of Latin America. "I do not question Mr. Lincoln's conscientious belief that the negro was made his equal, and hence is his brother," Douglas sneered, "but for my own part, I do not regard the negro as my equal, and positively deny that he is my brother or any kin to me whatever." When Lincoln emphatically disclaimed any desire to confer political and social equality upon Negroes, Douglas accused him of hypocrisy, complaining that he offered one set of principles in northern counties and another to audiences farther south. The cry of Negro equality pursued Lincoln, despite all his protestations, throughout the campaign and no doubt affected its outcome. White supremacy, a doctrine that scarcely needed defending in nineteenth-century America, was not the central theme of Douglas's argument, but he used it with great effectiveness to buttress his plea for a multiform society, resting on sturdy local autonomy, as the alternative to sectional strife.

For Lincoln, it was vitally necessary to throw off the imputation of radicalism. Hence he dissociated himself from the incipient Republican movement of 1854, renewed his pledge to support recovery of fugitive slaves and to oppose interference with slavery in the Southern states, disavowed racial equality, and rejected the individual inferences which Douglas drew from the House Divided speech. But it was not enough merely to defend himself against the thrusts of his opponent. As the challenger, Lincoln needed to mount a vigorous offensive. His greatest task was, in the apt words of Harry V. Jaffa, to "destroy Douglas' credentials as a free-soil champion," credentials won in the fight against the

Lecompton constitution. This meant accentuating the fundamental differences that still separated Douglas from the Republican party despite their recent collaboration in Congress. Such strategy, already embodied in the House Divided speech, was not entirely compatible with Lincoln's efforts to absolve himself from antislavery extremism; for the latter required conservative utterances that actually reduced the distance between him and Douglas. The resulting ambivalence in his argument exposed him to the charge of being inconsistent and inspired conflicting historical interpretations of his essential outlook and purpose.

Lincoln's case against Douglas may be summarized as follows: The divisive influence of slavery was the one great threat to the American union, and the policy inaugurated in the Kansas-Nebraska Act had only intensified the sectional conflict. On the moral issue posed by slavery there could be no middle ground; the neutralism preached by Douglas was calculated to dull the Northern conscience and thus clear the way for legalization of the institution everywhere in the nation. Only the Republican program, which accorded with the views of the founding fathers, offered a feasible alternative to this grim eventuality. Slavery must be recognized as an evil and, within the bounds of the Constitution, treated as an evil. Specifically, it must be confined to its existing limits and marked for ultimate extinction.

There were obvious risks attached to this line of argument, but Lincoln had good reason for accepting them. The territorial question by itself simply did not present enough contrast between Douglas and the Republicans, especially since their joint anti-Lecompton effort. A much sharper distinction could be drawn if the discussion were shifted to the more expansive domain of moral principles. And so, as the debates progressed, Lincoln laid increasing emphasis upon the fundamental conflict between those who believed, and those who did not believe, that slavery was wrong. "That is the real issue," he said at Alton. "That is the issue that will continue in this country when these poor tongues of Judge Doug-

las and myself shall be silent. It is the eternal struggle between these two principles—right and wrong—throughout the world."

Along with his main assault upon Douglas's position, Lincoln was quick to undertake any collateral maneuver that promised advantage. For example, the first two questions that he asked at Freeport were designed to aggravate the quarrel between Douglas and the Buchanan-Southerner wing of the Democratic party. One of them forced the Little Giant to repudiate a significant provision in the English compromise. The other elicited his famous "Freeport doctrine," summed up in the phrase "unfriendly legislation," with which he proposed to rescue popular sovereignty from the effects of the Dred Scott decision. Both replies aroused anger in the South, but since the slaveholders had by now written off Kansas as a lost cause, the Freeport doctrine soon became the primary focus of their hostility to Douglas. Here, then, was the raw material for a familiar legend: that Lincoln, with a single well-placed blow, split the Democratic party and deprived Douglas of the presidency.

This second Freeport question was actually tangential to Lincoln's principal line of attack, which, after all, stressed the *affinity* between Douglas and the slave interest, not their disagreements. Yet because of the prodigious consequences attributed to it, the question has come to be regarded as the very crux of the debates and as a major turning point in American history.

The vigor with which Lincoln and Douglas belabored one another tended to magnify the distance separating their respective points of view. Neither man was an extremist; both offered reasonable solutions to the slavery problem; and they were frequently closer to agreement than either would admit. But these are facts that should qualify, not dominate, any description of their relationship. The distortion that results from emphasizing consensus instead of conflict in the Lincoln-Douglas debates can be seen in the writings of James G. Randall. A biographer who fully appreciated Lincoln's greatness, but whose sympathies, as a "revisionist" historian, were primarily with Douglas, Randall found his way out of an awkward dilemma by minimizing the differences between the two rivals. Lincoln and Douglas, he was fond of repeating, had "much in common." They thought alike on many problems that went unmentioned throughout the debates, and even in their discussion of slavery they *"seemed to differ* while actually agreeing on many points." Indeed, a reading of Randall leaves one with the impression that no vital principles were at stake in the campaign, that the candidates, merely to satisfy the demands of partisanship, put on an exciting show which obscured the underlying similarity of their aims and methods.

What Randall seemed to overlook was that differences may be far from absolute and yet historically important. The debates do not reflect the ultimate conflict between abolitionist and slaveholder. They embody instead the principal cleavage in Northern thought, which, though narrower, had its own profound influence upon the course of events. A brief review will show that Lincoln's disagreement with Douglas was broad enough and deep enough to be significant.

1. *Negro slavery in the territories.* Here, beyond any question, the debaters supported different policies. It is the contention of Randall and others, to be sure, that the difference was inconsequential because freedom would have been as well served by popular sovereignty as by the Republican program of restriction. But this argument ignores certain compelling facts. First, the recent history of Kansas had demonstrated that popular sovereignty could easily be perverted to the service of slavery. Second, many Northerners feared that the Douglas doctrine would be combined with new annexations—of Cuba, for instance—to enlarge the domain of slavery. And finally, the territorial issue was not separable from the larger problem; for the legal status of slavery in the federal territories had become a measure of its moral acceptability in the nation as a whole.

2. *Negro slavery.* The great difference here was not in the category of immediate objectives but in certain general commitments which would surely influence future action. Lincoln, holding that slavery was a "moral, social and political

wrong," proposed to yield it only the minimum protection guaranteed by the Constitution and looked forward to its eventual abolition. Douglas refused to pass any judgment upon slavery and would let it compete for public approval in every locality on an equal basis with the antislavery principle. He professed indifference to the ultimate fate of the institution, but saw no reason why the republic could not "exist forever divided into free and slave states, as our fathers made it." Furthermore, whereas Douglas maintained that the problem was one to be dealt with exclusively by the states, Lincoln contended that the presence of slavery affected the whole nation and was therefore a proper subject of concern to the federal government, within the limits of its powers. Whatever contemporary merit there may have been in Douglas's argument, history has vindicated Lincoln's nationalism, as well as his verdict against slavery.

3. *The Negro.* According to Randall, the debaters "did not fundamentally differ" in their views on racial relations. The accuracy of this assertion must be challenged, however, because it was when they discussed fundamentals that the two men disagreed most sharply. For one thing, Douglas subscribed unequivocally to the belief that the Negro race was innately inferior to the white, but Lincoln never went beyond the acknowledgment that the belief might be true. In speaking of Negroes, moreover, the Little Giant did not attempt to hide a strong personal repugnance which contrasted noticeably with Lincoln's tone of detachment. The fact remains, it is true, that Lincoln explicitly approved all the social arrangements of his day (except slavery) that were based upon the theory of Negro inferiority. In words that grate harshly upon the modern ear, he declared his opposition to Negro citizenship, Negro suffrage, and racial intermingling. "I have no purpose," he protested under Douglas's goading, "to introduce political and social equality between the white and black races. There is a physical difference between the two, which . . . will probably forever forbid their living together on the footing of perfect equality."

The whole texture of American life compelled

such a pronouncement in 1858, and the Lincoln of history would not exist if he had failed to comply. But it is what Lincoln *claimed* for the Negroes, not what he was willing to *deny* them, that retains significance, namely: "All the rights enumerated in the Declaration of Independence." No doubt Lincoln failed to see everything that was implied in confirming the Negro's inalienable right to life, liberty, and the pursuit of happiness. His eyes were fixed upon the problem of slavery. Yet he must have known that for Negroes, no less than white men, the Declaration promised much more than freedom from bondage. The first steps toward fulfillment of that larger promise were taken during his presidency. Lincoln's first principle of racial relations—that the Declaration of Independence belongs to all Americans—was actually subversive of the existing order which he endorsed. It has become increasingly meaningful in the twentieth century, while the doctrine embraced by Douglas is on its way to the scrap-heap of error. There was that difference, if none other, between the two debaters.

Not the least curious feature of this extraordinary campaign was the fact that neither candidate had the full support of party leaders outside the state. In Lincoln's case, the defection of certain Eastern Republicans went no further than periodic declarations of neutrality regarding the Illinois contest. The New York *Post* of July 13, for instance, said that the cause of freedom would benefit substantially from either man's election. Such impartiality, exasperating to Illinois Republicans, was prompted largely by the desire to court anti-Lecompton Democrats in several critical states. It implied no disparagement of Lincoln, whom Republican newspapers everywhere treated with the utmost respect. Douglas, on the other hand, faced the venomous opposition of the Buchanan administration, which, not satisfied with editorial assaults and patronage reprisals, attempted to undermine his strength in Illinois by setting up a rival Democratic organization there.

The separate Buchanan party in Illinois began to take shape during the spring of 1858 when it became apparent that Douglas would retain firm command of the regular Democratic machinery. Invested with control of federal patronage in the state, and warmly supported by administration newspapers like the Washington *Union,* this motley group of political castoffs, misfits, and placemen proposed to enter its own slate of candidates in the contest for legislative seats. Even a few victories might give the "Buchaneers" a decisive voice in the balloting for senator and thus assure the defeat of Douglas. Illinois Republicans were naturally delighted at the prospect of facing a divided opposition. More than that, they found it desirable to foster the schism by lending encouragement to the weaker faction. The result was one of the strangest situations ever to develop in American politics. At the very time that an alliance of Republicans and Douglas Democrats in Washington was waging a desperate fight against the Administration and the Lecompton constitution, the Republicans of Illinois were entering into collaboration with pro-Lecompton Democrats for the purpose of unseating Douglas.

The Little Giant repeatedly denounced this "unholy and unnatural combination" of his adversaries, but Republican spokesmen met all such complaints with protestations of innocence. "There is not now, has not been, and will not be, any union . . . expressed or implied, between the Republicans of Illinois and the Lecomptonites here or elsewhere," declared the Chicago *Tribune.* Lincoln's own disclaimers were equally emphatic. "I have no objection to the division in the Judge's party," he said at Galesburg, "but I defy the Judge to show any evidence that I have in any way promoted that division." Yet it is a matter of record that Lincoln held several consultations with John Dougherty, the Buchaneer candidate for state treasurer, and that negotiations produced at least a working agreement, if not a formal alliance, between Republicans and Administration Democrats.

"It is our true policy to nurse the Buchanan men," Joseph Medill informed Trumbull in April. From the editor of the *State Journal* came a similar report: "All along, as you are aware, we have been encouraging the Buchanan men as much as possible and stimulating them to orga- nize." Republicans not only conferred and corre- sponded with the Buchaneers but wrote editorials praising them, published notices of their meet- ings, and augmented the size of those meetings by attending them in force. In Chicago, John Went- worth worked openly with the Administration men, filling columns of his newspaper with exhor- tations and advice. Republicans of the Springfield area kept in close touch with Buchaneer activities through William Herndon, whose father and brother were local leaders of the movement. The latter served on the editorial staff of the *Illinois State Democrat,* a newly established Administra- tion organ which apparently expected financial help from the Republicans and hired a Republi- can journalist in Chicago to write some of its political articles.

Hoping to promote mass desertions from Douglas by predicting them, Republican newspa- pers published fantastic estimates of Buchaneer strength in the state. The *Press and Tribune* said that a "general stampede" of Democrats to the Buchanan side was developing. Douglas would be "driven from the field" or left with less than ten supporters in the new legislature. On October 7, less than four weeks before election day, the same sheet described the Administration forces as "hopeful, enthusiastic and defiant," with "flatter- ing prospects of success" in many of the Demo- cratic strongholds. When the election was over and the Buchaneers had polled a miserable 2 per cent of the popular vote, *Tribune* editors sourly confessed the truth: "There is not now and never has been a Buchanan party in Illinois. . . . every shrewd politician in the state has known it for a month at least."

The spectacle of Republicans cooperating with Lecompton Democrats offended Horace Greeley, and James G. Randall has called it "one of the least inspiring aspects" of the 1858 campaign. Whether the Illinois strategy was reprehensible or justified by circumstances must remain a mat- ter of opinion, but the results certainly failed to vindicate its wisdom. Douglas lost only a few thousand votes to the Buchaneers, and for this cheap price he freed himself from much of the

burden that the slavery issue had placed upon Northern Democrats. The fierce hostility of the Buchaneer faction was his best answer to the con- spiracy charge in Lincoln's House Divided speech. By exploiting the break between Douglas and the Administration, Illinois Republicans weakened their case against him as a tool of the slaveholding interest.

Although a heavy rain fell over much of the state on November 2, more voters went to the polls than in the presidential contest two years earlier. The election proved to be so close that even the losers could claim a measure of victory. With a popular plurality of about four thousand votes in a quarter of a million (but not quite a majority, since the Buchanan faction polled five thousand), the Republicans elected their candi- dates for state treasurer and superintendent of public instruction. The Democrats carried off the major prize, however, by winning enough seats in the legislature to ensure Douglas's re- election, fifty-four to forty-six. Just a few hun- dred votes in several critical counties had made all the difference. For Lincoln and his disap- pointed followers there was frustration as well as comfort in having come so near. And while the exultant Democrats, like most victors, hailed the outcome as a simple triumph of vir- tue, Republicans mournfully catalogued every specific factor that might have tipped the scales against them. Their list included such items as the rainy weather and the malign influence of the Catholic church, but according to the three most common complaints, Lincoln had been victimized by dishonesty at the polls, treachery from abroad, and an unfair apportionment of legislative seats.

Lax enforcement of defective laws permitted much trickery and fraud in the election proce- dures of the 1850's. There were, for example, no official ballots. Local party organizations usually printed their own, and it was common practice to run off, in addition, a supply of spurious opposi- tion tickets for distribution in the enemy camp. More serious was the lack of a general registra- tion law, which made it relatively easy to evade the residence requirement. As a consequence, voters were frequently "colonized," that is, moved on the eve of an election from safe or hopeless districts into doubtful ones. Here the Democratic party had a distinct advantage because it commanded the loyalty of Irish railroad workers, whose semi-transient existence fitted them admirably for such maneuvers.

During the final weeks of the Lincoln-Douglas campaign, Republican leaders became increasingly alarmed about reports of Irish movements into the central counties. Newspapers described the invasion in detail and issued frantic warnings against a plot to steal the election for Douglas with "border ruffian tactics." Late in October, the state central committee sent out a circular letter with careful instructions on how to prevent illegal voting. Charles H. Ray proposed that a secret army of vigilantes be organized to guard the polls with revolvers protruding from their pockets. Herndon, almost beside himself, confided to Theodore Parker that bloodshed might be necessary to "maintain the purity of the ballot-box." "What shall we do?" he demanded. "Shall we tamely submit to the Irish, or shall we rise and cut their throats?"

The trouble was that an illegal voter, even when challenged, could swear to his eligibility and cast a ballot. He ran the risk of prosecution for perjury, of course, but convictions were hard to get. Lincoln, who had himself encountered at Naples "about fifteen Celtic gentlemen, with black carpet-sacks in their hands," suggested an additional piece of strategy. To Norman B. Judd, the state chairman, he wrote:

> When there is a known body of these voters, could not a true man, of the "*detective*" class, be introduced among them in disguise, who could, at the nick of time, control their votes? Think this over. It would be a great thing, when this trick is attempted upon us, to have the saddle come up on the other horse.

With his usual prudence, Lincoln did not specify the means by which the "control" was to be established.

Despite Republican precautions, some "colonized" Irishmen undoubtedly did vote on election day, but whether their number was large enough to affect the outcome is impossible to determine. The Republicans, in their post-election grumbling on the subject, were far less frenzied, however, than they had been a few weeks earlier. Their fears, though not groundless, had apparently been exaggerated.

Lincoln men reserved their bitterest reproaches for the Eastern Republicans who had given aid and comfort to Douglas. "I say d—n Greely & Co.," exclaimed an Edgar County leader. "They have done more harm to us in Ills. than all others beside not excepting the d—n Irish." From Quincy, Lincoln's friend Jackson Grimshaw reported that it had rained "rain and rail road Irish and Pro Slavery K.N.'s and worse than all Seward and Greely Republicans who voted for Douglas." Similar expressions of anger issued from David Davis, John M. Palmer, Ebenezer Peck, and other prominent Republicans, as well as from the party press. Whatever its merits as a diagnosis of Lincoln's defeat, this renewed outcry against betrayal from the East had important consequences, primarily because the Illinoisans were disposed to blame William H. Seward almost as much as they did Greeley.

Seward, unlike Greeley, had never openly advocated the re-election of Douglas, but at the same time he had not lifted a finger to help Lincoln. Many Illinois Republicans resented his aloofness and, more than that, mistrusted it. Remembering his cordial relations with Douglas during the Lecompton struggle, the rumors of a personal alliance, and the course followed by Thurlow Weed's newspaper, they were convinced that the New York senator had been covertly hostile to their cause. More than one looked ahead to 1860 as a time of reckoning and echoed the sentiments of the Chicagoan who declared: "If the vote of Illinois can nominate another than Seward, I hope it will be so cast." This was an abrupt change from the situation at the beginning of 1858, when Seward had been, to all appearance, the favorite choice for the presidency among Illinois Republicans. The decline of his popularity in the state left an empty space which Lincoln soon filled. That at least one Illinoisan nursed his grudge for two years is revealed in a congratulatory letter addressed to Lincoln on May 28, 1860. "It is a double satisfaction to me," wrote the Chicago banker, J. Young Scammon, "that you should have been nominated over Seward and New York dictation; and when I recollected how much Seward did to favor Douglas and prejudice you and us in Illinois, I could but feel that it was a very righteous retribution that he should be defeated by you."

In the opinion of some Illinois Republicans, however, the worst blow had been struck by the respected Whig-American leader, Senator John J. Crittenden of Kentucky, with help from Lincoln's old friend, T. Lyle Dickey. The latter, having persuaded himself that the Republican party was falling into radical hands, went over to the Democrats in the summer of 1858 and campaigned actively for Douglas. He managed to draw a letter from Crittenden praising the Little Giant and, after waiting for the most favorable moment, published it shortly before election day. The maneuver undoubtedly hurt Lincoln most in the very places where he was beaten—that is, in the old Whig strongholds of central Illinois. Lincoln himself bluntly told Crittenden that the use of his name had "contributed largely" to the Republican defeat.

Pointing to their plurality in the popular vote, Republicans also charged that Lincoln had been cheated by an unjust distribution of legislative seats. It had required four votes in the northern counties, they complained, to offset three in the south, and the new General Assembly would have forty-six Republicans who represented a larger total population than the fifty-four Democrats. Douglas, the advocate of popular sovereignty, had been re-elected under a system that thwarted the will of the majority.

Historians tend to agree. With uncritical vehemence they label the apportionment "unfair," "antique," "gerrymandered," and even "infamous." Yet the statute in question actually dated back only to the "antiquity" of 1852 and

was based upon the latest federal census. True, a state census taken in 1855 supplied fresher data, but a Republican bill deriving from it had been killed in the Democratic legislature, and a Democratic bill had been vetoed by the Republican governor. The word "gerrymander" is singularly inappropriate because the Republican party did not even exist when the law was passed, and Illinois politics had not yet become thoroughly sectionalized. Any gerrymandering undertaken in 1852 would have had little force by 1858. Furthermore, even though Lincoln did unquestionably labor under some disadvantage, the Illinois law, compared with other apportionments past and present, was actually somewhat better than the average.

One thing often overlooked is that not every legislative seat was at stake in the 1858 contest. There were thirteen state senators holding over, eight of them Democrats, and so the Republicans needed more than a minimal victory to place Lincoln in the United States Senate. Altogether, the voters elected 87 legislators: 46 Democrats and 41 Republicans. This means that Lincoln, whose party polled about 50 per cent of the popular vote, received only 47 per cent of what we may call the electoral vote, while Douglas, with just 48 per cent of the popular vote, was given 53 per cent of the electoral vote—an inequity, to be sure, but hardly an unusual or outrageous one. If the results had mirrored the popular vote exactly, the Republicans would have won 44 seats instead of 41, still two less (counting their holdovers) than the number necessary to elect Lincoln.

As an additional test, however, let us suppose that the Republican apportionment bill had become law. When the 1858 votes are redistributed according to its provisions, Lincoln naturally fares better, but the issue is still in doubt. With the total number of seats increased by the bill to 105, it appears that the Republicans would have controlled 53, the barest possible majority. It is therefore less than certain that the popular will of 1858 was thwarted by the apportionment of 1852. The closeness of the race made a relatively minor injustice seem decisive. But under that same law, after all, a Republican named Lyman Trumbull twice won election to the Senate.

The Lincoln-Douglas campaign of 1858 proved to be a contest without a real loser. Lincoln, despite his defeat, emerged as a national figure; Douglas with a hard-won victory preserved and consolidated his leadership of Northern Democrats. The most obvious consequence of this anomalous election, in which the voters of a state virtually appropriated the power to choose a senator, was that it produced not one, but two nominees for the presidency. The startling swiftness with which Lincoln rose to party leadership by 1860 should not obscure the fact that Douglas, too, climbed higher than ever before. Both men profited immensely from their strenuous efforts in 1858.

It is often said, however, that Douglas paid a high price for his re-election—that in order to win he was compelled to take a position which alienated the South and widened the split in the Democratic party. The statement is true, and yet it is not the whole truth; for a politician must choose from possible alternatives. Election results in other Northern states, where the Democratic party met nothing but defeat, testified eloquently to the soundness of Douglas's judgment in 1858. No one realized better than Lincoln that the Little Giant had adopted the strategy best calculated to prevent a Republican victory in 1860. His ultimate failure only verified the fact that in some circumstances even the best strategy is not good enough. The momentum gathered in their contest for a Senate seat carried both Lincoln and Douglas to the threshold of the White House, but only one could enter.

26

FORMING A FREE BLACK COMMUNITY

ELIZABETH R. BETHEL

The end of the Civil War in 1865 opened the question of the position of the freedman in American society. Now that they were no longer slaves, would black Americans be allowed the same rights as white citizens? Should black males be allowed to vote? To serve on juries? To hold office? To own property? The Fourteenth and Fifteenth Amendments to the Constitution provided one answer to these questions; they gave the freedman all the rights of American citizenship including the right to vote.

But constitutional principle was one thing and southern practice another. Through intimidation and violence, southern whites sought to maintain the old system of racial domination and white supremacy that had prevailed in the prewar South. As Elizabeth Bethel documents in this essay, southern blacks were beaten for attempting to vote, black political leaders were assassinated, and the Ku Klux Klan was organized with the object of keeping blacks "in their place." By the late 1860s it was clear that white southerners were determined to prevent any change in their system of racial privilege and power.

But the history of Reconstruction was not only a story of black suppression and white domination. Individually and collectively, southern blacks challenged the power and racialist assumptions of their white neighbors. Wherever they could, freedmen reestablished the family and kinship ties they had lost during slavery. Thousands of ex-slaves flocked to urban areas to find employment and establish their economic independence. Others, such as those whose story is told in this essay, purchased land, established communities, and provided for their family's well-being. The story of black reconstruction, as Bethel ably shows, is a story of courage and a single-minded search for freedom.

What do you think accounts for the solidarity shown by the people of Promiseland in the face of white terrorism? How does the solidarity of the small farmers of Promiseland compare with that of the Shawnee who followed Tecumseh and Tenskwatawa in their campaign against encroaching white settlers as discussed by R. David Edmunds in Reading 17?

Promised Land was from the outset an artifact of Reconstruction politics. Its origins, as well, lie in the hopes, the dreams, and the struggles of four million Negroes, for the meaning of freedom was early defined in terms of land for most emancipated Negroes. In South Carolina, perhaps more intensely than any of the other southern states, the thirst for land was acute. It was a possibility sparked first by General William T. Sherman's military actions along the Sea Islands, then dashed as quickly as it was born in the distant arena of Washington politics. Still, the desire

Reprinted from Elizabeth R. Bethel, *Promiseland: A Century of Life in a Negro Community* (Philadelphia: Temple University Press, 1981), 17–40. © 1981 by Temple University. Reprinted by permission of Temple University Press.

for land remained a goal not readily abandoned by the state's freedpeople, and they implemented a plan to achieve that goal at the first opportunity. Their chance came at the 1868 South Carolina Constitutional Convention.

South Carolina was among the southern states which refused to ratify the Fourteenth Amendment to the Constitution, the amendment which established the citizenship of the freedmen. Like her recalcitrant neighbors, the state was then placed under military government, as outlined by the Military Reconstruction Act of 1867. Among the mandates of that federal legislation was a requirement that each of the states in question draft a new state constitution which incorporated the principles of the Fourteenth Amendment. Only after such new constitutions were completed and implemented were the separate states of the defeated Confederacy eligible for readmission to the Union.

The representatives to these constitutional conventions were selected by a revolutionary electorate, one which included all adult male Negroes. Registration for the elections was handled by the Army with some informal assistance by "that God-forsaken institution, the Freedman's Bureau." Only South Carolina among the ten states of the former Confederacy elected a Negro majority to its convention. The instrument those representatives drafted called for four major social and political reforms in state government: a statewide system of free common schools; universal manhood suffrage; a jury law which included the Negro electorate in county pools of qualified jurors; and a land redistribution system designed to benefit the state's landless population, primarily the freedmen.

White response to the new constitution and the social reforms which it outlined was predictably vitriolic. It was condemned by one white newspaper as "the work of sixty-odd Negroes, many of them ignorant and depraved." The authors were publicly ridiculed as representing "the maddest, most unscrupulous, and infamous revolution in history." Despite this and similar vilification, the constitution was ratified in the 1868 referendum, an election boycotted by many white

voters and dominated by South Carolina's 81,000 newly enfranchised Negroes, who cast their votes overwhelmingly with the Republicans and for the new constitution.

That same election selected representatives to the state legislature charged with implementing the constitutional reforms. That body, like the constitutional convention, was constituted with a Negro majority; and it moved immediately to establish a common school system and land redistribution program. The freedmen were already registered, and the new jury pools remained the prerogative of the individual counties. The 1868 election also was notable for the numerous attacks and "outrages" which occurred against the more politically active freedmen. Among those Negroes assaulted, beaten, shot, and lynched during the pre-election campaign months were four men who subsequently bought small farms from the Land Commission and settled at Promised Land. Like other freedmen in South Carolina, their open involvement in the state's Republican political machinery led to personal violence.

Wilson Nash was the first of the future Promised Land residents to encounter white brutality and retaliation for his political activities. Nash was nominated by the Republicans as their candidate for Abbeville County's seat in the state legislature at the August 1868 county convention. In October of that year, less than two weeks before the general election, Nash was attacked and shot in the leg by two unidentified white assailants. The "outrage" took place in the barn on his rented farm, not far from Dr. Marshall's farm on Curltail Creek. Wilson Nash was thirty-three years old in 1868, married, and the father of three small children. He had moved from "up around Cokesbury" within Abbeville County, shortly after emancipation to the rented land further west. Within months after the Nash family was settled on their farm, Wilson Nash joined the many Negroes who affiliated with the Republicans, an alliance probably instigated and encouraged by Republican promises of land to the freedmen. The extent of Nash's involvement with local politics was apparent in his nomination for public office; and this same nomination brought him to the forefront of county Negro leadership and to the attention of local whites.

After the attack Nash sent his wife and young children to a neighbor's home, where he probably believed they would be safe. He then mounted his mule and fled his farm, leaving behind thirty bushels of recently harvested corn. Whether Nash also left behind a cotton crop is unknown. It was the unprotected corn crop that worried him as much as his concern for his own safety. He rode his mule into Abbeville and there sought refuge at the local Freedman's Bureau office where he reported the attack to the local bureau agent and requested military protection for his family and his corn crop. Captain W. F. De-Knight was sympathetic to Nash's plight but was powerless to assist or protect him. DeKnight had no authority in civil matters such as this, and the men who held that power generally ignored such assaults on Negroes. The Nash incident was typical and followed a familiar pattern. The assailants remained unidentified, unapprehended, and unpunished. The attack achieved the desired end, however, for Nash withdrew his name from the slate of legislative candidates. For him there were other considerations which took priority over politics.

Violence against the freedmen of Abbeville County, as elsewhere in the state, continued that fall and escalated as the 1868 election day neared. The victims had in common an involvement with the Republicans, and there was little distinction made between direct and indirect partisan activity. Politically visible Negroes were open targets. Shortly after the Nash shooting young Willis Smith was assaulted, yet another victim of Reconstruction violence. Smith was still a teenager and too young to vote in the elections, but his age afforded him no immunity. He was a known member of the Union League, the most radical and secret of the political organizations which attracted freedmen. While attending a dance one evening, Smith and four other League members were dragged outside the dance hall and brutally beaten by four white men whose identities were hidden by hoods. This attack, too, was an act of political vengeance. It was, as well, one

of the earliest Ku Klux Klan appearances in Abbeville. Like other crimes committed against politically active Negroes, this one remained unsolved.

On election day freedmen Washington Green and Allen Goode were precinct managers at the White Hall polling place, near the southern edge of the Marshall land. Their position was a political appointment of some prestige, their reward for affiliation with and loyalty to the Republican cause. The appointment brought them, like Wilson Nash and Willis Smith, to the attention of local whites. On election day the voting proceeded without incident until midday, when two white men attempted to block Negroes from entering the polling site. A scuffle ensued as Green and Goode, acting in their capacity as voting officials, tried to bring the matter to a halt and were shot by the white men. One freedman was killed, two others injured, in the incident which also went unsolved. In none of the attacks were the assailants ever apprehended. Within twenty-four months all four men—Wilson Nash, Willis Smith, Washington Green, and Allen Goode—bought farms at Promised Land.

Despite the violence which surrounded the 1868 elections, the Republicans carried the whole of the state. White Democrats refused to support an election they deemed illegal, and they intimidated the newly enfranchised Negro electorate at every opportunity. The freedmen, nevertheless, flocked to the polls in an unprecedented exercise of their new franchise and sent a body of legislative representatives to the state capitol of Columbia who were wholly committed to the mandates and reforms of the new constitution. Among the first legislative acts was one which formalized the land redistribution program through the creation of the South Carolina Land Commission.

The Land Commission program, as designed by the legislature, was financed through the public sale of state bonds. The capital generated from the bond sales was used to purchase privately owned plantation tracts which were then subdivided and resold to freedmen through long-term (ten years), low-interest (7 percent per annum) loans. The bulk of the commission's transactions occurred along the coastal areas of the state where land was readily available. The labor and financial problems of the rice planters of the low-country were generally more acute than those of the up-country cotton planters. As a result, they were more eager to dispose of a portion of the landholdings at a reasonable price, and their motives for their dealings with the Land Commission were primarily pecuniary.

Piedmont planters were not so motivated. Many were able to salvage their production by negotiating sharecropping and tenant arrangements. Most operated on a smaller scale than the low-country planters and were less dependent on gang labor arrangements. As a consequence, few were as financially pressed as their low-country counterparts, and land was less available for purchase by the Land Commission in the Piedmont region. With only 9 percent of the commission purchases lying in the up-country, the Marshall lands were the exception rather than the rule.

The Marshall sons first advertised the land for sale in 1865. These lands, like others at the eastern edge of the Cotton Belt, were exhausted from generations of cultivation and attendant soil erosion; and for such worn out land the price was greatly inflated. Additionally, two successive years of crop failures, low cotton prices, and a general lack of capital discouraged serious planters from purchasing the lands. The sons then advertised the tract for rent, but the land stood idle. The family wanted to dispose of the land in a single transaction rather than subdivide it, and Dr. Marshall's farm was no competition for the less expensive and more fertile land to the west that was opened for settlement after the war. In 1869 the two sons once again advertised the land for sale, but conditions in Abbeville County were not improved for farmers, and no private buyer came forth.

Having exhausted the possibilities for negotiating a private sale, the family considered alternative prospects for the disposition of a farm that was of little use to them. James L. Orr, a moderate Democrat, former governor (1865 to 1868), and family son-in-law, served as negotiator when

the tract was offered to the Land Commission at the grossly inflated price of ten dollars an acre. Equivalent land in Abbeville County was selling for as little as two dollars an acre, and the commission rejected the offer. Political promises took precedence over financial considerations when the commission's regional agent wrote the Land Commission's Advisory Board that "if the land is not bought the (Republican) party is lost in this district." Upon receipt of his advice the commission immediately met the Marshall family's ten dollar an acre price. By January 1870 the land was subdivided into fifty small farms, averaging slightly less than fifty acres each, which were publicly offered for sale to Negro as well as white buyers.

The Marshall Tract was located in the central sector of old Abbeville County and was easily accessible to most of the freedmen who were to make the lands their home. Situated in the western portion of the state, the tract was approximately sixty miles northwest of Augusta, Georgia, one hundred and fifty miles northeast of Atlanta, and the same distance northwest of Charleston. It would attract few freedmen from the urban areas. Two roads intersected within the lands. One, running north to south, linked those who soon settled there with the county seat of Abbeville to the north and the Phoenix community, a tiny settlement composed primarily of white small scale farmers approximately eighteen miles to the south. Called New Cut Road, Five Notch Road, and later White Hall Road, the dirt wagon route was used primarily for travel to Abbeville. The east-west road, which would much later be converted to a state highway, was the more heavily traveled of the two and linked the cluster of farms to the village of Greenwood, six miles to the east, and the small settlement of Verdery, three miles to the west. Beyond Verdery, which served for a time as a stagecoach stop on the long trip between Greenville and Augusta, lay the Savannah River. The road was used regularly by a variety of peddlers and salesmen who included the Negro farmers on their routes as soon as families began to move onto the farms. Despite the decidedly rural setting, the families who bought land there were not isolated. A regular stream of travelers brought them news of events from well beyond their limited geography and helped them maintain touch with a broader scope of activities and ideas than their environment might have predicted.

The Marshall Tract had only one natural boundary to delineate the perimeter of Negro-owned farms, Curltail Creek on the north. Other less distinctive markers were devised as the farms were settled, to distinguish the area from surrounding white-owned lands. Extending south from White Hall Road, "below the cemetery, south of the railroad about a mile" a small lane intersected the larger road. This was Rabbit Track Road, and it marked the southern edge of Negro-owned lands. To the east the boundary was marked by another dirt lane called Lorenzo Road, little more than a trail which led to the Seaboard Railroad flag stop. Between the crossroads and Verdery to the west, "the edge of the old Darraugh place" established the western perimeter. In all, the tract encompassed slightly more than four square miles of earth.

The farms on the Marshall Tract were no bargain for the Negroes who bought them. The land was only partially cleared and ready for cultivation, and that which was free of pine trees and underbrush was badly eroded. There was little to recommend the land to cotton farming. Crop failures in 1868 and 1869 severely limited the local economy, which further reduced the possibilities for small farmers working on badly depleted soil. There was little credit available to Abbeville farmers, white or black; and farming lacked not only an unqualified promise of financial gain but even the possibility of breaking even at harvest. Still, it was not the fertility of the soil or the possibility of economic profit that attracted the freedmen to those farms. The single opportunity for landownership, a status which for most Negroes in 1870 symbolized the essence of their freedom, was the prime attraction for the freedmen who bought farms from the subdivided Marshall Tract.

Most of the Negroes who settled the farms knew the area and local conditions well. Many were native to Abbeville County. In addition to Wilson Nash, the Moragne family and their in-laws, the Turners, the Pinckneys, the Letmans, and the Williamses were also natives of Abbeville, from "down over by Bordeaux" in the southwestern rim of the county which borders Georgia. Others came to their new farms from "Dark Corner, over by McCormick," and another nearby Negro settlement, Pettigrew Station—both in Abbeville County. The Redd family lived in Newberry, South Carolina before they bought their farm; and James and Hannah Fields came to Promised Land from the state capitol, Columbia, eighty miles to the east.

Many of the settlers from Abbeville County shared their names with prominent white families —Moragne, Burt, Marshall, Pressley, Frazier, and Pinckney. Their claims to heritage were diverse. One recalled "my grandaddy was a white man from England," and others remembered slavery times to their children in terms of white fathers who "didn't allow nobody to mess with the colored boys of his." Others dismissed the past and told their grandchildren that "some things is best forgot." A few were so fair skinned that "they could have passed for white if they wanted to," while others who bought farms from the Land Commission "was so black there wasn't no doubt about who their daddy was."

After emancipation many of these former bondsmen stayed in their old neighborhoods, farming in much the same way as they had during slavery times. Some "worked for the marsters at daytime and for theyselves at night" in an early Piedmont version of sharecropping. Old Samuel Marshall was one former slave owner who retained many of his bondsmen as laborers by assuring them that they would receive some land of their own—promising them that "if you clean two acres you get two acres; if you clean ten acres you get ten acres" of farmland. It was this promise which kept some freedmen on the Marshall land until it was sold to the Land Commission. They cut and cleared part of the tract of the native pines and readied it for planting in anticipation of ownership. But the promise proved empty, and Marshall's death and the subsequent sale of his lands to the state deprived many of those who labored day and night on the land of the free farms they hoped would be theirs. "After they had cleaned it up they still had to pay for it." Other freedmen in the county "moved off after slavery ended but couldn't get no place" of their own to farm. Unable to negotiate labor or lease arrangements, they faced a time of homelessness with few resources and limited options until the farms became available to them. A few entered into labor contracts supervised by the Freedman's Bureau or settled on rented farms in the county for a time.

The details of the various postemancipation economic arrangements made by the freedmen who settled on the small tracts at Dr. Marshall's farm, whatever the form they assumed, were dominated by three conscious choices all had in common. The first was their decision to stay in Abbeville County following emancipation. For most of the people who eventually settled in Promised Land, Abbeville was their home as well as the site of their enslavement. There they were surrounded by friends, family and a familiar environment. The second choice this group of freedmen shared was occupational. They had been Piedmont farmers throughout their enslavement, and they chose to remain farmers in their freedom.

Local Negroes made a third conscious decision that for many had long-range importance in their lives and those of their descendents. Through the influence of the Union League, the Freedman's Bureau, the African Methodist Church, and each other, many of the Negroes in Abbeville aligned politically with the Republicans between 1865 and 1870. In Abbeville as elsewhere in the state, this alliance was established enthusiastically. The Republicans promised land as well as suffrage to those who supported them. If their political activities became public knowledge, the freedmen "were safe nowhere"; and men like Wilson Nash, Willis Smith, Washington Green, and Allen Goode who were highly visible Negro politicians took great risks in this exercise of freedom. Those risks were not without justification. It was probably not a coincidence that

loyalty to the Republican cause was followed by a chance to own land.

Land for Sale to the Colored People

I have 700 acres of land to sell in lots of from 50 to 100 acres or more situated six miles from Abbeville. Terms: A liberal cash payment; balance to be made in three annual payments from date of purchase.

J. Hollinshead, Agent
(Advertisement placed by the Land Commission
in Abbeville Press, 2 July 1873)

The Land Commission first advertised the farms on the Marshall Tract in January and February 1870. Eleven freedmen and their families established conditional ownership of their farms before spring planting that year. They were among a vanguard of some 14,000 Negro families who acquired small farms in South Carolina through the Land Commission program between 1868 and 1879. With a ten-dollar down payment they acquired the right to settle on and till the thin soil. They were also obliged to place at least half of their land under cultivation within three years and to pay all taxes due annually in order to retain their ownership rights.

Among the earliest settlers to the newly created farms was Allen Goode, the precinct manager at White Hall, who bought land in January 1870, almost immediately after it was put on the market. Two brothers-in-law, J. H. Turner and Primus Letman, also bought farms in the early spring that year. Turner was married to LeAnna Moragne and Letman to LeAnna's sister Francis. Elias Harris, a widower with six young children to raise, also came to his lands that spring, as did George Hearst, his son Robert, and their families. Another father-son partnership, Carson and Will Donnelly, settled on adjacent tracts. Willis Smith's father Daniel also bought a farm in 1870.

Allen Goode was the wealthiest of these early settlers. He owned a horse, two oxen, four milk cows, and six hogs. For the other families, both material resources and farm production were modest. Few of the homesteaders produced more than a single bale of cotton on their new farms that first year; but all, like Wilson Nash two years earlier, had respectable corn harvests, a crop essential to "both us and the animals." Most households also had sizeable pea, bean, and sweet potato crops and produced their own butter. All but the cotton crops were destined for household consumption, as these earliest settlers established a pattern of subsistence farming that would prevail as a community economic strategy in the coming decades.

This decision by the Promised Land farmers to intensify food production and minimize cotton cultivation, whether intentional or the result of other conditions, was an important initial step toward their attainment of economic self-sufficiency. Small-scale cotton farmers in the Black Belt were rarely free agents. Most were quickly trapped in a web of chronic indebtedness and marketing restrictions. Diversification of cash crops was inhibited during the 1870's and 1880's not only by custom and these economic entanglements but also by an absence of local markets, adequate roads, and methods of transportation to move crops other than cotton to larger markets. The Promised Land farmers, generally unwilling to incur debts with the local lien men if they could avoid it, turned to a modified form of subsistence farming as their only realistic land-use option. Through this strategy many of them avoided the "economic nightmare" which fixed the status of other small-scale cotton growers at a level of permanent peonage well into the twentieth century.

The following year, 1871, twenty-five more families scratched up their ten-dollar down payment; and upon presenting it to Hollinshead obtained conditional titles to farms on the Marshall Tract. The Williams family, Amanda and her four adult sons—William, Henry, James, and Moses—purchased farms together that year, probably withdrawing their money from their accounts at the Freedman's Savings and Trust Company Augusta Branch for their separate down payments. Three of the Moragne brothers —Eli, Calvin, and Moses—joined the Turners and the Letmans, their sisters and brothers-in-law, making five households in that corner of the

tract soon designated "Moragne Town." John Valentine, whose family was involved in A.M.E. organizational work in Abbeville County, also obtained a conditional title to a farm, although he did not settle there permanently. Henry Redd, like the Williamses, withdrew his savings from the Freedman's Bank and moved to his farm from Newberry, a small town about thirty miles to the east. Moses Wideman, Wells Gray, Frank Hutchison, Samuel Bulow, and Samuel Burt also settled on their farms before spring planting.

As the cluster of Negro-owned farms grew more densely populated, it gradually assumed a unique identity; and this identity, in turn, gave rise to a name, Promised Land. Some remember their grandparents telling them that "the Governor in Columbia [South Carolina] named this place when he sold it to the Negroes." Others contend that the governor had no part in the naming. They argue that these earliest settlers derived the name Promised Land from the conditions of their purchase. "They only promised to pay for it, but they never did!" Indeed, there is some truth in that statement. For although the initial buyers agreed to pay between nine and ten dollars per acre for their land in the original promissory notes, few fulfilled the conditions of those contracts. Final purchase prices were greatly reduced, from ten dollars to $3.25 per acre, a price more in line with prevailing land prices in the Piedmont.

By the end of 1873 forty-four of the fifty farms on the Marshall Tract had been sold. The remaining land, less than seven hundred acres, was the poorest in the tract, badly eroded and at the perimeter of the community. Some of those farms remained unsold until the early 1880's, but even so the land did not go unused. Families too poor to consider buying the farms lived on the state-owned property throughout the 1870's. They were squatters, living there illegally and rent-free, perhaps working a small cotton patch, always a garden. Their condition contrasted sharply with that of the landowners who, like other Negroes who purchased farmland during the 1870's, were considered the most prosperous of the rural freedmen. The freeholders in the community

were among the pioneers in a movement to acquire land, a movement that stretched across geographical and temporal limits. Even in the absence of state or federal assistance in other
regions, and despite the difficulties Negroes faced
in negotiating land purchases directly from white
landowners during Reconstruction, by 1875
Negroes across the South owned five million
acres of farmland. The promises of emancipation
were fulfilled for a few, among them the families
at Promised Land.

Settlement of the community coincided with
the establishment of a public school, another of
the revolutionary social reforms mandated by the
1868 constitution. It was the first of several public
facilities to serve community residents and was
built on land still described officially as "Dr. Marshall's farm." J. H. Turner, Larkin Reynolds,
Iverson Reynolds, and Hutson Lomax, all
Negroes, were the first school trustees. The families established on their new farms sent more than
ninety children to the one-room school. Everyone
who could be spared from the fields was in the
classroom for the short 1870 school term. Although few of the children in the landless families
attended school regularly, the landowning families early established a tradition of school attendance for their children consonant with their new
status. With limited resources the school began
the task of educating local children.

The violence and terror experienced by some
of the men of Promised Land during 1868 recurred three years later when Eli and Wade Moragne were attacked and viciously beaten with a
wagon whip by a band of Klansmen. Wade was
twenty-three that year, Eli two years older. Both
were married and had small children. It was rumored that the Moragne brothers were among
the most prominent and influential of the Negro
Republicans in Abbeville County. Their political
activity, compounded by an unusual degree of
self-assurance, pride, and dignity, infuriated local
whites. Like Wilson Nash, Willis Smith, Washington Green, and Allen Goode, the Moragne
brothers were victims of insidious political reprisals. Involvement in Reconstruction politics for
Negroes was a dangerous enterprise and one

which addressed the past as well as the future. It
was an activity suited to young men and those
who faced the future bravely. It was not for the
timid.

The Republican influence on the freedmen at
Promised Land was unmistakable, and there was
no evidence that the "outrages" and terroriza-
tions against them slowed their participation in
local partisan activities. In addition to the risks,
there were benefits to be accrued from their alliance with the Republicans. They enjoyed appointments as precinct managers and school trustees. As candidates for various public offices, they
experienced a degree of prestige and public recognition which offset the element of danger they
faced. These men, born slaves, rose to positions of
prominence as landowners, as political figures,
and as makers of a community. Few probably had
dared to dream of such possibilities a decade earlier.

During the violent years of Reconstruction
there was at least one official attempt to end the
anarchy in Abbeville County. The representative
to the state legislature, J. Hollinshead—the former regional agent for the Land Commission—
stated publicly what many local Negroes already
knew privately, that "numerous outrages occur
in the county and the laws cannot be enforced by
civil authorities." From the floor of the General
Assembly of South Carolina Hollinshead called
for martial law in Abbeville, a request which did
not pass unnoticed locally. The Editor of the
Press commented on Hollinshead's request for
martial law by declaring that such outrages
against the freedmen "exist only in the imagination of the legislator." His response was probably
typical of the cavalier attitude of southern whites
toward the problems of their former bondsmen.
Indeed, there were no further reports of violence
and attacks against freedmen carried by the
Press, which failed to note the murder of County
Commissioner Henry Nash in February 1871.
Like other victims of white terrorists, Nash was
a Negro.

While settlement of Dr. Marshall's Farm by
the freedmen proceeded, three community residents were arrested for the theft of "some oxen

from Dr. H. Drennan who lives near the 'Prom-iseland.' " Authorities found the heads, tails, and feet of the slaughtered animals near the homes of Ezekiel and Moses Williams and Col-bert Jordan. The circumstantial evidence against them seemed convincing; and the three were ar-rested and then released without bond, pending trial. Colonel Cothran, a former Confederate officer and respected barrister in Abbeville, repre-sented the trio at their trial. Although freedmen in Abbeville courts were generally convicted of whatever crime they were charged with, the Wil-liamses and Jordan were acquitted. Justice for Negroes was always a tenuous affair; but it was especially so before black, as well as white, qual-ified electors were included in the jury pool. The trial of the Williams brothers and Jordan signaled a temporary truce in the racial war, a truce which at least applied to those Negroes settling the farms at Promised Land.

In 1872, the third year of settlement, Promised Land gained nine more households as families moved to land that they "bought for a dollar an acre." There they "plow old oxen, build log cabin houses" as they settled the land they bought "from the Governor in Columbia." Colbert Jor-dan and Ezekiel Williams, cleared of the oxen stealing charges, both purchased farms that year. Family and kinship ties drew some of the new migrants to the community. Joshuway Wilson, married to Moses Wideman's sister Delphia, bought a farm near his brother-in-law. Two more Moragne brothers, William and Wade, settled near the other family members in "Moragne Town." Whitfield Hutchison, a jack-leg preacher, bought the farm adjacent to his brother Frank. "Old Whit Hutchison could sing about let's go down to the water and be baptized. He didn't have no education, and he didn't know exactly how to put his words, but when he got to singing he could make your hair rise up. He was a num-ber one preacher." Hutchison was not the only preacher among those first settlers. Isaac Y. Mo-ragne, who moved to Promised Land the follow-ing year, and several men in the Turner family all combined preaching and farming.

Not all of the settlers came to their new farms

as members of such extensive kinship networks as the Moragnes, who counted nine brothers, four sisters, and an assortment of spouses and children among the first Promised Land residents. Even those who joined the community in relative isola-tion, however, were seldom long in establishing kinship alliances with their neighbors. One such couple was James and Hannah Fields who lived in Columbia before emancipation. While still a slave, James Fields owned property in the state capitol, which was held in trust for him by his master. After emancipation Fields worked for a time as a porter on the Columbia and Greenville Railroad and heard about the up-country land for sale to Negroes as he carried carpet bags and listened to political gossip on the train. Fields went to Abbeville County to inspect the land be-fore he purchased a farm there. While he was visiting, he "run up on Mr. Nathan Redd," old Henry Redd's son. The Fieldses' granddaughter Emily and Nathan were about the same age, and Fields proposed a match to young Redd. "You marry my granddaughter, and I'll will all this land to you and her." The marriage was arranged before the farm was purchased, and eventually the land was transferred to the young couple.

By the conclusion of 1872 forty-eight families were settled on farms in Promised Land. Most of the land was under cultivation, as required by law; but the farmers were also busy with other activities. In addition to the houses and barns which had to be raised as each new family arrived with their few possessions, the men continued their political activities. Iverson Reynolds, J. H. Turner, John and Elias Tolbert, Judson Rey-nolds, Oscar Pressley, and Washington Green, all community residents, were delegates to the county Republican convention in August 1872. Three of the group were landowners. Their politi-cal activities were still not received with much enthusiasm by local whites, but reaction to Negro involvement in politics was lessening in hostility. The *Press* mildly observed that the fall cotton crop was being gathered with good speed and "the farmers have generally been making good use of their time." Cotton picking and politics were both seasonal, and the newspaper chided local Negroes for their priorities. "The blacks have been indulging a little too much in politics but are getting right again." Iverson Reynolds and Washington Green, always among the community's Republican leadership during the 1870's, served as local election managers again for the 1872 fall elections. The men from Promised Land voted without incident that year.

Civic participation among the Promised Land residents extended beyond partisan politics when the county implemented the new jury law in 1872. There had been no Negro jurors for the trial of the Williams brothers and Colbert Jordan the previous year. Although the inclusion of Negroes in the jury pools was a reform mandated in 1868, four years passed before Abbeville authorities drew up new jury lists from the revised voter registration rolls. The jury law was as repugnant to the whites as Negro suffrage, termed "a wretched attempt at legislation, which surpasses anything which has yet been achieved by the Solons in Columbia." When the new lists were finally completed in 1872 the *Press,* ever the reflection of local white public opinion, predicted that "many of [the freedmen] probably have moved away; and the chances are that not many of them will be forthcoming" in the call to jury duty. Neither the initial condemnation of the law nor the optimistic undertones of the *Press* prediction stopped Pope Moragne and Iverson Reynolds from responding to their notices from the Abbeville Courthouse. Both landowners rode their mules up Five Notch Road from Promised Land to Abbeville and served on the county's first integrated jury in the fall of 1872. Moragne and Reynolds were soon followed by others from the community—Allen Goode, Robert Wideman, William Moragne, James Richie, and Luther (Shack) Moragne. By 1874, less than five years after settlement of Dr. Marshall's farm by the new Negro landowners began, the residents of Promised Land remained actively involved in Abbeville County politics. They were undaunted by the *Press* warning that "just as soon as the colored people lose the confidence and support of the North their doom is fixed. The fate of the red man will be theirs." They were voters, jurors,

taxpayers, and trustees of the school their children attended. Their collective identity as an exclusively Negro community was well established.

Only Colored Down in This Old Promised Land

Abbeville County, South Carolina
Mr. John Lomax passed through the Promised Land yesterday, and he thinks the crops there almost a failure. The corn will not average two bushels to the acre, and the cotton about 300 pounds [less than one bale] to the acre. A large quantity of sorghum cane was planted. It was almost worthless. The land appeared as if it had been very well cultivated.
Abbeville Press
30 September 1874

The forty-eight men and women who established conditional ownership of the farms at Promised Land between 1870 and 1872 were required by law to place at least half of their land under cultivation within three years of their purchase. There was, however, no requirement about the crops to be planted. The men who established that cultivation standard probably assumed that cotton would be the major cash crop, as it was throughout the Piedmont. At Promised Land cotton was indeed planted on every one of the farms, but not in overwhelming amounts. The relatively small cotton fields were overshadowed by fields of corn, peas, and sorghum cane; and the sense of permanence among the settlers was clearly evident when "they planted peach trees and pear trees and had grape vines all over" the land, which only a few years before was either uncleared of native pine forests or part of the upcountry plantation system. Cotton, the antebellum crop of the slaves, became the cash crop of freedom. It would never dominate the lives of the farmers at Promised Land.

The 1870's were economically critical years for the new landowners. They had mortgage payments to meet and taxes to pay, but they also had families to feed. In 1870, when the price of cotton reached twenty-two cents a pound, all this was possible. In the following years, however, cotton prices declined dramatically. This, combined with generally low cotton yields, resulted in economic hardship for many of the farmers. Poverty was their constant neighbor, and their struggle for survival drew them into a cycle of indebtedness to white "lien men."

In those depression years there was little credit in the Piedmont. "The poor people wasn't able to buy their fertilize. That's what makes your cotton." Storekeepers and merchants reserved their resources for the local white planters, and the Negro farmers were forced to find credit from other sources. They turned to their white landowning neighbors and in some cases their former masters, the Devlin family in Verdery; the Tuck family, nearby farmers; and the Hendersons, Verdery merchants. To them the Promised Land farmers paid usurious interest rates for the fertilizer they needed "to make a bale of cotton" and the other supplies and foodstuffs they required to survive the growing season.

It was during this decade that the community farmers learned to maintain a skillful balance between a small cotton cash crop and their subsistence fields. Careful in the management of debt, most landowners probably used their cotton crop to meet their mortgage payment to the Land Commission and their tax bill to the county. There was never any surplus on the small farms, and a crop failure had immediate and personal consequences. At best a family would go hungry. At worst they would lose their farm.

Times were hard; and, despite generally shrewd land and debt management, twenty of the original settlers lost title to their land during the early 1870's. All migrated from Promised Land before the 1875 growing season. An advertisement in the *Press* attracted some new purchasers to the vacated farms, but most buyers learned of the land through friends and relatives. New families once again moved on to the land. Wilson Nash bought the farm originally purchased by John Valentine; both men were church leaders and probably discussed the transaction in some detail before the agreement was finalized.

Allen Goode, Wells Gray, and James Fields added to their holdings, buying additional farms from discouraged families who were leaving. Moses Wideman's younger brothers, William

and Richmond, together bought an eighty-five-acre farm and then divided it, creating two more homesteads in the community. J. H. Turner, who secured a teaching position in an Edgefield County public school, sold his farm to his brother-in-law Isaac Y. Moragne. Each of the landowners had a brother, a cousin, or a friend who was eager to assume the financial burden of landownership; and none of the twenty vacated farms remained unoccupied for long. Promised Land quickly regained its population. The new arrivals strengthened and expanded the kinship bonds, which already crisscrossed and united individual households in the community.

Marriage provided the most common alliance between kinship groups. The Wilson and Wideman families and the Fields and Redds were both so related. The use of land as dowry, first employed by James Fields to arrange his granddaughter's marriage to Nathan Redd, provided a convenient and viable bargaining tool. When Iverson Reynolds bought his thirty-acre farm he also purchased a second, twenty-acre tract in his daughter's name, looking forward to the time of her marriage. "When Oscar Pressley married Iverson Reynolds' daughter, Janie, Iverson Reynolds give him that land or sold it to him. But he got that farm from old Iverson Reynolds when he got married." The Moragnes, Turners, Pinckneys, and Letmans were also united through land-based dowry arrangements. "The Moragne women is the ones that had the land. All them, the Turners, the Pinckneys, and the Letmans— all them got into the Moragnes when the women married these men."

Marriage did not always accompany kinship bonds, for at Promised Land, like every place else, "some folks have childrens when they not married. Things get all mixed up sometimes." Still, the community was a small and intimate place, woven together as early as the 1880's by a complex and interlocking series of kin ties, which were supplemented by many other kinds of personal relationships. The separation of public and private spheres blurred; and, married or not, "when the gals get a baby" everyone was aware of the heritage and family ties of new babies.

"Andrew Moragne supposed to been his daddy, but his momma was a Bradley so he took the name Bradley." Even so, promiscuity and illegitimacy were not casually accepted facts of life. Both were sinful and disgraceful not just to the couple but to their families as well. For women a pregnancy without marriage was particularly painful. "Some might be mean to you then," and many refused to even speak publicly to an unmarried women who became pregnant. "All that stop when the baby is born. Don't want to punish an innocent baby." Legitimate or not, babies were welcomed into families and the community, and the sins of the parents were set aside. Ultimately, the bonds of kinship proved more powerful than collective morality, and these bonds left few residents of the community excluded from an encompassing network of cousins, aunts, uncles, and half-brothers and sisters.

As the landowning population of Promised Land stabilized, local resources emerged to meet day-to-day needs. A molasses mill, where the farmers had their sorghum cane ground into molasses by Joshuway Wilson's oldest son Fortune, opened in the community. Two corn and wheat grist mills opened on Curltail Creek. One, the old Marshall Mill, was operated by Harrison Cole, a Negro who subsequently purchased a vacant farm in the community. The other, the former Donalds Mill, was owned and operated by James Evans, an Irish immigrant whose thirst for land equaled that of his Negro neighbors. North Carter, the youngest son of landowner Marion Carter, opened a small general store at the east-west crossroads, where he sold candy, kerosene, salt, and other staples to his neighbors, extending credit when necessary, knowing that they would pay when they could. Long before the final land purchase was completed, the freedmen at Promised Land had established a framework for economic and social self-sufficiency.

The farms, through hard work, decent weather, and an eight-month growing season, soon yielded food for the households. A pattern of subsistence agriculture provided each Promised Land family a degree of independence and self-reliance unknown to most other Negro families in the area. Cows produced milk and butter for the tables, and chickens eggs and fresh poultry. Draft animals and cash money were both scarce commodities, but "in them days nobody ever went hungry." Hogs provided the major source of meat in the community's subsistence economy. "My mother and them used to kill hogs and put them down in salt in wood boxes and cover them so flies couldn't get to them for about five or six weeks. Take it out and wash it, put on red pepper and such, hang it up to dry, and that meant be *good.*" The absence of an abundant cotton crop was not a sign of lack of industry. Prosperity, as well as productivity, was measured against hunger; and, in the never-ending farm cycle, fields were planted according to the number of people in each household, the number of mouths to be fed.

Community and household autonomy were firmly grounded in the economic independence of the land. Both were strengthened with the establishment of a church in Promised Land. In 1875, fully a decade before the final farms were settled, James Fields sold one acre of his land to the Trustees of Mt. Zion A.M.E. Church. It was a sign of the times. At Promised Land, as elsewhere in the South, freedmen withdrew from white churches as quickly as possible. Membership in the Baptist and Methodist denominations increased tenfold between 1860–1870 as the new Negro churches in the South took form. Mt. Zion was relatively late in emerging as a part of that movement for independence from white domination, but the residents of Promised Land were preoccupied for a time with more basic concerns. The fields had to be established as productive before community residents turned their energies to other aspects of community development.

The Field's land, located squarely in the geographical center of Promised Land, was within a two-mile walk of all the houses in the community. On this thinly wooded tract the men carved out a brush arbor, a remnant of slavery days; and Isaac Y. Moragne led everybody in the young settlement in prayers and songs. From the beginning of their emancipation schools and churches were central components of Negro social life; and at Promised Land religion, like education, was established as a permanent part of community life while the land was still being cleared.

Newcomers and Community Growth

Most families survived those first settlement years, the droughts and crop failures, Ku Klux Klan attacks, and the violent years of Reconstruction. They met their mortgage payments and their taxes, and the years after 1875 were relatively prosperous ones. Promised Land was well established before the Compromise of 1877, the withdrawal of federal troops from the state, and the election of Wade Hampton as governor. The political squabbles among the white Democrats during the years after Hampton's redemption of South Carolina touched the folks at Promised Land only indirectly. The community was, for the most part, preoccupied with internal events.

By 1880 the community had expanded from forty-nine to eighty-nine households, an average growth of four new families each year for the previous decade. Fifty of those families were landless, attracted to Promised Land for a combination of reasons. Probably at least some of them hoped to acquire land there. Promised Land was the only place in the area where Negroes had even minimal hope of buying land after 1877. Local farmers and planters, never eager to sell land to Negroes, now grew even more recalcitrant as Democratic white rule was re-established. Sharecropping dominated farming arrangements between whites and Negroes throughout the Cotton Belt. The landowners at Promised Land, "well, they was wheels. They *owned* their farms." And the respect and prestige they commanded within the county's landless Negro population were another kind of attraction for landless families.

The violence of Reconstruction was moderated only slightly, and a concern for personal safety was surely another reason Negroes moved to Promised Land. Few of the early settlers, those who came before the mid–1880's, could have escaped that violence, even if their contact was indirect. Wilson Nash, Willis Smith, Allen Goode, Washington Green, Wade and Eli Moragne all

headed landowning households. For any who might forget, those men were constant reminders of the dangers which lay just beyond the community's perimeter.

The men at Promised Land still exercised their franchise, fully aware of both the dangers and the benefits which they knew accompanied political activity. Together they walked the three miles to Verdery and collectively cast their ballots at the post office "where Locket Frazier held the box for the niggers and Red Tolbert for the whites." Perhaps they walked together as a symbolic expression of their solidarity, but much more likely it was because of a practical concern for their own safety. They were less vulnerable to attack in a group. As it had in the past, however, this simple exercise of citizenship enraged the local whites; and, once again, in the early 1880's the men at Promised Land faced the threat of violence for their partisan political activities.

> Them old Phoenix rats, the Ku Klux, come up here to beat up the niggers 'cause they went to Verdery and voted. Them old dogs from Phoenix put on red shirts and come up here to beat the poor niggers up. Old George Foster, the white man, he told them "Don't go down in that Promiseland. Josh Wilson and Colbert Jordan and them got some boys up there, and they got shotguns and Winchesters and old guns. Any white man come in to Promiseland to beat the niggers up, some body going to die. They'll fight 'til hell freezes over. You Phoenix rats go back to Phoenix." So they went on down to Verdery, and they told them the same thing.

Their reputation, their readiness, and their willingness to defend their land were clearly well-known facts about the people at Promised Land. The "Red Shirts" heeded the warning, and white terrorists never again attempted to violate Promised Land. This, too, must have been a part of the community's attraction to landless families who moved there.

Promised Land in 1880 was a community which teemed with activity. Most of the newcomers joined in the brush arbor worship services and sent their children to the community schools. Liberty Hill School and the white schoolmaster were replaced by "schools scattered all around the woods" taught by Negro men and women who lived at Promised Land. Abbeville County maintained a public school. Crossroads School for Colored was taught by H. L. Latimer. The Mill School, maintained by the extensive Moragne family for their children, was held in James Evans' mill on Curltail Creek and was taught by J. H. Turner, Moragne brother-in-law. The Hester School, located near the southern edge of the community, was so named because it met in the Hester family's home. All three private schools supplemented the meager public support of education for Negro children; and all were filled to capacity, because "folks had big families then—ten and twelve childrens—and them schools was crowded."

The representatives to the 1868 South Carolina Constitutional Convention who formulated the state's land redistribution hoped to establish an economically independent Negro yeomanry in South Carolina. The Land Commission intended the purchase and resale of Dr. Marshall's farm to solidify the interests of radical Republicanism in Abbeville County, at least for a time. Both of these designs were realized. A third and unintended consequence also resulted. The land fostered a socially autonomous, identifiable community. Drawing on resources and social structures well established within an extant Negro culture, the men and women who settled Promised Land established churches and schools and a viable economic system based on landownership. They maintained that economic autonomy by subsistence farming and supported many of their routine needs by patronizing the locally owned and operated grist mills and general store. The men were actively involved in Reconstruction politics as well as other aspects of civil life, serving regularly on county juries and paying their taxes. Attracted by the security and prestige Promised Land afforded and the possible hope of eventual landownership, fifty additional landless households moved into the community during the 1870's, expanding the 1880 population to almost twice its original size. Together the eighty-nine households laid claim to slightly more than four square miles of land, and within that small territory they "carved out their own little piece of the world."